Lucius Annaeus Seneca

Epistles of Seneca

Lucius Annaeus Seneca

Epistles of Seneca

ISBN/EAN: 9783743335066

Manufactured in Europe, USA, Canada, Australia, Japa

Cover: Foto ©Thomas Meinert / pixelio.de

Manufactured and distributed by brebook publishing software
(www.brebook.com)

Lucius Annaeus Seneca

Epistles of Seneca

THE EPISTLES OF *LUCIUS ANNÆUS SENECA.*

EPISTLE I.

On the Value and Use of Time. (a)

THIS do, my *Lucilius*; vindicate the dignity of man: be your own master: and such hours as have hitherto been forcibly taken from you, or stolen unawares, or have slipped by inadvertently, recollect, and for the future turn to some account. You may be assured what I say is true: part of our time we are obliged to sacrifice to office and power; friendship and common occurrences steal another part; and another slides away insensibly: but most scandalous is the loss of it when owing to negligence and dissipation: and yet small attention will evince, that great part of life (b) is spent in doing ill, a greater in doing nothing, and too often the whole in doing little or nothing to the great purpose of being. Where will you find (c) a man who sets any value upon time? who rates a day, or seems to understand that *he dies daily*? (d) For herein are we deceived; we look forwards at death; whereas death, in a great measure, is already passed: all the lapsed years of life are in the tenure of death (e). Act therefore, my *Lucilius*, as you inform me you do. Embrace every hour (f): the stronger hold you have on to-day, the less will be your dependance on to-morrow. Life, however unimproved, still glides away. There is nothing (g) we can properly call our own, but *Time:* all other things are foreign to us: nature hath put us in possession of this one fleeting transitory boon;

which any one deprives us of at pleaſure *(b)*: and ſo great is the folly of mortals, that, when by entreaty they have obtained things of the loweſt value, mere trifles, at leaſt ſuch as are payable again, they ſuffer them to be ſet to their account; but no one thinks himſelf indebted, who hath borrowed *Time*; whereas this is the only thing that the moſt grateful heart cannot repay.

You will aſk, perhaps, how I act myſelf, who am giving you this advice? I will confeſs ingenuouſly; it is with me, as with thoſe who are luxurious, and yet not quite negligent of their affairs. I ſtill keep an account of my expences; I cannot ſay, I loſe nothing; but I can tell you what I loſe, and why, and in what manner. I am not aſhamed *(i)* to own the cauſe of my poverty: but it happens to me, as to many who have been reduced to indigence, not merely by their own miſconduct: all men are ready to excuſe and pity, but none to aſſiſt them. What then? I can by no means think him a poor man, who hath ſtill enough *(k)*, however ſmall a portion it be, wherewith to be content. But may you, my friend, ſtill keep your own; and ſeize the opportunity to uſe it properly. For as our anceſtors wiſely judged,—Sera parſimonia in fundo eſt,—*It is too late to be ſparing, when the veſſel is almoſt out* (*l*). As not only a little (*m*) but the worſt of every thing generally remains at the bottom.

ANNOTATIONS, PEFERENCES, &c.

(a) The antients had ſeveral curt and wiſe ſentences among them, which they ſuppoſed ſome *God* the author of, (as if they had been always ſenſible of the neceſſity of divine revelation, and were ready to acknowledge the obligation,) ſuch were, *Know thyſelf*, *Obey God*, *Nothing too much*, and the like; but one of the moſt celebrated among them, is, χρόνου φείδου, Tempori parce, *Huſband well your Time*. (*See* Cic. de Fin. l. 3. Clem. Alex. Strom. I. Stobæ l. III. Eraſm. Adag. Muret. in loc) This then *Seneca* makes the ſubject of his firſt Epiſtle: and parallel to it, is the exhortation of his cotemporary, our Apoſtle, *Epheſ.* 5. 16. *Col.* 4. 5. *Redeeming our Time*, &c. (See Ep. 117. Plin. Ep. l. 9.

(b) That great part of life] Opſopæus from four MSS. reads it, Maxima vitæ pars elabitur malè agentibus, magna nihil agentibus, tota vita aliud agentibus. (See this paſſage explained in Alciat Parergon Juris, l. 4, c. 14.

(c) Where will you find——

On all-important Time, through every age,
Tho' much and warm the wiſe have urg'd; the man
Is yet unborn, who duly weighs an hour.
I've loſt a day; the prince who nobly cried,
Had been an Emperor without his crown.——*Young*.

(d) He

(d) He dies daily] 1 Cor. xv. 31. Καθ' ἡμέραν ἀποθνήσκω.

(e) In the tenure of death] Ἡμεῖς ἐκ τότε ἀρχόμεθα ζῇν τότε ἀποθνήσκομεν. Theophraſt. *As ſoon as we begin to live, we die.* Or, *When to live, we then begin to die.* Οὕτως καὶ ἡμεῖς γεννηθέντες ἐξελίπομεν, *ſo we as ſoon as we were born, began to draw to our end.* Wiſdom. v. 13. (See Epiſt. 12. 24. 58. 120.)

(f) Embrace every hour] ——Throw years away!

Throw empires, and be blameleſs. Moments ſeize;
Heav'n's on their wing: a moment we may wiſh,
When worlds want wealth to buy.——*Id.*

——Sapere aude:
Incipe. Qui rectè vivendi prorogat horam
Ruſticus expectat, dum defluit amnis, at ille
Labitur, et labetur in omne volubilis ævum.——*Hor.*

Dare to be wiſe: begin. By virtue's rule
Whoſo defers to live, is like the fool,
Who ſtays, expecting the whole river gone;
Which flows, and will for ever ſtill flow on.

(g) There is nothing—] All ſenſual man, becauſe untouch'd, unſeen,
He looks on Time as nothing; nothing elſe
Is truly man's; 'tis fortune's——*Young.*

(h) Which every one deprives us of at pleaſure]

Ex quâ nos expellit, quicunque vult.

Where is that thrift, that avarice of Time,
(O glorious avarice!) thought of death inſpires;
As rumour'd robberies endear our gold!—
O Time, than gold more ſacred!——*Young.*

But we are ſo perverſe, that however avaritious and tenacious we are of other things, we are extremely prodigal of Time; we freely grant, at leaſt, part of it to any one that aſks it, and are never upon our guard againſt thoſe thieves, that in a friendly way ſteal it from us. *The pilferer of a ſixpence upon the road is without remorſe committed to the gallows, whilſt he who ſteals* my Time, *is under no obligation to apologize for his conduct.* May we not complain here of the inequality of the legiſlature? For ſurely nothing is more precious than *Time.* Nullâ re ita nos egemus ut tempore. *There is nothing we are ſo much in want of as Time.* Zeno——And *Theophraſtus* was uſed to ſay, Πολυτελὲς ἀνάλωμα χρόνος, *Nothing is more expenſive than the loſs of Time.*—And this, according to *Gronovius*, is undoubtedly the ſenſe of the place: but ſome read it, Ex quâ non expellit—i. e. *No one is deprived of this treaſure, but he that will not uſe it aright,* or *who ſuffers it to be taken, or ſtolen from him.*——*Opſopæus* from a MS. Ex quâ non expellitur—and *Eraſmus* ſtill differently, Ex quâ expellit quemcunque vult; i. e. *Nature hath given man this poſſeſſion, but reſumes it at pleaſure.* And ſo the old French, *De laquelle elle chaſſe quiconque elle veut.*

(i) I am not aſhamed] Alluding to his attendance at court.

(k) Who hath ſtill enough] Old as I am, I complain not of the few days that remain for me in this life, but am ſatisfied with them, and am determined to improve them to the beſt advantage.——Happy reſolution!

(l) It is too late] From Heſiod, c. 366.

Ἀρχομένου δὲ πίθου καὶ λήγοντος κορέσασθαι·
Μεσσόθι φείδεσθαι· δειλὴ δ' ἐνὶ πυθμένι φειδώ.
The barrel full, drink deeply, if you pleaſe;
Then ſpare: 'twill be too late, when on the lees.

Perſius alludes to the ſame in Sat. II.

— Donec deceptus et exſpes
Nequicquam fundo ſuſpiret nummus in imo.
Thus vainly dreams the wretch, and ſtill ſpends on,
'Till a poor deſperate guinea left alone
In ſilence mourns his dear companions gone.

And not unlike this is our proverb, *When the ſteed is ſtolen, he ſhuts the ſtable door.* Quandoquidem accepto claudenda eſt janua damno. *Juv.* Sat. III. Προμηθεύς ἐστι μετὰ τὰ πράγματα. *Lucian.* And that of the French. Apres la mort le medicin. *After death the doctor.* (*See* Eraſm. Adag. 2. 2. 64.)

(*m*) *As not only a little*] *Antiphanes* ſpeaking of life, ſays,

Σφοδρ' ἐστὶν ἡμῶν ὁ βίος οἴνῳ προσφερής·
Ὅταν ᾖ τὸ λοιπὸν μικρὸν, ὄξος γίνεται.
Our life like wine, when but few years are paſt,
Is briſk and ſtrong; but vinegar at laſt.

EPISTLE II.

On Study; and true Riches. (*a*)

I AM happy, *Lucilius*, in conceiving great hopes of you, both from what you write, and from what I hear of you: it ſeems, you are no wanderer, nor apt to diſquiet yourſelf in vain with change of place; a reſtleſſneſs which generally ſprings from ſome malady in the mind. The chief teſtimony, I apprehend, of a mind truly calm and compoſed, is, that it is conſiſtent with, and can enjoy itſelf.

Be pleaſed likewiſe to conſider that the reading many authors, and books of all ſorts, betrays a vague and unſteady diſpoſition. You muſt attach yourſelf to ſome in particular, and thoroughly digeſt what you read, if you would entruſt the faithful memory with any thing of uſe. He that is every-where, is no-where (*b*). They who ſpend their time in travelling, meet indeed with many an hoſt, but few friends. This is neceſſarily the caſe of thoſe, who apply not familiarly to any one ſtudy, but run over every thing curſorily and in haſte. The food profits not, nor gives due nouriſhment

nouriſhment to the body, that abides not ſome time therein. Nothing ſo much prevents the recovery of health, as a frequent change of ſuppoſed remedies. A wound is not ſoon healed, when different ſalves are tried by way of experiment. A plant thrives not, nor can well take root, that is moved from place to place. What profits only accidentally, *in paſſing*, is of little Uſe. Variety of books diſtracts the mind; when you cannot read, therefore, all that you have; it is enough to have only what you can read (*c*). But you will ſay, you have a mind ſometimes to amuſe yourſelf, with one book and ſometimes with another: it is a ſign, my friend, of a nice and ſqueamiſh ſtomach, to be taſting many viands, which, as they are various and of different qualities, rather corrupt than nouriſh. Read therefore always the moſt approved authors, and if you are pleaſed at any time to taſte others, by way of amuſement, ſtill return to thoſe as your principal ſtudy. Be continually treaſuring up ſomething to arm you againſt poverty, ſomething againſt the fear of death and other the like evils, incident to man. And when you have read ſufficiently, make a reſerve of ſome particular ſentiment for that day's meditation.

Such is my own practice: of the many things I read, I generally ſelect one for obſervation: for inſtance, to-day I have been reading *Epicurus* (*d*): (for you muſt know I ſometimes make an excurſion into the enemy's camp, not by way of deſerter, but as a ſpy;) *chearful poverty*, ſays he, *is an excellent thing*. Now I cannot conceive, how that ſtate can be called *poor*, which is *chearful*. The man, whoſe poverty ſits eaſy upon him, is rich (*e*). Not he that hath little, but he that deſireth more, is the poor man. For what avails it, how much a man hath in his cheſt, or in his barns; what ſtock he has in the field, or what money at intereſt; if he is ſtill hankering after another's wealth: if he is ever counting, not what he has got already, but what he may get (*f*)? Do you aſk me, what I take to be the proper *mean of wealth?* I will tell you:—firſt, a *ſupply of neceſſaries*; 2dly, *an eaſy competency* (*g*).

ANNO-

ANNOTATIONS, &c.

(a) Was I to have inscribed this Epistle to any one, according to my first design, it would have been to a Rev. D. D. whom I know to have read as many books as any one of the present age; and wrote not a few: and yet he is thought very deficient in his manner, and elegance of style: but he is my friend;—and so I will take the censure upon myself, as conscious of having richly deserved it. In 1725, of the first sermon I preached upon a publick occasion, I submitted the MS. to my friend Doctor Gretton, who returned it with the following compliment. —

" In polite writings we use no parentheses; in philosophical the fewer the better. You do not want " invention; your thoughts crowd upon you; but I think a little classical arrangement is wanting, " and a few connecting particles; or rather a more perpetuated thread of discourse: you come nearer *Seneca* than *Tully*; the *Arena sine calce.*"

And, I fear, I cannot boast any great improvement in 1780: the reason, (as Seneca here expresseth it) because Nullius me ingenio familiariter applicavi, sed omnia cursim et properans transmisi. The courteous reader will excuse an old man's talking of himself. Perhaps it may have some use.—— N. B. The 28th Epistle turns upon much the same argument with this.

(b) He that —] Quisquis ubique habitat, Nævole, nusquam habitat.—*Martial.*

Fig: Οξυμωρον—Reviviscentis imperii spes Fabius fuit. Qui novam de Hannibale victoriam commentus est, *nolle pugnare.*

(c) When you cannot —] Fig. Antimetathesis —So *Pliny. Paneg.* Non ideo vicisse videris, ut triumphares, sed triumphare, ut vinceres.

(d) You will recollect here that *Seneca* was not an *Epicurean* but a *Stoic.*

(e) The man whose—] So in the foregoing Epistle,

Non puto pauperem, cui quantulumcumque superest, sat est. *I cannot think him poor, who hath wherewithal to be content.*

(f) Is ever counting—] Non quod habet numerat tantum quod non habet optat. *Manil.*

(g) Quod sat est.] *Lucilius,* the old Roman poet, argues thus——

Nam si, quod satis est homini, id satis esse potisset,
Hoc sat erat: nunc cum hoc non est, qui credimus porro,
Divitias ullas animum mi explere potisse?

No wealth can satisfy the man, who thinks,
What is sufficient, not enough for him.

EPISTLE

EPISTLE III.

On Friendſhip.

YOU inform me, *Lucilius,* that you have ſent letters to me by your *friend,* and then deſire me not to communicate with him all that I know of you; for this, you ſay, is not what you would chuſe to do yourſelf: and is not this to own, and deny him, at the ſame time, to be your friend (*a*)? You ſeem to uſe the word as a common appellation, and to call him *friend,* as we call all candidates for an office, *good men*; and accoſt thoſe whoſe name does not immediately occur, with, *Dear Sir* (*b*). Be this as it will; yet know, that if you think any one your friend, whom you dare not truſt as far as you would your ownſelf, you are greatly miſtaken, and know not the importance of true friendſhip.

It may be neceſſary to conſult and adviſe with a friend in everything, but it is proper firſt to know him (*c*). After friendſhip contracted all truſt is due; but a judicious choice muſt precede it. They ſtrangely blend the duties relating to friendſhip, who, contrary to the precept of Theophraſtus, when they have fixed the fancy, think it time enough to judge, rather than, having judged, embrace the friend. Conſider with yourſelf, for ſome time, whether ſuch a one is worthy to be received into your boſom, and if he ſeems a proper perſon, admit him with your whole heart. Converſe as frankly and boldly (*d*) with him, as you would with your ownſelf. Yet live ſo, *Lucilius,* as to commit but what you dare truſt even with an enemy.

However, as many things may intervene, which, from their own nature or cuſtom, are termed *ſecrets*; theſe belong to the province of a friend; with whom you muſt communicate all your cares, and all your counſels. This is the way to make him faithful (*e*) indeed: for many have taught others to deceive by an apprehenſion of being deceived themſelves; and, by an unjuſt ſuſpicion, given others a right, as it were, to offend in this point.

 Why

Why then ſhould I be upon the reſerve with my friend? Why ſhould I not think myſelf alone, even in his preſence?

Some people are apt to blab to every one they meet what ought to be entruſted only with friends; and to diſburthen themſelves of whatever may chance to wring them, by teazing every ear with the doleful tale: there are others, who are afraid of the conſciouſneſs of their deareſt converſants; nay, they are ſo obſtinately cloſe, with regard to every ſecret, that, if poſſible, they would not truſt their own conſciences with them. They are both in the wrong; it is no leſs a fault to truſt every one, than to truſt no one (*f*): only the former I take to be a more generous error, the latter a more ſafe one.

In like manner are they worthy reprehenſion, who are always reſtleſs, or always indolent: for to delight in buſtle and tumult is not *induſtry*, but the conflict of a diſorder'd mind; nor is it to be called *eaſe*, that thinks every the leaſt motion irkſome, but rather languor, and diſſipation. I will therefore recommend to you what I read in *Pomponius* (*g*). *There have been thoſe*, ſays he, *who have ſo devoted themſelves to ſolitude, in ſome dark corner, as to think every thing* without *to be trouble and confuſion.* Theſe two things are to be interwoven, as it were, together, *Reſt* and *Labour*. If you examine Nature; ſhe will tell you, ſhe made both the Day and the Night.

ANNOTATIONS, &c.

(*a*) *To be your friend*] In this double ſenſe of the word is that of *Socrates*, Ω φίλοι οὐδεὶς φίλος, *ye are all my friends, and yet I have no friend.*

(*b*) *Sir*] Dominum. So, *Martial.*

Cum te non noſſem, Dominum Regemque vocabam.
Cum voco te Dominum, noli tibi, Cinna, placere,
Sæpe etiam ſervum ſic reſaluto meum. *Id.*
Be not proud, Cinna, *that I call you*, Sir;
Oft hears my ſlave the ſame, an idle cur!
Or thus:
I call you Sir, *yet ſmile not at the name,*
For, Cinna, *oft my ſervant hears the ſame.*

Muretus likewiſe quotes a Greek epigram, but as all the wit lies in the pun, it is not worth tranſlating.

Ην ὁ φίλος τι λαλῇ, δόμινε φράτερ αὖθις ἀκούει·
Ην δὲ λαλῇ μηδὲν, τὸ φράτερ ἴσθι μόνον.
Οἶμαι γὰρ καὶ ταῦτα τὰ ῥήματα· αὐτὰρ ἔγωγε
Οὐκ ἐθέλω δόμινε· οὐ γὰρ ἔχω δόμινον.

(*Vid. Torrent. in Suet. Aug.* 33. *Claud.* 39. *Lipſ. in l.* 2. *Tac. Ann. Briſſon. l.* 8. *de Form.*

(c) First to know him] Sidonius, p. 304. Est enim consuetudinis meæ, ut eligam ante, post diligam. *It is my way, to chuse first, and love afterwards.*—The precept of *Theophrastus* here referred to, is, ὅτι δεῖ κρίναντα φιλεῖν, ἀλλ' ὀ φιλοῦντα κρίνειν, *It is proper to judge, before we fix our affection, rather than to fix it before we have formed our judgment.* An excellent precept for the young of both sexes, but especially for the fair sex!

(d) As boldly] This has not always been thought true policy, Ita crede amico, *saith* Publius, ne sit inimico locus. *So trust a friend, as to leave no room for his becoming your enemy. And* Sophocles Aj. 690.

—— Ἐς τε τὸν φίλον
Τοσαῦθ' ὑπουργῶν ὠφελεῖν βουλήσομαι
Ὡς αἰὲν οὐ μενοῦντα· Τοῖς πολλοῖσι γὰρ
Βροτῶν ἄπιστος ἐσθ' ἑταιρίας λιμήν.

And so assist and love my friend, as if
One day he would forsake me; for to many
The hav'n of friendship proves a faithless hav'n.

(e) To make him faithful] So *Livy*, Vult sibi quisque credi et habita fides ipsam obligat fidem. *Every one is desirous of credit; and to trust, is the way to be trusted.* And *Plutarch*, in his *Connubial* Precepts, Ποιεῖ καὶ τὸ πιστεύειν δοκεῖν πιστεύεσθαι, καὶ τὸ φιλεῖν φιλεῖσθαι· *To believe, is an inducement to be believed; and to love, to be beloved.*

(f) To trust no one] So, *Phædrus*, Periculosum est credere et non credere. *To believe, and not to believe, are alike dangerous.* Πίστεις δ' ἄρα ὁμῶς καὶ ἀπιστίαι ὤλεσαν ἄνδρας.

Both trust, and diffidence, are alike destructive. Hesiod.

(g) Pomponius] There was a tragic poet of this name, and others; but as this sentence has not a poetical turn, *Lipsius* reads it *Pompeius*, the philosopher.

(h) Osborne, in his discourse, *On the greatness and corruption of the Church of Rome*, having just before spoken of *Seneca*, seems to have fallen into his style; so widely different from any other part of his writings.—" There is nothing, says he, idleness and peace makes not worse; labour and exercise " better: the tree that stands in the weather, roots best and deepest: the running water and air that is " agitated are most wholesome and sweet. The cause of this, must be deduced from God's eternal " decree, that nothing in nature should remain idle and without motion."

EPISTLE IV.

On the Study of Philosophy; from whence the Contempt of Death, and also of Wealth and Grandeur.

PErsevere, *Lucilius*, as you have begun; and be as expeditious as possible; that, being once master of a regular, and well-informed mind, *(a)* you may the longer enjoy it. There is a pleasure indeed in endeavouring to regulate

regulate and reform the mind, but how much more exquiſite is that, which ariſes from the contemplation of a mind ever innocent and pure? You yet remember the joy of heart you felt, when, laying aſide *the veſt and tunic*, you put on the *manly robe*, and was introduced to the *Prætor*. Expect ſtill greater joy, when you ſhall have caſt off all puerile inclinations, and philoſophy has ranked you in the claſs of *men*. We may have paſſed indeed our childhood, when what is more grievous, childiſhneſs ſtill remains: and, what is yet worſe, we are old men in authority, but boys in vices and imperfections; not only boys, but meer infants *(b)*. As thoſe are afraid of the moſt light and trivial things, and theſe of vain bugbears; ſo we are afraid of both.

Only purſue your ſtudies; and you will find, that ſome things, the more they are dreaded, are the leſs to be feared: the laſt evil is nothing: Death approaches: what then? you might have been afraid of him, could he abide with you; but he no ſooner comes, than he is gone *(c)*. It is hard however, you ſay, to bring your mind to a contempt of life. See you not upon what frivolous occaſions it is often contemned? One hangs himſelf, at the door of his cruel miſtreſs; another breaks his neck from the top of an houſe (*d*), to avoid the threatening wrath of his maſter; and another, when he has played the runaway, ſtabs himſelf, to prevent his being carried home.

Think you that Virtue cannot as effectually diſſipate the fear of Death, as baſe timidity? No man can enjoy life with complacency, who is too ſollicitous to prolong it, and eſteems as the greateſt happineſs the number of Conſuls he lives to ſee. Let ſuch be your daily meditation, as will enable you, with an equal mind, at any time, to let go your hold of life; which ſome are ſo tenacious of, as to embrace it with painful endurance: like thoſe, who, being carried along by a torrent, catch at briars, or any thing, be it ever ſo ſharp, that is within their reach. Moſt men are apt to waver, miſerably, between the fear of death, and the torments of life. They are unwilling to live, and know not how to die (*e*). Render life therefore pleaſant to you, by caſting away all ſollicitude about it. No good can truly delight the poſſeſſor, unleſs his mind be prepared againſt the loſs of it: and no loſs is eaſier to be borne, than of that which cannot be recalled, or again expected. Against all accidents therefore, which even the most mighty are subject to, exhort and harden yourself continually. Consider that a fatherless child (*f*), and an eunuch, bore sentence against the life of *Pompey*, and put it in execution. A cruel and insolent *Parthian* slew *Crassus* (*g*). *Caius Cæsar* (*h*) commanded *Lepidus* to bow down his neck to the stroke of *Decimus* the tribune; and he did the same himself to the rake *Chærea*. Fortune hath advanced no one so high, as not to threaten him with the same treatment, with which she had permitted him to treat others. Trust not your present tranquillity. The sea in a moment is ruffled into a storm; and the ships that were dancing in safety upon the wave, are, in that instant, wrecked, and swallowed up. Consider that a robber as well as an enemy may cut your throat: and supposing you are safe from any higher power; life and death (*i*) are at the will of a menial servant: yes; let any one not fear death, and he is master of your life. Recollect the instances you have known of those, who have fallen by domestic treachery, either by open force, or surprize; and you will find that as many have perished by the resentment of slaves, as of kings. What avails it therefore to you, how powerful he is, whom you are afraid of; if what you fear, is in every one's power to execute? Or if you should be taken by an enemy, and he should command you to be led where he pleases, even to death; why do you deceive yourself, and think this the first time of your suffering that, which you have daily undergone! For I affirm that, from the hour you was born, Nature led you the same way (*k*). In these and the like considerations the mind must be continually exercised; if, with a pleasing satisfaction, you would expect that last hour, which makes all the rest disagreeable.

But to conclude this epistle; be pleased to accept a sentence, which, this very day, gave me no small delight; and which flower I likewise stole from another's garden. Magnæ divitiæ sunt lege naturæ composita paupertas. *Poverty measured by the law of Nature is great riches.* Now, do you know what this law of nature requires? Only not to hunger, not to thirst, or be cold for want of clothing. To expel hunger and thirst, there is no necessity of sitting in a palace, and submitting to the supercilious brow, and contumelious favour of the rich and great: there is no necessity of sailing upon the deep, or of following the camp. What nature wants is every-where to be found, and attainable without much difficulty: whereas ſuperfluities require the ſweat of the brow; for theſe we are obliged to dreſs anew; are compelled to grow old in the field; and driven to foreign ſhores. A ſufficiency is always at hand.

ANNOTATIONS, &c.

(a) See Ep. 1. Traditi boni perpetua poſſeſſio eſt, &c. *The poſſeſſion of good is everlaſting; no one who hath once learned virtue can forget it*, &c.

(b) See Ep. xxiv. cxv. Lucret. ii. 54.

Nam veluti pueri trepidant, atque omnia cæcis
In tenebris metuunt: ſic nos in luce timemus.
Interdum nihilo quæ ſunt metuenda magis, quam
Quæ pueri in tenebris pavitant ſinguntque futura.
For like as children in the dark of night
Tremble and ſtart; ſo we ev'n in the light;
Fearful like them, of ſhadows, light and vain,
The idle fancies of a childiſh brain.

(c) *Than he is gone*] How deep implanted in the breaſt of man
The dread of death! I ſing its ſovereign cure.
Why ſtart at death? Where is he? Death arriv'd,
Is paſt; not come, or gone; he's never *here*.
Imagination's fool, and *Error's* wretch,
Man makes a death which Nature never made;
Then on the point of his own fancy falls,
And feels a thouſand deaths in fearing one. *Young.*

(d) *Another breaks his neck*] Hic ſe præcipitem tecto dedit, ille flagellis
Ad mortem cæſus. *Hor.*
A deſperate leap one luckleſs caitiff tries;
Torn by the flagrant laſh another dies. Francis.

(e) *Unwilling to live*] Such the rebuke of *Epictetus*. Θαυμαςοὶ ἄνθρωποι, μήτε ζῆν θέλοντες, μήτε αποθνήσκειν. *Strange men as ye are, who are neither willing to live, nor to die.*

(f) *A fatherleſs child*] A ſtronger inſtance of the inſtability of human greatneſs is ſcarce to be found in hiſtory than this, the fall and death of *Pompey* the Great: having fled to Egypt for protection in his laſt diſtreſs, where reigned young *Ptolemy*, (who was juſt come of age, and had been highly obliged to *Pompey*, for the friendſhip and favour which he had ſhewn his father) he was there aſſaſſinated, (by order of the young King, and one *Pothinus*, his tutor, and prime miniſter of ſtate) his head cut off, and his body thrown and expoſed upon the ſhore.——But not long after, the generous *Cæſar* ordered *Pothinus*, and *Achillas* the aſſaſſin, to be ſlain; and the young King, having been overthrown in battle, fled away in diſguiſe, and was never heard of afterwards. *See Plutarch's* Life of *Pompey*.

(g) *M. Craſſus* killed in a tumult by a Parthian, called *Pomaxaithres*. His ſon was before ſlain by the Parthians; and his head brought to his father by way of inſult. *See his Life in* Plutarch.

(h) *Caius Cæſar*] *Caligula*, Emperor, ſlain by *Caſſius Chærea*, tribune of the Prætorian Cohort, in the 29th year of his age, and the 4th of his reign. *See his Life by* Suetonius.

(i) *Life and Death*] Contempſit omnes ille, qui mortem prius. *Sen.*
Nihil eſt difficile perſuadere, perſuaſis mori. *Juſtin.*
There is nothing ſo difficult but what you may perſuade a man to do, who is not afraid to die.

(k) *Nature led you the ſame way*] See Epiſt. l, xxiv.

EPISTLE V*.

Against the Affectation of Singularity—On Hope and Fear.

IT demands my approbation, and gives me infinite pleaſure, to find, *Lucilius*, that you purſue your ſtudies with attention, and make it the chief, to improve daily in goodneſs and virtue. I not only exhort, but earneſtly beſeech you, to perſevere. But this too I muſt adviſe you, that you affect not to be ſingular, either in your dreſs, or manner of life; like thoſe who are ambitious, not with a deſign of doing any good, but of being taken notice of *(a)*. Pretend not to an uncouth habit, ſlovenly to neglect the hair and beard, to declare a ſworn averſion to a piece of plate, to lie on the ground, or to exhibit any other extraordinary mark of perverſe ambition *(b)*. The very name of *Philoſophy*, however modeſtly and decently purſued, is inviduous enough, and ever ſubject to calumny. What if we have determined to withdraw ourſelves from the ordinary converſe of men; let all the difference lie *within*, but let our outward appearance *(c)* be the ſame with that of other people. Let not the outer garment be either gawdy, or mean and ſordid: let us not ſigh after plate, ſilver or gold, emboſſed, and decorated with arms and mottos; nor think it a ſign of frugality to be quite deſtitute either of gold or ſilver: let us act upon this principle, not to lead a life *contrary* to the generality of men, but a better *(d)*: otherwiſe, they, whom we propoſe to inſtruct and reform, will fly from and avoid us; beſides, our converſants will think nothing worthy their imitation, when they are afraid they muſt imitate all we do. Now this is what philoſophy chiefly recommends to her pupils, *ſound ſenſe, common humanity*, and the *ſocial virtues*; ſo as to converſe with thoſe, whom the diſparity of our profeſſion ſeparates us from.

Let us alſo beware, leſt intending to be admired, we make ourſelves ridiculous and odious. Our buſineſs is to live according to Nature *(e)*; but it is contrary to Nature, to afflict the body, to hate decency and cleanlineſs, and to diet one's ſelf, not only with cheap food, but with ſuch as is groſs and horrid *(f)*. As it is luxury to covet dainties, it is folly and madneſs to reject ſuch things as are in common uſe and eaſily to be obtained. Philoſophy preaches temperance and frugality, not ſevere mortification: and frugality may be decent, and not inelegant. This then is the mean that I ſhould chuſe, a life tempered between politeneſs and vulgarity; let all men admire it, but at the ſame time ſee and acknowledge, that there is nothing ſo extraordinary in it, but what is practicable. What then? Muſt we act, in all reſpects, like other men? Shall there be no difference between us and the commonalty? Yes ſurely; he will find a great difference, who more narrowly inſpects our conduct. Whoever comes into a houſe of ours, let him admire the *man*, and not the furniture. He is great, who uſeth his earthen veſſels as contentedly as if they were ſilver; nor leſs to be eſteemed is he, who uſeth ſilver not more proudly than if it was earthenware. It betrays a weak mind not to be ſufficient for the ſupport of wealth.

But to make you a ſmall preſent of the fruit I gathered to-day, know, that I have learned from our *Hecaton* (*g*), that to ſet bounds to our deſires is a ſure remedy againſt fear. Deſines timere, ſi ſperare deſieris. *If you ceaſe to hope*, ſays he, *you will ceaſe to fear*. But you will ſay, how can things ſo very diſſimilar have any effect upon each other? I will tell you; diſſimilar as they ſeem to be, there is a connection between them. As the ſame chain holds both the priſoner and his guard (*h*), ſo do theſe two affections, however contrary they may ſeem to each other, march linked together: and fear follows hope. Nor do I wonder at this; ſince both belong to a mind in ſuſpenſe; and anxious concerning what may happen. But the principal cauſe of both is, that we diſregard the preſent, and extend our views to things at a diſtance. Forecaſt therefore, an indiſputable good to man, is turned into evil. Brute beaſts fly ſuch dangers as they are ſenſible of; and, having eſcaped them, reſt ſecure. But we are tortured, both with what is paſt, and with what is to come. Thus many things, really good in themſelves, hurt us: for, memory recalls, and forecaſt anticipates, the torment of fear. No one is wretched from what is preſent only.

ANNO-

ANNOTATIONS, &c.

* According to my first design, I had inscribed this Epistle to my late friend Dr. Rawlinson: the propriety of it, I believe, would not be doubted by those who knew him.

(a) Of being taken notice of] Conspici. In Scripture language, πρὸς τὸ θεαθῆναι τοῖς ἀνθρώποις, *To be seen of men.* Matth. xxiii. v.—*Horace* ridicules some of his time, who in like manner affected to be thought poets.

> Nanciscetur enim nomen pretiumque poetæ—
> Si tribus Anticyris caput insanabile nunquam
> Tonsori Licino commiserit.——
> *A poet's fame and fortune sure to gain,*
> *If long their beards; incurable their brain.* Francis.

(b) Muretus observes, that not only wisdom, but oftentimes ambition affects a sordid garb; nor are any men more sollicitous for fame and glory, than they who pursue it under a pretence of flying from it.

So when *Diogenes*, the cynic, told *Plato*, " that he despised and trampled upon his pride," " *True, said* Plato, *you do so; but with more pride.*"—And *Aristotle* imputes the sordid and negligent dress of the *Lacedæmonians* to pride and arrogance.

(c) Our outward appearance] Though the Apostle says *our conversation is in heaven*, Phil. iii. 20, *yet he condescends to be made all things to all men, that, at least, he might save some.* 1 Cor. ix. 18, 22.

(d) But a better] I should be sorry, if any of my brethren, who may chance to read this Epistle, did not effectually feel this, and other excellent precepts exhibited herein.

(e) According to Nature] See Epist. 41. De vit. beat. c. 3.

(f) Erasmus justly thinks this applicable to the beastly crew of monks and friers, and all such as affect singularity and unnecessary wretchedness in dress and diet. And the ingenious *Francis Osborne* reckons this among the causes of the defection from the church of *Rome.* " The seeking to maintain a greater " shew of piety, than was suitable to human frailty and the comforts of life." The frier's habit being no less nasty than unseemly, and therefore shunned by nicer judgments, and those of parts, not so capable of temptation from any thing, as pleasure and profit. Or if such austerity was called for, in relation to external zeal, (the parade of all religions, and fit to be mustered up often in the eyes of the people) yet the generality might have been left to more decent accoutrements, by which they had become sociable unto others, and not loathsome to themselves.

(g) Hecaton, the Stoic philosopher, a disciple of *Panætius.* He lived at *Rhodes.*

(h) And his guard] This sort of military guard *Manilius* supposed born under the influence of the constellation *Andromeda.*

> Vinctorum Dominus, sociusque in parte catenæ,
> Interdum pœnis innoxia corpora servat *l.* 5.
> *The prisoner's keeper, partner of his chain,*
> *Oft saves the guiltless from the threaten'd pain.* See Ep. 70 and 78.

EPISTLE

EPISTLE VI.

On Friendſhip and Converſation. (*a*)

I AM very ſenſible, *Lucilius*, that I am not only improved (*a*), but, as it were, transformed (*b*); and yet I pretend not to ſay, or expect, that there is nothing, in the common courſe of life, that requires further improvement. There are many things that ſtill call for reformation: ſome affections to be checked and lowered, others to be encouraged and raiſed. And indeed I think this is a ſign of the mind's being improved, when it can ſee thoſe faults, of which it was ignorant before. In ſome maladies, a ſenſibility of pain gives hopes of recovery. I was therefore deſirous to acquaint you with my ſudden change; as I then began to have more confidence of our friendſhip; *that* true friendſhip, which neither hope, nor fear, nor any intereſted view can diſunite; *that*, which men carry to the laſt, and for which they would not ſcruple to die. I could name ſeveral, who wanted not a friend (*c*), but friendſhip. Now this cannot happen, where minds are poſſeſſed with an uniformity of will, to act honourably. And why can it not? Becauſe they know that all things, and more eſpecially adverſity, are to be held in common.

You cannot imagine what new improvements I collect every day. "Inform me, you ſay, of the means, which you have experimentally found of ſo great efficacy." It is my deſire ſo to do: I will tranſmit every thing to you; and am glad to learn, in order to inſtruct (*d*). Nor indeed would any thing give me pleaſure, however excellent and ſalutary it might be, was I to keep the knowledge of it to myſelf. Was wiſdom offered me under ſuch reſtriction, as to be obliged to conceal it, I would reject it. No enjoyment whatever can be agreeable without participation. I will therefore lend you the books themſelves; and that you may not waſte much time, in ſearching after the uſeful and profitable, as it lies ſcattered in ſeveral places, I will ſet ſome mark, *(in the margin, or otherwiſe)* whereby you may immediately recur to thoſe paſſages, which I both approve and admire.

Yet

Yet after all (*e*), converſation and familiarity will have better effect than any thing written, or a formal ſpeech. You muſt come hither, and be preſent with us; firſt, becauſe men give greater credit to their eyes, than to their ears; and ſecondly, the way by precept is long and tedious; whereas that of example is ſhort and powerful. *Cleanthes* had never reſembled *Zeno*, if he had been ſatisfied only with his lectures. He was intimate with him, privy to all his ſecrets, and diligently obſerved, whether he lived up to his own rule. *Plato* and *Ariſtotle* (*f*), and the whole tribe of philoſophers of various ſects (*g*), learned more from the morals of *Socrates*, than from his preachments. It was not the ſchool of *Epicurus*, but familiarity that made *Metrodorus* (*h*), *Hermachus*, and *Polyænus*, ſo eminent in the world. Nor do I invite you hither, merely for *your* good, but my own; as in conference each may aſſiſt the other in many points. In the mean while, as, according to cuſtom, I owe you every day ſomething by way of a ſmall preſent, I will inform you, wherein *Hecaton* to-day gave me great pleaſure: " *Do you aſk*, ſays he, *what improvement I have made of late?*— Amicum eſſe mihi cœpi; *I have learned to be a friend to myſelf*. Great improvement this indeed! Such a one can never be ſaid to be alone: for know, that he, who is a friend to himſelf, is a friend to all mankind.

ANNOTATIONS, &c.

(*a*) There is an excellent commentary on this ſubject in *Plutarch*, entitled, *How a man may know the improvement he makes in virtue.*

(*b*) *Transformed*] Tran-figurari, which relates entirely to the *mind*, or *inner man*. So the Apoſtle— *Circumciſion availeth nothing, nor uncircumciſion, but a new creature.* Gal. 6. xv. If a man be in Chriſt, he is *a new creature. Old things are paſſed away, behold, all things are become new.* II Cor. 5. 17.

(*c*) *A friend*] i. e. A common friend. *See* Epiſt. iii.

(*d*) *I am glad to learn, in order to inſtruct*] Cato ap. Cic. de Fin. 3.——Impellimur natura ut prodeſſe velimus, imprimiſque docendo rationibuſque prudentiæ tradendis. Itaque non facile eſt invenire, qui quod ſciat ipſe, non tradat alteri. *A natural impulſe directs every man to do good to as many as he can, and eſpecially by inſtructing and forming them to the purpoſes of wiſdom. And indeed it is not eaſy to find a man who is not communicative to another of the knowledge he poſſeſſes himſelf. We therefore have a propenſity to teach as well as to learn.*

So the old Poet *Lucilius* ——Id me.

Nolo ſcire mihi, cujus ſum conſcius ſolus,
Ne damnum faciam. Scire eſt neſcire, niſi id me
Scire alius ſcierit.——

Which *Perſius* in fewer words——

Scire tuum nihil eſt, niſi te ſcire hoc ſciat alter.
For it is nothing worth that lies conceal'd:
And ſcience is not ſcience till reveal'd. Dryden.

(*e*) *Yet after all*] Plus tamen tibi viva vox—proderit.
—Præterea multo magis, ut vulgo dicitur, *viva vox* afficit.
Nam licet acriora sint quæ legas, altius tamen in animo
Sedent quæ pronuntiatio, vultus, habitus, gestus etiam dicentis affigit.
Plin. Ep. iii. l. 2.

Besides, according to the proverb, what the ear hears stands in no need to be guessed at. *And suppose what you read in itself more affecting, yet certainly the pronunciation, the countenance, the dress, the gesture, of an orator, imprint his lessons more deeply upon the mind.*

(*f*) *Aristotle*] *Lipsius* observes here that there must be some mistake, or that *Seneca* wrote too hastily; for so far was *Aristotle* from conversing with *Socrates*, that he never saw him: as *Socrates* died in the first year of the 95th *Olympiad*, or according to *Diodorus* in the 97th; and *Aristotle* was born in the first year of the 99th, according to *Laertius*, *Dionysius*, *A. Gellius*, *Eusebius*, and others. And consequently *Ammonius* is likewise mistaken; when in his life of *Aristotle* he talks of his living three years with *Socrates*.

(*g*) *Of various sects*] Hæc autem, ut ex Appennino, fluminum, sic ex communi sapientiam jugo sunt doctrinarum facta divortia.—Cic. de Orat. l. 3. 19. *From this common source of philosophy (the Discourses of* Socrates) *as rivers from the* Appenines, *learning began to run in different channels*; &c. You know, says *Aristides* to *Socrates*, that I never learned any thing from you professedly; yet great benefit did I reap from you while in the same house; still greater, if at any time in the same room; and much more when my eyes were fixed upon you, as you was speaking; but most of all, when I was sitting by you, and hung as it were upon your garment. *Plato* in *Theage*.

(*h*) *Metrodorus*] There were two of this name, disciples of *Epicurus*: the one *Metrodorus*, of *Stratonica*; who left *Epicurus*, and followed *Carneades*: the other, the Athenian, who still kept with *Socrates*, and in many treatises propagated his doctrine; who is the person here spoken of.

Hermachus) The son of *Agemarchus*, of *Mitylene*, who succeeded *Epicurus* in his school.

Polyænus) The son of *Athenodorus* of *Lampsaca*. He was the disciple of *Epicurus*, but died before him.

(*i*) *I have learned*] Cæpi. This word not in the MS. nor the last sentence, Qui sibi amicus est.—So in the old French, which renders the place thus: sçhaches que chacun peut avoir un tel amy. *Know that it is in the power of any one to have such a friend.* But it is a stoical maxim, *That he who loves himself*, i. e. who studies wisdom and goodness, *will also love others*. Nec sibi, sed toti genitum se, credere mundo, *Not born as for himself, but all the world.*

EPISTLE VII.

On public Shows, particularly the Gladiators (a)*—and Converse with the World.*

Do you ask, *Lucilius*, what I would have you principally to avoid? The rabble. You are not yet strong enough to be safe among the many. I will confess to you my own weakness: when I venture abroad, I never return the ſame moral man I went out. What I ſettled before, is diſcompoſed; or ſomething that I rejected returns. It is with us, who are juſt recovered from ſome inveterate diſorder, as with thoſe who, by long indiſpoſition, are ſo weakened, that the being brought into the air, gives them a diſagreeable ſenſation.

Intercourſe with the world (*b*) is prejudicial: ſome one or other, either by example or diſcourſe, will paint vice in ſuch agreeable colours, as to taint the mind inſenſibly; ſo that the more company we keep, the greater is our danger. But nothing is more hurtful to a good diſpoſition than to while the time away at ſome public ſhew: for then vice ſteals upon us more eaſily under the maſque of pleaſure. Would you think it? I really return from ſuch entertainments, more covetous, more ambitious, more diſſolute, nay, even more cruel and inhuman, from having converſed with men. By chance, I fell in with a public ſhow at *mid-day*; expecting ſome ſport, buffoonery, or other relaxation, when the eyes of the ſpectators had been ſatiated with the ſight of human gore. Nothing leſs: all the bloody deeds of the morning were mere mercy: for now, all trifling apart, they commit downright murder: the combatants have nothing to ſhield the body: they are expoſed to every ſtroke of their antagoniſt; and every ſtroke is a wound: and this ſome prefer to their fighting in pairs, matched, and well accoutred; or of ſuch as were men of great art and experience in the profeſſion: and why ſhould they not? There is no helmet or ſhield to repel the blow: no defence, no art: for theſe are but ſo many balks and delays of death. In the morning men are expoſed to lions and bears: at noon to the ſpectators themſelves. Menſlayers are ordered out againſt one another; and the conqueror is detained for another ſlaughter. Death alone puts an end to this buſineſs; while fire and ſword are employed as inſtruments. And all this is carried on after the ordinary ſlaughter of the day is over. But ſome one hath committed a theft: what then? He deſerves to be hanged: another ſlew a man; it is but juſt he ſhould be ſlain himſelf. And what haſt thou deſerved, O wretch, who canſt take delight in theſe horrid ſolemnities (*c*)? "*Kill, burn, ſcourge,*" is all the cry. "*Why is be ſo afraid of the ſword's point? Why is be ſo timorous to kill? Why does be not die more manfully?*" They are urged on with ſtripes, if they refuſe to encounter; and are obliged to give and take wounds with a forward and open breaſt. Is the appointed ſhow at a ſtand, that ſomething may be doing, they are called out to cut one another's throats. But, do you not conſider, that bad examples often recoil to the prejudice of thoſe who ſet them? Thank the immortal gods, that you are inſtructing him (*d*) to be cruel, who cannot learn.

Hence it is manifeſt, that a mind, that is tender and not over-tenacious of what is right, is not to be entruſted with the converſe of *the many*. Vice is catching. The varying populace can ſhake a *Socrates*, a *Cato* or a *Lælius*, from his purpoſe; ſo that none of us, however poliſhed the diſpoſition, can ſtand againſt the violence of vices, that aſſail us in ſuch a numerous body. Nay, even one example of luxury, or avarice, is capable of doing much miſchief. A delicate coxcomb by degrees ſoftens and effeminates his converſants: a rich neighbour incites covetouſneſs: an ill-minded man is apt to taint with malignity his companion, however ſimple and candid.

What then, think you, muſt be the conſequence when a man ſubjects himſelf to every public attack? You muſt either imitate, or hate the aſſailants: both are to be avoided; leſt, you become like the bad, becauſe they are many; or inimical to many, becauſe unlike them. Retire therefore into thyſelf, as much as poſſible: converſe with thoſe, who are capable of making you better; and admit thoſe, whom you think yourſelf capable of inſtructing. Theſe are reciprocal duties. Men often learn, while they teach. There is no reaſon however, that the glory of publiſhing your ingenuity ſhould introduce you to the public, either by way of recital, or diſpute: which indeed I ſhould not be averſe to, was your art adapted to the level of the vulgar: ſcarce any one can underſtand you: or if one or two of better parts than ordinary, ſhould by chance fall in your way, it will demand ſome pains to inſtruct them, and bring them to your taſte. "For whom then, you will ſay, have you taken ſo much pains to learn?" Fear not; your time was not thrown away; if it was for yourſelf only.

But, that I may not have learned all that I have picked up to-day for myſelf alone; I will communicate with you three ſentences of great importance, though almoſt in the ſame ſenſe. One of which I ſhall pay you, as the uſual debt; and I beg your acceptance of the other two beforehand. *Democritus* ſaith, unus mihi pro populo eſt et populus pro uno, *One is to me*

 a thouſand,

a thouſand, and a thouſand as one. And well hath he ſpoke, (whoever he was, for the author is not known) who to one that aſked him, "*why beſpent ſo much diligence in an art, which but few could be the better for?*" replied, ſatis ſunt mihi pauci, ſatis eſt unus, ſatis eſt nullus, *A few are enough for me, nay, one is enough, or no one at all.* And more excellent is the third: when *Epicurus* was writing to one of his fellow-ſtudents, *Theſe things*, ſays he, *I write not to the many, but to you alone*; ſatis enim magnum alter alteri theatrum ſumus, *for we are to each other a theatre large enough.* Theſe, my *Lucilius*, are the things which I would have you treaſure up in your mind, that you may deſpiſe the vain pleaſure, that accrues from the approbation of the world (*e*). Many praiſe thee: but are you ſatisfied with yourſelf, if you are what they take you for and applaud? Let your goodneſs be approved *within*.

ANNOTATIONS, &c.

(*a*) *The gladiators*] The firſt ſhow of gladiators exhibited at *Rome*, was that of *M.* and *D. Brutus*, upon the death of their father, A. U. C. 489, ante Chriſtum, 264. But the honour of removing this barbarity out of the Roman world, was reſerved for *Conſtantine* the Great, A. U. C. 1096, about 600 years after their firſt inſtitution; yet under *Conſtantius*, *Theodoſius*, and *Valentinian*, the ſame cruel humour began to revive; 'till a final ſtop was put to it by the Emperor *Honorius*, A. D. 396. —There were ſeveral orders or kinds of gladiators who owed their diſtinction to their country, their arms, their way of fighting, and the like. The three kinds mentioned in this Epiſtle, are the *Meridiani*, who engaged in the afternoon; the *Poſtulatitii*, commonly men of great ſkill and experience, whom the people particularly deſired the Emperor to produce; and the *Ordinarii*, ſuch as were preſented according to the common manner, and at the uſual time, and fought the ordinary way. *Kennett's Roman Antiq.*

(*b*) *Intercourſe with the world*] When I who paſs a great part, very much the greateſt part of my life alone, ſally forth into the world, I am very far from expecting to improve myſelf, by the converſation I find there; and ſtill further from caring one jot for what paſſes there.

Bolingbroke, Letter 212, vol. ii.

In driving me out of party, they have driven me out of curſed company; and in ſtripping me of titles, rank, and eſtate, and ſuch trinkets, which every man, that will, may ſpare, they have given me that which no man can be happy without. *Id.* vol. ix. p. 45.

(*c*) *Horrid ſolemnities*] Dr. *Kennett* concludes his account of the gladiators with the following paſſage from *Cicero*.—Crudele Gladiatorum ſpectaculum et inhumanum nonnullis videri ſolet, &c. *The ſhows of the gladiators may poſſibly to ſome perſons ſeem barbarous and inhuman; and indeed, as the caſe now ſtands, I cannot ſay that the cenſure is unjuſt: but in thoſe times, when only guilty perſons were the combatants, the ear perhaps might receive better inſtructions; but it is impoſſible that any thing which affects the eyes, ſhould fortify us with more ſucceſs againſt the aſſaults of grief and death.* Tuſc. Qu. 2. See Epiſt. xcv.

(*d*) *Inſtructing him*] He is ſuppoſed to mean the Emperor *Nero*, who at the beginning of his reign was far from being cruel. His predeceſſor *Claudius*, when addreſſed by ſome of theſe poor wretches, as they paſſed before him, with, *Ave, Imperator, morituri te ſalutant*, returned in anſwer. *Avete vos!* which when they would gladly have interpreted as an act of favour, and a grant of their lives, he ſoon gave them to underſtand, that it proceeded from the contrary principle of barbarous cruelty and inſenſibility *Suet. Tacit* Ann. xiv.

(*e*) *The approbation of the multitude*] Or do I ſeek, ſaith the Apoſtle, *to pleaſe men? for if I yet pleaſed men, I ſhould not be the ſervant of Chriſt.* Gal. i. 10.

EPISTLE VIII.

On Temperance, and the Benefit of Philosophy.

YOU feem, *Lucilius*, to be furprized, that I fhould command you to fhun the public, to retire, and reft fatisfied with the complacency of your own confcience: as if I was regardlefs both of my own, and the precepts of my principals *(a)*, who recommend an active life: know then it is for this purpofe I conceal myfelf, and fhut my doors; that I may fee no one, in order to profit many. No day, I can affure you, paffes by unemployed: and even part of the night I claim for ftudy. I lie down indeed, but keep my eyes, tired and heavy as they are, ftill at work. Moreover, I have withdrawn myfelf not only from men, but from all manner of worldly affairs, even my own: I am at work for pofterity *(b)*: I am continually writing fomething, I hope for their benefit; intending to treat them with fome falutary prefcriptions, and the compofition of certain medicines, that I myfelf have happily experienced, in my own malady; which if not perfectly cured, hath been prevented from growing worfe. I am endeavouring to fhew to others the right path, which I am perfuaded I have found, after much wearinefs and travail.—Beware of thofe things, I fay, which are apt to pleafe the vulgar, and are merely accidental; be fufpicious and diftruftful of every cafual good. It is for wild beafts, and fifh, to be deceived by fome alluring bait. Think ye that fuch and fuch things are the effects of fortune (*c*)? No; they are fnares. Whofoever would lead a fafe and pleafant life, let him avoid fuch falfe and treacherous benefits, which thinking to catch, we are miferably deceived; and caught ourfelves, as with birdlime (*d*). An ambitious courfe of life leads to a precipice: the end of an high ftation is, to fall: for it is not in our power to ftop, when our feeming happinefs hath taken a wrong bias. Either abide firm in your ftation, or confide in yourfelf (*e*). So fhall not Fortune overthrow you, but only dafh againft you, like a wave, and be beat back again.

Maintain therefore this found and falutary way of living: fo far only to indulge the body, as to preferve it in good health *(f)*. It muft be treated more roughly, if you would have it obedient, or ferviceable, to the foul (*g*). Food fatisfies hunger; let drink affuage thirft; clothes keep off the cold, and

and an houſe defend you, from whatever elſe might injure the body: it matters not whether the houſe be of turf, or foreign marble: a man may be as ſafe and happy under a thatched, as under a golden roof. Deſpiſe the ſuperfluities, which needleſs labour acquires, by way of ornament or credit. Think, there is nothing admirable in thee, but the ſoul (*b*). Nothing ſo great, as to be compared with the greatneſs of it. Now, while I am meditating on theſe reflections, and am deſirous to convey them to poſterity, ſeem I not to be doing more good, than in being ready, when called upon, to bail my friend, or to be witneſs to his will, or to give him my hand and ſuffrage in the ſenate, when a candidate for ſome public office? Believe me, they who ſeem to be doing little or nothing, are ſometimes engaged in matters of the greateſt moment, while they are employing themſelves on things, at the ſame time, both human and divine.

But to conclude this Epiſtle, and therein diſcharge my uſual payment; not out of my own ſtock I confeſs; for I have ſtill in hand *Epicurus*; in whom I this day read, Philoſophiæ ſervias oportet, ut tibi contingat vera libertas; *you muſt be the ſlave of philoſophy, if you deſire to enjoy true liberty.* He that hath once ſubjected and delivered himſelf up to her, is inſtantly made free: for, this her ſervice, I ſay, is perfect freedom (*i*). Perhaps, you may aſk me, why I am ſo fond of reciting the excellent ſayings of *Epicurus*, neglectful of thoſe of my own ſchool? Are not theſe then of *Epicurus* ſpoken in general, and ſuitable to every ſect? How many things occur which are ſaid or might have been ſaid by the philoſophers? Not to mention the tragedians, or our *togatæ*, which are ſometimes ſerious, being a ſort of a tragi-comedy? How many excellent ſentences do we find even in a *Mime* or farce? There are ſeveral in *Publius* full worthy the buſkin: one I ſhall quote, which belongs to philoſophy and the ſubject before us; where he denies all caſual things to be properly our own:

> Alienum eſt omne, quicquid optando venit.
> *What we muſt wiſh for, is a foreign good.*

But I remember one from you, *Lucilius*, which I think better, and more terſe;—

> Non eſt tuum, fortuna quod fecit tuum.
> *That is not thine, which you to fortune owe.*

And

And I cannot paſs by another ſaying of your's, which I ſtill prefer to the foregoing—

> Dari bonum quod potuit, auferri poteſt.
> *The good that's giv'n, may be taken from us.*

Obſerve, I expect no acquittance for theſe; what I now ſend you, is your own.

ANNOTATIONS, &c.

(*a*) *The precepts of my principals*] *Zeno, Chryſippus*, and others of the Stoics aſſert, that a wiſe man ſhould not be ſo reſerved, as, when called upon, to refuſe the management of public affairs; knowing that he may be the means to prevent the growth of vice; and to excite his fellow citizens to virtuous actions: nay, that they are the only perſons fit for magiſtracy and judicature. *Diog. Laert.*

(*b*) *At work for poſterity*] The great *Cato*, invincible as he was, and often the leader of armies, thought however that he could be of more ſervice to the commonwealth by the publication of his military diſcipline in writing: ſince brave actions benefit only the preſent age; but ſuch things, as are wrote for the public good, laſt for ever. *Veget. de re Mil.* l. 2. —What Engliſhman can read this, without being put in mind, to his great ſorrow and deteſtation, of the horrid tranſactions of laſt week (June 12, 1780), when the houſe of that great and good man, Lord Mansfield, Chief Juſtice of England, was cauſeleſsly attacked; and, with the rich furniture, all the notes and obſervations of ſo conſummate a lawyer and judge, (the whole work and labour of a long life, contained in a number of manuſcript volumes and papers) were all committed to the flames with undiſtinguiſhing rage, and conſumed, by the moſt villainous crew of inſurgents that ever diſgraced a people!

(*c*) *Such gifts*] *Pliny* has an excellent Epiſtle to this purpoſe (l. ix. ep. 30) *My opinion is, that a man who would be truly bountiful ought to exert his liberality, towards his country, his neighbour, his relations, his friends, and let me ſay, by way of diſtinction, his* friends in the greateſt indigence. (Such a precaution Lord *Orrery* obſerves, was neceſſary in an age, where liberality ſeldom was directed by innate goodneſs of heart, but often ſkulked under the maſk of craft and deſign) *not like thoſe perſons who chuſe to apply their gifts, only where they ſee a probability of finding a moſt ample return. Such gifts are like baited hooks. They are not meant to beſtow your own property, but the property of others.* Alluding to the *Hæredipetæ* or *Captatores*, who were ſo numerous a band of miſcreants in the days of *Pliny*, that they are mentioned with ridicule and abhorrence, by all the ſatyriſts of that time; and particularly by *Martial*—To *Gargalianus*, (l. iv. 56.)

> Munera quòd ſenibus viduiſque ingentia mittis
> Vis te munificum Gargaliane vocem?
> Sordidius nihil eſt, nihil eſt te ſpurcius uno,
> Qui potes inſidias dona vocare tuas.
> Sic avidis fallax indulget piſcibus hamus:
> Callida ſic ſtultas decipit eſca feras.
> Quid ſit largiri, quid ſit donare, docebo;
> Si neſcis: dona Gargaliane mihi.

> *For gifts you to the old and widows ſend,*
> *Would you,* Gargal. *be deem'd a generous friend?*
> *Nothing can be more ſordid or more baſe,*
> *To think ſuch baits will for kind preſents paſs:*

Anglers thus hooks for greedy fish prepare;
And silly beasts are driv'n into a snare.
How to be truly generous would you know,
Something on me, for friendship sake, bestow.

(*d*) *And caught themselves*] Vid. Ep. 119. Valer. l. 9. c. 4. Proculdubio hic non possedit divitias, sed a divitiis possessus est.—*Plin.* Ep. sup. cit. Ea invasit homines habendi cupido ut possideri magis quam possidere videantur. *The thirst of gain is so excessive, that men seem to be possessed by their wealth, not to possess it.*—Bionys vetus dictum ad avarum, Ουκ οὗτος τὴν οὐσίαν κέκτηται, ἀλλ' ἡ οὐσία τοῦτον. Sic D. Cyprian. ad donat. l. 2. Vid. Not. ad Sidon. Apoll. p. 512.

(*e*) *Or confide in yourself*] I read this passage with *Gronovius*, Aut statum rectus, aut temet tene. *Remain firm in your place or station, without being allured by any blandishment of fortune*; or, if you have been so already, check your pursuit, so as still to be master of yourself, and not subject altogether to her caprice. *So, the old French*, Il faut donc se contenter de choses quò sont bounes et certaines, ou plutôt de soi meme.—*Muretus*, Aut rectus sta, aut semel fuge.—*Malherbe*, Il faut savire teste, ou s'ensuir.

(*f*) *In good health.*] Our divine precept runs much higher, *Take no thought for your life what ye shall eat; neither for the body what ye shall put on.—But rather seek ye the kingdom of God, and all things shall be added to you.* Matth. vi. 31.

(*g*) *To the soul.*] *If thine eye offend thee pluck it out*; Matth. 5. 19. And let Christians also remember what the Apostle saith, *If ye live after the flesh ye shall die; but if, through the spirit, ye mortify the deeds of the body, ye shall live.* Rom. 8. 3. *Therefore*, says he, *I keep under my body and bring it into subjection.* 1 Cor. 9. 27. *And who indeed is the perfect man*, saith St. James, *but he that is able to bridle the whole body?* 8. 2.

(*h*) *But the soul*] *For what is a man profited, if he should gain the whole world, and lose his own soul? or, what shall a man give in exchange for his soul?* Matth. 16. 26.

(*i*) *Perfect freedom*] *Ye shall know the truth, and the truth shall make you free.* John 8. 32.—*Stand fast in the liberty, wherewith Christ hath made you free.* Gal. 3. 1. *If then the Son shall make you free, ye shall be free indeed.* John 8. 56.—See Ep. 75. ad fin.

EPISTLE IX.

On Friendship; Self-Complacency, and Contentment.

YOU desire, *Lucilius*, to know, whether *Epicurus* justly reprimands those, who are pleased to affirm, *that a wise man is satisfied in himself, and consequently wants no friend.* This is objected (*a*) by *Epicurus* against *Stilpo*, and all those who place their *summum bonum* (or, *chief good*) in a certain

 indifference

indifference of ſoul. We cannot help being obſcure, while we endeavour to expreſs the Greek ἀπάθειαν *(apathy)* in one word, and call it *impaſſibility*; for the contrary to what we mean may be underſtood thereby *(a)*. We mean one, who denies any ſenſe or feeling of any kind of evil; but it may likewiſe be underſtood of one, who cannot *bear* any kind of evil. Conſider therefore, whether we may not better define it, *A ſoul invulnerable*, or *beyond the reach of ſufferance*. Now this is the difference, between us *(Stoics,)* and them, (the *Epicureans*.) Our wiſe man gets the better of every evil, but yet he feels it: whereas their wiſe man pretends not to feel it. In this however we agree, A wiſe man is contented and ſatisfied in himſelf: and yet, as ſufficient as he is in himſelf, according to our tenets, he deſires to have a friend, a neighbour, a companion. And as to the contentment we are ſpeaking of, he is contented with a part, as it were, of himſelf: for ſhould he have loſt a hand by any diſeaſe, or by the ſword of an enemy; or ſuppoſe, by ſome accident, an eye; he is contented with that which is left; and will live as chearfully with his maimed body, as if it were entire. What is wanting, he will not ſigh for in vain; though at the ſame time, no doubt, he had rather not want it. And thus is a wiſe man ſatisfied in himſelf, not that he deſires to have no friend, but he knows how to be content without one: I mean, he can bear the loſs of a friend patiently; though perhaps he will not be long without one; as it is in his power to repair the loſs when he pleaſes. As when *Phidias (b)* hath loſt, or diſpoſed of, a ſtatue, he will ſet about making another; ſo the wiſe artiſt, in forming friendſhips, will ſubſtitute another friend in the room of him he hath loſt. You may aſk, perhaps, what method a man muſt take, ſo ſoon to gain a friend? I will tell you, provided you accept of this in full payment of the debt I owe you in the epiſtolary way.

Saith *Hecaton*, "*I will diſcloſe to you an excellent philtre; without the uſe of love-powder, herb, or bewitching charm,*—ſi vis amari, ama; *love, that you may be beloved (c).*" Now, there is a pleaſure, not only in the habit of a ſure and laſting friendſhip, but alſo in the acquiſition and beginning of a new one: the ſame difference that is between the huſbandman, who hath got in his crop, and him that ſoweth, is there between him who hath got a friend, and him who is endeavouring to get one. *Attalus*, the philoſopher, was wont to ſay, Jucundius eſſe amicum facere, quàm habere; *there*

is

is more pleaſure in making a friend, than in having one. As the artiſt takes more delight in the act of painting, than in having painted: for why? that earneſtneſs and anxiety with which he purſued his work, gives a more pleaſing ſenſation, than what he taſtes in having finiſhed his piece: he now enjoys indeed the fruit of his art, but while he was painting, he enjoyed the art itſelf: to have our children grown up, ſuppoſe to twenty years of age, may be of more ſervice indeed; but their prattling infancy is ſweeter and more entertaining. But to return to our purpoſe—

The wiſe man, I was ſaying, however ſatisfied in himſelf, is yet deſirous to have a friend; and for this reaſon, was there no other; that ſo great a virtue, as the exerciſe of friendſhip, may not lie dormant: not, as *Epicurus* ſays (*e*) in the Epiſtle before me, that he may have a friend to comfort him on the bed of ſickneſs, or relieve him, when poor, or in priſon; but that he may have ſome one, on whom to diſplay the like merciful diſpoſition, whether by comforting him in ſickneſs, or delivering him from inimical durance. He thinks very wrong, who regards only himſelf, and makes ſelf-intereſt the ground of friendſhip: he will end as he begun: he profeſſes to ſerve his friend even in bonds, but as ſoon as he hears the clinking of the chain, deſerts him. Theſe are what are commonly called *temporary* (*f*) friendſhips; which laſt no longer than to ſerve a turn. Hence the proſperous are ſurrounded with a number of friends; while the wretched bemoan themſelves in ſolitude: for then is the time of flight, when put to the trial. From whence we ſee ſo many ſcandalous examples of friends, either deſerting, or betraying one another through fear: whereas the end of friendſhip ought to correſpond with the beginning. He that hath undertook to be a friend, becauſe it is expedient, or dreams of other gain than what naturally ariſes from friendſhip, will never be true to the obligation, but will be tempted, upon the leaſt view of intereſt, to act contrary to the laws of friendſhip. To what purpoſe then have I choſe a friend? Why, to have one whom I would ſerve to the utmoſt in caſe of neceſſity, would follow him into baniſhment; and for whoſe life and preſervation I would expoſe myſelf to danger and death (*g*). What you are pleaſed to call friendſhip, is not friendſhip, but mere traffick (*h*), having regard only to ſome advantage that may accrue therefrom. No doubt, the affection of lovers hath ſomething in it very like friendſhip: but it is ſtill

 imperfect,

imperfect, and may be called a sort of *insane* friendship. Is it then founded on the views of profit, of ambition, or of glory? No; love of its own pure motive, neglectful of all other considerations, incites the mind to the desire of beauty, not without hopes of mutual endearments. And what then? Does a vile affection spring from, or form an alliance upon, a more honourable cause? But this, you say, is not the point in question; whether friendship is desirable merely upon its own account: for if so, the man who is satisfied in himself, may well accede thereto, as to the most lovely object; not allured by any hope of gain, or disheartened at any change of fortune. He detracts from the majesty of friendship, who enters upon it merely as a preservative against evil accidents. The wise man (dreads no accident, he) is satisfied in himself. But this quality, my *Lucilius*, is generally misinterpreted: men are apt to exclude the wise man from all community with the world; contracting him, as it were, within his own skin. It will be proper therefore to distinguish, and explain what we mean, by *self-complacency*.

Now, a wise man is satisfied in himself, not merely with regard to life, but to his living happily: the former indeed wants many things, but the latter nothing more than a sound, elevated mind, contemptuous of the power of fortune. Accept also of a nice distinction (*i*) made by *Chrysippus*: he affirms, *that a wise man can want nothing; yet many things are necessary for him:* on the contrary, *A fool stands not in need of any thing, for there is nothing he knows how to use; but he wants every thing.* The wise man stands in need of eyes and hands, and other requisites for daily use; but he *wants* nothing; for *to want* is to be necessitous; but a wise man is a stranger to necessity. However satisfied therefore he may be in himself; he may still make use of a friend; nor does he act against principle, if he desires more than one; not that he thereby may live happily, for he can be happy without a friend. The *summum bonum* seeks not any external provision, it is maintained within, and is entire in itself; if it looks out for any foreign accession, it becomes subject to the caprice of fortune. But what sort of life must a wise man lead, when, without a friend, he is cast into prison, or left destitute in a foreign country, or is detained in a long voyage by contrary winds, or cast ashore upon a desert island? Why as *Jupiter*, (when, at the conflagration of the world, all the rest of the gods

are

are confounded, in the wreck of nature,) will acquiesce in himself, taken up entirely with his own ideas: somewhat like this is a wise man disposed, through life: he is collected within himself: there he dwells: and notwithstanding, so long as it is in his power, he orders, and busies himself with, worldly affairs, he is contented in himself; he marries a wife, still contented; he brings up his children, still contented; and perhaps had rather not live at all, than live without a companion: it is not however with a view to advantage, that invites him to cultivate friendship (*l*), but a sort of instinct, or natural inclination: there is a certain innate sweetness in friendship; as solitude is generally odious and distasteful, the desire of society is pleasant and agreeable: as nature ingratiates man with man, such is our incitement to friendship. The wise man however, though he proves the most affectionate of friends, to such as he hath acquired, nay, though he equals, and sometimes prefers them to himself, yet terminates all good in himself, and assumes the words of *Stilpo (m)*; that *Stilpo*, whom *Epicurus* here attacks in the Epistle before me; and whom (when his country was taken, and he had lost his children, and his dearer wife, and had escaped from the flames, alone; and yet seemed happy,) being asked by *Demetrius Policrates* (so called from his having destroyed many towns) *whether he had lost any thing*; *No*, says he, *all the goods I have I carry with me*. Behold a truly brave and great man; he is victorious over victory itself. *I have lost nothing*, says he: he makes *Demetrius* even doubt of his conquest: *I carry every thing with me*, viz. justice, virtue, temperance, prudence, and the disposition, to think nothing to be really good that can be taken from us. We admire some animals in that they can pass through fire without detriment: how much more admirable is this philosopher, who without loss or harm, made his way, through fire, sword, and ruin! You see how much easier it is to conquer a whole nation than one man.

The like noble sentiment and language holds the *Stoic* (*n*). He carries his *all*, undamaged, through a city on fire; for he is contented in himself; and under this character rates his happiness. Yet think not that the *Stoics* alone fling out such generous expressions; even *Epicurus*, who is here reprimanding *Stilpo*, says something not dissimilar thereto; which I beg your acceptance of, though I had before paid you the debt of the day.—Si cui sua non videntur amplissima, licet totius mundi dominus sit, tamen miser est.

If, says he, *what a man possesseth seems not amply sufficient, was he master of the world, he would be wretched:* or perhaps it may seem better expressed in this manner, (for we are to regard the sentiment, rather than the expression) Miser est qui se non beatissimum judicat licet imperet mundo; *He who does not think himself happy, is miserable, though he command the world.* And that you may know this to be the common voice of nature, you will find in the comic poet;

> Non est beatus, esse qui se non putat (*o*).
> *He is not bless'd, who thinks himself not bless'd.*

It matters not what condition you are in, if you think it a bad one. What if that villainously rich man; or, that lord of many, but slave to more, call themselves happy, will this their declaration make them so? No: it avails not what a man says of himself, but what he thinks: nor what he thinks to-day, but continually. Nor need you be concerned that any one hath amassed great wealth, which he is unworthy of: for no one but the wise man is capable of self-complacency: and a fool will be disgusted at his own condition, be it what it will.

ANNOTATIONS, &c.

(*a*) *For the contrary*] So in *Cicero*, explaining the tenets of the Stoics. The word *inestimable*, which is generally used for something so great, as to be invaluable, signifies a thing of *no value*, and not worthy of any esteem.

(*b*) *Phidias*] The celebrated statuary of *Athens*: he flourished, A. M. 3511. Or, suppose, any other statuary.

(*c*) So in the Epigram—Marce, ut ameris ama.

And Theocritus——Στεργετε τὸς φιλεοντας, ἱν' αν φιλεητε, φιλῆσθε.

> Quisquis amatur amet, ut et ipse ubi amarit, ametur.
> *Love those who love you; if you fain would prove*
> *The kind and mutual tenderness of love.*

(*d*) *Attalus*] A Stoic philosopher, in the time of *Tiberius*. See Epist. 108.

(*e*) Epicurus *says, these creatures, (brutes,) upbraid the remorselessness of humanity,—in not being capable of gratuitous love, nor knowing how to be a friend without profit. Well therefore might the comedian be admired, who said,* For reward only man loves man. Epicurus *thinks that after this manner children are beloved of their parents, and parents of their children. But if the benefit of speech was allowed to brutes, and if horses, cows, dogs and birds, were brought upon the stage, the song would be changed; and it would be said, that neither the cow loved the calf for gain, nor the mare her foal, nor fowls their chicken, but that they*

were

were beloved gratis, *and by the impulse of nature*, &c. Plutarch. de amore in Liberos.—Vid. Lipf. Manuduct. l. 3. Diff. 16.

So Horace, *Sat.* I. 1. 81. At fi aliquis cafus lecto te affixit, habes qui
Affideat, fomenta paret, medicum roget, ut te
Sufcitet, ac reddat natis, carifque propinquis.
If, by a cold fome painful illnefs bred,
Or other chance, confine me to my bed,
My wealth will purchafe fome good-natur'd friend
My cordials to prepare, my couch attend;
And urge the doctor to preferve my life,
And give me to my children and my wife.——Francis.

(f) Temporary] Ονομα γαρ, εργω δ' ουκ εχουσι οἱ φιλοι,
Οἱ μη 'πι ταισι συμφοραις εισι φιλοι.——Eur.
They're friends by name, but not in deed,
Who are not friends in time of need.

(g) Danger and death] *And greater love hath no man than this, to lay down his life for his friend.* John 15. 13. *See* Epift. 6.

(h) Traffick] Negotiatio. *So* Cicero (II. De Nat. Deor.) Amicitiam fi ad fructum noftrum referremus, non erit ifta amicitia; fed *mercatura* quædam utilitatum fuarum.

(i) A nice diftinction] *Muretus* obferves that *to want*, δεισθαι, *egere*, here fignifies, fo to *want* a thing, as to be anxious after, and not able to bear the lofs of it: and that ενδεισθαι, *indigere, to ftand in need of*, means, to *want* a thing that is abfolutely ufeful and neceffary, and which a man knows how to make a right ufe of. *Cicero* has treated on this queftion in his firft book of *Tufculan Queftions*: but *Plutarch* with more perfpicuity hath ridiculed it, in his treatife, *Of Common Notions againft the Stoics.*

(*k*) The Stoics fuppofed that *Jupiter*, or Nature, and the firft principle of all things, was *fire*; that part of it, being of a groffer confiftence, was turned into animal life: and the ftill groffer part was made water, and of water earth: but that at a certain time all things fhall again be reduced into their firft principle, *fire*. And this they called εκπυρωσις, or *the conflagration of the world*. Vid. Lipf. Phyfiol. l. 2. Diff. 22.

Chryfippus fays, that *Jupiter* is like to man, as is alfo the world and Providence to the foul. When therefore the conflagration fhall be; *Jupiter*, who alone of all the gods is incorruptible, will retire into *Providence*, and they being together, will both perpetually remain in one fubftance of the æther.——*Plutarch*. Ib.

(*l*) *To cultivate friendfhip*] *Epicurus* publickly profeffed, that all friendfhips were founded on a view to pleafure or intereft; and this they carried fo far, as to maintain, that fathers had no other love for their children than what fprung from the profit or pleafure they enjoyed, or expected to enjoy from them. But the *Stoics* thought much better; that not only parental love was a natural affection, but that man is formed by nature for fociety; and that they have an inftinctive love and relationfhip for each other; and confequently that the friendfhips of all wife and good men are pure and difinterefted, without the leaft view to any recompence whatever. *See the above quotation from* Plutarch.

(*m*) *Stilpo*] See this ftory related differently in *Laertius*' Life of *Zeno*, who was the difciple of *Stilpo*, p. 177.

(*n*) This ftoical doctrine is what *Horace* ridicules, Ep. 1. 1. 106.
Ad fummum fapiens uno minor eft Jove, dives,
Liber, honoratus, pulcher, rex denique regum,
Præcipue fanus, nifi cum pituita molefta eft.
In fhort this Stoic, this wife man, is all
That free and beauteous, good, and great, we call.

A king

A king of kings, inferior to none
But to the Ruler of the skies alone;
As strong in health too;—could he but take off
The painful grievance of a cursed cough.

(c) Non est beatus, &c. But it is equally true from what follows in *Seneca*, that
Non est statim beatus, esse qui se putat.
He is not always happy, who thinks himself so.
Vid. Lipf. Manuduct. L. 2. Diff. 32.

EPISTLE X.

On Solitude and Prayer. * (a)

BE assured, *Lucilius*, that I have not alter'd my opinion. Shun, I say, the rabble: shun a few; nay, every one: I know not whom to recommend to you as a proper conversant; and upon this I form my judgment; I dare trust you with yourself (*b*). *Crates* (as they say) a follower of that *Stilpo*, (*c*) whom I mentioned in my former epistle, when he saw a young man walking in private by himself, asked him, " *what he was doing there alone? I am conversing with myself*, says he: to whom *Crates* replied, *take care, young man, I beseech you, and diligently consider with yourself, whether you are not conversing with a bad man.* We are apt to set a watch upon the melancholy in distress; lest they should make a bad use of solitude: and, indeed, no imprudent person should be left alone; for then it is, that his thoughts are ever busy: he lays schemes to endanger himself or others; and plans his wicked purposes; then it is, he utters what the mind before concealed, either through fear or shame; he emboldens his courage; he enflames the lustful passions; and, in his wrath, meditates revenge. In a word, the only advantage, that solitude pretends to, in trusting no one, and not fearing to be betrayed, is lost upon a fool; he betrays himself.

Know

Know then, *Lucilius*, what I hope of you; rather what I am confident of, (for hope belongs to an uncertain good) I cannot, I say, find any one, with whom I had rather you should converse, than with yourself. I well remember, what noble words, and full of energy, you once poured forth with great spirit; when I immediately congratulated myself and said, *surely such excellent things come not from the lips only; they must be founded on sincerity, and a good heart: this young man is not one of the vulgar; he regards salvation:* so *speak*; so *live*.

Be careful ever to maintain this greatness of soul: and though you have reason to thank the gods for the success of your former vows, cease not to pray; and ask particularly for *wisdom*, (*e*) a *sound mind*, and *health of body*. Why should you not often pray for these blessings? Fear not to importune a gracious God, (*f*) when you ask not for any foreign good, or what belongs to another person.

But, according to custom, I shall subjoin to this epistle a small present: it is from *Athenodorus*; and I think it a just and excellent observation: Tum scito esse te omnibus cupiditatibus solutum, cùm eo perveneris, ut nihil deum rogas, nisi quod rogare possis palam. *Know*, says he, *that you have discharged every irregular passion, when you are arrived to such goodness, as to ask of God nothing, but what you care not if all the world should hear*. But, alas! how great is the folly and hypocrisy of the present age! men are continually whispering and muttering to God some villainous prayer (*g*); was any one to listen, they are immediately silent; and thus what they are unwilling men should hear; they presume to offer up to God. Consider then, whether you may not take this maxim for a wholesome rule of life: so *live among men, as if the eye of God was upon you; and so address yourself to God, as if men heard your prayer*.

ANNOTATIONS, &c.

* (*a*) It has been said of *Socrates*, that he was *half a Christian*; I think this epistle of *Seneca* will carry *him* somewhat farther.

(*b*) *Antisthenes* being asked what benefit he had reaped from philosophy, made answer—τὸ δύνασθαι ἑαυτῷ ὁμιλεῖν. *To be able to converse with himself.*

(*c*) *The follower*] Stilponis auditor—but not of the same sect or party: his proper master was *Diogenes* the *Cynic*. Indeed the lectures of *Stilpo* were so sweet and eloquent, that he drew to them many of the studious and learned at *Megara*, and particularly this *Crates*, and *Zeno* himself.

(*d*) *He regards salvation*] Ad salutem spectat. *Gall.* Il regarde au salut. But if *salvation* seems too strong a word to come from the mouth of an heathen, though there is no necessity for taking it in the Christian sense, it may be rendered, *he has regard to his own good and welfare.*

(*e*) *For wisdom*] So *Juvenal* x. 356. Orandum est, ut mens sit sana, in corpore sano.

Pray we for health of body, and of mind.

—— The prayer of *Solomon* is so pertinent to this place, that I could not omit it, though so well known to every one.——

"*Give me, O Lord God, an understanding heart, to judge thy people, that I may discern between good and bad.—Give me wisdom and knowledge.*" And God said to *Solomon*, "*Because this was in thine heart, and thou hast not asked riches, or honour, nor the life of thine enemies, neither yet hast asked long life for thyself, but hast asked wisdom and knowledge:—Lo! wisdom and knowledge are granted thee, and I will give thee both riches and honour, such as none of the kings have had before; neither shall any after thee have the like.*"- 1 Kings, ii. 9. 2 Chron. i. 10.

. To which let me add from St. *James*, i. 5. *If any of you lack wisdom, let him ask of God that giveth all men liberally, and upbraideth not, and it shall be given him: but let him ask in faith, nothing wavering.*

(*f*) *To importune God*] See Luke 18, 1. where is set forth the parable of the importunate widow.— *To the end, that men ought always to pray, and not to faint. Pray without ceasing.* 1 Thess. 5, 17.

(*g*) *Some villainous prayer*] *I wonder* (says *Plutarch*) *that*, Hercules, *or some other god, has not long since plucked up and carried away* the tripod, *whereon is offered such base and villainous questions to* Apollo: *some applying themselves to him as a mere paltry astrologer, to try his skill, and impose upon him by subtle questions: others asking him about treasures buried under ground, others about marrying a fortune: so that* Pythagoras will here be convinced of his mistake when he affirmed that, the time when men are most honest, is, when they present themselves before the gods: *for those filthy passions, which they dare not discover before a grave mortal man, they scruple not to utter to* Apollo. *De defect. orat.*

This is finely touched upon by *Horace*, Ep. l. 16, 57.

Vir bonus omne forum quem spectat, et omne tribunal
Quandocunque Deos vel porco vel bove placat.
Iane pater, clarè, clarè cum dixit, Apollo.
Labra movens metuens audiri, pulchra Laverna,
Da mihi fallere, da sanctum justumque videri;
Noctem peccatis, et fraudibus objice nubem.
Your honest man, on whom with aweful praise,
The Forum and the courts of justice gaze:
If e'er he make a public sacrifice,
Dread Janus, Phœbus, *clear and loud he cries,*
But, when his prayer in earnest is prefer'd,
Scarce moves his lips, afraid of being heard;
Beauteous Laverna, my petition hear,
Let me with truth and sanctity appear:
Oh, give me to deceive, and, with a veil,
Of darkness and of night, my crimes conceal.——*Francis.*
Haud cuivis promptum est, murmurque humilesque susurros,
Tollere de templis et aperto vivere voto:
Mens bona, fama, fides, hæc clarè, et ut audiat hospes:
Illa sibi introrsum, et sub lingua immurmurat! O si
Ebullit patrui præclarum funus!
——Pupillumque utinam, quem proximus hæres
Impello, expungam!——

Thus boldly to the gods mankind reveal,
What, from each other, they for ſhame conceal;
Give me good fame, ye powers, and make me juſt,
Thus much the rogue to public ears will truſt:
In private then—*when wilt thou*, mighty *Jove*,
My wealthy uncle from this world remove?—
O were my pupil fairly knock'd o' th' head!
I ſhould poſſeſs th' eſtate, if he were dead, &c.——Dryden.

EPISTLE XI.

On Modeſty, Baſhfulneſs, and natural Habit.

I HAVE had the pleaſure, *Lucilius*, of converſing with a friend of yours, of a moſt excellent diſpoſition; his very firſt ſpeech ſhewed ſuch ingenuity, ſtrength of mind, and proficiency in learning, as to give me a taſte of what we may one day expect from him. What he ſaid, was by no means premeditated, as I came upon him unawares. As ſoon as he had recovered the ſurprize, it was with difficulty that he ſhook off that decent modeſty, which is a very good ſign in a young man (*a*); ſo deep a bluſh was ſpread over his face: and this, I think, will not leave him, even when he hath ſtrengthened his mind with virtue, thrown off all vices, and commenced the *wiſe man*.

It is not in the power of wiſdom entirely to ſurmount the natural imperfections of mind or body: whatever is innate and inbred may be corrected by art, but cannot be quite rooted out. Even ſome, of the moſt ſteady temper, when obliged to ſpeak in public, have been known to ſweat, as if they had been fatigued with running a race; while others have been ſo affected on the like occaſion, as to have their knees tremble, their teeth chatter, their tongue faulter, or their lips ſo cloſe, that they cannot open their mouth. And this baſhfulneſs, neither diſcipline, nor uſe can ſhake off: nature will ſtill prevail, and admoniſh, even the ſtrongeſt, of this

their

their weakneſs (*c*): for ſuch I reckon the bluſh which ſpreads itſelf over the face of the graveſt perſons. It is more common, indeed among youth, who have more heat, and a delicate conſtitution; but it ſpares not even veterans and ſages. There are ſome, indeed, who are never more to be dreaded, than when they redden (*d*); as if they had, at once, thrown from the heart all decency and modeſty. As *Sylla* was always moſt violent, when the blood roſe in his face: but nothing could be more ſoft and pleaſing than the countenance of *Pompey*; he always bluſhed, when in company, and eſpecially when he made a public oration; and I remember to have ſeen *Fabian* (*e*) bluſh, upon being called upon in the ſenate, only as a witneſs, and I thought it became him admirably well. This was not owing to any infirmity of mind, but to ſurprize and accident: which, though they do not always embarraſs the unexperienced, yet naturally affect ſuch as, from the conſtitution of the body, are apt to bluſh. For as there are ſome whoſe blood is ſo well-tempered as not to be moved extraordinarily; there are others in whom it is ſo lively and active as to be continually flying into the face: and this, as before obſerved, no wiſdom can get the better of; otherwiſe it would ſubject nature to its command, and eradicate every imperfection. Whatever ariſeth from the condition of birth, or the temperature of the body, it will ſtick by us; how much, or how long ſoever, the mind has been endeavouring to fix and compoſe itſelf upon right principles, none of theſe things can be avoided, any more than they can be acquired. The greateſt artiſts on the ſtage, who mimick all kinds of paſſion; who can expreſs fear and trembling, and diſplay all the ſigns of heartſore grief; when they are to expreſs baſhfulneſs, can do no more than exhibit a dejected countenance, ſpeak low, and caſt their eyes upon the ground; they cannot bluſh when they would: it is in vain either to forbid or command a bluſh: wiſdom neither promiſes, nor can perform any thing in this reſpect; they are their own maſters; and come, and go, as they pleaſe.

But this epiſtle demands a ſentimental clauſe: accept then of this, which I take to be a ſalutary and uſeful maxim, worthy of being engraved upon the heart: aliquis vir bonus nobis eligendus eſt, ac ſemper ante oculos habendus, ut ſic tunquam illo ſpectante vivamus, et omnia tanquam illo vidente faciamus. *We muſt fix upon ſome good man* (*f*), *and have him always before*

before our eye, as a witneſs of our life and actions. And this likewiſe, my *Lucilius*, was the precept of *Epicurus*; he would have a guardian, or cenſor, continually ſet over us; and with great propriety: for ſure, many ſins would be prevented, was ſome witneſs to be preſent at the commiſſion. Let the mind, therefore, ſuppoſe ſome one preſent, whom it may revere; and from whoſe authority every ſecret may receive ſanction. Happy the man, who not only by his preſence, but by being thought upon, has ſuch influence upon another perſon, as to induce him to act decently! And happy the man, who ſo reverences another, as upon only calling him to mind, forms and regulates his own conduct. He, that ſo reverenceth another, will ſoon be reverenced himſelf. Chuſe therefore *Cato*; or if *Cato* ſeems ſomewhat too rigid, chuſe *Lælius*, a man of not ſo ſevere a temper; or chuſe ſome one, among your acquaintance, whoſe life and manner of addreſs, charm you; and having in view either the underſtanding or preſence of ſuch a one, look upon him, either as your guardian or model: there muſt be ſome one, I ſay, according to whoſe plan we muſt form our morals: without ſome certain rule, you will never correct what is amiſs.

ANNOTATIONS, &c.

(a) *A good ſign in a young man*] So *Pliny*, ſpeaking of *Calpurnius Piſo*, the younger, ſays,—Commendabat hæc voce ſuaviſſimâ, vocem verecundia; multum ſanguinis, multum ſollicitudinis in ore magna ornamenta recitantis: etenim neſcio quo pacto magis in ſtudiis homines timor quàm fiducia decet. *Theſe beauties were extremely heighten'd by a moſt harmonious voice, which a very becoming modeſty rendered ſtill more pleaſing. Confuſion and concern, in the countenance of a ſpeaker, throws a grace upon all he utters; for there is a certain decent timidity, which, I know not how, is infinitely more engaging than the aſſured, and ſelf-ſufficient air of confidence.* M.—*Diogenes*, the Cynic, ſeeing a young man bluſh, ſaid to him, Θάρρει, τοιοῦτόν ἐστι τῆς ἀρετῆς τὸ χρῶμα. *Take courage, youth; you need not be aſhamed; this is the colour of virtue*—Πᾶς ἐρυθριῶν γε χρηστὸς εἶναί μοι δοκεῖ. Menander

A bluſh points out the goodneſs of the heart. See Ep. 25.

(b) *To ſpeak in publick*]. *Plutarch*, ſpeaking of *Alcibiades*, obſerves, that, *though he was as ſagacious, and happy in his thoughts as any man whatever; yet, for want of a little aſſurance, he very often miſerably loſt himſelf in his pleadings; and would faulter and make pauſes in the middle of an oration; purely for the want of a ſingle word, or ſome neat expreſſion that he had in his papers and could not preſently recollect.*—And there have been two remarkable inſtances, partly in our memory, of this inability to ſpeak in publick; notwithſtanding the greateſt capacities and accompliſhments that could be required in ſuch a province: I mean, in that elegant writer, Philoſopher, and ſtateſman, Mr. *Addiſon*: and our late worthy provoſt of King's college, *Cambridge*, Dr. *Roderick*; who never attempted to preach but once, in a country

village,

village, (*Milton*, near *Cambridge*) and even there, had not courage enough to go half through his ſermon.

(*c*) *This weakneſs*] —Il. ω. 44.—οὐδέ οἱ αἰδὼς

Γίνεται, ἥ τ' ἄνδρας μέγα σίνεται, ἠδ' ὀνίνησι.
Shame is not of his ſoul; nor underſtood,
The greateſt evil, and the greateſt good.

Vid. Plutarch. (de vitioſo pudore. c. n.)

(*d*) *When they redden*] *Tacitus*, in his life of *Agricola*, ſpeaking of *Domitian* ſays, *His countenance was cruel, being always covered with a ſettled red: in which he hardened himſelf againſt all ſhame and bluſhing.*

(*e*) *Fabian*, the philoſopher, and rhetorician, (ſee Ep. 100.) He flouriſhed in the reign of *Tiberius*, when *Seneca* was a young man.

(*f*) *We muſt fix upon*] See Ep. 25. *Lipſ.* Manud. III. Diſſ. ult.

—— Κᾂν ἀπῶθεν ᾖ

Ἀνὴρ ὁ χρηστὸς, δυστυχοῦντας ὠφελεῖ. Eur.
Thus good men, in ſome meaſure, can attend,
Ev'n in their abſence, a diſtreſsful friend.

Xenophon (Dict. et Fact. I. 4.) attributes this to *Socrates*; *that even in his abſence the remembrance of him was of great ſervice to thoſe who were converſant with him and heard his lectures.*

And *Plutarch* (de Sign. Profectûs) adviſeth, *when we go upon any buſineſs, or undertake any office, to ſet before our eyes ſome excellent perſon, either alive or dead, and conſider with ourſelves, what* Plato *would have done in this affair; what* Epaminondas *would have ſaid; how* Lycurgus, *or* Ageſilaus *would have behaved; that addreſſing ourſelves, and adorning our minds at theſe mirrors, we may correct every diſagreeing word and irregular paſſion.—And if the conſideration and remembrance of good men being preſent and entertained in our minds, preſerve the* proficiency, *in all affections and doubts, regular and unmoveable; you may judge that this alſo is a token of* a proficient in virtue.

But a ſerious *Chriſtian* need not to be reminded to place a *Cato*, a *Lælius*, or even a St. *Paul* in his view for this purpoſe; he cannot but know, that he hath infinitely a more powerful guardian, and more cloſe inſpector, ever over him, or rather in him.—For *know ye not, that ye are the temple of God, and that the Spirit of God dwelleth in you?* 1 Cor. 3. 16. 6. 19. See alſo Rom. 8. 9. Epheſ. 4. 30. 1 Theſſ. 5. 19.

EPISTLE XII.

On Life and Old Age.

GO where I will, Lucilius, or do what I will, I meet with ſomething that reminds me of old Age. I went the other day to my *villa* without the city, and was complaining, that it ſeemed greatly out of repair, notwithſtanding my continual expence. *I cannot help it*, ſays my bailiff, *it is no fault of mine; I have done all I can, but it is very old.* Now, you muſt know, that this *villa* is of my own building. What then muſt I expect, if the ſtone wall, of my own time, is decayed! So much for that; but ſtill more out of humour; *ſurely,* ſays I, *thoſe plane-trees have been much neglected; how knotty and crooked are the branches! there is ſcarce a leaf upon them: and the trunks how wretched and ſquallid! This could never have happened, if they had been properly dug about, and well watered.* Upon this, my bailiff ſwears heartily, that *he has done all he could, that no care has been wanting in him, but the trees are very old.* True enough; for I planted them myſelf, and ſaw their firſt foliage. Turning to the door, *What old decrepit fellow is this,* ſaid I, *whom you have properly enough placed here, with his face pointed to the door? (a) where did you get him? what was your fancy for bringing a ſtrange corpſe to my houſe?—Do you not know me?* ſays the old man; *I am* Felicio, *to whom formerly you was wont to bring play-things; I am the ſon of* Philoſitus, *your late bailiff; your favourite play-fellow.* " Surely, *ſays I,* the man doats; what does he talk of being a little boy, and my play-fellow? But it may be ſo indeed; for he is ſhedding his teeth.

This is what I am obliged to my *villa* for; that, look where I will, I am put in mind of my old age. Be it ſo; let me enjoy it; let me love it. It is replete with pleaſure, when we know how to uſe it. Fruit is then more grateful, when at the end of the ſeaſon. The bloom of youth is then moſt comely, when paſſing into manhood. Your wine-bibbers reliſh beſt the laſt bottle, even that which overſets them, and gives the finiſhing ſtroke to the debauch. Whatever is exquiſite in pleaſure is reſerved to the laſt. Even age is moſt pleaſant, when the decay is not too rapid, but comes gently on; nor can I think it deſtitute of pleaſure, even on the verge of life: or, this may be reckoned inſtead of pleaſure, that it wants none. How ſweet is life, when all anxious deſires have taken their leave of us!

But it is very irkſome, you will ſay, to have death always before our eyes. Death, my friend, ought to be placed before the eyes of the young, as well as of the old. For we are not ſummoned according to the pariſh regiſter. And beſides there is no man ſo old, as to make it ſinful to expect another day *(b)*. Now, every day is another ſtep in life. Our whole time consists of parts, and circles circumscribed within circles of different dimensions; some one of which takes in and compasseth the rest: and this is what includes the life of man: another compriseth the years of youth, and another those of childhood. There is also a complete year, which contains in itself all those times, that by multiplication, form the course of life: a month is confined in still narrower bounds; and a day consists of yet a smaller compass: and this hath also a beginning and ending, a circuit from east to west. *Heraclitus* therefore, (who from the obscurity of his style got the nickname of *Scotinus*, (*Darkling*) saith, "Unus dies omni par est," *One day is par to another*. This some interpret, as if he had said, They are equal with regard to hours; which is certainly true; for if a day consists of twenty-four hours, every day is equal; for what is lost in the day is made up in the night. Others interpret it, that one day is equal to any other, by way of resemblance; as the longest space of time exhibits no more than what you have seen in one day, *viz.* light and darkness, frequently repeated in the alternate changes of the heavens; and is no otherwise different than in not being always of an equal length. Every day therefore is to be so ordered and regulated, as if it closed the rear, set bounds to, and completed life (*c*).

Pacuvius, (*d*) the debauchée, who had lived so long in *Syria*, that he made it, as it were, his own; when, with wine and costly dainties, he banquetted as at a funeral, would order himself to be laid out with the usual solemnities, and carried upon a bier from supper; while amidst the applause of his boon companions, this was sung to music; Βεβίωκε, βεβίωκε, *He hath lived, he hath lived indeed*. This was his practice almost every night. Now, what *he* did wantonly, and from a bad turn of mind; let us do, from a good one: and as we go to sleep, let us, in a pleasant and chearful temper, say,

Vixi, et quem cursum dederat fortuna peregi.
I've liv'd; I've run the destin'd course of fate.

If God is pleased to add to our days *the morrow*; let us accept it with thanksgiving. He is a most happy man, and truly enjoys himself, who expects the morrow, without the least anxiety; whoever hath said over night, *I have lived*, rises the next morn to gain.

But

But it is time to conclude this Epiſtle. " What then, *you will ſay*, will it come without the uſual preſent, ſome peculiar ſentiment?"—Never fear, it ſhall bring ſomething; yes, and ſomething of conſequence. For what can be more excellent than the words I here ſubjoin? *It is wretched to live in neceſſity, but there is no neceſſity for living ſo* (*e*).—Let us thank God that no one is *long* detained in wretchedneſs: neceſſity is really to be overcome. But theſe, you will ſay, are the words of *Epicurus*; why do you continually refer me to others? Give me ſomething of your own.—What is true, Lucilius, is my own. And I ſhall go on, in quoting Epicurus and others; that they, who enliſt themſelves in any ſect, and regard not *what* is ſaid, but *by whom* it is ſaid, may know, that, when any thing is ſaid, perfectly good, all the world have a right to it.

ANNOTATIONS, &c.

(*a*) *With his face to the door*] This alludes to the antient cuſtom of their *laying out* the dead body, (Πρόθεσις, *conlocatio*), which was always near the threſhold at the entrance of the door. *Hom. Il.* τ. 212, on the death of *Patroclus*.

> Ὅς μοι ἐνὶ κλισίῃ δεδαϊγμένος ὀξέϊ χαλκῷ
> Κεῖται, ἀνὰ πρόθυρον τετραμμένος—
> *Pale lies my friend, with wounds disfigur'd o'er,*
> *And his cold feet are pointed to the door.*——Pope.

So *Virgil* (11. 30.)—Recipit qua ad limina greſſum

> Corpus ubi exanimi poſitum Pallantis Acœtes
> Servabat ſenior—
> *Then to the gates* Æneas *paſs'd, and wept,*
> *Where old* Acœtes Pallas' *body kept.*—Lauderdale.

And they took particular care, in placing the body, to turn the feet and face towards the gate; which cuſtom *Perſius* has elegantly deſcribed (Sat. iii. v. 103.)

> ———tandemque beatulus alto
> Compoſitus lecto, craſſiſque lutatus amomis
> In portam rigidos calces extendit—
> *Our dear departed brother lies in ſtate,*
> *His heels ſtretch'd out and pointing to the gate.*——Dryden.

The reaſon of this poſition (ſays Bp. *Kennet*) was to ſhew all perſons whether any violence had been the cauſe of the perſon's death. *Vid. Lipſ. Elect.* 1. c. 6.

(*b*) *Another day?* why not another year, with *Cato* in *Cicero*; Nemo eſt tam ſenex, qui ſe *annum* non putat poſſe vivere? *No one is ſo old who does not think he can live another year.*—Lipſ.

(*c*) *Every day*] This precept from *Horace*, Omnem crede diem tibi diluxiſſe ſupremum. Grata ſuperveniat quæ non ſperabitur hora.

> *Believe that ev'ry morning ray*
> *Hath lighted up the lateſt day:*
> *Then if to-morrow's ſun be thine,*
> *With double luſtre ſhall it ſhine.* Francis.

Muſonius,

Mosonius,—non est præsentem diem bene transigere, nisi qui proponit velut ultimam illam transigere. *No one can be said to pass his day well, who did not propose to pass it as his last.*

(*d*) *Pacuvius*] Qui voluptatibus dediti, quasi in diem vivunt vivendi causas quotidie finiunt. *Plin. Ep.* *The sons of sensuality who have no views beyond the present hour, terminate with each day the whole purport of their lives.* Melmoth. *Those who are entirely devoted to pleasure, live as if their lives were to end with the day, and every day convinced the world they deserve to die.* Orrery.

(*e*) Nullum malum est in necessitate vivere, sed in necessitate vivere necessita nulla est, &c. However these words might become a *Roman* or *Epicurean*, they could not but be shocking to a Christian reader, if translated in the sense *Seneca* intended: I have therefore given them another turn, and adapted them, as well as I could, to more sound doctrine. Besides, if every *morrow*, as *Seneca* here saith, *is to be looked upon as gain, and to be received with thanksgiving*; how ungrateful, how wicked must we be, to abridge ourselves voluntarily of that favour, when we know not what *the morrow* may bring forth by the providence of God, for our relief, (multis viis, saith *Seneca*; true, if he had said) by *patience*, *industry* and *prayer*.

EPISTLE XIII.

On Magnanimity in Distress. Certain Remedies against Fear.

I KNOW, *Lucilius*, your magnanimity: for even before you was instructed in the sound precepts of philosophy, in order to surmount all difficulties; you was pleased to exert yourself strenuously against the power of fortune; and much more, when you had grappled with her, and experienced your strength: which indeed cannot be well known, 'till the difficulties that surround us on every side make a closer attack. Then it is, that a soul, truly noble and unconquerable, gives proof of its abilities: this is the only test: the wrestler cannot enter the lists with true courage, who has not been seasoned, as it were, with bruises. He, that hath often seen his own blood unterrified,—who has had his teeth beaten out with the fist,—who hath been tripped up, and pressed with the whole weight of his antagonist, and hath still kept up his courage;—who, as often as he hath been thrown, hath rose more fierce and stubborn; he it is, that, at any time, engages, full of hope. Therefore to carry on the metaphor, I must observe, that Fortune hath often thrown, and fallen upon you; but you scorned to yield:

you

you ſtill ſtarted up, and more reſolutely ſtood your ground: for valour, when provoked, grows the ſtronger. Yet, if you are pleaſed to accept of my advice, I will point out ſome proper aid for your better defence.

There are more things, my *Lucilius*, that frighten, than which preſs hard upon us: and we are often more diſtreſſed from opinion, than in reality. I am not ſpeaking to you in the language of *Stoiciſm*, but in an humbler ſtrain. For *we* indeed think all thoſe afflictions, that are apt to extort ſighs and groans, light and deſpicable. Laying aſide theſe big words, (but, O ye Gods, how true!) I only require this of you, that you would not anticipate miſery; ſince the evils, you dread as coming upon you, may perhaps never reach you, at leaſt they are not yet come. Thus ſome things torture us more than they ought; ſome, before they ought; and ſome which ought never to torture us at all. We heighten our pain, either by preſuppoſing a cauſe, or anticipation. This however we ſhall defer at preſent, as it is a controverted point *(a)*: what I think to be light, you will contend to be very grievous: I have ſeen ſome laugh under the ſcourge, while others have cried at a box o' the ear. But we ſhall preſently ſee, whether thoſe you think ſo inſupportable are of any weight in themſelves, or formidable only through our weakneſs. Grant me only this, that, when you are ſurrounded by thoſe who would perſuade you, that you are miſerable, you would reflect not upon what you hear, but what you think, and feel yourſelf; and conſulting with your patience, as you certainly know yourſelf beſt, aſk yourſelf the following queſtions: "Whence is it that theſe my friends "ſo bewail my condition? Why do they keep at ſuch a diſtance; fearing "contagion, as if calamity was catching? Is there any thing really bad "in the caſe? or, is it only what has got a bad name?" Examine further, whether you are tortured, or grieve cauſeleſſly, making that an evil, which is not ſo? But you will ſay, "How ſhall I know, whether my afflictions "are real or not?" Obſerve then what I ſay upon this point.

We are afflicted with ſuch evils, as are preſent or future, or both. Concerning preſent evils, it is eaſy to form a judgment; if the body be ſtill free, in ſound health, and in no pain from external injury; ſay with yourſelf, "I am well to-day, be the morrow as it will."—But you are afraid of ſome future evil.——Conſider well, whether the grounds upon which your fear of ſome evil to come is founded, are warrantable. We generally labour

 under

under unjust suspicions, and are often deceived by report: which may well be supposed to affect individuals, when it has been known to put an end to a battle. 'Tis certain, *Lucilius*, we lie open to impression, without duly weighing the things that strike us with sudden fear (*b*); we will not give ourselves time to examine them; we tremble; and then turn our backs, like those soldiers, whom the dust raised by a flock of sheep have drove from the camp; or, whom some false story, without knowledge of the author, hath terrified and put to flight. Things, false and vain, I know not how, are apt to disturb us more than such as are true; for these have their certain measure; whereas the former are the effects of blind conjecture, and the fancies of a coward mind. No sort of fear therefore is so pernicious, and remediless, as that we call *panic:* other fears are irrational, but this quite senseless. Let us therefore diligently examine into this affair.

It is probable such an evil may happen.—It will take up some time therefore before it is true, if ever. How many things happen unexpectedly! and how many have been expected that have not happened? But suppose such a thing should certainly happen; what avails it to anticipate sorrow? it will be time enough to grieve when it comes: in the mean while, promise yourself better things: at least, there will be so much time gained: and many things may intervene; whereby the impending evil, however near it is supposed, may rest where it is, or vanish, or fall upon another person. Fire hath given time for flight of those within: some, falling from on high, have been gently laid upon the ground without hurt: sometimes the sword, when at the very throat, hath been withheld: and the condemned criminal hath outlived the appointed executioner (*c*). — Bad fortune hath also its inconstancy: perhaps it may happen, perhaps not; while it does not happen, think for the best. It is not uncommon for the mind, even when there is no apparent sign of distress, to afflict itself with vain imaginations; to make the worst interpretation of some doubtful word; or, looking upon a person to be more offended than he is, to consider, not how great his anger, but what may be the consequences of it. How vain is life, or what end can there be of misery, if fear is thus to have its full scope! Here then let prudence step in to your assistance; here let strength of mind throw off all fear, however manifest the cause: at least let one foible repel another: temper fear with hope (*d*): nothing that we fear

fear is so certain, as that it is not more certain, what we dread may not happen, and what we hope for deceive us. Let fear and hope be put to the test: and because all things are uncertain, be kind to yourself, and fancy what you like best. If fear prompts any uncouth surmise, still incline to the better part, and give yourself no further trouble.—Now and then reflect upon this; that the greater part of mankind, when there is no evil present, nor like to happen, are upon the fret, and under continual alarms; for no one resists the impulse, when it hath once taken effect, or endeavours to reduce to truth the object of fear: no one thus reflects with himself; "The author is mistaken; he hath certainly feigned such a report, or has been too credulous." No; we give ourselves up to the reporter; with dread we look upon uncertain things as certain; we observe no mean; and therefore simple doubt is turned into real fear.

I am almost ashamed, *Lucilius*, to address you in this manner, and presume to comfort you with such weak arguments. But, should any one tell you, that such a thing will not happen; do you, on the contrary, say, "It will happen; and what then? Let it happen; it may turn to my good: death by being contemned makes life honourable: the juice of hemlock, by which the great *Socrates* fell, completed his character: and when *Cato* was determined to die, had the conqueror taken the sword out of his hand, he would have robbed him of great part of his glory *(e)*."—But too tedious are my exhortations, when you need rather a remembrancer than a counsellor; for I have said nothing against the bent of your own nature: you was born to great accomplishments: so much the more therefore study to raise, and adorn your good disposition.

I shall now conclude this Epistle; when I have set the usual mark to it, by subjoining some excellent saying or other, as thus: *Among the many evils that attend on folly, this is one, It is always beginning to live (f)*. Consider well, my *Lucilius*, best of men, the full purport of this sentence; and you will learn, how vile and ridiculous is the levity of men, who are ever projecting, and laying new foundations of life, and building their fond hopes thereon. Look on all around you, and observe with what anxiety even old men are making great preparations, either with some ambitious view, or for travel, and merchandise. Now what can be more abſurd than to ſee an old man beginning to live *(g)*? I ſhould not have added the name of the author of this ſentiment, had it been ſo well known, as ſome other of the common ſayings of *Epicurus,* which I have taken upon me to quote, and adopt for my own.

ANNOTATIONS, &c.

(a) A controverted point] Between the *Stoics* and the *Epicureans*, with others who think pain an evil; whereas to the former it is an indifferent thing.

(b) 'Tis certain] See Ep. 24.

Ητὸ μέλλον ἐκφοβεῖ καθ' ἡμέραν,
Ὡς τῶ γε πάσχειν τ' ὑπὲρ μεῖζον κακόν.——Eur.
The future terrifies, with daily fear,
Than real ills to ſuffer, more ſevere.

(c) I remember two particular inſtances of this: one, at *Eton*, of a labourer falling from a very high ſcaffolding: the other, at *Cambridge*, of a young gentleman's falling from the upper ſtory of *Chriſt*-College, unhurt. But what is more extraordinary and to the purpoſe; in the late horrid riot beforementioned, the inſurgents ſet fire to *Newgate*, and delivered, among the other priſoners, three unhappy wretches that were to have been executed the next morning. And within a few days,—— *Dennis*, (alias *Jack Ketch)* was capitally convicted, and condemned; for being concerned in the ſaid riot.

(d) Fear with hope] See Epiſt. 104.—But it is obſervable here, that there were ſome philoſophers, called by the Greeks, *Elpiſticks*, i. e. *Hopers*; who maintained that the chief happineſs in life conſiſted in hope; and that were we deprived of this, and the delight attending it, life would be an inſupportable burthen. *See* Plutarch. *Sympos.* 4. 4.

(e) Had robbed him] As *Seneca* might think; but no true Chriſtian can be of the ſame opinion, though *Cato* acted upon principle, even the chief principle of *Stoiciſm*; ſince it may eaſily be proved a falſe one, from the fitneſs of things, and had been proved by the forementioned great philoſopher, *Socrates*. Vid. Plato. See alſo the foregoing Epiſtle.

(f) Beginning to live] See Ep. 20. Lipſ. Manud. l. ii. c. Diſſ. 15.

(g) An old man] Juvenes adhuc confuſa quædam et quaſi turbata non indecent: ſenibus placida omnia et ordinata conveniunt; quibus induſtria ſera, turpis ambitio eſt. Plin. Ep. l. 3. 1. *In young men perhaps ſome irregularity and diſorder may not be unbecoming.* But in the downhill of life; all things ſhould be carried on ſmoothly and methodically: induſtry is ill-timed, and ambition a reproach.— *Orrery.*

EPISTLE XIV.

On Caution, and Security.

I Confess, *Lucilius,* that an affection for, as also the care and preservation of, the body, is natural: nor do I deny but that sometimes it may be indulged: yet I cannot allow, that one should be a slave to it. He that is a slave to his body,—is over-anxious for its welfare,—and refers every thing thereto,—is a slave to many masters. We ought so to comport ourselves, not as if we lived for the body, but as if we could not live without it. Too great a love for it, racks us with perpetual fears, burthens us with unnecessary anxieties, and subjects us to contumely. He that sets too high a value upon his body, can never have a due sense of what is great and honourable. It is worthy indeed of our most diligent care; yet if reason exacts, or dignity and fidelity *(a)* require it to be committed to the flames, we are to submit. At the same time, I say, we must endeavour, as far as lies in our power, not only to avoid danger (*b*), but all manner of annoyance: we must make ourselves as secure as possible, by frequently reflecting on the means, whereby those things, that are to be feared, may be repelled: and of such things, if I am not mistaken, there are three sorts; *indigence, diseases,* and *oppression from some superior.* Of these nothing can be more terrible than the last, *tyrannical oppression:* it rushes upon us with uproar and violence; whereas the natural evils I have mentioned, silently creep upon us, nor strike with terror either the eyes or ears: but how great the pomp of an execution! Chains, fire, the sword, and wild beasts, gaping for a feast on human entrails: let the imagination add to these a dungeon, a cross, iron whips, hooks, the being sawed asunder, impaled, or torn in pieces by horses, or having the clothes dawbed with pitch, or other the like inflammable matter, and then set on fire, or whatever else the most shocking cruelty hath invented (*c*). Is it any wonder we should be afraid of these tortures, whose variety is so manifold, and apparatus so terrible? For as the executioner afflicts more severely the person condemned, the more instruments of pain he sets in view, (whereby patience itself is overcome:) so, in other

other reſpects, among all thoſe evils that are apt to damp the ſpirits, and ſubdue the courage of man, *they* have the greateſt effect that are moſt viſible. Other plagues indeed are not leſs grievous, I mean, hunger and thirſt, an inflammation in the bowels, or a burning fever, but then they are not ſeen: they ſhake no weapon at us, nor preſent any thing terrible to the eye: whereas the former, like vaſt armies in array, ſubdue the mind with the appearance and tremendous preparation. What have we to do then, but to take all poſſible care to give no offence (*d*)?

There are times, when, in a popular government, the rabble are to be feared (*e*): or if the government be ſuch, that the chief executive power is in the ſenate, then are the leading men therein moſt to be dreaded: and ſometimes the people have delegated their power to particular perſons even againſt themſelves. Now as in theſe caſes it is very difficult to have every one our friends, we may reſt ſatisfied in not having them our enemies. The wiſe man therefore will be cautious not to provoke the reſentment of thoſe in power; nay, he will ſhun it, as he would a ſtorm, if he was at ſea. When you ſailed to *Sicily*, you paſſed through the Straits; you know the place therefore: now a raſh pilot never regards a ſouth wind, though it be that which harraſſeth the *Sicilian* ſea, and forms thoſe dreadful whirlpools: he never minds to ſteer on the larboard, but ſails on into the very mouth of the boiſterous *Charybdis* (*f*). Whereas one of more caution is continually enquiring of the more experienced, how the tide flows---what ſigns of a ſtorm are in the clouds,---and keeps on his courſe, at a wary diſtance from the places notorious for whirlpools and ſhipwrecks. Such is the conduct of the wiſe man, in life. He avoids as much as poſſible the power that can hurt him; without diſcovering his deſign; as there is ſome ſort of ſecurity even in this, not to fly profeſſedly; becauſe what a man flies from, he tacitly condemns.

How to be ſafe from the populace in general requires circumſpection. Firſt then let me adviſe you, to avoid party; to aim at nothing that is apt to raiſe ſtriſe (*g*) among the competitors;—and 2dly, not to be greedy of amaſſing ſo much wealth as might enrich the ſpoiler: the leſs you carry about you ſo much the ſafer: no one, or very few, are ſuch villains as to ſpill human blood, for the ſake of ſpilling blood: more men act upon a view

view of intereſt than from malice *(b)*: the robber paſſeth by a man in rags; and the poor man finds quarter in a place beſet with thieves. Laſtly, three things, from antient preſcription, are to be avoided: *Hatred*, *Envy*, and *Contempt*: and the way to effect this, wiſdom alone can ſhew. It is a very nice point, and to be treated with great caution, leſt the fear of envy ſhould throw us into contempt; leſt ſeeming unwilling to trample upon others, we diſcover that we may be trampled on ourſelves. The being to be feared, hath cauſed many to be afraid for themſelves. We muſt retire, and lower, as it were, ourſelves, as much as poſſible, yet not ſo as to be contemptible: for envy and contempt are alike dangerous. In ſhort, we muſt have recourſe to philoſophy: as this ſort of learning commands reſpect, like (that badge of honor) the ſacred *Fillet*: I do not ſay among good men only, but among ſuch as are not extremely bad. For, eloquence at the bar, and what other arts are uſed to move the people, commonly create an adverſary: but philoſophy is ever quiet, and, minding its own buſineſs, is above contempt: and ſo far above other arts as to be reſpected even by the worſt of men: wickedneſs will never get to ſuch an height, will never ſo conſpire againſt virtue, as not to leave the name of *Philoſopher* venerable and ſacred. But philoſophy itſelf muſt behave with candour and moderation.

" What then, you will ſay, muſt we think of *Cato*? Was his philoſophy " ſo calm and gentle, when he exerted himſelf, in order by his counſel, to " repreſs the civil war, and intervened between two princes, furious in " arms; and, while ſome oppoſed *Pompey*, and others *Cæſar*, dared to pro- " voke them both himſelf?" It is doubtful indeed, whether, at that time, it was proper for a wiſe man to take charge of, or concern himſelf with, public affairs. Some one might ſay, " what is your intention, *Cato*? The " buſineſs now is not concerning *Liberty*; for that has long ſince been loſt: " the diſpute is, whether *Cæſar* or *Pompey* ſhall be maſter of the common- " wealth: what have you to do with this contention? You have no part " here: the point is already ſettled; a lordly governor is to be choſen; and " what matters it to you which of them conquers? The better man can- " not: he indeed may be the worſe who is overcome; but he cannot be the " better who overcomes; when, to conquer in ſuch a cauſe, is in itſelf " diſhonour."

I have only touched upon the laſt part of *Cato's* behaviour: but the foregoing times were ſuch as would not properly admit of a wiſe man's interfering in the ruinous ſtate of the republic. What could *Cato* do more, amid the many plunders, than bawl, and make a vain outcry; when at one while he was dragged from the *Forum*, through a lane of people, who lifted up their hands againſt him, and even ſpit upon him; and at another time was hurried out of the Senate-houſe to priſon? But we ſhall ſee hereafter the propriety of a wiſe man's concerning himſelf with government affairs, and whether it be worth his while to riſque the loſing his labour: for the preſent I ſhall recommend to you thoſe philoſophers, who, being excluded from every public office, have retired, to ſtudy and adorn life; and form laws for the good government of mankind, without any offence to thoſe in power.

The wiſe man will not give any diſturbance to the public as a reformer; nor endeavour to be pointed at for ſingularity in the conduct of life: what then? will he certainly be ſafe, who follows this maxim? I can no more promiſe you this, than a ſound ſtate of health to a temperate man; and yet nothing contributes more to health than temperance. A ſhip may ſometimes be loſt in the haven; but what various accidents is it ſubject to in the midſt of the ſea? How great then muſt be the danger of the man, who is ever buſy, and forming great deſigns, when it is ſcarce poſſible to be ſafe even in retirement? I do not deny but that ſometimes the innocent may ſuffer, but much oftener the guilty: a man may not want ſkill, though he may chance to be wounded, through his armour. Laſtly, the wiſe man regards the intent of every action, without being concerned for the event: the outſet is in our own power; the event belongs to fortune; whom I will not allow to paſs ſentence upon me (ſubmitting herein to no other judge but Reaſon and the fitneſs of things) though ſhe may perhaps bring trouble and vexation; the robber is not condemned before the fact.

But now I ſee you are holding out your hand for your daily ſtipend. I will fill it with gold: and becauſe I mention gold, learn from hence how to make the uſe of it the more agreeable. Is maximè divitiis fruitur qui minime divitiis indiget. *He moſt of all enjoys riches, who wants them the leaſt.* "Tell me, you ſay, who is the author of this ſentence?" Well; to ſhew

ſhew you how liberal we are, we have determined to give *(i)* you more than is our own. It is the ſentiment of *Epicurus*, *Metrodorus*, or ſome other of that ſchool. But what ſignifies who ſaid it? It is ſaid to all. He that wants riches, is anxious after them, but no good is enjoyed with anxiety. He is always ſtudying to make ſome addition to his ſtore, who thinks of nothing but an increaſe of his wealth: ſuch a one forgets the ight uſe of what he has got; he is ever buſy at his account-books; or attending the Forum; he daily conſults the almanack; and, inſtead of being a proprietor, becomes his own factor.

ANNOTATIONS, &c.

(a) Fidelity] *Fides*. The Chriſtian word is *faith*. Gall. *La Foy*.

(b) To avoid danger] And can there, good Mr. Stoic, be any greater danger, any greater annoyance, dreaded, than death? How then can it be taking care of the body, or obſerving the firſt rule of nature, ſelf-preſervation, ſo highly commended elſewhere, to ruſh voluntarily on death? But thus Stoiciſm often contradicts itſelf. *See* Epiſt. 24.

(c) The moſt ſhocking cruelty] Vid. Brodæ. Miſcell. l. 2. c. 9. Turneb. Adverſar. l. 15. c. 15 Sigon. de Judiciis, l. 3. c. 18.

(d) To give no offence] The Apoſtle's advice in this reſpect, as in all other, far tranſcends the Stoic; eſtabliſhing a doctrine which the wiſeſt philoſopher of them all had not yet advanced. *Recompenſe*, ſays he, *no man evil for evil. Provide things honeſt in the ſight of all men; and if it be poſſible, as much as lieth in you, live peaceably with all men.* Rom. 12. 17.

(e) The rabble] See Ep. 8. Note *(b)*.

(f) Charybdis] Dextram Scylla latus, lævum implacata Charybdis obſidet.---*Virgil.* iii. 420.

For on the right, her dogs, foul *Scylla* hides;
Charybdis roaring on the left preſides,
And in her greedy whirlpool ſucks the tides.---*Dryden.*

(g) To raiſe ſtrife] For *where envy and ſtrife is, there is confuſion, and every evil work.*---Jam. 3, 16.

(h) More men] Plures computant quam oderunt.---al. occiderint. *From whence* Pincianus *conjectures*, plures compilant, quam occiderint: *More commit robberies than murders.* So the old French, La plus part demande la bourſe, que la vie.

(i) To ſhew you] Vulg. ut ſcias quam benigni ſimus propoſitum eſt aliena laudare: *Others*, dare, *which I follow, as beſt anſwering to* benigni ſimus, *carrying on the metaphor.*

EPISTLE XV.

On Diet and Exercise.

IT hath been, *Lucilius*, an ancient cuſtom to begin an Epiſtle, with this compliment, *I am glad to hear you are well (a)* : and I will ſay, (I think with propriety) *I am glad to hear you ſtudy philoſophy :* for this is *to be well :* without this, the ſoul is ſick ; and even the body, though ever ſo ſtrong and vigorous, without this, hath but the ſtrength of a frantic madman. Be this ſort of health then your principal care, nor let the other be neglected ; which indeed will not coſt you much pains, if you are deſirous to procure it : for it would be ridiculous, and by no means convenient for a ſtudious man to be engaged in any laborious exerciſe, in order to make the arms more pliant, to widen the ſhoulders, or harden the ribs : was you to be crammed like a gladiator, to make your muſcular parts more brawny, you will never equal a fed ox in weight and ſtrength. Beſides, the more large and groſs the body, the more will the mind be cramped and inactive. Straiten therefore and lower the body, in order to give the mind fairer play. Many inconveniences attend on thoſe who devote themſelves to the care of the body ; firſt in ſome laborious exerciſe that exhauſts the ſpirits, and makes them unfit for more intentive ſtudies : and ſecondly, the ſubtilty of the mind *(b)* is checked by nothing more than by repletion. Add to this the ſlavery of the loweſt kind *(c)* grown into an habit, among men, who devote their whole time to the bagnio or tavern ; who have ſpent the day according to their wiſh, if they have been almoſt diſſolved in ſweat ; and to ſupply the place of the juices thereby exhaled, have poured down large draughts of liquor upon an empty ſtomach. To ſweat and to drink, what is this but the life of a porter *(d)* ?

There are ſome gentle exerciſes, which ſufficiently recreate the body and take up but little time, the principal thing to be regarded. An eaſy run, the ſwinging the hands to and fro with weights in them, leaping in length or height, or dancing (if I may ſo call it) like the *Salii (e)* ; or (to ſpeak leſs courtly) like a fuller or weaver. Chuſe any one of theſe ; it is eaſy, and requires

requires no art. But in whatever you are pleaſed to divert yourſelf, tarry not long, before you return to the exerciſe of the mind. This may be employed both night and day: it is ſtrengthened and maintained by moderate labour: neither heat, nor cold, nor even old age can hinder this ſort of exerciſe. Cheriſh this good, which is improving every day. Not that I would have you always poring over a book; or at your writing deſk: ſome reſpite *(f)* is to be given to the mind; yet not ſo as to enfeeble, but only to refreſh it. Taking the air on horſeback, or in a chariot, keeps the body in exerciſe, and prevents not the ſtudy of the mind. In walking alſo, with a friend, you may read, dictate, ſpeak, and hear. Sometimes to ſtrain the voice, at a certain pitch, without raiſing or lowering it, as in ſingſong *(g)*, is an exerciſe *(h)* not to be deſpiſed: and then if you deſire to learn in what manner you muſt walk; take along with you, one of thoſe merry fellows, who are put upon finding out new devices for bread *(i)*; you may get one, who will teach you a right ſtep, and other ceremonies, in eating or ſpeaking; and be as impudent, as the credulity of your patience will permit him. *What then?* you will ſay: *Muſt I begin at once to ſpeak aloud, and with vehemence?* No: it is ſo very natural for the voice to be raiſed and wound up gradually, that the greateſt wranglers begin with a common accent, and ſo proceed to vociferation. No gladiator *(k)* bawls out for *help and mercy* at the firſt onſet. However therefore the impulſe of your mind may perſuade you, you may upbraid a fault, ſometimes with more earneſtneſs, and ſometimes with more lenity, as may beſt ſuit your voice and lungs: and when you are to recover your voice to the uſual pitch, let it gradually deſcend, and not drop at once: let it be managed with the temper and diſcretion of a judicious orator, and not rage in the ſtyle of a blockhead or ruſtic: for it is not our intention to exerciſe the voice, but that the voice ſhould exerciſe us. Thus then *(l)* I have ſaved you from ſome trouble and expence; (in giving you my advice *gratis)* to which let me add a ſmall preſent which cannot but be acceptable to you.

An excellent ſentence that; Stulta vita ingrata eſt, trepida eſt, tota in futurum fertur; *The life of a fool is made up of chagrin, anxiety, and diſmal apprehenſions of what may happen.* You will aſk me, who is the author of it? The ſame as before. And what life do you think he calls the *life of a fool?* Such a one as that of *Baba* and *Ixion (m)?* No: it is ſuch a one as

 we

we ourſelves lead, whom blind ambition and fond deſires hurry upon acquirements that may be hurtful, and yet never ſatisfy; who, if any thing could ſatisfy *(n)*, have enough already; who never conſider, how ſweet it is to have nothing to aſk; and how noble it is to be fully content, without any the leaſt dependence upon Fortune. Think therefore now and then, *Lucilius*, upon your own acquiſitions; and when you obſerve how many are above you, think alſo how many are below you: if you would be grateful to heaven, for the happineſs of life, think how many you ſurpaſs therein. But why do I compare you with others? you have even ſurpaſſed yourſelf *(o)*.

Set yourſelf then ſome bounds, which, if you would, you cannot, paſs. Thoſe inſidious bleſſings we are ſo fond of, and which are much more ſweet in expectation, than in enjoyment, will ſoon paſs away *(p)*: was there any ſolidity in them, they would ſatisfy: but by their ſpecious appearances they only provoke and incite the thirſt. As to what remains for me in the currency of time, why ſhould I rather aſk Fortune to give it me, than prevail on myſelf not to aſk it? Or, why ſhould I be ſollicitous after it, unmindful of human frailty? Shall I amaſs? What? Labour and toil. Behold, this day is my laſt: if not, my laſt is very near.

ANNOTATIONS &c.

(a) Vel ſolum illud ſcribe, unde priores incipere ſolebant, ſi vales bene eſt, ego valeo, *Or let your letter conſiſt only of that old-faſhioned compliment*, In hopes that you are well; as I am at this preſent writing. *Plin.* L. 1. Ep. 11.

(b) The ſubtilty of the mind] *Diogenes*, the Cynic, being aſked *why the wreſtlers* (in the games) *were generally very ſtupid and ſenſeleſs*; anſwered, *Becauſe they are ſtuffed with beef and bacon*; alluding to the animals, as well as to the eaters. To which *Galen* adds that proverbial ſaying, Παχεῖα γαςὴρ λεπτὸν ὐ τίκτει νόον, Pinguis venter non gignet tenuem ſenſum.---Eraſm. 3. 6. 18.---The Engliſh ſay, *Fat paunches make lean pates*.

(c) Peſſimæ notæ mancipia in magiſterium (*al.* in magiſtratum) recepta. Or, it may be rendered, *Slaves of the loweſt ſort, admitted into office, and familiarity*; alluding to the *Græculi Magiſtri*, mentioned below.

(d) Cardiaci] One ſubject to the *heart-burn*. Plin. 23. 25. Juv. v. 33.

(e) Like the Salii] An order of prieſts, inſtituted by *Numa*; who when they carried the ſacred *Ancilia* in proceſſion, kept juſt meaſures with their feet, and ſhewed great ſtrength and agility in the various and handſome turns of their body.

(f) Some reſpite] See Ep. 84.

(g) As in ſing ſong] Per gradus et certos modos. Lipſius *obſerves, that by* Gradus *is to be underſtood, the riſing or falling of the voice*; *and that* modi *relates to the tone*.

(h) An

(h) *An exercise*] This was also reckoned an exercise of great utility. (Vid. Hieron. Mercurial. l. 6. Artis Gymnasticæ: Plutarchi *γ.ει.α*, c. 26.)

(i) *For bread*] Græculus esuriens, in cœlum, jusseris, ibit. *Juv.* 3. 76.
All things the hungry Greek *exactly knows,*
And bid him go to heav'n, to heav'n he goes.---Dryden.

(k) *The gladiator*] Alluding to the gladiator's appeal to the people when in the utmost distress; as they had it in their power to save him, if they pleased.

(l) *They then*---] Various are the readings here; from one (Pincian.) it may be rendered: *A certain* Greek *hath saved me some trouble in this affair, who hath enabled me to add to the foregoing a small present.* The life, &c.

(m) Baba *and* Ixion] Two silly fellows of those times. But *Erasmus* reads, Babys et Ixionis---That *Babys* the brother of *Marsyas*, who challenged *Apollo* in singing; and the poet's *Ixion*, who embraced a cloud instead of *Juno*.

(n) Ep. 2. (N. g.)

(o) *Surpassed yourself*] Having been advanced from a Plebeian to the Equestrian order; and now *Cæsar's Procurator*; an officer, sent by the Emperor into some province, to receive and regulate the public revenue, and to dispose of it at the Emperor's command. *See* Ep. 19. (N. c.)

(p) Ah think, my friends, how swift the minutes haste!
The present day entirely is our own.
Then seize the blessing ere 'tis gone:
To morrow! fatal sound! since this may be our last.

Yalden on human Life.
Dryden's Miscell. v. iii.

EPISLE XVI.

On the Study of Philosophy.

I KNOW, *Lucilius*, that it is your opinion, no one can live happily, or indeed scarce tolerably, without the study of philosophy: and that wisdom, when perfected *(a)*, makes life completely happy, and, without having made any great progress, satisfactory. But this opinion, clear as it is, must be established and fixed deeper in the heart, by daily meditation. It is more difficult to abide by good resolutions, than to form them. You must persevere, and by continual application so strengthen the mind, that it may be as truly good, as the will is to have it so. You need not, therefore, give yourself the trouble of many words, and protestations to me; I am perfectly satisfied in the progress you have made; I know too, that what you write is upon good principles, not feigned, nor coloured over: yet give me leave

leave to ſay, that though I have great hopes of you, I am not quite confident: I would have you think the ſame yourſelf. Preſume not, too ſoon and eaſily, on your own ſtrength: examine well yourſelf *(b)*: make different ſcrutinies and obſervations, but more eſpecially conſider this; whether you have made a progreſs in philoſophy, or in life itſelf; in knowledge, or in practice.

Philoſophy is no popular artifice; nor made for ſhew, and oſtentation(*c*): it conſiſts not in words, but in deeds. Nor is it to be applied to, only as an amuſement, to take off the tediouſneſs of the day: no; it forms and faſhions the mind; ſets life in good order; directs the conduct; ſhews what is to be done *(d)*, and what to be left undone; it ſits at the helm, and ſteers our courſe through the wide ſea of doubt; in ſhort, no man can live in ſafety without it. Innumerable accidents happen every hour, which muſt have recourſe to philoſophy, as a faithful counſellor. But ſome one will ſay, " What avails philoſophy, if fate (or *deſtiny as the* Stoics *think*) will take " its courſe *(e)*: if God is the ſupreme governor of the world? or if (ac" cording to the *Epicureans) Chance* is all in all; For, things certain can" not be altered; and no preparation can be made againſt what is uncer" tain; if either God hath prevented my purpoſes, and hath decreed what " I ſhall do; or if every event is in the diſpoſal of Fortune?" Be this as it will, *Lucilius*, let any, or all of theſe opinions take place; philoſophy is nevertheleſs neceſſary, and to be diligently ſtudied: whether Fate, I ſay, binds us by an inexorable law; or God, the ſovereign of the world, diſpoſeth all things; or Chance impels, and toſſeth about at random, human affairs; ſtill philoſophy muſt be our defence; this will exhort us to obey God with a willing mind; and more ſtrenuouſly to reſiſt the power of Fortune; this will teach you to truſt in providence *(f)*, and humbly ſubmit to caſualties. But there is no need at preſent to launch out further into diſpute, concerning our free-agency, if Providence holds the reins of government; or we are bound and dragged by the chain of deſtiny; or the ſudden changes in the courſe of things depend upon mere *Chance*. I return therefore, *Lucilius*, to adviſe and exhort you, not to ſuffer the ardour of your mind to become faint and languid by any ſuch ſurmiſes; reſolve and perſevere, 'till ſuch impulſe becomes an habit.

Now,

Now if I know you well, *Lucilius*, you have been musing, from the beginning, upon what sort of present I would send with this Epistle. Peruse it, and you will find something; wherein indeed you will have no reason to admire my judgment; for I am still liberal of what is not my own: but why do I say, not *my own?* whatever is *properly* said by any one, I make bold to call it *mine*; as that saying of *Epicurus*, si ad naturam vives, nunquam eris pauper: si ad opinionem nunquam dives: exiguum natura desiderat, opinio immensum. *If you live according to nature, you will never be poor; if according to opinion, never rich: what nature demands, is little; what opinion, immense.* Let the possessions of many rich men be heaped upon you; let fortune exalt you far above any private condition of life; let her cover you with a roof of gold, clothe you with purple, surround you with delicacies, and so enrich you, as to have the ground, whereon you walk, paved with marble, and bestow upon you not only money enough for use, but to squander away: add to these, statues, pictures, and whatever else art can supply the most luxurious fancy with; the issue of all will be, only an inducement, still to covet something more. The desires of nature have their limits: but those that arise from false opinion, have not where to rest; for they know no bounds. He that walks in a straight and beaten path will soon find an end; but he that wanders out of his way, will long wander; for error is infinite. Withdraw yourself therefore from vain superfluities, and when you would know, whether what you are sollicitous after, ariseth from a natural or a fond and blind desire; consider whether such thing, if obtained, can give you solid contentment; if not,--if as far as you have gone, you must still go further; you may be assured that the path you walk in, is not the right path of nature.

ANNOTATIONS, &c.

(a) The Stoical wise man exists not but in description; for as *Plutarch* observes, ἔστι δ' οὔτε οὐδαμοῦ γῆς, οὐδὲ γέγονεν. De pugn. Stoic.) *There is no such one upon earth, nor ever was.* And *Cicero*, Stoicam sapientiam interpretantur, quam adhuc nemo mortalis est consecutus. *(in Lœl.) The Stoics give you such a definition of virtue as no mortal man ever yet attained to.* However, he may be look'd upon as set forth by way of example; as, in the *Gospel*, Christians are required *to be* perfect, *even as their father which is in heaven is perfect.* Matth. 5. 48. And as *Plato* (in Phæd.) says, *Pure wisdom is not attainable on this side the grave*; no Christian can properly assume the character, 'till *he comes to the general assembly, and church of the first-born, which are enrolled in heaven, and to the throne of God, who* is *is the judge of all, and to the spirits of just men, made* perfect. Heb. 22. 23. See 1 King. 8. 46. Job. 9. 20. Ps. 51. 5 Prov. 20. 9 Eccles. 7. 20. 1 Cor. 13. 11 Phil. 3. 12. Col. 4. 12. 2 Tim. 3. 17. 1 John. 1. 8. See also, *Sen.* de Ben. 1. Ep. 42. (N. a) *Lips.* Manud. 11. 8.

(b) Examine yourselves whether ye be in the faith; prove your ownselves, &c. 2 Cor. 13. 5. 1 Cor. 11. 28. See Ep. 25. (N. e.)

(c) Lipsius ex *Lactantio.* Mendacium incongruum et ineptum est, non in pectore, sed in labiis habere bonitatem, ne ergo---Virtutem verba putes, ut Lucum ligna,---Hor. Ep. 1. 6. 31.

'Tis ridiculous to think,
(As heedless minds the weakest things approve)
That words make virtue, just as trees a grove.——Creech.

Be ye doers of the word, not hearers only, deceiving your own selves; Jam. 1. 22. See also, Matth. 7. 21. Rom. 2. 13.

(d) As we say of the scriptures, *all scripture is given by inspiration of God, and is profitable, for doctrine, for reproof, for correction, for instruction in righteousness,* that the man of God may be perfect, thoroughly furnished unto all good works. 2 Tim. 3. 16.

(*e*) Fatalism, an old thread of doctrine, of late twisted anew, by a most ingenious, and indefatigable *spinner*; but *happily* untwisted by one of the same breed; forasmuch as, instead of carrying us through the extensive labyrinth of doubt, it fixeth us like statues, on the spot, merely passive; or (without a metaphor) will lead us to the following conclusion: that, since no action or event could possibly be different from *what it has been, is, or will be,* repentance becomes an idle ejaculation, and every application to Heaven for mercy and forgiveness, unnecessary, &c. *N. Dict.*

(f) Trust in the Lord with all thine heart; and lean not unto thine own understanding. In all thy ways acknowledge him, and he shall direct thy paths. Prov. 3. 5.—*I will trust and not be afraid; for the Lord Jehovah is my strength, and my song, and he is become my salvation.* 11. 12. 2.—*Trust not in uncertain riches, but in the living God, who giveth us richly all things to enjoy.* 1 Tim. 6. 17.

EPISTLE XVII.

On the same; and concerning Poverty.

THROW away all these vanities, *Lucilius,* if you are wise, or rather that you may be wise. Strive with all your might to attain sound wisdom. If any thing withholds you, either untie the knot or cut it. But *family-affairs,* you say, *detain you; which you would fain so order, as, without any further trouble, to arrive at an easy competency; so that poverty may be no burthen to* you; *nor* you *to any one.* When you say this, *Lucilius,* you seem not to know the whole strength and power of the *good* in question; you see indeed the excellency of philosophy in the gross; but as yet you consider confider not minutely enough its feveral parts; you know its great utility, at all times, and in all refpects; forafmuch as, (to ufe the words of *Cicero)* in maximis opituleter, et in minima defcendat; *it affifts us in affairs of the higheft confequence, and defcends even to the loweft (a).* Believe me, if you confult philofophy, fhe will perfuade you not to fit fo long at your counting-defk.

But this is your fcheme; this the chief avocation from your ftudies: *to fhun that dreadful thing, poverty.* And what if, after all, poverty fhould prove defirable? Riches have prevented many from the ftudy of philofophy: poverty is always free, and always fecure. If an enemy's trumpet founds an alarm, the poor man knows it to be of little confequence to him *(b)*: if there is an outcry of fire, he is at the trouble of faving nothing but himfelf: if he muft go aboard, he makes no buftle in the port; nor does he difturb the fhore with a fingle attendant, much lefs with a crew of fervants, for whom it might be difficult to find provifion in a foreign country. Not but that it is an eafy matter to fupply a few mouths, efpecially of thofe that are orderly, and require nothing more than a common meal. Hunger cofts not much to be fatisfied; but a nice palate is expenfive. Poverty is contented with the fatisfaction of her prefent defires. Why therefore do you contemn fellowfhip with *her*, whofe manner every rich man in his fenfes, or who would fain live happily, defires to imitate? Would you be at leifure to improve, and attend the duties of the mind, you muft either be poor, or act as fuch. Study will turn to little account, where there is no refpect had to frugality; and frugality is a fort of voluntary poverty.

Lay afide, therefore, thefe frivolous excufes; *I have not yet got enough; when I have, I will give myfelf up entirely to philofophy.* Nothing is to be fought before this, which you defer, and poftpone to every thing. You muft begin here. But you fay, *I would fain get wherewithal to live.* Learn then how to get it. If any thing hinders you from living well, let it not hinder you from dying well. There is no reafon that poverty, or even want fhould recall you from the ftudy of philofophy; for even hunger is to be endured while we are in purfuit of this, as patiently as in a ſiege. And what is the reward of patience at ſuch a time; but the not falling into the hands, and ſubmitting to the diſcretion of the conqueror? But how much greater the reward that *this* promiſeth, even perpetual liberty; a liberty out of the reach of men or gods to deſtroy! *(c)* Hunger hath been driven to ſuch extremes, that whole armies have wanted neceſſaries, and been forced to eat the roots of herbs *(d)*, and ſuch offals as are not fit to be named *(e)*. And for what did they ſuffer all this? for a kingdom *(f)*, and, what is ſtill more ſurpriſing, for a kingdom not their own. And will any one ſcruple to endure poverty, that he may free his mind from all hurtful paſſions, *and be king of himſelf?*

There is no neceſſity therefore for being rich, before you enter upon this ſtudy. You may apply yourſelf to it without a viaticum, and attain it, without proviſion, or ſupplies. But ſo it is, *Lucilius,* when you ſhall have got every thing elſe, you will then look after philoſophy. You ſuppoſe this the laſt neceſſary of life, or, if I may call it ſo, an additional accompliſhment. But I beg of you, whatever you are in poſſeſſion of, to ſtudy philoſophy: for how do you know but that you have too much of worldly goods already? Or, if you have nothing, make the attainment of this your firſt ſtudy.

But neceſſaries will be wanting. What neceſſaries? All that nature aſks is very little; and a wiſe man will accommodate himſelf to nature. If he is driven to the laſt extremity, *he knows his time here is but ſhort (g).* And if he has ſtill enough to keep body and ſoul together, he is thankful for it, and makes the moſt of what he has got: not being ſollicitous or anxious after any thing more than mere neceſſaries, food and rayment. He ſits himſelf down contentedly, and laughs at the hurry and fatigues of the rich; and the many vexations and perplexities of thoſe who are ſtriving to be ſo; ſaying, *Why are ye ſo long about it? why do ye plague yourſelves with the expectation of intereſt-money; or of ſome great return in trade; or the death of an old miſer; when ye may ſoon be rich in a more compendious way? Wiſdom ſupplies the place of wealth; and where ſhe hath made riches ſeem ſuperfluous ſhe hath given*

 them.

them. But this argument belongs not properly to you, *Lucilius*, who may be ranked among the rich; change but the times *(b)*, and you have a great deal too much. But in every age there is enough to ſupply nature.

And here I might have ended this Epiſtle, had I not uſed you to a bad cuſtom. As no one can ſalute or addreſs the *Parthian* kings without a preſent; ſo there is no taking leave of you *gratis*. Well then, I will ſtill borrow from *Epicurus*,---Multis paraſſe divitias, non finis miſeriarum fuit, ſed mutatio;---*The acquiring much wealth hath proved to many, not an end, but only a change, of their miſeries.* The fault however lies not in the things acquired, but in the mind itſelf. That which made poverty grievous, makes alſo riches irkſome. As it matters not, whether you place a ſick man, on a wooden, or a golden couch; ſince he ſtill carries his diſeaſe along with him; ſo whether a diſcompoſed mind be placed in wealth or poverty, it is the ſame thing. The diſtemper will ſtill attend it.

ANNOTATIONS, &c.

(a) *Lipſius* gives theſe words to *Hortentius* rather than to *Cicero*.

(b) The rich only are in danger. So *Petronius*;

Cum cecinère tubæ, jugulo ſtat divite ferrum.

(c) Or, *the being ſubject to no fear either of man or God.* This may be looked upon as a Stoical rant; but *St. Peter* ſays, *Who is he that will harm you, if ye be followers of that which is good?*—1. Pet. 3. 13.—See alſo Ep. 38. (N. x.)

(d) See *Sen.* de ira. c. 20. *Sidon. Apoll.* viii. 7. No. P. 437.

(e) Dictu fædam]—ad inſames jam jamque coegerat eſcas. ib.

(f) The Apoſtle argues in like manner. *Every one that ſtriveth for the maſtery is temperate in all things: now they do it to obtain a corruptible crown, but we an incorruptible.* 1 Cor. 9. 25.

Pro toto hoc argumento, pulchrè Manilius,
Quæremus lucrum navi, mortemque ſequemur
Ad prædas. Pudeat tanto bona velle caduca.
Quid cœlo dabimus! quantum eſt quo veneat omne?
Impendendus homo eſt, Deus eſſe ut poſſit in ipſo.
Pulchra, inquam, hæc magis, an pia? *Lipſ.*
—*From food and clothes from eaſt to weſt we run,*
And ſpendthrifts *often ſweat to be undone.*
Are periſhing goods *worth ſo much pains and coſt,*
Hard to be got and in enjoyment loſt?
Then what muſt heaven deſerve? That gold, that buys
The reſt, how diſproportionate a price!
It aſks a higher value, and to gain
The God, *lay out* thyſelf, *the price is* man. Creech.

(*g*) Exiliet e vita] This, I think, is the ſecond paſſage which required to be ſoftened, in order to avoid a certain doctrine of the Stoics, which could not but be ſhocking to a Chriſtian reader; and which *Seneca* himſelf ſeems not to approve of, in what follows;—*Si verò exiguum fuerit, et anguſtum, quo vita produci poſſit*, id boni conſulet. *See* Ep. 12. 14. 24. 65. (N. i.)

Beſides, the turn here given, and which the words will bear in ſome meaſure, is conſonant to that moſt comfortable doctrine of the Apoſtle; *Our light affliction* which is but for a moment, *worketh for us a far more exceeding, and eternal weight of glory.* 11 Cor. 4. 17.

(*h*) Saculum muta, nimis habes Vulg.—Sæculum muta—*Lipſ. Opſop.* i. e. If we look back to the times of the *Fabricii*, and the *Curii*, before luxury grew into faſhion, *you have already too much.*

EPISTLE XVIII.

On the Behaviour of a Philoſopher at certain Seaſons. On Poverty; and immoderate Anger.

DECEMBER is a month, in which the city ſeems in full employ. Public feaſting and luxury are allowed, and every place reſounds with the noiſe of preparation: as if there was no difference between the feaſt called *Saturnalia* (*a*), and the common working days; ſo that he was not wide of the mark, who was pleaſed to ſay, that December now laſted all the year!—I ſhould have been glad, *Lucilius*, if you had been here, that I might have conferred with you, and heard your opinion, concerning what is to be done; whether we muſt go on in our uſual way; or, leſt we ſhould ſeem too far to diſſent from the humour of the times, we ſhould likewiſe unrobe, and give a looſe to joy, banquetting and wine. For what was not uſual but on ſome uproar and diſturbance, or when any calamity befel the city (*b*), we now change our dreſs for the ſake of pleaſure and feaſting. If I am not miſtaken in you, were you appointed arbiter in this affair, you would not have us act altogether like the rabble, nor altogether unlike them: unleſs perhaps the mind, on theſe feſtival days, is to be reſtrained, in order to exhibit a ſingle example of abſtinence, while every one elſe is indulging himſelf in the moſt luxurious pleaſures. He gives a ſure token of his ſteadineſs, who is not to be drawn into ſoftneſs and luxury at ſuch a time; and ſo much

ſtronger

ſtronger is he, if he keeps himſelf ſober and thirſty, when all the people are drunk and overcharged. But the more moderate way is, not to be particular at this time, ſo as to be taken notice of; nor yet to give into all their meaſures; but to do what others do, though not in the ſame manner. A man may celebrate a feſtival without luxury and exceſs of riot.

But I have an inclination to try the firmneſs of your mind; by giving you ſuch precepts as have been given, and followed too, by great men. Set apart certain days, in which taking up with the meaneſt and vileſt diet, and the moſt coarſe and rough cloathing, you may ſay to yourſelf; *And is this all that I was afraid of?* While in ſecurity, let the mind prepare itſelf againſt difficulties; and amidſt the favours of fortune, be ſtrengthened againſt any injurious treatment. The ſoldier, in the time of peace, exerciſes himſelf; throws up trenches, and, in fruitleſs labour, takes a great deal of pains, to inure himſelf againſt the time, when it may become neceſſary. Whom you would not have tremble in the time of action, you muſt harden before the time comes. In like manner ſome have continually ſo inured themſelves to poverty, as almoſt to proceed to want; that they may never be ſurprized with what they have learned to bear.

Think not that I am inviting you to a mean repaſt *(c)*, or the hovel of a poor man *(d)*, or whatever elſe it is, whereby luxury ſometimes relieves itſelf, and ſmooths over the irkſomeneſs of riches by way of change: no; I deſire that your bed may be really hard; your clothes rough, your bread ſtale, and of the vileſt ſort: endure this three or four days, or ſometimes longer, that it may not be whim only by way of variety, but a fair tryal *(e)*; and then, believe me, *Lucilius*, you will exult in being ſatisfied with what coſts a trifle: and you will learn, that you are under no ſuch great obligation to fortune, for a maintenance; for let her be as ſpiteful as ſhe pleaſes, ſhe cannot but ſupply you with ſuch things as are abſolutely neceſſary.

Yet after all, there is no reaſon to think you have done a great thing: it is no more than what many thouſand ſlaves, and poor wretches do daily. All that you can boaſt of is, that you do it voluntarily. And then it will be as eaſy for you to endure it always *(f)* as ſometimes to undergo the trial. Let us be exerciſed, as it were, at the poſt; leſt fortune ſhould come upon us unprepared. Let poverty be familiar to us. We ſhall more ſecurely enjoy wealth, if we know that it is not grievous to be poor. That great maſter of pleaſure, *Epicurus*, obſerved certain days, wherein he very ſparingly ſatisfied hunger, to prove whether there was any thing that did not contribute to the enjoyment of full and conſummate pleaſure: or if any thing was wanting thereto, what it was; and whether it deſerved all that care and pains, that are generally beſtowed in the acquiring it. This is what he ſays of himſelf in the Epiſtle he wrote to *Polyænus*, when *Charinus* was governor of *Athens*. And he even glories in it; that he could dine at leſs expence than three farthings *(g)*; when *Metrodorus*, who had not made ſo great a proficiency in philoſophy, would ſpend the whole. Do you think that he found only ſatiety in his meal? yes, and pleaſure too; a pleaſure not light and tranſitory, and to be at times repeated, but ſtable and certain. Not that mere water is ſo pleaſant a thing, or a coarſe cake, or a piece of barley bread; but the chief pleaſure conſiſts in being able to extract even ſatisfaction from theſe, and to arrive at ſuch a paſs, as to bid defiance to the inclemency of fortune. What if the allowance of a common priſon is better; and even the executioner ſupplies the criminals under ſentence of death with a larger portion: how great muſt that mind be, to ſubmit to that condition voluntarily, that is decreed for thoſe who are reduced to the laſt extremity! This is to raiſe, as it were, a counter-battery to Fortune. Begin therefore, *Lucilius*, to practiſe theſe things; ſet apart ſome particular days to quit, as it were, the world; and make the loweſt condition familiar to you: accept the fellowſhip of poverty.

> Aude hoſpes contemnere opes, et te quoque dignum
> Finge Deo. Virg. 8. 364. *(h)*

Not that I would debar you from the poſſeſſion of riches, but would have you ſo poſſeſs them, as not to be afraid of loſing them. Which

intrepid

intrepid ſecurity you may attain by this ſimple method; only by perſuading yourſelf that you can live happily without them; and looking upon them as ever ready to take wing.

I ſhall now begin to fold up my letter. But pay me firſt, *you ſay*, the uſual debt. Well then, *Epicurus* ſhall pay you. Immodica ira gignit inſaniam, *Immoderate anger turns to madneſs*: You cannot but know this truth, if ever you was maſter of a ſtubborn ſlave, or had an enemy *(i)*. But indeed this paſſion is apt to afflict all ſorts of perſons: it ariſes as well from love as from hate; it breaks out not only in ſerious affairs, but amidſt ſport and jeſting; nor does it ſignify ſo much from what provocation it ſprings; as what ſort of mind it affects; as it is not to be conſidered how great a fire is, but whereon it happens to light: be it ever ſo great, it hurts not ſolid bodies; while ſuch as are dry and combuſtible ſoon raiſe a ſpark into a mighty flame. Thus it is, *Lucilius*, the event of an extraordinary paſſion is madneſs; and therefore anger is to be avoided, not only for moderation-ſake, but for the health, *both of the mind and body (k)*.

ANNOTATIONS &c.

(a) This feſtival is ſuppoſed to have been inſtituted in memory of the liberty enjoyed in the golden age under *Saturn*, before the names of maſter and ſervant were known in the world. For among other mirthful ceremonies to be obſerved on this feſtival, ſervants were allowed to be ſo free with their maſters, as to change clothes with them, and make them wait upon them at table:

Exercent epulas læti famuloſque procurant
Quiſque ſuos.—*Attius*.
Feſtaque ſervorum, cùm famulantur heri. *Auſonius*.

And even to ridicule them to their faces:

Hor. Sat. II. 7. 4.—Age, libertate Decembri,
Quando ita majores voluêrunt, utere; narra.
Go to, and as our antient laws decree,
Uſe boldly thy December's liberty,
Speak fairly what thou wilt, thou mayſt be free. Creech.

This feſtival at its firſt inſtitution was kept only one day, (the 14th of the kalends of *January*) which continued to the time of *Auguſtus*, when two more days were added; and by *Caligula* two more; according to *Martial*,

Et jam Saturni quinque fuêre dies.
Hæc ſignata mihi quinque diebus erant. *Id.*

Which soon after were encreased to seven days;

Sic *Novius*, Atellanarum scriptor,
Olim expectata septem veniunt Saturnalia.
Et *Mummius* quidam,—Nostri majores veluti bene
Multa instituère, sic hoc optimè, frigore
Fecère summo dies septem Saturnalia.

See Ep. 47.—*Lucian*, (who in his *Saturnalia* recites the forms and ceremonies observed on this festival. *Macrob.* ii. 10. *Alex. ab Alex.* ii. 22. *Lips.* Saturn. i. 2, 3.

(b) Ergo ubi concipiunt quantis sit cladibus urbi
Constatura fides superûm, ferale per urbem
Justitium; latuit *plebeio tectus amictu*
Omnis honos; nullos comitata est purpura fasces.—Lucan. ii. 18.
While thus the wretched citizens behold
What certain ills the faithful gods foretold:
Justice suspends her course in mournful Rome,
And all the noisy Courts at once are dumb:
No honours shine in the distinguish'd weed,
No rods the purple magistrate precede.-----Rowe.

(c) Ad modicas cœnas. *Al.* medicas. *Al.* monas. *Al.* moneas. From whence *Muretus* conjectures *Timoneas*, such an entertainment, as one might expect from *Timon*, the Misanthrope, in his reduced state. *Opsop. Lips.*

(d) Pauperum cellas. Vid. *Sen.* ad Helviam. c. 12.
Mundæ que, parvo sub lare pauperum,
Cœnæ, sine aulæis et ostro,
Sollicitam explicuère frontem. Hor. Od. iii. 29. 14.
To frugal treats and humble cells,
With grateful change the wealthy fly;
Where health-preserving plainness dwells
Far from the carpet's gaudy eye.
Such scenes have charm'd the pangs of care,
And smooth'd the clouded forehead of despair. Francis.

(e) The like Precept is given by *Epictetus*. Diss. 13.

(f) Or, *for the ring of wrestlers*. Ad palum, a la luite, *Vet. Gall.* a la Quintaine. *Malherbe.*

(g) Non toto asse. Timocrates objected to Epicurus, *that he spent daily above a pound in meat and drink*. This *Laertius* denied, who, with many others, alledged, *that* Epicurus *lived upon the most simple and mean diet*, according to his own words; *I exult in bodily pleasure, with the enjoyment only of bread and water; I despise all manner of sumptuous delicacies, not for their own sake, but on account of the disorders that attend them.* Stobæ. Serm. 17.—So in his Epistle to *Menæcius*, *Bread and water, says* Epicurus, *give consummate pleasure to a man when dry and hungry.*

(h) *Mean as it is, this palace and this door,*
Receiv'd Alcides, *then a conqueror:*
Dare to be poor; accept our homely food,
Which feasted him; and emulate a God. Dryden.

(i) Cùm habuerint servum et inimicum. *Muretus* thinks these words to be suspected; but why I cannot conceive: for what things are apt to exasperate a man more than *a disorderly slave*, or *a malicious enemy?*

(k) He

(k) *He that is ſlow to wrath, is of great underſtanding; but he that is of an haſty ſpirit, exalteth folly.* Prov. 14. 29. *He that is ſlow to wrath, is better than the mighty; and he that ruleth his ſpirit, than he that taketh a city.* 16. 32. *Ceaſe from anger, and forſake wrath.* Pſ. 37. 8. *For wrath killeth the fooliſh man, and indignation ſlayeth the filly one.* Job. 5. 2. *Be not haſty in thy ſpirit to be angry, for anger reſteth in the boſom of fools.* Eccleſ. 7. 9. *Let every one be ſwiſt to hear, ſlow to ſpeak, ſlow to wrath.* Jam. 1. 19. *Be ye angry, and ſin not; let not the ſun go down upon your wrath.* Epheſ. 4. 26. *Let all bitterneſs and wrath, and anger, and clamour, and evil-ſpeaking, be put away from you, with all malice.* 34.

EPISTLE XIX.

On Solitude and Retirement *.

I Exult, *Lucilius*, at the reception of every letter from you confirming my hopes; as they not only promiſe but engage for you. Go on, I pray you; for what can I aſk of my friend better, than what I would aſk *of the gods* in his behalf? Withdraw yourſelf from your preſent employments, if you can, gracefully; if not, force yourſelf from them. We have flung away time enough already; let us begin in our old age to decamp. Seems it a diſagreeable taſk? We have lived in a ſtormy ocean, let us die in a quiet harbour. Not that I would have you affect ſingularity, or think to gain a name, by retirement; which you ought not, either to boaſt, or to conceal. For I ſhall never deſire to prevail upon you ſo far, as that, condemning the madneſs and folly of mankind, you ſhould retire into ſome ſecret place, forgetting and forgot. Act ſo, that your retreat, though not talked of, may yet be ſeen. Such as have not yet entered upon a public life, may do as they pleaſe, and ſtill live in obſcurity; but you are not at liberty herein. The ſtrength of your genius, your elegant writings, and great and noble alliances, have every where publiſhed your name: ſo well are you known, that was you to ſhut yourſelf up in the remoteſt part of the

 world,

world, it would be in vain: no darkneſs can ſo ſcreen you, but that the luſtre of your former actions would betray you.

But I think, you may now demand ſome reſt, without reſentment, anxiety or remorſe. For what do you leave behind you that you can poſſibly regret? Clients? Not one of them follows you for your ſake, but for what they can get.—Friends? Friendſhips indeed were ſought formerly; but now intereſt is all *(a)*. Or are you afraid that ſome old man in your abſence will alter his will? Or that your viſiters will ſeek ſome other levee? *Lucilius*, any thing extraordinary, and eſpecially liberty, is not to be purchaſcd for nothing; conſider, whether you had rather loſe yourſelf, or your connections. For my part, I wiſh you had grown old in as private a ſtation, as you was born; and that fortune had never introduced you into high life. Your rapid ſucceſs hath carried you quite beyond the proſpect of healthful happineſs. A province, a government, and all its appendages! and then follow other offices, and ſtill other after them! What end will there be? What do you expect before your ambition will be ſatisfied? To have all you deſire? That will never be. As we ſay of the ſeries of cauſes, of which fate is compoſed, the ſame we ſay of deſires, from the attainment of one ſtill ſprings another. You are involved in a ſtate of life; which, of itſelf, can know no end of miſery and ſlavery. Withdraw your neck from the yoke; it were better broke at once, than to be always oppreſſed †. If you reduce yourſelf to a private ſtate, every thing indeed will be leſſened, but there will be enough left for a reaſonable mind: whereas now, though vaſt ſtores are heaped upon you, there is yet no ſatisfaction. Had you rather then enjoy contentment with a little, or ſuffer hunger amidſt plenty? Proſperity is not only covetous itſelf, but expoſed to the covetouſneſs of others; and it is not poſſible to ſatisfy others, if you cannot ſatisfy yourſelf.

But you will ſay, How ſhall I extricate myſelf? In every way you can. Think how many things you have raſhly undertaken to get money; what toils you have undergone for honour. Something muſt be attempted for the ſake of eaſe and retirement; or you muſt wear out yourself in the fatigues of office; live in a continual hurry of business, amidst a storm, which no moderation can fly from, nor any proposed enjoyment of life escape. For what avails it how much you desire ease yourself, when your fortune will not suffer you to enjoy it? And what if you still advance in life? As much as you add to your success, you add to your fears. Give me leave to remind you of a saying of *Mecænas'*, when the torture of his dignity *(b)* forced the truth from him; Ipsa enim altitudo attonat summa: *The greater the height, the more subject to the effects of thunder.* This is what he hath advanced in his treatise called *Prometheus*; and his meaning is, *that too great height astonishes and confounds the happy person.* Can there be any power of so great worth, as to make you talk thus idly, as if you were drunk *(c)*? *Mecænas* indeed was an ingenious man, and would have set a noble example of Roman eloquence, if prosperity had not enervated, nay, quite unmann'd him *(d)*. And such, *Lucilius*, must be your fate, unless, (what he too late desired) *(e)* you lower your sails, and make to shore.

With this saying of *Mecænas*, I might here have discharged my account with you, but that I fear you will dispute it, and not accept of payment in such *new coin.* No; as things are, *Epicurus* must pay the usual debt; well then, he says, Ante circumspiciendum est, cum quibus edas et bibas, quàm quod edas et bibas. Nam sine amico visceratio, leonis ac lupi vita est. *You must rather have regard to the persons with whom you eat and drink, than to what you eat and drink. For good cheer without a friend, is the life of a lion or a wolf (g).* Now this is what you can never do but in retirement. At present, you will have guests enough, whom your secretary is pleased to pick out from your leveè; but he greatly errs, who looks for a friend in his crouded drawing-room; or who only tries him at an entertainment *(h)*. For no greater evil attends the man of business, and much employ, than that he takes those to be his friends, to whom he is no hearty friend himself; and thinks nothing of greater efficacy in promoting friendship, than conferring benefits. Whereas there are some men, who the more they stand indebted to your generosity, the more they hate you. A small favour

indeed

indeed makes a debtor, but a large one an enemy. What then, do not benefits procure friendſhips? yes, when you are allowed to chuſe the perſon you would oblige; not when they are conferred promiſcuouſly. Therefore when you have any ſuch intention, or till you are your own maſter, embrace this opinion of the wiſe: *It is of more conſequence to conſider, on whom the benefit is conferred, than what it is.*

ANNOTATIONS, &c.

* "There is a difference between *retirement* and *ſolitude*: the former may be ſocial, and filled up "with all the endearments of life; we carry with us into *retirement*, the affections of nature: but "we drop them in *ſolitude*: in the one we fly from the incumbrance, in the other, from the de-"lights of ſociety."

(a) "Sincerity, conſtancy, tenderneſs, are ſeldom to be found; they are ſo much out of uſe, that the man of mode imagines them to be out of nature. *We meet with few friends*: the greateſt part of thoſe, who paſs for ſuch, are, properly ſpeaking, nothing more than acquaintance: and no wonder; ſince *Tully's* maxim is certainly true; that friendſhip can ſubſiſt, non niſi inter bonos, *(only among the good)* at that age of life, when there is balm in the blood, and that confidence in the mind, which the innocency of our own heart inſpires, and the experience of other men's de-ſtroys." *Bolingbroke* Lett. p. 148.

" Believe me, (ſays the ſame Philoſopher) there is more pleaſure, and more merit too, in culti-vating friendſhip, than in taking care of the ſtate. Fools and knaves are generally beſt fitted for the laſt; and none but men of ſenſe and virtue are capable of the other." Lett. 200.

† See Ep. 22. (N. 6.)

(b) Mecænatis vera in ipſo eculeo elocuti. – Ponit eculeum pro dignitate torquente poſſidentem. *Vet. Schol.*—Eculeo, i. e. dignitate, et Aula, ubi aſſidua tormenta. *Lipſ.* Or perhaps by *eculeo*, ſays *Muretus*, *Seneca* means, the three laſt years of *Mecænas'* life, wherein he could ſcarce ever get any ſleep.

(c) *Lipſius* thinks this not ſaying too much, as applied to *Mecænas*. See a ſpecimen of his ſtyle, and the flouriſh of a *Maccaroni*, Ep. 114.

(d) Ep. 92. Habuit (Mecænas) grande et virile ingenium, niſi ipſe illud diſcinxiſſet.

(*e*) Not being in ſo high favour, at that time, with *Auguſtus*, as was his wife *Terentia*.

(f) In aſpero et probo. Nummus *probus*, qui non peccat in materia; *aſper*, quum nondum eſt detritus uſu. *Eraſm.* Sed vid. *Muret.* et Lipſ. *Hodiè apud Turcas*, Aſpri, *nummuli ex argento.*

(*g*) See Ep. 73.—Εῤῥ' ἐς κόρακας μονοφάγε καὶ τοιχωρύχε. *Alexis.*

Go and be hang'd, thou ſolitary glutton,
An houſebreaker is a better man.

The Romans *give us the ſaying of a pleaſant man, and a good companion, whoever he was, who, having ſupped alone, ſaid,* that he had eat indeed, but not ſupped, *as if a ſupper always wanted company and converſation, to make it palatable and pleaſing.* Plutarch, Sympos. vii. Prol.—Hence the Latins uſe the words *convivium*, and *cœna*, quaſi κοινή. *Lipſ.*

(*h*) See Sen. de Benef. vi. 34.

EPISTLE XX.

True Philosophy consists not in Words, but in Actions.

On the Contempt of Wealth.

IF you are well, and think yourself worthy of, one-day, becoming your own master, I rejoice: for it will be my glory, to have extricated you from that state wherein you so long wavered, without hopes of being made free. But this, my *Lucilius*, I shall beg and require of you: that you would permit philosophy to sink deeper into your heart;---that you would often make trial of your proficiency; not by speech or writing, but by the firmness of mind, and the diminution, at least, of all fond desires. Some propose to gain the applause of an audience by declamation; others to entertain the ears of young men, and such as are at leisure to attend their lectures, with variety of matter, and volubility of speech. But philosophy teaches to act, not to speak; and requires that every one should live according to the law prescribed; and that his conduct should agree with his discourse *(a)*; and that without any discordant action, it should be of one and the same colour throughout, for this is the whole duty and proof of wisdom; that deeds should correspond with words; and that the man should be every where, and at all times, consistent with himself. But where shall we find such a one? There are few, indeed; but there are some. However, it must be own'd a difficult task; though I do not say that a wise man should always walk with the same step, but in one and the same path. Observe, therefore, whether your dress be different from your furniture; whether you are liberal to yourself, and sordid to those who belong to you; whether you sup frugally, and build prodigally. Enter, at once, upon one certain rule of life, and square your whole life by the same. Some are very sparing, and even niggardly, at home, but are very generous and expensive abroad. Such different behaviour is faulty, and betrays a mind a mind ſtill wavering, without any certain tenour of life. Moreover, I will ſhew you, from whence this inconſtancy, this contrariety, proceeds. No one ſeriouſly purpoſes what he really would have; or if he does, he perſeveres not therein, but paſſes on to ſomething elſe; nor is this the only change of mind; for he ſoon returns even to that, which he had before caſt off and condemned. Therefore, laying aſide all former definitions of wiſdom, and comprehending the whole meaſure of human life, we may reſt ſatisfied with this: *What is wiſdom? It is always to will, or always not to will, the ſame thing.* (b) I think I need not add any ſuch exception, as that the thing any one wills, muſt be what is right: for nothing but what is right, can pleaſe always. Men, therefore, know not what they would have, but at the very moment when they would have it. No one ſeems to have the power of fixing, poſitively, what he wills or not, upon the whole. The judgment is daily altered, and is, at one time, oppoſite to what it is at another; ſo that many ſpend their whole lives, as it were, in play. (c) Preſs on, therefore, *Lucilius*, as you have begun; and, haply, you will either reach your journey's end, or, at leaſt, know, that you have not, as yet, reached it, nor can reach it, but by your own induſtry.

What then, you ſay, muſt become of your domeſtics? When they are no longer maintained by you, they will learn to maintain themſelves. And what you could not know from your own courteſy, and good-nature, poverty will teach you. This will retain your true and ſure friends; when *they* will deſert you, who honoured you not for your ſake, but their own intereſt. Is not poverty itſelf therefore amiable, when it points out the perſons who love you unfeignedly? O! when will that day come, that no one ſhall commend you more than you deſerve; or preſume to honour you with falſe praiſe! Hither let all your thoughts tend; regard this; wiſh for this; remitting all other affairs to the guidance of Providence, that you may be ſatisfied with yourſelf, and happy in your own endowments. What felicity can be more divine? Reduce yourſelf to a low degree; from whence you need fear no fall. And that you may the more willingly do this, I hope the tribute, which this epiſtle will immediately pay you, will prove an inducement.

ducement. Nay, though perhaps you may dislike it, *Epicurus* is even now ready to pay it for me. *Your discourse, believe me, would appear more magnificent from a truckle-bed and a patched coat; for things delivered under these circumstances are not only well expressed, but well proved.* (*d*) And, for my part, I am never more affected with what I hear from our *Demetrius* than when I see him laid upon straw, and so badly equipped as to appear rather naked, than clothed. What then? May not a man despise riches, even when it is in his power to enjoy them? (*e*) Certainly he may: And he shews a noble mind, who seeing them flow around him, and wondering with himself at his good fortune, laughs; and rather knows them to be his own from what he hears, than from any alteration they make in his conduct. It is extraordinary for a man not to be corrupted by the communication of wealth. He is great, who, amidst his riches, can humbly look down upon himself as a poor man; but much more secure is he who has none. I know not, you say, how such a one, was be reduced to poverty, would bear it. And I say (for *Epicurus*) I know not how a poor man would despise riches, were they to fall to his lot. The mind therefore in both is to be regarded; and we must consider, whether the one affects poverty, and the other despiseth riches: Or otherwise a straw bed, and ragged clothes are but a light proof of the will, unless it shall appear, that a man acts, not by necessity, but choice. But the good disposition I am speaking of, is not the looking upon these things as preferable; but because by such preparation, they become easy to be borne. And indeed, my *Lucilius*, they are easy; nay, by being thought upon long before, should they fall to your lot, they will be pleasant too. For they have that in them without which there can be no pleasure, *security*.

I think it necessary therefore, what I wrote to you concerning the practice of some great men; to set apart certain days for the exercise of an imaginary poverty, which is the rather to be practised, because we are apt to become effeminate by delicacies, and to think all things hard and irksome. The mind requires to be roused and forced from its lethargic disposition; and to be often reminded of what a little portion we have by the appointment of nature. No man is born rich in himself; as soon as he enters upon life, he is obliged to be contented with milk and ſwadling clothes; ſuch a beginning promiſeth not kingdoms, *though kings are not exempt from it.*

ANNOTATIONS, &c.

(*a*) See Ep. 16 (N. c.)

So *Chaucer*, in the character of the Parſon.

" This noble enſample to his ſchepe he yaff.
" That firſt he wrought, and afterwards he taught;
" Out of the Goſpel he the wordis caught:
" And this figure he added thereunto;
" That if gold ruſted, what ſchuld yryn do?"

Thus rendered by *Dryden:*

His preaching much, but more his practice, wrought;
A living ſermon of the truths he taught:
If they be foul on whom the people truſt,
Well may the baſer *braſs contract a ruſt.*

(*b*) This is *Zeno's* ὁμολογία, *conſiſtency*, the end of philoſophy. *Cato* (ap. *Cic.* De Fin. iii.) ſummum hominis bonum poſitum eſt in eo, quod ὁμολογίαν ſtoici, nos appellamus *convenientiam*, ſi placet.

See Ep. 35. (N. c.) 74. (N. h.) 95. 120. *Lipſ.* Manud. II. 15.

(*c*) They are reſtleſs in body, as in mind:

Tanta mali tanquam moles in pectore conſtat.——
Quid ſibi quiſque velit, neſcire et quærere ſemper:
Commutare locum, quaſi onus deponere poſſit.——
Hoc ſe quiſque modo fugit, et quod ſcilicet, ut fit,
Effugere, haud potis eſt ingratis hæret et angit.

Lucret. III, 1070.

Oh! if the fooliſh race of man, who find
A weight of cares, ſtill preſſing on their mind,
Could find as well the cauſe of this unreſt,
And all this burden, lodg'd within the breaſt;
Sure they would change their courſe; not live as now;
Uncertain what to wiſh, or what to vow:——
——*Thus every one o'erworks his weary will,*
To ſhun himſelf, and to ſhake off his ill:
The ſhaking fit returns, and hangs upon him ſtill.—Dryden.

(*d*) *Lipſius*, doubts whether theſe are the words of *Epicurus*; and ſeems rather to think them the words of *Seneca*, in anſwer to what *Epicurus* is ſuppoſed to have ſaid.

(*e*) I cannot but think that *Seneca* is here drawing his own picture, notwithſtanding what has been ſaid of his wealth and covetouſneſs.—" To deſpiſe riches with *Seneca's purſe*, (ſays Lord Bolingbroke) is to have at once all the advantages of fortune and philoſophy."

EPISTLE

EPISTLE XXI.

The Honour of Philoſophy.

DO you think, *Lucilius*, that the contents of your laſt are of any great importance? Indeed you give yourſelf much unneceſſary trouble. You know not what you would have: you rather approve of virtue, than follow it. You ſee wherein true felicity is placed, yet have not the courage to make any advance thereto. Give me leave then to ſhew you what prevents it, becauſe you ſeem but little to conſider it yourſelf. You have a great opinion of thoſe things you are ſuppoſed to leave; and when the ſecurity you would wiſh to enjoy is ſet before you, the ſplendor of the life you muſt retire from, dazzles and retains you, under an apprehenſion of falling into a ſordid and obſcure condition. You are miſtaken, *Lucilius*; the way propoſed, and which you ought to purſue, is rather an aſcent. As is the difference between ſplendor and light, when *this* has a certain origin in itſelf, but *that* ſhines with borrow'd rays; the ſame is there between this, your ſort of, life and the philoſopher's: the life you lead, becauſe it ſhines but by reflection, is ſoon eclipſed, when any thing intervenes; whereas the life propoſed is ever bright in its own luſtre: your philoſophical ſtudies will render you famous and noble: I will give you an inſtance of it from *Epicurus*. When he was writing to *Idomeneus (a)*, and endeavouring to recall him from a ſpecious way of life, to more ſolid and laſting glory, at a time when he was the miniſter of royal power *(b)*, and tranſacting the affairs of ſtate; if, ſays *Epicurus*, *glory is your purſuit; know, that my Epiſtles will make you more famous than all thoſe things you adore, or for which you are adored.* Did he ſpeak falſely herein? Who would have known *Idomeneus*, had not *Epicurus* regiſtered and engraved him in his Epiſtles? All thoſe potentates and princes from whom *Idomeneus* held his titles, are buried in oblivion. *Cicero's* Epiſtles ſtill preſerve the name of *Atticus* or otherwiſe *Agrippa's* being his ſon-in-law, *Tiberius* his grand-daughter's huſband, and *Druſus Cæſar* his great-grandſon, would have been of little advantage to him. He had been loſt among ſo great names, had not *Cicero* ſet him in view *(c)*. The vaſt deluge of time will flow in upon us; and though ſome great geniuſes may raiſe their heads above it, and for a while exert themſelves againſt oblivion; yet muſt they one day fall like thoſe who have gone before them.

What *Epicurus* promiſed his friend, I in ſome meaſure promiſe you, *Lucilius*; I flatter myſelf, that I ſhall have ſome favour with poſterity; and can at leaſt preſerve for a time ſuch names as I think proper to take with me. Our *Virgil* promiſed immortal honour to two perſons, and ſtill makes good his promiſe;

> Fortunati ambo, ſi quid mea carmina poſſunt.
> Nulla dies unquam memori vos eximet ævo;
> Dum domus Æneæ capitoli immobile ſaxum
> Accolet, imperiumque pater Romanus habebit *(d)*.

Whomſoever fortune hath exalted, and all ſuch as are the limbs, as it were, and partakers of another's greatneſs, flouriſh for a while, are greatly careſſed, and have a full levèe, while they continue in office; but no ſooner are they gone, than every remembrance of them is loſt for ever. Whereas the work of learning and ingenuity is ever encreaſing, nor are the poſſeſſors of them honoured only in themſelves, but whatever has any connection with them.

That I may not make mention of *Idomeneus gratis*, he ſhall pay for himſelf. It was to him that *Epicurus* wrote that noble ſentence, in which he exhorts him to make *Pythocles* rich in no doubtful or common way: *If*, ſays he, *you would make* Pythocles *rich, you muſt not add to his wealth, but ſubtract from his deſires (e)*. A ſentence too clear in itſelf to need explanation, and too eloquent to be heighten'd: but this I muſt adviſe you, not to think this ſpoken, with relation only to riches; for apply it to what you pleaſe, it is ſtill of the ſame force. *If you would make* Pythocles *more honourable, you muſt not add to his titles, but ſubtract from his deſires. If you would have* Pythocles *to enjoy perpetual delight, you must not add to his pleasures, but subtract from his desires. If you would make* Polythocles *the happy old man, and fill up the measure of life; it is not to be done, by adding more years, but by retrenching his desires.* Nor is there any reason to think, these are merely the words of *Epicurus*, for they are the voice of Nature. And what is usually done in the senate, we must do the same in philosophy: when any one hath delivered his opinion, and in some measure it demands assent, I immediately desire a division, and I follow him *(f)*. I the more willingly relate these sayings of *Epicurus*, that I may prove to those who have recourse to him under false hopes to find some cloak for their vices; that go where they will, they must still lead a good and sober life. When you visit his gardens and read this inscription; *Stranger, you may live well here: here pleasure is the* summum bonum; *the master of this house is ready to entertain you: he is humane and hospitable: he will give you a cake to eat, and water to drink; and in the end he will say to you, have you not been well entertained?* Know, that these gardens provoke not hunger, but assuage it. Nor do they enflame the thirst by the very draught, as some liquors do, but quench it, by a natural and easy remedy. In this sort of pleasure I am grown old. But observe, that I am speaking to you of such desires, as are not to be soothed by mere words, but such as require something, easily attainable, for their satisfaction. For with regard to the extraordinary, which may be deferred, corrected, or suppressed; I must remind you of this one thing; that such pleasure is not natural, is not necessary. If you bestow any thing upon it, it is merely voluntary *(g)*. *The belly hath no ears (h)*, either to receive precepts, or admit excuse: it makes its demands indeed, and often calls upon us; and yet is no troublesome creditor, as he is dismissed contentedly with a little; if you only give what you owe him, not all that is in your power to give.

ANNO-

ANNOTATIONS &c.

(*a*) That *Epicurus* flattered *Idomeneus* is objected to him by *Laertius*, in his Life of *Epicurus*. And *Athenæus* c. vii. observes that *the good man* (Epicurus) *flattered both* Idomeneus *and* Metrodorus, τῆς γαστρὸς ἕνεκεν, *for belly-timber.*

(*b*) To *Lysimachus*, or some other of *Alexander's* successors.

(*c*) "Neither his son *Agrippa*, nor grandson *Tiberius*, nor great grandson *Drusus*, would have been of any service to him, if *Cicero's* name by drawing *Atticus'* along with it, had not given him an immortality.—Dr. *Middleton's* Life of *Cicero*.

(*d*) In that beautiful Episode, of *Nisus* and *Euryalus*; l. ix. v. 446.

O happy friends! for if my verse can give
Immortal life, your fame shall ever live:
Fix'd as the capitol's foundation lies;
And spread, where-e'er the Roman Eagle flies.—Dryden.

(*e*) The words of *Epicurus* (Stob. Serm. 17.) are, Ει βουλει πλουσιόν τινα ποιῆσαι, μὴ χρημάτων προστιθει, της δ' ἐπιθυμιας ἀφαιρει. So *Plato* (Stob. Serm. x.) to one who was ever hankering after wealth, said, *Thou wretch, if thou wouldst be happy, endeavour not to encrease thy store, but to diminish thy desires.* And *Socrates*, to one, that asked him, how a man might become rich, answered, *By being contented to be poor.*

Pythocles was an handsome young man, whom, though but of 18 years of age, *Epicurus* was pleased to extol for his extraordinary genius, above all the learned of *Greece*, for which extravagant adulation he is blamed both by *Laertius* and *Plutarch*.—Lips.

(*f*) Sen. *de vit. beat.* c. 3. Brisson. *de Form.* c. 2. Kennett's *Rom. Antiquities*, p. 103.

(*g*) Epicurus dividebat cupiditatum genera, non nimis fortasse subtiliter, utiliter tamen. Partim esse naturales et necessarias; partim naturales et non necessarias; partim neutrum.—Naturales, satiari pœnè nihilo; nec secundum genus difficile ad potiendum; tertias, planè inanes et ejiciendas funditus putavit. *Cic.* Tusc. v.——*Nemesius* (de Anima c. xviii.) in like manner divides pleasures into three kinds; *Natural and necessary, for the support of life; as food and rayment: Natural, but not absolutely necessary; as marriage, and a communion of the sexes; neither necessary nor natural; as drunkenness, petulance, luxury.*

(*h*) "Discourse to, or call upon, hungry persons, they will not mind you, or leave their meat to attend, or, as Erasmus, ubi de pastu agitur, non attenduntur honestæ rationes. (Λιμῳ γαρ οὐδ' ἐστιν αντειπειν ἐπος *Hunger cannot bear contradiction.*) Nothing makes the vulgar more untractable, fierce and seditious, than scarcity and hunger.—Nescit plebes jejuna timere.—There is some reason the belly should have no ears, because words will not fill it." *Ray.* Prov. p. 100.

Οὐ γάρ τι στυγερῆ ἐπὶ γαστέρι κύντερον ἄλλο
Επλετο, ἥ τ' ἐκέλευσεν ἕο μνήσασθαι ἀνάγκῃ.—Od. 4. 116.
Spent with fatigue, and shrunk with pining fast,
My craving bowels still require repast,—
Necessity demands our daily bread,
Hunger is violent, and will be fed.—Pope.

EPISTLE

EPISTLE XXII.

On Retirement; for the Study of Philosophy.

YOU are now ſenſible, *Lucilius*, that you muſt diſengage yourſelf from thoſe ſpecious and vain avocations, that take you from your ſtudies: and you deſire to know by what means you can effect this. There are ſome things which cannot be communicated but by a perſonal conference. The phyſician cannot preſcribe a proper diet, or a proper time for bathing, by letters only: He muſt know the conſtitution of his patient, and feel his pulſe. According to the old proverb, Gladiatorem in arenâ capere conſilium *(a)*, *The gladiator conſults his advantage when actually engaged.* The eye or countenance of his antagoniſt, his manner of parrying, and the attitude of his body, direct his obſervation. What is uſual or ought to be done in certain caſes, may be preſcribed, and ordered in writing: ſuch counſel is given to perſons abſent, and to poſterity: but at what time a thing is to be done, and in what manner, no one can teach at a diſtance: circumſtances muſt be well weighed; nor is the being preſent alone ſufficient, a man muſt be prudent, and watchful to obſerve the fleeting opportunity: diligently, I ſay, obſerve this; and lay hold on it, as ſoon as it is perceived; and with your whole ſtrength and mind extricate yourſelf from your preſent employ: I will give you my opinion in plain terms:

You muſt either quit your manner of life, or it is not worth while to live: but this I alſo think, that the gentleſt methods to extricate yourſelf muſt firſt be uſed; endeavour to looſen your bonds, before you proceed to violence: not but that it may be thought more brave to fall at once than to live in continual ſuſpenſe *(b)*. But what I now particularly require is, that at length you entangle yourſelf no further, but reſt ſatisfied with ſuch buſineſs, as you have involved yourſelf in, or which, as you would rather have it thought, hath fallen upon you.

You muſt by no means look out for more: if you do, you can have no manner of excuſe; nor can you plead it accidental. What is uſually ſaid on this occaſion, is generally falſe: *I could not do otherwiſe; however unwilling I was, it was abſolutely neceſſary.* There is no neceſſity for puſhing forwards unadviſedly; it is ſomething, if not to repugn, yet to ſtand one's ground, and not preſs too much upon the favour of fortune. You muſt excuſe me, therefore, if I not only differ from you in opinion, but appeal to more prudent perſons than myſelf, as is my cuſtom, when in doubt. I have read an Epiſtle from *Epicurus* much to the point in hand: it is written to *Idomeneus*; whom he adviſeth to fly, and make all the haſte he can, before ſome ſuperior power intervenes, and deprives him of the liberty to act as he pleaſes. Yet he ſubjoins that nothing muſt be attempted but at an apt and proper ſeaſon; and that when ſuch ſhall offer, it muſt immediately be embraced: he forbids any one that is meditating his flight, to dream; and gives hopes of a ſalutary eſcape from the moſt difficult diſtreſs, if we neither prevent, nor neglect a proper opportunity.

I ſuppoſe you would be glad to know the Stoical doctrine in this matter.—There is no reaſon then that any one ſhould accuſe them of temerity: they are rather cautious, than raſh. Perhaps you expect to hear, that *it is cowardly to yield to affliction; we muſt ſtrive hard to go through with the taſk impoſed upon us; and perform the duty enjoined; he is neither ſtrenuous, nor brave, who ſhuns labour, but he whoſe mind gathers ſtrength from the difficulties that ſurround him.* Theſe things indeed will be ſaid, and rightly too, if perſeverance can find its reward; and nothing is required to be ſaid or done, but what becomes a good man; otherwiſe, he will never wear himſelf out in any fruitleſs or diſhonourable toil; neither will he buſy himſelf in any thing that deſerves not the name of buſineſs. He will not act as you ſuppoſe, ſo as, being involved in the extravagant views of ambition, to ſuffer himſelf to be hurried away with the tide; no; being convinced of his dangerous ſituation: how uncertain and ſlippery his ſtate is; he will withdraw his foot, and without turning his back, make a gradual retreat.

It

It is an eafy matter, *Lucilius*, to efcape toil and trouble, when you once defpife the profits propofed thereby: thefe are what detain us in flavery. *What then*, you will fay, *fhall I caft off thefe precious hopes? fhall I leave the crop in the field? fhall I live deferted? no lacqueys behind my coach? no levèe in my hall?* Thefe indeed are the things which men unwillingly forego; and, however they deteft trouble, are fond of the perquifites thereof. They complain of ambition as they would of a miftrefs; and if you fearch into their true affection, they do not hate it, but only quarrel with it now and then. Examine thofe who are frequently deploring their condition, and lamenting their difappointment of thofe things they cannot live without; and you will find their continuing in a ftate, of which they fo grievoufly complain, is merely voluntary. Indeed, my *Lucilius*, few are flaves, but who are fond of flavery; which if you really deteft, and *bonâ fide* defire to be free; and for this purpofe you afk time to confider *(c)*; that without perpetual anxiety you may obtain your liberty; know, that the whole tribe of Stoics are ready to ferve you: every *Zeno*, every *Chryfippus* will advife you, what is moderate, juft and true: but if you draw back, and ftay to confider what you may carry with you, and with what ftock of money you may charge your retirement, you will never extricate yourfelf while you live. A man cannot fwim with a load about him. Emerge to a better fort of life, the gods being propitious to you: but think them not propitious to thofe, whom they load with fplendid mifery; and yet are to be excufed in this refpect, forafmuch as thofe things that rack and torture thefe happy mortals, were given at their own requeft.

I had folded up my letter and fealed it, but muft open it again, in order to fend you the ufual prefent of fome excellent fentence, worthy your notice. And lo! one occurs; whether more true or eloquent I cannot fay. If you enquire after the author, it is *Epicurus*; for I am ftill for fetting off my budget with another's property. Nemo non ita exit e vitâ, tanquam modo intraverit, *Every one goes out of life, as if he was juft come into it*. Take whom you will, old or young, or of middle age, you will find him, equally, afraid of death, and ignorant of life. Nothing is left finifhed; as our proper bufinefs is ftill deferred to another day. But nothing pleases me more in this sentence, than that i chargeth old men with infancy. But let me consider; *No one, say Epicurus, goes out of life, but as he came into it:* this, with his leave, i not true. We die worse than we were born. Nor is this the fault c Nature; she may justly complain of us, and say, *What is the meaning c this? I brought you into life, void of vain desire, of idle fears, of supersti tion, of perfidiousness, and the like pests of society. As you came into th world, so go out of it.* Happy the man who has found true wisdom who dies as free from anxiety, as when he was born! But, alas! w now tremble at the apprehension of every danger; we have no courage no colour left; we shed unprofitable tears: yet what can be more ab surd and scandalous, than to be troubled on the very brink of security But the reason is plain; though destitute of every good in life, we stil desire life, and its enjoyments, such as they are. But it is gone; for n part of it stays long with us; it is in a perpetual flow *(d)*; it is n sooner transmitted to us, but it vanisheth; yet no one regards how wel he lives, but how long: when every one has it in his power to liv well, but no one to live long.

ANNOTATIONS, &c.

(*a*) Gladiatorem in arenâ capere consilium.—Quod plerumque iis accidere consuevit qui in ip negotio *consilium capere* coguntur. *Cæs. de Bell. Gal.*—Dicimus et e re nata *consilium capere.*— Erasm. Adag. 1. 6. 41.

(*b*) *Seneca* often breaks in upon us with this *Heroical Stoicism*; (as in Ep. xix. Subdue cervice jugo tritam: semel illam incidi, quàm semper premi, satius est) but generally with such hesitatio as to seem rather to speak from his profession, than his conscience.

(*c*) Advocationem petis, i. e. moram. *Lips.*—Vetus poeta,

Cur differs, mea lux, rogata semper,
Cur longam petis *advocationem.*

Vid. Sen. ad Merciam, c. 10.

(*d*) Epp. 1, 24, 29.

EPISTL

EPISTLE XXIII.

The Wiſe Man only enjoys true Pleaſure.

YOU expect, perhaps, that I ſhall give you an account, how agreeably we have ſpent the winter, which hath been ſhort and mild; and how uncomfortable, and more than ordinarily cold, the ſpring; and the like trifles, ſought after by thoſe, who admire nothing more than tattle. No, *Lucilius*; what I propoſe to treat of, will, I doubt not, be of ſervice, both to you and myſelf. And what ſhall that be, but to recommend to you *Goodneſs* and *Virtue!* Do you aſk wherein to lay the foundation? *Take no pleaſure in vanities*. And do I call this the foundation? It is the pinnacle. He hath reached the ſummit of perfection, who knows wherein true joy conſiſts; and who hath not placed his happineſs in any foreign power. That man muſt be always in anxiety and doubt, who fondly depends upon hope *(a)*, though what he deſires be at hand, is eaſily attainable, and though he be ſeldom diſappointed in his views. Learn this therefore, my *Lucilius*, before all things, wherein to rejoice *(b)*. You may think, perhaps, that I intend to abridge you of many pleaſures, when I fling out all fortuitous things, and adviſe you not to indulge even Hope itſelf, the ſweeteſt of all delights: quite the contrary, I aſſure you. I would have you always enjoy pleaſure: but I would have it originate at home: it will find a place there, if it be dependent on yourſelf alone. Other enjoyments affect not the mind; they only ſmooth the brow, and are merely ſuperficial *(c)*; unleſs perhaps you think a man enjoys pleaſure, becauſe he laughs. The mind ought to be earneſt and confident, and in a ſpecial manner raiſed above the world. Believe me, true joy is a ſerious thing. *(d)* Do you think any one with a merry countenance, or, as your coxcombs phraſe it, with *a laughing eye (e)*, can deſpiſe death? can open his door to poverty? can reſtrain pleaſure, as it were, with a bridle? or meditate patience, under pain and affliction? He that can do all this, enjoys a great pleaſure, though it be a ſevere one. And ſuch is the pleaſure I would put you in poſſeſſion of. It will never leave you, when you have found the way to attain it *(f)*. The lighter and baſer metal lies at the top of the mine; *that* is of moſt value, the vein of which runs deep, and ſufficiently pays the encreaſed labour of the miner. Such things as delight the vulgar, carry with them a light and perfunctory ſatisfaction; and whatever joy is adventitious, wants a foundation: whereas the joy I am ſpeaking of, and whereunto I would fain bring you, is truly ſolid, and will manifeſt itſelf *within*.

Purſue, my *Lucilius*, the only thing that can make you happy *(g)*; throw down, and trample upon thoſe ſpecious baubles, which have only an extrinſic ſplendor, and depend upon a promiſe. Regard the true good; and rejoice in your own. Do you aſk what I mean by *your own*? Yourſelf; at leaſt, the better part of you. If your body claims ſome regard, and indeed nothing can be done without it, think it rather what is neceſſary, than any thing great. The pleaſures it ſuggeſts are vain, and of that duration, often to be repented of, and unleſs uſed with great moderation they turn to the contrary: yes, I ſay, pleaſure is apt to run headlong, and fall into miſchief, unleſs reſtrained in due meaſure; and it is very difficult to keep due meaſure in what you firmly think to be good. There is no ſafety, but in the deſire of what is *truly* good. Do you aſk what that is, and whence it ariſeth? I will tell you: *From a good conſcience, from honeſt thoughts and juſt actions*, from a contempt of fortuitous things, and from a conſtant tenour of life in one and the ſame pleaſing track *(g)*. For how can they, who ſkip from one deſign to another, and not voluntarily, perhaps, but are forced thereto by mere accident, enjoy any thing that is ſure and laſting, being thus in continual ſuſpenſe and ever wavering? There are ſome few, it is to be hoped, who order themſelves, and their relatives, with deliberation, and judgment: the reſt, like things floating on a river, go not of themſelves, but are carried along; of which things ſome are carried in a ſmoother ſtream, or ſtopped in an eddy, and others are hurried down by the torrent into the main ſea. We muſt therefore fix upon ſome good deſign and perſevere therein.

But it is time to pay my uſual debt; and a ſentence from your own *Epicurus* ſhall diſcharge this Epiſtle. Moleſtum eſt ſemper vitam inchoare: *It is a tedious thing to be always beginning to live:* or, perhaps, it may be better expreſſed in this manner; Malè vivunt, qui ſemper vivere incipiunt; *They lead a wretched life who are always beginning to live.* But why? you will ſay, for this wants explanation. Why, becauſe ſuch a life muſt neceſſarily be always imperfect. *That* man can never be prepared for death who is juſt beginning to live. This then is what muſt engage our endeavour: to live to the ſatisfaction of ourſelves and of the world. But no one can have done this, who has ſcarce begun to live. Think not there are few ſuch; it is the common practice of almoſt all mankind. Some indeed begin to live, juſt at their latter-end; and if you think this ſtrange, I ſhall add what will more ſurpriſe you; many ceaſe to live, before they begin.

ANNOTATIONS, &c.

(*a*) Hope is neceſſarily attended with fear: but the ſecurity and confidence of a Stoic know no fear.

(*b*) *Cicero* (IV. *Tuſc.*) from *Laertius* takes notice of the Stoical diſtinction, between (gaudium et lætitiam) *joy and pleaſure.* Cùm ratione animus movetur, placidè atque conſtanter, *gaudium* dici: cùm autem inaniter et effusè exſultat, *Lætitiam*, (τὴν ἡδονὴν *Laert.*) quam ita definiunt (*Stoici*,) ſine ratione animi elationem, (ἄλογον ἔπαρσιν. *Laert.*) *There is a placid and calm motion conſiſtent with reaſon, called joy, and there is likewiſe a vain wanton exultation, or* tranſport, *which they define to be* an elation of the mind without reaſon.

Auguſtinus in Iſ. 57. *Non eſt gaudere impiis*, dicit Dominus; tanquam impii potius *lætari* poſſint, quàm *gaudere*. Lipſ. Manud. III. 5. See Epp. 27, 52, 59, 72, 98.

Let thy prieſts, O Lord God, be clothed with ſalvation; And let thy ſaints rejoice in goodneſs. 2 Chron. 6. 41. *The ſtatutes of the Lord are right and rejoice the heart.* Pſ. 19, 8. 119, 111. *Our rejoicing is this, the teſtimony of a good conſcience,* &c. 2 Cor. 1. 12. *As ſorrowful, yet always rejoicing.* 6. 10. *Rejoice evermore.* 1 Theſſ. 5. 16. Yet believing, *ye rejoice, with joy unſpeakable, and full of glory.* 1. Pet. 1. 8.

(*c*) *The triumphing of the wicked is ſhort, and the joy of the hypocrite but for a moment.* Job. 20. 5.

(*d*) It is that internal *peace and harmony, which flows from a greatneſs of ſoul mixed with manſuetude*; Pax et concordia animi, et magnitudo cum manſuetudine. *Sen.* de beat. vit. c. 3. *Serve the Lord with fear*, and rejoice with trembling. Pſ. 2. 11.

(*e*) *Hilariculo*, MSS. As affectedly ſpoken, by the Fribbles of the age, for *hilari oculo*. See Ep. 53.

(*f*) *Your heart ſhall rejoice, and your joy no man taketh from you*; John, 16. 22. *The fruit of the Spirit, is love, joy, peace.* Gal. 5. 22.

(*g*) *But one thing is needful.* Luke, 10. 42. See Ep. 53.

(*h*) *Our rejoicing is this; the teſtimony of a good conſcience; that in ſimplicity, and godly ſincerity, not with fleſhly wiſdom, but by the grace of God, we have our converſation in the world.* 2 Cor. 1. 12.

EPISTLE

EPISTLE XXIV.

On the Fear of Evils to come.

YOU write, *Lucilius*, that you are greatly embarraſſed, concerning the event of a *proceſs*, with which you are threaten'd by an implacable enemy; and you expect, I ſuppoſe, that I ſhould perſuade you to think better, and to acquieſce in the pleaſing hope: for what neceſſity is there to anticipate evil, and to preſuppoſe *that*, which it will be time enough to ſuffer when it happens; and ſo loſe the enjoyment of the preſent, through fear of what is to come? Without doubt it is ridiculous to make yourſelf miſerable at preſent; becauſe this may be your lot ſome day or other. But I ſhall lead you *another way (a)* to reſt in ſecurity.

In order to get rid of (or at leaſt to alleviate) your preſent anxiety, I would adviſe you to ſuppoſe, whatever you are afraid will happen, really to happen: and whatever the misfortune may be; weigh it well with yourſelf; and tax your fear: from whence you will find, that ſuch miſfortune will not either be very great or of long duration *(b)*. And to ſtrengthen you the more, you may ſoon collect many examples of perſons in the like diſtreſs. Every age abounds with them. On whatever accidents you reflect, either domeſtic or foreign, you will meet with inſtances, where a good diſpoſition, great proficiency in learning, and the ſtrongeſt efforts of nature, have not been wanting. And after all, ſhould you chance to be condemned in this ſuit, can any thing harder be expected, than baniſhment, or a priſon? Or has the body any thing worſe to fear, than to be hanged or burned? Now ſuppoſe any one of theſe to be your lot; and you may ſummon to your aid thoſe, who have deſpiſed them all; men, who will give you no great trouble in looking out for them; you need only make choice of them for your purpoſe. *Rutilius (c)* ſo took his condemnation, as to think nothing irkſome to him, but the being condemned wrongfully. *Metellus (d)* ſuffered baniſhment with a courageous, but *Rutilius* even with a willing mind; the former

former aſſured the commonwealth of his return to ſerve them; the latter, when *Sylla* ordered him to return, refuſed it, at a time when no one dared to deny *Sylla* any thing. *Socrates* read lectures in priſon, and when there were thoſe who promiſed him an eſcape, he refuſed to accept it, and ſtill continued there, to take off from men, by his example, the fear of the two greateſt evils, baniſhment and death *(e)*. *Mutius* thruſt his hand into the fire *(f)*: 'tis a ſevere thing to be burned; but how much more ſevere to inflict it upon one's ſelf! You ſee here a man of no letters, nor inſtructed with any philoſophical principles againſt pain and death, but only ſupported by a military courage, exacting puniſhment of himſelf, for having miſcarried in a bold attempt. He ſtood calmly looking on his right hand, while it melted away in the flame, nor withdrew it, though burnt to the naked bone, 'till his enemy ordered the fire to be taken away. He might have done ſomething of more happy conſequence in the field, but nothing braver. You ſee alſo how much readier valour is to ſuffer and deſpiſe torture, than cruelly to impoſe it. *Porſenna* more eaſily pardoned *Mutius* for his intention to kill him, than *Mutius* would pardon himſelf for not having killed him. *But theſe examples*, you ſay, *are known to every ſchool-boy, and, no doubt but, in ſpeaking of the contempt of death, you will bring in* Cato. And why not? Indeed I cannot paſs by ſo ſtriking an example, as that he exhibited, when, on his laſt night, he was reading *Plato*, with his ſword lying by him. Theſe were the two inſtruments he caſt his eye upon in his extremity; the one to teach him to be willing to die, the other to put it in execution. Having ſettled therefore his affairs, as well as they could be ſettled in that his diſtreſſed condition, he thought this only remained to be done; that no man might either have the power to kill, or the opportunity of making *Cato* obliged to him for his ſafety: and then taking up his drawn ſword, which to that day he had kept pure from murder, *Fortune*, ſays he, *weak has been thy power in oppoſing my endeavours; hitherto you have done nothing; I fought not for my own liberty, but the liberty of my country: nor have I acted with ſuch ſtubborn perſeverance to live free myſelf, but to live among a free people; but now, ſince all is loſt, and the affairs of mankind* are *deſperate*, Cato *is determined to retire out of your reach in ſafety*. Whereupon he gave himſelf a mortal wound: but it was dreſſed

dreſſed and bound up by the phyſicians; when having loſt much blood, and being weaker in body, but not in ſpirit, enraged not only at *Cæſar*, but at himſelf too; he tore open his wound with his naked hands, and did not diſmiſs, but throw out his noble ſoul, indignant, and ever ſcornful of ſuperior power *(g)*.

I bring not theſe examples by way of exerciſing the fancy, but to arm you againſt whatever may ſeem moſt terrible. It may poſſibly however have a better effect, was I to ſhew you, that not only great men have deſpiſed death, but even ſome, who in all other reſpects ſeem to have wanted ſpirit, yet in this have equalled the braveſt: like that *Scipio*, (the ſon-in-law of *Cneius Pompeius)* who, being carried by a contrary wind into *Africa*, when he found his ſhip was taken by the enemy, fell upon his ſword; and to thoſe who enquired after the General; *the General*, ſays he, *is well*. Which ſpeech, in my opinion, makes him as great as any of his anceſtors, and permits not the glory, ſo fatal to the *Scipios* in *Africa*, to be interrupted. It was great to conquer *Carthage*, but greater ſtill to overcome death. *The General*, ſays he, *is well*. Could a General, and *Cato's* General, die more nobly? (rather *more cowardly)*.

I need not appeal to the hiſtories of former times for more inſtances of thoſe, who have ſhewed a contempt of death: even in theſe our own, ſo much complained of for effeminacy, and luxury, you will find ſeveral of every age, condition, and degree. Believe me, *Lucilius*, death is not ſo terrible, but that it may ſometimes be deemed a deſirable bleſſing. Without any great anxiety therefore you may hear the threats of your adverſary: and though the conſciouſneſs of your innocence may give you ſome aſſurance; yet as a cauſe may be over-ruled, hope for juſtice, but at the ſame time be prepared againſt all that injuſtice can do.

More eſpecially be mindful to throw aſide the terrors and confuſion of report; and look upon things ſimply as they are; ſo ſhall you find, there is nothing dreadful in them, but the fear itſelf. What you ſee among boys, happens to us who are ſtill but older boys *(h)*. They are afraid

afraid of even thofe they love, their companions, and playfellows, when they come upon them mafked and difguifed. Not only from men, but from things the mafk muft be taken off; and the naked countenance reftored.

Why do you tell me of fwords and fire, and a crowd of executioners muttering around you? Take away this pomp, this frightful mafk, and you will terrify none but fools. Death is all: and what is death? My flave, and even a maid fervant have defpifed it. Or, why again do you make fuch a horrible parade of fcourges, and iron whips; and a feveral engine adapted to the torture of a feveral joint; and a thoufand other inftruments for the excruciating every part of the body? Lay afide thefe terrifying objects; filence the groans, the bitter exclamations, and outcries, extorted by the rack. The pain is but little more than what fome one defpifes in a fevere fit of the gout; and another endures in the cholic by mere indigeftion; or the tender young woman goes through with in childbirth. It is light, if I can bear it; and if it be more than I can bear, there is an end of it. Revolve thefe things in your mind, which you have often heard, and often mentioned: whether you have heard, or fpoke to the purpofe, let the effect determine; for nothing can be more fcandalous than what is objected to us. *We fpeak, indeed, but do not* act, *like Philofophers.*

And what think you? Is this the firft time you fancied yourfelf in danger of death, or banifhment, or pain? You are miftaken; thefe are what you have been fubject to, ever fince you was born. Whatever may happen, we muft think will happen. You have hitherto taken my advice; I therefore now exhort you not to fuffer your mind to fink under this difquiet, left it fhould grow dull, and lofe its vigour, when it is moft wanted, and ought to exert itfelf. Carry thefe reflections from a private caufe to a more general one. Say, this body is frail and mortal; not only liable to pain from injuries and tyrannical power, but to have its very pleafures turned into torments: feaftings create furfeits; drunkennefs brings on a weaknefs and trembling of the nerves; luftfulnefs a diftortion of the hands, feet and joints. Say likewife, muft I be poor? I ſhall find companions enough. Muſt I be baniſhed? I will look upon where I am ſent to, as my native place. Muſt I be bound? what then? am I now free? Nature hath enchained me with this heavy load of fleſh *(i)*.. Muſt I die? I ſhall be no more ſick, or bound; I ſhall feel the ſtroke of death no more. I am not ſo ſilly as to dwell here upon the idle chant of *Epicurus*; and tell you that vain are all our fears of puniſhment below; that there is no *Ixion* rolling round upon a wheel; no *Siſyphus* forcing with main ſtrength a huge ſtone up a hill; nor that the bowels of *Tityus* are daily fed upon, yet growing ſtill afreſh. No one is ſuch a child as to fear *Cerberus*, dark holes, or goblins as we ſee them pictur'd with naked bones! Death either quite conſumes us, or ſets us free *(k)*. If the latter; what a better ſtate may we not expect, when diſencumbered from this load of fleſh? if the former, there is an end of all; we are equally deprived of good and evil. But permit me here to remind you of a verſe of your own, having firſt premiſed, that you muſt not think it wrote for others, but for yourſelf alſo: it is vile to ſpeak one thing, and think another; how much more vile to think one thing and write another! I remember you one day ſpeaking to this point, and obſerving, that we die not at once, but are gradually approaching thereto, we *die daily (l)*; for every day ſome part of life is taken from us: even while we are growing, life decreaſeth: we firſt loſe infancy, then childhood, then youth; even all that is paſt to yeſterday incluſive, is loſt for ever; nay, this very day we now live, we divide with death: as it is not the laſt drop of water, or grain of ſand, that exhauſts the hour-glaſs, but all thoſe that continually flowed before; ſo in the laſt hour of life, it is not that alone which creates death, but which alone finiſhes it. We then arrive there, but have been long on our journey. I remember when you was commenting upon this ſubject with your uſual eloquence, always indeed great, but never more ſtriking, than when you adapt words to the like ſolemn truths, you was pleaſed to ſay,

Mors non una venit, ſed quæ rapit, ultima mors eſt *(m)*.

I had rather therefore, *Lucilius*, you ſhould read yourſelf, than my Epiſtle; from whence it will be manifeſt, that *the death we fear is really the laſt, but not the only one.*

But

But I know what you now expect, ſome noble or ſpirited ſaying; or ſome uſeful precept by way of ſupport, or ornament of this Epiſtle. Well then; I will give you ſomething that relates to the matter in hand. *Epicurus* chides not thoſe leſs, who court death, than thoſe who fear it, *(n)* and ſays, *it is ridiculous to have recourſe to death, becauſe life is irkſome; when we ourſelves have made life ſo irkſome, as to make death deſirable.* And in another place he ſays, *what can be ſo abſurd, as to wiſh for death, when you have made life burthenſome, only through fear of death!* To theſe you may add that alſo which is of the ſame import: *ſo great is the folly or rather madneſs of mortals, that ſome for fear of dying ruſh on death (o).* Whichſoever of theſe ſentences you reflect upon, you will ſtrengthen your mind with patience, in the ſufferance either of life or death: for indeed we are to be exhorted, and confirmed in both theſe points, ſo as not to be too much in love with life, nor too much to loath it. Nay, even when reaſon perſuades us *(p)*, it would be happier for us to die; we muſt not be raſh *(q)*, and hurry precipitately on a ſuppoſed relief. A truly brave and wiſe man ought not cowardly to fly from life, but to make a decent exit. And above all things he muſt not indulge that ſickly paſſion, which hath ſeized on many, of luſting after death. For know, *Lucilius*, there is a certain indiſcreet inclination to death, as well as to other things; which oftentimes prevails on men of a noble and truly generous ſoul, as well as on the indolent and deſponding. The former deſpiſe life, and the latter are overborne with it. A ſatiety of ſtill ſeeing and doing the ſame things, hath ſtrangely affected ſome, not through any hatred, but a mere diſdain of life; into which they unhappily fell, and not indeed without ſome impulſe from philoſophy itſelf *(r)*; as we are apt to cry, Quouſque eadem? *What, always the ſame thing?* I wake, I ſleep, I am full, I am hungry; I am cold, and now warm; there is no complete end of any thing; but all things return, and are connected in a circle: they fly, and they purſue: the day preſſes upon the night, and the night upon the day *(s)*: the Summer ends in Autumn, and Autumn is ſucceeded by Winter; which itſelf ſoon gives way to the Spring; and thus they paſs away but to come again: I ſee nothing new; I can do nothing new. Hence, I ſay, ſome are ſick of life; and there are many, who do not think life irkſome, but ſuperfluous.

ANNOTATIONS &c.

(*a*) See Epp. 13, 74.—*another way*, i. e. *on the contrary*, omnem fortunæ licentiam in oculis habere, tanquam quidquid poteſt facere, factura ſit. Quicquid exſpectatum eſt diu, levius accidit. *To ſuppoſe that fortune will do all that lies in her power to oppreſs you. Whatever has been long expected, falls the lighter.* Ep. 78. *Lipſ.* Manud. II. Diſſ. 1.

(*b*) According to what follows. Levis eſt ſi ferre poſſum; brevis eſt ſi ferre non poſſum. From Æſchylus.

Θαρσει, πονυ γᾶρ ακρον ὐκ εχει χρονον.

Take courage; pain is ſhort when moſt ſevere.

(*c*) *P. Rutilius Rufus*, of an illuſtrious family at *Rome*; Conſul with *Mallius*, U. C. 648. He was a learned hiſtorian, and to his integrity *Cicero* bears witneſs. Being baniſhed by *Sylla* the Dictater, he went to *Smyrna*, where he was made a citizen; and, being recalled, refuſed to return, ſaying, *He had rather his country ſhould be aſhamed of his baniſhment, than have any cauſe to grieve at his return.* Epp. 67. 79. *Sen.* de Provid. c. 3. Ad Marc. c. 22. Tac. Ann. IV. 43. Val. Max. 6. 4. 4. Ov. de Ponto. l. 3. 63.

Et grave magnanimi robur mirare Rutili,
Non uſi reditûs conditione dati.
Admire the brave Rutilius, *whoſe diſdain*
Refus'd the favour to return again.

(*d*) *Metellus*, the ſurname of the family of the *Cæcilii*, from whom were deſcended many illuſtrious perſons. The *Metellus* here mentioned was called *Numidicus*, from having conquered *Jugurtha*, King of *Numidia*; he was Cenſor and Conſul U. C. 648. but was baniſhed for refuſing to ſwear againſt the laws of *Apulcius Saturninus*, the Tribune. He was reſtored at the earneſt entreaty of his ſon, who was therefore honoured with the name of *Pius*.

(*e*) And ſmiling aſked his friends who propoſed his eſcape, *whether they knew any region out of* Attica, *οὐ προσβατον θανατῳ*, *inacceſſible to death.* Xenoph. Apol.

"*Mutius*, (ſays *Plutarch*), was a perſon endowed with every virtue, but moſt eminent in war. He reſolved to kill *Porſenna*, the moſt powerful Prince in *Italy*, but not knowing him among his nobles, he ſlew one of them, who looked moſt like a King. He was taken in the fact, and a pan of fire having been ſet before the King, who intended a ſacrifice, *Mutius* thruſt his right hand into the flame, and while it was burning, beheld *Porſenna* with a ſteady and undaunted countenance: *Porſenna* admiring the man, diſmiſſed him; and returned him his ſword, which he received with his left hand, (from whence he was called *Scævola, i. e.* left-handed) and out of gratitude aſſured him, there were 300 Romans lurking in his camp, all as reſolute as himſelf; and that being deſtined by lot, to make the firſt attempt, he was not concerned at having miſcarried, ſince he found *Porſenna* to be ſo good a man, as to deſerve rather to be a friend to the *Romans*, than an enemy; and accordingly he was accepted as ſuch." Plut. Life of Poplicola. *Sen.* Ep. 66.

(*g*) This *Cato* (ſays Lord *Bolingbroke*) ſo much ſung by *Lucan* in every page, and ſo much better ſung by *Virgil* in half a line, ſtrikes me with no great reſpect, when I ſee him painted in all the glorious colours which eloquence furniſhes, when I call to mind that image of him that *Tully* gives in one of his letters to *Atticus*, in ſubmitting *to be made a tool to his party*, &c. See Ep. 71. (N. g.)

And even *Plutarch* ſays of him, "that in ſuch outrageous virtue, Humour often gets the upper hand, and inſinuates itſelf under the maſk of equity and reaſon." (See his Life.)

And

And as to this last action of his life, so often repeated, and so highly commended in this Epistle, I can scarce refrain from saying with old *Syphax* (in Mr. Addison's *Cato*)

> " *'Twas pride, rank pride, and haughtiness of soul.*
> " *I think the Romans call it Stoicism.*"

(*b*) *Older boys.*] See Epp. 4. (N. b) 115. De Const. Sapien. c. 120. *Diogenes* the Cynic being asked, *in what part of* Greece *he had seen good men?* *Men,* says he, *no where; but I saw some boys at* Lacedæmon.

> Men are but children of a larger size.——*All for Love.*

(*i*) *O wretched man that I am, who shall deliver me from the body of this death!* al. *from this body of death!* al. *from the death of this body!* Rom. 7. 24. See the foregoing verse.

(*k*)
> Aut nihil est sensus animis a morte relictum,
> Aut mors ipsa nihil.—*Lucan.* III. 39.
> *Or endless apathy succeeds to death,*
> *And sense is lost with our expiring breath;*
> *Or if the soul some future life shall know,*
> *To better worlds immortal shall she go:*
> *Whate'er event the doubtful question clears,*
> *Death must be still unworthy of our fears.*—Rowe.

(*l*) *We die daily*] See Epp. 1. (d) 58 (o) 120.

> The bell strikes one, we take no note of time,
> But from its loss. To give it then a tongue,
> Is wise in man. As if an angel spoke
> I feel the solemn sound; if heard aright,
> It is the knell of my departed hours.
> Where are they? with the years beyond the Flood.—*Young.*
> Is Death at distance? No; he has been on thee,
> And given sure earnest of his final blow.
> Those hours, &c. Ib. See Ep. 49. (b)

Αλλ' ἡμεῖς ἕνα φοβέμεθα γελοίως θάνατον,—κ. τ. λ. Plutarch. De Ei ap. Delph. c. 23. *We ridiculously fear our death having so often died; and are continually dying. For not only, as* Heraclitus *said, the death of fire is the generation of air; and the death of air is the generation of water; this is more plainly visible in man: man terminates in the aged; as the youth in man; the child in the youth; the infant in the child: so yesterday died in to-day; and to-day dies in to-morrow.*

My worthy and ingenious friend, the late Mr. *Donaldson*, observed upon this passage, *that Death may be supposed to have a mortgage upon life: he does not enter upon the premises, on the fall of this or that grain of sand, but forecloses on the last.*

(*m*)
> *There are more deaths than one, but that the last,*
> *That takes us off*——

So *Muretus*; all the former copies,

> Mors non ultima venit, quæ rapit, ultima mors est.

Which *Lipsius* approves and thus explains: Non quæ venit et jam præteriit, mors est, sed illa propriè quæ rapit ultima, et nos aufert. *Gronovius* likewise retains the old reading, but explains it in another manner: Falsum est, mortem, ultimam rerum venire, vel venisse, multis mortibus conficimur, et sæpe ad nos venit, antequam rapiat; sed illa mors, quæ nos rapit et aufert, mortium est ultima.—La mort a degrez et celle ne premiere, qui nous vient a ravir, mais c' est bien la derniere. *Vet. Gall.* L'homme a plus d'un trespas, mais le dernier l'importe. *Malberbe.*

Among Christians, indeed, *a second death* is to be feared, but only by those who come under the description in Rev. 21. 8. See c. 2. v. 11.

(*n*) From

(*n*) From whence that excellent precept in *Martial*;

Summum ne metuas diem, nec optes.
Nor fear, nor wish, this day may be your last.

(*o*) Hostem dum fugeret se *Fannius* ipse peremit;
Hic rogo, non furor est ne moriare, mori? *Ib.*
Himself the coward Fannius *slew,*
When from his foe he fain would fly;
But greater madness can you shew,
Than thus, for fear of death, to die? M.

Stultitia est timore mortis, mori. See Ep. 7. (N. e.)

(*p*) i. e. according to the doctrine of the Stoics. See Ep. 12. 13. 72. *Lips.* Manud. III. 22. 23.

(*q*) *We must not be rash*] I can go no further without recommending this, and what follows, to those, who (if any such there be) think there is any weight in what *Seneca* hath elsewhere advanced, in the language of *Stoicism*, on the other side of the question: (see Epp. 30. (N. b.) 69. (N. d.) To which let me add, that just reply of a certain *Rhodian* (Ep. 70.) who under the most severe oppression, was advised to starve himself: *No*, says he, Omnia homini dum vivit, sunt speranda; *While there is life there is hope.*

Lucretius (*r*) ~~*Laertius*~~ introduces Nature herself, saying,

Nam tibi præterea quod machiner inveniamque
Quod placeat, nihil est; eadem sunt omnia semper,
Si tibi non annis corpus jam marcet, et artus
Confecti languent; eadem tamen omnia restant;
Omnia si perges vivendo vincere secla. III. 958.
To please thee, I have emptied all my store,
I can invent, I can supply no more,
But run the round again, the round I ran before.—Dryden.
Yet I can find no new, no fresh delight;
The same dull joys must vex the appetite.
Altho' thou couldst prolong thy wretched breath
For numerous years; much more, if, free from death.—Creech.

(*s*) Hor. Od. II. 18. 15.—Truditur dies die,

Novæque pergunt interire lunæ.
Day presses on the heels of day;
And moons encrease to their decay.—Francis.
Of man's miraculous mistakes, this bears
The palm; *that all men are about to live.*—
All *promise* is poor dilatory man,—
And that through every stage.——
At *thirty* man *suspects* himself a fool:
Knows it at *forty*; and reforms his plan;
At *fifty* chides his infamous delay;
Pushes his prudent purpose to *resolve*;
In all the magnanimity of thought
Resolves; and re-resolves; then dies the same.—*Young.*

EPISTLE

EPISTLE XXV.

On Contentment: and Solitude.

COncerning the two friends mentioned in your laſt, we muſt proceed a different way. The vices of one (the elder) are to be corrected, of the other to be quite broken off. I ſhall be very free with the former; for I cannot be ſuppoſed to love the man whom I ſhould be afraid to offend in this reſpect. And *what?* you will ſay, *do you intend to keep a pupil of* 40 *years old under guardianſhip? Conſider his age; it is now become hardy and intractable; tender minds only, are to be worked upon to any purpoſe (a)*. I know not what good I ſhall do; but I had rather fail in ſucceſs than in my duty. Nor muſt we deſpair of the poſſibility of healing thoſe who have been ill a long time, provided we can keep them from intemperance, and they will ſubmit to do, and ſuffer many things againſt their wills. Nor indeed can I promiſe much concerning the younger, but that he ſtill bluſhes, as aſhamed of doing wrong *(b)*. This baſhfulneſs is by all means to be kept up: for as long as this remains, there will be room to hope for amendment. With the veteran we muſt go more cautiouſly to work, leſt he fall into a deſperate way: nor can there be a better time for taking him in hand, than in ſome interval, when he ſeems inclined to a good diſpoſition. Such an interval indeed hath impoſed upon ſome; but it cannot deceive me: I expect that thoſe vices, which have ſlept for a while, but are not dead, ſhould break forth again, with more malignity. However I ſhall beſtow a few days on this affair, and try whether any thing can be done or not.

In the mean time, do you, *Lucilius*, continue to act ſtrenuouſly as uſual; and contract your budget. Scarce any of thoſe things we happily enjoy are neceſſary *(c)*. Let us return to the law of Nature. We ſhall be rich enough. All that we fancy we want is gratuitous, or of little conſequence. Nature aſks for bread and water *(d)*: no one is ſo poor, but he can anſwer this demand; and whoever confines his deſires to theſe, may contend with *Jove* himſelf in happineſs *(e)*, as ſaith *Epicurus*. From whom, as uſual, I ſhall conclude with an excellent ſentence;—Sic fac omnia tanquam ſpectat aliquis; *Do every thing, as before a witneſs (f)*.

Without doubt it is of great advantage to have a conſtant guardian over you, whom you reverence, and think concerned in all your deſigns. Yet it is more magnificent ſo to live, of yourſelf, as under the inſpection, and in the preſence of ſome good man; and with this I ſhould be ſatisfied that whatever you do, you do it, as before a witneſs; foraſmuch as ſolitude is apt to prompt all manner of evil. When you have made ſo great progreſs as to reverence yourſelf, you may diſmiſs your tutor; but 'till then, look upon yourſelf as under the inſpection of ſome one in authority: ſuppoſe a *Cato*, or *Scipio*, or *Lælius*, or any other, in whoſe preſence the moſt abandoned would ſcruple to commit a crime; or rather confer this honour upon yourſelf *(g)*.

When you have done this, and you begin to think worthily of yourſelf, I will recommend to you the advice of *Epicurus*; Tunc præcipuè in te ipſe ſecede, cùm eſſe cogeris in turba; *Then eſpecially retire, as it were, into yourſelf, when you are obliged to be in much company.* It behoves you to be unlike the many. But ſhould it not be ſafe for you thus to retire; examine all around; there is no one with whom a man had not better converſe than with himſelf. *Then eſpecially* (ſays Epicurus) *retire into yourſelf, when you are obliged to be in a mixed company*; that is, if you are a good man; of a calm, and ſober diſpoſition; otherwiſe it would be better to go into company; where you would ſcarce find a more dangerous man to be with, than with yourſelf.

ANNO-

ANNOTATIONS, &c.

(a) Tenera finguntur] Hor. Ep. I. 2. 64.

Fingit equum tenerâ docilem cervice magister
Ire viam quam monstrat eques.
The jockey trains the young and tender horse;
While yet soft-mouth'd he breeds him to the course.—Creech.

And *Plato* says, *young men*, κηρινυς εἶναι, *are to be moulded like wax.*

(b) See Ep. 11. (N. a.)

(c) "Nothing is more certain than this truth; that all our wants beyond those which a moderate income will supply are merely imaginary; and that his happiness is greater, and better assured who brings his mind up to a temper of not feeling them, than his who feels them, and has wherewithal to supply them." *Bolingbroke*, Lett. 191.

(d) Panem et aquam] Lucan. IV. 377.

Discite quam parvo liceat producere vitam
Et quantum natura petat—
—— Satis est, populis fluviusque ceresque.
Behold how little thrifty nature craves,
And what a cheap relief the lives of thousands saves.—
When all we want, thus easily we find;
The field and river can supply mankind.—Rowe.
Επεὶ τί δεῖ βροτοῖσι, πλὴν δυοῖν μονον,
Δημητρος ἀκτῆς πωματος θ' ὑδρηχου. *Eurip.*
Nature demands for mortals but two things,
Bread-corn from Ceres, and sweet water-springs.

(e) Ep. 110. Habeamus aquam, habeamus polentam; Jovi ipsi de felicitate controversiam faciamus.—Sic Επικυρος.

(ap. Stobæ.) Ελεγε ἑτοιμος ἔχειν καὶ τῷ Διῒ ὑπὲρ
Ευδαιμονίας αγωνίζεσθαι, μαζαν ἔχων καὶ ὕδωρ.

(f) However this injunction from *Epicurus* may be interpreted; as if "there was no villainy, which a man may not commit, if he can but persuade himself, that he shall not be detected or punished by men," the gods being out of the case: (see *Leland*, Vol. II. p. 94.) *Seneca*, I think, intends no more, than that a sense of shame, as well as fear of punishment, is a sufficient restraint, on an ingenuous mind, capable of distinguishing between good and evil, from acting contrary to moral duty. See Ep. 11. (N. f.)

(g) ——Παντων δὲ μαλιστα—αισχυνεο σ'αυτον.

Above all things, (says *Pythagoras*) *reverence yourself.*

"The first and leading disposition to engage us on the side of virtue was, in this sage's opinion, to preserve above all things a constant reverence of our own mind; and to dread nothing so much as to offend against its native dignity." *Fitzosborne's* Lett. 19.

EPISTLE XXVI.

On a good old Age. Meditation on Death.

I HAVE heretofore told you, *Lucilius*, that I was within ſight of old age. I now fear I have paſſed it by, and left it behind me: ſome other word better agrees with my years, at leaſt the ſtate of my body; for indeed old age is properly a name belonging to one weary of life, rather than to one broken down with years as I am. You may reckon me, if you pleaſe, decrepit, and in the laſt ſtage. But I congratulate myſelf with you, that, whatever my body may feel, my mind or underſtanding is not ſenſible of any decay or injury from time *(a)*. Vices only are grown old, and whatever is inſtrumental thereto: the ſoul ſtill flouriſheth, and rejoiceth that ſhe hath ſo little to do with the body: having partly diſrobed herſelf, ſhe glories in it, and makes me even doubt concerning old age. She calls this the *flower* of age; let us believe her, and let her enjoy her proper good. It is a pleaſure to me to conſider, and examine, what I owe of this tranquillity, this correctneſs of morals, to wiſdom, and what to old age: and diligently to enquire, what it is I cannot do, and what I would not do; and if what I cannot, be alſo what I would not; I have reaſon to rejoice in my inability. For, what cauſe is there of complaint, what great inconvenience, if what muſt one day end, be now upon the decay? Perhaps you will ſay, it is the greateſt inconvenience imaginable, to be infirm, to languiſh, or, to ſpeak properly, to be melted down: for, we are not forcibly laid low on a ſudden; we gradually waſte away; every day purloins ſomething from our ſtrength: and what exit can be happier, than to be diſſolved, as it were, by a gentle decay of nature? Not that there is any thing very grievous in a ſtroke, or ſudden departure out of life; but becauſe it is eaſy, and natural thus to ſteal away by degrees *(b)*.

For

For my own part, as if I was now about to make the experiment, and the day approached, that muſt paſs ſentence on the foregoing years, I thus obſerve and commune with myſelf. " All that I have ſaid or " done hitherto is nothing: vain and deceitful are the aſſurances of the " mind, all involved in chicane and flattery: what advance I made in " wiſdom, death alone can ſhew: I therefore calmly compoſe myſelf " againſt that day, when all ſhifts and ſubtleties laid aſide, I muſt pro- " nounce truly concerning myſelf; whether I ſpeak and think, what " is truly great and noble: whether the big and contemptuous words " thrown out againſt fortune were mere diſſimulation and artifice, to " engage applauſe. Regard not the opinion of men *(c)*; 'tis at beſt " doubtful, and generally partial: regard not particular ſtudies; our " buſineſs relates to the whole of liſe; death will pronounce ſentence " on the man: yes, I ſay, diſputations and learned conferences, and " collections from the ſayings of wiſe men, and eloquence of ſpeech, " all theſe ſhew not the true fortitude of mind: the moſt baſe and " cowardly may yet be bold in ſpeech. How you have acted in general, " *Seneca*, will then appear when you come to die. I accept the terms. " I am not afraid of judgment." Thus I commune with myſelf; yet ſuppoſe me ſpeaking likewiſe to you, *Lucilius*. You indeed are younger: but it matters not; years are not reckoned: it is uncertain when or where death expects you; and therefore expect *him* every where.

I was about to conclude, and indeed folding my paper; but the whole ceremony muſt be obſerved; and this Epiſtle have its paſſport. I need not tell you from whence the loan; you know whoſe cheſt I generally make free with. I hope in a little time to pay you out of my own ſtock; in the mean while *Epicurus* ſhall ſtand my friend: Meditare utrum commodius ſit, vel mortem tranſire ad nos vel nos ad eam; *Conſider whether it be better, that Death ſhould come to us, or we go to him*. The ſenſe is plain. It is an excellent thing to know what Death is, and how to die: you perhaps may think it unneceſſary, to learn that, which can but once be of any uſe: now this is the very reaſon, why we ought to ſtudy it: we muſt always be learning that, which we never can be aſſured we rightly know. Think upon Death. He that commands this, bids you think upon liberty. He that hath learned to

 die,

die, hath unlearned to be a slave. Death is above every power upon earth: at least beyond it. What is a prison, or guards, or bars, to him? The passage is still free and open *(d)*: but there is a strong chain, which still binds us down; the love of life *(e)*: which as it is not to be thrown off at once, may yet be eased and lessened; that, when an exigency requires, nothing may detain or hinder us from being prepared, and ready to submit to that which we must one day certainly undergo.

ANNOTATIONS, &c.

(*a*) This I think every one will give him credit for who is conversant in his writings. According to *Menander*,

> Εἶ τ' ἄλλ' αφαιρειν ὁ πολὺς ει ωθε χρονος
> Ημῶν τό γε φρονεῖν ασφαλεστερον ποιεῖ.
> *Of whate'er else depriv'd by length of time,*
> *Wisdom we find as firm as in its prime.* M.

(*b*) Subduci] Senectus leniter emittit, non repente avulsum vitæ, sed minutatim *subductum*. Ep. 33. (N. g.)—According to THE OLD MAN'S WISH in *Dryden's* Miscell. III. 178.

> *May I govern my passion with an absolute sway,*
> *And grow wiser and better as my strength wears away,*
> *Without gout or stone by a gentle decay.*

(*c*) *But with me it is a very small thing*, says St. Paul, *that I should be judged of you or of man's judgment; yea, I judge not my own self*. 1 Cor. 4. 3.

(d) According to the Stoical doctrine, (too) often repeated. But see Ep. 24, &c. but particularly Ep. 70.

(*e*) *But there is a strong chain*] Sc. *the love of life*;—Amor vitæ, qui non est abjiciendus.—But consider, O Christian, how much stronger is the chain that binds *thee* down; however painful it may be at present to endure it, viz. *the will of God*.

" That it is the intention of the Deity we should remain in this state of being 'till his summons calls us away seems as evident, as that we at first entered into it by his good pleasure; for we can no more continue, than we could begin to exist without the concurrence of the same supreme interposition. *Fitzosborne's* Lett. 13.

EPISTLE

EPISTLE XXVII.

Virtue only is ſecure.

YOU ſay, *Lucilius*, that I may well take upon me to adviſe you; foraſmuch as having corrected myſelf, I am now at leiſure to attend the amendment of others. No, my friend, I am not ſo vain or unjuſt, as, being ſick myſelf, to pretend to cure others *(a)*; but, as lying in the ſame infirmary, I am talking to you of our common illneſs, and communicating with you ſuch remedies, as I think will be of ſervice. Suppoſe me then, to admit you into my privacy, and thus, in your preſence, expoſtulate with myſelf. "Number your years, *Seneca*, and "you will be aſhamed to deſire, and be hunting after, thoſe things, "wherein you delighted when a child *(b)*. And be it your particular "care on this ſide the grave, that your vices may all die before you. "Forego thoſe turbulent and dear-bought pleaſures, that hurt, not "only before, but after enjoyment; as crimes though not found out "when perpetrated, ſtill carry anxiety with them: all unlawful plea-"ſures are attended with remorſe: there is no ſolidity in them; nor "any thing worthy of confidence; even though they hurt not, they "ſoon paſs and are gone. Look out rather for ſomething more ſub-"ſtantial and laſting: but alas! there is no ſuch thing, except what "the mind can find within itſelf: virtue only can give perpetual joy "and ſecurity *(c)*; whatever may ſeem to obſtruct it, paſſeth over like "a cloud, which for a moment darkens, but cannot hide the day. O, "when ſhall I enjoy ſo great happineſs! You have not indeed been "idle, *Seneca*; but this is not enough; you muſt ſtill exert yourſelf; "a great deal remains to be done: conſequently you muſt be vigilant, "and ſpare no pains, as you expect ſucceſs. This depends upon your-"ſelf; it is an affair that accepts of no delegate, nor admits of any "aſſiſtance, as in other kinds of learning;" which puts me in mind of *Calviſius*

4

Calvisius Sabinus; one, who, in our memory, was rich, having a free and gentleman-like patrimony, and underſtanding; but I never ſaw a man ſo ridiculouſly happy. He had ſo treacherous a memory, that he often forgot the names of *Ulyſſes*, *Achilles*, and *Priam*; names, which every well-educated man remembers as well as we do our firſt ſchool-maſters. No old Nomenclator, who is apt to impoſe upon his maſter with a falſe name, ever made ſuch blunders, as when he pretended to talk of the *Greeks* and *Romans*. And yet he affected to be thought a profound ſcholar *(d)*. He took therefore this compendious method; he bought ſervants at an extravagant price; one who underſtood *Homer*; another, who was maſter of *Heſiod*; and to the nine lyric poets, he aſſigned a ſeveral ſervant. You need not wonder at his great expence, for if he could not find ſuch as were ſuitable at hand, he placed them out to be inſtructed, and duly qualified: and having thus made up his family, he was continually making entertainments, and impertinently troubling his gueſts with his ſecond-hand learning; for he had always ſome one at his feet to prompt him every now and then with verſes, which endeavouring to repeat, he would often break off in the middle of a line or word. Whereupon *Satellius Quadratus*, a ſmell-feaſt, or ſharker on ſuch fools, and who conſequently was a jeſter, and, as it generally follows, a ſcoffer, adviſed him one day to hire ſome Grammarians as his ſcrap-gatherers, or remembrancers: when *Sabinus* told him that every ſervant he had ſtood him in an hundred pounds; "you might have "bought, ſays he, for leſs money, ſo many caſes of books," as he took it in his head that he knew all that any of the family knew, or was contained in his houſe. The ſame *Satellius* therefore would fain have perſuaded him, to enter himſelf in the liſt of wreſtlers, thin, pale, and ſickly as he was. And when *Sabinus* anſwered, "how is that poſſible, when I am ſcarce alive?" "Never mind that, ſays *Satellius*, do you not ſee what ſtrong and brawny ſervants you have got?—A good underſtanding is not to be hired or purchaſed; and I really think was it put to ſale, there would be but few bidders; whereas a bad one is often purchaſed, and paid dearly for.

But

But take what I owe you, and farewell; Divitiæ ſunt, ad legem naturæ, compoſita paupertas; *Poverty ſettled by the law of nature, is wealth (e).* This *Epicurus* often repeats: but that cannot be ſaid too often, which is ſcarce ever learned. It is enough to point out remedies to ſome, while others require them to be frequently applied.

ANNOTATIONS, &c.

(a) *Ye will ſurely ſay unto me this Proverb*, Phyſician, heal thyſelf. *Luk.* 4. 23. Ἄλλων ἰατρὸς αὐτὸς ἕλκεσι βρύων.—Etenim qui multorum cuſtodem ſe profitetur, cum ſapientes ſui primum aiunt cuſtodem eſſe oportere. Cic.—Eraſm. 2. 5. 38.—4. 4. 32.

(b) *When I was a child, I ſpake as a child, I reaſon'd as a child; but when I became a man I put away childiſh things.* 1 Cor. 13. 11.

(c) See Epp. 23. (N. e) 72. 92. *Sen.* de Beat. Vit. c. 3. *Lipſ.* Manud. III. Diſſ. 5. And in Sacred Writ, *Wiſdom* ſpeaking of herſelf ſays, *Whoſo hearkeneth unto me ſhall dwell ſafely, and ſhall be quiet from fears of evil.* Prov. 1. 33.

(d) According to that in *Euripides* (Heracl. 745)

—— εἰώθαμεν γὰρ
τὸν εὐτυχοῦντα πάντ' ἐπίστασθαι σαφῶς.
—— *'Tis common, to ſuppoſe,*
There is no lore, but what the rich man knows.

(e) See Epp. 4. 25. (N. e.)

EPISTLE XXVIII.

Change of Place makes no Alteration in the Mind.

YOU think it ſtrange, *Lucilius*, and as happening to yourſelf alone, that after ſo long a journey, and the viſiting ſo many different places, you could not throw off your chagrin and melancholy diſpoſition. The mind muſt be changed for this purpoſe, and not the climate *(a)*. Tho' you croſs the ocean; tho' (as our *Virgil* ſays) terræque urbeſque recedant *(b)*. Whitherſoever you fly, your vices will ſtill follow. *Socrates*, to one complaining after the ſame manner, ſays, "*Why do you wonder that travelling does you no good, when, go where you will, you carry your-*

ſelf

self along with you? The same cause, that sent you out, lies still at heart. What can the novelty of foreign lands avail? what the knowledge of divers cities and countries? It is all a fruitless labour. And do you ask, why this your flight is to so little purpose? It is because, as *Socrates* said, *you cannot fly from yourself.* The mind's burthen must be left behind, or you will no where find complacency and delight. Think your condition such as *Virgil* gives his prophetess. When roused and instigated, she is replete with spirit not her own;

> Bacchatur vates, magnum si pectore possit
> Excussisse Deum *(d).*

You travel here and there to shake off the inward load; which by such agitation only becomes more troublesome. As in a ship, a burthen that is fixed and immoveable, strains it the less; while such as are moveable are apt to sink the side to which they roll, by their unequal pressure. In every thing you do, you are still acting against yourself. The very motion cannot but hurt you; it is shaking a sick man. Get rid of this internal evil, and every change of place will be agreeable. Though you are driven to the utmost parts of the earth, or confined to some corner in a strange land; be what it will, you may still find entertainment. It matters not where you come, but what sort of man, you come thither. The mind is not to be devoted to any particular place. We must live in the world under this persuasion. *I am not born for one corner of it more than another; the whole is my native country.*

Was this manifest to you, you would be no longer surprized at not finding any benefit from the difference of place, when weary of one you fly to another. For the first would have pleased you, if you had thought it your own. You do not travel, but wander, and are driven about from place to place; whereas what you are in search of, *a good life,* is to be found any where. What place can be more turbulent, than the Forum? yet if you was obliged to live there, even there might you find tranquillity: not but that a man, if he was at his own disposal, would fly as far as possible from the sight, and much more from the neighbour-

neighbourhood of ſuch a noiſy place. For as a damp and foggy air affects even the moſt firm and healthy conſtitution; ſo there are places, if not dangerous, yet very inconvenient, to a mind well-diſpoſed, but not fully accompliſhed. I diſſent from thoſe who defy a ſtorm; and not diſliking a public and buſy life, are continually exerting their courage, in ſtruggling with, and getting through, difficulties. A wiſe man would endure this, if it fell to his lot; but he would by no means make it his choice. He had rather live in peace, than amidſt the din of war: for it is of little avail to him, to have thrown off his own vices, if he muſt be perpetually contending with thoſe of other men. Thirty tyrants, you ſay, environed *Socrates*, yet could not break, or bend the ſteadineſs of his mind: it matters not how many maſters you have, ſlavery is one and the ſame: he, that deſpiſes *this*, let his governours be as many as they will, is ſtill free.

But it is time to conclude, having firſt paid my toll: Initium eſt ſalutis, notitia peccati, *The acknowledgment of a crime is the firſt ſtep to reformation.* This is an excellent ſaying from *Epicurus:* for he, that knows not when he treſpaſſeth, can never deſire to be reformed. You muſt accuſe yourſelf, before you can mend. There are ſome who even glory in their ſins; and do you think they will ever be ſollicitous for a remedy, who account their vices as ſo many virtues? As much as poſſible therefore reprove yourſelf; examine yourſelf thoroughly *(e)*: firſt, do the office of an informer, then of a judge, and laſtly of an interceſſor, though a little wholeſome puniſhment may be ſometimes not amiſs *(f)*.

ANNOTATIONS, &c.

(*a*) Hor. Ep. I. 11. 27.

Cœlum non animum mutant qui trans mare currunt,
Strenua nos exercet inertia; navibus atque
Quadrigis petimus bene vivere; quod petis hic eſt;
Eſt Ulubris; animus ſi te non deficit æquus.
If they, who through the vent'rous ocean range,
Not their own paſſions, but the climate change;
Anxious through ſeas and land to ſeek for reſt,
Is but laborious idleneſs at beſt:

In desert Ulubræ *the bliss you'll find,*
If you preserve a firm and equal mind.—Francis.

Græcè suavius, τον τοπον, ου τον τροπον.—*Muretus.*

They change *the place, but not the natural disposition.*

(*b*) Virg. 3. 72. *Cities and land are seen no more.* Ep. 72.

(*c*) See Ep. 104.

(*d*) Virg. 6. 79.

Struggling in vain, impatient of her load,
And lab'ring underneath the pond'rous god,
The more she strove to shake him from her breast,
With more and far superior force he press'd.—Dryden.

(*e*) *See* Ep. 16. (N. b) And if self-examination, with the following, may, by a fair construction, be deemed Christian principles; let *Seneca* have the honour of them, exclusive of his party; for *self-conviction, self-condemnation,* and *imploring pardon of God,* are, by no means, in general, *Stoical* requisitions. There is a spiritual pride and self-sufficiency running through their whole scheme of philosophy; very incompatible with that humble frame of mind, which Christianity requires as a necessary ingredient, in the piety and virtue of such imperfect creatures, as we are in this present state.

(*f*) "I have sometimes thought, that if preachers, and moral writers, keep vice at a stand, or so much as retard the progress of it; they do as much as human nature admits: a real reformation is not to be brought about by ordinary means; it requires those extraordinary means, which become *punishments* as well as lessons."—*Bolingbroke,* Lett. 46.

And indeed *Seneca* himself looks upon repentance as the greatest punishment a man can suffer. Nec quicquam gravius afficitur quàm qui ad supplicium pænitentiæ traditur. *See* Leland, Pt. II. c. 9.

EPISTLE XXIX.

On popular Applause.

YOU are pleased to enquire, *Lucilius*, after our friend *Marcellinus*, and desire to know how he goes on. Know then, he very seldom comes near me: and the reason of this is, he dreads to hear the truth: not that he is in any great danger of it from me; for truth, I think, is not to be thrown away upon those who will give no attention. It is questioned therefore whether *Diogenes* and such other cynics, as were perpetually reprimanding every one they met, acted wisely and commendably

ably in ſo doing: for what can it avail to reprimand thoſe, who are deaf and dumb, either naturally, or by ſome vicious habit? "But why, "you ſay, need I be ſparing of words? They coſt nothing: I may "not know perhaps whether I can do any good with the perſon I ad-"moniſh; but this I muſt know, that in admoniſhing ſeveral, it would "be ſtrange indeed if I did not reform ſome one. Let the hand be "liberal *(a)*, and, no doubt, but in attempting many things, in ſome "it will ſucceed."—Indeed, *Lucilius*, I cannot think ſuch behaviour would become a man of any note; for his authority would hereby be leſſened; and his remonſtrances, by being made ſo cheap, not have weight enough to carry a reformation. An archer muſt ſometimes miſs, as well as hit, the mark; and you cannot call it art that takes effect by chance: but wiſdom is an art, which muſt aim at a certain end: it muſt look out for thoſe whom it thinks capable of inſtruction; and leave others to themſelves, where there are little hopes of ſucceſs; however, we are not to quit them immediately, but to try every friendly remedy, to the laſt hour of deſperation.

I have not quite given *Marcellinus* over; even yet, I think, he may be recovered; if a hand be ſtretched out, in time, to ſave him. Indeed there is ſome danger leſt he ſhould expoſe his friend; for he is a man of parts, and great wit, though depraved at preſent. But I ſhall diſregard the danger, and not be afraid to tell him his faults: I ſuppoſe he will play his uſual game, have recourſe to his facetiouſneſs, and provoke the eye of lamentation to laugh: he will firſt cut his jokes upon himſelf, and then take the ſame liberty with us; with his buffoonry he will prevent all that I have to ſay; he will ſift out the ſchools, and charge the philoſophers with drinking, whoring, and gluttony. Such a one, he will ſay, lives with an adultreſs; another in a tavern; and another is perpetually *dangling at court:* he will tell me of that merry philoſopher, *Ariſto*, who affected to diſpute as he was carried along in his litter; for ſuch was the time he choſe for acting his part: it being enquired of what ſect he was, *Scaurus* anſwered, "*I am ſure he is no Peripatetic.*" And when *Julius Græcinus (b)*, an excellent man, was aſked, what he thought of him; "*Indeed,* ſaid he, *I cannot tell you;*

for I know not how he behaves on foot;" as if he was talking of a charioteer. *Marcellinus,* I ſay, will fling in my teeth ſuch mountebanks as theſe; who had much better quite diſown philoſophy, than pretend to ſell it. I am determined however to put up with ſuch affronts. He may make me laugh; but perhaps I ſhall make him weep: but if he ſtill keeps his laughing mood, I will laugh too, as if pleaſed with the misfortune, that he is poſſeſſed with ſuch a merry kind of madneſs. But ſuch forced jollity ſeldom laſts long: obſerve, and you will find the ſame man laughing extravagantly, and within a little while as extravagantly raving *(c)*. I am reſolved, I ſay, to addreſs him, and remonſtrate to him how much greater he would be, if he appeared leſs in the eyes of the vulgar. If I am not ſo happy as to cut down every vice, I may perhaps check them in their growth. I cannot expect them to ceaſe altogether, but they will intermit, and perhaps one day ceaſe entirely, when they have got an habit of intermiſſion. This then is in no wiſe to be diſdained: as a pleaſing remiſſion of ſickneſs is a ſort of recovery.

But while I am preparing for *Marcellinus,* do you, *Lucilius,* (who can command yourſelf, and, who, well knowing from whence you ſet out, can from thence conjecture where your journey will end,) ſettle well your morals; raiſe your ſpirit; ſtand up boldly againſt every thing that is formidable; nor perplex yourſelf with numbering thoſe whom you have any reaſon to fear. Would you not think a man a fool, who is afraid of a multitude in a place where but one can paſs? Many have it not equally in their power to put you to death, though many at the ſame time may threaten it. We are ſo formed by nature, that one only may as eaſily take away thy life, as one gave it.

But, *Lucilius,* I think you ought to be aſhamed of not remitting me my laſt *payment;* however, that I may not behave myſelf ſo meanly towards you with regard to intereſt-money, and throw upon *you* what I owe myſelf, be pleaſed to accept of this; Nunquam volui populo placere; nam quæ ego ſcio, non probat populus; quæ probat populus, ego neſcio; *I had never any ambition to pleaſe the people; for the things*

that

that I am concerned to know, they diſlike; and what they like, I know not. Do you aſk who ſays this; as if you knew not whom I make ſo free with? *Epicurus.* But all, in every ſchool, ſay the ſame thing, *Peripatetics, Academics, Cynics.* For who that delights in virtue can pleaſe the vulgar *(d)*? Popular favour is ſought by vileſt artifices *(e)*. You muſt level yourſelf with the vulgar to pleaſe them; they will never approve what they do not own. But it is of much greater concernment, to conſider how you appear to yourſelf, than how you appear to others; the affection of the mean and baſe cannot be purchaſed but by ſome mean and baſe action. Wherein then can philoſophy (ſo much commended above other things, and ſo much to be preferred before all other ſciences) be of ſervice to you? Why it will teach you rather to be agreeable to yourſelf, than to the populace; to eſtimate judgment and opinions, not by the number of their abettors, but their genuine worth; to live without fear; and to overcome misfortunes by *patience and courage.*—But if I hear you celebrated by the mobility; if when you enter the theatre, you are received with acclamations, applauſe, and pantomimic geſtures; if idle boys and women ſing your praiſes through the ſtreets, how is it poſſible that I ſhould not pity you, when I know the way that leads to ſuch extraordinary favour?

ANNOTATIONS, &c.

(*a*) *Let the hand be*] Spargenda eſt manus—Alluding perhaps to fencers; whoſe ſucceſſive ſtrokes are called by *Quintilian*, prima, ſecunda, tertia, &c. manus.—Or to an army beſieging a town, when the attack is to be made in ſeveral places.—Or to a generous mind, diſpoſed to do all the good in its power.

(*b*) Julius Græcinus] Whom *Caligula* put to death out of mere malice to his virtue. *See* Sen. de Benef. II. 21.

(*c*) *Lipſ.* rabire—Sic *Varro*, Quid blateras? quid rabis?—*Pincian.* reads it *rudere*, and quotes *Perſius* (III. 9.)

—— Ut Arcadiæ pecuaria rudere credas.
He mutters firſt, and then begins to ſwear;
And *brays* aloud with a more clamorous note
Than an *Arcadian Aſs* can ſtretch his throat.—*Dryden.*

(*d*) Diogenes, the Cynic, as the people were coming out of the Theatre endeavoured to get in; and being aſked, *what he intended?* *Only*, ſays he, *to act according to the whole tenour of my life.* It being a conſtant maxim in philoſophy, not to walk in the ſame track with the common people. The ſame

ſame being told, that the people laughed at him, *Perhaps*, ſays he, *the aſſes laugh at them; now I no more mind the people than they do the aſſes.*

(*e*) "*Popularity, if purchaſed at the expence of baſe condeſcenſion to the vices or follies of the people, is a diſgrace to the poſſeſſor: but when it is the juſt and natural reſult of a laudable and patriotic conduct, it is an acquiſition which no wiſe man will ever contemn.*" *Cic.* Læl. p. 93.

I have made bold to give another turn to this ſentence, and to leave to the enlightened Stoic his, Ut ſine metu deorum hominumque vivas; ut aut vincas mala, aut finias. "The Stoics, through an affectation of greatneſs of mind, deſtroyed, as far as in their power, *the influence of fear in* mortals, by taking away the fear of the gods, of pain, ſickneſs, diſgrace and death; which tends to ſubvert one of the main principles of government, both human and divine.—It is evident, that this is one way by which the Author of Nature deſigned Mankind ſhould be governed, viz. by *fear*; which gives force to the ſanctions of law, and without which they would have ſmall effect. See *Leland*. II. 9.

EPISTLE XXX.

On the Contempt of Death.

I HAVE ſeen *Baſſus Aufidius* (*a*), a very excellent man, ſhaken, and ſtruggling with age: but now he is too low to be ever raiſed. Old age preſſeth him down with all its weight: you know, *Lucilius*, he was always of a weak, and conſumptive conſtitution: he has ſuſtained it a long while, or rather patched it up, but now can hold out no longer.—As in a ſhip, by the help of a pump, a leak or two is eaſily-remedied; but when it begins to be ſhattered, and to gape in many places, all remedies are applied in vain: ſo, an old and crazy body may for a while be ſupported, and propped up; but when, as in an old edifice the joyces are all ſtarted, and, as ſoon as one crevice is cloſed, another breaks out, nothing can be done, but *patiently to wait its fall* (*b*).

Our *Baſſus* however is ſtill chearful in mind. This is the fruit of philoſophy: it makes a man brave in every habit of body; in the ſight of death eaſy and chearful; and not faint-hearted, though in full decay. (*c*) A ſkilful pilot ſtill navigates the ſhip, though the ſails be rent, and keeps

keeps on his courſe with ſuch broken tackling as the ſtorm has left him. Thus does our *Baſſus*; he looks upon his end with ſuch a ſteady mind and countenance, that was he to look ſo upon the end of another man, you would think he had loſt all feeling. This, *Lucilius*, is a great virtue, and, however neceſſary, not ſoon or eaſily learned,—when the inevitable hour is come, to depart without murmur or regret. Other kinds of death admit of hope to the laſt: a diſeaſe may be got over; a fire be extinguiſhed; a falling houſe hath thrown, on one ſide, thoſe, whom it was likely to have cruſhed in pieces: the ſea hath caſt ſome ſafe aſhore, at the inſtant it was like to ſwallow them up: the ſoldier has withdrawn the ſword from the neck of thoſe he was about to kill: but they, whom extreme age is conveying to death, have no reſource; no interceſſion can be of ſervice here. And though it be a longer ſort of death, there is none more mild and gentle. Our *Baſſus* ſeems to attend, and, as it were, inter, himſelf *(d)*; nay, to live as if he had ſurvived himſelf, and without concern made a report of his own departure. For he talks much of death, and this continually; in order to perſuade us, that whatever inconvenience or fear, there may be in this matter, it is the fault of the perſon dying, not of death; and that there is no more trouble in it, than after it, [*to a good man.*] It is as abſurd for a man to fear what he cannot be ſenſible of, as to fear what will never happen: for can a man think, that he ſhall be ever ſenſible of that, which deprives him of all ſenſation, [*ſuppoſing that Death did ſo?*] Therefore, ſays he, Death is ſo far beyond every evil, that it is beyond all fear of evil. I know theſe things are often ſaid, and cannot be ſaid too often; but neither when I have read them, had they ſo good an effect upon me; nor when I have heard them from thoſe who, when they ſpoke of them, were in no danger themſelves of the things which they told us we ought not to fear.

But *Baſſus* had authority, when he ſpake of approaching death. For I will freely tell you my mind: a man is generally more brave at the very point of death, than when it is at ſome diſtance from him: for Death, juſt at hand, hath given courage enough even to the unlearned, not to think of eſcaping what is inevitable. So the gladiator who was afraid of of death during the combat, yields his neck to his victorious adverſary and even guides the point of his ſword to the moſt mortal place. Bu the death which is not ſo near but that it gives us leiſure to ſee it advancing towards us, requires a more compoſed firmneſs of mind; which i very rare, nor can be attained but by a wiſe man. I moſt attentivel therefore heard *Baſſus* paſſing ſentence upon death, and, as upon a neare inſpection, giving an account of it.*(f)* No doubt was one to riſe from th dead and inform you upon his own experience, that there was no evi in death, he would find more credit, and have greater weight with you yet what terror is to be apprehended at the approach of death, they ca well inform you who have ſtood near it; who have ſeen it coming, an gave it welcome.

Among theſe you may reckon *Baſſus*; who would by no means deceiv us; and he ſays that *a man is as great a fool who fears Death, as he tha fears old age; for as old age follows manhood, Death follows old age.* He ſhould not deſire to live, who is afraid to die. Life is given us on theſe conditions; it is the path that neceſſarily leads to Death: how ridiculous therefore to fear it! Things doubtful are to be feared; things certain are to be expected. Equal and alike invincible is the neceſſity of death to all: who then can complain of not being exempt? The firſt part o equity, is equality. But it is idle to pretend to plead the cauſe o Nature, who would not have our condition to differ from her own: whatever ſhe hath framed, ſhe breaks, and in time diſſolves; and whatever ſhe hath broken and diſſolved, ſhe frames anew. Now if any one is ſo happy as to be gently taken off by old age; not ſuddenly torn from life; but having ſtolen away *(g)* gradually by an eaſy decay: ſurely he hath great reaſon to thank all the gods; that, being full of days, he now retires to reſt, ſo neceſſary to man, ſo grateful to one that is weary and fatigued.

You ſee ſome wiſhing for death, and indeed with more earneſtneſs than others wiſh for life. I know not which to think will inſpire us with a nobler mind; they who wiſh for and demand death, or they who chearfully and contentedly *wait its coming*: the former ſometimes happens from

from ſuddden indignation or a fit of paſſion; but the latter is a tranquillity founded on reaſon and ſound judgment *(b)*: it is common to receive death angrily; no one receives him chearfully but ſuch as have been a long while prepared for his coming.

I confeſs therefore I made frequent viſits to my dear old friend; to know whether I ſhould find him ſtill the ſame, or whether the vigour of his mind decayed with the ſtrength of his body: but I found it rather encreaſed *(i)*, like the joy of a racer, when, in the ſeventh and laſt round, he drew near the prize. He ſaid indeed that conforming himſelf to the precepts of *Epicurus*, he from the firſt had no great apprehenſions of pain at the laſt moment; or, if it was ſo, his comfort was, it could be but ſhort; as no pain can laſt long that is exquiſite: and ſtill a greater comfort, that if in the ſeparation of ſoul and body, there muſt be torture, he had no reaſon to fear any other pain after that: yet that he did not doubt but that the ſoul of an old man was juſt ſitting, as it were, upon his lips, and had no need of being forced from him by a painful violence: the fire that meets with fuel, muſt be extinguiſhed by water, and ſometimes not without the fall of the houſe: but where fuel is wanting, it goes out of itſelf. I am attentive, *Lucilius*, to theſe things, not as if they are new to me, but as what I muſt ſoon make proof of myſelf. What then? Have I not ſeen many forcibly breaking the thread of life? Indeed I have: but I eſteem them more, who welcome death, not out of any hatred, or indignation to life; and who rather receive him as a viſiter, than force him to them.

Baſſus moreover ſaid, that it was entirely from ourſelves that we were tortured with the apprehenſion of death's being near: for to whom is he not near, being ready to ſtrike in all places, and at every moment? But let us conſider, ſays he, even then, when there is an apparent cauſe of death, ſome cauſe may be nearer, which we do not dread. An enemy has threatened ſome one with death, and behold a ſudden indigeſtion prevents the ſword. If we were to diſtinguiſh the cauſes of our fear, we ſhould find that ſome are real, and others only imaginary. We fear not Death, but on'y the thoughts of Death: for we are not further from it at one time than another; ſo that if Death is to be feared, he is always to be feared: for, what hour is exempt from death?—But I am afraid you ſhould hate ſo long an Epiſtle worſe than death; and therefore ſhall conclude with this caution; *The beſt way, never to fear Death, is to be often thinking of it (k).*

ANNOTATIONS, &c.

(a) Baſſus, an eminent hiſtorian in the time of *Auguſtus* and *Tiberius*.

(b) Circumſpiciendum eſt, quomodo exeas. The Stoic again, according to cuſtom. *See* the laſt Note in the foregoing Epiſtle. And I cannot but think that *Seneca* himſelf hath ſufficiently contradicted that favourite tenet in this Epiſtle; as when he commends the ſkilful pilot for endeavouring to work his ſhip, and keep on his courſe, though the veſſel is almoſt a wreck: and in what follows with regard to *Hope*, and the extraordinary eſcapes from danger and death. Vid. infr. (N. h. i.) Ep. 24.

(c) " Let us fence againſt phyſical evil by care, and the uſe of thoſe means which experience " muſt have pointed out to us: let us fence againſt moral evils by *philoſophy*.—We *may*, nay (if we " will follow *Nature*, and do not work up imagination againſt her plaineſt dictates) we *ſhall* of courſe " grow every year more indifferent to life, and to the affairs and intereſts of a ſyſtem out of which we " are ſoon to go. The decay of *paſſion* ſtrengthens philoſophy."—*Bolingbroke*, Lett. 47.

(d) Sc. componere] Thus Horace (Sat. I. 9. 27.)

Haud quiſquam; omnes compoſui.—
Not one (remains)—*I ſaw them all by turns*
Securely ſettled in their urns.—Francis.

(e) The belief of a *particular providence* indeed is founded on ſuch probable reaſons as juſtly to demand our aſſent: and to preſume, in this our imperfect ſtate, to point out any particular inſtances of an immediate divine interpoſition, would be meer weakneſs and folly. (*See* Fitzoſborne's Lett. 48.) Yet the paſſage before us in *Seneca* was exemplified in ſo extraordinary a manner, ſome years ago, in my neighbourhood, that to *ſome* at leaſt the hand of providence could not but be manifeſtly viſible. I mean in the preſervation of two young gentlemen, (the ſons of Sir *Richard Mill*, Bart.) and others of the ſame ſchool at *Kenſington*; when, in a high wind, *November* 1, 1740, part of the houſe fell, and the Rev. Mr. *Dorman*, the worthy maſter, (æt. 42) and his amiable and induſtrious conſort (æt. 38) were both killed: and of the two young gentlemen beforementioned, one, who was, in turn, attending on Mr. *Dorman*, was *thrown out of the room*, as by report, rolled up in the carpet; and the other, who was ſtanding by Mrs. *Dorman*, was thrown down into the cellar, and dug out of the ruins, both unhurt. And the reſt of the young gentlemen, near ſixty in number, it being *Saturday*, were happily in the yard at play; who, with the reſt of the family within, received no injury. *See* the excellent Preface to Mr. *Dorman's* poſthumous Sermons.

(f) Was one to riſe from the dead] Whatever effect this might have had upon *Lucilius*; of the Jew, and unbelieving Chriſtian we are told by divine authority, *that if they hear not Moſes and the Prophets, neither would they believe, though one roſe from the dead.* Luke 16. 31.

(g) Minutatim ſubductum. See Ep. 26. (N. b) *Alexis*, the comic poet, when he was decrepit and could ſcarce crawl along, being aſked, *τί ποιεῖς; How do you do? or, what are you doing?* anſwered, *Κατὰ σχολὴν ἀποθνήσκω, I am dying leiſurely.* (Stob. Serm. 115.)

4 *(h)* Founded

(*b*) *Founded in reason and sound judgment*] Here speaks *Seneca* indeed and not the Stoic: as also in what follows; Animus non magnâ vi distraheretur; *The soul is not to be forced from the body by painful violence.* Sophocles.

Σμικρὰ παλαιὰ σώματ' εὐνάζει ῥοπή.

The aged with small impulse rest in peace.

(*c*) "When the body instead of acquiring new vigour, and tasting new pleasures, begins to decline, and is sated with pleasures, or growing incapable of taking them, the mind may continue still to improve and indulge itself in new enjoyments. Every advance in knowledge opens a new scene of delight; and the joy that we feel in the actual possession of one, will be heightened by that which we expect to find in another: so that before we can exhaust this fund of successive pleasures, Death will come to end our pleasure and pains at once. In his studiis laboribusque viventi, non intelligitur quando obrepit senectus ita sensim sine sensu ætas senescit, nec subito frangitur sed diuturnitate extinguitur. [*In fine, he who fills up every hour of his life in such kind of labours and pursuits as these I mentioned, will insensibly slide into old age without perceiving its arrival; and his powers, without being suddenly and prematurely extinguished, will gradually wear away by the gentle, and natural effect of accumulated years.* Melmoth.]——Bolingbroke on Retirement.—See Ep. 26.

(*d*) I cannot but subjoin to this Epistle that excellent imitation of *Martial's* Epigram, De M. Antonio, (x. 24.) by Mr. *Pope*.

At length, my friend, (while Time with still career
Wafts on his gentle wing his eightieth *year)*
Sees his past days, safe out of Fortune's pow'r,
Nor dreads approaching Fate's uncertain hour:
Reviews his life, and, in the strict survey,
Finds not one moment he could wish away,
Pleas'd with the series of each happy day.
Such, such a man extends his life's short space,
And from the goal again renews his race.
For he lives twice, who can at once employ,
The present well, and ev'n the past enjoy.

Be pleased to add to the foregoing Note the conclusion of Ep. 61. from *Seneca* himself, Mortem plenus expecto. *Having had the full enjoyment of life,* I wait for *Death.* Supr. (N. b.)

EPISTLE XXXI.

Labour necessary for the Attainment of Virtue, the only Good.

YOU are now my own, *Lucilius,* since you begin to be what you promised. Follow that impulse of mind, which despising and trampling under foot all popular good, will lead you to the fountain-head. I do not desire to have you greater or better, than what you really endeavour to be. The foundation you have laid is large; only finiſh what you have begun: let the building completely anſwer the deſign. After all, you will ſhew yourſelf a wiſe man if you ſtop your ears; I do not mean with wax, but with ſomething cloſer than what *Ulyſſes* is ſaid to have ſtopped the ears of his companions *. The voice he was afraid of was ſoft and ſoothing, not a public one: but this that you have to fear, comes not from one rock alone, but reſounds from every part of the globe. Pleaſure ſpreads not her ſnares peculiarly in one place; there is not a city, but is to be ſuſpected: but eſpecially, where they ſhew moſt fondneſs, be moſt upon your guard: however good their intention, if you would be happy, it will be requiſite, to pray to the gods, that none of thoſe things that are generally prayed for, may be your portion: the things, which theſe pretended friends deſire may be heaped upon you, cannot be called *good:* there is but one *good*, the cauſe and foundation of an happy life, and that is, *a ſure confidence in virtue (a)*. Now this cannot be attained, except labour be deſpiſed; and ranked with thoſe things that are neither good nor evil. For it is impoſſible the ſame thing ſhould be good and bad; ſometimes to be light and ſufferable, or ſometimes to be dreaded. Labour therefore is not a *good*. What then is good? the contempt of labour, (i. e. not to be concerned, when it is required.) Therefore have I blamed all ſuch as labour, and are induſtrious, to no good purpoſe: but as to thoſe, who ſtrive at what is juſt and good, the more pains they take, and the leſs they ſuffer themſelves to be overcome, and ſtop for breath, I admire and encourage them, ſaying, *Riſe ye ſo much higher, and then take reſpite; but gain the top of this hill, if you can, in one breath.* Labour ſtill whets a generous mind. There is no neceſſity therefore, that you ſhould ſelect from the old formal prayer of your parents, what you would have, or wiſh for: and much leſs, having atchieved great things, that you ſhould be continually importuning the gods: make yourſelf happy, which you certainly will do, if you have a right apprehenſion that all ſuch things are good as appertain to virtue; and all vile and baſe wherein vice is concerned. As nothing is ſplendid without a mixture of light, and nothing black, but with a mixture of ſhade and darkneſs; or, as nothing, without the help of fire, is warm; and without air nothing cold; ſo, the conjunction

tion of virtue and vice makes things either good or bad, ſcandalous or honourable.

What then is good? The knowledge of things. And what is evil? ignorance *(c)*. The prudent obſerver of times will reject ſome things, and will chooſe others; but if he has a truly great and noble ſoul, he neither fears what he rejects, nor too fondly admires what he has choſen. I beg of you, not to give out, or be diſcouraged in your purſuits; it is not enough, not to refuſe labour, you muſt demand it. What labour, you will aſk then, is vain and frivolous? That which is laid out in trifles; not that it is bad in itſelf, any more than what is ſpent upon things of fairer account; 'tis only the ſufferance of the ſame mind, that exhorts to arduous and difficult undertakings, ſaying, *Why do you ſtop? It is not the part of man, to fear the ſweat of his brow.*

Add to this, that perfect virtue conſiſts in an equality and honour of life, always conſiſtent with itſelf; and well-ſkilled in the knowledge of things both human and divine *(d)*. This is the *ſummum bonum*, which if obtained you are no longer a ſupplicant, but *a companion of the gods (e)*. And how, you ſay, is it to be obtained? Not by paſſing over the *Alps*, or the *Graius (f)*, or through the deſerts of *Candavia*; or by the *Syrtes*, or *Scylla* and *Charibdis*; all which you have done for the ſlight recompence of a petty government. The way is ſafe and pleaſant which Nature hath pointed out to you: ſhe hath given you thoſe things which, if you decently retain, you will riſe a god. Now it is not money that can thus exalt you; for God has not money: nor is it the outward robe, for God is not clothed: nor fame, nor oſtentation, or notoriety among mankind; no one knows God *(g)*: many entertain ſtrange and prepoſterous opinions of him, and are overlooked *(h)*. Nor is it that you have a crowd of ſervants, ready to carry you in a litter, in town or country: God, the moſt high and powerful, himſelf upholdeth all things *(i)*. Nor is it beauty or ſtrength that can make you happy: all theſe things are ſubject to decay. We muſt therefore look out for ſomething, which is not to be impaired by length of time; ſomething which fears no lett or hindrance, and

and than which nothing better can be desired. And what is that? A soul, that is truly just, and good, and great. For what else can you call this, *but a Deity within (k)?* And which a freed-man, or a slave, may be master of, as well as a Roman knight. For what is a Roman knight? what a freed-man or a slave? names, that have sprung from ambition, or oppression. From any obscure corner of the world you may rise to heaven. Rise then,

— Et te quoque dignum finge Deo. (Virg. 8. 365.)
— *And shew yourself full worthy the divine abode.*

A god, not made of gold, or silver; nor of such materials indeed can the likeness of God be made *(l)*. Remember that such, as have heretofore been propitious to Rome, *had their images made of clay (m)*.

ANNOTATIONS, &c.

* Hom. Od. p. 39. Σειρῆνας μὲν πρῶτον ἀφίξεαι, κ. τ. λ.

Next where the *Sirens* dwell you plow the seas;
Their song is death, and makes destruction please.——
Fly swift the dangerous coast; let every ear
Be stopp'd against the song; 'tis death to hear.—
Then ev'ry ear I stopp'd against the strain,
And from access of phrenzy lock'd the brain.—*Pope.*

This celebrated story of the *Syrens*, (said to have been invented by the *Phœnicians*,) seems best accounted for, if, with the Annotator, we suppose the whole merely allegorical; or a fable containing an excellent moral; applicable not only to idleness and dissipation, (according to *Horace*, Vitanda est improba Siren desidia—) but to all pleasures in general, *which by being too eagerly pursued, betray the uncautious into ruin; while wise men, like* Ulysses, *making use of their reason, stop their ears against their insinuations.*—The Annotator likewise observes a great similitude between this passage in *Homer* and the words of (his cotemporary) *Solomon*, in the Proverbs, c. vii. 6.—27. c. ix. 13. 18. a most beautiful description of an harlot, and her silly devotees.—*I beheld among the simple ones*, &c.

(*a*) " The school of *Zeno* placed this *sovereign good* in naked virtue, and wound the principle up to an extreme beyond the pitch of nature and truth. (See N. e.) A spirit of opposition to another doctrine, which grew into great vogue while *Zeno* flourished, might occasion this excess. *Epicurus* placed the sovereign good in pleasure. His terms were wilfully or accidentally mistaken. His scholars might help to pervert his doctrine, but rivalship enflamed the dispute; for in truth there is not so much difference between *Stoicism*, reduced to reasonable intelligent terms, and genuine orthodox *Epicurism*, as is imagined. The felicis animi immota tranquillitas (*the steady tranquillity of an happy mind*) and the voluptas (*pleasure*) of the latter are near akin. And I much doubt whether the firmest hero of the *Stoics* would have borne a fit of the stone, on the principles of *Zeno* with

greater

greater magnanimity and patience than *Epicurus* did, on thoſe of his own philoſophy. However *Ariſtotle* took a middle way, and placed *Happineſs* in the joint advantages of mind, of body and of fortune." See *Bolingbroke* on Exile, *inf.* Ep. 41.

(*b*) Air, (in the opinion of the Stoics) the coldeſt of all bodies. Vid. *Plut.* περὶ τῦ πρώτυ Ψυχρῦ. *Lipſ.* Phyſiol. ii. 15.

(*c*) The doctrine of Socrates. See Ep. 81. 118.

(*d*) *Conſiſtent with itſelf*] See Ep. 20. (N. b.) 35.

So *Marcus Antoninus* Emp. adviſes,—" to do every thing, even the moſt minute, as mindful of the connection there is between divine and human things; for (ſays he) you will neither rightly diſcharge any duty to man, without a due regard to divine things; nor, on the other hand, any duty to God, without a regard to human things. L. 3. c. 16.

(*e*) Socius Deorum] The common boaſt of the Stoics; which originates from ſuppoſing *Virtue* to be the ſame as in God. Ep. 87. Quæris quæ res ſapientem efficit? Quæ Deum. *Do you aſk what conſtitutes a wiſe man? The ſame that conſtitutes a God.* There is a bolder rant in Ep. 73. *Sextius*, &c. was wont to ſay that Jupiter *could not do more than a wiſe and good man.* *Lipſius* indeed very juſtly condemns this, but ſoftens the ſentiment before us, by ſuppoſing *Seneca* to ſpeak not abſolutely, but comparatively, as in Ep. 59; Sapiens cum Diis *ex pari* vivit. And elſewhere, Diis ſocii ſumus et membra, (de Prov. c. 1.) ſapiens vicinus proximuſque Diis; excepta mortalitate, *ſimilis Deo*; this is not only admiſſible, but commendable, when it goes no further than *Homer's* ἀντίθεοι, θεοείκελοι, ἰσόθεοι, (*godlike*) or, Ep. 73. nulla ſine Deo mens bona, *'Tis the Divinity within that forms the wiſe man.* Thus St. John, 1 Ep. 4. 16. *Hereby we know that we dwell in God, and God in us. God is love; and he that dwelleth in love, dwelleth in God, and God in him.* See Epp. 41. 73. Lel. i. 295.

(*f*) Alluding to the paſſage of *Hannibal*, and *Hercules*.

(*g*) Nemo novit Deum] *Canſt thou by ſearching find out God? Canſt thou find out the Almighty to Perfection? It is as high as heaven, what canſt thou do? deeper than* Hades, *what canſt thou know?* Job 11. 7. *What man is he that can know the counſel of the Lord? Or who can think what the will of the Lord is? for, the thoughts of mortal man are miſerable, and our devices are but uncertain.* Wiſd. 9. 14. *No man knoweth the things of man, ſave the ſpirit that is in him; even ſo knoweth no man the things of God, but the ſpirit of God.* 1 Cor. 2. 11.

(*h*) Multi de Deo malè exiſtimant, et impune] *And the times of this ignorance God winked at*, &c. Act. 17. 30.

(*i*) *Upholding all things by the word of his power.* Heb. 1. 3.

> Omnia fers; oneri tamen haud obnoxius ulli es. Vida. H. 1.
> *Eternal reſt is thine, and ſoft repoſe,*
> *That bearing all things, yet no preſſure knows.*
> Omnia ſuſtentas, procuras omnia, aliſque
> Dum præſens ades; ipſa tua eſt præſentia vita,
> Omnibus ipſa ſalus—Ib.
> *Thy preſence keeps, directs, preſerves the whole;*
> *Kind guardian of the world, its life and ſoul.*—M.

(*k*) Deum in humano corpore hoſpitantem] A remarkable expreſſion, which ſeems to border upon that of *St. John* (i. 4.) *And* the Word *was made fleſh and dwelt among us*, &c. though it implies little more than what is expreſſed in the foregoing Note (*e*). To which let me add from Ep. 74, Miraris hominem ad Deos ire? Deus ad homines venit, imò, quod propius eſt, in homines venit. Ep. 41. Bonus vir ſine Deo (interno, *Lipſ.*) nemo eſt. *Vid. Loc.*

(*l*) " *Numa*,

(*l*) "*Numa* (A. M. 3237. U. C. 40.) forbad the *Romans* to represent God in the form of man or beast; nor was there any graven image admitted among them formerly. The first 160 years they built temples and chapels, but made no statue or image; thinking it great impiety to represent the most excellent of beings by things so base and unworthy; as there was no access to the Deity but *by the mind*, raised and elevated by divine contemplation." *Plutarch's* Life of *Numa*.

Forasmuch as we are the offspring of God, we ought not to think the Godhead is like unto gold or silver, or stone graven by art and man's device; &c. Act. 17. 29.—*To whom then will you liken me, or shall I be equal?* says the Holy One; *Lift up your eyes on high, and behold who hath created these things*; &c. Isaiah, xl. 18. 28.

(*l*) Fictiles fuisse] See Epp. 95. 98. cv.—Or perhaps the words will bear another sense; *the Gods, to whom we are so much obliged, were but men, made of clay like ourselves.*

EPISTLE XXXII.

On Retirement, and Perseverance in Virtue.

I AM always enquiring after you, *Lucilius*, and asking every one that comes from your way, how you do, and where, and with whom you converse. You cannot deceive me; I am with you. Live then as if I was a constant inspector of your actions. Do you ask, what pleases me most concerning you? Why, that I hear nothing of you; and that most of those I enquire of, can give me no information. This, I say, is what is right and salutary: to converse as little as possible with men of a different sentiment. 'Tis true I have so good an opinion of you, that I am persuaded you cannot be warped, or drawn from your purpose, though a crowd of sollicitors stood around you. What then do I fear? not that they can work any change in you, but lest they should hinder you in your progress.

Now nothing can be more prejudicial, than to be dilatory; especially as life is so short, and made much shorter by inconstancy. Still ever beginning with some new employ or other, we cut it out as it were into small parcels, and so make waste of it. Hasten therefore, my dearest

dearest *Lucilius*, and think how you would accelerate your ſpeed, was an enemy purſuing you; as when a troop of horſe are coming and preſſing upon ſuch as fly: for this is really the caſe: you are preſſed upon, make haſte, and eſcape. Convey yourſelf into ſafety; and now and then conſider with yourſelf, how excellent a thing it is to finiſh life before death; and then to wait ſecure, and ſelf-dependent, in the poſſeſſion of an happy life; which cannot be happier be it ever ſo long *(a)*. O, when will you ſee the day, when you ſhall know that time does not belong to you; when in a pleaſing tranquillity, and the full enjoyment of ſelf-complacency you are regardleſs of to-morrow *(b)*!

Would you know what it is that makes men ſo deſirous of length of days, and ſollicitous after futurity? No one is a friend to himſelf *(c)*. Your parents wiſhed other things for you than what I do; for I recommend the contempt of all thoſe things, which they prayed you might enjoy in plenty. Their deſires were to rob many, to enrich you; as what was transferred unto you, was to be taken from others. I only wiſh you to be maſter of yourſelf: that your mind long agitated with vain imaginations, may reſiſt them, and be ſteady: that it may ſatisfy itſelf, and underſtanding what is the *true good* (which being underſtood is eaſily attainable) it may not want any aſſiſtance from Time *(d)*. In ſhort, the man has got the better of all wants,—is diſmiſſed and abſolutely free,—who lives when he hath finiſhed life *(e)*.

ANNOTATIONS, &c.

(a) Self-dependent] I read this paſſage with *Gronovius*,—inniti ſibi in poſſeſſione beatæ vitæ—As in the preceding Epiſtle, Beatæ vitæ cauſa eſt—*Sibi fidere*. And Ep. 92. Tenet ſumma, et ne ulli quidem, niſi ſibi innixus.—Though, by the way, this Stoical paradox is by no means a Chriſtian doctrine; and what *Solomon* condemned, long before the name of a Stoic was in being. *He that truſteth to* (himſelf, or) *his own heart, is a fool.* Prov. 28. 26. But perhaps the *vita beata* may likewiſe be referred to another ſtate after this; eſpecially if we read it, as ſome do, *ſed* (inſtead of *ſi*) *longior*.

(b) Take therefore no thought for the morrow, &c. Matth. 6. 34. Do your duty, as in the foregoing verſe, and leave the reſt to Providence.

(c) Nemo ſibi contingit. *No one is himſelf*, or *for himſelf*.—*Eraſmus* (Adag.) interprets it, Neminem ſibi naſci, *No one is born for himſelf*, which interpretation *Lipſius* juſtly diſapproves; and underſtands it, of not being diſtracted by various purſuits, or the direction of other people; much

the ſame with what follows; Opto tibi tui facultatem, *I wiſh you to be maſter of yourſelf.* C'eſt qu'il ne ſe trouve perſonne, qui *ſe veule aider.* Vet. Gall.—*Malherbe,* Il ne point d'homme, qui *ſoit a ſoi.*

(d) From time to time] Since according to the Stoics, *Happineſs is always one and the ſame.* See Ep. 92.

(e) O that bleſt ſon of foreſight! Lord of Fate!
That awful independent on to-morrow!
Whoſe work is done: who triumphs in the paſt,
Whoſe yeſterdays look backward with a ſmile;
Nor wound him, like the Parthian, as they fly;
That common, but opprobrious lot!—*Young.*

EPISTLE XXXIII.

On Reading and Study. Sentimental Stoiciſm.

YOU deſire, *Lucilius,* that in theſe, as in my former Epiſtles, I ſhould tranſcribe ſome particular ſentence from our maſters (the *Stoics,* as well as from the *Epicureans).* Give me leave to tell you, they buſied not themſelves with flowery ornaments. Their whole context is equally ſtrong and nervous: it would betray an inequality, were ſome parts to ſhine more conſpicuous than other: one tree is not admired particularly where the whole grove ſhoots up to an equal height.—With ſuch wiſe ſayings as you require, both the Poets and Hiſtorians abound; therefore I would not have you think they are only to be found in *Epicurus:* they are public enough, eſpecially among us Stoics: but they are taken more particular notice of in *him,* as *they* are rarely interſperſed, and 'tis unexpected for *him* to exhibit any thing that is bold and ſtrong; who is the profeſſed maſter of ſoftneſs and delicacy: for ſuch is the opinion moſt men entertain of him; though to me I own he ſeems quite the contrary, even brave, notwithſtanding his long ſleeves *(a).* Fortitude and induſtry and a warlike diſpoſition are as well

well found among the *Perſians* as among the *Romans*, and other ſhort-ſkirted *(b)* nations. There is no reaſon therefore to require from us ſelect repetitions of choice things: you will find among our writers the choiceſt things in a continued ſtrain: but we make no parade of ſuch things: nor do we deceive the buyer, as if nothing was to be found in the ſhop, but what is exhibited in the ſhew-glaſs: he is permitted to chuſe what pattern he pleaſes. And what if we deſired to diſtinguiſh ſome particular ſentences; to whom ſhould we aſſign them? * To *Zeno*, or *Cleanthes*, or *Chryſippus*, or *Panætius*, or *Poſſidonius?* No; we are under no ſuch reſtriction; every one claims his own privilege; is King of himſelf; whereas among the *Epicureans*, whatſoever *Hermachus* ſays, or *Metrodorus*, it is ſtill referred to one; whatever doctrine is advanced in *that* ſchool, it is under the conduct and auſpices of one, *(Epicurus.)* With us, there is ſo great plenty of things, and all of the ſame tenor, that, if we would, we could not, extract any thing in particular;—Pauperis eſt numerare pecus, (Ov. Met. 13, 824.) *He is a poor man who can count his flock.*—Wherever you turn your eye, ſomething occurs, that would appear eminent, were it not read among its peers.

Wherefore think not, *Lucilius*, that you can taſte ſummarily, and by ſcraps, the writings of our greateſt men: the whole muſt be read, and thoroughly digeſted. It is one finiſhed piece; and by the due proportion of the whole, according to the plan of the projector, the work is ſo connected that you cannot ſpare a part, without detriment: not that I diſpute your conſidering the ſeveral parts one after another, ſo that you take in the whole man. As it is not a fine arm, or a fine leg that ſpeaks a beautiful woman, but the graceful ſymmetry of the whole, that takes off your admiration of any ſingular part. However, if you require it, I will not deal ſo niggardly with you as I pretend, but will wait upon you with a full hand. There are plenty of beauties, ſcattered up and down; but we muſt take them, I ſay, all together, and not pretend to pick and chuſe: for they do not drop one after another, but flow connected in a perpetual ſtream: and I doubt not but they will be of great ſervice to thoſe, who are yet ignorant, and admitted only to the *Exoteric* doctrine. For things circumſcribed, and, like verſes, confined to meaſure, are more eaſily fixed upon the mind; and therefore we give boys certain ſentences to learn, and what the Greeks call χρεῖαι *(c)*; becauſe their tender minds can better comprehend them, and are not yet capable of further proficiency.

But it is ſcandalous for a man to catch at fine ſayings, and to depend upon his memory for a few of the beſt note. He ought now to ſtand upon his own bottom; and to ſay ſuch things as of himſelf: not as having heard them from others. It is ſcandalous, I ſay, for an old man, or one bordering upon age, not to be wiſe beyond the reach of his note-book. *This is what* Zeno *ſaid*; *or this is what* Cleanthes: but what do you ſay yourſelf? How long muſt you be under tutorage? Exert yourſelf, and exhibit ſomething worthy of notice, and from your own ſtock. I can have no great opinion of the generoſity and greatneſs of ſoul in thoſe, who are for ever ſkulking under the protection of another, and whoſe ambition reaches no further than to read or interpret; without daring to publiſh, as an Author, what they have been learning all their lives. They have exerciſed indeed their memories in the writings of others; but memory is one thing, and knowledge another: to remember, is to retain a thing entruſted with the memory; but to know, is to exhibit ſomething of one's own; and not to depend upon example; and be continually referring to a maſter; as thus *ſaith* Zeno, or thus ſaith *Cleanthes:* let there be ſome difference made between *you* and a book. How long muſt you be learning? Preſcribe ſomething yourſelf: what avails it for me to hear, what I may read, perhaps better expreſſed elſewhere? But we are told a living voice can do much! It may be ſo; but not *that*, which utters only what another hath ſaid, and ſo performs the part of a Notary *(d)*.

Add now, what belongs to thoſe who are ſtill mere pupils: firſt, they follow thoſe who have gone before them, in that, wherein every one hath diſſented from his predeceſſor: 2dly, they follow them in that, which is ſtill to be ſought, and will never be found, if we content ourſelves with what is already attained; and laſtly, he that follows another, invents nothing; nay he ſeeks nothing. What then? muſt I not follow the

the ſteps of thoſe who have gone before me? Yes; I will walk in the old path *(e)*; but if I chance to find one nearer and plainer, I ſhall be inclined to take it, and direct others thereto. Truth is open to all men; but as yet hath not been engroſſed: much is left to future generations.

ANNOTATIONS &c.

(a) Long ſleeves]: Licet manuleatus ſit.]

Et tunicæ manicas, et habent redimicula mitras. Virg. 9. 616.
Your veſts have ſweeping ſleeves; with female pride
Your turbans underneath your chins are ty'd.—Dryden.

Vid. Gell. 7. 12. Arceſilaus, interrogatus, cur ex aliis ſectis ad Epicureas tranſirent multi, nemo ex illis ad alias? Nam, *inquit*, ex viris Galli fiunt *(eviratì)* ex Gallis viri nunquam. *Lipſ.*

(b) Malchinus tunicis demiſſis ambulat, eſt qui
Inguen ad obſcenum ſubductis uſque facetus. Hor. Sat. I. 2. 25.
Malchinus *trails his robe along the ground,*
Another humouriſt *tucks it up around*
His waiſt, how filthily obſcene!

* *Zeno*, the founder of the ſect of the Stoics.

Cleanthes, the Stoic, ſcholar to *Crates*, and ſucceſſor to *Zeno*: by his firſt profeſſion a wreſtler, and forced to work by night, to keep him from hunger and ſcorn in the day-time.---His phyſicians enjoining him to faſt two days, for the cure of an ulcer under his tongue, he refuſed to comply, taking it unkindly, that they would offer to bring him back, being two days onward on his journey; ſo continuing to faſt two days longer, he died, *æt.* 80. Vid. Juv. II. 5. Perſ. v. 64.

Chryſippus, ſcholar to *Zeno*, and ſucceſſor to *Cleanthes*, having ſpent what his father left him, he took to the ſtudy of philoſophy, and became ſo incomparable a logician, that it grew to a proverb, *If the gods would ſtudy logic, they would read Chryſippus.* He died, of a violent laughter with ſeeing an aſs eat thiſtles, as ſome ſay, but, according to *Hermippus*, of a vertigo, æt. 73. *Hor.* freq.

Panætius, a *Rhodian* by birth, mentioned and imitated by *Cicero*, in his Offices. He was tutor to *Scipio Africanus*, and *Lælius*. Nobiles libros Panæti. *Hor.*

Poſidonius, the diſciple of *Zeno*, and an eminent hiſtorian.

(c) χρεία] A ſhort and facetious ſentence: the word is likewiſe applicable to fact; as, *Crates* cum indoctum puerum vidiſſet, pædagogum ejus percuſſit; Crates *ſeeing a blockhead, did not puniſh the boy, but his maſter.*

(d) This, and great part of the Epiſtle, I own, militates againſt the Annotations here offered to the public. I have endeavoured to make ſome apology for them in my Preface, to which I refer the reader; and if he pleaſes he may take in the three or four laſt lines of this Epiſtle.

(e) Walk in the old path] Ego vero utar via veteri.—Thus ſaith the *Lord, Stand ye in the ways, and ſee, and aſk for the old paths, where is the good way, and walk therein, and ye ſhall find reſt for your ſouls.* Jer. 6. 16.

EPISTLE

EPISTLE XXXIV.

It is Part of Goodneſs, to deſire to become Good.

I THRIVE, I exult, and ſhaking off old age, am warm again, as often as I underſtand what you do, and what you write, and how much you excel yourſelf, (for it is ſome time ſince you left, and roſe above the populace). If a well nurtur'd tree, bearing fruit, delights the huſbandman; if a ſhepherd takes pleaſure in the increaſe of his flock: if a foſter-father looks upon the youth, his ward, as his own, what pleaſure muſt it be to one, who hath tutored a good underſtanding, to ſee it anſwer his hopes when grown to maturity? I claim you to myſelf; you are my work *(a)*; when I firſt ſaw your good diſpoſition, I laid my hand upon you; I exhorted you; I ſpurred you on; nor would ſuffer you to loiter; but frequently puſhed you forward; and do ſo ſtill; but now I encourage you in your ſpeed; and am myſelf encouraged by you.

And what (you ſay) would you have more? Truly this is doing a great deal; but it is not with the affairs of the mind as with common things, where the beginning of every work is ſaid to be half *(b)*. It is a great part of goodneſs to deſire to become good. But do you know whom I call *good?* One that is abſolutely perfect *(c)*; whom no power, no neceſſity can force to do a bad thing: and ſuch a one I ſee in you; if you endeavour, and perſevere, ſo to behave, that all you ſay and do may tally and be conſiſtent with itſelf; and all alike ſterling. The mind of one, whoſe words and actions diſagree, can never be right and perfect *(d)*.

ANNOTATIONS, &c.

(*a*) Opus es meum] *You are my work*; ſo St. Paul to the Corinthians; *are not you my work in the Lord?* 1 Cor. 9. 1.

(*b*) *To be half*] Operis dimidium.] So *Horace*, Ep. 1. 2. 40.

Dimidium facti, qui bene cœpit, habet; ſapere aude
Incipe——
Who ſets about, hath half his work performed:
Dare to be wiſe; begin——

Well begun is half done, *Prov.*

(*c*) See Ep. 16. N. (a).

(*d*) See Ep. 20. N. (a).

EPISTLE XXXV.

On Love and Friendſhip.

WHEN I ſo earneſtly intreat you, *Lucilius*, to ſtudy philoſophy, it is to ſerve myſelf: I am in queſt of a friend, which I cannot expect, unleſs you go on to poliſh yourſelf as you have begun. I am perſuaded you love me, and yet you are not what I call a friend. *What then, are love and friendſhip different qualities?* Certainly. He that is a friend, loves; but not every one that loves, is a friend. Therefore friendſhip is ſomewhat more than love; and always does good: whereas love is ſometimes prejudicial. Go on then with your ſtudies, were it only that you may learn to love truly; and be as expeditious as you can, leſt while you intend my advantage, another ſhould reap the benefit.

Indeed I already ſeem to enjoy the fruit of amity; while I fancy to myſelf, that we ſhall be of one mind; and that all the vigour which age hath taken from my years, will be reſtored me in yours; though I confeſs they fall not much ſhort of mine: however I long effectually to enjoy this pleaſure. There is a certain complacency that reacheth us from thoſe we love, even in their abſence; but it is light and tranſitory: the ſight, the preſence, the converſation of a friend, give a more ſenſible and lively pleaſure; eſpecially when we ſee not only *him* we deſire to ſee, but ſuch a one as we would wiſh him to be. Bring me therefore yourſelf, nothing can be a more acceptable preſent, *(b)* and to haſten you the more, conſider that I am old, and yourſelf mortal. Proceed then upon my account, not regardleſs of your own: and above all things take care that you be conſiſtent *(c.)*

As often as you would make trial of your proficiency, *Lucilius*, obſerve whether you deſire the ſame thing to-day as yeſterday; a change of the will ſhews the mind to be reſtleſs, and fluctuating juſt as the wind ſits; what is fixed and ſteady will abide ſo. This is abſolutely the caſe of one perfectly wiſe; and in ſome meaſure of a proficient *(d)* in the way of wiſdom. *Wherein conſiſts the difference?* The one is moved indeed, but without quitting his place, only nods a little; whereas the other is not in the leaſt moved.

ANNO-

ANNOTATIONS, &c.

(*a*) See Ep. 2. Friendſhip derives all its ſtrength and ſtability from virtue and good ſenſe. There is not, perhaps, a quality more uncommon in the world, than that which is neceſſary to form a man for this refined commerce; for however *ſociableneſs* may be eſteemed a juſt characteriſtic of our ſpecies, friendlineſs, I am perſuaded, will ſcarce be found to enter into the general diſpoſition. *Fitzoſborn.* Lett. iv.

(*b*) Ingens munus, Sen. de benef. c. 8. *He that gives me himſelf,* (if he be worth taking) *gives a great benefit* (magnum). And this is the preſent which *Æſchines,* a poor diſciple of *Socrates* made his maſter; *others may have given you much,* ſays he, *but I have nothing left to give but myſelf. This gift,* ſays *Socrates, you ſhall never repent of, for I will take care to return it better than I found it.* L'Eſtrange.

(*c*) See Ep. 20 (N. b.)

(*d*) This diſtinction between (proficientem et conſummatum; ſtudioſum, et doctum) the *Proficient,* and the *Adept,* in wiſdom is frequent; Ep. 72. Hoc intereſt inter conſummatæ ſapientiæ virum et alium procedentis.—De vit. beat. c. 24. Noſtrum vitium eſt, quo quod dicitur de *ſapiente* exigimus de *proficiente.*—De conſtant ſap. c. 98. Aliud eſt *ſtudioſus* ſapientiæ, aliud jam *adeptus* ſapientiam. Vid. Ep. 92. *Lipſ.* Manud. 11. diſſ. 9.

EPISTLE XXXVI.

The Opinion of the Vulgar to be deſpiſed.—No Annihilation.

ENCOURAGE your friend, *Lucilius,* ſtrenuouſly to contemn thoſe, who pretend to chide him for ſeeking ſolitude and retirement, forſaking his dignity; and when he had it in his power ſtill to riſe, preferring to every thing elſe a quiet life. How well he hath managed for himſelf, will be viſible every day. They, who now ſeem ſo much to be envied, will ſoon paſs away; ſome be ſtricken down; others fall of courſe. Proſperity is often turbulent and reſtleſs; it torments itſelf; it racks the brain in more ways than one; it incites men to different

4 purſuits;

purſuits; ſome to ambition; others to luxury; it puffs up ſome, and renders others effeminate and totally involved in diſſipation. *But may not ſome bear their proſperity well?* Yes, as ſome do wine (*a*). There is no reaſon, therefore, they ſhould perſuade you he is a happy man, who is ſurrounded with clients; they run to him as to a lake of water, which they, who drink, at the ſame time diſturb.—But they ſay your friend is an idle trifler? what then? you know how perverſely ſome ſpeak, and mean the contrary.

And what, if they once called him, when in power, a happy man? (*b*) was he *ſo?* Nor ſhould I any more regard their thinking him of a ſour churliſh diſpoſition. *Ariſto* was wont to ſay, that he had rather ſee a young man ſedate and grave, than gay and agreeable to the populace. The wine (*c*) that at firſt was rough and hard, becomes in time good and palatable; but that which is ſoft and ſmooth at firſt barrelling, will ſeldom bear age. Or let them call him ſtupid, if they pleaſe, and an enemy to his own preferment; this ſolidity will turn out well in the end; let him only perſevere in the way of virtue, and drink deep in the *liberal* ſtudies, properly ſo called, not ſuch as it is enough to be ſprinkled with, but thoſe wherewith the mind ought to be thoroughly embued. This is the proper time to learn: *what then, is there any time improper?* No; but though at all times it is right and decent to ſtudy, it is not right to be always under a maſter. It is a mean and ſcandalous thing to ſee an old man at his A. B. C. (*d*) It is for young men to learn; and old men to make a right uſe of what they have learned.

It will turn out, therefore, to your advantage, to make him as great and as good as you can. Theſe are the benefits, which are profeſſedly to be required, and in return beſtowed; theſe undoubtedly of the firſt claſs, which it is as honourable to give as to receive. (*e*)

Laſtly, He is not now at his own liberty; having promiſed and vowed, he muſt go on. It is leſs ſcandalous for a man to become a bankrupt, than to deceive the hopes of a friend in his goodneſs. To pay a common debt, the merchant hath need of a proſperous voyage;

and the husbandman of a fertile soil, and a good season; but all that is demanded of your friend, a good will alone can pay.

Fortune hath no jurisdiction over morals. Let him rightly order these, that the tranquil mind may arrive at perfection: as when a man is not sensible of any deprivation or addition, but continues in the same even temper let what will happen; who, if the common goods of life are heaped upon him, still soars above them; or if any, or every thing of the like kind be taken from him, he is as great as ever. Had he been born in *Parthia*, he would have handled his bow from his infancy; if in *Germany*, he would have brandished his little spear, *(f)* while yet a boy; if he had lived in the time of our ancestors, he would have learned to ride, and to close in with the foe. Thus is every one disciplined by the custom of his country. What is it then your friend must make the chief employment of his meditation? Even that which will be of service to him, against all the arrows of fortune, and the attack of every enemy; *to despise death.*

I grant there is something terrible in death, and shocking to our minds, that are formed by nature for self-love. There is no need therefore of being prepared and disciplined to that which we are voluntarily carried to by a certain natural instinct, as all men are inclined to self-preservation. No one need be instructed, if occasion was, to lie on a bed of roses; but a man must be hardened and well fortified, to retain his fidelity on the rack; to stand his ground when covered over with wounds; to watch before the trenches, and not so much as to lean upon his pike, because sleep is apt to creep upon a reclined posture. But after all, death is no evil; that which is really an evil, must have been proved such by some one *(g)*.

But if you have so great a desire to prolong life; consider that none of those things that are taken from our sight, and are hid in the bosom of nature, from whence they come and go, are entirely consumed. They go off the stage, but do not perish; and death, which we so much dread and detest, puts off life for a while, but does not deprive us of it it entirely: a day will come, which ſhall raiſe us again to light; *(h)* and which many indeed would refuſe, had they not forgot all that was paſt *(i)*. But hereafter I ſhall more fully explain to you, how things that ſeem to die and be loſt, are only changed. If then we are to return, we ought to make our exit with a willing mind. Obſerve the circling courſe of things, you will ſee that nothing in this world is extinguiſhed, but riſes and ſets alternately. The ſummer paſſeth away, but another *March* reſtores it again; the winter is gone, but returns again in its uſual months. Night hides the ſun under the earth, but day ſoon brings him back again: the ſtars in their courſes go the ſame round, and one hemiſphere is depreſſed while the other riſes.—But I ſhall conclude at preſent with this obſervation, that as neither infants nor children, nor the infirm of mind, fear death; it is ſcandalous for reaſon, not to afford that confidence and ſecurity which mere ignorance animates us with.

ANNOTATIONS, &c.

(a) Without being intoxicated; or according to *Lipſius*, drink it with moderation. But he thinks the place to be ſuſpected, and that ſomething is wanted.

(b) Unhappy man] *Lipſius* doubts, whether *Seneca* here means himſelf, when in proſperity, or *Comitius Sylla*.

(c) Frequent compariſon is made, between man and wine; which, when new, ferments and is turbid: ſo in a young man, the ſpirits are apt to riſe and boil, but become calm and ſettled by age. Thus *Alexis* the comic poet,

Ὁμοιοτατον ανθρωποις οινον την φυσιν. κ. τ. λ.

The compariſon is likewiſe transferred to fruit;

When *Accius*, the poet, had read his tragedy called *Atreus*, to his friend *Pacuvius*, *Pacuvius* told him, that there were many great and ſublime things in it, but that they ſeemed to him a little too harſh and ſtiff; it may be ſo, ſays, *Accius*, and *I am not ſorry for it; for from hence, I hope, I ſhall write better hereafter; for it is with a man's genius as with fruit: that which is hard and ſour at firſt, becomes mild and pleaſant; but ſuch as is at firſt ſoft and inſipid, ſeldom ripens properly, but grows mealy and rotten.* Agell. 13. 2.

(d) To ſet about habits of meditation and ſtudy late in life, is like getting into a go-cart with a grey beard, and learning to walk when we have loſt the uſe of our legs. In general the foundation of an happy old age, muſt be laid in youth; and in particular, he who has not cultivated his reaſon young, will be utterly unable to improve it old. Maneat ingenia ſenibus, modo permaneat ſtudium et induſtria. Cic de Seneɑ.—See *Bolingbroke* on Retirement and Study.

(e) To give as to receive] Like all other acts of charity, of which we are told by divine authority, *it is more bleſſed to give than to receive.* Acts. 20, 36.

(f) Tenerum haſtile, i. e. Framea, *A Javelin.*

(g) The undiſcovered country, from whoſe Bourne no traveller returns. Hamlet.

(h) This is not to be underſtood of the *παλιγγενεσία*, the *renovation* or *regeneration* of the *Pythagoreans*, but of the *Stoics*, ſomewhat like that of the *Millenians*. To the former of which *Lucretius* alludes. l. 3. v. 168.

Nec ſi materiam noſtram collegerit ætas,
Poſt obitum rurſum que redegerit, *ut ſita nunc eſt.*
Atque iterum nobis fuerint data lumina vitæ
Pertineat quidquam tamen ad nos id quoque factum.
Nay grant the ſcattered aſhes of our urn
Be join'd again, and life and ſenſe return;
Yet how can that concern us, when 'tis done,
Since all the memory of paſt life is gone? Creech—Vid. *Lipſ.* Phyſiol. Diſſ. 22.

(i) Forget all that was paſt] This ridiculous opinion prevailed amongſt many, even the wiſeſt of the Heathens, from the time of *Pythagoras*, that *after a certain revolution of years, we ſhould live in the world again, without the leaſt reminiſcence of a former life.* How much more then are we Chriſtians obliged to divine revelation, that hath delivered us from this and the like errors, with regard to futurity, that, *we ſhall not all ſleep*, or die, *but we ſhall all be changed, in a moment, in the twinkling of an eye at the laſt trump; for the trumpet ſhall ſound, and the dead ſhall be raiſed incorruptible and we ſhall be changed, &c.* 1 Cor. 15. 52.

EPISTLE XXXVII.

In Praiſe of Philoſophy.

YOU have promiſed, *Lucilius*, to ſhew yourſelf a good man; which is the greateſt tye and obligation imaginable upon a good diſpoſition: you are hereby as ſtrongly bound as upon oath: and ſhould any one tell you, this warfare is ſoft and eaſy, he would impoſe upon you; but be not deceived: the words of this honourable indenture run in the ſame ſtrain with thoſe of the vileſt ſort *(a)*; Uri, Virgis, ferroque, necari: *to be burned, ſcourged to death, or ſlain by the ſword.* All the difference is that the wretches, who hire themſelves for gladiators, and eat and drink what they muſt repay with their blood, ſuffer theſe things perforce; but from you it is required, that you ſuffer willingly and freely: it is lawful for them, to lay down their arms, and beg for mercy of the people

people *(b)*: but it is not for you to ſubmit, and beg your life: you muſt ſtand your ground, and die unconquer'd. Beſides, what avails it to gain a few days or years? We are born without any particular time of diſcharge. *How then*, you will ſay, *ſhall I get off?* You cannot indeed avoid neceſſities; but you may overcome them. There is a way to do this; and the only way is philoſophy. Apply yourſelf to this, if you would be well, if you would be ſecure, if you would be happy; in a word, what is the greateſt of all, if you would be free.—It muſt be ſo.—Folly is mean, abject, ſordid, ſervile; ſubject to many, and the moſt cruel, paſſions: and from theſe lordly maſters, which ſometimes govern by turns, and ſometimes all together, nothing can deliver you but wiſdom, which is the only true liberty. There is but one path *(c)* that leads to this, and that a ſtraight one; you cannot wander from it; only march boldly on.

If you would ſubject all things to you, ſubject yourſelf to reaſon: you will govern many, if reaſon governs you: you will learn from her, what to attempt, and the manner how; you need not fear a ſurprize: whereas it is difficult to find a man, who can give a rational account for what he wills; he is not led thereto by any previous deliberation, but driven by a certain impulſe, or whim: we as often attack Fortune, as Fortune us; but it is ſcandalous not to go of ourſelves; but to be continually hurried along, and, on a ſudden, being ſurprized in the middle of a ſtorm, to ſtand amazed, and aſk, *How came I hither?*

ANNOTATIONS, &c.

(a) *Of the vileſt ſort*] viz. The oath of the Gladiators. The form of which we have in a fragment of *Petronius Arbiter*, In verba Eumolpi juravimus, *Uri vinciri, verberari, ferroque necari*; et quiquid aliud Eumolpus juſſiſſet, tanquam legitimi Gladiatores, domino corpora animoſque religioſiſſimè addicimus. *We engaged in an oath* to be bound, ſcourged, burned, or killed by the ſword, *or whatever elſe* Eumolpus *ordained*; *and thus like free-born Gladiators ſelling our liberty, we religiouſly devote both ſoul and body to our new maſter.*

> Quid refert, uri vergis ferroque necari? Hor. Sat. II. 7. 56.
> *What difference is there, whether you engage,*
> *Be cut and flaſh'd, and kill'd upon the ſtage?*——Creech.
> *Or*, &c.————See Epp. 7. 71. *Lipſ.* Saturn. II. c. 5.

(b) Of the Gladiators the party that was worſted (ſubmiſit arma) *laid down his arms*, and acknowledged himſelf conquered: yet this would not ſave his life, unleſs the people pleaſed, and therefore he made his application to them for pity. Vid. *Lipſ.* Saturn. II. 22. 23.

(c) viz. *Wiſdom*, or the guidance of right reaſon.

EPISTLE XXXVIII.

On Epiſtolary Correſpondence.

YOU juſtly deſire, *Lucilius*, to keep up this epiſtolary correſpondence. The inſtruction is generally of ſervice, which is gradually inſtilled into the mind. Prepared harangues, poured forth among the people, make indeed more noiſe, but they want familiarity. Philoſophy is good counſel; and counſel is not given with clamour. Sometimes indeed the former preachments, if I may call them ſo, are neceſſary; where he that heſitates, hath need to be driven; but where this is not the caſe, *viz.* to enkindle in a man a deſire only to learn; but that he may learn to ſome purpoſe; words in a lower tone will ſuffice: they enter more eaſily, but they take good hold: nor is there need of many words, but only ſuch as promiſe efficacy. They are to be ſcattered, like ſeed, which, however ſmall, having found a proper ſoil, unfolds its powers, and from a ſmall grain (*a*) expands itſelf marvellouſly all around. The ſame doth ſpeech; you ſee not the effects at firſt; but it dilates in its gradual working: few things are ſaid, but if the mind gives them good reception, they gather ſtrength, and ſhoot out to perfection: the condition of good precepts, I ſay, is the ſame with that of ſeeds; they have a great effect, though in a narrow compaſs, let the mind be prepared to receive, and harbour them properly: the mind itſelf will likewiſe generate more; and give back with encreaſe what it hath received.

ANNOTATIONS, &c.

(*a*) *Which from a ſmall grain,* &c.] Seminis modo; quod quamvis ſit exiguum, cum occupavit idoneum locum, vires ſuas explicat, &c. *The kingdom of heaven is like a grain of muſtard-ſeed, which indeed is the leaſt of all ſeeds, but when it is grown it is the greateſt among herbs, and becometh a tree.* Matth. 13. 31. Where likewiſe in the parable of the Sower, it is written, *He that received ſeed into the good ground, is he that heareth the Word, and underſtandeth it; which alſo beareth fruit; and bringeth forth, ſome an hundred-fold, ſome ſixty, ſome thirty.* See Ep. 73. (N. h.)

EPISTLE XXXIX.

On the Contempt of Superfluities.

THE commentaries you desire carefully digested and reduced to a narrower form, I will in truth send you, *Lucilius*; but consider, whether the common form of address would not be of more advantage to you than what we now vulgarly call (breviarium) a *breviary*: but formerly when we spoke *Latin* (summarium) a *summary*: the former is more necessary for a learner; the latter for one who already knows something: *that* teacheth, and this exhorteth; but I will furnish you with both: tho' I think there is no necessity for my quoting any one by way of authority; for he that acts by his proctor *(a)*, or gives security, argues himself unknown. However I will write on the subject you desire, but it shall be in my own way. Among many, perhaps you will find those whose writings may seem not so well drawn up, and digested as they ought to be: but look into the list of philosophers; this will oblige you to rouse yourself; and, when you see how many have laboured for *you*, make you wish yourself one of the party: for a generous mind hath always this good quality, to be easily incited to do what is just and honourable. A man of a truly noble soul delights not in any thing that is base and mean; nothing but what has the appearance at least of something great, can attract him and call him forth to action.

As the flame rises on high in straight lines, nor sinks, any more than it can rest, while there is fuel to maintain it; so the mind is ever in motion, and the more in earnest it is, so much the more lively and active: but happy is the man who applies this impulse, to things that are lovely and of good report: he will soon set himself out of the power and reach of fortune: he will moderate prosperity, lessen adversity, and despise those things that are generally most admired: as it is the part of a great mind to contemn grandeur; and rather to wish for a genteel competency than store of wealth; for that is useful and lasting *(b)*; but this,

this, in being ſuperfluous, is often prejudicial: as the corn is laid, when the ears are overcharged by too rich a ſoil, the branches are broke down by their load of fruit; and too great fertility ſeldom comes to perfection: thus it happens to the mind, when broke by immoderate proſperity, men employ it in not only injuring others, but themſelves.

What enemy was ever ſo outrageous againſt any man, as their very pleaſures are againſt ſome; whoſe weakneſs and mad luſtings you may pardon upon this very account; that they themſelves greatly ſuffer from their own doings.

Nor undeſervedly does this vile paſſion torment them. The deſire can never be ſatisfied, that tranſcends the bounds of nature: Nature hath her limits; but vain and libidinous deſires ſcorn a boundary. Neceſſary things are meaſured by utility; but where will you put a ſtop to ſuperfluities? Beſides ſuch men plunge themſelves in pleaſures, which, becoming habitual to them, they cannot diſengage themſelves from: and in this, they are moſt miſerable, that they are come to ſuch a paſs as to make even ſuperfluities neceſſary. They are ſlaves therefore to their pleaſures, they do not enjoy them: and they are in love with their own diſtreſſes, which is ſure the greateſt of all: for then indeed is their wretchedneſs complete, when baſe and vile things not only amuſe, but pleaſe them; and there is no room left to hope for a cure, when what were the moſt deteſtable vices, are become (habitual, or) the manners of the age.

ANNOTATIONS, &c.

(a) Notorem. *Cic.* Cognitorem. *Sen.* γνωστῆρα. *One to whom application is made, concerning the condition or quality of another perſon.* *Sen.* in Lud. *de morte Claudii*—Si quis a me notorem petiſſet, te fui nominaturus, *If any one had aſked me to recommend to him a* proctor, or advocate, *I ſhould have named you.*

(b) Uſeful and laſting] Illa enim utilia vitaliaque ſunt.

—— Amicum
Mancipium domino, et frugi quid ſit ſatis, hoc eſt
Ut vitale putes—Hor. Sat. II. 7. 3.
Thy faithful, thrifty, ſervant, ſir,
Who fancies that *ſufficient ſtore,*
Which Nature's wants ſupplies, and aſks no more.

EPISTLE XL.

On Elocution *.

I AM obliged to you, *Lucilius*, for your frequent Epiſtles: it is the only way I have to know you, when at ſuch diſtance: I never receive one from you, but I ſuppoſe you preſent. If the pictures of our abſent friends are agreeable to us, by calling them to our minds, and alleviating the diſcomfort of abſence, however falſe and illuſory the conſolation; how much more agreeable are the letters, that convey a lively repreſentation of thoſe, for whom we have an affection? For the moſt pleaſing part of an interview with a friend is effected by his hand-writing; we ſee and acknowledge him.

You ſay, you have heard that *Serapion* the philoſopher, when he came to *Sicily*, and, as uſual, harangued the people, was wont to roll out his words with great impetuoſity, preſſing and crowding them together; as more things roſe to his imagination, than one mouth could ſuffice to utter diſtinctly. I can by no means approve of this in a philoſopher: whoſe pronunciation ſhould be as regular and well-compoſed as his life: no oration can be decently exhibited that is hurried and gabbled over. Therefore in *Homer* a ſpeech delivered with vehemence, and coming over us like the fall of ſnow, is attributed to the orator *(Ulyſſes)*: *(a)* while ſuch as flows more mildly, and ſweeter than honey, comes from the old man *(Neſtor)*. *(b)* Think therefore that a rapid and verboſe way of ſpeaking, rather becomes a mountebank *(c)*, than one who is treating of any great and ſerious ſubject; and whoſe buſineſs it is to give inſtruction. Nor would I have the delivery too ſlow any more than too ſwift: to give it out drop by drop is as diſagreeable, as pouring it out all at once: we muſt not keep the ear upon the ſtretch, nor oppreſs it with tediouſneſs. A barrenneſs of thought and imbecility of ſpeech takes off the attention of an audience, by reaſon of the diſguſt that arises from unnecessary pauses, and a sleepy sort of language: tho' I must own that what is waited for, is more easily impressed upon the mind, than what flies by promiscuously: and lastly, men are said to *deliver* precepts to their pupils: but that cannot be said to have been *delivered*, which hath escaped unnoticed.

We may add to the foregoing, that a discourse, designed to convey truth, ought to be plain and simple, not too much laboured. A popular harangue seldom aims at truth; it is calculated to move the passions of the vulgar, and to please, with its rapidity, the unthinking ear; it gives no time for recollection: it is gone. And how can that be supposed to direct others, which is under no direction itself? Besides a discourse, intended for the cure of a sick mind, ought to sink deep into us: no remedy can have any effect unless it be well digested. There is nothing therefore more vain and idle than an hasty and careless delivery; it is nothing more than mere sound. My fears are to be assuaged, my passions are to be curbed; my doubts are to be cleared; luxury restrained; and avarice reproved: and how can any of these things be done in a violent hurry? Can a physician cure his patient by passing by him? or can a din of words rushing on us, without any select meaning, give us any more pleasure than it does profit? As it is sufficient once to have seen and known a thing which you did not think possible; so to have heard *once* the men, who thus exercise their lungs, is full enough. For what can any one learn, what can he follow; or how judge of the mind of those, whose oration is confused, and always upon the gallop, so as not easily to be stopped? As when we are running down a hill, we cannot halt, just where we please; but the body is carried along by its own impulsive weight; so, such volubility of speech cannot command itself; and is especially indecent in philosophy; which ought calmly to lay down its well-chosen words, and not fling them out at random, but proceed gravely step by step. *What then? must it never exert itself, and raise its voice?* Yes certainly, provided that grace and dignity are still preserved; which too great earnestness and violence are sure to destroy: let it have strength and energy, but in a moderate degree; let it flow in a perpetual stream, but not rush down like a torrent. I would scarce allow

allow a public orator ſuch a velocity of ſpeech, and much leſs a philoſopher, as not to be able to recover himſelf, and keep within bounds. For how can a judge keep pace with him, and eſpecially the rude and unſkilful, when oſtentation, or an affected paſſion has worked him up beyond his ſtrength? He ought to ſpeak no faſter, nor throw in any thing, but what the ear can patiently imbibe.

You would therefore, *Lucilius*, do right, if you would not mind thoſe who regard not what is ſaid, or in what manner, but how much: and if, when neceſſity requires it, you had rather ſpeak like *Publius Vinicius*, concerning whom, when it was required, how he declaimed, *Aſellius* anſwered, *Slow enough:* for *Geminus Varus* ſaid of him, *He could not conceive how ſuch a one could be called eloquent, who could not join three words together*. Yet why ſhould you not ſtill prefer the manner of *Vinicius*; though ſome ſuch fellow ſhould interrupt you, as ſaid to him, parcelling out his words, as if he was dictating, not declaiming, *Pritbee, ſpeak, or not*. For I am far from thinking the method of *Quintus Haterius*, a celebrated orator in his time, to be what a man in his ſenſes would chuſe. He never pauſed, he never heſitated, but ended in the ſame ſtrain as he began. Different nations however are of a different taſte: and though among the Greeks this manner of ſpeaking might be faſhionable enough, yet it is our cuſtom when we write to ſtop every word *(d)*. And even *Cicero*, who brought the Roman eloquence to perfection, kept but a gentle pace *(e)*. The Roman dialect is ſomewhat vain-glorious; it ſets a value upon itſelf, and would be valued by others. *Fabian*, a moſt excellent man, in life and literature, and, what comes after theſe, in eloquence, diſputed rather dexterouſly than earneſtly; you might call it eaſe, rather than volubility. This then is what I recommend in a wiſe man, though I do not inſiſt upon it; that his ſpeech ſhould run on without any let or impediment; yet I had rather the pronunciation ſhould be diſtinct than fluent. But what makes me the more urgent in this affair, is, that it is a trade you cannot enter upon, without loſing, in ſome meaſure, your credit: you muſt brazen your face, and bawl ſo, as ſcarce to hear yourſelf ſpeak; and ſuch a rapid courſe of ſpeech will be apt to fling out many things, which you would by no means approve of: I ſay therefore you cannot well enter upon it, without loſing, at leaſt, a part of your wonted modeſty. Beſides it will require daily application, and take you off from the ſtudy of more eſſential things, for that of mere words: which if you were a maſter of, and extremely fluent, yet are they ſtill to be tempered with care and diſcretion. For as a grave and modeſt gait becomes a wiſe man, ſo does a ſmooth and compact diſcourſe, without an air of intrepid boldneſs. The ſum of all is, I command you, ſpeak, rather ſlow and diſtinctly.

ANNOTATIONS, &c.

* *Muretus* prefaces his notes on this excellent Epiſtle, with a reflection concerning the pſeudo-philoſopher *Serapion*, as here ſet forth by *Seneca*.—" Many, ſays he, and very notable examples " have I found of the *Serapion* kind among the preachers, and interpreters of the moſt ſacred " writings: whoſe diſcourſes, inſtead of being ſo ſpruce and curled, (like themſelves,) ought to be " full of gravity, authority, majeſty, ſanctity: but the whole has been ſo beſprinkled with the " flower of poppy and ſeſame; and wound up in ſo ſweet and honied a ball of words; that the " people have ran to them, as to hear ſome jeſter or comedian, rather than a maſter of morals, and " a corrector of vice. They ſet themſelves in ſome mimic attitude, and then twice or thrice ſtroak- " ing the face downwards, they ſtretch out their hands to the vulgar, (under which I comprehend " both great and ſmall) who are gaping after ſomething wonderfully great and divine: this done, " they let looſe the tongue, in a perpetual flow of words, without much reſpect to either ſtop or " cadence; heaping together a vaſt number of ſimilies, and pretty antitheſes; and having ſaid a " thing properly enough *once*, they know not when to have done with it; but repeat it over and " over again, with various turns, in a moſt puerile manner: all the while toſſing their arms about, " as if they were dancing; and adapting their geſticulations to ſomething they fancy very arch, tho' " ridiculouſly abſurd; allowing not the leaſt reſpite to themſelves or their audience; among whom " the ignorant and unſkilful are rapt with admiration; while the wiſer ſort nauſeate and are ſhocked " at the unmeaning ſtuff."—" I ſhould adviſe therefore, ſays *Muretus*, all ſuch modern *Serapions* " to read this Epiſtle, and conſider whether they do not border upon the foibles that are here ſo " ſmartly reprehended by *Seneca*."———He alſo refers them to what *Muſonius* ſays on this point in *Gellius*.—Noct. Att.

And I cannot help recommending the ſame to the many young *Serapions* in our great metropolis; who affect fine and florid diſcourſes *on the ſocial and moral virtues*, (as they are called) in preference to, and even excluſive of, the ſound doctrines and exalted precepts of Chriſtianity. But more eſpecially let me recommend it to thoſe, who unmindful of decency, as well as duty, either drawl, and dream over, *the Common Prayers*, or gabble them over ſwifter than ever lawyer did his brief. I have heard of one not long ago, who vaunted that "*he would give any parſon in town to the Second Leſſon, and read prayers with him.*" He was one day chid for this fancied excellency by one of ſome authority (whom he had given pain to, during the whole ſervice) in the following odd manner of expreſſion, though it wants not its meaning; "*Sir, you have a good voice and would read very well, but that you always read the word GOD with a little g.*" This is ſo well known, that perhaps it may point

point out the gentleman; if it does, let him take shame to himself, and others warning by it.

☞ This note was wrote some years ago when I first thought of translating these Epistles; and I fear it is not *now* out of date.

I have lately met with something so apropos to the foregoing, by way of contrast, in a sermon by the Rev. Mr. *Lamot*, that the transcribing it, I think, will need no apology, even to those who had read it before.—" By a good preacher, (says Mr. Lamot) I do not mean a man of noise and gesture; who preaches up himself and not his subject, and goes to the pulpit as many go to the church to be seen of men. The action of the Theatre, and the bombast of the Romances, are unworthy of the pulpit, and disgrace its solemnity. But by a *good preacher*, I understand, a man, who from his original good sense, improved by a good education, enters deep into the spirit of the sacred text, speaks what he feels, and feels what is just, who in his lectures is clear and copious; in his sermons, accurate and persuasive; in both more attentive to sense than to sound, to dignity of sentiment, than loftiness of style; who manages his discourses with such propriety, that in each there is as much simplicity as will render it instructive to the vulgar, and as much sublimity as will render it acceptable to the refined."

(*a*)——ἔπεα νιφάδεσσιν ἐοικότα χειμερίῃσιν. Il. γ. 222.

But when *Ulysses* rose in thought profound,
His modest eyes he fix'd upon the ground:
As one unskill'd or dumb, he seemed to stand,
Nor rais'd his head, nor stretch'd his scepter'd hand,
But when he speaks, *what elocution flows!*
Soft as the fleeces of descending snows;
The copious accents fall with easy art;
Melting they fall, and sink into the heart. *Pope.*

(*b*) Τοῦ καὶ ἀπὸ γλώσσης μέλιτος γλυκίων ῥέεν αὐδή. Il. α. 249.

——Slow from his seat arose the *Pylian* sage,—
Experienced *Nestor* in persuasion skill'd;
Words, sweet as honey, from his lips distill'd. Id.

(*c*) Circulanti. Ep. 88. Appion, qui tota circulatus est Greciâ.

(*d*) As, QUAMQUAM. TE. MARCE. FILI.

(*e*) Gradarius fuit.] So, *Lucilius* speaking of a horse, Ipse equus non formosus, gradarius, optimus vector. *The horse indeed was not very handsome, but an* excellent pacer, *and carried one exceeding well.*

EPISTLE XLI.

There is a certain Divinity in good Men. A man is not to be esteemed for any external and foreign Good.

NOTHING, *Lucilius*, can be more commendable and beneficial; if, as you write me word, you persevere in the pursuit of wisdom. It is what would

would be ridiculous to wiſh for, when it is in your power to attain it (*a*). There is no need to lift up your hands to Heaven, or to pray the Ædile to admit you to the ear of an image, that ſo your prayers may be heard the better. God is near thee; he is with thee (*b*). Yes, *Lucilius*, I ſay, a holy ſpirit reſides within us, the obſerver of good and evil (*c*), and our conſtant guardian. And as we treat him, he treats us (*d*). At leaſt no good man is without a God. Could any one ever riſe above the power of fortune without his aſſiſtance? It is he that inſpires us with thoughts, upright, juſt and pure. We do not indeed pretend to ſay *what God*; but that a God dwells in the breaſt of every good man, is certain (*e*).

When you enter ſome grove (*f*), peopled with ancient trees, ſuch as are higher than ordinary, and whoſe boughs are ſo cloſely interwoven that you cannot ſee the ſky; the ſtately loftineſs of the wood, the privacy of the place, and the awful gloom, cannot but ſtrike you, as with the preſence of a deity; or, when we ſee ſome cave at the foot of a mountain, jutting over it with a ragged load of ſtone; not made with hands, but hollowed a great depth by natural cauſes; it fills the mind with a religious fear: we venerate the fountain-heads of great rivers: the ſudden eruption of a vaſt body of water, from the ſecret places of the earth, obtains an altar: we adore likewiſe the ſprings of warm baths; and either the opaque quality, or immenſe depth, hath made ſome lakes ſacred (*g*). And if you ſee a man, unterrified with danger, untainted with luſtful deſires, happy in adverſity, calm and compoſed amidſt a ſtorm, looking down as from an eminence, upon man: and on a level with the Gods; (*h*) ſeems he not a ſubject of veneration? Will you not own, that you obſerve ſomething in him, too great and noble to bear any ſimilitude to the little body of the man, that it inhabiteth? Yes; a divine power deſcendeth hither from above: a ſoul of ſuch excellence and moderation, as to look down with a noble ſcorn on earthly things, and to laugh at thoſe trifles we are apt to wiſh for or fear, cannot but be enkindled by the deity within; ſo great a quality cannot ſubſiſt but by the help of God: he is there in *part*, though ſtill remaining above in the Heavens. As the rays of the ſun reach, and with

with their influence pierce the earth, and yet are ſtill above, in the body from whence they proceed; ſo, a *mind*, great and holy, and thus humbled, to give us a more adequate knowledge of divine things, dwells indeed with us, but ſtill adheres to its original; it depends upon that; thither tend all its views and pious endeavours, vaſtly ſuperior to, however concerned in, human affairs.

And what is this, I ſay, but a *mind* that depends upon its own excellence, and ſhines by its own native ſplendour? For, what can be more abſurd, than to extoll in man, what is not properly his own? What greater folly, than to admire in man, what can and muſt be transferred to another? The golden trappings makes not the horſe a whit the better. It is one thing to ſee a Lion under obedience, and tamely ſuffering himſelf to be ſtroked and dreſſed by his keeper; and another thing, to ſee him wild in the deſert, and of untamed ſpirit: how much to be admired is this, while fierce and impetuous as nature formed him, and deck'd with terror, in which chiefly conſiſts his beauty; than the other, weak and faint, and ſpangled with plates of gold to make a ſhew? No one ought to glory in what is not his own. We praiſe the vine, whoſe branches are ſo loaded with fruit, as to bend the very props to the ground, with their burthen. And would you prefer to this a vine, with golden leaves, and golden fruit? Fertility is the proper virtue of a vine: in man likewiſe that alone is commendable, which is from himſelf. He has a beautiful family, ſuppoſe; a noble houſe, large farms, and money at intereſt: what then? None of theſe things are in him, but about him. Commend *that* in him, which cannot be taken away from, nor made a preſent to, him.

Do you aſk what that is? The *mind*, and reaſon perfected therein. For man is a rational animal; he has therefore compleated his own proper good, if accompliſhed according to the end for which he was born. And what is it that reaſon requires of him? The eaſieſt thing in the world; only to live up to the dignity of his nature (*i*). But I own, the common madneſs of the world makes this difficult: we puſh one another on to vice: and what hopes can there be of being reſtored to ſanity, while the people continue to drive us on, and there is no friend to ſtop us in our career?

4 ANNO-

ANNOTATIONS, &c.

(*a*) *When it is in your own power to attain it.*] So in Ep. 31. Unum bonum eſt. Sibi fidere.—Fac te ipſe felicem. This may be looked upon as a very proper ſentiment, *goodneſs depends upon a man's own will and endeavours*; conſidering man merely as a free-agent. But it rather ſeems a ſtoical boaſt, which ſtands refuted by what follows in this excellent epiſtle.——For ſuch was the abſurd and impious opinion of the Stoics. They had heard, that by the conſent of all nations, the Gods were called *the givers of all* good *things*, but they would not allow any thing to be *good*, but *virtue*, a *ſound mind*, *perfect reaſon*, and the like; and theſe, they fondly imagined, were attainable by man, without any favour of the Gods.

According to that of *Horace*, Ep. 1. 18. ult.

Sit mihi quod nunc eſt, etiam minus; ut mihi vivam
Quod ſupereſt ævi, ſi quid ſupereſſe volunt di.
Sit mihi librorum, et proviſæ frugis in annum,
Copia, ne fluitem dubiæ ſpe pendulus horæ;
Hæc ſatis eſt orare Jovem: qui donat et aufert,
Det vitam, det opes; *æquum mi animum ipſe parabo.*
Let me enjoy but what I have, or leſs,
'Twill not abridge me of my happineſs;
So that I've ſtore of books, ſweet mental cheer,
And in my purſe proviſion for the year,
Leſt I dependent on the future hour,
Subject myſelf to Fortune's wayward pow'r;
While thus for life and moderate wealth I pray,
If mighty Jove, *who gives and takes away,*
Will hear my pray'r; I, in myſelf will find
The bleſſing of a firm and tranquil mind.
Monſtro quod ipſe tibi poſſis dare; ſemita certè
Tranquillæ per virtutem patet unica vitæ. Juv. x. ad fin.
The path to peace is virtue, what I ſhew,
Thyſelf may freely on thyſelf beſtow. Dryden.

To be conſiſtent with themſelves therefore the Stoics were obliged to affirm that the Gods gave them nothing that was truly *good*. It is our happineſs to know better, from Truth itſelf, that, *every good gift is from above, and cometh down from Heaven*. Jam. 1. 17. 2 Cor. 3. 5. See Ep. 52. (N. b) *It is God that worketh in you both to will and to do of his good pleaſure*. Phil. 2. 13.—Nay, *Seneca* himſelf, ſo great is the force of truth, here acknowledgeth, that *God inſpireth us with good counſels, and the moſt exalted thoughts*, and that *no man can properly be ſaid to be maſter of his own fortune*; and accordingly adviſes his friend to pray for *bonam mentem*, and a good ſtate, *firſt of the* ſoul, and then of the body, Ep. 10. Vid. Lipſ. Phyſiol. *Leland*. II. c. 9.

(*b*) Prope eſt a te Deus, tecum eſt intus eſt.] How truly chriſtian is this, and what follows to the end of the paragraph! particularly bonus vir ſine Deo nemo eſt. As it is ſaid of *Abraham*, *God is with thee in all thou doeſt*, Gen. 21, 22. And of *Samuel*, *God is with thee*. 1 Sam. 10. 7. The *Lord*, ſaith St. *Paul*, *is not far from every one of us*; *for in him we live, move, and have our being*. As certain of your *own poets have ſaid* (Aratus, τοῦ γὰρ καὶ γένος ἐσμὲν) we are his offspring. Acts 17, 27.

17, 27. *I have said ye are God's, and the children of the most High.* Pf. 86. 6. *Partakers of the divine nature,* ii Pet. 1. 4. Sen. *de Prov.* c. 1. Vir bonus eft Dei proximus. Ep. 92. Quid eft autem cur non exiftimas *in eo divini aliquid exiftere, qui Dei pars eft?* Cic. Tufc. II. Humanus animus decerptus ex mente divina.—Hor. Sat. II. 2. 79. Divinæ particula auræ.

Quis poffet cœlum, nifi cœli munera poffet
Et reperire Deum nifi *qui pars ipfe Deorum eft.* Manilius.
Who can know Heav'n, but by the gift of Heav'n;
Or find out God, but who of God is part?—

Vid. Ep. 31. (N. d.) Lipf. Phyfiol. III. Diff. 8.

(*c*) Sacer intra nos fpiritus fedet,—obfervator et cuftos.] *Nebuchadnezzar* fpeaking of *Daniel,* fays, *In whom is the spirit of the holy Gods.* Dan. 4. 8. And thus the Evangelift to all good Chriftians; *God shall give you another Comforter, that he may abide with you for ever; even the Spirit of Truth, whom the world cannot receive becaufe it feeth him not, neither knoweth, but ye know him,* for he dwelleth with you, and fhall be in you. John 14, 17. The Apoftle frequently to the fame purpofe, *His fpirit dwelleth in you.* Rom. 8. 11.---*Know ye not that ye are the temple of God* and that *the Spirit of God dwelleth in you?* 1 Cor. 3, 16. 6, 15. *That good thing which was committed unto thee, keep,* by the Holy Ghoft which dwelleth in us. 2 Tim. 1. 14. God *is a difcerner of the thoughts, and intents of the heart, neither is there any creature that is not manifeft in his fight.* Heb. 4, 12. *I know their works and their thoughts,* faith the Lord. If. 66, 18.

(*d*) *If any man defile the temple of God, him fhall God deftroy; for the Temple of God is holy, which temple ye are.* 1 Cor. 3. 17. as in the foregoing verfe, quoted above. *Hereby know we, that we dwell in God, and God in us, becaufe he hath given us of his Spirit.* 1 John 4, 3. And, *as many as are led by the Spirit of God, they are the fons of God.* Rom. 8, 14. Wherefore, *grieve not the holy Spirit, whereby ye are fealed to the day of redemption.* Ephef. 4. 30.

(*e*) Quis Deus incertum eft] habitat Deus. Virg. 8. 352.

—— here makes abode
What God,—not known, but fure it is a God. See Ep. 73. (N. g.)

(*f. g.*) Lucos, atque in iis filentia ipfa adoramus. *Plin.* 12. 1. *We venerate the groves and their awful filence.* He mentions likewife the river *Clitumnus,* and the lake *Vadimon,* nulla in hoc navis, facer enim eft; *in which no fhip is allowed to fail, for it is facred,* &c. Vid. *Lipf.* ad Tac. Ann. 14.

(*h*) The conftant boaft of the Stoics. See above, and Ep. 31. (N. d.)

(*i.*) Sic eft faciendum ut contra *univerfam* naturam nihil condemnamus, et eâ tamen confervatâ *propriam* fequamur. Cic. Off. 1. *We ought to manage fo as never to counteract* the general fyftem of nature; but having taken care of that, we *are to follow the fway of our conftitution.* Quæ ea eft? in nobis ratio. *Quid autem eft ratio?* (Sen. Ep. 66.) Naturæ *imitatio.* *Quid eft fummum bonum? Ex naturæ voluntate fe gerere.* Vid. Loc. (N. 2.) *Lipf.* Manud. II. Diff. 17.

EPISTLE XLII.

There is scarce to be found a good Man.

YOU are persuaded, you say, *Lucilius*, that such a one is a good man: believe me, a good man is not soon accomplished, nor so easily known. Whom do you think I here call *a good man?* One but of the second class; for, of the first, you will scarce find such a phœnix in a thousand years *(a)*. No wonder; great things appear but in distant ages. Mean and ordinary things are the common produce of Fortune; but it is their scarceness that recommends all excellencies. The man you point out, is very far from being what he professes; and if he really knew what a *good man* was, he would by no means think himself one at present; and perhaps despair of ever arriving to that honour. *He has a bad opinion*, you say, *of all bad men*. What then? even bad men have the same. Nor is there a greater punishment of wickedness, than that it displeaseth itself, and all that are concerned with it. You also alledge, that *he abhors those who insolently abuse the authority and power they are entrusted with*; yes, and would do the same thing had he the same power.

The vices of many lie concealed in their imbecility (*b*): they would dare as great things, did their strength suffice, as they, whom a more prosperous fortune hath exposed to view: they only want the proper instruments for displaying their iniquity: so, even venemous serpents may be safely handled, while benumbed with cold; not that they now want venom; but it is frozen up, and consequently inactive. Cruelty, and ambition, and luxury, in divers persons, want nothing more than the favour of Fortune to make them attempt as bad offices as the basest men: give them their full scope, and you will easily perceive their inclination. You remember, when you told me, that you had now got such a one in your power, and could treat him as you pleased; my answer was, that he was light and volatile, and that you had not hold of his foot

foot but of his wing: I was miſtaken; you had hold indeed of a quill, but it was ſlipped out, and he fled.(c) You know what pranks he played afterwards, and what miſchiefs he intended for you, that were more likely to fall upon his own pate. He did not ſee, that he was himſelf ruſhing upon the dangers, which he deſigned for others: he did not conſider, how burthenſome thoſe very things would prove, which he wiſhed to enjoy, although they were not ſuperfluous.

This then is principally to be obſerved concerning thoſe things which we affect and labour after with great induſtry; either that there is no advantage in them, or more diſadvantage. Some things are altogether ſuperfluous; and ſome but of little value. We do not foreſee this, and think we have thoſe things for little or nothing, which we pay moſt dearly for: from hence appears our ſtupidity, we look upon thoſe things only as bought, for which we pay down our money; and fancy we receive thoſe *gratis*, for which we pay no leſs than our very ſelves: what we ſhould be unwilling to buy, were we to give our houſe for it, or a pleaſant and fruitful farm, we are ready to purchaſe, with anxiety, with danger, with the loſs of liberty and time: ſo that nothing ſeems of ſo little value to man, as man himſelf. In all our deſigns therefore and affairs, we ſhould act as when we apply to a merchant's factor for wares, we muſt conſider the price that is ſet upon what we intend to purchaſe; we oftentimes pay a high price for what we think coſts nothing: I could mention many things which having been agreed for and received, have extorted from us our liberty; things, which if we were not in the poſſeſſion of, we ſhould ſtill be maſters of ourſelves.

Weigh theſe things therefore with yourſelf; not only when the queſtion relates to gain, but alſo when it relates to loſs: *may ſuch a thing be loſt?* Certainly, as it was merely caſual; and you will live as well without it now, as before: *Have you had it long in poſſeſſion?* you may the more eaſily ſpare it, being ſatiated: *have you had it but a little while?* you loſe it, almoſt before you had time to reliſh it: *have you leſs money?* you have the leſs trouble: *have you leſs favour?* you will be leſs envied: look into thoſe things, which drive us almoſt to madneſs; and which we cannot part from but with a flood of tears: you will find, that it is not any real loſs, that gives you all this uneaſineſs, but only the opinion of loſs: no one really feels that they are gone, but only thinks ſo: he that truly poſſeſſeth himſelf, hath loſt nothing; but how few enjoy ſo goodly a poſſeſſion?

ANNOTATIONS, &c.

(a) *Plutarch* (de Pugn. Stoic.) juſtly obſerves, that there is not, nor ever was a man, who had reached to what the Stoics call *perfect wiſdom*; they talk indeed of ſuch a one, but he is only to be found in idea: as *Cicero* has painted a perfect orator, though no ſuch had ever exiſted. See Ep. 16. (N. a.)

(b) The late Mr. *Donaldſon*, a friend and neighbour obſerved to me, that he did not think it improbable that Mr. *Gray* had this paſſage in his eye when he wrote thoſe excellent lines in his Elegy on a Country Church-yard.

Perhaps in this neglected ſpot is laid
Some heart, once pregnant with celeſtial fire;
Hands, that the rod of Empire might have ſway'd,
Or wak'd to ecſtacy the living lyre.

But Knowledge to their eyes her ample page,
Rich with the ſpoils of Time did ne'er unroll;
Chill penury repreſs'd their noble rage,
And froze the genial current of the ſoul, &c.

(c) Te non pedem ejus tenere, ſed pennam, mentitus ſum; plumâ tenebatur. *Malherbe* has given this metaphor another turn, that *inſtead of taking hold of his foot, you only took hold of his ſleeve; which he ſlipped from and fled.* The perſon here intended is ſuppoſed to be the adverſary mentioned in Ep. 24.

EPISTLE XLIII.

On Report; and Conſcience.

YOU wonder, *Lucilius*, how I came to be ſo particularly informed of your affairs; who could poſſibly tell me your thoughts, which you had diſcloſed to no one? He who knows almoſt every thing, *Rumour.*

What

What then, you ſay, *am I of ſuch conſequence as to be the ſubject of rumour?* It may be ſo; but there is no reaſon why you ſhould judge of yourſelf from what is ſaid of you here (at *Rome)* but what is ſaid of you where you dwell. Whatever is eminent in a neighbourhood is of conſequence, where it is eminent: but greatneſs has no certain meaſure; compariſon either raiſes or depreſſeth it. A veſſel that ſeems large in a river, looks very little in the wide ocean. The rudder is large in one ſhip, and ſmall in another: though you think not ſo highly of yourſelf, you are really a great man in the province where you dwell: how you live, how you ſup, how you ſleep, is enquired after, is known.

You muſt live therefore with the more care, and circumſpection; and eſteem yourſelf a happy man, when you can thus live, as it were, in public; when the roof and the walls indeed cover you, but do not hide you: whereas there are many who think themſelves happily encloſed therein, not that they may live more ſafely, but that they may ſin more ſecretly. I will tell you how to judge of the morals of men: you will ſcarce find any one who dares to live with open doors: it is ſelf-conſciouſneſs, not pride, that ſets the porter there: we live, as if we were in fear of being caught, or ſeen, unawares: but what avails it to hide ourſelves, and eſcape the eyes and ears of men? a good conſcience calls a crowd around it, undiſmayed; a bad one even in ſolitude is anxious and uneaſy *(a)*. If what you do be juſt and honourable, let all the world know it; if it be vile and ſcandalous, what ſignifies that no one knows it, when you know it yourſelf? Wretched art thou, O man, who deſpiſeſt this witneſs *(b)*!

ANNOTATIONS, &c.

(a) It is finely ſaid by *Tertullian*, Nullum maleficium ſine formidine eſt, quia nec ſine conſcientia ſui. *There is no evil doing but what is attended with dread, becauſe there is none but what is attended by conſcience.*

(b) Polybius.—Οὐδεὶς οὕτως οὔτε μάρτυς κ. τ. λ. *There is no evidence ſo formidable, no judge ſo ſevere, as conſcience that ſits upon the mind of every evil doer.*

Conſcientia mille teſtes.—

Juv. 13. 192.—Cur tamen hos te
Evaſiſſe putes, quos diri conſcia facti
Mens habet attonitos, et ſurdo verbere cædit,

Occultum quatiente animo tortore flagellum.
Pœna autem vehemens, ac multo ſævior illis,
Quas et Cæditius gravis invenit aut Rhadamanthus,
Nocte dieque ſuum geſtare in pectore teſtem.
But why muſt theſe be thought to 'ſcape, that feel
Thoſe rods of ſcorpions, and theſe whips of ſteel
Which conſcience ſhakes, when ſhe with rage controuls;
And ſpreads amazing terrors through their ſouls?
Not ſharp Revenge, nor Hell itſelf can find
A fiercer torment than a guilty mind;
Which day and night will dreadfully accuſe;
Condemns the wretch, and ſtill the charge renews.—Creech.

EPISTLE XLIV.

Virtue and Philoſophy confer Nobility.

DO you ſtill make yourſelf ſo little, *Lucilius*, as to complain, that Nature firſt uſed you hardly, and then Fortune? I am aſtoniſhed at ſuch language; when it is in your own power, not only to raiſe yourſelf above the vulgar, but to aſcend the higheſt ſtep of human felicity. This good, if any, we owe to philoſophy, that it pays no peculiar regard to geneaolgy. If we look back into the origin of mankind, we ſhall find that all are alike deſcended from the gods (*a*). You are a Roman knight, and your own induſtry hath advanced you to this honour: this however is an honour few can boaſt: the Court or Senate admits not every one; and even the Camp, that calls men to toil and danger, is very nice in its choice of officers (*b*): but Virtue opens her doors to all: in this reſpect all are alike noble. Philoſophy makes no diſtinction of perſons, but finds ſufficient ſplendour for all. *Socrates* was no patrician; *Cleanthes* worked at the well, and earned his living by watering gardens; philoſophy did not find *Plato* noble (*c*), but made him ſo. Why ſhould you deſpair of being equal to theſe great men? They were all your anceſtors, if you behave worthy of them: and you *will* ſo behave, if you can perſuade yourſelf that no one excels you in nobility:

and why not; ſince ſo many have gone before us, that every one's origin is loſt, beyond the reach of memory? *Plato* ſaith, *there is no King but who* (in all probability) *is deſcended from a ſlave, and no ſlave but who may be deſcended from a King (d)*. Such is the confuſion of things in proceſs of time; and ſo various the perpetual exerciſe of Fortune.

Who then is noble? He who hath a natural diſpoſition to virtue. This is the chief thing to be conſidered; otherwiſe there is no one, but who may carry his claim back to the firſt principles of things *(God and matter.)* From the birth of the world to the preſent day, an alternate ſeries of good and evil, hath rendered us either ſplendid or vile. The hall decorated with ſtatues, black with age and ſmoke, makes not the nobleman: no one hath lived for our glory; nor have we any claim upon what was done before we were born: it is the *mind* that ennobleth a man *(e)*; which as well from a cottage, as a palace, exalts him above the power of Fortune.

Suppoſe then you were not a Roman knight, but a plebeian, the ſon of a freed-man; you may yet attain the honour of being the only free man among many of the beſt-born. Do you aſk by what means? By diſtinguiſhing good and evil, not according to vulgar eſtimation; you muſt conſider, not from whence they ſpring, but whither they tend; not what they are in themſelves, but in their conſequences. Whatever can make life truly happy, is abſolutely good in its own right, becauſe it cannot be warped into evil. *From whence then comes error?* In that, while all men wiſh for a happy life, they miſtake the means for the thing itſelf; and, while they fancy themſelves in purſuit of it, they are flying from it: for, when the ſum of happineſs conſiſts in ſolid tranquillity, and an unembarraſſed confidence therein, they are ever collecting cauſes of diſquiet, and not only carry burthens, but drag them painfully along, through the rugged and deceitful path of life: ſo that they ſtill withdraw themſelves from the good effect propoſed; the more pains they take, the more buſineſs they have upon their hands: inſtead of advancing they are retrograde; and as it happens in a labyrinth, their very ſpeed puzzles and confounds them.

ANNO-

ANNOTATIONS, &c.

(a) Τυ γὰρ γενος εσμεν. See Ep. 31.

(b) As to the Roman levies; every tribe being called out by lot, was ordered to divide into their proper centuries; out of each century were ſoldiers cited by name, with reſpect had to their ſtate and claſs; for this purpoſe there were tables ready at hand, in which, the *name*, age, and wealth, of every perſon was exactly deſcribed, &c. See *Kennet*. *Lipſ.* Milit. l. 1.

(c) This is contradicted by *Laertius, as* Ariſto *was ſaid to have been his father, and* Perictione *the daughter of* Glaucus *his mother: which ſpake his nobility on both ſides; as his father was deſcended, through* Codrus, *from* Neptune *himſelf, and his mother's family from the wiſeſt of men,* Solon. *And* Apulius *remarks that when* Plato *was a boy, he wore gold rings in his ears,* the token of nobility.—Be that as it will, it was philoſophy and learning that truly ennobled and rendered him famous.

(d) If *Plato* has any where ſaid this, he likewiſe ſays, *Kings deſcended from Kings may be traced up to* Jupiter. Though the former may certainly be true in the circle and courſe of things.

(e) According to *Euripides*,

——Τὺς γὰρ ανδρειυς φυσει
Καὶ τὺς δικαιυς, τῶν κενῶν δοξασματων
Κἂν ὦσι δυλων ευγενεστερυς λεγω.
The juſt and well-diſpos'd put in their claim,
Tho' born of ſlaves, for ſome high-honour'd name.

EPISTLE XLV.

Of Books. The Mind is to be employed on Things and not on Words. The happy Man.

YOU complain, *Lucilius*, that, where you at preſent reſide you want books: it matters not, how many you have, but how good they are. Reading, with ſome point in view, profits a man; but variety only amuſeth *. He that hath fixed upon the end of his journey, muſt purſue one path, and not wander out of his way: this would not be called a journey, but rambling. You had rather, you ſay, I ſhould give you books than counſel. Such as I have I am ready to ſend you, and even my whole ſtock; nay, I would, if poſſible, tranſport myſelf to you;

and indeed did I not expect that you soon will have fulfilled your commiſſion, old as I am, I ſhould have undertaken the voyage: nor would *Charybdis*, *Scylla*, or any fabulous ſtories relating to this ſea, have deterred me from it. I would have ſwam over it, inſtead of being carried; to have enjoyed your preſence, and learned what progreſs you have made in the accompliſhments of the mind. But as for your deſiring me to ſend you my books, I think myſelf not a whit the more ingenious, than I ſhould think myſelf handſome, becauſe you deſired my picture. I know you make this requeſt more out of complaiſance than judgment; but if it be from judgment, I muſt tell you, your complaiſance hath impoſed upon you. However, ſuch as they are, I will ſend them; and entreat you to read them, as the writings of one, who is ſtill ſeeking after Truth; not preſuming to have found it; and ſeeking it with earneſtneſs and reſolution: for I have not given myſelf up to any particular maſter; I have not enliſted myſelf ſolemnly in any ſect †: I truſt indeed much to the judgment of great men, but at the ſame time deſpiſe not my own. They have ſtill left us many things for future inveſtigation; and perhaps might have ſupplied us with many things neceſſary, had they not attached themſelves to things vain and ſuperfluous: they loſt much time in cavilling about words, and in captious diſputations, which ſerve only to exerciſe and amuſe vain minds. They ſtart knotty queſtions, and then ſolve them, by the help of a few words of doubtful meaning: and have we leiſure for all this? do we yet know how to live, or how to die? Thither ſhould our utmoſt care and diſcretion be directed, in order to be provided againſt being deceived by things, as by words: what avails it to perplex yourſelf and me, with the diſtinction of words of like ſound, when no one can be deceived by them but in ſubtle diſputations?

Things themſelves deceive us: let us learn to diſtinguiſh them: we embrace evil for good; we wiſh for things contrary to what we wiſhed for before; our vows impugn our vows; and our purpoſes thwart and oppoſe one another: how nearly does flattery reſemble friendſhip? It not only imitates friendſhip, but ſeems to overcome and excel it *(a)*; it is ſucked in with favourable ears; deſcends into the heart; and is then moſt grateful, when moſt pernicious: teach me to diſtinguiſh this like-nefs: a fawning enemy fometimes attacks me in the name of a friend: vice impofes upon us under the mafk of virtue; temerity lies concealed, under the title of valour; indolence is taken for moderation; and the coward for a cautious man. Now, error in this refpect is very dangerous; fet therefore a particular mark on thefe things: but was you to afk a man if he has got horns, no one would be fo foolifh as to rub his brow for conviction; nor fo dull and ftupid as not to know, he has not got that which, by the moft fubtle inferences you would perfuade him he has. Thefe then deceive without any detriment; like the cups and balls of jugglers (*b*), in which the very fallacy delights us; make me to underftand how the feat is done, and all the pleafure of it is loft: I may fay the fame of all idle queftions, properly called *Sophiftry*; which to be ignorant of is by no means prejudicial; nor is there any profit or delight in knowing them.

Throw afide the ambiguity of words, and teach us this important truth; that he is not the happy man, whom the vulgar efteem fo, on account of his great wealth, but he whofe mind is all goodnefs; upright, and noble, trampling upon what the world holds in admiration; who fees no one, with whom he would change condition; who reckons a man happy, only in that he preferves the dignity of man; who takes Nature for his guide; conducts himfelf by her laws; and lives up to her prefcriptions; whofe truly good poffeffions are fuch, as no external power can take away; who turns evil into good; fure and fteady in point of judgment, without prejudice, without fear; whom no external force can difturb, though perchance it move him; whom, when Fortune hath pointed at him her fharpeft arrow, and with her whole ftrength, fhe only rakes, but cannot wound him; and *that* but feldom; for her other weapons, with which fhe affails mankind, rebound from him like the hailftones, which falling on our houfes, without any inconvenience to the inhabitants, make a little rattling, and are diffolved (*c*).

Here then exert yourfelf, for why fhould you detain me with fuch ftuff as you yourfelf call *pfeudomenon* (i. e. *fallacious reafoning:*) and of which fo many idle books are compofed? Behold, the whole of life deceives

deceives me; reprove this; if you are ſo acute, reduce this to truth. We judge thoſe things neceſſary the greateſt part of which are merely ſuperfluous; and even thoſe things, which are not ſuperfluous, have not ſufficient weight in them to make a man rich and happy: nay, though a thing be neceſſary, it is not immediately to be pronounced good: we proſtitute this title if we give it to bread, or other viands, without which no one can ſupport life: what is good, is neceſſary; but not every thing that is neceſſary is good; becauſe ſome things are abject and mean, which however are abſolutely neceſſary.

There is no one, I think, ſo ill informed of the importance of *good*, as to apply this term to the neceſſaries of the day: why then will you not rather transfer your care, to ſhew to all men, that with great loſs of time they are ever ſeeking ſuperfluities; and that many ſpend their whole life in queſt of the means to live. Conſider the whole world; reconnoitre individuals; who is there, whoſe life is not taken up with providing for to-morrow? Do you aſk what harm there is in this? An infinite deal: for ſuch men do not live, but are about to live: they defer every thing from day to day; however circumſpect we are, life will ſtill outrun us *(d)*: but now, while we are ſo dilatory, it paſſeth away as if it did not belong to us; it ends indeed at its laſt day, but is loſt every day.

But that I may not exceed the bounds of an epiſtle, and fill the reader's hand with a load of paper; I ſhall defer to another opportunity this diſpute with the Logicians; who generally ſpin their reaſonings ſomewhat too fine; and are ſtudious to exhibit little elſe than *this* and *that (e)*.

ANNOTATIONS, &c.

* See Ep. II. † Nullius addictus jurare in verba magistri. *Hor.* Ep. I. l. 14.

(a) Thus *Horace* (A. P. 431.)

Ut qui conducti plorant in funere, dicunt
Et faciunt prope plura dolentibus ex animo.
As hirelings, paid for the funeral tear,
Outweep the sorrows of a friend sincere.

(b) This rub on the logicians comparing their trifling argumentation to the tricks of jugglers, was from *Arcesilaus*, who said, τοὺς διαλεκτικοὺς ἐοικέναι τοῖς ψηφοπαίκταις οἵτινες χαριέντως παραλογίζονται.

(c) This is a most admirable character or description of *a good man*; but how greatly it may be heightened under the Christian scheme, we may see exemplified in that incomparable fiction, entitled *Sir Charles Grandison*. Fiction did I say? Be it so. It seems to me so replete with sentimental truths, and elegant diction, that I know no book, next to those of a religious tenour, that I would sooner recommend for perusal to a young man, and especially one of a superior rank.—According to my first plan I had inscribed the following Epistle to Mr. *Richardson*; and desired his acceptance of my application of it to his the said history, as coming from one of his many just admirers.

(d) Life will still outrun us] —— Life speeds away,

From point to point, tho' seeming to stand still;
The cunning fugitive is swift by stealth:
Too subtle is the moment to be seen:
Yet soon man's hour is up and we are gone.
Too prone's our heart to whisper what we wish;
'Tis later with the wise than he's aware;
The wisest man goes slower than the sun;
And all mankind mistake their time of day,
Ev'n age itself.——*Young.*

(e) This and *that*] Hoc solum curantibus, non et hoc. Alluding to the usual forms of their syllogisms; *a thing must be either* this *or* that; *it cannot be* this; *therefore it must be* that; or, it *cannot be* this *and* that; *it is* this, *therefore not* that. This puts me in mind of two lines, which a modern wit hath set by way of *moral* to a burlesque tragedy.

From such examples as of *this* and *that*,
We all are taught to know—I know not what. *Covent-Garden Tragedy.*

EPISTLE XLVI.

Concerning a Book which Lucilius *presented him with of his own Writing.*

I HAVE received, *Lucilius*, the book you promised me; I opened it, intending just to have a taste of it, and to read it at my leisure: but I was

was ſo delighted with it, that I could not help reading on: and my opinion of its being well wrote, will be manifeſt from hence; that I thought it ſhort, though it be too voluminous to be either of your writing or mine *(a)*; and ſeems at firſt ſight to be the works of *Livy*, or *Epicurus (b)*; but ſo entertaining and alluring was all that I read, I was reſolved without delay to finiſh it. And though it was late in the evening, hunger pinched me, and the clouds threatened a ſhower *(c)*, yet I read the whole: nor was I only amuſed but quite charmed: what judgment! what ſtrong ſenſe! what forceful energy! Was there any pauſe given, or did it riſe by ſtarts? No: it was not any peculiar ſtroke, but the whole tenour of it, that pleaſed me, as a maſterly and divine compoſition: yet, however ſtrong, it did not want grace and ſweetneſs in its proper place. You are indeed great and ſublime: this is what I would have you maintain and perſevere in: the ſubject matter is alſo of conſequence; eligible, and copious; ſo as to pleaſe the fancy, and exerciſe the genius.

I ſhall write more concerning this book, when I have again peruſed it: my judgment is not yet ſettled; it is as if I had only heard and not read it: permit me therefore to re-examine it: you have no reaſon to fear that I ſhall flatter you with an untruth. How happy are you, in giving no room for any one to ſay a falſe thing of you, even at ſuch a diſtance; except that where no cauſe is given, we ſometimes flatter for cuſtom's ſake.

ANNOTATIONS, &c.

(a) Cum eſſet nec mei nec tui *temporis*. *So* Lipſius, Salmaſius, *and others*. *But* Gronovius Gruter. et al. read it, *Corporis*. The antient way of writing was in long rolls, which when too large for the hands, were put under the chin, to be enrolled by degrees; or when too voluminous for this, they were laid upon a deſk, and ſuch as was gone through with, was puſhed forward and hung down from it. According therefore to the latter reading, the book here mentioned is ſuppoſed ſuch as neither of them could conveniently read without the like aſſiſtance.

(b) Epicurus is ſaid to have wrote more books than any one among all the philoſophers, not excepting *Chryſippus*.

(c) Though it was almoſt ſupper time, and he was afraid a ſhower would prevent his taking his uſual walk before it.

EPISTLE

EPISTLE XLVII.

On the Treatment of Servants.

IT by no means difpleafes me, *Lucilius*, to hear from thofe you converfe with; that you live in fome fort of familiarity with your fervants: this becomes your prudence, your erudition *(a)*. *Are they flaves?* No; they are men; they are comrades; they are humble friends: *Are they flaves?* Nay, rather fellow-fervants; if you reflect on the equal power of Fortune over both you and them. I therefore laugh at thofe, who think it fcandalous, for a gentleman, to permit, at times his fervant to fit down with him at fupper: why fhould he not? but that proud cuftom hath ordained, that the mafter fhould fup in ftate; furrounded at leaft by a dozen fervants; with greedinefs he loads his diftended paunch, now difufed to do its proper office (of digeftion.) So that it cofts him more pains to evacuate than to gormandize; while the poor fervants are not allowed to open their lips, fo much as to fpeak: the fcourge reftrains every murmur; nor are mere accidents excufed, fuch as a cough, a fneezing, an hiccup; filence interrupted by a word is fure to be punifhed feverely: fo that they muft ftand, perhaps the whole night, without taking a bit of any thing, or fpeaking a word. Whence it often happens, that fuch as are not allowed to fpeak before their mafters, will fpeak difrefpectfully of them behind their backs *(b)*: whereas they who have been allowed not only to fpeak before their mafters, but fometimes with them; whofe mouths were not always fewed up, have been ready to incur the moft imminent danger, even to the facrificing their lives, for their mafter's fafety; they have talked at an entertertainment; the rack cannot extort a word from them. Befides, from the forementioned arrogance, arifes the proverbial faying, Totidem effe hoftes, quot fervos: *As many fervants, fo many enemies* *(c)*; not that they are naturally enemies, but we make them fuch.

I pafs

I paſs by the more cruel and inhuman actions, wherein we treat ſervants, not as men, but as beaſts of burthen *(d)*; and need only mention, that while we are indulging our appetites, one is employed to wipe up our ſpawlings; another, down upon his knees, gathers up the ſcraps and broken bottles; another carves up ſome choice birds, and, diſſecting them with a dexterous hand, lays the breaſts and rumps in delicate order *(e)*; wretched is the man, who lives to no other purpoſe, than to cut up with dexterity a fat fowl; unleſs he is more wretched who teaches this art out of mere voluptiouſneſs, than he who learns it to get his bread; another ſerves as ſkinker, and *** is ſubject to the vileſt and moſt ſcandalous offices! Another who is allowed the freedom of playing the buffoon, (*f*) and cenſuring the gueſts, goes on in his wretched ſtate of life, expecting every day, that his ability to flatter, to drink, and prattle, will induce ſome one to invite him again to-morrow; add to theſe the caterers, who have an exquiſite knowledge of their maſter's taſte; what reliſh beſt provokes his appetite; what will moſt pleaſe his eye; what dainty will ſuit his ſtomach; what he loaths from ſatiety; and what ſuch a day he will eat greedily; and yet their maſter diſdains to ſup with them, thinking it a diminution of his grandeur to admit a ſervant to the ſame table. The Gods are moſt juſt, who to repay their wonted arrogance, have ſometimes given *them* maſters, even from thoſe whom they ſo much deſpiſed. Before the door of *Caliſtus*, (*g*), have I ſeen his former Lord waiting; and even the man, who once fixed a label on his breaſt, and ſet him to ſale among his rejected ſlaves, excluded, while others were admitted: the ſervant, who was put in the firſt rank of abject ſlaves, whom to make vendible the cryer was obliged to exert his voice (*h*), hath now returned the compliment (*i*); in his turn rejected his maſter, and thought him not worthy to enter his houſe. His maſter ſold *Caliſtus*, but how many things ſince hath *Caliſtus* ſold his maſter?

Were you to conſider, that he, whom you call your ſlave, is ſprung from the ſame origin, enjoys the ſame climate, breaths the ſame air, and is ſubject to the ſame condition of life and death, you might as well think it poſſible for you to ſee *him* a gentleman, as he to ſee *you* a ſlave.

ſlave. In the fall of *Varus (k)*, how many born of the moſt ſplendid parentage, and not unjuſtly expecting, for their exploits in war, a ſenatorial degree (*l*), hath fortune caſt down? She hath made of one a ſhepherd, of another a cottager. And can you now deſpiſe the man, whoſe fortune is ſuch, into which, while you deſpiſe it, you may chance to fall?

I will not enter into ſo large a field of diſcourſe, as to diſpute on the uſe of ſervants, whom we are apt to treat with contumely, pride and cruelty: but this is the ſum of what I would preſcribe; *live ſo with an inferior, as you would have a ſuperior live with you* (*m*). As often as you think on the power you have over a ſervant, reflect on the power your maſter has over you. But you ſay you *have no maſter*: be it ſo; the world goes well at preſent (*n*); it may not do ſo always; you may, one day, be a ſervant yourſelf. Do you know at what time *Hecuba* became a ſlave? as alſo *Crœſus*; and the mother of *Darius*(*o*); and *Plato*, and *Diogenes* (*p*)? Live therefore courteouſly with your ſervant; vouchſafe him conference; admit him to counſel, and even to your table. I know the whole band of fops will cry out upon me, alledging, that nothing can be more mean, nothing more ſcandalous: and yet I have caught ſome of theſe kiſſing the hand of another's ſervant.

See you not by what means our anceſtors withdrew all manner of envy from maſters, and contumely from ſervants? They called a maſter, *pater familias*, *the father of a family*; and ſervants, *Familiares*, (as the word is ſtill uſed in our *Mimes*) their *familiars* (*q*). They inſtituted certain feſtivals, when the ſervants not only ſat at table with their maſters, but were allowed to bear honourable rule in the Houſe, and enact laws; in ſhort they looked upon a family as a little commonwealth. What then, ſhall I admit all ſervants to my table? Yes, as well as all your children: you are miſtaken if you think I would reject even thoſe of the meaner ſort; ſuppoſe, the groom, or the cowkeeper; I eſteem them not according to their vocation, but their manners: the manners are a man's own; his vocation, ſuch as it is, is the gift of Fortune; let ſome ſit down with you, becauſe they are worthy, and others that they may become ſo; what remains in them of low and ſervile converſation, may be thrown off by converſing with their betters.

There is no reaſon, my *Lucilius*, that you ſhould ſeek a friend only in the *Forum*, or at Court; if you ſearch diligently, you may poſſibly find a truer friend at home: good materials are often loſt for want of a workman; for once make the experiment: as he is a fool, who, when buying a horſe, inſpects or examines nothing more than the bridle and ſaddle, he is as great a fool who eſteems a man from his dreſs, or his condition in life, which is alſo a ſort of dreſs. *Is he a ſlave?* His mind may yet be free: *is he a ſlave?* Why ſhould this prejudice you againſt him? Shew me the man who is not a ſlave (*r*). One is a ſlave to luſt; another to covetouſneſs; another to ambition; and all to fear. I can ſhew you a man of conſular dignity, a ſlave to an old woman; a very rich man a ſlave to his handmaid; and many a young nobleman, who are the very bond-ſlaves of players. No ſlavery is more infamous than that which is voluntary: there is no reaſon, therefore, that ſome over-nice perſons ſhould deter you from ſhewing yourſelf affable and good-humour'd to your ſervants; inſtead of carrying yourſelf proudly as their ſuperior: let them rather honour you than fear you *(s)*.

Some one now will ſay that I am inviting every ſlave to aſſume the cap *(of Liberty)*, and degrading every maſter from his proper ſtation, becauſe I have ſaid, rather let them reſpect, than fear you; what, ſays he, muſt they only reverence him, as his clients, and ſuch as attend his leveè? He that will ſay this, forgets, that what ſatisfies God, may well ſatisfy a maſter: God is reverenced and loved: love cannot accord with fear. I think therefore you act juſtly in not requiring your ſervants to fear you; and in chaſtizing them with words only; it is for brutes to be corrected by the ſcourge; not every thing that offends, hurts us: daintineſs compells us to outrage; ſo that the leaſt thing that thwarts our inclination can put us in a paſſion; we take upon us to act like Kings *(t)*; who not conſidering their own ſtrength, and the weakneſs of others, are cauſeleſsly enraged as if they re-

 ceived

an injury; when the greatneſs of their ſtate hath rendered them quite ſecure againſt any ſuch danger: this they know, but by an unjuſt complaint, they pretend to have received an injury, in order to commit one themſelves. I am unwilling to detain you any longer; for I think you have no need of exhortation. Good morals, among other advantages, have this quality; they enjoy ſelf-complacency, and are always ſteady; but a wicked diſpoſition is ever light and changeable; no matter whether the change be for the better, a change is enough.

ANNOTATIONS, &c.

(*a*) Erudition, with the Stoicks is the ſame as wiſdom. Vid. *Lipſ.* Manud. II. diſſ. 1.

(*b*) Like him in the old comedy. (Ariſtoph. Ran. 737)

—— *μαλα γ' ἐποπτευειν δοκῶ,*
Ο῞ταν καταρασωμαι λαθρα τῶ δεσποτῃ.
—— *Nothing gives me greater pleaſure*
Than privily to abuſe and curſe my maſter.

(*c*) From *Cato.*—But ſurely they muſt be either very bad ſervants, or bad maſters.—See this proverbial ſentence, and other paſſages of this epiſtle fully treated of in *Macrob.* Saturn I. c. 11. It is notorious, that the Lacedæmonians not only, in their general conduct treated their ſlaves with great harſhneſs and inſolence, but even maſſacred them, on ſeveral occaſions, in cold blood, and without provocation; leſt from growing too numerous or powerful, they might endanger the State.

But as M. de Monteſquieu very properly obſerves, their danger was owing to this inhuman treatment; whereas among the *Athenians,* who treated their ſlaves with great gentleneſs, there is no inſtance of their proving troubleſome or dangerous to the public. *Leland* Vol. II. p. 45, l. 4.

(d) There is a pertinent reflection in Lord *Orrery's* obſervations (on Plin. Ep. l. 3. 14.) "What "can be baſer, what more inhuman, than to oppreſs ſervants and ſlaves, miſerable by their ſituation, and only to be made leſs ſo, by that *proper* indulgence, which is due to the meaneſt of our "fellow-creatures, and which will always be allowed them by thoſe, who ſpring from the ſeeds of "virtue, and who ſcorn to wear honours, they have not deſerved? When we behold a barbarous "maſter and an ill-natured Lord, it is no unjuſt preſumption, notwithſtanding his load of titles, "to conclude, that by ſome accident or another he certainly ſprouts from the refuſe of the people, "and the dregs of mankind.

(*e*) Theſe dextrous carvers were called *Chironomontes,* Juv. V. 121.

—— Et Chironomonta volanti
Cultello, donec peragat dictata magiſtri.
Meanwhile thy indignation yet to raiſe,
The carver, dancing round each diſh, ſurveys
With flying knife; and as his art directs,
With proper geſture, every fowl diſſects. Bowles.

Sen. de beat. Vit. c. 17. *Carpi, Carptores*; Petron. *Scindendi opſonii Magiſtri.*—*Vid.* Sidon. Apoll. l. 4. Ep. 7. Ib. 2. 12. Quantâ arte ſcindantur aves in fruſta non enormia.

(*f*) Such a one was Calliodorus, to whom *Martial*,——

Festivè credis te, Calliodore, jocari,
Et solum multo permaduisse sale;
Omnibus arrides, dicteria dicis in omnes,
Sic te convivam posse placere putas,
At si ego non bellè, sed verò, dixero, quiddam,
Nemo propinabit, Calliodôre, tibi.
You think it smart, my friend, to cut your jests,
And with your gibes bespatter all the guests;
At all you laugh, censure, abuse, and tease;
And think by such accomplishments to please;
But were I only to speak truth of you,
You'd find no House to be invited to. M.

(*g*) *Calistus* was the freed-man of *Claudius*, yet this is said not of *Claudius*, but of some former master. Infra domino quam multa] Sc. by the favour of *Claudius*. *al leg.* domini; i. e. *of his master's*; viz. *Claudius*.

(*h*) As *Apuleius* says jocosely of himself, Tunc præco diruptis faucibus et rancâ voce saucius, in meas fortunas ridiculos construebat jocos; *The cryer then strained his jaws, and tore his throat, till he was quite hoarse, in setting me off with his ridiculous jests.*

(*i*) Apologavit.] A word in use among the vulgar, but from a Greek original. Ἀπολέγειν. Our *to apologize*, from the same.

(*k*) Variana clade. *So*, Lipsius. Al. *Marianâ* clade. But I think the former preferable; as it happened in the time of *Augustus*, and the effects were still visible. *Quinctilius Varus*, with three legions, was overthrown, and slain, by *Arminius*.

(*l*) Having served three years, as a military Tribune, according to the institution of *Augustus*. Vid. *Lips.* Milit. II. c. 20.

(*m*) *Whatsoever you would that men should do unto you, even so do unto them; for, this is the law and the prophets.* Matth. 7, 12. *Masters give unto your servants, that which is equal and just; knowing that ye also have a master in Heaven.* Col. 4. 1.

(*n*) Bona ætas.] Or, *you are young*, as, mula ætas, signifies *old age*.

(*o*) *Hecuba*, the wife of *Priam*, the last King of Troy. *Crœsus*, the last King of *Lydia* taken prisoner by *Cyrus*. The mother of *Darius*, taken prisoner by *Alexander*.

(*p*) *Plato*, having given some offence to Dionysius in *Sicily*, he ordered him to be sold; and accordingly he was carried to *Ægina*, and there sold for twenty pounds, to *Anniceris*, the *Cyrenaic*; who very readily gave him his liberty, and restored him to his friends at *Athens*.

When *Diogenes* was to be sold for a slave, he cry'd, *Who will buy a master?* And to him that bought him, *you must dispose yourself to obey me*, (said he) *as great men do their physicians*.

(*q*) Familiares. *See* Ep. 77. Sidon. Apol. l. 4. Ep. 8.

(*r*) Hor. Sat. I. 4. 25.—Quemvis media erue turba

Aut ab avaritia, aut miserâ ambitione laborat
Hic nuptarum insanit amoribus.——
Take me a man, at venture from the crowd,
And he's ambitius covetous, or proud;
One burns to madness for a wedded dame.—Francis.

Whosoever committeth sin is the servant of sin. 1 John. 8. 92. *Know ye not that to whom ye sold yourselves servants to obey, his servants ye are to whom ye obey.* Rom. 6. 16.

(*s*) *There is no fear in love, but perfect love casteth out fear, because fear hath torment: he that feareth is not made perfect in love.* 1. John, 4. 18.

(*t*) *Sen.* (de ira. l. ii. c. 31.) Regis quisque intra se habet animam, ut licentiam sibi dari in alterum velit, in se nolit.---We have too many instances of this tyranny even in our own history; such were Rich. II. Edw. IV. Henry VIII. upon particular occasions.

EPISTLE XLVIII.

On social Virtue, and the Trifling of Sophistry.

THE Epistle which you favoured me with, *Lucilius*, on your journey, almost as long as the journey itself, I shall answer at another opportunity. I must retire awhile, and consider what counsel it will be proper to give you: for as you, when you applied to me, took time to consider of it; have I not a right to claim the same indulgence; when the question is of such a nature *(a)*, as to require more time to solve, than to propose it; especially as one thing may be expedient for you, and another for me? I am speaking again as an *Epicurean (b)*: for indeed what is expedient for me, is also expedient for you; or I am not your friend, if what concerns you, is not of like concern to me.

Friendship makes a mutual interchange of things necessary, be it either in prosperity or adversity: true friends have all things in common *(c)*: nor can any one live happily who lives to himself alone, and considers nothing further than his own advantage: you must live for others if you would live honourably for yourself. This social virtue is to be diligently and religiously observed, which blends us all one with another, and points out one common right to mankind; but has most efficacy in cultivating the interior society of friendship: for he will certainly have all things in common with a friend, who knows that he hath many things in common with man, as his fellow-creature. Therefore, *Lucilius*, best of men, I had rather these subtle disputants would direct me, in diſtinguiſhing what I owe my friend, and what to mankind in general; than pretend to ſhew me how many ways a man may be ſaid to be a *friend*; and to what different ſenſes the word *man* may be applied.

Lo! wiſdom and folly take different paths: on which do I attend? or which do you recommend to me? Wiſdom looks upon man as a common friend: Folly regards not a friend in man. The former (the *Stoic*) deſigns a friend for himſelf; the latter (the *Epicurean*) himſelf for a friend: (i. e. *referring all things to himſelf alone.*)

You are apt, *Lucilius,* to wreſt the meaning of words; and amuſe yourſelf in the arrangement of ſyllables: indeed, unleſs I contrive the moſt artful queſtions, and by a falſe concluſion built upon true premiſes, affirm a lye, I can ſcarce ſeparate what is to be followed, from what is to be eſchewed: I am really aſhamed, that, old as we are, we ſhould thus trifle in ſerious affairs—

Mouſe is a ſyllable,
But a mouſe gnaws cheeſe;
Therefore, a ſyllable gnaws cheeſe.

Suppoſe now I was not maſter enough of logic to find out the fallacy of this ſyllogiſm, how dangerous would be my ignorance? what inconvenience would ariſe therefrom? Surely, I ought to be afraid, leſt I ſhould catch ſyllables in my mouſetrap; or, were I not to take more care, leſt a book ſhould eat my cheeſe. But perhaps the following ſyllogiſm is more acute and better formed:

Mouſe is a ſyllable;
But a ſyllable does not gnaw cheeſe:
Therefore a mouſe does not gnaw cheeſe.

What childiſh trifling! Is this the effect of all our gravity! Does our beard grow for this? Does all our labour and ſtudy tend to teach ſuch wretched ſtuff, with a grim and melancholy viſage?

Would you know what true philoſophy promiſeth all mankind? I will tell you, *good counſel.* We ſee one man ſtruggling in the jaws of death; another rack'd by poverty; another is tortured by riches, either his own or his neighbour's: one man dreads bad fortune, another is diſſatiſfied with good; one thinks himſelf hardly uſed by man, another by by the gods: ſeeing all this, why do you offer me ſuch ſilly trifles as the abovementioned? Here is no room for jeſting; you are called upon to ſuccour the diſtreſſed; you are under an obligation to lend all poſſible aſſiſtance to the ſhipwreck'd, to the priſoner, to the ſick, to the poor and needy, and to the unhappy under ſentence of death. Whither do you turn away? what are you doing? The man you ſport with is in great fear and trouble; rather aſſiſt him; beſtow your eloquence in favour of thoſe, who from real pains are ready to periſh; ſee how on every ſide they all ſtretch out their hands to you, and implore your aſſiſtance, with regard to the life that is paſt, and is ſtill decaying; in you is all their hope and ſtrength; they beſeech you to deliver them from this ſtorm of trouble and vexation, and ſhew the clear light of truth to ſuch as are diſtracted with error *(d)*. Diſtinguiſh to them what *Nature* hath made neceſſary from what is vain and ſuperfluous; what eaſy laws ſhe hath impoſed upon mankind; how pleaſant life may be made; how free and eaſy to ſuch as follow her laws; and how ſevere and intricate to thoſe, who rather truſt to opinion than nature. But, pray, what do theſe ſubtle diſputants with all their art? Do they drive out the luſtful paſſions? Do they even reſtrain them? I could wiſh that theſe diſputes only did no good: they really do hurt: I will make this manifeſt to you when you pleaſe; and that good natural parts are cramped and weakened by ſuch quirks and ſubtleties. I am aſhamed to ſay, what uſeleſs weapons they put into the hands of thoſe who are warring againſt fortune; and how poorly they equip them. This (the way you are in) is the only way to obtain the chief good; in the other the exceptions to philoſophy are intricate and vile, ſuch as engage the young ſtudents that attend the Prætor *(e)*. For, what elſe do ye, when you draw into error him, whom ye interrogate, but cauſe him to appear nonſuited? But as the Prætor reſtores the one to his right, ſo does Philoſophy the other. Why do ye depart from your large promiſes? and having ſpoke big words, that ye would cauſe that the glittering of gold ſhould no more dazzle my eyes than that of a ſword;—that with great conſtancy I ſhould deſpiſe and trample upon all that either men wiſh or fear;—do ye deſcend to the A, B, C, of grammarians? Is this the way to heaven? For this is what philoſophy promiſeth, that it will make me equal to the powers above. To this was I invited: for this purpoſe

I came:

I came: perform your promise. As much as possible, therefore, *Lucilius*, withdraw yourself from these exceptions and prescriptions of sophists. Plain and simple arguments best become and set forth truth. Even had we more time in life, it must be sparingly laid out, that we might have enough for necessaries: but now what madness is it to learn trifles, when life is so very short *(f)*?

ANNOTATIONS, &c.

(a) There seems to have been a consultation between *Seneca* and *Lucilius* concerning the latter's remaining in the province, when *Seneca* wished for his return to *Rome*.

(b) According to the Epicurean principle of measuring friendship by profit and advantage. See Epp. 3. 20. and the following Note.

(c) Aristotle being asked, Quid esset Amicus? *What was a friend?* answered, *μια ψυχὴ δυο σωμασιν ἐνοικοῦσα*, *One soul inhabiting two bodies*. Amicum qui intuetur, tanquam exemplar aliquod intuetur sui, &c. *Cic.* Læl. c. 7. "Whoever is in possession of a true friend, sees the exact counterpart of his own soul. In consequence of this moral resemblance between them, they are so intimately *one*, that no advantage can attend either, which does not equally communicate itself to both." And "surely, nothing can be more delightful than to live in a constant interchange and vicissitude of reciprocal good offices." "Not that a good man's benevolence is by any means confined to a single object: he extends it to every individual. For true virtue incapable of partial, and contracted exceptions to the exercise of her benign spirit, enlarges the soul with sentiments of universal philanthropy." *Melmoth*.—And such, from indisputable authority, were the primitive Christians; *The multitude of them that believed were of one heart and one soul, neither said any of them, that ought of the things he possessed was his own; but they had all things in common.* Acts 4. 32.

And here I cannot but acknowledge, (as every Christian reader will acknowledge) an obligation to the translator of *Cicero's Lælius*, for his admirable remark (N. 68.) on this subject, concluding as follows; "Upon the whole then, it appears, that the divine Founder of the Christian Religion, as well by his own example, as by the spirit of his moral doctrine, has not only encouraged, but *consecrated* FRIENDSHIP.

(d) This is what the philosophers promise, and perform according to *Lucretius*, V. 12.

——Deus ipse fuit, Deus—
Qui princeps vitæ rationem invenit eam, quæ
Nunc appellatur sapientia; quique per artem
Fluctibus e tantis vitam tantisque tenebris,
In tam tranquillo, et tam clarâ luce locarunt.
He was a God, who first inform'd our souls
And led us by philosophy and rules,
From cares and fears, and melancholy night,
To joy and peace; and shew'd us splendid light.——Creech.

But we learn from the most authentic records, that the wisest and best of the antient philosophers, when they undertook to settle the great foundations of religion, were at a loss, and so strangely puzzled, that the most knowing among them renounced all knowledge; and so far were they from being able to point out the way to happiness, that scarce any two of them could agree in what that happiness consisted: wherefore, I should not think it much amiss, if a Christian looked upon these lines of *Lucretius* as prophetical, and applied them, with a grateful heart, to the Christian scheme.

(e) The

(*e*) The Prætorship was the second office for dignity in *Rome*. Their principal business was to administer justice to the citizens, and strangers; and to make edicts as a supplement to the civil law.

(*f*) Our want of time and the shortness of human life are some of the principal commonplace complaints, which we prefer against the established order of things. The man of business despises the man of pleasure, for squandering his time away; the man of pleasure pities or laughs at the man of business for the same thing, yet both concur superciliously and absurdly to find fault with the Supreme Being for having given them so little time. The philosopher, who mispends it very often as much as the others, joins in the same cry and authorises the impiety. *Theophrastus* thought it extremely hard to die at ninety, and to go out of the world, when he had just learned to live in it: his master *Aristotle* found fault with Nature, for treating man, in this respect, worse than several other animals: both very unphilosophically! And I love *Seneca* the better for his quarrel with *Aristotle* on this head." *Bolingbroke* on Retirement.

EPISTLE XLIX.

On the Brevity of Life. Useful Things only to be studied.

I OWN, my *Lucilius*, that he is supine and negligent, who is no otherwise put in mind of a distant friend, than by an advertisement from such a place: but so it happens that places, which have been familiar to us, often call forth the affection reposited in our bosom; and not suffering the remembrance of a friend to be quite extinguished, rouse it from its dormant state; as the grief of those who have lost a friend or relation, though lulled for a while, is renewed at the sight of an old servant, or of the clothes, or place of residence of the deceased. You cannot imagine what an affection for you, at our present distance, *Campania*, and particularly *Naples*, hath raised in me at the sight of your beloved (villa) *Pompeii*: your whole self stands, as it were, before my eye, especially at the time of my taking leave of you; I see you restraining the tear just starting from your eye; and labouring in vain to stifle those affections, which, from being suppressed, discover themselves the more: even *now* methinks I must part from you.

For

For what may not this *now* be applied to, upon reflection? It was but just *now* when I was fitting at the feet of *Sotio (a)* the philosopher; just *now* I began to plead at the bar; just *now* I was desirous to leave off; and but just *now* the task was too much for me. O the infinite velocity of time, which is more apparent, when we look back upon what is past: for it deceives us, when we are intent upon the present. So swift is the course of its precipitate flight, we have not leisure to consider it *(b)*. Shall I give you a reason for this? All that is past of time, is in one place: it is at once beheld, and gone at once. Hence all things fall into the vast abyss: otherwise there could not be such long intervals in a thing, so entirely short in itself: we live, comparatively, but a moment; nay less than a moment; but this, little as it is, Nature hath divided into the specious appearance of a longer space: of one part she hath formed what we call *infancy*; of another, *childhood*; of another, *youth*; of another, *manhood*, still inclining to old age; and of another, *old age* itself. How many degrees hath she comprehended in a narrow compass! It was but just *now*, when I began a friendship and correspondence with you; and yet this *now* hath proved a great part of life; whose brevity we must one day become sensible of.

I was not used to think the flight of time so swift; which now seems to me incredible *(c)*; either because I am got as it were upon the last line of it *(d)*; or because I have of late began to reflect and compute my loss of it; and consequently am more vexed, that any one should spend the greater part of it in vanities and trifles, when the whole, though attended to with the most diligent care and circumspection, sufficeth not for doing, what is necessary to be done.

Cicero affirms, that were his days to be doubled, he should not find time enough to read the Lyric Poets; I say the same of the Logicians: the more demure and wretched triflers! The former professedly wanton away their time; but these fondly imagine they are doing something of importance: not but that they are sometimes to be looked into; but nothing more than with a transient view; a salute, as it were, at the door; to the intent only that we may not be imposed upon; and fancy more good couched under them than is apparent. But why should you perplex yourſelf and me with a queſtion, which it is more prudent to deſpiſe than to ſolve? It is for one who is idle, and can make a miſtake without much detriment, to enquire into theſe minute things. As when the alarm is given, and the ſoldier is commanded to march; neceſſity obliges him to quit the fardels he had collected in the time of peace; and with proper accoutrements to take the field: I have no leiſure to ſift the meaning of doubtful words, or to try my ſkill in unriddling them.

Aſpice qui coeunt populi, quæ mænia clauſis
Ferrum acuant portis.—(Virg. 8, 385.)
[*Behold what nations join, and ſhut their gates*
'Gainſt me and mine!]

The horrid din of war reſounding on every ſide muſt be attended to with great preſence of mind; I ſhould juſtly be thought a madman if, when even the women and old men were piling up ſtones to fortify the wall; when the young men within were expecting or demanding an order to ſally out; when hoſtile weapons ſhook the gates, and the ground under foot trembled, by being dug and undermined; I ſhould then ſit idle and at eaſe propounding queſtions of this ſort:

What you have not loſt, you have got,
But you have not loſt horns,
Therefore you have horns.

Or inventing others conſtructed in the form of this acute dotage. Nor ſhould I ſeem leſs mad, was I *now* to beſtow my time upon ſuch traſh; for I am even *now* beſieged: in the former caſe I was threatened only with danger from without; and was defended from the enemy by ſtrong walls; but my preſent danger is from within, even the danger of death; I am not at leiſure therefore to trifle; I have a great work in hand. What ſhall I do?

Death purſues me; life is fleeting; inſtruct me with regard to theſe points; teach me ſomething, that I may not fly from death, nor life from me *(e)*: exhort me, againſt theſe difficulties, to put on æquanimity; ſtrengthen me with conſtancy, againſt theſe inevitable evils; make me content with the time I have to live; teach me that the good of life, conſiſts not in the duration, but in the right uſe of it. That

it

it is poſſible, nay, that it often happens, for a man, who hath been long in the world, to have lived but a little time. Remind me, as I am going to ſleep, that it may be I ſhall wake no more; or rather, when I awake that I ſhall ſleep no more. Tell me when I go out, that poſſibly I may not return; and, when I return, it may be I ſhall go out no more. You are miſtaken, if you think that upon the wide and dangerous ſeas only, there is the ſmalleſt line or interval between life and death; it is the ſame in all places; Death indeed does not ſhew himſelf every where ſo near, yet every where he is as near. Take away this darkneſs from me *(f)*, and you will the more eaſily diſcover to me theſe things, for which I am prepared.

Nature hath endowed us with ſufficient docility: and though as yet our reaſon may be imperfect, it is what may be perfected. Let us confer together concerning juſtice, piety, frugality, and particularly chaſtity; both that which teaches me from violating the body of another, and that which inſtructs me in the due care of my own. If you would not lead me into any by-path, I ſhall ſooner attain to the wiſh'd-for end of my journey. For as the Tragedian ſaith, *The ſpeech of truth is ever plain and ſimple (g)*. It ſhould not therefore be rendered intricate or obſcure; nor can any thing be more diſagreeable than ſuch wily and ſubtle craftineſs, to a generous mind that hath great things in view.

ANNOTATIONS, &c.

(a) Euſeb. Chron. *(extremis Augusti annis)* Sotio philoſophus Alexandrinus, præceptor Senecæ, clarus habetur. *At the end of the reign of* Auguſtus *flouriſhed* Sotio, *the philoſopher of* Alexandria, *tutor to* Seneca.—See Ep. 24.

(b) Thoſe hours which lately ſmil'd, where are they now?
Pallid to thought, and ghaſtly! drown'd, all drown'd,
In that great deep, which nothing diſembogues!
The reſt are on the wing—how fleet their flight!
Already has the fatal train took fire:
A moment, and the world's blown up to thee,
The ſun is darkneſs, and the ſtars are duſt.—*Young.*

(c) Time in advance behind him hangs his wings,
And ſeems to creep, decrepit with his age.
Behold him when paſt by, what then is ſeen,
But his broad pinions, ſwifter than the winds!
And all mankind in contradiction ſtrong,
Rueful, aghaſt! cry out on his career.—*Id.*

(d) Quia admoveri lineas sentio.——

Linea was a trench drawn round the *Arena* to mark the course for those who entered the lists.

Admoveri lineas, *is the same with* decrepitos et extrema tangentes, Ep. 26. *Upon the last stage of life.*

Or metaphorically for the last line on the chess-board, as Hor. Ep. I. 16, ult.—Mors ultima linea rerum est.

Death is that goal the poet here intends,
The utmost course, where human nature bends.

This does not mean that Death is an end of all things, but of all our misfortunes. Rerum *for* rerum malarum, *as in* Virgil, fessi rerum,—sunt lacrymæ rerum,—trepidæ rerum.

— Επ' ἄκραν ἥκομεν γραμμὴν κακῶν. Eur. Antig.
Reduced to the last extremity.
Μή μοι, τὸ πρῶτον βῆμ' ἐὰν δράμῃ καλῶς,
Νικᾶν δοκείτω τὴν δίκην, πρὶν ἂν πέλας
Γραμμῆς ἵκηται καὶ τέλος κάμψῃ βίου. Id. Elect. 954.
Let no one dream of victory,
Howe'er successful his first round,
'Till he hath reach'd the goal, and end of life.

(e) i. e. live in indolence, and doing nothing to the purpose of being.

(f) Has tenebras discute.—

Through this opaque of nature and of soul,
This double night, transmit one pitying ray,
To brighten and to chear.—*Young.*

(g) Απλοῦς ὁ μῦθος τῆς ἀληθείας ἔφυ. Eur. Phæn. 472.

EPISTLE L.

Tender Minds are the more easily wrought upon, but it is not impossible to get the better of an inveterate Habit.

AFTER some months, *Lucilius,* I have received the letter you sent me: I therefore thought it of little avail to enquire of the person who brought it, any news relating to you: for he must have had a good memory to have recollected every thing. And yet I hope you live so, as in whatever place you are, I may be informed of what you are doing: but what else can you be doing, than studying every day, to make yourself a better man? casting off some error or other; and particularly learning that your vices are your own, and not to be imputed to circumstances;

ſtances; for ſome we aſcribe to times and places; but wherever we go, they are ſuch as ſtill follow us.

The ſimpleton, *Harpaſte*, that attends my wife, hath continued an hereditary burthen in my family; for I own I am much diſguſted at ſuch prodigies. If I would divert myſelf with a fool, I have not far to look for one; I laugh at myſelf. This ſilly girl went blind on a ſudden; and what I tell you, is very ſtrange, but true: ſhe does not ſeem to know, that ſhe is blind: ſhe often aſks her governeſs to walk out; for ſhe ſays, the houſe is ſo dark ſhe cannot ſee *(a)*. Now tho' we are apt to laugh at her, we all lie under the ſame predicament: no one will own himſelf covetous; no one, luſtful: yet the blind deſire a guide; but we ſtill wander on without a guide, and ſay, "*I am really not ambitious, but no one can live otherwiſe at Rome. I am not expenſive, but it is impoſſible to be penurious while we live in the city: it is not my fault that I am paſſionate; for I have not yet fixed upon a certain rule of life: it is the failing of youth.*" Why do we thus deceive ourſelves? The evil that infects us comes not from without; it is internal, it reſides in the very breaſt: and therefore it is the more difficult to be reſtored to health, becauſe we know not, or pretend not to know, that we are ſick.

Were we to undertake a cure, how long would it be before that of ſo many pains and diſeaſes could be effected? But we do not ſo much as ſeek a phyſician; who certainly would have much leſs trouble was he to be called in, upon the firſt ſymptoms. Young and tender minds are ſoon prevailed upon to attend to thoſe, who ſeriouſly point out to them the right path: no one is brought back with difficulty to the ſtandard of Nature, but ſuch as have quite deſerted her: but the misfortune is, we are aſhamed to learn wiſdom; we ſeem to think it diſgraceful to look out for a maſter in this reſpect; and yet we can never hope ſo great a good will flow in upon us merely by chance: ſome pains muſt be taken; and to ſay the truth, no great pains are required, if, as I before obſerved, we only begin to correct and reform the mind before it is too harden'd in depravity; nor, be it harden'd as it will, ſhould I quite deſpair.

despair. There is nothing but what perseverance, assiduity, and diligent care may overcome *(b)*. The hardest oak, however bent, may be made streight; heat will unbend the crooked beam; and things, however designed by Nature for other purposes, are applied to such services as our use requires. How much easier will the mind take any form you please? it is flexible, and more pliant than either air or water; for what is the mind, but a certain indwelling spirit? And a spirit is the more easily worked upon than matter, as it is more fine and subtile.

There is no reason then, my *Lucilius*, that you should entertain the less hopes of any one, because the malignity of evil hath laid hold of him, and had him long in possession: no one learns virtue before he hath unlearned vice: in this respect we are all pre-engaged *(d)*: but we ought to apply ourselves more strenuously to amendment; because the possession of good is everlasting. No one that hath once learned virtue, can forget it *(e)*: for, the contrary evils are of foreign growth, and therefore may easily be extirpated and expelled. Such things as are in their proper place, abide there constantly: Virtue is according to Nature *(f)*; Vice is ever her foe, and ever prejudicial. But as virtues once truly received into the breast, cannot again depart; and consequently the conservation of them is easy; so the first entrance upon them is arduous; because it is the common part of a weak and sick mind, to dread what it has not yet experienced. Therefore the mind must be compelled to make a first essay; and then the medicine will not prove disagreeable, when it gives delight at the time it effects a cure: the pleasure of the remedies is seldom tasted before health is procured; but philosophy is at the same time both salutary and pleasant.

ANNOTATIONS, &c.

(a) Muretus (in his Note) makes mention of a friend of his under the like delusion, though a sensible and learned man: he was grown deaf with age, being near fourscore; but would not acknowledge his infirmity: he fancied every one spoke in a lower tone than they used to do formerly; and whispered, that he might not hear them.

(b) This is a principal maxim of the Stoics, that, *virtue is to be acquired by erudition:* Nemo enim per se satis valet, ut emergat, &c. Ep. 52. *No one is sufficient of himself to emerge*, &c. Vid. *Lips.* Manud. II. Diss. X.

(c) Thus

(c) Thus *Horace*, Ep. I. 1. 38.

Invidus, iracundus, iners, vinofus, amator,
Nemo adeò ferus eft, ut non mitefcere poffit
Si modo culturæ patientem commodet aurem.

Is fame thy paffion? wifdom's pow'rful charm,
If thrice read over fhall its force difarm;
The flave to envy, anger, wine or love,
The wretch of floth, its excellence fhall prove.——Francis.

(d) *The imagination of man's heart is evil continually.* Gen. 8. 21. *Out of the heart proceed evil thoughts, &c.* Matth. 15. 19. *Ceafe to do evil, learn to do well*, &c. If. 1. 16. 1 Pet. 3. 11.

(e) *Virtue*, fays *Socrates*, *like truth, admits not either addition, or diminution.* Ep. 72. *See alfo* Epp. 74. 75. *Lipf.* Manud. III. Diff. 3.

(f) See Epp. 92. 95.

EPISTLE LI.

Such Places are to be avoided as effeminate the Mind.

EVERY one muft do as they can, my *Lucilius:* it is your lot to be near *Ætna*, that celebrated mountain of *Sicily*; which I am furprized that *Meffala* and *Valgius* fhould take to be the only one of the kind, for fo they both write; whereas *vulcanos* are to be feen, not only in high places (where indeed they are more frequent, as it is the nature of fire to afcend) but alfo in the low: for our part, we muft be content with *Baiæ* (*a*); though, I own, I was induced to leave the place the day after I came thither: a place, not the more to be defired becaufe nature hath endowed it with certain qualities, which the voluptuous take delight in, and the luxurious have made their theme of praife.

And what then? Is any place to be cried down at pleafure? No; but as one drefs is more becoming to a wife and good man than another; nor has he an averfion to any particular colour, but that he thinks fome one lefs decent for a man who profeffes frugality; fo there may be a country, which a wife man, or one in purfuit of wifdom, may difapprove of, as tending to the corruption of good morals: thinking therefore on a place of retirement, he would never fix upon *Canopus (b)*, (though as diſſolute a place as it is, it hinders no one from being ſober and temperate) nor on *Baiæ*, now become the very hoſtrie of vice: where luxury takes her full ſwing; and the people, as if by permiſſion, grow more and more diſſolute: whereas would we live happy, we ſhould reſort to a place, that is not only productive of health for the body, but conducive alſo to ſound morals. As I would not live among the executioners; ſo neither would I live in a tavern or a cook's-ſhop. Is there any neceſſity for ſeeing men drunk and reeling about the ſtreets; or hearing the riotings of ſailors; and the lakes reſounding with looſe ſongs, and concerts of muſick; with many the like entertainments; which luxury, as if altogether lawleſs, not only offends in, but makes public profeſſion of. It is our buſineſs to fly as far as poſſible from all allurements to vice: the mind is to be withdrawn from the ſoft blandiſhments of pleaſures, and inured to hardſhips. One winter-quarters pulled down the ſtrength of *Hannibal*; and the delights of *Campania* quite enervated that great man, who was impenetrable to the cold and deep ſnows of the *Alps*: he conquered in arms, but was conquered by luxury and vice. Our condition likewiſe is a warfare (*d*), and ſuch a one wherein no reſt, no leiſure-time is allowed. Pleaſures in the firſt place are to be ſubdued; which (as you ſee) have drawn in the moſt ſavage tempers. If any one ſhould propoſe to taſk himſelf, let him know, that nothing is to be done of a ſoft and delicate caſt.

What have I to do with warm baths or hot houſes, where the reeky air exhauſts the juices of the body (*e*)? If I muſt ſweat, let it be by exerciſe. Were we to do as *Hannibal* did; and, during the interruption in the courſe of affairs, or in the time of a truce, give up ourſelves to the pampering the body; no one would unjuſtly reprehend ſuch an indulgence, dangerous to a conqueror, much more to him who hopes to conquer. We are not allowed ſo much liberty as thoſe who followed the *Carthaginian* ſtandard: more danger remains for us, if we yield; and even more work, if we perſevere in duty. Fortune wages perpetual war againſt me; I have no mind to yield; I take not her yoke upon me; nay,

nay, what requires still greater courage and virtue; when imposed upon me, I throw it off; the mind is not to be thus shattered with delicacies. If I yield to pleasure, I must submit to pain, to trouble, to poverty: ambition would claim the same right over me; and also anger: I shall be distracted with a sad variety of passions, nay, torn in pieces. Liberty is proposed to me; this is the prize to be contended for: do you ask, what is liberty *(f)*? it is to be a slave to nothing; not even to necessity, or accidents; to bring fortune to reason; from the day that I was sensible of my superior power, she could do nothing; and shall I suffer her to triumph over me, *while my mind is still free (g)*?

To a man reflecting on these things no places are proper but such as are serious and sacred: too much pleasantness effeminates the mind, and no doubt but some climates more than others corrupt the internal vigour of the soul. Any road is tolerable to our pack-horses, whose hoofs are hardened and grown callous, by travelling in rough and craggy ways; while such as are fed in soft and marshy pastures are soon fretted and worn out. The hardships of a country life (as in the *Highlands)* generally make better soldiers *(h)* than the idle and tender breeding of the city. The hands that are transferred from the plough to the pike refuse no labour: the spruce and well-oiled boxer gives out at the first onset: it is the more severe discipline of the place that strengthens the disposition, and renders it fit for great enterprizes. *Scipio (i)* thought *Linternum* a more proper place for his voluntary banishment than *Baiæ:* his fall was not to be so pleasantly accommodated. And those great men whom fortune had raised to the highest honours, and conferred on them the treasures of *Rome, Caius Marius, Cneius Pompeius*, and *Cæsar, (k)* built themselves indeed country-seats, in the *Baian* territory, but they placed them on tops of hills: this seemed more soldier-like, to live, as it were, in a watch-tower, that commanded the country far and wide. Behold what situations they chose; in what places they raised their buildings; and what manner of edifices they preferred! you would not call them villas but fortresses. Do you think *Cato* would have chose some pleasant shore for his dwelling-place, that he might count the harlots as they sailed by, and see variety of pinnaces painted with divers colours; or a lake ſtrewed over with flowers; or to have heard the nocturnal revels of jovial ſongſters? Had he not rather, do you think, remain within the trenches (*l*), than ſpend a night amidſt ſuch merriment (*m*)? Who that is a man, had not rather be awakened with the ſound of the trumpet calling to arms, than with a midnight ſerenade!

We have quarrelled long enough with *Baiæ*; but never can enough with our vices; which I beſeech you, my *Lucilius*, to perſecute everlaſtingly: throw away from you every thing that tears the heart; and if you cannot otherwiſe get rid of it, ſpare not the heart itſelf (*n*). But eſpecially diſlodge pleaſures; and have as great ſpite againſt them as againſt the thieves, whom the Ægyptians call *Philetas* (*o*), who hug that they may trip up, and embrace, in order to ſtrangle us.

ANNOTATIONS, &c.

(*a*) *Baiæ*, a city of *Campania*, near the ſea, ſituated between *Puteoli* and *Miſenum*, famous for its warm baths: from whence it is ſuppoſed all other baths of the like kind are called *Baiæ*.

> Nullus in orbe ſinus Baiis prælucet amœnis.—Hor. Ep. I. l. 83.
> Ut mille laudem, Flacce, verſibus Baias;
> Laudabo dignè non ſatis tamen Baias:
> Baias ſuperbæ blanda dona naturæ. Mart. xl. 81.
> *The muſe, however copious in the praiſe*
> *Of* Baiæ's *healing ſprings, can never raiſe*
> *The theme above its merit, from where flow*
> *The kindeſt gifts that nature can beſtow.*—M.

(*b*) *Canopus*, a city in *Ægypt*, 12 miles from Alexandria. It was built by *Menelaus* in memory of his pilot *Canopus* who died there; and wherein he left all his men who were unfit for ſervice.——*Where the ſhores*, ſays *Strabo*, *inceſſantly reſound, night and day, with the noiſe of pipes and feaſting, in all manner of luxury and intemperance, among both men and women, on ſhipboard*: ſo that *Canopea luxuria* was become a proverb. *Eraſm.* Adag. p. 1346.

> Prodigia et mores urbis damnante Canopo.——*Juv.* VI. 84.
> ——— Luxuriâ quantum ipſe notari
> Barbara famoſo non cedit turba Canopo. *Id.* XV. 45.

(*c*) *Livy* 23, 18. Itaque quos nulla mali vicerat vis, perdidère nimia bona ac voluptates immodicæ; et eo impenſiùs quo avidiùs ex inſolentiâ in eas ſe immerſerant, &c.

And thus, they, whom no hardſhips, no forces in the field had conquered, were deſtroyed by luxury and voluptuouſneſs, to which fatal evils the more they were ſtrangers, the more eagerly they plunged themſelves into them.

(*d*) Στρατεία τίς ἐστιν ὁ βίος ἑκάστου καὶ αὐτὴ μακρὰ καὶ ποικίλη. *Life is a warfare long and various.* Epict. III. 24. *The weapons of our warfare*, ſays St. *Paul*, *are not carnal, but mighty towards God, to the pulling down of ſtrong holds*, &c. 2 Cor. 10. 4. And of himſelf, *I have fought a good fight*, &c. 2 Tim. 4. 7. See alſo Ep. 6. 14. 17.

(*e*) In

(e) In fudoribus---corpora exhaufturus.] Ep. 108. Decoquere corpus atque exinanire fudoribus,---inutile fimul delicatumque credimus. *Suppofing it to be a nice and ufelefs cuftom to feeth the body, and weaken the folids by extravagant fweating.*

(f) Epict IV. 21. *Sen.* Ep. 75.

(g) Ego illam feram, cum in manu mors fit.] I am again, you fee, obliged to give another turn to the fentence, in order to avoid the horrid ftoicifm, fo often advanced in thefe Epiftles, and yet fo often refuted by *Seneca* himfelf.

(h) Hor. Od. I. 12. Fabritium que
Hunc, et incomptis Curium capillis,
Utilem bello tulit, et Camillum
Sæva paupertas et avitus apto
Cum lare fundus.

Form'd by the hands of penury fevere,
In dwellings, fuited to their fmall domains,
Fabritius, Curius, *and* Camillus *rofe*
To deeds of martial glory. Francis.

(i) I muft beg leave here to tranfcribe, at leaft an abftract of the character of this great man (often mentioned in thefe Epiftles), as moft elegantly drawn up by Mr. *Melmoth* in his *Cato* (or *Cicero* on old age) N. 27. " The military talents of the firft *Scipio Africanus*, although in no refpect excelled by any of the moft famous captains, in *Roman* or *Grecian* annals, were by no means fuperior to the more amiable virtues of his heart." And to crown all, this illuftrious *Roman* was impreffed with a ftrong fenfe of religious duties, and a firm belief of a fuperintending providence.---But " the important fervices he had rendered his country, in conjunction with thofe eminent private virtues which he had upon every public occafion difplayed, feem to have given him fuch an afcendancy in the ftate, as to have raifed, in fome of the moft diftinguifhed patriots of that age, a ftrong jealoufy of his credit and power."---And accordingly " they commenced a profecution againft him."---But *Scipio*, " inftead of vindicating his character from the charges of his impeachment, treated the accufation with difdain; and refufing to comply with the fummons for his appearance, withdrew to his villa at *Liternum*,---by a fort of voluntary exile;---where he fpent the remainder of his days, amufing himfelf in the cultivation of his farms, and without difcovering the leaft regret at being excluded from a fcene, in which he had figured with fo much honour to himfelf, and advantage to his country." See Epift. 86.

(k) Viam Miseni propter et villam Cæfaris, quæ fubjectos finus editiffima profpectat. *Tac.* Ann. 14. 9. The wretched *Agrippina*, mother to *Nero*, from the benevolence of her domeftics, received a flight and vulgar grave, *upon the road to Cape* Mifenum, adjoining to a villa of *Cæfar's* the *Dictator*; *which from its elevated ftation overlooks the coafts and bays below.*

(l) Among the various readings here I have followed *Gronovius*; in actâ. Baias, actas, convivia, commiffationes. *Cic.* pro Cato.---Et in actâ cum fuis accubuiffet. *Cornel. Nep.*

(*m*) Quàm unam noctem inter talia duxiffe] al. Quod (vallum) in una nocte manu fuâ ipfe duxiffet. So, the old Englifh, *which in one night's fpace he had digged and caufed to be inclofed.*

(*n*) *If thy right eye offend thee, pluck it out, and caft it from thee, &c.* Matth. 5. 29. 18. 8 Mark, 9. 47. *See* Ep. 71, 8.

(*o*) Philetus] qu. *Kiffers.* a Gr. φιλεῖν, ofculari, amplecti.

Ὅς γε γυναικὶ πέποιθε, πέποιθ᾽ ὅγε φιλήτῃσι. Hef. 1. 373.

Too fatirical on the fair fex to be tranflated!

Hefychius. Φιλήτης, Κλέπτης λῃστής, fur, latro.

EPISTLE LII.

The Necessity of having a good Tutor. Philosophy despiseth the vain Applause of the Populace.

WHAT is it, *Lucilius*, that, as we are intentionally going one way, ſtill drives us another? What is it detains us there, where we have no inclination to ſtay? What is it, that thwarts our ſpirit nor permits us to determine upon any one thing ſeriouſly? Our thoughts are ever wavering; we *will* nothing freely, nothing abſolutely, nothing always. It is *folly*, you ſay; which is conſtant in nothing, and pleaſed with nothing long *(a)*.

But how or when ſhall we get cured of this malady? No one has ſtrength enough of himſelf to emerge *(b)*. *Epicurus* ſays, that *ſome*, (including himſelf among them) have been ſo happy, as to find out for themſelves a path, that leads to truth. And theſe he greatly commends; whoſe ſtrength of genius hath uſher'd them into the world; while others want help, and can never make any figure, unleſs ſome one goes before them, whom they follow with ſucceſs: ſuch a one, he ſays, was *Metrodorus*. This likewiſe is excellent; tho' a genius but of the ſecond claſs. Now we pretend to no more than this ourſelves: and we ought not to deſpiſe a man, becauſe he has been obliged to a friend, for putting him into a good way; the very deſire to be ſo obliged is of no ſmall conſequence.

Beſides theſe, you will find a third ſort of men, whom yet we ought not to diſdain, who require to be forced and compelled to good *(d)*; who want not only a leader, but an aſſiſtant with power irreſiſtible: if you deſire an example of this ſort; *Epicurus* offers you *Hermachus*; therefore he congratulates the one *(Metrodorus)* and admires the other: *(Hermachus:)* for tho' both arrive at the ſame end, yet greater praiſe ſeems due to him, who had the greater difficulty to encounter: as in building two houſes of equal ſtrength and ſplendour; where the ground was firm and good, the work hath roſe preſently; but where the foundation is laid in a watery or ſandy ſoil, much labour and time muſt be ſpent before it comes to be ſettled: in the one caſe, the whole work that hath been done appears in ſight; in the other, a great and more difficult part of it lies concealed: I have therefore called him the happier man, who had little or no trouble with himſelf, but I think him the more deſerving, who hath overcome the malignity of his nature, and did not wheedle but force his inclination to attend wiſdom. Know then that ſuch is the hard and laborious taſk, impoſed upon us; we are continually meeting with impediments; we muſt engage therefore, as it were, in battle; and call in ſome ally *(e)*; but whom, you ſay, muſt I call? this man or that? It matters not; call whom you pleaſe: but I would have you regard the principals, who are at your ſervice; both among thoſe who now are or have been.

Of theſe who now are, we muſt not chuſe ſuch as with great fluency pour out their words, *(f)* and deal in common place ſtuff; and ſtrole from company to company: but ſuch, whoſe life itſelf is a lecture; who not only preſcribe what is to be done, but give proof of it in their own practice *(g)*; and who in teaching what is to be avoided, are never found guilty, of what themſelves condemn. Chuſe him for your guide, whom you admire more when you ſee his actions than when you hear his doctrine; nor do I altogether forbid you to attend on thoſe alſo, whoſe cuſtom it is to admit the populace, and to entertain them with an harangue, provided they do it with this view; to make both themſelves and others better men; and not on account of ambition: for what can be more ſcandalous than a philoſopher affecting popularity and applauſe! Does a patient ever *praiſe* the phyſician while he is uſing the knife or lancet *(h)*? Be ſilent, be patient, and give yourſelves up to proper direction for your cure: ſhould you exclaim, and be noiſy, I ſhould pay no regard thereto, except it were, that I thought I had touched you ſo, as to make you bewail your ſins; or, if it be only to ſhew, how much you attend to, and are moved with the ſublime: there is no harm in it; or be it to give your vote and approbation of what is conducive to your amendment, this too I permit.

The

The ſcholars of *Pythagoras* were enjoined ſilence for five years: think you then they were allowed to make their remarks, and give their plaudit? Beſides, how great muſt be his folly, who when he diſmiſſeth his audience is highly pleaſed with the acclamations of the unſkilful? What cauſe hath a man to rejoice at being praiſed by thoſe, whom he cannot praiſe himſelf! *Fabian* harangued the people; but he was heard with decency and modeſty: ſometimes indeed a loud applauſe would burſt forth, but it was at the ſublimity of his ſentiments, not at the charming ſound of his ſweet-flowing elocution. There is a great difference between the applauſe of the theatres and that of the ſchools: and there may be abuſe and an impropriety in giving praiſe. Things are known by certain ſigns and tokens if well obſerved; and a very little circumſtance will give proof of a perſon's diſpoſition: an immodeſt perſon is ſometimes known by his gait, by a motion of the hand, by a ſingle repartee, by ſcratching the head with one finger *(i)*, or a lear of the eye: laughter betrays a fool; and the countenance, or dreſs, a madman: theſe, I ſay, are common tokens; and you may alſo know what a man, is, by obſerving in what temper he receives praiſe, and by whom it is given: An auditor will ſometimes ſtretch out his hands to a philoſopher, and a crowd of admirers riſing up, hover, as it were, over his head. Now ſuch a one is not praiſed hereby; if you underſtand the thing rightly, it is nothing more than a mere hubbub. Let ſuch acclamations as theſe be given to thoſe arts, that have nothing more in view than to pleaſe the populace. Let philoſophy be adored in ſilence. Young men indeed may ſometimes be allowed to follow the impulſe of the mind; but then only, when the impulſe is ſo ſtrong, that it is not in their power to refrain: this ſort of praiſe carries with it an exhortation to the whole audience, and particularly encourageth the minds of youth: but let them be moved with the ſubject propoſed, and not merely with the compoſition: otherwiſe eloquence is prejudicial to them, if it only ſtirs up a deſire of the like accompliſhment, and not of virtue.

But I ſhall defer this matter for the preſent, for it requires a ſingular and long diſcuſſion, to ſhew how the populace are to be addreſſed, and what liberties are to be taken on each ſide. There is no doubt but that philoſophy

philoſophy is injured when it is proſtituted to any ſiniſter purpoſe: but it may be drawn in its proper colours and native beauty, when exhibited by a *Sage*, and not a mere pedlar.

ANNOTATIONS, &c.

(*a*) But what does the *Chriſtian* ſay? Why, that it is the internal depravity of mankind (entailed by *Adam* on his poſterity) of which the antient philoſophers not knowing the cauſe in vain ſought a remedy in their frantic ſchemes of philoſophy. Nor were the antient poets leſs ſenſible of the evil, though alike ignorant of the cauſe.

> Τὰ χρηστ' ἐπιστάμεσθα, καὶ γιγνώσκομεν,
> Οὐκ ἐκπονοῦμεν δ'·---Eur. Hippol. 380.
> *Our duty well we know, and underſtand,*
> *But practiſe not.*

Euripides likewiſe introduces *Medea* ſpeaking thus of herſelf. *Med.* v. 1078.

> *Καὶ μανθάνω μὲν, οἷα δρᾶν μέλλω κακά.*
> *Θυμὸς δὲ κρείσσων τῶν ἐμῶν βουλευμάτων.*
> *Full well I know the ills by me deſign'd,*
> *But paſſion over-rules the lab'ring mind.* M.

Thus expreſſed by *Ovid.* Met. l. 7.

> ———Si poſſem ſanior eſſem:
> Sed trahit invitam nova vis: aliudque Cupido,
> Mens aliud ſuadet: video meliora, proboque:
> Deteriora ſequor.——
> *Smit by new pow'rs, my heart unwilling bleeds;*
> *Diſcretion there, and here affection pleads:*
> *I ſee the right, and I approve it too;*
> *I blame the wrong, and yet the wrong purſue.*

Such were the Heathens. Comp. Rom. i. 22. II. 14. 15. Such the Scribes, Mark xii. 32. Such the Jew, Rom. x. 2. II. 17. 18. And ſuch, alas! the Chriſtian, according to the acknowledgment of St. *Paul*; *For the will is preſent with me, but how to perform that which is good I find not; for the good that I would, I do not; but the evil which I would not, that I do: Now if I do that I would not, it is no more I that do it, but ſin that dwelleth in me.* Rom. vii. 18. Where note, the Apoſtle's expreſſions of *not willing the evil he doth*, &c. are not intended here to leave any innocence, or excuſe upon himſelf, as not acceſſary to his fault: but partly to acknowledge the good effect of the law upon him; partly the tyrannical and powerful operation of ſin *before grace*. *See* M. Fell. Rom. viii. 3. &c. Gal, i. 14, &c.

(*b*) Nemo per ſe ſatis valet, ut emergat. *Not that we are ſufficient of ourſelves* (ſo much as) *to think* (and much leſs to act) *any* (good) *thing, as of ourſelves; but our ſufficiency is of God.* Cor. iii. 5. *For by grace are ye ſaved through faith; and that not of yourſelves: it is the gift of God.* Epheſ. ii. 8. Phil. ii. 18. *See* Epp. 4, (N. a) 45.

(*c*) *Cicero* (de Nat. Deor.) *ſays that* Epicurus (gloriabatur, ut videmus, in ſcriptis, ſe magiſtrum habuiſſe nullum) *gloried, as we ſee in his writing, that he was* ſelf-taught: Laertius *affirms the ſame, though ſome ſuppoſe him to have been a pupil of* Xenocrates.

(*d*) *Forced*

(*d*) *Forced and compelled to good*] as is the ſuppoſed caſe of a *Calviniſt*.

(*e*) *Finally, my brethren, be ſtrong in the Lord, and in the power of his might, and put on the whole armour of God: for we* Chriſtians wreſtle (or contend) *not againſt fleſh and blood* (viſible enemies) *but againſt principalities, againſt powers, againſt the rulers of the darkneſs of this world, againſt ſpiritual wickedneſs in baſe ſlaves.* Epheſ. vi. 10. See the foregoing Epiſtle.

(*f*) *For when they ſpeak great ſwelling words of vanity, they allure, through much wantonneſs,* thoſe *that were for a while eſcaped from them who live in error; while they promiſe them liberty, they themſelves are the ſervants of corruption.* ii Pet. 2. 18.

(*g*) *For yourſelves know, how you ought to follow us; for we behaved not ourſelves diſorderly among you.* ii Theſſ. 3. 7.——

A living ſermon of the truths he taught.——*Chaucer's* Good Parſon.

(*h*) It is obſervable that the phyſicians in thoſe days profeſſed ſurgery, and prepared their own medicines, which is not reckoned ſo reputable among us as in foreign countries, where it is the general practice. See Ep. 75.

(*i*) This was looked upon as a ſure ſign of an effeminate coxcomb; Τῷ δακτύλῳ τὴν κεφαλὴν κνᾶσθαι (Lucian.) *To ſcratch the head with the top of one finger,* ſo as not to diſcompoſe the order of the curls. Of whom Juvenal, IX. 133.

Conveniunt et carpentis et navibus omnes
Qui digito ſcalpunt uno caput——
——— *All will throng*
To Rome, by boat or coach, to make this match,
Their heads who neatly with one finger ſcratch.——Stapylton.

EPISTLE LIII.

The great Power and Value of Philoſophy.

WHAT can I not be perſuaded to when I have been prevailed upon to attempt a voyage? I ſet ſail in an unruffled ſea, but the ſky look'd heavy as overcharged with dark clouds that generally turn to rain or wind: yet doubtful and blowing as the weather ſeem'd, I thought, *Lucilius*, I ſhould ſoon be convey'd ſo few miles as from your *Parthenope*, to *Puteoli* (*a*): and to get thither the ſooner, we launched out into the deep in a direct courſe for the iſland *Neſis*, without coaſting it along the ſhore. But when I had got ſo far, as to be indifferent, whether I went

on,

on, or returned, the ſmoothneſs of the ſea which firſt tempted me out *(b)*, was gone off: it was not indeed as yet a ſtorm, but the ſea began to roll and the ſurges to ſwell and claſh. Whereupon I deſired the maſter of the veſſel to ſet me ſomewhere aſhore; but he told me it was impoſſible; as there was no haven near; and that he feared nothing ſo much in a ſtorm as the land. But I was too much vexed, to be apprehenſive of any danger; for I was terribly ſea-ſick, and could get no relief by evacuation: I therefore inſiſted upon it whether he would or not, that he ſhould bear to ſhore; which as ſoon as we drew nigh to, I waited not, till, as *Virgil* ſays *(c)*, obvertunt pelago proras, *(they turn the prow of the ſhip to the ſhore)* aut, anchora de prora jaciatur *(or caſt anchor)*. But mindful of my old cuſtom, I flung myſelf into the ſea in my looſe robe, as when we go into the cold bath: And you cannot imagine what I ſuffer'd, when I ſprawled among the rocks, ſeeking or making what way I could: I then perfectly underſtood, why mariners are ſo juſtly afraid of land: and it is incredible to think what I further ſuffer'd, when I could not bear my own load: know this, that the ſea was not ſo great an enemy to *Ulyſſes*, either from ſickneſs, or frequent ſhipwreck, as it is to me; ſo that was I oblig'd to ſail again, I ſhould think it twice ten years before I finiſh'd my voyage.

However as ſoon as I was a little recover'd (for, this ſickneſs, you know, ſoon goes off upon landing,) and had refreſh'd my body with anointing it in the ſun, I began to reflect with myſelf, how forgetful we are of our infirmities, not only thoſe of the mind, which the greater they are, the more they lie concealed; but of the body, which now and then admoniſh us, and make us ſenſible of them. A ſlight diſorder is apt to deceive us; but when it gathers ſtrength, and a real fever burns up the body, it forces acknowledgment, be the patient ever ſo hardy, and ſubject to ſuch diſtempers. The feet ach, the joints prick and ſhoot; but as yet we diſſemble *(d)*, and ſay, we have ſprained our ancle, or overtired ourſelves by ſome violent exerciſe, or in ſhort, we know not what it is; but when the knots are formed, and the nervous fibres grown ſo ſtiff as to diſable one from walking, it is then acknowledg'd to be the gout (*e*). It is not ſo with the diſeaſes of the mind, which the worſe they are, are the leſs perceived. Nor need you wonder at this, deareſt

Lucilius; for he that dozes, or takes a nap, ſometimes thinks that he is ſleeping, even in his ſleep: whereas a ſound ſleep extinguiſheth all dreams, and ſinks the mind ſo deep, as to deprive it of its intellectual faculties. Why is not a man ready to acknowledge his faults? becauſe he is as yet plunged in them *(as in a ſound ſleep.)* To tell a dream is the part of one awake; and to confeſs our imperfections, is a token of ſanity.

Let us awake therefore *(f)* that we may be ſenſible of, and correct our errors. Now, it is philoſophy alone that will rouſe us; tis ſhe alone that will ſhake off a ſound ſleep: dedicate yourſelf entirely to her; you are worthy of her, and ſhe of *you*: embrace her moſt cordially: deny yourſelf to all beſides, boldly, publickly. There is no reaſon that a philoſopher ſhould be at the will and pleaſure of any one elſe. If you were ill, you would not concern yourſelf with family-affairs; nor with the buſineſs of the Forum; nor would you have ſo great a value for any one, as to appear an advocate in court for him: your whole attention would be taken up, in endeavouring to get rid of your diſorder: and will you not do the ſame now?

Let every impediment be thrown aſide, while you attend only to the attainment of a ſound mind. No one can attain this, who is buſied about other things (*g*). Philoſophy exerciſeth a regal power: ſhe grants time; but accepts it not: ſhe is no ſubſtitute; ſhe is the principal, in waiting, and gives commands (*h*). *Alexander*, to a certain ſtate that promiſed him part of their lands, and half their property, ſaid, *that he came into Aſia with this reſolution; not to accept of what they would be pleaſed to give him; but that they might enjoy what he ſhould think proper to leave them (i)*. Philoſophy uſeth the ſame *language* in all reſpects. *I will not accept the time of you, which ſeems ſuperfluous, and you know not how to employ; but you ſhall have that, which I ſhall think proper to ſpare you.*

Give up yourſelf entirely to her: ſit cloſe by her; worſhip her; ſo ſhall there be a wide difference between you, and the commonalty; you ſhall far excel other mortals; nor ſhall the gods themſelves far excel you. Do you aſk in what the difference between you ſhall conſiſt? they will continue longer. But it is the glory of a ſkilful artiſt to include much in a little compaſs: the few days of a wiſe man are as much to him, as his eternity is to God: nay, there is ſomething wherein the wiſe man has the advantage of the gods themſelves (*k*), *They* are what they are by nature, *the wiſe man* is what he is by his own induſtry: behold, a wonderful thing, to have the weakneſs of a man and the ſecurity of God. Incredible is the ſtrength of philoſophy in repelling every violent attack from without: not one of fortune's darts can fix itſelf in her: ſhe is every where guarded and impenetrable: ſome ſhe wearies out; the lighter ſort ſhe retains in the folds of her outer robe: and others ſhe ſhakes off unhurt, and even returns them on him from whom they came.

ANNOTATIONS, &c.

(*a*) *Parthenope*, the birth-place of *Lucilius*; now called *Naples*. *Puteoli*, a city in *Campania*; now *Pozzuola*. *Neſis*, an iſland in *Campania*, al. *Neſſis*. Unde malignum aera reſpirat pelago circumflua Neſſis, *Stat*. II. 2. 78,—now called *Niſita*.

(*b*) me corruperat] induced me to forego the reſolution I had in common with *Cato*, Mari non ire quo terra poſſem; *not to go by ſea, where I could go by land.*

(*c*) Virgil. Æn. III. 277. VI. 3.

(*d*) So *Lucian*——

Απας γὰρ αὐτὸν βεκαλεῖ ψευδοστομῶν
Ως ενστραφεὶς, ἢ προσκόψας τι βάσιν,
Λεγει φιλοισιν, μὴ φράσας τὴν αἰτίαν.
Ὁ μὴ λεγει γάρ, ὡς δοκῶν λαθεῖν τινας,
Χρονος δέ γ' ἕρπων μηνύει κἂν μὴ θελῃ
Κάι τότε λαμαδεις ονομάσας με τοὔνομα,
Πᾶσι θρίαμβος, ἐμβεβάσταχθαι φίλοις.

Fain would a man deceive himſelf, and friends,
Aſham'd of his diſorder, (if the gout)
And feigns ſome accident, a wrench, or ſprain:
But owns ere long the ſore diſeaſe, by name,
When carried *by his friends, as 'twere in triumph.* M.

I indeed, happily, know nothing of the gout; and cannot conceive why any one ſhould have been aſhamed of it; unleſs the *Romans* ſuppoſed it not *hereditary*, but always acquired by luxury and high-living. (Locuples podagra, *Juv*. 13. 96—turpeſque podagras *Virg*. E. 3. 299.) but, I believe, there are many inſtances to the contrary.

(*e*) utraſque

(*e*) utrosque pedes *dextros fecit*] l. distorserit vel detorserit. *Lips.*

Lucian, ib.

Ἐπὰν δὲ καὶ τὸν ἕτερον ἀλγήσῃς πόδα
Στενῶν δακρύεις, ἐν δὲ σοὶ φράσαι θέλω,
Ταῦτ' ἔστ' ἔχεις, κἂν θέλῃς, κἂν μὴ θέλῃς.
But when both feet are swoln, you then cry out;
And pain obliges you to own, with me,
Whether you will or not, it is the gout.

(*f*) This metaphor is frequent in Scripture——*Awake, ye drunkards,* Joel, i. 5, *knowing, that it is high time to awake out of sleep, for now is our salvation nearer than when we believed.* Rom. xiii. 11. *Awake to righteousness and sin not.* I. Cor. xv. 34, &c.

(*g*) Martha, *Thou art careful and troubled about many things, but one thing is needful.* Luke x. 41. See Ep. xxiii. (N. f.)

(*h*) Ordinaria est] So the chief or principal Consuls, who were elected in January were stiled *Ordinarii,* as distinguished from the *Honorarii,* and *Suffecti*; the *honorary, or such as were elected at other times.* See Ep. 110. Sidon. Apol. p. 86. Sueton. *Jul.* c. 26.

(*i*) When *Darius* offered to surrender *Lydia, Ionia, Æolis,* to *Alexander,* he answered, *that he came not out with the view of so small a recompence, but for the conquest of his kingdom, and the empire of the east.* Qu. Curt. l. iv.

(*k*) Nothing, with our author's leave, can be more impious and intolerable than this arrogance of the Stoics; who were not satisfied with making their *wise man* equal to the gods, but even in some cases gave him the preference! Though this indeed might seem excusable, if they really believed some facts related of the gods, (for which they were rallied by the poets, and particularly the comedians, *Aristophanes, Plautus, Terence*) which a truly good man would abhor to harbour in his thoughts, and much more to perpetrate. See Epp. 31. 59. 73. 87. 102.

EPISTLE LIV.

Against the Fear of Death.

MY malady, *Lucilius,* hath given me a long respite (*a*), but is now come upon me on a sudden. Do you ask, what malady? really you may well ask; for there is none, I think, but what I am afflicted with. Yet I seem destined to one in particular, which why I should honour with a *Greek* name, I know not (*b*): for I think I may properly call it, suspirium, (*a cough,* or *shortness of breath:*) the violence of it, indeed, lasts not long: like a storm, it is generally over within the hour. For who can long want breath? all other infirmities or dangers of the body have

have paſſed by me unregarded; none ſeeming more troubleſome to me than this: for any other is nothing more than *being ſick*, but this is to expire: therefore the phyſicians call it, *the exerciſe of death* (*c*). The breath will ſome time or other go off, as it frequently attempts ſo to do.

You may perhaps think me chearful, in now writing to you, becauſe I have eſcaped; but was I to rejoice at this, as if I now enjoy'd a complete ſtate of health, I ſhould act as ridiculouſly, as one who thinks he has gained his cauſe, by forfeiting his recognizance. Indeed while I was almoſt choaked, I was not the leſs chearful and courageous in thought: what is this, I cried? does death make ſo many trials of me? he is welcome; I have long ſince made trial of *him:* do you aſk how long? why, before I was born. To die, *is not to be (d):* and what that is I already know: it will be the ſame after I am gone, as it was before I was in being. Was there any torment in this, we muſt have experienced the ſame before we came into the world; but we were not then ſenſible of any pain or trouble. I aſk, whether you would not call him a fool, who thinks a candle in a worſe condition when it is put out, than before it was lighted up? We are alſo lighted up, and *(to all appearance)* put out: in the interval indeed we ſuffer ſomething; but before and after all is ſecure. For in this, my *Lucilius*, *(if I am not miſtaken)* we deceive ourſelves, in thinking that death only follows life, whereas it both goes before and will follow after it: for where is the difference in not beginning, or ceaſing to exiſt? the effect of both is, *not to be (e)*. With theſe and the like tacit remonſtrances I communed with myſelf, (for I had not breath to ſpeak,) till my fit by degrees began to go off, and I enjoy'd ſtill longer intermiſſions; not that as yet, does my breath flow in a natural and eaſy courſe: ſtill I feel my diſorder hanging upon me; and let it do what it will, provided I labour not nor ſigh in my *mind*.

And be aſſur'd of this; that I ſhall not tremble at the laſt gaſp, being already prepared, and quite regardleſs of the day *(f)*. But let me particularly recommend to your praiſe and imitation ſome one, whom it grieves not to die, when it is a pleaſure to live: for what virtue is there in in going off when you are forced *(g)*? Yet even here there is room for virtue: I am oblig'd indeed to quit the ſtage, but I will make a willing and decent exit: and therefore the wiſe man can never be ſaid to be forced off, becauſe to be forced off, is to be expelled from whence you retire unwillingly: but the wiſe man does nothing unwillingly: he is not ſubject to neceſſity: for what *muſt be done*, that he alſo wills *(h)*.

ANNOTATIONS, &c.

(a) Commeatum] More properly *a furlow*: for it is a military term.

(b) Gr. ἆσθμα, aut Ὀρθόπνοια, *an aſthma*. Vid. Mercurial. Var. Lect. vi. 16.

(c) Meditationem Mortis.] Which *Hieron. Mercurial.* not knowing a reaſon for, alters it to Exercitationem. And another learned phyſician writes it Modulationem; but *Gronovius* proves the right reading to be, Meditationem, in the ſame ſenſe with Exercitationem; from ſeveral paſſages in *Plautus*, *Cicero*, &c. Vid. Gronov. in loc.

(d) Mors nos in illam tranquillitatem, in qua, antequam naſceremur, jacuimus, reponit. *Sen.* ad Marc. c. 19. ad Polyb. c. 27.

The Tragedian in the ſame ſtrain:

Quæris, quo jaceas poſt obitum loco?
Quo non nata jacent.—*Sen.*

So *Andromache* in Eur. Troad. 631.

Τὸ μὴ γενέσθαι, τῷ θανεῖν ἴσον λέγω.

And *Cicero*, Hoc ſaltem in maximis malis boni conſequamur, &c. Ep. V. 21. *This advantage we may at leaſt derive from our calamities; that they will teach us to look upon death with contempt; which even if we were happy we ought to deſpiſe*, as a ſtate of total inſenſibility: *but which under our preſent afflictions, ſhould be the object of our conſtant wiſhes.* And elſewhere, Si non ero, ſenſu carebo.—Una ratio videtur, quicquid evenerit ferre moderatè; præſertim cum omnium rerum mors ſit extremum. But the ingenious and learned tranſlator obſerves, that, *theſe paſſages, without any violence of conſtruction, may be interpreted as affirming nothing more than that death is an utter extinction of all ſenſibility with reſpect to human concerns.* (Somewhat like this we meet with in Eccleſ. ix. v. *The living know that they ſhall die, but the dead know not any thing.* It follows, v. 6. *Their love, and their hatred and their envy is now periſhed*, neither have they any more a portion for ever in any thing that is done under the ſun.) Moreover, "that *Cicero's* real ſentiments and opinions are not to be proved from the foregoing; as it was uſual with him to accommodate his expreſſion to the principles or circumſtances of his correſpondence: that in a letter to *Atticus* he expreſsly mentions his expectation of a future ſtate, Tempus eſt nos de *illa perpetua* jam, non de hac exiguâ vitâ, cogitare; *it is time for us to conſider, not the ſhort life we are allotted here, but* life everlaſting: and, that his philoſophical writings abound with various and full proofs, that he was firmly perſuaded of *the immortality of the ſoul.*" (Vid. loc.) And I think we may ſay the ſame, in all reſpects, of our Author, notwithſtanding what he hath advanced in this Epiſtle, when in contradiction thereto he hath elſewhere alledged, that *the ſouls of the good and virtuous, after death, are carried up into heaven, and live in a ſtate of bliſs.* Ep. 63. Cogitemus ergo, Lucili cariſſime, citò nos eo perventuros, &c. *Let us conſider, deareſt Lucilius, that we ſhall ſoon arrive there, where he is gone whom we bewail;*

bewail: and perhaps (if according to the opinion of some wise men there is a place prepared for our reception hereafter) that he, whom we fondly imagined to have perished, is sent before us to that happy mansion. And more expresly, Ep. 102. Dies ista, quam, tanquam extremum reformidas, æterni natalis est. *The day, which men are apt to dread as their last, is but the birth-day of an eternity.* Nothing surely can heighten more the obligation we Christians owe to the good pleasure of God, in giving us certainty in these high matters concerning himself, and *the immortality of the soul*; wherein the antient philosophers, even the wisest of them, *Socrates, Cicero, Seneca,* were so perplexed and bewildered with doubt and error. Not but that in the more poetical part of Scripture, we have similar passages before us concerning death; as, *Why died I not from the womb?* (says *Job* in the paroxism of grief) *for now should I have been still and quiet; I should have slept with Kings and Counsellors of the earth; I should have been as infants that never saw light.* Job. iii. 11, 19. And Eccles. iii. 19. 20. *That which befalleth the sons of men, befalleth beasts; as the one dieth, so dieth the other. All go to one place, all are of the dust, and all turn to dust again:* which is contradicted, or rather answered in the next verse, if the whole be a dialogue; *who knoweth the spirit of man that goeth upward, and the spirit of a beast, that goeth downward to the earth.*—Blessed therefore be God for the vouchsafement *of his gracious purpose by the appearing of our Saviour, who hath abolished death, and brought life and immortality to light through the Gospel.* II. Tim. 1. 10.

(*e*) *Seneca* repeats the same thought in *Consol. ad Polyb.* c. 7. as also in *Consol. ad Marc.* where he absolutely rejects the notion of future punishments, &c. *See* Leland, II. p. 289.

(*f*) Here again *Seneca* seems to speak like a Christian philosopher: so that if any thing is wanting here, as *Muretus* conjectures, we may regret the loss.

(*g*) I would recommend to you the example of some young man, who in the prime of life *is not afraid to die:* as for me, I am old, and therefore it is no virtue.

(*h*) And thinks, in Mr. *Pope's* language, that *whatever is, is right.*

EPISTLE LV.

A true Friend is never absent.

I Often return from taking the air in my chariot, as much tired, as if I had walked as far as I had rode; for it is a pain to me to be carried far; and perhaps the more so, because it is not natural: Nature hath given us feet, to walk withal, as well as eyes to see with, for ourselves. I know that an indulgence of this kind is apt to weaken one; and we may leave off walking, 'till by disuse we cannot walk at all; but a little shaking was at present necessary for me, that either I might throw off such phlegm as was troublesome to me, or that by such gentle exercise I migh

I might extenuate the difficulty of breathing; and indeed I found great benefit therefrom, which made me persist in it the longer; especially being invited, by the pleasantness of the shore, that winds between *Cumæ* and the villa of *Servilius Vatia*; forming a neck of land, with the sea on one side, and the lake on the other: the ground too at this time was more firm and solid, by reason of a late tempest; as the waves, you know, by frequent overflowing, level or smooth it; whereas a calm or long ebb, loosens it, when the moisture that cemented the sands is all drained from them.

But, according to custom I was looking round to see, if I could find a proper object for some useful reflection: when I happen'd to cast my eyes upon the villa, that sometime since belong'd to *Vatia.*—In this villa, that rich *Prætorian*, who had signalized himself in nothing but his indolence, spent his days; and living to a good old age, was from this circumstance alone accounted an happy man. For as often as a connection with *Asinius Gallus (a)*, or the hatred (and sometime after, the love) of *Sejanus (b)*, (for it was alike dangerous to be his aversion or favourite) had brought any one to ruin; all men would cry, *O happy* Vatia, *you alone know how to live:* he indeed knew how *to lie concealed*, but not *to live:* for there is a great difference, between a retired life and an idle one: I never passed by his villa in my life, but I cried, *Vatia hic situs est*, *Here lies* Vatia.(c) But, philosophy my *Lucilius*, is so sacred and venerable a thing, that whatever pretends to be like it, must rest upon a falsity: for the vulgar think a man who has retired from business must necessarily be free from all care and trouble; well satisfied in and living altogether for, himself: whereas nothing like this can be applied to any one, but to the *wise man:* he indeed is a stranger to anxiety, and knows how to live for himself: such a one, I say (which is the principal good) knows how *to live*; whereas the man, who flies from men and business, whom the ill success of his ambition hath banished from conversation, who cannot bear to see another happier than himself: who like a timorous and silly animal hides himself for fear---such a one lives not to himself, but to luxury, to sleep, to lust: he lives not always to himself who lives

to

to no one elſe: yet there is ſomething ſo valuable in conſtancy and perſeverance, that even the moſt ſtubborn indolence gains ſome credit.

I can write nothing of certainty concerning the *Villa* itſelf; for I know nothing more than the front and outſide, as it appears to us on the road. There are two grottos of curious workmanſhip, each of whoſe floors are of equal dimenſions with the court yard; the one of which never admits the ſun; the other is expoſed to it all day long: A river that runs into the ſea, and the *Acheruſian* lake, divides, like a canal, a grove of plane trees: and this river, tho' frequently drawn, is ſtill ſupplied with ſtore of fiſh; but the fiſhermen ſpare it when the ſea is open to them; and when ſtormy weather gives them an holyday, every one catches the fiſh as they can. But what makes this *Villa* moſt commodious, is, that it hath *Baiæ* on the other ſide the wall; enjoying all the pleaſures of it without its inconveniences. So much I know due to its praiſe: and indeed it is a *Villa* I think habitable all the year: for it fronts the weſt wind, and receives ſo much of it as to keep it off from *Baiæ*.

Vatia therefore ſeems not injudiciouſly to have choſen this Villa, wherein to retire, and wear out his days in indolence, and a quiet old age. But in truth, it is not the place, be it where it will, that can confer true tranquillity; it is the mind that is all in all. I have ſeen chagrin and melancholy in the moſt pleaſant and chearful *Villa*; and I have ſeen men, in the midſt of ſolitude, fatigued, as it were, with buſineſs.

There is no reaſon therefore you ſhould complain of your ſituation, becauſe you are not in *Campania*. And why ſhould I ſay, you are not there? Send us your thoughts: a man may very well converſe with his abſent friends; indeed as often and as long as you pleaſe: nay, we enjoy this pleaſure great as it is, the more, on the account of abſence: for the being preſent is apt to make us ſomewhat ſhy: and becauſe, having an opportunity to talk, and walk together, when we ſit down, or are parted, we think no more of thoſe we ſaw ſo lately; and what may make us bear abſence the more patiently is, there is no one, who is not often abſent, to his friend or neighbour: for conſider the many abſent nights, and the different employs of the day on either ſide and the different purſuits, the different ſtudies, and frequent calls out of the city; and you will find, that a voyage or a journey does not deprive us of ſo much of our friend's company as you imagined. A friend is to be enjoy'd, by the *Mind*; this is never abſent; it daily ſees whom it pleaſes. Therefore, ſtill ſtudy with me, ſup with me, walk with me: we ſhould live in very narrow bounds, could any thing be excluded our thoughts: I ſee you ſtill, my *Lucilius*, I ever hear thee; in ſhort, I am ſo much with you, that I am in doubt, whether I ſhall ſend you any more epiſtles or only a complimental billet.

ANNOTATIONS, &c.

(*a*) *Tiberius* had long hated him, for that *Gallus* had married *Vipſania*, daughter of *Marcus Agrippa*, and formerly wife of *Tiberius*; who ſuſpected that by this match he meant to ſoar above the rank of a ſubject; he poſſeſſed alſo the bold and haughty ſpirit of *Aſinius Pollio* his father. That *Gallus* periſhed through famine was indiſputable; but whether of his own accord or by conſtraint was uncertain.

(*b*) The character of *Sejanus*, as drawn by *Tacitus*, is, that he was alike deſtructive to the ſtate, when he flouriſhed and when he fell. His perſon was hardy and equal to any fatigue; his ſpirit daring but covered; ſedulous to diſguiſe his own counſels, dextrous to blacken others; alike fawning and imperious; to appearance exactly modeſt, but in his heart foſtering the luſt of domination. No acceſs to honours but through his favour, and this purchaſed. He was at length executed, and his body drawn through the ſtreets; and not only his children, but all thoſe under accuſation of any attachment to him, were put to the ſlaughter.

(*c*) —— A man "may retire and drone life away in ſolitude, like a Monk, or like him, over the door of whoſe houſe ſomebody wrote, *Here lies ſuch a one*. But no ſuch man will be able to make the true uſe of retirement." See *Bolingbroke* on Retirement.

EPISTLE LVI.

On Tranquillity—(a).

LET me die, if I think ſilence ſo abſolutely neceſſary for a ſtudious man as it ſeems at firſt to be: variety of noiſe ſurrounds *me* on every ſide: I lodge even over a bath. Suppoſe now all kinds of ſounds that can be harſh and diſagreeable to the ears; as when the ſtrong boxers are exerciſing themſelves, and fling about their hands loaded with lead (*b*), or when they are in diſtreſs, or imitate thoſe that are, and I hear their groans; or when ſending forth their breath, which for ſome time they held in, I hear their hiſſing, and violent ſobs; or when I meet with an idle varlet, who anoints the ordinary wreſtlers for their exerciſe, and I hear the different ſlaps he gives them on their ſhoulder, with either a flat or hollow palm; or if a ball-player (*c*) comes in, and begins to count the balls, it is almoſt over with me. Add to theſe the rank (*d*) and ſwaggering bully, the taking a pickpocket, or the bawling of ſuch as delight to hear their voice echo through the bath (*e*); add alſo thoſe, who daſh into the pond with a great noiſe of the water; and beſides theſe, ſuch whoſe voices at leaſt are tolerable: ſuppoſe a hair-plucker (*f*) every now and then ſqueaking with a ſhrill and effeminate tone, to make himſelf the more remarkable, and is never ſilent but when he is at work, and making his patient cry for him: add to theſe the various cries of thoſe that ſell cakes and ſauſages, the gingerbread baker, the huckſter, and all ſuch as vend their wares about the ſtreets with a peculiar tone. *Sure you have no ears*, you ſay, *or muſt be made of iron, whoſe mind is not diſturbed with ſuch various and diſſonant ſounds; when our* Chryſippus (*g*) *is almoſt killed, with only the common ſalutations of the morning.* I aſſure you, *Lucilius*, I regard all this noiſe no more than the ebbing and flowing of the water: though I hear that a certain people, near the River *Nile*, gave this as a reaſon for changing the ſite of their city; becauſe they could not bear the noiſe of the waterfalls (*h*).

 But

But as for me, I own a voice diſtracts me more than any noiſe whatever; for that draws off the mind, but this only ſtrikes, and fills the ear: and I will moreover tell you what I reckon among thoſe things that give me no diſturbance, the rattling of the carriages in the ſtreets *(i)*; a ſmith's forge in the houſe, a ſawyer's yard next door; and the horrid noiſe a fellow makes, who, by the *Temple of Peace*, is ever trying his new-made hautboys and trumpets, and does not ſing but bawl: the ſound indeed, which ſtartles me after intermiſſions, is ſomewhat more troubleſome to me than that which is continued; but I am ſo inured to theſe things, that I could even hear a boatſwain *(k)* giving orders to his crew, with the moſt harſh and hoarſe vociferation, without being in the leaſt diſcompoſed.

The truth is; I force my mind to be ſo intent upon itſelf, as not to be drawn off by any thing from without. Whatever noiſe is abroad, I care not, while all is calm and quiet within; no jarring between deſire and fear; no diſſenſion between avarice and luxury: in ſhort, no one paſſion thwarting another; for what availeth all imaginable ſilence, if the paſſions are at variance?

> Omnia noctis erant placidâ compoſta quiete;
> *All things were lull'd, by night, in pleaſing reſt,*

ſaith the poet *(Varro)*; but 'tis falſe; there can be no pleaſing reſt, but what is the effect of reaſon *(l)*: the night rather promotes than prevents trouble, and only changes one ſcene of anxiety for another: for even the dreams of thoſe that ſleep, are as turbulent as all the accidents of the day. There can be no true tranquillity, but what ariſeth from a ſound mind. Behold the man, who endeavours to ſleep, while the whole houſe is ſilent; and, that the leaſt noiſe may not reach his ears, all the ſervants are order'd not to ſpeak a word: and, if they approach near his bed, to tread as ſoftly as poſſible; yet is he turning from one ſide to another, and would fain get a nap; ſtill complaining, that he hears noiſes, while not the leaſt is made. Now, what do you think is the reaſon of this? why, his mind is diſturb'd; this muſt be appeaſed; the ſedition within muſt be calm'd; the noiſe is there; for you muſt

not

not think the mind is at peace; tho' the body were to lie as ſtill as in the arms of death.

Even reſt itſelf is ſometimes reſtleſs; and therefore it is proper we ſhould be rouſed to action, and employ'd in ſome of the liberal ſciences, as often as liſtleſſneſs ſeiſeth us impatient of its own weight. Great generals when they ſee a ſoldier diſobedient to orders, condemn him to ſome hard labour; nor will permit him to join his company. They have no time to play and wanton, who are tied down to buſineſs; and nothing is more certain, than that the vices of idleneſs are thrown off by proper employ.

We often ſeem to retire, when fatigued with public affairs, and chagrin'd at ſome unhappy and diſagreable ſtation; yet even amidſt this retirement, which fear and diſguſt have induced us to ſeek, ambition ſometimes rankles at the heart: for it was not quite cut off, but only tired, and ſore vexed at things not ſucceeding to its wiſh: I ſay the ſame of luxury, which ſometimes ſeems to give way: but ſoon again revives, ſolliciting thoſe who have profeſſed frugality; and in the midſt of parſimony purſues the pleaſures it had not entirely condemn'd, but only left for a time; and purſues them now the more vehemently, as the more ſecretly it can obtain its deſires; for the more public all vices are, they are the leſs daring: diſeaſes likewiſe are more eaſily curable, when they break out, and ſhew themſelves what they are: and you may be aſſured that avarice, ambition, and all the evils of the human heart are the moſt dangerous, when they ſubſide, and are patched up by a pretended cure. We may ſeem at eaſe, but are far from being ſo; were we really ſo;—if we have ſounded a retreat;—if we have deſpiſed all ſpecious trifles,—nothing, as I have before obſerv'd, can recall us; or withdraw our attention; not even the harmony of men or birds, could interrupt our ſerious thoughts, now become ſure and ſolid. The diſpoſition is light and wavering, which can be moved by any accidental ſound: it ſtill retains anxiety, and a dread of ſomething that excites its curioſity and care, as ſays our *Virgil*, (2, 726).

A. me:

A me quem dudum non ulla injecta movebant
Tela, neque adverſo glomerati ex agmine Graii;
Nunc omnes terrent auræ, ſonus excitat omnis
Suſpenſum, et pariter comitique onerique timenti.

I who ſo bold and dauntleſs juſt before
The Grecian darts and ſhocks of lances bore,
At every ſhadow now am ſeiz'd with fear,
Not for myſelf but for the charge I bear (Dryden).

In the former part of theſe lines *Æneas* reſembles a wiſe and brave man, whom not the brandiſhing of ſpears, nor the claſhing arms of an engaged troop, nor the outcries of a beſieged city, can terrify; in the latter, a meer coward, wrapt in fear, and ſtartled at every noiſe; whom a ſingle voice, taken for the din of a multitude, quite caſts down; and the lighteſt motions drive to deſpair: his burthen *(his aged father)* makes him timorous.—Take whom you will, of thoſe rich men who gather much, and load themſelves therewith, you will ſee him *(like* Æneas*)* *fearful for his charge*. Know therefore you are then only truly compoſed, when no alarm can move you; when no voice can ſhake you from yourſelf, whether it flatters, or threatens you; or pours forth a variety of idle ſounds. What then? is it not more convenient ſometimes to be free from noiſe and brawling? No doubt of it. Therefore I intend ſoon to change my quarters; I had a mind, once to try and exerciſe myſelf; but what neceſſity is there for tormenting myſelf any longer; when *Ulyſſes* found ſo eaſy a remedy, for preſerving his companions from the ſweet melody of the *Syrens*? *(Ep. 31.)*

ANNOTATIONS, &c.

(*a*) It is impoſſible to read this humorous Epiſtle, without being reminded of the late Mr. Hogarth's excellent print, *The enraged Muſician*, who cannot be ſuppoſed ſo great a philoſopher as *Seneca*; when ſurrounded with ſuch a variety of external noiſe as is therein expreſſed.

(*b*) Cum laſſata gravi ceciderunt brachia maſſâ. Juv. vi. 423. See Ep. 15.

(*c*) Pilicrepus. So *Turneb.* Adverſ. vii. 4. But *Mercurial.* Art. Gymnaſt. i. 12. (where is explained this whole Epiſtle) ſuppoſes it to be the *ſtoker*, or he that ſupplies the fire under the baths with pitchy balls.—al. Pellicrepus. al. Pilicerpus.—*Vid.* Cœl. Rhodig. xxx. 19. Sidon. Apoll. p. 109.

(*d*) Scordalum

(*d*) Scordalum, *qu.* Scorodalum. *Erasm. Turneb.* One that stinks of garlick. Ep. 84. Or, *one of a rank smell after exercise*, qu. scordylum.—al. *One that cleans the baths from all filth and ordure*, a Gr. [illegible].

(*e*) According to *Horace*, (Sat. i. 4. 75)—In medio qui

> Scripta foro recitent sunt multi: quique lavantes;
> Suave locus voci resonat conclusus.——
> *But many bards the public forum chuse,*
> *Where to recite the labours of their muse;*
> *Or vaulted baths, that still preserve the sound,*
> *While sweetly floats the voice in echoes round.*—Francis.

(*f*) Alipilum, al. alipilarius, i. e. qui alas depilat. *Juvenal* speaking of one as yet a boy;—nec vellendas jam præbuit alas. (11. 157.)

(*g*) *Lipsius* thinks this by no means applicable to *Chrysippus* the philosopher; and therefore reads it, *Crispus*, a friend of *Seneca's*.

(*h*) Quem (strepitum) perferre gens ibi a Persis collocata non potuit, obtusis assiduo fragore auribus, et ob hoc sedibus ad quietiora translatis. *Natural Quest.* iv. 2.

(*i*)

> Stridentum et moderator essedorum,
> Curvorum, et chorus Helciariorum,
> i. e. *of those who tow the barge.*

Sidon. Apoll. x. 2.——Sic *Claudian*. de gallicis mulis,

> Consensuque pares, et fulvis pellibus hirtæ
> Esseda concordes multisonora trahunt.
> *Drawn by mules, match'd in colour and in size,*
> *Loud-rattling through the streets the chariot flies.* M.

And *Martial*, iv. 64.

> Ne blando rota sit molesta somno;
> Quem nec rumpere nauticum celeusma
> Nec clamor valet helciariorum.

(*k*) Pausarium] properly one who gave the (celeusma) *command*) or *orders*, to the rowers. *Ovid.* Met. III. 617.

> ——— Qui requiemque modumque
> Voce dabat remis, animorum hortator Epopeus.

(*l*) The opinion which is said to be *Zeno's* is somewhat quaint, but may deserve our consideration: he said, that any one may give a guess at his *proficiency*, from the observation of his dreams, thus: *if when asleep he fancied nothing that was immodest, nor formed to consent to any wicked actions, or dishonest intentions, but found his fancy and passions of his mind undisturbed, in a constant calm, as it were always serene and enlightened with the beams of divine reason.* Plut.

EPISTLE

EPISTLE LVII.

On Fear, and the Immortality of the Soul.

WHEN I was obliged to leave *Baiæ* again for *Naples*, I easily persuaded myself, that we should meet with another storm, so determined to go by land. But the roads were so bad, and full of sloughs, that I was as much rocked as if I had gone by sea (*a*). I underwent the whole ceremony of wrestlers (*b*); wanting neither the *ceroma (anointing)* nor the *baphe (being sprinkled over with dust)*, especially in the hollow way that leads to *Naples*. Nothing can be more tedious than travelling through that dungeon-like vale; nothing more disagreeable than the narrow passage, which is darkness itself: so that it was impossible to see our way: or had the place admitted any light, the dust itself would have blinded us, which is troublesome enough in the high and open road; but what must it be, when enclosed, without a breath of air to carry it off; and we only kick it up upon one another? Thus I say we were plagued with two contrary evils; and the same road, on the same day, covered us with mud and dust. Yet even this darksome way yielded matter for reflection; I felt a certain stroke upon my mind, and a change, though without fear, which the novelty and hideousness of the place brought upon me.

I am not speaking, *Lucilius*, as if this was applicable only to myself; who am far from pretending to a tolerable sufficiency, and much less to perfection; let it be applied to one, over whom Fortune hath lost all her power; and you will find that even such a one may be sensible of an attack, and change his colour. For there are certain sensations which even a virtuous man cannot avoid; as when Nature seriously reminds him of his mortality: wherefore his countenance occasionally puts on a gloomy sorrow; he is startled with surprize; and his head as dizzy, as if he looked down into the deep from a lofty precipice. Now, this is not fear, but a natural affection, which Reaſon itſelf cannot diſcard (*d*). Whence it happens that ſome brave men, who are ready to ſhed their own blood in their country's cauſe, yet cannot bear to ſee the blood of another perſon; ſome have even ſwooned away at the ſight of a freſh wound; and ſome at the dreſſing of an old and purulent ſore; others had rather receive a ſtroke from a ſword, than ſee one given. Therefore, as I ſaid before, I felt a certain alteration, but no perturbation of mind.

And now, as ſoon as the light began to break in upon us, I felt an alacrity, which came upon me, unthought of, uninvited: I began then to ſay with myſelf; how ridiculous is it to fear any thing, more or leſs, when there is one common end of all? for what matter is it whether a man be killed by the falling of a tower, or of a mountain? it is ſtill but death; nothing more: yet there are ſome who are more afraid of one thing than another, tho' they are both alike fatal: fear is therefore more apprehenſive of the cauſe, than of the effect. You perhaps may think I am now ſpeaking of thoſe little *Stoics*, who ſuppoſe the ſoul of man, when violently preſſed down by an enormous weight, cannot make its way any where, but is totally cruſhed and demoliſhed, becauſe it had not a free *exit*: no (*c*) ſuch matter; they who advance this doctrine ſeem to me much miſtaken: as the flame cannot be ſuppreſſed, but ſtill flies round that which would preſs it down; and as the air is not hurt by any ſtroke you give it; nor indeed divided, but that by its elaſticity it pours back again upon the place it has quitted; ſo the ſoul, which is of the fineſt and moſt ſubtile quality, cannot be ſurpriſed and cruſhed within the body, but by reaſon of its ſubtilty, breaks forth from whatever ſeems to overwhelm it.

As the lightning having darted its influence far and wide, returns through a ſmall crevice; ſo the ſoul which is far more ſubtile than flame, takes its flight through every pore of the body. From whence ariſeth a queſtion concerning immortality: and this, you may be aſſured of, *Lucilius*, that, if it ſurvives the body, it can by no means periſh, becauſe it is not periſhable: ſince no immortality admits an exception, nor can any thing deſtroy what is naturally *eternal* (*f*)

ANNOTATIONS, &c.

(*a*) There is the like metaphor in *Statius* (Silv. iv.)

> Nutabat cruce pendulâ viator,
> Sorbebatque rotas maligna tellus;
> Et plebs in mediis Latina campis
> *Horrebat mala navigationis.*

(*b*) *See* Faber Agoniſt. III. 22.

(*c*) Crypta Neapolitana.] A dark way, cut through the mountain *Poſtlypo*; by whom, or at what time is unknown: it is now about a mile long, leading to *Naples*. The windows, if there were any, might have been ſtopped up, by time and neglect in *Seneca's* days; but *Alphonſus* I. king of *Navarre* and *Arragon*, Ann. 1105, cut two new ones, and ſmoothed the road.

(*d*) See this whole affair elegantly treated of in *Agell.* xix. 1. and more fully in *Lipſ. Manuduct.* iii. 7. Ep. 85. 116.

(*e*) *Lipſius* does not recollect meeting with this ſtoical poſition any where elſe but in *Statius* (Theb. VI.) where ſpeaking of a miner, whom the earth fell in upon, and cruſhed to death, he elegantly, as in general, ſays,

> —— jacet intus
> Obrutus; ac penitus fractum obductumque cadaver
> Indignantem animam propriis non reddidit aſtris.
> *Acres o'erwhelm him, as he lifeleſs lies,*
> *Nor ſuffer the indignant ſoul to riſe*
> *From the deep load, and claim her native ſkies.* M.

The ſame opinion was held concerning a perſon's being drowned. When (Virg. Æn. I. 95.) *Æneas* terrified at the approach of a dreadful ſtorm at ſea, ſighed, not, as *Servius* obſerves, for fear of death merely, but of ſuch a death, as prevented the ſoul from making her eſcape and ſurviving the body: for being of the ſame quality with *fire*, it muſt neceſſarily be extinguiſhed by the ſurrounding waters. Thus *Homer*, (Od. δ. 511) deſcribing the death of *Ajax Oïliades*, ſays

> Ω'ς ὁ μὲν ἔνθ' ἀπόλωλεν, ἐπεὶ πίεν ἁλμυρὸν ὕδωρ.
> *And thus he periſh'd, in the briny ſea*
> *For ever buried* —

And *Seneca* himſelf, (de ira iii. 19.) ſpeaking of that haughty and moſt inhuman tyrant, *Caius Caligula*, ſeems to lament the caſe of thoſe, who were proſcribed, more bitterly, foraſmuch as *Caius* ordered all their mouths to be ſtopped, at the execution, with a ſpunge, or part of their own clothes; *What horrid cruelty!* ſays he, *not to give the ſoul the liberty of departing, freely and naturally from the loathſome carcaſe!* but theſe are vulgar notions, built on too weak a foundation, to impoſe upon the wiſdom of *Seneca*; as is manifeſt from what follows,—*they who advance this doctrine*, &c.

(*f*) Hoc quidem certè habe, ſi (*animus*) ſuperſtes eſt corpori, *propter hoc* illum nullo genere poſſe perire, *propter* quod non perit. But various are the readings here; *Lipſius* is for diſcarding the latter *propter*, or changing it for the adverb, *propterea*; whence *Gronovius* only ſtrikes out the *propter hoc*; and alludes to the foregoing opinion of ſome *Stoics*, which *Seneca* thinks abſurd, unleſs it could be proved that the ſoul is mortal.

Here we ſee our author, *Seneca*, like the greateſt men among the ancients before him, *Socrates*, *Plato*, *Cicero*, &c. ſtill wavering in his opinion concerning *a future ſtate*; yet they all ſeemed inclined to believe the affirmative: no wonder; for though the *immateriality* of the ſoul, (which none but a

rank

rank Atheist, or a modern P——y, would deny) is certainly a good argument for its *immortality*; as having no divisible parts, no contrary qualities, no principles of death and corruption in it, as our bodies, and other material compositions have: yet this argument, strong as it is, is still subject to objections; as indeed all arguments are in these abstruse points, when drawn merely from the light of unassisted reason: and this serves greatly to enhance the Christian's obligation to his blessed *Saviour*; *who hath brought life and immortality to light through the Gospel.* As before mentioned, Ep. 54. (N. d.)

EPISTLE LVIII.

On the Poverty of the Latin *Tongue.*

Of Genus, Species, Ideas, Being, and other Logical Terms.

I NEVER yet well understood, before to-day, the great poverty of our language, and extreme want of words *(a)*. There are a thousand things, *Lucilius*, when we are talking of *Plato*, which require names, but have them not; and some which had names, but have now lost them, through a scrupulous disgust: but who will allow disgust in a case of necessity? the *gad-fly*, for instance, which drives the cattle madding about the fields, and disperseth them through the woods, was called by the Greeks, *Oestram*, and by our ancestors *Asilum*, as appears from *Virgil* (G. 3. 147.)

> Est lucos Silari juxta, ilicibusque virentem
> Plurimus Alburnum volitans, cui nomen *Asilo*
> Romanum est *Oestron* Graii vertêre vocantes:
> Asper, acerba sonans, quo tota exterrita silvis
> Diffugiunt armenta:—
> *About th' Alburnian groves, with holly green*
> *Of winged insects mighty swarms are seen;*

This

This flying plague to mark its quality,
Oestrus *the* Grecians *call*; Asylus, *we:*
A fierce loud-buzzing breeze; their stings draw blood,
And drive the cattle gadding through the wood. Dryden.

I think he understood this word to be now lost. And not to detain you long, there were some simple words in use, as *Cernere* ferro *(b)*, in *Virgil*, for which we now use the compound, *decernere*; and the use of the simple seems to be lost;

(12.709)—Stupet ipse Latinus
Ingentes genitos diversis partibus orbis
Inter se coiisse viros et cernere ferro.

So they formerly said, *Jusso (c)*, instead of *Jussero*: and in this likewise I would have you believe *Virgil* rather than take my bare word for it—Cætera qua Jusso, mecum manus inferat arma. 11. 467. I say not this with an intention to shew you, how conversant I am with the Grammarians, but that you may understand from hence, how many words, made use of by *Ennius* and *Attius*, are now grown obsolete; when even from *Virgil*, who is daily in the hands of every one, some word or other is continually lost.

What means, you say, this preamble? whither does it tend? I will tell you. I desire to make use of the word, *Essentia (d)*, *(Essence)*, whether it does or does not offend your ear: I have the authority of *Cicero* for it; and I think you will not dispute *that* being a rich one: but if you require a more modern example, I can produce you *Fabian (f)*; that eloquent and graceful orator, sometimes so very nice in the choice of his words, as to create disgust. For what must we do, my *Lucilius*? How otherwise shall I express the Greek word ουσια, *(i)* *something necessary, comprehending nature, and the foundation of all things?* I beg your permission therefore to use this word; and I will endeavour to be as sparing as possible of such permission, and perhaps be contented with that alone. But be as kind, and easy as you will, what will it signify, if, after all, I cannot sufficiently express the word in *Latin*, and therefore have started this quarrel with our tongue? And you will condemn the scantiness of it the more, when I tell you there is a word of

one

one ſyllable, which I know not how to tranſlate; would you know what it is? Τὸ ὄν, (*Being*)—you may think me perhaps a little too nice, or ſomewhat dull; ſince it may be done very eaſily by rendering it, *Quod eſt*, (*what is*). But I plainly perceive there is a difference; ſince I am oblig'd to make uſe of a verb for a noun: but if it muſt be ſo take it as it is; *Quod eſt*. Now a friend of mine, a moſt learned man, told me, this very day, that *Plato* had applied this word ſix different ways: I will explain them all to you having firſt premiſed, that it is a *Genus*: now a *Genus* is that upon which the ſeveral *Species* depend; from which every diviſion is formed, and under which all things are compriſed. And if we enquire after the firſt *Genus*, we ſhall find it by proceeding upwards from the ſeveral particulars; as thus, man is a *Species*; horſe is a *Species*; dog is a *Species*. Therefore ſome common tye or connexion is to be ſought, which comprehends them all, and ſubjects them to itſelf; and what is that? *Animal:* therefore *Animal* is the *Genus* of all the things aforementioned, man, horſe, dog. But there are ſome things that are *Animated*, and yet are not *Animals*. For plants and ſhrubs have an *Anima*, (*a principle of life*) in them; and accordingly we ſay, they *live*, they die. Therefore *animantia*, *things having life*, will hold ſuperior rank, becauſe both *Animals* and *Plants* are in this claſs. Other things want this principle of life, as ſtones: therefore there is ſomething that claims a place before the *Animantia*, and that is *Body*; and this too is diviſible into bodies *Animate*, and *Inanimate:* there is even ſomething before *Body*; for we ſay ſome things are *Corporeal* and ſome *Incorporeal:* what is it then from whence all things are deduced? Why it is that, to which we have given but an improper name, *Quod eſt*, (*what is*): for thus may it be divided into *ſpecies*; *whatever is*, is *Corporeal* or *Incorporeal*; this then is the firſt, moſt ancient, and, if I may ſo ſpeak, *General Genus*.

There are other kinds of *Genus*, but they are *Special*; as, *man* is a *Genus* (*b*); for he contains in himſelf the *Species* of nations; as *Greeks*, *Romans*, *Parthians*;—of colours, as black, white, brown;—of individuals, as, *Cato*, *Cicero*, *Lucretius*: therefore as it contains many things it is a *Genus*; but as ſubject to ſomething elſe, it comes under the name

of

of *Species*. The *Genus*, that I call *General*, hath nothing above it; it is the beginning of all things; it has all things under it. Some ſtoics indeed are for raiſing another *Genus* above this, ſtill more principal; of which I ſhall ſpeak preſently, having ſhewn you that the *Genus* I am treating of, deſerves abſolutely the firſt rank, ſince it is ſo capacious, as to compaſs all things in itſelf. I divide *Quod eſt*, (*that which is*), into two *Species*, corporeal and incorporeal: there is no third. I divide *Body* into animate or inanimate: again, I divide *Animantia* (*things having life*) into ſuch as have *Animum*, (*a mind* or *ſoul*) and ſuch as have only *animam*, (*a principle of life*): or thus, ſome things have a faculty, whereby they walk, and paſs along; while other are fixed in the earth, and grow, and are nouriſhed by their roots: again, I divide *Animals* into mortal, and immortal. But ſome ſtoics ſeem to ſuppoſe a ſtill higher *Genus*, τί τι quiddam, *Somewhat* or *Thing*), which is thus accounted for: they ſay, in the nature of things, ſome have a being, and ſome have not; and that ſuch as have not, are ſtill in the nature of things which occur to the mind; as *Centaurs*, *Giants*, and whatever elſe is formed by a falſe imagination, and find a reſemblance in the mind though in reality it hath no ſubſtance.

I now return to what I before promiſed; to ſhew you the ſix ſeveral modes or ways into which *Plato* divides *the things that are:* the firſt kind of *Quod eſt*, *(that which is)* is not to be comprehended by the touch, or ſight, or any of the ſenſes, but only in *Mind* or *Thought*; becauſe taken *generally*; as man *in general*, is not an object of ſight, but a *ſpecial* or particular man is, as *Cæſar*, or *Cato*. *Animal*, is not ſeen but in the imagination, but the ſpecies is ſeen *(i)*; in an horſe, or dog. In the next place of *the things that are*, *Plato* ſubjoins that which excels and tranſcends all other things; this, he ſays, is *by way of eminence*; as the word, *Poet:* which indeed is the common name of all verſifiers, but among the Greeks it dignifies but one man; as when it is ſaid, *the poet*, you muſt underſtand thereby *Homer (k)*. And what is this? GOD, who is greater than, and far above, all things *(l)*. A third kind is of thoſe things, which are properly *in being*; and theſe are innumerable, but placed far beyond our ſight: they are the peculiar furniture of *Plato*; he he calls them ideas (*m*); from whence all things were made that are made, and according to which they haveall their form; and theſe are immortal, immutable, inviolable. Now, an *Idea*, or rather what *Plato* calls by this name, is this: *the eternal exemplar of all the things that are made in nature:* but I will explain this definition, to make the thing ſtill clearer to you: I have a mind, ſuppoſe, to draw your picture: I take *you* then as a pattern of what I intend to draw; and from this pattern the *mind* gets a certain form, upon which it frames its work: now, this form or pattern which inſtructs me, and from which all imitation is borrowed, is an *Idea*.

Such exemplars are infinite in the nature of things, as of men, birds, fiſhes; according to which every thing ſhe intends to make, or that is to be made, is formed.—The εἶδος (idos, *image or reſemblance)* hath the fourth place: pray attend to what is meant by this word, and impute it to *Plato*, not to me, if you find any difficulty in comprehending theſe matters: there muſt needs be ſome difficulty, in all ſuch abſtruſe and ſubtil points. I before made uſe of a pourtrait by ſome painter, who when he would draw a *Virgil*, to the life, ſuppoſe in colours, looked ſtedfaſtly at him: now, the face or form of *Virgil*, the pattern of the work to be formed was an *Idea*; but what the artiſt took from him, and delineated upon the canvas, is the εἶδος *(idos)*. Do you deſire to know the difference? The one is the pattern; the other is the form, taken from this pattern, and joined to the piece in hand: the artiſt imitates the one; but forms the other. A ſtatue likewiſe hath a certain face or appearance; this is the *Idos*; and the pattern itſelf hath a certain face or appearance, which the ſtatuary obſerving, he from thence makes the ſtatue; this is an *Idea*. Or, to give you another diſtinction; the *Idos* is *in* the work; the *Idea* is *out* of it; nor is it only out of it, but *before the work was*.—The fifth kind is of thoſe things that are in common, pertaining to us; they are indeed all things as men, cattle, and the like. The ſixth is of thoſe things, which ſeem, or are, but, as it were, in being; as a *Vacuum*, *Time*, &c.

Whatever we ſee, or touch, *Plato* reckons not among thoſe things that can properly be ſaid *to be:* becauſe they are upon the continual float, and are ſubject to daily diminution and addition. No one is the *ſame* man, in old age, as he was in youth; no one is the ſame in the morning, that he was yeſterday; our bodies are carried away as a river: all that you ſee runs down with time: nothing ſtill remains the ſame: even while I ſay theſe things are changed, I am changed myſelf. This is what *Heraclitus* means, when he ſays, *we go not twice into the ſame River (n)*. The River ſtill keeps its name, but the water paſſeth away. This indeed is more manifeſt in a river than in man; but yet as ſwift a courſe carries us likewiſe away; and therefore I am ſurpriſed at our folly in being fond of ſo fleeting a thing as is the body; and in perpetual fear, leſt we ſhould die one day or other, when every moment is the death of our former habit of body *(o)*; and can you be afraid, *Lucilius*, leſt that ſhould happen ſome time or other, which happens every day? What I have ſaid, relates to man, compoſed of matter, fleeting, frail, and ſubject to variety of accidents. But the world likewiſe, eternal as it may be and invincible, is ſtill for ever changing, and remains not the ſame a moment; for tho' it may have all things in it, it ever had; it poſſeſſeth them not in the ſame manner; the whole order is continually changed *(p)*.

Do you aſk me what all this ſubtilty profits a man? Truly, I think, nothing: but as an engraver, when he has long been poring over his work, and tired his eyes; takes them off, and gives them reſt a while; in order to indulge, and ſtrengthen them, as they ſay; ſo we ought ſometimes to unbend the mind and refreſh it with certain amuſements: not but that amuſements may be work; and even from theſe, due obſervation may pick out ſomething that may be turned to good account. This my, *Lucilius*, is what I practiſe myſelf: from whatever I read, however remote it may be, from philoſophy *(q)*, I endeavour to extract ſomething that may be uſeful. But what, you will ſay, do I gain from the dry ſubjects I have been treating of, ſo diſtant from a reformation of manners? How can *Platonic Ideas* make me a whit the better man? What can I extract from theſe towards reſtraining my paſſions? Why, this; foraſmuch as *Plato* denies, that all ſuch things as are ſubſervient to the ſenſes, and which incite and provoke the paſſions, are of a claſs with thoſe which come under the name of truth: they are all imaginary

3 therefore,

therefore, and only make their appearance for a time; there is nothing ſtable, or ſolid: and yet we deſire them as if they were always permanent, and we could have them always in poſſeſſion.

Weak and frail, we ſubſiſt, as it were by intervals: let us ſet our minds then upon the things that are eternal *(r)*: let us admire the univerſal forms of things, flying on high; and *God* in the midſt of them; diſpoſing all things as it ſeemeth beſt, and providing, (as he could not make them immortal, becauſe formed of matter) *(s)* that they periſh not in death, but through his wiſdom overcome the malignity of body: for all things remain, not becauſe they are eternal, but becauſe they are under the care and protection of an Almighty governour: things immortal in their own nature ſtand not in need of a guardian; but mortal things are preſerved by the hand that made them, ſurmounting the frailty of the materials by his almighty power (*t*).

Let us deſpiſe the things, which are ſo far from being precious that it is a doubt whether they are at all: at the ſame time let us think, that, if divine providence is pleaſed to deliver the world, (not leſs mortal than ourſelves) from danger and deſtruction, our own care and forecaſt may in ſome meaſure contribute to prolong our days, and keep up this little tenement; provided we can govern and reſtrain the fond paſſions, that bring untimely ruin on the greater part of mankind. *Plato* lived to a good old age by his prudence: he was favoured indeed with a ſtrong conſtitution, and took his name from the breadth of his cheſt (*u*); but voyages and perils had greatly lower'd his ſtrength; temperance however, and moderation of thoſe things that are apt to provoke deſire, and a diligent regard for the preſervation of health, lengthen'd his days, notwithſtanding the many rubs he had met with in the courſe of his life: for, I think, you know this, that he lived exactly to complete his *eighty firſt year*, dying on his birth day (*w*): wherefore certain magi or *Wiſemen*, who were then at *Athens*, did ſacrifice to him after his deceaſe, thinking him ſomething more than man, who had ſo completely finiſhed the moſt perfect *climacteric*, nine multiplied by nine: tho' I believe *Plato* would not have ſcrupled to have remitted a few days of that ſum, as alſo

 the

the ſacrifice. frugality and temperance are, no doubt, the great preſervatives of old age; which, as I think it is not greatly to be coveted, is not to be refuſed *(x)*: it is pleaſant to dwell as long as poſſible with one's ſelf; eſpecially when a man has rendered himſelf worthy of ſelf-enjoyment.

Therefore let us examine this point *(y)*: whether it be right to diſdain the extremities of old age, and not wait the iſſue, but forcibly cloſe the ſcene. He is not far from a coward, who chuſes to linger out his fate; as a man muſt be a ſot, who drains the pitcher, and drinks up the very dregs; yet this muſt likewiſe be enquired into; whether the laſt ſtage of life can properly be called the *dregs (z)*; and whether it may not be the moſt pure, and cleareſt part of it; at leaſt if the intellect hath received no injury; and the ſenſes, ſtill perfect, entertain the mind; or the body hath no paralytic diſorder, or other extraordinary defect: but there is ſome difference between a man's prolonging his life, or his death: for if the body is become uſeleſs, and incapable of its functions, why ſhould any one deſire to retain the reluctant ſoul? *Perhaps* it ought to be let looſe, before it comes to this paſs, leſt you ſhould not then be able to do it, when you were ſo inclined. If there is greater danger of living wretchedly than of dying ſoon, I ſhould think him a ſilly man, who would not ſtand the chance of ſo great a benefit, at the expence of a few days. Few come to their death-bed, even in very old age, without having received ſome injury: a liſtleſs indolence of no ſervice to itſelf or others hath affected many: how then can you think it hard or cruel to loſe ſomething of life, were it to be put an end to? Hear me not with regret, as if this my opinion had any reference to you; but weigh well what I ſay. I will not quarrel with, or forſake, my old age, ſo long as it preſerves me whole to myſelf; I mean whole in that better part of me, the mind. But if it hath begun to impair my underſtanding, and to dull my ſenſes; if it hath ſcarce left any life, but a ſoul only, I ſhould gladly leap out of ſuch a rotten and ruinous tenement *(aa)*: neither would I ſeek death, to eſcape a diſeaſe, provided it were curable, and not prejudicial to the mind: nor ſhould pain alone, make me have recourſe to violence; for, ſo to die would be to own

myſelf

myſelf conquered; but if I *know* I muſt for ever ſuffer ſuch a violent diſeaſe *(bb)*; I ſhould deſire to go, not on account of the diſeaſe, but becauſe it proved a let or hindrance to the enjoyment of every thing for which we live. He is a weak man and a coward who dies for fear of pain; and he is a fool, who chuſes to live in the certain ſufferance of it.

But I grow tedious; tho' I have matter enough on this ſubject to ſpin out the whole day. And how can he pretend to talk of putting an end to his life who knows not how to put an end to an epiſtle? So, *farewell.* Which I fancy you had rather read, than a diſcourſe concerning nothing but death.

ANNOTATIONS, &c.

(a) Quanta verborum nobis *paupertas*, imò *egeſtas* ſit.——So *Pliny* (Ep. IV. 18.) Inopiâ ac potius ut Lucretius ait, hac *egeſtate* patrii ſermonis.—*And by the* want, *or rather the* poverty *of our native tongue.* Orrery. Where I would chuſe, by his Lordſhip's leave, to tranſpoſe the words *want* and *poverty*; as the former is by much the ſtronger word. Ep. 17. Non eſt quod *paupertas* nos a philoſophiâ revocet, nec *egeſtas* quidem. A man may be *poor*, and yet not in *want*.

Non eſt paupertas, Neſtor, habere nihil. *Martial.*

The words referred to in *Lucretius* are,

Nunc et Anaxagoræ ſcrutemur Homœomeriam
Quam Græci memorant, nec noſtrâ dicere linguâ
Concedit nobis patrii ſermonis egeſtas. l. 830.
Next let's examine with a curious eye,
Anaxagoras's philoſophy,
By copious *Greece*, term'd *Homœomery*;
For which our Latin language, poor in words,
Not one expreſſive ſingle voice affords. *Creech.*

The like in III. 260——rationem reddere aventem
Abſtrahit invitum patrii ſermonis egeſtas.
Fain would I give the cauſe, was not my ſong
Check'd by the poorneſs of the Latin tongue.

(b) Cernere ferro. *Servius* acknowledgeth, and confirms this reading; and *Muretus* proves the uſe of the word *cernere* from *Attius* and *Plautus.* *Pierius*, however, and ſome moderns contend for *decernere*; abſurdly enough! (was the verſe to have continued ſound) againſt the teſtimony of *Servius*, and even this of *Seneca* himſelf.

* The Roman King beholds with wond'ring ſight
Two mighty champions match'd in ſingle fight;
Born under climes remote, and brought by Fate,
With ſwords to try their title in the ſtate.—*Dryden.*

(c) So,

(c) So, capsis, for capueris. *Cic.* (de Leg. II.) noxit for nocuerit. *Lucilius*, &c. See Turneb. Adverf. XV. 15.

(d) Essentiam.] It seems we owe this word to the sagacity of *Muretus*, all the books before having it *quid sentiam*.

(e) Sidon. Apoll. Lecturus es hic novum verbum *essentiam*; sed scias hoc ipsum dixisse Ciceronem.

(f) Fabian.] The same whom *Fabius* means by *Flavius*;—Usiam, quam *Flavius Essentiam* vocat.—His name was, *Serv. Flavius Papinius Fabianus*.

(g) All things spring from Ουσία (Usia) i. e. *God* and *Nature*. Lipf.—*Perionius* thought the word *Natura* would sufficiently express the Greek Ουσία, which, if suitable in some instances, can never be allowed in philosophical disputations, as Ουσία and φυσις, strictly speaking, signify very different things. Nor would it be better expressed by the word *Substantia*: for when rightly distinguished ὕπαρξις, i. e. Substantia, and Ουσία, (εἶναι and ὑπάρχειν) have a several meaning. No *Latin* word therefore seems more proper to express the Gr. Ουσία than *Essentia*. Muret.

(h) Homo genus est] Nay, rather *the most special* species. εἶδος εἰδικώτατον. For neither are these, here mentioned, *Greeks, Romans, Parthians*, different *species* of men; nor does the difference of individuals consist in a difference of species, but of number. *Seneca* therefore we must own is somewhat deficient in these niceties; nor indeed were the writings of *Aristotle*, who alone is exquisitely accurate in these points so generally known, or studied, in those days as they have been since. *Muret.* And *Lipsius* thinks that *Seneca* most probably here follows the logic of *Chrysippus*; which is now quite out of date.

(i) Neither is the *species* properly said to be seen: but *this* horse or *this* dog.

(k) Cicero (in topicis)—*Homerus'* propter excellentiam, commune poetarum nomen effecit apud Græcos suum.

(l) For *God* alone is Πηγὴ πάσης τῆς οὐσίας, *the Fountain of all Being*. According to the name *God* is pleased to assume in Holy Writ, Ἐγώ εἰμι ὁ Ὤν. *I am That I am*. Exod. III. 14.

(m) Ep. 65. Hæc exemplaria rerum omnium Deus intra se habet, &c. *The exemplars of all things in the world God hath in his mind,——which* Plato *calls* Ideas, *immortal, immutable, indefatigable*.—Boethius (de Consol. III.)

O qui perpetua mundum ratione gubernas
Terrarum cœlique fator,—Tu cuncta superno
Ducis ab exemplo, pulchrum pulcherrimus ipse
Mundum menté gerens, similique in imagine formans,
Perfectasque jubes perfectum absolvere partes.

O thou Father, Soveraine of heaven,
And of erthes, that governest this world
By perdurable reason——Thou that art elder fairest,
Bearing the fayre world in thy thought,
Formedst this world to thy likeness-sembable,
Of that fayre world in thy thought;
Thou drawest all things on thy soveraine ensemplar,
And commandest that this world perfectly ymakid,
Have freely and absolute his perfite parties. Chaucer.

Ideas] Plato; *Originales rerum species* Macrobius; *Principales formas* Claud. Mamertus dixit; et Ausonius *datas formas*, i. e. rebus a Deo impressas. Vid. Lipf. Phyf. II. 3.

(n) Plato in Cratylo. Λέγει που Ἡράκλειτος, ὅτι πάντα ῥεῖ, καὶ οὐδὲν μένει· κ. τ. λ.

(o) See Ep. 1. 8. 24. (N. I.)

(p) And

(*p*) *And they that use this world as not abusing it; for the fashion of this world passeth away.* I Cor. 7. 41.

(*q*) Philosophy, *viz. moral.* Which is always meant by way of eminence.

(*r*) *Set your mind on things above, not on things on the earth.* Col. iii. 2. *While we look not at the things that are seen, but at the things which are not seen; for the things which are seen are temporal, but the things which are not seen are eternal.* 2 Cor. iv. 18. See Ep. 17. 65.

(*s*) 'Twas an absurd and wicked opinion of the ancients, *that God of his goodness would have all things immortal, but that it was not in his power so to do, on account of the perishable nature of the materials.* As if that God who made all other things had not likewise created matter. More rightly therefore *Lactantius*, Idem materiæ fictor est, et rerum materiâ constantium; *The same God, who formed things of matter, formed likewise matter itself.* Ps. 148. 1, 6. Is. 40. 26, 42. 5. 43, 12, 19. 1. 16. Rev. 10, 6.

(*t*) *Thou sendest forth thy spirit, they are created, and thou renewest the face of the earth.* Ps. 104, 30.

(*u*) He was before called by his grandfather's name, *Aristocles*, but *Plato* from the Gr. Πλατὺς (*broad*) Epp. 47. Much the same that is here said of *Plato*, is recorded of *Herodicus Selimbrianus* by *Plato* himself, and by *Aristotle* and *Plutarch*. And *Muretus* likewise tells us of one *Alvisius Cornelius*, a *Venetian*, who by temperance and sobriety restored his constitution, though miserably shattered by a loose and debauched life, and given over by his physicians; but by a steady resolution in the observation of a regular and moderate diet, gentle exercise, freedom from anxiety, chearful conversation with his friends, and other innocent amusements, he so recovered as to outlive the physicians themselves, and to reach an extreme old age. But the most extraordinary instance of this kind is the famous *Cornaro* of the same country; whose history is well known.

(*w*) Thargelioris septimo die, (*May* 7th) A. M. 3522.) al. *February* 7th. Plut. Sympos, viii. 1.

(*x*) Happy is the man, who, by the blessing of God, can say, *Experto credite.*

(*y*) See it more fully examined in *Lips.* Manud. III. 22, 23. And as *Seneca* here at least speaks doubtfully, but seems rather to reprove the false courage of the Stoic, in this respect, than encourage it, we need not be apprehensive of any mischief: I shall reserve what I have farther to say on this subject 'till we meet with something more flagrant, (Epp. 70. 78) in the mean while referring the reader to Epp. 24. q.) 26. (N. d.) 30. 50.

(*z*) See Ep. I. (N. m.)

(*aa*) And who would not, *if providence so willed?* The same is quoted, both by *Muretus* and *Lipsius*, of Gorgias *Leontinus* in *Stobæ.* Serm. cxviii.

(*bb*) But what mortal can know that? Who can tell what God, with whom nothing is impossible, may be pleased to do for one, even in the last extremity? The Christian therefore would scorn to make such a supposition.

EPISTLE

EPISTLE LIX.

On Joy and Pleasure. A good Conscience the only true Joy.

I RECEIVED great *pleaſure, Lucilius,* from your epiſtle: for, give me leave to uſe the word in its common acceptation, without wreſting it to a ſtoical ſenſe; according to *their* doctrine indeed *pleaſure* is *vice:* it may be ſo; but the word is commonly uſed to ſignify *a chearful diſpoſition of the mind.* I know, I ſay, that the word pleaſure, (if brought to *our* ſtandard) is uſed in a bad ſenſe, and *joy* only allowed to *the wiſe man (a):* for 'tis the elevation of a mind, that confides in its own ſuperlative worth and ſtrength: yet, vulgarly ſpeaking, we ſay, we had great *joy* in ſuch a one's being choſen conſul, or in a marriage, or at the birth of a ſon; which are ſo far from deſerving the conſtant name of *joy,* that they often prove the beginnings of ſorrow. It is the property of true *joy,* never to ceaſe, or to be changed into the contrary. Therefore our *Virgil,* when he ſays,—*Et mala mentis gaudia (b)* may ſpeak elegantly, but not very accurately, becauſe there can be no *joy* in what is *evil:* he gave this name to certain *pleaſures,* and hath expreſſed what he intended; for he meant to ſhew that ſome men are joyous in their *evil* doings. I did not however ſpeak improprely when I ſaid, I received *pleaſure* from your epiſtle. For tho' a plain ſimple man may well rejoice occaſionally, yet as this affection is irregular and changeable, I call it *pleaſure* indeed, but ſuch a one, as, being raiſed upon the opinion of imaginary good, may be immoderate, unreaſonable.

But to return: I will tell you what pleaſed me in your epiſtle. You have words at your command; yet are not proud of ſpeech, or apt to run on further than you deſigned; there are many, who are induced to write more than they intended, being tempted by the elegance of ſome pleaſing phraſe: but it is not ſo with you: all is cloſe, and to the purpoſe: you

you ſay as much as you think proper; and yet mean more than you ſay: this is a ſign of great ſufficiency; it ſhews that the mind delights in nothing that is ſuperfluous; nothing that is vain, or bombaſt: I find indeed ſome metaphorical expreſſions; but they are not too bold, nor inelegant; having ſtood the teſt of the judicious; I find alſo ſome ſtrong images and compariſons; which if any one forbids us to uſe, and thinks them allowable only to *poets*; he ſeems to me not to have read any of thoſe ancient authors, who had not as yet affected a ſmooth and plauſible way of ſpeaking: they who ſpoke in a ſimple ſtyle, and aimed at demonſtration generally uſed *parables (c)*; which I think neceſſary, not only as the poets uſed them, for decoration, but as helps to our weakneſs, and to tie down, as it were, both the hearer and the ſpeaker to the point in queſtion. But eſpecially when I read *Sextius (d)*, a ſmart writer, philoſophically diſplaying *Roman* morals in the *Greek* Tongue *(e)*, I am pleaſed with that *ſimile* of his; that as an army forms itſelf into a ſquare *(f)*, when an attack is expected from an enemy on every ſide; ſo, ſays he, ought a wiſe man to act; he muſt draw out all his virtues on every ſide (*g*); that whenever any danger threatens, he may be provided with a defence; and that without any diſorder they may obey the word of command: as we ſee in a well-diſciplined army, how attentive all the forces are to the orders of their principal officers; being ſo diſpoſed, that a ſignal given by one of them, immediately takes place both in horſe and foot: this, ſaith *Sextius*, is much more requiſite in our conduct: for in the field, it often happens, for men to be afraid of an enemy without cauſe; and nothing turns out ſafer than a way that has been moſt ſuſpected: but folly is always under alarms: terror attacks it both from above and below: it trembles on every ſide; dangers both purſue and meet it; every thing is dreaded; it is alway unprepared, and even terrified at the beat of its allies.

Whereas the *wiſe man*, guarded and prepared againſt every attack, draws not back his foot, whether poverty or ſorrow, or ignominy, or pain, aſſail him: undaunted he ſtands amidſt all theſe, and ſtrenuouſly oppoſes them. For our parts, many things chain us down; many things enfeeble us; we have been long dead in ſin (*h*): it is a difficult matter to waſh and be clean; for we are not ſtained, but infected.

But not to run on in this manner, from one metaphor to another, I ſhall now enquire into what I have been long conſidering, *whence it is that Folly gets ſuch ſtrong hold of us,*—And it muſt be, *firſt*, becauſe we do not valiantly repel it, nor exert our whole ſtrength for our recovery. And next, becauſe thoſe things, which the ſons of wiſdom in former times deviſed for our good, have not obtained ſufficient credit with us; we receive them not cordially; paying but a ſlight regard to things of ſo great importance: how can any one acquire ſufficient ſtrength to oppoſe the whole band of vices, who makes it his ſtudy only at leiſure hours? We none of us go to the bottom, but ſtill dwell upon the ſurface: and think we have taken full pains enough if we have beſtowed a little time on the ſtudy of philoſophy. And this moreover is a particular hindrance to us; *we are ſoon ſatisfied with ourſelves*;—if we meet with thoſe who are pleaſed to compliment us with the appellations of *good men*, prudent and devout, we really think we are ſo; nor are we contented with moderate commendation; but whatever encomiums ſhameleſs flattery thinks proper to beſtow upon us, we think them all our due *(i)*. We eaſily give our aſſent to thoſe who affirm that we are the wiſeſt and beſt of men, though we know they are not always given to ſpeak truth: and are even ſo indulgent to ourſelves, as to wiſh to be praiſed for that, the contrary of which we know ourſelves to be extremely guilty of: are we cruel? we would fain be cried up for our humanity: do we live upon rapine? we deſire to be thought liberal; and temperate, though ever ſo great ſots and debauchees. *Alexander*, when he was roving through *India*, and laying waſte, by war, nations, that were ſcarce known to their neighbours, as he was beſieging a certain city, and looking out for the eaſieſt place to make a breach, was ſtruck with an arrow; yet, while warm, he perſevered, and went on with his enterprize; but ſoon after, (when, the blood being ſtaunched, the wound began to feſter and grow painful; and his leg, as it hung down from the horſe was gradually benumb'd) being forced to alight, he thus exclaimed; *All men ſwear, I am the ſon of* Jupiter, *but this wound ſufficiently teſtifieth that I am no more than man* (*k*). Let us do the ſame thing, when flattery, according to our quality, plays the fool with us; and congratulates us upon our abilities: let us ſay; *you indeed are pleaſed to call me wiſe and prudent; but I know*

know myſelf better; I covet many uſeleſs, I wiſh for many hurtful things; and while every brute animal knows from ſatiety the due meaſure of eating and drinking, I know it not myſelf with all my wiſdom.

I will now ſhew you, *Lucilius*, how you may know whether you are truly wiſe, or not. A wiſe man is one who full of joy, lives as happy in *his* condition, as the gods can do in *theirs*, ever chearful, placid, and unſhaken (*l*). Now conſult your own boſom; if you are never depreſſed with ſorrow; nor elevated with hope, in painful expectation of ſome future good; if both night and day you enjoy an equal tenour of mind; ſublime, and full of complacency; you are then arrived at the ſummit of human felicity.

But if you covet pleaſures and purſue them every where, and in every manner; you are as far eſtranged from *wiſdom*, as from *joy*: this is what you propoſe and deſire to attain, but you are miſtaken if you think it attainable by riches: or do you ſeek *joy* amidſt the higheſt honours, I ſhould rather ſay, amidſt cares and troubles? Purſuits of this kind as productive of mirth and pleaſure, are generally the cauſes of pain and grief. All men, I ſay, are in purſuit of *joy*, but are quite ignorant how to attain that which is truly great and laſting. One man thinks to find it in banquetings and luxury: another in the flights of ambition, and a fawning crowd of clients; another from a kind miſtreſs; another from a vain oſtentation of learning, and ſuch ſtudies as avail nothing towards healing the ſoul. Short and treacherous delights deceive the heart, like drunkenneſs; which pays for the merry madneſs of an hour, with ſickneſs and irkſome loathing of a day or more: or like the popular and vulgar acclamations, which are not to be purchaſed or made ſatisfaction for, but with great loſs and pains. Think therefore O *Lucilius*, and be aſſured that the effect of wiſdom is conſtant *joy*: ſuch is the mind of a wiſe man, as is the region above the moon, perpetually fair and ſerene (*m*).

This is therefore a ſufficient inducement to ſtudy wiſdom: becauſe it is never without joy; *that joy* which ever ſprings from a conſciouſneſs of virtue: no one can taſte *joy* but the brave, the juſt, the temperate.

What then, you will ſay, do fools and bad men never *rejoice?* Yes, as the lions do, over their prey. When men have fatigued themſelves with a debauch, when they have ſpent the whole night in drinking,—when their pleaſures, having charged the little body with more than it can hold, begin to ſuppurate; then it is the wretches exclaim, in that verſe of *Virgil,* (6. 513.) Namque ut ſupremum falſa inter gaudia noctem.

Egerimus noſti:—

You know, that diſmal night in joys we paſt,
And never thought it was to be our laſt.

Thus the luxurious ſpend their time *amid falſe joys,* and pretend to indulge every night as if it were their laſt. But the joy which the gods, and godlike-men taſte, is never interrupted, never ceaſeth: it would ceaſe, if it were borrowed from without; but as it is not dependent upon the bounty, ſo neither is it upon the will, of another. Fortune cannot take away, what ſhe hath not given.

ANNOTATIONS, &c.

(*a*) With regard to this diſtinction between gaudium (*joy*) and voluptas aut lætitia (*pleaſure* or *mirth*) *Cicero* (Tuſc. IV.) ut confidere decet, timere non decet, ſic quidem gaudere decet, lætari non decet. *As a rational aſſurance becomes a wiſe man, but not fear; ſo does* joy, *but not* merrineſs. And *Muretus* quotes a verſe from *Afranius* (*if it is not his own,* ſays Lipſius)

Gaudebit ſapiens, lætabuntur cæteri.
Others are merry, but the wiſe rejoice.——See Ep. 23. (N. b.) 72.

(*b*) Virg. 6. 278.—*The guilty joys of a perturbed mind.*

(*c*) Thus beſides thoſe things which our *Saviour* concealed under types and figures, he was pleaſed to expreſs others in *parables,* as the calling of the Gentiles in the parable of the houſholder. Matth. x. 5. 6. And the rejection of the *Jews,* under the parable of perſons invited to a marriage feaſt, who would not come. Matth. xxi. 1.

(*d*) *Q. Sextius.* There were two of this name, both very eminent philoſophers, father and ſon. The father born in the reign of *Auguſtus,* and ſuppoſed the author of a new ſect; but was rather the reſtorer of the *Pythagorean* doctrine. *See* Lipſ. Man ud. I. 5, 18. *Plutarch* mentions his *quitting all offices and places of honour, that he might the more freely, and without diſturbance apply himſelf to the ſtudy of philoſophy.* (On man's progreſs in virtue.)—See alſo Ep. 64, 73. Plin. xvii. 28.

(*e*) He ſtudied and wrote while at *Athens.*

(*f*) See this fully explained in *Lipſ.* de Militia, l. v.

(*g*) Something like this we meet with in that beautiful metaphor of St. *Paul: Take unto ye the whole armour of God, that ye may be able to ſtand in the evil day, having your loins girt about with truth; and having on the breaſt-plate of righteouſneſs. Take the helmit of ſalvation and the ſword of the Spirit, which is the word of God.* Epheſ. vi. 11, 18.

(*h*) Dia

(*h*) Diu in istis vitiis jacuimus.] *And you hath he quickened who were dead in trespasses and sins, wherein in time past we walked according to the course of this world*, &c. Ephes. ii. 1, 5. Col. ii. 13.

" (*i*) There is no turn of mind so liable to be tainted by this sort of poyson as a disposition to entertain too high conceit of one's merit, &c. *Cic.* Læl. p. 132.——" But into snares of this kind, those men can never fall, who in obedience to the famous Oracle, study to *know themselves*. They will discover such mixture of frailties, follies and vices, blended with their virtues; and will find upon a review of their conduct, so many humiliating occasions of self-condemnation, as cannot fail of rendering them firm and inaccessible against the dangerous approaches of adulation. It was, from this just sense of human imperfections, that *Alexander* used to say, his animal appetites, together with his constantly standing in need of being *repaired* by sleep, were two circumstances (*to which we may add a third from this Epistle*) that sufficiently secured him from the flattery of those base courtiers, who endeavoured to persuade him *he was more than man*. Plut. ib. N.

(*k*) Q. Curtius, l. viii.—*Arrian* says, he was wounded (in malleolo pedis) in the *ankle*. *Curtius*, (in surâ) in *the calf*.

(*l*) See Epp. 9. 31. 68. 71. *Lips.* Manud. iii. 14.

(*m*) *Sen.* de Ira. iii. 6. *Lucan* ii. 269,

Fulminibus propior terræ succenditur aër,
Imaque telluris ventos, tractusque coruscos
Flammarum accipiunt: nubes excedit Olympus
Lege Deûm. Minimas rerum discordia turbat,
Pacem summa tenent.———

So in eternal steady motion, roll
The radiant spheres around the starry pole:
Fierce lightnings, meteors, and the winter's storm,
Earth and the lower face of heav'n deform,
Whilst all by nature's laws is calm above;
No tempest rages in the court of Jove.——Rowe.

EPISTLE LX.

On vulgar Wishes and Luxury. *

I COMPLAIN, I wrangle, I am quite angry. Do you still wish, *Lucilius*, for what your nurse, or your tutor, or a fond mother wished for you? Alas! you know not what evils they pray'd for; how inimical to our peace and happiness are the wishes of our friends; and the more so,

 when

when they happily ſucceed *(a)*? I do not at all wonder, that all manner of evils attend us from our very childhood. We grow up, under the *involuntary* curſes of our parents.

Let the gods at length hear our diſintereſted prayer *(b)*: how long muſt we importune them for ſomething *extraordinary*, for our ſupport? How long ſhall we fill all the fields around our great cities with tillage? How long muſt a whole province mow for us? How long ſhall a fleet of ſhips, from more than one ſea, be ſcarce ſufficient to ſupply the table of one man? The ox is ſatisfied with the paſture of a few acres: one foreſt ſufficeth for the maintenance of many elephants: but men muſt be pamper'd with the produce both of ſea and land.—Hath nature then given us ſuch an inſatiable paunch, with ſo ſmall a body, that we ſhould ſurpaſs the greedineſs of the largeſt and moſt voracious animals? No: for how little falls to the ſhare of nature! and indeed ſhe requires but little. It is not the hunger of the belly, that puts us to this expence, but ambition, pride and luxury. Theſe belly-mongers, therefore, as *Salluſt* ſays *(c)*, let us rank among the number of beaſts not of men; and ſome of them not even among animals; but among the dead. *That* man only lives who is employ'd in ſome uſeful exerciſe: ſuch as conceal themſelves in indolence, make a grave of their home: you may very juſtly fix an inſcription in marble over their doors; *(hic ſitus eſt—)* for they have foreſtalled their own death.

ANNOTATIONS, &c.

* This Epiſtle and the two following *Muretus* ſuppoſes not to be entire, but only mere fragments of Epiſtles. *Lipſius* on the contrary thinks them entire, and looks upon them as certain thoughts or reveries of *Seneca*, which he was pleaſed to publiſh under the title of Epiſtles. And, ſurely, as far as they go, they are equal to the reſt.

(a) ——— Pauci dignoſcere poſſunt
Vera bona, atque illis multum diverſa, remotâ
Erroris nebulâ. Quid enim ratione timemus
Aut cupimus? Quid tam dextro pede concipis, ut te
Conatûs non pœniteat votique peracti?
Evertêre domos totas *optantibus* ipſis
Dii faciles.—*Juv.* x. 3. (f. operantibus.)

Look round the habitable world; how few
Know their own good, or knowing it pursue!
How void of reason are our hopes and fears!
What in the conduct of our lives appears,
So well design'd, so luckily begun;
But when we have our wish, we wish undone?
Whole houses of their whole desire possest,
Are often ruin'd at their own request. Dryden.

(*b*) —— Si consilium vis
Permittes ipsis expendere numinibus, quid
Conveniat nobis, rebusque sit utile nostris.
Nam pro jucundis aptissima quæque dabunt Dii.
Carior est illis homo, quam sibi. *Juv.* x. 346.

Receive my counsel, (and your wisdom prove)
Intrust thy fortune to the powers above:
Leave them to manage for thee, and to grant
What their unerring wisdom sees thee want.
In goodness as in greatness they excell;
O that we lov'd ourselves but half so well! Dryden.

And what says St. *Peter* in this respect? *Humble yourselves therefore under the mighty hand of God, that he may exalt you in due time, casting your care upon him, for he careth for you.* i. Pet. v. 6. See also Ps. lv. 22. Matth. vi. 25. Sam. iv. 10.

(*c*) Omnes homines qui sese student præstare cæteris animalibus summâ ope niti decet. Ne vitam silentio transeant, veluti pecora, quæ natura prona, atque ventri obedientia finxit. *Sall.* Bel. Civ. *It is necessary for all men, who would fain excel other animals, strenuously to avoid passing their lives in obscurity and silence, ever groveling and intent upon their food.* For *they that are such serve not our Lord* Jesus Christ, *but their own belly.* Rom. xvi. 18. *Whose God is their belly; whose end is destruction.* Phil. iii. 19. See the foregoing verse.

(*d*) See Ep. 55.

EPISTLE LXI.

On Old Age and Death.

LET us no longer indulge the will. I follow this maxim, *Lucilius*, that, now being old, I may not seem to hanker after those things which pleased me when I was a boy (*a*). Night and day this is my task, at least this is my intention; to reform every evil way. And this I do, that one day may be as a whole life; not that I indeed take it for my last; but look upon it, as what possibly may prove so. In such a disposition of mind, I now write this epistle to you, as if death was to call upon me before I had finished it. Be it so; I am ready to attend him; and therefore truly enjoy life; because it is of little concern to me, how far death is off.—Before old age, my study and care was to live well; and now in old age, it is to die well; but to die well, is to die willingly.

Endeavour, *Lucilius*, to bring yourself to such a pass, as to do and suffer nothing unwillingly: *what must be, must be:* necessity is applicable to one that maketh resistance, not to the willing: there is no necessity, where the will submits: he that willingly receives a command, takes off the severest part of servitude, *viz.* the doing that which he would not: it is not obedience to a command, that makes a man miserable, but repugnancy. Therefore let us so compose the mind, that whatever exigence happens, we may meet it willingly; and especially let us think on our latter end without regret or sorrow (*b*). We must provide for death sooner than life: life is sufficiently provided for; but we are still greedy of further means: something seems still to be wanting, and will ever seem so: it is not in the power of days or years to satisfy us with life (*c*); this depends upon the disposition of the mind. I have lived, dearest *Lucilius*, *enough*, and to my satisfaction: and now, satiated, as it were, with life, I expect, and with calm resignation, *wait for death*.

ANNOTATIONS, &c.

(*a*) So St. *Paul*; *When I was a child, I spake as a child, I understood as a child, I thought as a child; but when I became a man I put away childish things.* 1 Cor. 13, 11.

(*b*) *O that they were wise, that they understood this, that they would consider their latter-end!*— Deut. xxxii. 29.

(*c*)
Sed omnia perfructus vitai præmia, marces:
Sed quia semper aves quod abest, præsentia temnis:
Imperfecta tibi elapsa est, ingrataque vita,
Et nec-opinanti mors ad caput adstitit ante
Quàm Satur, ac plenus possis discedere rerum. Lucr. iii. 970.

If old, thou hast enjoy'd the mighty store
Of gay delights, and now canst taste no more.

But

But yet, becauſe you ſtill deſir'd to meet
The abſent, and contemn'd the preſent ſweet,
Death ſeems unwelcome, and thy race half run;
The courſe of life ſeems ended when begun:
And unexpected haſty death deſtroys,
Before the greedy mind is full of joys. Creech.

Inde fit ut raro, qui ſe vixiſſe beatum
Dicat, et exacto contentus tempore vitæ
Cedat, *uti* conviva ſatur, reperire queamus. Hor. Sat. I. 1. 117.

From hence how few, like ſated gueſts, depart
From life's full banquet with a chearful heart? Francis.

Who adds by way of Note, "Perhaps our poet had in view an expreſſion of *Ariſtotle, we ſhould "go out of life, as we ought to riſe from a banquet, neither thirſty nor full of wine.*" See Ep. 30. N. h. i.)

EPISTLE LXII.

On Buſineſs and Study.

THEY talk at random, *Lucilius*, who ſay, that a multiplicily of affairs prevents their application to the liberal arts: they only pretend to buſineſs, or encreaſe it voluntarily, by continually making buſineſs for themſelves. But I am happily diſcharged, my *Lucilius*; I am quite at leiſure; and be where I will, I am my own maſter: for I give not myſelf up to common affairs, but attend them occaſionally: I hunt not after excuſes for loſing my time: and wherever my ſituation is, there I continually exerciſe my meditations, and reflect upon ſomewhat that may prove ſalutary to the mind. When I join my friends, I am not the more abſent from myſelf: nor do I tarry long with thoſe, whom I chance to meet at any time, or whom duty obliges me to attend. I am with all good men: theſe I make my companions in whatever place, or in whatever age they live. I always carry *Demetrius*, beſt of men, along with me; and leaving thoſe that are array'd in purple, I converſe with him half-naked, as he is, and admire him. Why ſhould I not? I ſaw that he wanted nothing.

Any

Any one may *despise* all things; but no one can *have* all things. The shortest way to riches then, is to despise them (*a*). But our *Demetrius* lives so, not as if he despised all things, but as if (*being a King or master of them*) he grudged not others the use of them.

ANNOTATIONS, &c.

(*a*) See Ep. 73. (N. b.)

EPISTLE LXIII.

Consolatory on the Death of a Friend.

I AM sorry to hear, that your friend *Flaccus* is dead; but would not have you afflict yourself, *Lucilius*, beyond measure: I dare not require of you not to grieve at all; tho' I think it would be better: but who is master of such firmness of mind, except the man, who is greatly superior to the power of fortune? And even such a one cannot but be pinched by such an accident, but then it will be no more than a pinch. Fears are very excusable, if they run not down immoderately, and we endeavour ourselves to suppress them: our eyes ought not to be dry on the death of a dear friend; neither should they stream; 'tis decent to weep, but useless to bewail. You may perhaps think this a hard injunction; but remember, that the prince of the Greek poets, allows, as it were, but one day for a flow of grief (*a*), and says that even *Niobe* bethought herself of food (*b*).

But from whence come lamentations and immoderate wailings! why, by tears we endeavour to express our loss; but, we *persevere* in grief only

only to make the more ſhew of it. No one thus ſorrows to himſelf (*c*). O wretched folly! there is even ambition and vanity in grief. What? then you ſay, "*Shall I forget my friend?* "Truly, the remembrance of him, which you propoſe, will be but ſhort, if it laſts no longer than your apparent grief: for ſome occurrence, or other, will ſoon change the contracted brow into a ſmile; nor do I think it will require much longer time, ere the loſs will in ſome meaſure be forgot; and the ſevereſt ſorrows ſubſide: as ſoon as ever you ceaſe to be a ſpy upon yourſelf, that ſhew of ſorrow will be no more: you are now the keeper of your ſorrow, but know, that it often eſcapes from its keeper; and generally, the more violent it is, the ſooner. Let us endeavour to make the remembrance of a loſt friend as eaſy and agreeable as poſſible: no one returns willingly to that, which he cannot reflect upon without great pain: but if it needs muſt be, that we cannot hear the name of thoſe whom we loved and have loſt, without a certain pang of affliction, it is ſtill ſuch a pang as is not always deſtitute of pleaſure: for, as our *Attalus* was wont to ſay, "the remembrance of a departed friend hath ſomething grateful "in it; as ſome fruits have a pleaſing tartneſs; or as in old wine the "bitterneſs is not diſreliſhed: it is but for a while, when all that was "diſagreeable goes off, and pure pleaſure reviſits its habitation." If then we believe *Attalus*, to think our friends ſafe and well, is to feed on cakes and honey; but the remembrance of them, when gone, however ſweet, is intermixed with a certain acid. Be it ſo: who knows not that acids and bitters whet the appetite? I beg leave however to differ from him in opinion: to me the remembrance of a friend is altogether pleaſant and agreeable: I enjoyed them while living, as if I was one day to loſe them: and I parted from them as if I ſtill enjoy'd them in contemplation, *(or was to meet them again)*.

Act then, my *Lucilius*, as becomes your diſcretion; put not a bad conſtruction on the favours of fortune: ſhe hath taken away, but ſhe firſt gave. Let us therefore the more eagerly enjoy our friends while we may; becauſe it is uncertain how long it will be in our power. Conſider too how often we muſt leave them, being oblig'd, ſuppoſe, to take a long journey; nay, that even dwelling in the neighbourhood we muſt be often abſent from them; ſo that we loſe them alſo while among the living. But can you bear the mockery of thoſe, who, having before treated their friends with great neglect, now bewail them moſt miſerably; or who pretended not to have any love for a friend before they have loſt him? Then indeed they mourn bitterly; being afraid it ſhould be doubted, whether they loved or no: but methinks they give too late proof of their affection. Beſides, if we have other friends remaining, we pay them but an indifferent compliment, in diſcovering, that they cannot make up, and comfort us, for the loſs of one; if we have none, we have more reaſon to complain of ourſelves, than of fortune; ſhe hath taken one from us; and we would not be at the pains of a recruit. Again, it is to be doubted if he truly loved *one*, who could not love more than one *(d)*: if a man who was robbed of his only coat, ſhould chuſe to ſit down, and weep, rather than look about him for ſomewhat to cover his ſhoulders, and keep off the cold; would you not take him for a fool? You have loſt one friend; look out for another: it is much better ſo to repair your loſs, than to ſit down and weep.

I know, that what I am going to ſay, is trite and common, I ſhall not however paſs it by. Time generally puts an end to grief, where a man will not do it intentionally: but nothing can be more ſcandalous in a prudent man, than to expect a remedy for grief in being tired of it: I had much rather that you ſhould leave grief, than that grief ſhould leave you: deſiſt then as ſoon as poſſible from that, which, if you would, you cannot go on with much longer. Our anceſtors allowed women to mourn a year; not that they were obliged to mourn ſo long, but no longer: but I do not find there was any time fixed for the mourning of men: for the leſs they mourn, the better. But where will you point me out a widow (even from among thoſe whom you could not pull away from the corpſe, and ſcarce keep from leaping upon the funeral pile) who hath ſhed tears above a month? Nothing creates diſguſt ſooner than grief; while freſh and decent indeed, it meets with abettors and comforters; but when extravagant, and of long duration, it is to be laughed at; for it is either feigned or ridiculous.

Even

Even I, who write this to you, mourned ſo immoderately for my deareſt relation, *Annæus Serenus (f)*, that (even againſt my will) I may juſtly be number'd among thoſe, who have been overcome with grief. But I now condemn myſelf for it; and underſtand that the principal cauſe of my mourning ſo bitterly, was, that I never reflected on the poſſibility of his dying before me: I thought of nothing more, than his being younger, indeed much younger than myſelf; as if the deſtinies regarded the order of our birth. Let us therefore continually reflect upon our own, as well as upon the mortality of thoſe we love. I ſhould have ſaid, "my *Serenus* is younger than myſelf; and what then? He "ought in the courſe of nature to die after me, but may chance to die "before me." Having made no ſuch reflection as this,—fortune ſurprized me, and ſtruck me unprepared. But now, I think all things mortal; mortal without any reſtriction: whatever may happen at any time, may happen this very day. Let us conſider therefore, my deareſt *Lucilius*, that *we* ſoon muſt be, what he is, whom we now bewail: and perhaps (if the opinion and report of ſome wiſe men be true, that there is a *place prepared for our reception hereafter)* he, whom we fondly imagined to have periſhed, is ſent before us to that happy manſion *(g)*.

ANNOTATIONS, &c.

(*a*) Hom. Il. τ. 228. Where *Ulyſſes* endeavours to reſtrain the immoderate grief of *Achilles*, on the death of *Patroclus*:

Αλλὰ χ'ρη τὸν μὲν καταθάπτειν ὅς κε θάνῃσι
Νηλέα θυμὸν ἔχοντας, ἐπ' ἤματι δακρύσαντας.
Eternal ſorrows what avails to ſhed?
Greece honours not with ſolemn faſts the dead:
Enough, when death demands the dead, to pay
The tribute of a melancholy day. Pope.

(*b*) Hom. Il. ω. 601. where *Achilles*, to comfort the good old King *Priam*, when he comes to beg the corpſe of his ſon *Hector*, reminds him of the well known hiſtory of *Niobe*.

——— Νῦν δὲ μνησώμεθα δόρπου·
Καὶ γάρ τ' ἠΰκομος Νιόβη ἐμνήσατο σίτου,
Τῇ περ δώδεκα παῖδες ἐνὶ μεγάροισιν ὄλοντο ———
——— *But now the peaceful hours of ſacred night*
Demand reflection, and to reſt invite.
Nor thou, O father, thus conſum'd with woe,
The common cares that nouriſh life forego.

Not thus did Niobe, *of form divine,*
A parent once, whose sorrows equall'd thine;
Six youthful sons, as many blooming maids,
In one sad day beheld the Stygian shades. Pope.

But how much more interesting and to the purpose is that admirable description of David's lamentation for his child?—*Then said his servants unto* David, *what thing is this that thou hast done? Thou didst fast and weep for the child while it was alive, but when the child was dead, thou didst rise and* eat bread! *And he said, while the child was yet alive, I fasted and wept, for I said who can tell whether God will be gracious to me, that the child may live? But now he is dead, wherefore should I fast?* Can *I bring him back again?* I shall go to him, *but he cannot return to me.* ii Sam. 21. See the last Note.

(*c*) Nemo tristis sibi.—Thus *Martial.*

Amissum non flet, cum *sola* est Gellia patrem;
Si quis adest, jussæ prosiliunt lacrymæ:
Non dolet hic, quisquis laudari, Gellia quærit;
Ille dolet verè, qui sine teste dolet.

Gellia, *not even her father mourns, alone;*
When seen, the ready tears run trickling down:
They mourn not, who in wish'd-for praise succeed;
Who weeps without a witness, weeps indeed. M.

(*d*) Because friendship is a social virtue, not so confined as true affection between the sexes. Et quoniam res humanæ fragiles caducæque sunt, &c. *Cic.* Læl. ad fin. "And since man holds all his possessions by a very precarious tenure, we should endeavour, as our friends drop off, to repair their loss by new acquisitions, lest one should be so unhappy as to stand, in his old age, a solitary, unconnected individual, bereaved of every person whom he loves and by whom he is beloved: for without a proper and particular object upon which to exercise the kind and benevolent affections, life is destitute of every enjoyment that can render it justly desirable." *Melm.* Fitzosborn's Lett.

(*e*) A year, i. e. the old year of *Romulus*, or the space of ten months: for when *Numa* afterwards added two months more, he did not alter the time he had before settled for mourning; which was also the time appointed unto widows to lament the loss of their deceased husbands; before the expiration of which time, they could not decently marry again. *Plut.* in vitâ Numæ. *Brisson.* de jure Connub. l. 10.

(*f*) To whom *Seneca* inscribed his treatise *on Tranquillity.* He was *Præfectus Vigilum*, an officer somewhat like our *high-constable*, but of more authority. He died, with some other great men of his time, by eating mushrooms. *Plin.* l. 22.

(*g*) *Solonis* quidem sapientis elogium est, quo se negat velle suam mortem dolore amicorum et lamentis vacare. Vult, credo, se esse carum suis sed haud scio un melius *Ennius*,

Nemo me lacrymis decoret, neque funera fletu
Faxit——

Non censet lugendam esse mortem quam immortalitas consequatur. *Cic.* (de Sen.) It is natural, I confess, (*with Solon*) *to desire to be remembered with regret by our particular friends; but I am inclined to give the preference to the sentiment of* Ennius:

Nor loud lament nor silent tear deplore
The fate of Ennius, *when he breathes no more.*

In the poet's estimation, Death, which opens the way to immortality, is by no means a subject of reasonable lamentation. Melmoth.

"Under

" Under the influence of ſuch a perſuaſion to indulge unreſtrained grief, would be a proof, not of a generous affection to one's friend, but of too intereſted a concern for one's ſelf. *Id.* And again, to bewail an event attended with ſuch advantageous circumſtances, would, I fear, have more the appearance of envy than of friendſhip. *Id.*

However, with regard to two real friends, I will venture to affirm, that in deſpite of death, they muſt both continue to exiſt, ſo long as either of them ſhall remain alive; for the deceaſed may, in a certain ſenſe be ſaid ſtill to live; whoſe memory is preſerved with the higheſt veneration, and the moſt tender regret in the boſom of the ſurvivor; a circumſtance which renders the former happy in death, and the latter honour'd in life." *Id.*

Socrates ſteadily and firmly aſſerted, that the human ſoul is a divine and immortal ſubſtance; that death opens a way for its return to the celeſtial manſions; and that the ſpirits of thoſe *juſt* men, who have made the greateſt progreſs in virtue, find the eaſieſt and moſt expeditious admittance. This was alſo the opinion of my departed friend, *Scipio Africanus.* Cic. de Amic. Somn. Scip. *Id.* Cato, N. 86.

The ſouls of the righteous are in the hand of God; and no torment ſhall touch them. In the ſight of the *unwiſe, they ſeemed to die, and their departure is taken for miſery, and their going from us to be utter deſtruction*; but they are in peace. *Wiſd.* iii. 1.

In my father's houſe (ſaith our Saviour) *are many manſions*; *I go to prepare* a place for you; I will come *again, and receive you to myſelf, that where I am, ye may be alſo.* John xiv. 2.

But ye are come (and have acceſs by the New Covenant as fellow citizens, and members of the ſame ſociety) *unto the* (celeſtial) *mount* Sion; *and unto the city of the living God, the heavenly* Jeruſalem, *and to an innumerable company of angels, and to the general aſſembly and church of the firſt-born, which are written* (and enrolled) *in heaven, and to* (the throne of) *God, the judge of all, and to the ſpirits of juſt men made perfect.* Heb. xii. 22. *See* Epp. 54. (N. d.) 65. (N. g.) Lipſ. Phyſiol. iii. 11, 14.

EPISTLE LXIV.

On Authors; eſpecially Qu. Sextius; *and the Reſpect due to great Men.*

YOU was yeſterday with us. If I had ſaid only *yeſterday, Lucilius*; you might complain; and therefore I added *with us*; for with me you are always. Some friends came in; ſuch, as for whom we generally make a larger fire; not like that, which ſmokes from the kitchen of the

the wealthy, and is wont to ſcare the watchmen; but a middling one; enough to ſhew that I had company. Our converſation turned upon various topics, bringing nothing to a point, but tranſultory from one thing to another, as it generally happens in a mix'd aſſembly. At length it was agreed upon, to read a treatiſe, wrote by *Qu. Sextius, (a)* the father; believe me, a great man, and, let who will deny it, a *ſtoic*. Good Gods! how full of energy, and ſpirit! ſuch as you will ſcarce find in the whole tribe of philoſophers: ſome of their writings indeed have a great name, but in all other reſpects are weak and languid, in compariſon. They propoſe; they debate; they cavil. They inſpire us not, with courage and conſtancy, becauſe they have them not themſelves. Whereas when you read *Sextius*; you will ſay, *this man is alive, he exults, he is free, he is ſomewhat more than man:* he ſends me away full of conviction and confidence: whatever diſpoſition of mind I am in, when I read him, (I will own to you) I am ready to defy all accidents, and to cry out; *why do you loiter, fortune? Come on; you ſee, I am prepared:* for I wrap myſelf in a mind like his, which ſeeks an opportunity to try its ſtrength, and diſplay its valour.

Spumentemque dari pecora inter inertia votis
Optat aprum, aut fulvum deſcendere monte leonem *(b)*.

I long, methinks, to have ſomething for cauſe of triumph, in the exerciſe of patience. For this excellency likewiſe hath *Sextius*; he ſets before you the tranſcendency of a happy life, and gives you hopes of obtaining it. He placeth it indeed on high, yet ſhews it to be attainable by a willing mind: and virtue herſelf will teach you, not only to be charm'd with ſuch a life, but to hope for it *(c)*.

For my own part nothing takes up more of my time, than this contemplation of wiſdom. I look upon it with admiration and ſurprize, as on the world itſelf; which I often behold with wondring eyes, as if juſt entered upon the wide ſcene, and I now firſt ſaw the heavens. On this account I venerate the diſcoveries of wiſdom, and not leſs the ingenious diſcoverers: it delights me, as if entering on a large eſtate: ſuch are the acquiſitions prepared for me; ſuch the fruits of their labour. But let us act herein like a diſcreet houſholder: let us continually im-

4 prove

prove what we have got; that our posterity may be ſtill oblig'd to *us* for an acceſſion. Much remains to be done; and will ſtill remain: Nor will any one, born a thouſand generations hence, be precluded an opportunity of ſtill making ſome improvement. And what if the ancients may be ſaid to have found out every thing? yet the application, the knowledge, and the right ordering of ſuch their diſcoveries will ever be new.

Suppoſe certain remedies had been found out for every complaint in the eye: there would be no occaſion indeed to ſearch for more; but diligence muſt be uſed in adapting theſe to the ſeveral diſorders and as the occaſion may require. If the eye lack moiſture, it is to be ſupplied by one method; by another, the eye-lids, when too thick, are to be attenuated; by another, a ſudden flux, or humour is reſtrained; by another, the ſight is ſharpen'd; now, the remedies muſt firſt be properly prepared; and the time for the application of each, in their reſpective caſes, muſt be obſerv'd. So, the ancients have found out proper remedies, for the ſeveral maladies of the mind, but how they are to be applied, and when, it is the buſineſs of the party concern'd to enquire.

They who have gone before us have done a great deal, but not finiſhed the work: however, they are to be admired, and reverenced as Gods *(d)*. Why ſhould I not keep by me the ſtatues and pictures of great men, as ſo many remembrancers, and even celebrate their birth days? Why ſhould I not always mention them with honour? The ſame veneration that I owe my own tutors, I owe to theſe, the tutors of mankind; from whom the beginnings of ſo great good have been derived to us. If I meet a Conſul or a Prætor, I will ſhew him all the ſigns that are uſually made, in token of honour and reſpect: I will alight from my horſe *(e)*; I will pull off my bonnet; I will give him the way. And ſhall I not think upon the two *Cato's*, *Lælius* the wiſe, *Socrates* the good, *Plato*, *Zeno*, and *Cleanthes* with the utmoſt veneration? Yes, I will always reverence them and riſe up at the bare mention of ſuch great names.

ANNO-

ANNOTATIONS, &c.

(*a*) See Ep. 59. (N. d.) Lipf. Manud. l. 6.

(*b*) Virg. Æn. IV. 158.

Impatient he views the feeble prey,
Wishing some noble beast to cross the way;
And rather would the tusky boar attend,
Or see the tawny lion downward bend. Dryden.

(*c*) You will do right, says *Lipsius*, if you ascribe the whole of this description (of *Sextius*) to *Seneca* himself; for a truer picture of him cannot be drawn.

(*d*) Lucret. V. 52.——Nonne licebit

Hunc hominem * numero Divûm dignarier esse.
Therefore the man who thus reform'd our souls,
Who slew these monsters, not by arms, but rules;
Shall we, ungrateful we, not think a God? Creech.

* Either *Pythagoras*, or, (according to *Lactantius*) *Thales*.

(*e*) When the son of *Fabius* was chosen consul (A. U. C. 743) his father, by reason of age and infirmity, and perhaps from a design to try his son, came up to him on horseback; whereupon the young consul ordered him to alight, if he had any business with him. This infinitely pleased the old general; and though the standers-by seemed offended at the imperiousness of the son's behaviour towards a father, so venerable for his age and authority, yet he instantly alighted from his horse, and embraced his son with open arms, telling him, "Now, thou art my son indeed, since thou under-"standest the authority with which thou art invested, and well knowest whom thou art to command." *Plutarch. Livy, Val. Max.*

And it is reported of *Pompey*, that he, in like manner, commanded (by one of his lictors) *Tigranes*, King of *Armenia*, to alight from his horse, before he would permit him to speak to him. *Dion.* l. 36. See *Lips. Elect.* l. i. c. 23.

(*f*) Adeperiam caput] *I will uncover my head*; i. e. supposing it to be covered, either with the petasus, *broad-brimmed hat*, seldom or never wore but upon a journey; or the pileus, *a cap*, allowed to slaves (when made free, and their heads had been close shaved) as a defence from the cold, and as a badge of their liberty; and to other persons under some indisposition; or with lacinia togæ, *the lappet of their gown*; and this was not a constant cover, but only occasional, to avoid the rain, or sun, or other accidental inconveniencies. Hence it is that we see none of the ancient statues with any covering on their heads, except perhaps a wreath, or something of the like nature. *See* Lips. de Amphitheat. c. 20. *Potter's* Rom. Antiq. p. 320.

EPISTLE LXV.

On the First Cause.

YESTERDAY, my *Lucilius*, my day was divided between ſickneſs and ſelf-enjoyment: the former took poſſeſſion of the forenoon, and happily reſign'd the afternoon to the latter. I endeavour'd therefore to amuſe the mind with reading: this done, as I grew ſtronger, I impoſed a harder taſk upon it, and ſpurred it on: I ſat down to write, and indeed with more earneſtneſs than uſual, as when I undertake ſome knotty point and am reſolved to maſter it: but ſome friends coming in they laid a reſtraint upon me, and compell'd me as a ſick man, that knows not what is good for himſelf, to lay aſide the pen. We then fell into diſcourſe; part of which, ſtill under debate, I ſhall here ſend you; we have choſen you our umpire; and have cut out more work for you, I believe, than you imagine.

There are three different opinions relating to *Cauſe (a)*. I. Our ſtoics, you know, ſay there are two things from whence all other are derived; *viz. Cauſe*, and *matter (b): matter* lies inert, and helpleſs, ready for all purpoſes; but for ever continuing in the ſame ſtate, if not put into motion. *Cauſe*, i. e. Reaſon, *(c)* gives a certain form to matter, and ſhapes it at pleaſure: from whence proceed all the various works of nature: there muſt be ſomething therefore from whence a thing is made, and ſomething by which it is made: *this* they call *cauſe*; the other *matter*. Every art is an imitation of nature. What I have ſaid therefore of the univerſe, transfer to the works of man. A ſtatue, for inſtance, requires both *matter*, capable of being work'd upon, and an artiſt to give it form: therefore in a ſtatue braſs is the *matter:* and the ſtatuary the *cauſe*. The ſame is the condition of all things; foraſmuch as they conſiſt, or have their eſſence, from *that whereof* they are made and *that by which* they are made. The ſtoics then allow but of this one *cauſe*, *the* efficient, or that which makes a thing what it is.

II. *Ariſtotle* divides *cauſe* into three ſorts, (the *material*, the *efficient* and the *formal*). The *firſt*, ſays he, is *matter* itſelf, without which nothing can be made: the *ſecond*, is the *maker*; the *third*, the form, which is annexed to any work whatever, as, ſuppoſe, a ſtatue; and this he calls *Idos:* to theſe he adds a fourth, (called the *final*, or) the end, and deſign of the whole work.—Now to explain theſe; braſs is the *firſt cauſe* of a ſtatue, for it could never have been made, if there had not been that whereon to found, or give it being. The *ſecond cauſe* is the *workman*; for this braſs could never have been faſhioned into a ſtatue, had it not fallen into the hands of a ſkilful artiſt. *The third cauſe*, is the *form*; for it could not have been ſaid to be the ſtatue of a *doryphorus* (a *life-guard-man)* or a *diadumenos* (a King, or a Prince, wearing a diadem) if ſuch an appearance or form had not been given to it. The *fourth cauſe* is the *deſign* in making it; for without this it had not been made what it is: what then is *deſign?* Why, that which inviteth the artiſt, and which he conſtantly has in view in the proſecution of his work: whether it be money, if the artiſt intends what he makes for ſale; or glory, if he works for reputation; or devotion and piety, if he deſign'd it for a gift to ſome temple; therefore this alſo is a *cauſe*, whatever it be, for which a thing is made and without which it had not been made.

III. *Plato* adds a fifth to theſe, *the exemplar*, or what he calls an *Idea (d):* for it is by the obſervance of this, that an artiſt forms whatever he hath determined to form. Now it matters not, whether this exemplar be any thing *without*, whereon he may fix his eye, or only what he hath conceived and planned in his mind. The exemplars of all things in the world, God hath in himſelf: he comprehends in his omniſcient *mind*, the number and faſhion of all things that have been or ſhall be made; it is even full of theſe reſemblances which *Plato* calls *Ideas*, immortal, immutable, indefatigable. There are therefore, according to *Plato*, *five cauſes (e)*; that *from* which a thing is; that *by* which it is; that *whereby* it is what it is: that *for* which it is; that *according* to which it is: laſtly, that which conſiſts of all theſe: as in a ſtatue (for that is what we have choſe to exemplify our meaning by) that

that *from* which it is, is the braſs; that *by* which it is, is the artiſt; that *whereby* it is what it is, is the form; that *for* which it is, is the deſign of the maker; that *according* to which it is, is the exemplar; and ſo from all theſe is formed a ſtatue. And all theſe *Plato* applies to the great world: the maker, ſays he, is *God*; from what it is made, *matter*; the *form*, is the diſpoſition and order of things, viſible therein; the *exemplar*, that according to which God formed the immenſity of this moſt beautiful work; the *end*, that for which it was made; do you aſk, what end God could propoſe therein? To diſplay his goodneſs. For truly thus ſpeaks *Plato:* " what was the cauſe of God's making " the world? He is good; and all that he hath made is good; and being " good, he cannot envy any good to his creatures; and therefore he hath " made the world in its beſt faſhion; and furniſhed it in the beſt manner poſſible *(f)*. "

Now judge you, *Lucilius*, and give us your opinion; who ſeems to ſpeak with moſt probability, not who ſpeaks the exact truth; for that is as much above us, (in this our infirm ſtate,) as truth itſelf. In my humble opinion, the group of cauſes, as here collected by *Ariſtotle* and *Plato*, comprehends either too much, or too little: for if that is to be reckoned *a cauſe*, without which a thing cannot be made what it is; they have ſaid too little; becauſe they muſt reckon *time* a cauſe, ſeeing that without *time* nothing can be made. They muſt reckon *place*; for if there was not a *ſomewhere* for a thing to be, it could not be at all: they muſt reckon *motion*; for without this, nothing could either be formed, or come to decay: without *motion*, there can be no art, no change. But we are enquiring after one firſt and general cauſe: now, this ought to be ſimple, as matter is ſimple; what then is this firſt cauſe? Why, *active wiſdom*, i, e, GOD; ſo that there are not many, and particular *cauſes*, but one, upon which all other depend, and that is, *the efficient*. You will ſay, perhaps, *form* is a *cauſe*, being that which the artiſt adapts to his work; no; it is a *part*, but not a *cauſe:* the *exemplar* likewiſe is not a *cauſe*; but the neceſſary means to a *cauſe*; it is as neceſſary to the artiſt, as his chiſel or his file; without theſe art could not carry on the work; yet they are not part nor cauſes of the art itſelf.—But the *deſign*

Hh 2 for

for which an artist sets about any work, is said to be a *cause*: be it so; it is not however the *efficient*, but *adventitious*; and these are innumerable; but we are enquiring after *one* general cause. This also they have alledged, not according to their usual accuracy; that the whole world, and all its complete furniture is *a cause*: for, there is a wide difference between the work itself, and the cause of it. Either then, give us your opinion, *Lucilius*; or what is much easier in these cases, deny that it is in your power; being not quite clear in the matter; and so dismiss, and leave us to ourselves.

But why, you say, do I delight to spend my time in these futile enquiries, which check not any fond desire, nor drive from the bosom an irregular passion? Truly, I employ myself on these subjects in order to settle my mind, and fix my attention: I first pry into, and examine myself, and then turn my thoughts to the vast world: nor in this employ do I lose my time as you imagine: for all these things if they are not minced too minutely, and spun out in vain and useless subtilties, mightily raise and refresh the soul; which being heavily pressed down by its usual burthen, desires to be at large and to return thither, from whence it was taken. For this body is the load, and punishment of the soul: the soul perpetually labours under the weight of it; it is actually in bonds (*g*), till philosophy comes to its relief, permits it to breath awhile, and delight itself with the vast prospect of nature; and to transfer the affections from things below to things above; from the terrestrial to such as are *heavenly* (*h*). This is the liberty she from hence enjoys; this her pleasing flight; when she escapes from the guard that confined her here; and makes a tour to heaven. As your artificers, who have been intent upon some nice work that fatigues the eyes when they have only a dim and glimmering light in their shops; go out into the street or some open place, where the people are wont to disport themselves, and there feast the eye with the clear light of day: so the soul shut up in this sad and gloomy tabernacle, as often as it can, seeks ease and freedom, and pleasingly enjoys itself in the contemplation of the works of nature.—

The

—The wiſe man, and even the diſciple of wiſdom, remains indeed ſtill in the body, yet the better part of him frequently makes excurſions: all his thoughts are ſet upon ſublime things; and as if bound by the military oath, he looks on the gift of life as his preſent pay; and ſo reforms himſelf as to have neither love nor hatred thereto; and from hence patiently endures all that mortality is ſubject to; well knowing, that greater and more ſolid ſatisfactions are yet to come (*i*).

And would you, *Lucilius*, debar me from an inſpection into the works of nature; and confine me from a view of the *whole* to ſome ſcanty part of it? Shall I not enquire into the origin of things;--- who created the univerſe;---who firſt divided the maſs, and gave motion to inert and lifeleſs matter? Shall I not enquire, who formed this our world; by what wiſdom ſuch an immenſity of things came under rule and order; who collected the ſcattered, and ſeparated ſuch as were confuſed and blended together; and brought forth the wonderful beauty that lay concealed under one ſqualid deformity or chaos? Or, from whence ſo great light is poured all around upon us; whether it be from fire, or ſomething brighter than fire? Shall I not enquire, I ſay, after theſe things? Shall I remain for ever ignorant, whence I came; and whether I am to ſee this world but once, or often (*k*)? whether I am going, and what happy manſion waits the ſoul, when delivered from the ſervitude of the body (*l*)? Do you forbid me to concern myſelf with heaven, i. e. do you command me to live with my head ever bowed down to the earth? No; I am greater and born to nobler purpoſes, than to be the vile bondſlave of my body; which I conſider in no other light, than as the chain that deprives me of my native liberty. This body then let Fortune attack when ſhe pleaſes; ſhe cannot wound me through it: all that can ſuffer in *me* is the body: ſubject as this tabernacle is to injury, the ſoul, that dwells therein, is ſtill free. Nor ſhall this fleſh, however frail, compel me to baſe fear, or to hypocriſy, or to diſſimulation miſbecoming a good man; I would by no means ſay a falſe thing, were it to do honour to this inſignificant little body: if I think proper, I can withdraw myſelf from all fellowſhip with it; nor even now while we remain together, is our compa-

nionſhip

nionſhip upon equal terms; for the ſoul claims all dominion to herſelf; and on the contempt of the body founds her true and certain liberty.

But to return to our deſign: this inſpection into the nature of things, that I have been ſpeaking of, is what will contribute greatly to the liberty of the ſoul: foraſmuch as we learn from hence, that the univerſe conſiſts of *God* and *matter*; that God rules and governs all things, which being diſperſed around, follow Him their Ruler and their Guide. Now, the Maker, i. e. *God*, muſt be greater than the things made, i. e. *matter*, which is ever ſubject to his Almighty power. And what God is in the world, ſuch is the mind or ſoul in man; what in the world is *matter*, in us is body. Let the worſe then be ſubſervient to the better: let us be firm and ſtrong againſt accidents; let us not dread injuries, or wounds, or chains, or poverty, or death itſelf. For, what is death? It is either an end of life, or the paſſage into another; and why ſhould I fear to be no more, ſince that is the ſame as not to have been? much leſs I have reaſon to be afraid of paſſing elſewhere; for, wherever I go, I ſhall certainly be more at large than I am at preſent.

ANNOTATIONS, &c

(a) Between the *Stoics*, and *Ariſtotle*, and *Plato*.

(b) The ſame according to *Laertius*, called by *Plato*, Θεὸν καὶ ὕλην; which *Thales* calls, *Mentem* et *Aquam*. *Pythagoras*, Monas, *unio*, (mens, ſive Deus, *God)* Δυὰς, binio, (materia, *matter)* which *Lipſius* carries back to *Homer* δ. 366) under the allegorical characters of *Proteus*, and his daughter *Eidothea*, (al. *Theonomè*. Eur. al. *Eurynomè*, Zenod.) *Cicero*, Acad. Quæſt. 1. 6. Naturam dividebant (Stoici) in res duas, ut altera eſſet efficiens; altera autem quaſi huic ſe præbens, ex quâ aliquid efficeretur, &c. Explained by *Lactantius*, vii. 3. Stoici naturam in duas dividunt partes unam quæ efficiat, alteram quæ ſe ad faciendum tractabilem præſtat. Ita iſti uno naturæ nomine res diverſiſſimas comprehendèrunt, *Deum*, et *mundum*, artificem et opus, dicuntque alterum ſine altero nihil poſſe, tanquam natura ſit Deus mundo permiſtus: nam interdum ſic conſundunt, ut ſit Deus ipſa mens mundi, et mundus ſit corpus Dei. *The Stoics divide Nature into two parts*; the Maker and the thing made, i. e. *God*, and *the world*; *as if* God *was the ſoul of the world, and the* world the body of God. It were well (ſays *Leland*, l. 13.) if the abſurdity of this way of philoſophiſing were the worſt of it. But beſides that it gave occaſion to ſome of thoſe extravagant flights of the *Stoics*, ſo unbecoming dependent creatures, as if they had a divinity and ſufficiency in themſelves, which placed them in ſeveral reſpects on an equality with God (ſee Ep. 53.) this notion was made uſe of

for

for supporting Pagan idolatry, and was therefore of the most pernicious consequence to the interest of religion.

But the principal error, and what among the Greek philosophers, from the time of *Aristotle*, became the favourite opinion, was, *they all (Plato* perhaps excepted) *thought it impossible to admit the making any thing out of nothing, and consequently that* matter *was coeternal with the* eternal mind. A scheme which confounds God and the creature, and pursued to its genuine consequence is subversive of all religion and morality. But as a sufficient answer to these or the like absurd principles relating to the Deity, I shall refer the reader to the words of Mr. *Locke*, (vol. ii. p. 249.) "'Tis " an overvaluing ourselves to reduce all to the narrow measure of our capacities; and to conclude " all things impossible to be done, whose manner of doing exceeds our comprehension: this is to " make our comprehension infinite, or God finite; when what he can do is limited to what we can " conceive of it. If you do not understand the operation of your own finite mind, that *thinking* " *thing within you*, deem it not strange that ye cannot comprehend the operations of that eternal " infinite mind, who made and governs all things, and whom the heaven of heavens cannot con" tain." *Acts*, 14. 15. 24. 16. *Lips.* Physiol. l. 4. ii. 2. *Leland*, i. 280.

(c) In the language of the *Stoics*. Thus—*ad Helviam*, Quisquis formator universi fuit, sive ille Deus est potens omnium, sive incorporalis *ratio*, ingentium operum artifex, sive divinus Spiritus per omnia maxima minima, æquali intentione diffusus, &c. c. 8.—*Whoever was the maker of the universe, whether it was God omnipotent, or incorporeal* Reason, *the artificer of great works*, or the divine Spirit, pervading *all things, with equal efficiency*, &c. A remarkable passage, compared with *Genesis*, i. i. 2.

(d) Whatsoever the mind perceives in itself, or is the immediate object of perception, thought, or understanding, that I call *Idea*. Locke, vol. i. p. 97. See Ep. 57. (N. m.) *Lips.* Physiol. ii. 3.

(e) Plutarch contracts them for him into *three* (ὑφ' ὅ, ἐξ ὅ, πρὸς ὅ) the *efficient*, the *material*, and the *final*, including the *exemplary* and *formal* in the *efficient*.

(f) God saw every thing that he had made, and behold! it was very good. Gen. i. 31. *All the works of the Lord are exceeding good, and whatsoever he commandeth shall be accomplished in due season. A man need not say, what is this? wherefore is that? for he hath made all things for their uses. Good things are created from the beginning for the good; so to the sinner they are turned into evil.* Eccluf. xxxix. 16, 35.

(g) From whence *the body*, in Greek, is called ὡς δεσμὸς ὑπ' αὐτῆς τῆς ψυχῆς ἐνταῦθα κατὰ φύσιν) *as enchaining and confining the soul against its nature.* Lipf. *For we know that every creature groaneth, and bewaileth in pain together until now.* Rom. viii. 22. *For we that are in this* (ruinous earthly) *tabernacle, do groan being burthen'd therewith; not for that we would be* (utterly) *unclothed, but clothed upon,* (with our future habitation) *that* (our present) *mortality might be swallowed up of life. For we know, that if our earthly house of this tabernacle were dissolved, we have a building of God, an house, not made of hands,* eternal in the heavens. ii Cor. v. 1. 5. See Ep. 24. (N. i.)

(h) See Ep. 38. (N. r.) and the following note.

(i) Seneca again; not the *Stoic*, but the Christian, who considereth, that *our light affliction which is but for a moment, worketh for us a more exceeding, and eternal weight of glory.* ii Cor. 14, 17. See Ep. 17. 58.

(k) An sæpe? Nesciam quo iturus sim. *Vulg. Pincian.* But *Gronovius* and the antient MSS. an sæpe nascendum? quo—alluding either to (παλιγγενεσίας) the stoical doctrine of the soul, existing in a former state, or (μετεμψυχώσεως) the Pythagorean *Transmigration*; which by the way, *Lactantius* (iii. 18.) gives to the Stoics—superesse animas post mortem Pythagorici et Stoici dixerunt; easque non nasci, sed insinuari in corpora, et de aliis in alia migrare. But *Lipsius* not only doubts this, but proves

proves the contrary. (Physiol. iii. 12.) This doctrine however prevailed among our anceſtors, the *Gauls*, (as we learn from *Cæſar)* and eſpecially the Druids; whom *Lucan* thus addreſſeth:

——— Vobis auctoribus, umbræ
Non tacitas Erebi ſedes vitaſque profundi
Pallida regna petunt; regit idem ſpiritus artus
Orbe olio, longæ, canitis ſi cognita vitæ. i. 449.
If dying mortals dooms they (the Druids) *ſing aright,*
No ghoſts deſcend to dwell in dreadful night;
No parting ſouls to griſly Pluto *go,*
Nor ſink the dreary ſilent ſhades below. Rowe.

It is ſo antient a doctrine that it is diſputable, whether the Druids borrowed it from *Pythagoras*, or *Pythagoras* from them. And among the many nations who are ſaid to have held this doctrine, *Juſtin Martyr* mentions the latter Jews, according to St. Matth. xv. 16 ſome ſay, *that thou art* Elias, *and others* Jeremias, *or one of the Prophets.*

(l) Lipſius reſolves this queſtion in the words of *Seneca's* father *(Suaſor* vi.) Animus divina origine hauſtus, oneroſi corporis vinculis exſolutus, ad ſedes ſuas et cognata ſidera recurrit. *The ſoul, of divine origin, when releaſed from the bonds of this burthenſome body, returns to its native ſeat and kindred ſtars.* And from *Seneca* himſelf *(de Tranquill.* xi.) Reverti eo, unde veneris quid grave eſt? *Can it be in anywiſe grievous, to return to the place from whence you came?*

An dubium eſt habitare Deum ſub pectore noſtro
In cœlumque redire animas, cœloque venire. Manilius, l. 4.
For who can doubt that God reſides in man?
That ſouls from heav'n deſcend, and when the chain
Of life is broke, return to heav'n again!

EPISTLE LXVI.

Deformity no Hindrance to Virtue.---Whether all Good be equal.

I HAVE ſeen, after many years, *Claranus*, who was my ſchoolfellow: I need not therefore call him old. Truly he ſeems even yet in full vigour and ſtrength of mind, ſtruggling perpetually with the infirmities of his little body. For nature ſeems not to have uſed him well, in placing ſuch a ſoul in ſuch a frame; or perhaps ſhe had a mind to ſhew, that the moſt noble and happy qualities may be concealed under

der any outward ſhape whatever. But he hath ſurmounted all difficulties and diſcouragements; and from contemning himſelf, is come to contemn all other things. So that in my opinion *Virgil* ſeems miſtaken, when he ſays

Gratior eſt pulchro veniens e corpore virtus.

For ſprightly grace and equal beauty crown'd. (Dryden)

For virtue needs no foreign ornament, ſhe derives her dignity from herſelf; and conſecrates the body ſhe inhabits (*a*). The more I beheld our *Claranus*, the more comely I thought him, and as ſtraight in body as in mind. A great man may ſpring from a cottage; and a beautiful and great ſoul dwell in a deformed body. Nature ſeems to me, to have produced ſome ſuch men, in order to demonſtrate, that virtue is not confined to any particular place: could ſhe have exhibited ſouls in a naked and viſible ſtate, ſhe might have done it, but now ſhe does more; in producing them entangled, as it were, and encloſed with bodies, yet breaking through all obſtacles to the diſplay of their excellency and effects. *Claranus*, I ſuppoſe, is ſet forth as an example, whereby we may learn, that the ſoul is not polluted by the deformity of the body, but the body is adorned by the beauty of the ſoul. I had the pleaſure of his company but a few days, however we had frequent diſcourſe; and the ſubjects of our converſation I here tranſmit to you.

On the firſt day, the queſtion propoſed was, *how* all good *could be put upon an equality*, when it is generally divided into three kinds (*b*). Under this title, according to the ſtoics, ſome things are *primarily good*, as, joy, peace, and the welfare of our country: next to theſe are ſuch as originate from ſome infliction on this wretched material body; as, *patience* under pain, and torture; and *temperance*, and diſcretion in a ſevere fit of ſickneſs: the former we wiſh for abſolutely, and directly; the latter as neceſſity ſhall require. There is yet a third ſort of *good*, ſuch as, a decent gait, a ſedate countenance, and a behaviour every way ſuitable to the character of a prudent man.

Now, how can theſe things be ſaid to be equal in themſelves; when ſome of them are ſo very deſireable, and other ſo diſagreeable? To diſtinguiſh them aright, let us return to, and conſider the *firſt good*; what it is. It is a mind, or ſoul, regardful of truth; well knowing what to avoid and what to purſue; ſetting a value upon things, not according to fancy, but reaſon; intermixing herſelf with the great univerſe, and contemplating what is doing therein; intent alſo upon her own thoughts and actions; as truly great as zealous in her endeavours; alike invincible by proſperity and adverſity: ſubjecting herſelf to neither; eminently exalted above contingencies and accidents; diſplaying her beauty with gracefulneſs; and by her ſtrength her ſound diſpoſition; undiſturbed, intrepid; whom no violence can ſhake; no changes or chances can either lift up or caſt down; ſuch is the ſoul, when accompliſhed with virtue (*c*); ſuch her appearance, when, brought under one view ſhe exhibits all her charms: however, there are ſeveral ſpecies of it, diſplayed in different actions according to the different circumſtances of life, yet in herſelf ſhe is neither greater, nor leſs.

For, the ſummum bonum, or *chief good*, cannot decreaſe; nor can virtue ever recoil (*d*); however converted into different qualities, being faſhioned according to the complexion of the affair in hand; for whatever ſhe hath touched, ſhe reduceth to her own likeneſs, and paints of her own colour; ſhe decorates actions, friendſhips, and ſometimes whole families which ſhe herſelf had united and ſet in order: in ſhort, whatever ſhe hath the management of, ſhe renders amiable, conſpicuous, and worthy admiration: therefore her ſtrength, and greatneſs cannot riſe higher at one time, than at another: becauſe what is *greateſt* admits no increaſe. You can find nothing more right than what is right, more true than what is true; more temperate than what is temperate (*e*). Every virtue hath a proper mean; and a mean is a certain meaſure. Conſtancy cannot go beyond itſelf any more than juſt confidence, truth, and fidelity. Nothing can be added to that which is perfect; it was not perfect, if any thing could be added thereto: and therefore no addition can be made to virtue; if there can, it is as yet defective: ſo, what is fit and honourable admits of no acceſſion; becauſe it is of the ſame rank with the things abovementiond; as alſo what is decent, juſt, and lawful, foraſmuch as they are comprehended under certain limits.

To

To admit encreaſe, is a ſign of imperfection: *all good* falls under the ſame predicament. Public and private utility are conjoyned, and being inſeparable are alike to be commended and maintained by all. Therefore virtues are equal in themſelves, and the works of virtue (*f*), and the men converſant therein: the virtues of plants and animals, as they are mortal, frail, weak, and uncertain, riſe and fall; and therefore are not to be eſteemed of equal value: whereas human virtues are ſubject to one rule; foraſmuch as right and ſimple reaſon is one. Nothing is more divine than what is divine; nothing is more heavenly than what is heavenly. Mortal things are raiſed up and thrown down; they are worn away, and grow again; they are exhauſted, and again repleniſhed; and therefore in this their uncertain ſtate, there is an inequality: but the nature of divine things is one: and reaſon is nothing elſe but a particle of the divine ſpirit infuſed into the human body. If reaſon then be divine and no good is without reaſon; then *all good* is divine: but there is no difference between things that are divine, therefore none between things *good*; and conſequently joy and a ſtrong and ſtubborn ſufferance of fortune are equal: for, in both theſe is the ſame greatneſs of ſoul, tho' in the one it is ſomewhat free and relax; in the other intent and reſolute. For why? Do you not think, *Lucilius*, that the virtue of him who courageouſly beſiegeth a city, and of him, who endureth the miſeries of a ſiege, is equal? Great is *Scipio* who lays ſiege to, and blocketh up *Numantia*; and compels the invincible forces therein, to be their own executioners*: Great alſo is the undaunted ſpirit of the beſieged, who know no blockade, while the gate of death is open; and who expire in the arms of liberty.

Other virtues are alike, equal in themſelves (*g*), as, tranquillity, ſincerity, liberality, conſtancy, æquanimity, perſeverance: foraſmuch as in all theſe one and the ſame virtue ſubſiſts; which renders the mind firm and invariable. Is there then no difference between joy, and an inflexible endurance of pain? None, as to the virtues themſelves, tho' a great deal as to thoſe things, by which each virtue diſplays itſelf: as in the one, there is a natural remiſſion or relaxation of the mind; in the other an unnatural grief: theſe then are the means, or certain modifications, that admit a wide difference: but the virtue in both is equal: the object or circumstance alters not the virtue; as no distress or difficulty can make it worse, nor any mirth or joy make it better: either *good* therefore, as *good*, must necessarily be equal; as the virtuous man cannot behave himself better under joyous circumstances; nor if afflicted, under fortune; and two things, wherein nothing better can be done, than what is done, must be equal: for if any thing foreign or external can lessen or encrease the virtue, it ceases to be the *one good*, that is fit and honourable: and if so; there is an end of every thing that is honourable: but why? I will tell you: nothing is honourable which is done unwillingly and perforce. Every thing honourable is voluntary: now, suppose a man, idle, querulous, unsteady, timorous, he then hath lost one of the best qualities a man can have, *viz.* self-complacency: nor can any thing be honourable, that is not free: for what is in a state of fear, is in a state of slavery: every thing that is truly honourable, enjoys security and tranquillity; but if a man refuseth any thing, that is fit to be done, if he complains, if he thinks it evil or an hardship, he must necessarily be disturbed, and in great perplexity; for on the one hand a shew of what is right and fit invites him; on the other, the suspicion of evil draws him back; therefore he that is about to do a truly just and honourable action, should he meet with any opposition, he may think it an annoyance, but let him not think it an evil; let him do it willingly; every thing truly honourable, is neither done by command or compulsion: it is pure without any mixture of evil.

I know what will be objected to me here, that I would fain persuade you, *Lucilius*, that there is no difference, whether a man be in the height of decent joy, or is silent upon the rack (*h*), and has strength enough to weary out his tormentor; I might answer you in the words of *Epicurus* (*i*); a *wise man* says he, *tho' he is roasting in* Phalaris' *bull, will cry out*, it is pleasant, and does not at all concern me. Why then should you be surprized at my saying, the *good* is equal, of one rejoycing moderately at a banquet, and of another with amazing fortitude enduring torment; when (what is more incredible) *Epicurus* says, *it is pleasant to be tortured*. But here I answer as before, there is a wide difference

difference between joy and pain: were I put to my choice, I ſhould certainly deſire to enjoy the one, and eſcape the other: the one is natural, the other contrary to nature: and as long as they are conſider'd in this light, there is undoubtedly a great diſparity between them.

But when we come to conſider virtue, they are equal, both that which labours hard in a rough and that which glides along in a ſmooth path. Vexation, and pain, and whatever elſe ſeems irkſome and inconvenient, are of no conſequence; for they are ſwallow'd up in virtue. As the ſtars hide their diminiſh'd heads before the brightneſs of the ſun; ſo pains, afflictions and injuries are all cruſhed and diſſipated by the greatneſs of virtue: whenever ſhe ſhines, every thing but what borrows its ſplendor from her, diſappears; and all manner of annoyances have no more effect upon her, than a ſhower of rain upon the ſea. In confirmation of this, you may obſerve, with what earneſtneſs a *good* man will fly to do what is juſt and right; tho' the executioner ſtands in his way; and the rack and fire are before him; he will perſevere in his duty; nor will he conſider what he is about to ſuffer but what he is about to do; and will truſt himſelf to a good action, as to a friend and good man; under whoſe protection he is ſafe and happy (*k*): an honourable action, tho' attended with ſevere and painful circumſtances, will have the ſame place in his eſteem, as a good man, however poor, an exile, and pale through want and ſickneſs. Well then, ſuppoſe we, on one hand, a good man, abounding with wealth; and on the other hand, one deſtitute of every thing, but what he hath in himſelf; each of them will be equally *a good man*, however unequal in outward circumſtances.

The ſame judgment, as I have ſaid before, may be formed of things as of men: virtue is as commendable in a body that is healthful and at large, as in one that is ſickly and in priſon. Therefore even your own virtue, *Lucilius*, you will not think the more commendable, becauſe fortune hath hitherto preſerved your body, hale and ſound; than if by ſome accident it had been wounded and maimed: otherwiſe it would be judging of the maſter by the liveries of his ſervants; for all things, over which chance hath any influence, are, at beſt, but of a ſervile nature; as riches, the body, and worldly honours: they are weak, tranſitory, mortal, and of uncertain poſſeſſion; whereas the works of virtue are free, noble, and invincible; not to be admired the more, on account of being favoured by any flattering fortune; or the leſs, becauſe preſſed and oppoſed by the croſſeſt circumſtances that can happen.

What is friendſhip among men, *that* is affection with regard to things: I cannnot think you would love a rich good man, more than a poor one; nor one that is ſtrong and brawny better than one, who is lean and ſickly; therefore neither will you affect a thing that is honourable, becauſe pleaſant and eaſy, more than what is ſurrounded with trouble and difficulty: otherwiſe you will make me believe, that, of two men equally good, you will prefer him, that is ſpruce and clean, to him that is dirty and ſlovenly; and further, will rather delight in the man that is whole and ſound of limb, than in one that is lame and purblind; till by degrees your delicacy proceeds ſo far, as, of two men equally juſt and prudent, you would rather chuſe him whoſe hair is frizzled and curled, than one with a bald pate: but where virtue is equal in both, the inequality in all other reſpects will ſoon diſappear; for *that* is the principal, all other things are merely adventitious. And who, I pray, is ſo unjuſt in his judgment, and partial among his family, as to love a ſon in health, more than one that is ſick; or one that is tall and luſty, more than one who is ſhort and weak? Brutes make no diſtinction in their young, and we ſee this particularly exemplified in birds and fowl. *Ulyſſes* was in as great haſte to reach the rocky barren ſhore of *Ithaca*, as *Agamemnon* was to reach the lofty walls of *Mycenæ*. For, no one loves his country becauſe it is more ſpacious than another, but becauſe it is his own.

Now whither tends all this? Why to ſhew you that virtue looks on all her works, as her offspring, with an impartial eye; indulges them all alike; and indeed the more earneſtly, when they are in any wiſe diſtreſſed; as the love of a fond parent generally inclines to thoſe who ſtand moſt in need of pity *(l)*. Not that virtue loves ſuch her works,

works, as are afflicted and oppreſſed, the more; but only as a good and tender parent, ſhe is the more concern'd to cheriſh and comfort them.

But after all, why is not one *good* greater than another? Becauſe, if a thing be truly fit, nothing can be fitter; or plainer than what is abſolutely plain: you cannot ſay there is any difference where there is a parity; neither therefore can any thing be more juſt and honourable than what is ſtrictly juſt and honourable. If then the nature of all virtues be equal, the three kinds of good are upon an equality. From hence I ſay, to rejoice, or to grieve with moderation, is equal; nor does *that* joy excel *this* firmneſs of mind, ſtifling its groans upon the rack. The former *good* is indeed more eligible, but the latter more admirable; nevertheleſs both are equal; becauſe whatever annoyance there may be therein, it lies hid under the veil of greater good: whoever is pleaſed to think them unequal, turns away his eyes from the virtues themſelves, and beholds only the externals. True good hath always the ſame weight and meaſure; but the falſe are lighter than vanity itſelf; and, however great and ſpecious they ſeem, are, when brought to the balance, always found deceitful. Depend upon this, *Lucilius*, whatever true reaſon commends, is ſolid, is eternal: it ſtrengthens the mind, and lifts it up on high, there to remain for ever: but ſuch things as are injudiciouſly praiſed, and extolled by the opinion of the vulgar, puff up the mind with vain delight: on the other hand, thoſe things which are dreaded as evils, affect it as ſenſibly, as the apprehenſion of danger affects animals: theſe things therefore both delight and afflict the ſoul without cauſe; neither are thoſe worthy of joy, nor theſe of fear: reaſon alone is immutable; and tenacious of its opinion; for it does not ſerve but command the ſenſes. Now, reaſon is equal to reaſon, as right is to right; but all virtue is right reaſon; and if right, then equal. And as reaſon is, ſuch are its actions, and therefore all equal: being ſimilar to reaſon, they are ſimilar in themſelves: I mean all ſuch actions as are juſt and honourable: not but that there may be a great difference in them with regard to the object or circumſtance, which may be more enlarged or more confined; ſometimes illuſtrious, ſometimes ignoble; at one time appertaining to many, at another to few; yet in all theſe, the beſt or principal

cipal thing is ſtill the ſame; as of good men, all are equal as good men; (*m*) though their ages may be different, the one old, the other young; or their ſhape, the one beautiful, the other deformed; or their fortune, the one rich, the other poor; the one popular, powerful, and well known both in town and country; the other known to very few, or ſcarce known at all; but in that they are good, I ſay they are equal. The *ſenſe* is no proper judge of good and evil; it is ignorant of what may be uſeful or what not; it cannot give its opinion, but of the thing preſent; it neither forecaſts what is to come, nor remembers what is paſt: it cannot ſee to the length of a conſequence; though on this depend the order and ſeries of things, and that uniformity of life that leads to perfection.

Reaſon therefore is the ſole arbitreſs of good and evil: of any thing external or foreign ſhe makes no account; and looks upon ſuch things as are indifferent, as acceſſions of little or no importance. All *good* with her, ſubſiſts in the mind: ſome things however ſhe receives as primary, and purſues them earneſtly with deſign; ſuch as victory, good children, the welfare of one's country; there are other things as of a ſecond order, which diſplay not themſelves but in adverſity; as the patient ſufferance of a ſevere diſeaſe, or of baniſhment: and ſome of a mixed kind, no more conſonant to nature, than againſt it; as, to walk or ſit with a good grace; for to ſit is as natural as to ſtand or walk. The two former kinds are different; foraſmuch as the firſt are agreeable to nature; as the dutifulneſs of children, and the ſafety of our country; and the ſecond are contrary to nature; as, to ſuſtain torment with courage, and conſtancy; and patiently endure thirſt, while a fever is burning up the heartſtrings. *What then, can there be any good that is contrary to nature?* No, but that is ſometimes contrary to nature, wherein this *good* ſubſiſts; for, to be wounded, or afflicted with a ſore diſeaſe, or to be broiled to death, is contrary to nature; but to preſerve an unconquerable mind amidſt theſe torments, is agreeable to the dignity of nature. To expreſs what I mean, as briefly as poſſible; the object of *good* is ſometimes againſt nature, but *good* itſelf never: becauſe no *good* can be without reaſon; and reaſon always follows nature. *What*

then

then is reaſon? The imitation of nature (*n*). And what is the *ſummum bonum*, or *chief good* of man? The behaving himſelf agreeably to the dictates of nature. You ſay, no doubt, "that the peace is happier, "which hath never been diſturbed, than that which is obtained by "the blood of thouſands; and that it is an happier ſtate of health which "hath never been broken, than that which is recovered by art and "patience, from a violent diſeaſe that threatened death: in like manner "you ſay, that joy is a greater good than a mind capable of enduring "pain and torment from the ſword and fire." I deny all this: for, however thoſe things that are caſual may be ſubject to a wide difference, being eſteemed according to the benefit of the receiver; the only one purpoſe of good men is to agree with nature, and this is alike in all.

When the ſenate agree to the opinion of any member, we do not ſay, that ſuch a one aſſents more than another; as they all join in the ſame opinion. The ſame I ſay of virtues, they all aſſent to nature; the ſame I ſay of *good*; every *good* agrees with nature. Some go off the ſtage of life, in their youth; others in old age; beſide theſe, dies the little infant, who hath done nothing more than ſeen life. Now all theſe were equally mortal; though death ſuffered the life of one to run on longer, cut off the other in the bloom of youth, and nipt the other in the very bud. One man is carried off amidſt a jovial banquet; to another death is but a continued ſleep; another dies in the arms of his miſtreſs; oppoſe to theſe, ſuch as are pierced by the ſword, or kill'd by the bite of a ſerpent, or cruſhed under ſome ruins, or have died in extreme torture by a long contraction of the nerves: can the end of any among theſe be called better or worſe? Death is the ſame to all; the means indeed are very different; but the end, I ſay, is ſtill the ſame: no death can be ſaid to be greater or leſs; for it has the ſame quality in all; to put an end to life; the ſame is what I affirm to you, *Lucilius*, concerning *good*; one ſort is to be found in mere pleaſures; another amidſt pain and ſorrow; *that* with pleaſing moderation hath directed the indulgence of Fortune; *this* hath ſubdued her moſt violent animoſity; the *good* was equal in both; though one walked on in a ſmooth path, and the other was forced to climb a rock: the end of all is the ſame; they are good, they are commendable, in that they follow reaſon and virtue; and virtue reduceth to an equality whatever ſhe is pleaſed to acknowledge for her own.

But that you may not be ſurpriſed, *Lucilius*, at this among other our poſitions; be pleaſed to recollect, that even according to *Epicurus*, there are two bleſſings, of which the chief, and moſt happy *good* is compoſed, *a body without pain*, and *a ſoul without paſſion or perturbation*. Theſe bleſſings admit of no increaſe, if they are complete and perfect; for how can that receive more, which is full already? If the body be free from pain, what can you add to this indolence; if the mind be conſiſtent, and well pleaſed with itſelf, what can you add to this tranquillity? As a clear ſky, when the ſun ſhines out in his full glory, is not ſuſceptible of greater brightneſs; ſo the condition of a man, who, by his diligence and diſcretion, enjoys a ſound body and a ſound mind, and who builds upon theſe his *chief good*, is intirely perfect; he hath reached the end of his wiſhes; his mind knowing no diſorder, nor his body any pain. Whatever blandiſhments happen from without they augment not the *chief good*, but only give it, as it were, a pleaſing reliſh: for the abſolute good of human nature is fully and completely ſatisfied with the peace of body and ſoul.

But I will give you alſo from *Epicurus* a diſtinction of *good*, more like to this of the ſtoics. There is a ſort of *good*, which, he ſays, he had much rather ſhould be his portion, as, the eaſe of the body, free from every annoyance; and a relaxation of ſoul, rejoicing in the contemplation of its own felicity; and another ſort, which, though he would not wiſh them to be his lot, yet have their merit, and what he commends and approves, as, the patient ſufferance, before mention'd, of a bad ſtate of health, and conſtancy in the moſt grievous pain which *Epicurus* (*o*) himſelf labour'd under, upon a moſt happy day: for, he tells us, he was racked with an ulcer in the bladder, and an inflammation in the bowels; ſo that it was impoſſible to endure more pain: yet even this he called a bleſſed day to him: now, no one can enjoy a bleſſed

blessed day, without being in possession of the *chief good*. You see then that even with your *Epicurus* there is a sort of *good*, which no one indeed would chuse; but which, if necessity requires it, is still to be embraced, to be commended, and placed upon an equality with *sovereign good*; as the day which closed the happy life of *Epicurus*, and for which he gave thanks with his dying breath.

Give me leave, *Lucilius*, best of men, to speak somewhat more freely; if any *good* could be greater than another; I should prefer those that seem so very disagreeable to such as are of a more soft and delicate nature: for it is greater, to bear up against, and conquer difficulties, than to use good fortune with moderation: on this account, I know, the same judgment will incite men, to carry themselves well in prosperity, and not to be less patient in adversity: he may be alike brave, who stands sentinel in the trenches, before the enemy hath sallied to force the camp; with him, who having his legs cut off, fighteth upon his stumps, and scorns to throw away his sword. *Go on, and prosper, my brave lads*, is said to the men, who are cover'd with wounds and returning from the field of battle: I cannot therefore but highly recommend this *good*, that hath manifested itself upon trial, and in a firm defiance to the power of fortune. Can I make any doubt, whether I should praise the maimed hand of *Mucius* (*p*) when burnt to the bone, more than the sound one of the bravest general? He stood contemning both the enemy, and the flames; and looked with a steady eye upon his hand, while it was dropping away in the fire; till *Porsenna*, who at first took pleasure in his torture, now envied him the glory of it, and order'd the pan of fire to be taken from him without his consent. Now why should I not reckon this stubborn patience as a principal *good*; nay, think it greater, than such as are secure, and untried by torture; as it is more glorious to conquer an enemy with a hand that is useless, than with one arm'd with weapons? What then, you say, would I wish this good to be mine? Why not? For unless any one can also wish it, he would scarce put it in execution. Or must I rather wish effeminately to stretch out my limbs to my old servants to rub and soften them, or bid some old male-nurse to straiten my little toes?

toes? No, I think *Mucius* a happier man, in giving his hand to the fire, as to ſome friendly operator (*q*), whereby he made ample amends for his miſtake; when unarmed and maimed as he was, he put an end to the war; and with the ſtump only of an arm conquered two Kings (*r*).

ANNOTATIONS, &c.

(*a*) *Know ye not that the body is the temple of God, and that the ſpirit of God dwelleth in you?* i. Cor. iii. 16. vi. 9.

(*b*) See Lipſ. (Manud. iii. 6.)

(*c*) Various are the readings here, but *Gronovius* with all the MSS. and old editions, Talis *Animus* eſt virtus. So *Ep.* 113. Virtus nihil aliud eſt quàm animus quodammodo ſe habens. *Ep.* 78. Hæc ratio perfecta virtus vocatur. *Cic.* (Tuſc. Qu. l. v.) Hic igitur animus, ſi eſt excultus, et ſi ejus acies ita curata eſt, ut ne cæcetur erroribus, fit perfecta ratio, i. e. abſoluta ratio, quæ eſt idem quod virtus. The human mind as derived from the Divine Reaſon, can be compared with nothing, but with God himſelf, if I may be allowed the expreſſion: *This then when improved, and its ſight ſo preſerved as not to be blinded by errors, becomes a perfect underſtanding, i. e. abſolute reaſon, which is the very ſame as virtue.*

(*d*) *Cic.* (Parod. iii.) Una virtus eſt, conſentiens cum ratione et perpetua conſtantia: nihil huic addi poteſt quo magis virtus ſit, nihil demi ut virtutis nomen relinquatur. *Virtue is uniform, and its uniformity conſiſts in unwearied perſeverance, and agreement with reaſon; no addition of circumſtance can make it more than virtue, no diminution can make it leſs.*

(*e*) *Cic.* (ib.) Atqui pares eſſe virtutes, nec bono viro meliorem, nec temperante temperantiorem, nec forti fortiorem, nec ſapienti ſapientiorem poſſe fieri, facillimè poteſt percipi. *If virtues are equal among themſelves, it may very eaſily be conceived, that a man cannot be better than good, more temperate than temperate, braver than brave, nor wiſer than wiſe.*

(*f*) *Cic.* (ib.) Atqui quoniam pares virtutes ſunt, *recte facta*, quando a virtutibus proficiſcuntur paria eſſe debent;—*As all our virtues are equal,* all good actions, *being derived from virtue, ought to be equal likewiſe.*——

Thus runs the argument; Virtue is right; what is right, admits of no encreaſe; therefore virtue admits of no encreaſe: and if virtue admits of no encreaſe, neither do ſuch things as flow from virtue, and all things rightly done are equal. Such is the doctrine of the ſtoics; add *further*,—itemque peccata quoniam ex vitiis manant, ſint æqualia neceſſe eſt. *It neceſſarily follows, that evil actions ſpringing from vice ſhould be alſo equal.*

Now in what ſenſe the Chriſtian is to take this poſition we may learn from St. *James*, (ii. 2.)—*Whoſoever ſhall keep the whole law and yet offend in one point, he is guilty of all*; i. e. with reſpect to the obedience he ought to pay to the authority of the Legiſlator, which is violated by the tranſgreſſion of one point, as of all the reſt, becauſe there is an equal authority, or rather the ſame, which influences the whole, and which connects the one with the other. For (v. 11.) *He that ſaid do not commit adultery, ſaid alſo do not kill*; *now, if thou commit no adultery, yet if thou kill,* thou art a tranſgreſſor of the law.

* Though ſome of the philoſophers among the *Heathens* allowed, yet the beſt of them condemn'd this *ſtoical heroiſm*, as a raſh forſaking the ſtation in which the providence of their gods had placed them. *See* Epp. 24, 30, &c.

(*g*) However

(*g*) However the ſchoolmen and others may ſeem to differ from this doctrine of the *ſtoics*, with regard to a diſtinction in kind, and a ſuperior excellency, as to prefer *the moſt rational prudence* to *juſtice*, juſtice to fortitude, and fortitude to temperance; in a word, to think that each virtue riſes in value the nearer it accedes to, and the more it partakes of reaſon, yet conſidered in itſelf, (ſuppoſe *temperance*) they allow it to be equal: nor in reality do they contradict the doctrine of the *ſtoics*; foraſmuch as the *ſtoics* admit not of any *good* but what is in its higheſt perfection. See *Lipſ.* (Manud. iii. 4.)

(*h*) In equuleo taceat] Cic. (de fin. 5.) Si vir bonus, cæcus, debilis, morbo graviſſimo affectus, exul, orbus, torqueatur in equuleo: quem hunc appellas, Zeno? Beatum, inquit: etiam beatiſſimum? Quippe inquit, cùm tam docuerim gradus iſtam rem non habere, quam virtutem, in qua ſit ipſum beatum—(*al.* Etiam beatiſſimum? Quippini? cùm.)

If a wiſe man is blind, maimed, deſperately ſick, baniſhed, childleſs, a beggar, and tortured upon the rack; how will Zeno *term ſuch a man?* Happy. *What, ſupremely happy?* Why not? ſince I have all along declared that happineſs, *quà* happineſs, is the ſame, juſt as its efficient cauſe, virtue, is virtue.—If we are to appeal to the common ſenſe of mankind, you can never prove ſuch a man to be happy: if to *the thinking few*, one part of them perhaps will doubt whether *virtue* has ſo much power as to make a man happy even in *Phalaris'* bull. But the other will make no manner of doubt that the *ſtoics* ſpeak *conſiſtently*, &c. Ib.

(*i*) *Cic.* (Tuſc. v.) Epicuro dicere licebit nullum ſapienti eſſe tempus etſi uratur, torquatur, ſecetur, quin poſſit exclamare, Quam pro nihilo puto? *Denique etiam*, Beatam vitam in Phalaridis taurum deſcenſuram. *It is allowable for* Epicurus, (who only affects being a philoſopher, and who aſſumed that name to himſelf) to ſay, that *a wiſe man may at all times cry out, though he be burned, tortured, cut to pieces,* How little do I regard it?—nay, *that a happy life may deſcend into* Phalaris' *bull.*

(*k*) *We know that all things work together for good to them that love* God. Rom. viii. 28.

(*l*) So *Seneca* (Thebaid.) Speaking of *Jocaſta's* affection for her ſon, the wretched *Polynices*——

Quo cauſa melior, ſorſque deterior trahit
Inclinat animus ſemper infirmo favens:
Miſeros magis fortuna conciliat ſuis.

When unrelenting Fate denies ſucceſs
To a juſt cauſe, o'erwhelm'd with wretchedneſs,
Either of friend, or relative, the mind
To helpful pity is the more inclin'd. M.

(*m*) This is another paradox of the ſtoics. *Cic.* (de fin. iv.) Sapientes omnes ſummè beatos eſſe. *That all wiſe men are ſuperlatively happy.* (Ib. v.) Quid minus probandum, quàm eſſe aliquem beatum nec ſatis beatum? Quod autem ſatis eſt, eò quidquid acceſſerit nimium eſt, at nemo nimium beatus, et nemo beato beatior. *Nothing is eaſier to be proved than that if a man is happy he is ſufficiently happy; if any thing were added to what is ſufficient it would be too much, but no one can be too happy, nor any one happier than he that is happy.* Apud Stobæum Παντα τὸν καλὸν και αγαθὸν ανδρα τέλειον εἶναι, διὰ τὸ μηδεμίας απολειπεσθαι αρετῆς, διὸ καὶ παντως ευδαιμονα ἀεὶ τὸν ανθρωπον τὸν αγαθόν. If a man be truly juſt and good, he is *perfect, as wanting no kind of virtue:* and therefore the good are *altogether* and *always* happy. Now if all ſuch be *perfect*, they are *equal*; if they be *altogether* and *always* happy, there can be no addition or diminution of their happineſs. *Lipſ.* (Maund. iii. 3.) *See* Epp. 71, 72, 74, 85, 92.

(*n*) Obſerve here an explanation of that capital *dogma* among the ſtoics, Naturam ſequi, *follow Nature*, ſo frequently inculcated by our author. *See* Epp. 5, 16, 25, 41, (N. 1.) To which may be be added (De beat. vit. c. 8.) Idem eſt beati vivere, et ſecundum naturam. *It is the ſame thing to live happily, and according to nature.* For this is wiſdom, non a naturâ de-errare, et ad illius legem exemplumque formari, ſapientia eſt. *Epictetus* exhorts more than once, Ὁμολογουμένως—καὶ συμφώνως φύσει ζῆν, *to live conformably, and in perfect harmony with Nature.* Not only the Stoics but *Plato* and the *Academics* aſſerted that *in no other thing were we to look for the* ſummum bonum, nulla in re alia niſi *natura,* quærendum eſſe illud ſummum bonum, quo omnia referuntur, dicebant. *Cic.* (de Academ.) The *Cynics* alſo and other eminent philoſophers, according to *Philo Judæus,* maintained *this to be the end of happineſs.* Τὸ μὲν ἀκολουθίᾳ φύσεως ζῆν. Horace Ep. i. 10, 12.

Vivere naturæ ſi convenienter oportet.
Would you to Nature's laws obedience yield——

—— Hi mores, hæc duri immota Catonis
Secta fuit, ſervare modum, *finemque* tenere,
Naturamque ſequi, patriæque impendere vitam. *Lucan.* ii. 380.
Such Cato's *manners, ſuch their ſtubborn courſe,*——
The golden mean unchanging to purſue,
Conſtant to keep the purpos'd end in view.
Religiouſly to follow Nature's laws,
And die with pleaſure in his country's cauſe. Rowe.

(*o*) See Ep. 92.

(*p*) See Ep. 24. (N. f.)

(*q*) Tractatori] Martial iii. 81, 13.

(*r*) *Tarquin* (expelled *Rome* after he had reigned twenty-five years) and *Porſenna.*

EPISTLE LXVII.

Whether all Good *be deſirable.*

TO begin with the common topic of diſcourſe.—The ſpring has began to open (*a*), (*and ſhew its influence on the vegetable world*) and is now inclining to ſummer: but at what time we might expect it to be hot, it is ſcarce warm; nor is it yet ſo ſettled, but that it often turns to a wintry day. And indeed ſo variable is the weather, that I dare not venture upon cold water (*b*); and therefore have it ſomewhat warmed: this, you will ſay, is neither to endure heat nor cold. It is ſo, *Lucilius:* my time of life has now cold enough of its own: I am ſcarce unfrozen

unfrozen in the midſt of ſummer: great part of my time therefore I lie couched upon my mattreſs: however I thank my old age for thus confining me (*c*), ſeeing now I cannot do, what I ought not to wiſh to do. My chief converſation is with books: if at any time an epiſtle from you intervenes, I think myſelf with you: and ſuch my affection, that I fancy I am anſwering you, not by way of letter, but by word of mouth: therefore concerning what you enquire after, I will talk to you as if preſent; and we will ſift the matter together.

You deſire to know, if *all good be deſirable:* " If it be *good*, you ſay, " patiently to bear ſickneſs with a greatneſs of ſoul, to endure torment; " and to ſuffer burning with conſtancy and courage; it follows, that " theſe things are deſirable." No, I really think none of theſe things eligible: I know no one that ever wiſhed to be ſcourged with rods, to be diſtorted with the gout, or ſtretched upon the rack; you muſt make a diſtinction here, *Lucilius*, and you will ſee what I mean (*d*): I would by no means deſire torment; but if it ſhould be my lot to ſuffer, I would wiſh to behave myſelf with decency, courage, and ſpirit: I would not deſire to be engaged in war; but was I enroll'd, I would wiſh to bear wounds, hunger and all the cruel hardſhips that attend ſuch a ſituation, like a brave ſoldier. I am not ſo mad, as to wiſh to be ſick; but ſhould it ſo happen, I would wiſh not to be intemperate, ſtubborn, nor effeminately to make complaint.

Some of our ſect maintain, that a brave ſuffering of ſeverities, though not to be deteſted and abhorred, yet is by no means to be deſired; becauſe no *good* is deſirable, but what is pure, tranquil, and out of the reach of vexation. I am not of the ſame opinion: becauſe, firſt, it is impoſſible, that any thing can be really *good*, but what is deſirable. Secondly, if virtue be deſirable, and there is no *good* without virtue; then is every *good* deſirable: and further, if a brave enduring of torture be not to be wiſhed for, I would aſk, whether fortitude is to be wiſhed for? Now fortitude is what deſpiſeth all dangers, and defies them: the moſt beautiful part of it, and indeed the moſt admirable, is not to yield to either fire or ſword; ſometimes not to ſhun a dart, but to receive

it

it with open breaſt: if fortitude then be deſirable, even patiently to endure torture is deſirable; for this is a part of fortitude. Separate, I ſay, theſe things; and then you can make no miſtake. For to ſuffer torture, is not deſirable; but to ſuffer it manfully, is: and this is what I would wiſh for; for it is virtue. *But did ever any one wiſh for it?* Know, *Lucilius*, that ſome wiſhes and prayers are manifeſt, and profeſſedly ſuch, when they are made for any thing in particular; ſome lie concealed, when many things are comprehended in one wiſh, without being expreſſed; for inſtance, I wiſh myſelf an honourable life; now ſuch a life conſiſts in a variety of actions and ſufferings; the tub of *Regulus* (*e*); the wound which *Cato* tore open with his own hand (*f*); the baniſhment of *Rutilius* (*g*), and the cup of poiſon that raiſed *Socrates* from his priſon into heaven, are all comprehended in this: therefore when I wiſhed for an honourable life, I wiſhed for theſe, or the like hardſhips; without which it is ſometimes impoſſible for a life to be honourable.

——O terque quaterque beati,
Queis ante ora patrum Trojæ ſub mœnibus altis
Contigit oppetere (*h*)!——

And what difference is there in wiſhing this for another, or confeſſing it to be deſirable? *Decius* devoted himſelf to the good of the public (*i*), and ſpurring his horſe into the midſt of his enemies ruſhed upon death: his ſon, emulous of paternal virtue, having uttered a few ſolemn, and now familiar words, did the ſame, ſollicitous to appeaſe the gods by the ſacrifice of himſelf; and thinking it a deſirable thing to die an honourable death. And can any one doubt but that it is a moſt glorious thing, to die thus nobly in ſome great work of virtue, and to purchaſe thereby an everlaſting name?

When any one manfully endures torment, he perhaps ſupports himſelf with all the virtues, though but one diſplays itſelf above the reſt, which is *patience*. There is *fortitude* herein; of which patience, and ſufferance, and endurance, are but the branches: there is *prudence*, without which no great deſign can be carried on: and which perſuades us to bear that as decently as poſſible, which it is not in our power to eſcape: there is alſo, *conſtancy*, which cannot be thrown from her ſeat, nor will ever depart from her purpoſe, let whatever torment endeavour to force her: in ſhort there is the whole undivided train of virtues. Whatever is done handſomely, one virtue does it, but it is according to the advice of the whole aſſembly (*k*). Now, what is approved by all the virtues, though it may ſeem the effect of one only, muſt be *deſirable*. For why? Do you think thoſe things only deſirable, which came from eaſe and pleaſure; ſuch as are manifeſted by garlands at the door (*l*)? There are ſome pleaſures that have ſorrow enough: and ſome vows are offered up by way of adoration and worſhip, rather than of applauſe and thankſgiving. Do you not think that *Regulus* ſincerely wiſhed to return to the *Carthaginians*? Aſſume the ſpirit of a truly great man; and withdraw yourſelf awhile from the opinion of the vulgar; take to yourſelf, as you ought, a ſemblance of the moſt beautiful and magnificent virtue; and you will find it decorated, not with frankincenſe and garlands, but with ſweat and blood. Behold *Marcus Cato*, reaching out his moſt pure hands to that ſacred breaſt of his, and widening the too ſhallow wound: would you ſay to him, *I would do as you do, but am ſorry you have done it*? Or, *how happy are you*, Cato, in *what you have done*? I cannot help thinking here of our *Demetrius*; who calls a life that is ſecure, and unmoleſted by any attack of fortune, *a dead ſea*. To have nothing to incite and rouſe you to action; nothing by whoſe threatning and aſſault, you may try the ſtrength of your mind; but to live at eaſe, undiſturb'd, and unſhaken, is not tranquillity; but a dead calm, (*ſoftneſs and delicacy*). *Attalus*, the ſtoic, was wont to ſay, *I had rather torture ſhould carry me out into her camp than indulge me at home in all manner of delights. What if I am wounded, I bear it manfully; it is well. What if I am ſlain, I die bravely; it is well.* Hear *Epicurus*, amidſt his pains, *it is ſweet and pleaſant*. For my part, I know not how to beſtow a ſoft name upon what is ſo honourable, yet ſo ſevere. I am burned, but ſtill invincible. And why is not this a *deſirable* thing; I do not ſay, to have the fire burn me; but that it cannot conquer me? Nothing is more excellent than virtue; nothing more beautiful: it is *good*, it is *deſirable*, whatever is done by her authority and command.

ANNOTATIONS, &c.

——— (*a*) Se *aperire* cœpit] From whence comes the word *April*, qu. aperilis.—See my note on the first line of that sweet old poet *Chaucer*.

Whannè that *Apryl* with his schouris sote,
The drought of March had piercid to the rote,
And bathid every vein in swiche licoure,
Of which Virtu engendrid is the floure;
Eke whannè Zephyrus, with his sote breth,
Exspirede hath, in every holt and heth,
The tender croppys; and the yongè sonne
Hath in the rammè half his course yronne—&c.

(*b*) Either in bathing or washing. *See* Epp. 53, 83.

Horace Ep. l. 15. 4.—Gelida cum perluor unda
Per medium frigus.——
——*When I mean to bathe,*
The middle winter's freezing wave beneath.—Francis.

(*c*) Quod me lectulo affixit] Not a dormitory, but a room with a couch; such as they usually had who lived a retired life, or were given to study. Ep. 72. Quædam *Lectum* et *otium* desiderant. Juv. vii. 105.

Est genus ignavum quod lecto gaudet et umbrâ.
They are a lazy people, either laid
Upon their couch, or walking in the shade.—Stapleton.

Pers. l. 53.——Lectis scribitur in vitreis.
Them and their woeful works the muse defies,
Products of citron beds, and golden canopies. Dryden.

(*d*) *Maretus* observes that *Aristotle's* distinction (*Politic.* p. vii.) in this point is short and full. *Some things*, says he, *are good and to be desired* absolutely: *other*, (ἐξ ὑποθέσεως [illegible],) *only* hypothetically: *It is a good thing, and to be wished for, that there should not be a wicked man in the city, but if there are any such, it is a desirable good, that they should be punished: sickness is not to be wished for, but if it happens, it is good to bear it with fortitude and patience*; and so of other things.

(*e*) *Regulus*, having been taken by the *Carthaginians*, and sent to *Rome*, to advise a change of prisoners, there pleaded for the contrary; yet having promised to return, he would not break his word, and returned accordingly; where he was barbarously murdered; being put into a *tub* stuck full of nails, and rolled down a hill. Ep. 98. Sen. de Provid. c. iii. De Tranquil. l. 15. Valer. Max. ix. 2. Tertull. (ad Mart. c. 4.) in arcæ genus stipatus, undique extrinsecus clavis confixus tot cruces sensit.—Cum mult. al.—But I shall only refer the reader to *Horace* (Od. iii. 5.)

Atqui sciebat quæ sibi barbarus
Tortor parabat—&c.
Nor did he not the cruel tortures know,
Vengeful prepar'd by a barbarian foe,
Yet with a countenance serenely gay,
He turn'd aside the crouds, who fondly press'd his stay. Francis.

And

And especially to *Cic.* (Off. iii. 31.) where the whole story is related, and the propriety of his return, in obedience to his promise and oath, is fully argued; and particularly in the notes of the ingenious translator Mr. *Guthrie*.——See also N. 74 of *Cic.* on old age, by Mr. *Melmoth*; who observes, that it has been doubted, by some modern writers of considerable note in the republic of letters, whether *Regulus* really underwent those horrid tortures which he is said to have sustained on his return to *Carthage*. It were to be wished, indeed, for the honour of humanity, they have been misrepresented, but the pretence is very strong, from historians as well as poets.

(f) Cato, Ep. 24. See the Index.

(g) Ep. 24, (N. c.)—*Socrates*, Ep. 63, (N. h.)

(h) Virg. i. 90. *O thrice, and four times happy they, he cried,*
Who, under Ilian *walls, before their parents died.* Dryden.

(i) It was a superstitious fancy among the old Romans, that if a General *(Dictator, Consul,* or *Prætor)* would consent to be *devoted* or sacrificed to *Jupiter, Mars*, the earth, or the infernal gods, all the misfortunes which otherwise might happen to his party, would, by virtue of that pious act, be transferred on their enemies; (see the form of this solemnity in *Livy* (viii. 9.) *Cic.* (de Fin. ii. 15. de Nat. Deor. ii.) This opinion was confirmed in the most renowned family of the Decii, of whom the father, son, (and grandson) all devoted themselves for the safety of their armies. See *Melmoth's* Cato, or *Cic.* on old age. N. 51.

Phebeiæ Deciorum animæ Phebeia fuêrunt
Nomina, pro totis legionibus hi tamen, et pro
Omnibus auxiliis, atque omni pube Latina
Sufficiunt Diis infernis terræque parenti:
Pluris enim Decii quàm qui servantur ab illis.

From a mean stock the pious Decii *came,*
Small their estates, and vulgar was their name;
Yet such their virtues, that their *loss alone*
For Rome and all our legions did atone;
Their country's doom they by their own retriev'd,
Themselves more worth than all the hosts they sav'd. Stepny.

See Fitzosborn's Lett. 57.

(k) This stoical opinion of the concatenation or connexion of all the virtues, seems almost general among the ancient philosophers: thus *Menedemus* and *Aristo*, unam virtutem esse, etsi multis insignitam vocabulis, *There is but* one *virtue, though set off under various titles.* Cicero (de Fin. v.) Cùm sic copulatæ connexæque sint virtutes, ut omnes omnium participes sint, nec alia ab alia possit separari; tamen proprium suum cujusque munus. So *the Fathers*; *Ambrose*, Connexæ sibi sunt concatenatæque virtutes, ut qui unam habet, plures habere videatur. And *Gregory*, Una virtus sine aliis, aut omnino nulla est, aut imperfecta est. See Epp. 66, (N. f.) 95. *Lips.* (Manud. iii. 4.)

(l) Hic nostrum placabo Jovem, laribusque paternis
Thura dabo, atque omnes violæ jactabo colores.
Cuncta nitent; longos erexit janua ramos,
Et matutinis operitur festa lucernis. Juv. xii. 90.
And incense shall domestic Jove appease:
My shining houshold gods shall revel there,
And all the colours of the violet wear.
All's right; my portal shines with verdant bays,
And consecrated tapers early blaze. Power.

Pers. v. 181.——*Lips.* Elect. i. 5.

EPISTLE LXVIII.

On Eafe and Retirement.

I APPROVE of your defign, *Lucilius:* conceal yourfelf, if you pleafe, in eafe and retirement; but take care to conceal this too. Know that what you propofe, is allowed, if not from any precept of the ftoics; yet by example (*a*): nay, I doubt not, but that I could prove, if you defired me, that you might do the fame according to precept. We recommend not the being concern'd in the public affairs of every government (*b*), nor at all times (*c*), without paufe or intermiffion during life (*d*). Moreover, when we have given the wife man a republic, worthy of him, i. e. the world: * he cannot be faid to be abfent from the fame, though he has thought proper to retire; nay, perhaps having left a fmall corner, he enters a great and fpacious palace; where being feated, as it were, in heaven, he learns, in what a low and mean place he fate when he afcended the chair of ftate, or the tribunal (*e*). Believe me, *Lucilius*, a wife man is never more in action than when engaged in the contemplation of things both human and divine.

But to return to what I was faying in the beginning of this epiftle, in order to perfuade you to keep your retreat a fecret. There is no reafon, you fhould honour it with the name of *philofophy* (*f*); find out fome other pretext; afcribe it to an ill ftate of health, or a weak conftitution, or lazinefs: to glory in eafe, is an idle ambition. Some animals, the better to lie concealed, confound their tracks, round about the place where they lodge: you muft do the fame; otherwife there will be thofe, who will perfecute you: many pafs negligently over what is vifible; but fearch after what is hidden and abftrufe: things, when under feal, tempt a thief; what lies expofed feems vile and of no account: the houfebreaker paffeth by an open door. The common people have all

all the same sort of manners and every blockhead the same: they will desire to break in upon your privacy: it is good therefore not to boast of it: now, there is a kind of ostentation, in shutting one's self up too close, so as never to appear in sight. One man will keep himself close at *Tarentum*; another at *Naples*; another for some years hath not steoped over his own threshold. But such a one only calls a crowd about his door, who makes his retirement the subject of idle stories, and the common talk.

When you retire, it must not be with a design, that others should talk of you; but that you should commune with yourself. And what must the subject be? Why, that which men make the general subject of their conversation, in freely speaking of their neighbours, viz. your own character. Indulge not too good an opinion of yourself: accustom yourself to speak and hear the truth; but chiefly reflect upon whatever weakness you are most sensible of yourself. There is scarce any man but who knows his own infirmity; one man therefore finds an evacuation necessary to ease his stomach, another is continually eating to strengthen him; another thinks fit to lower his corpulency by abstinence: some who are afflicted with the gout abstain from the luxury of wine and the bath; regardless in all other respects, they are chiefly intent upon preventing the painful disorder they are most subject to. So in the mind there are some crazy parts (*g*), which in time must be taken care of in order for their cure. And what is my employ, think you, in my retirement? Why, I am endeavouring to cure this ulcerated part. Were I to shew you a swoln foot, a livid hand, or the dry nerves of a contracted ancle, you would permit me, to lie in one posture, and indulge my disease: but much greater is the complaint within, which I cannot shew you. There is a load and an imposthume in my breast. Prithee, do not praise me, do not say, "*what a great man! he hath despised all things, and having condemn'd the frantic errors of human life he is retired.*" I have condemned nothing but myself. There is no reason you should desire to come to me to learn somewhat for your good; you are mistaken, if you think any help is to be had here: I am not a physician, but a sick patient; I had rather you should say of me, as you are

are going away: *alas! I took this man for one very happy and learned; I was all attention to him; I have received nothing from him I deſired; nothing to make me wiſh to come again.* If ſuch your opinion, if ſuch your language, I ſhould think, you had made ſome progreſs: I had rather my retirement ſhould want an apology, than be envied. *Do you really then,* Seneca, *recommend eaſe and retirement? This ſounds as if coming from Epicurus.* Be it ſo; I ſtill recommend retirement to you; wherein you may be employed in greater and more commendable things than thoſe you have quitted. To knock at the proud doors of the great,—to note in your memorandum book ſuch old men, as have no heirs at law (*b*), to be in high reputation at court,—theſe are but invidious privileges, of no long duration; and, if you think right, beneath the notice of a man of honour. One man excells me in the buſineſs of the forum; another hath better pay for his ſervices, whereby he riſes to the dignity of the equeſtrian or ſenatorial order; another is attended with more clients; I cannot match this man in his train of followers, nor that in popularity; and what then? Provided I could conquer torture, I ſhould not ſo much regard the being excelled and conquered by man.

I wiſh, *Lucilius*, you had been ſo happy as to have taken this reſolution long ago. I wiſh we had not deferred to think of an happy life, till now we are come within ſight of death. But let us delay no longer. We have now learned many things, which we before thought would have proved vain and fantaſtical in the eye of reaſon. As they are wont to do, who ſet out late, and by their ſpeed would recover the time they have loſt, let us now ſpur on. This time of life beſt ſuits our ſerious ſtudies. It is now clarified: it hath quite maſter'd the vices that were untameable in the firſt heat of youth; there remains but little fire to be extinguiſhed: and *when*, you ſay, *will that profit you, which you propoſe to learn at the end of life? Or to what purpoſe do you learn it?* Truly, to make a better exit; to die a better man (*i*). There is no time of life more proper for the attainment of a ſound mind, than that which by a long experience and a well exerciſed patience, hath ſufficiently humbled itſelf; and, having aſſuaged the affections and paſſions, obliged it, ſeriouſly to think of what is good and ſalutary. This is the ſhort time allotted

allotted as for the attainment of wiſdom; and whatever old man is ſo happy as to attain it, let him own that he owes no ſmall obligation to his years.

ANNOTATIONS, &c.

(a) The chief of the ſtoics, though they maintained that the affairs of government were moſt properly entruſted in the hands of the wiſe; yet would never *voluntarily* engage therein themſelves. *Sen.* (de beat. vit. c. 28) non quo miſerint me illi, ſed quo duxerint, ibo. Wherefore *Plutarch* condemns them, as not ſuiting their lives to their own doctrine.

(b) *every government*] Such, for inſtance, as are in ſo deplorable a ſtate, as to give no hopes of their recovery.

(c) *nor at all times*] As ſome muſt neceſſarily be devoted to relaxation, or private ſtudies.

(d) *Nor during life.* Ως γαρ αθλητικῆς, ὅτω καὶ πολιτικῆς περιοδ8 καταλυσις τις ἐστι· *Political as well as athletical engagements have their proper periods.* At *Rome* a ſenator after the ſixtieth year of his age was not compelled to attend the houſe; and after the ſeventieth never ſummoned. And both *Plato* and *Ariſtotle* think old age more proper for the function of the *prieſtly office* than for any other. From whence that celebrated verſe———

Εργα νεων, βυλαι δ' ανδρῶν, ευχαὶ δὲ γεροντων.
In deeds let youth, *in council* men *engage,*
But prayer and ſacrifice beſt ſuit old age. M.

* A wiſe man looks upon himſelf as a citizen of the *world*; and, when you aſk him where his country lies, points, like *Anaxagoras*, with his finger to the heavens.

" To talk of our abſtracting ourſelves from matter, laying aſide body, and being reſolved, as it were, into pure intellect, is proud, metaphyſical, unmeaning jargon. But to abſtract ourſelves from the prejudices, habits, pleaſures, and *buſineſs of the world*, is what many, though not all, are capable of doing. They who can do this, may elevate their ſouls, in a retreat, to an higher ſtation, and may take from thence ſuch a view of the world, as *Scipio* took in his dream, *Cic.* ſomn. *Scip.*) from the ſeats of the bleſſed, when the whole earth appeared ſo little to him, that he could ſcarce diſcern that ſpeck of dirt, the *Roman* Empire. Such a view as this will encreaſe our knowledge," &c. *Bolingbroke* on Retirement.

(e) The wiſe man ſeems to abaſe himſelf when he mounts the chair of ſtate, being hereby compelled to forego the ſublime contemplation of heavenly things. There is an excellent Epigram wrote by the philoſopher *Themiſtius* (and not by *Pallas*, as ſome injudiciouſly imagined) who when advanced to the Conſulſhip, thus exhorts himſelf to deſpiſe theſe worldly vanities, and aſcend to the ſtudy of philoſophy:

Αντυγος αιθεριης ὑπερημενος, εις ποθον ἦλθες
Αντυγος αργυρεης, αἶσχος απειρεσιον·
Ησθα κάτω κρεισσων· αναβας δ' εγενε μεγα χειρων
Δεῦρ αναβηθι κάτω. νῦν γὰρ ἄνω κατέβης.
High mounted in a ſilver car I ride;
The wiſh'd-for ſummit of ambitious pride.
Greater before, and happier, in the end;
Let me, to riſe to what I was, deſcend. M.

(f) I ſee

(*f*) *I see your vanity*, said *Socrates* to *Antisthenes*, *in your threadbare coat, which you are so proud to shew*. See the like argument in Epp. 5. 14. 18. 103.

(*g*) Causariæ partes] A military term; so, in *Livy*, Causarii milites, & causaria missio, a *furlow*, or *passport* granted to a sick or wounded soldier. *Vid*. Mercurial. Var. Lect. vi. 1.

(*h*) See *Sen*. de Benefic. vi. 33.

(*i*) As *Solon*, when he was dying, desired something might be read to him, and being asked upon what account he made this request, answered, *that he might die a more learned man*.

EPISTLE LXIX.

On the Affections and Passions.

I WOULD by no means, *Lucilius*, have you rove from place to place (*a*) because such frequent moving bewrays an unstable and unsettled mind. You cannot improve your leisure time, till you cease to wander, and gape about you. You cannot bring your mind under any rule, before you put a stop to the rambles of your body. And then, by the constant application of proper remedies you may expect a cure: your retirement must not be broken in upon: your former life must entirely be forgot: let your eyes forego their usual practice and your ears be accustomed to more sound discourse: as often as you presume to go out, you will meet with something that will recall your desires: as one that intends to throw off his affection, must shun every thing that is likely to remind him of his beloved object; for nothing so soon revives and grows fresh again as *love:* so he that intends to cast off his inclination for such things as before inflamed his desire, must turn away both his eyes and ears from the object he would fain forsake. The affection is very apt to rebell: which way soever it turns, it will be invited to seize the tempting opportunity: there is no evil but what finds some excuse to authorise it: covetousness promiseth wealth;

luxury many and various pleaſures; ambition, purple, applauſe, and power and all that power can do. Vice ever tempts you with ſome reward; but know, you muſt live free and diſintereſted. There is ſcarce time enough in a whole age, to ſubdue, and bring under the yoke, vices, that are grown proud and ſtubborn with too long liberty; much leſs can we expect to do this, if we permit the little time we have to be interrupted: daily vigilance and application ſcarce ſuffice to bring any one thing to perfection.

If you would attend to me, *Lucilius*, meditate on this; be this your exerciſe; *calmly* to receive death; nay, if neceſſity required, to court it. There is little or no difference, whether Death comes to us or we go to him *(b)*. Perſuade yourſelf, that it is but an idle opinion of the moſt ignorant, that, bella res eſt, mori ſuâ morte, *it is right and fair for a man to die the death allotted him (c)*. Think moreover that no one dies, but *when his time is come:* when you die, you have had the time you could properly call *your own (d)*; what you leave behind you, belongs to another perſon.

ANNOTATIONS, &c.

(*a*) See Ep. ii.

(*b*) Undoubtedly, Death, conſidered as Death, is the ſame, come when, or from what hand it will. But the means or manner of it, with regard to a rational agent, admit of a wide difference; eſpecially among Chriſtians; as there is ſcarce one in the whole train of virtues, but what is rejected and deſtroyed by the horrid cuſtom of ſuicide; as, *Fortitude*, *Conſtancy*, *Patience*, *a truſt in God*, &c.

(*c*) *Suetonius* ſpeaking of thoſe who murdered Cæſar in the capitol, obſerves that, Nemo amplius triennio ſupervixit, neque ſua morte defunctus eſt, *No one ſurvived him more than three years or died a natural death.* As to the ſentence here exhibited, though *Seneca*, ſpeaking as a Stoic, ſeems to condemn this opinion, I doubt not but that every Chriſtian, learned or unlearned, will approve of it. And 'tis notorious that *Seneca* contradicts himſelf in nothing more than in this point.

(*d*) No one is a proper judge of what is here called *his own time*. The time indeed that a man hath cut off by laying violent hands on himſelf, is not *his own*; for he is gone, and now hath nothing to do with it: but neither was it *his own*, ſo as to diſpoſe of it at his pleaſure, or to abridge himſelf of it; for it belonged to his family, to his king, to his God. See the Notes on the following Epiſtle. See alſo Epp. 16. 24. 34. 41. 44. 51. 94. 98.

EPISTLE LXX.

On Life and Death †.

AT laſt, *Lucilius*, I have been to ſee your *Pompeii:* where ſomething or other reminded me of my youthful days: and ſo affected me, as to make me fancy myſelf as young and active as ever; at leaſt to think that few years had paſſed ſince that happy time.—We ſail, *my Lucilius*, along the coaſt of life, and as in the ſea, our *Virgil* ſays,

—Terræq; urbeſq; recedunt, *we ſoon loſe ſight of land*;—

ſo in the rapid flow of time, we firſt loſe ſight of childhood, then of youth, then of middle age, on the confines of both, and then the better years of old age; and at laſt the common end of mankind begins to ſhew itſelf.

And do we think this a terrible rock? we are arrant fools if we do: it is rather a deſirable haven (*a*), than to be dreaded; into which if any one is carried in his younger years, he has no more reaſon to complain, than he that hath made a ſwift voyage; for one veſſel, you know, is made the ſport of gentle winds, and is detained, 'till it is quite tired with the tediousneſs of an idle calm: another by a ſmart and conſtant gale is carried along impetuouſly to the end of its voyage: the ſame happens to us in life: ſome are violently hurried thither, where even the moſt tardy muſt come at laſt: others are quite macerated and waſted away with length of days, ſo as to make life by no means deſirable; for it is not a good thing merely to live, but to live well and happily (*b*): therefore a wiſe man will take care to live well, and as he ought to live, not concerning himſelf with the length of time: he will conſider where he is to live, with whom, in what manner, and to what purpoſe, regardleſs, I ſay, of *how long*. If many troubles afflict him and deſtroy his peace, *he deſires to be gone* (*c*): and not only in the laſt extremities, but as ſoon as ever Fortune begins to be ſuſpected by him; he will con-

ſult

ſult with himſelf, whether it were not better for him to die: he thinks it of no great moment to him, from what hand he accepts the fatal ſtroke; nor that it can be any detriment to him, whether ſooner or later. He cannot be any great loſer who has but a *drop* to loſe: it is of no great importance to die ſoon, or to die late, but to die well or ill: now to die well, is to eſcape the perils of an evil life: and therefore I think it too effeminately ſpoken by the *Rhodian*, who, when he was caſt into priſon by a tyrant, and there kept encaged like a wild beaſt, ſaid to a perſon that perſuaded him to ſtarve himſelf, Omnia homini dum vivit, ſperanda ſunt, *while there is life there is hope* (*d*). However true this maxim may be, I cannot think life is to be purchaſed at any rate: ſome things, however great, however certain, are not what I ſhould deſire to obtain, at the expence of confeſſing myſelf weak and faint-hearted. Muſt I think that Fortune can do every thing for him who lives, rather than that ſhe hath no power over him who knows how to die? Yet, I muſt own that, in *ſome* caſes, though certain death were inſtant, and a man knew his deſtined puniſhment, he ought not to accelerate it by his own preſumption (*e*). *It is folly to die for fear of death*. Is the executioner coming? wait for him: why do you prevent him? why would you take upon you the adminiſtration of another's cruelty? do you envy him, or ſpare him, the diſagreeable office? *Socrates* might eaſily have ended his life by abſtaining from any nouriſhment, rather than have died by poiſon; yet he lived thirty days in priſon, and in expectation of death: not becauſe he preſumed that every thing would be done that could be done to ſave him; or that he had any hopes in being reſpited; but in dutiful ſubmiſſion to the laws, and to give his friends the enjoyment of his converſation to the laſt. Nothing could be more abſurd than to ſuppoſe that he deſpiſed death, and yet was afraid of poiſon.

On the contrary, *Druſus Libo*, a young man, as ſilly, as he was noble by birth, expecting greater things than any man could expect in that age, or he in any; when he was brought from the ſenate in a litter very ſick (or pretending to be ſo) with no great attendance, (for all his friends and ſervants had uncharitably forſaken him, not now as an

 accuſed

accused person, but as one condemned, and already dead in law) began to ask counsel, whether he should wait for death, or hasten it himself; *Scribonia* his aunt, (the widow of *Augustus)* a woman of great sedateness and gravity, thereupon said to him, *what pleasure can you have in the enjoyment of a life not your own?* *Drusus* took the hint, and dispatched himself; and I think not without reason (*f*). For if he that is to die within three or four days, at the pleasure of an enemy, chuses to live out the time, it cannot properly be called *his own*. We cannot however absolutely declare in all cases alike, when any external power threatens certain death, whether it is to be anticipated, or waited for: for much may be said on both sides: for if on one hand death is to be attended with any grievous torture; and on the other it is simple and easy, why should not this be preferred? As I would chuse a ship to sail in, or a house to live in; so would I the most tolerable death, when about to die.

Moreover, though life is not the better, the longer it is; yet surely death the longer it is, is so much the worse. We ought in nothing to be more obsequious to the mind, than in death: let a man indulge it with whatever death it is pleased to chuse; let him rush on, according to the impulse within, and break his chains (*g*). In the affairs of life, let him study the approbation of others, but in death let him please himself (*h*). It is ridiculous for a man to trouble himself with the following reflexions; some one will say, *I have been too rash; I have acted cowardly; such a death would have shewed a more generous and noble spirit* (*i*). But would you accept of the advice that is in your power to put in execution, and with which fame or censure have no concern, (*at least that you will be sensible of*); let this be your principal view, to take yourself out of the power of Fortune as speedily as you can; otherwise there will be those who may disapprove and condemn the fact (*k*): you will find even among the professors of wisdom, (*the Peripatetics* or followers of *Aristotle's* philosophy) those who deny, that upon any account a man is at liberty to lay violent hands on himself; who judge it a most heinous crime; and solemnly assert, that *it is the duty of every one to wait the time appointed by Nature.* He that says this, seems not to to know that he hath barred up, againſt himſelf, the way to liberty: the eternal law hath done nothing better than that it hath given us but one way of entrance into life, but many ways of going out of it (*l*): muſt I wait for either the cruelty of a diſeaſe, or of man, when I have it in my power to eſcape from the greateſt torments, and ſet myſelf free from all adverſity? This is one reaſon why we ſhould not complain of life, it detains no one againſt their will (*m*): human affairs are in ſuch a happy ſituation, that no one need be wretched but by choice. Do you like to be wretched? Live (*n*). Do you like it not? It is in your power to return from whence you came. To eaſe the pain of the head, you ſcruple not to bleed a vein; now there is no need of a much greater wound to reach the heart; you may open to yourſelf a way to liberty by a ſingle bodkin (*o*).

What is it then that makes us cowards and afraid to die? It is becauſe no one reflects that he muſt leave this earthly tenement ſome time or other. Hence fondneſs for the place, cuſtom, and imtimacy, detain us here like ſome old cottagers, in ſpite of injuries. Would you be free in oppoſition to the body? Dwell therein as if always about to depart: ſuppoſe with yourſelf that you muſt one day forego this fellowſhip; and you will with greater courage break it off when neceſſity requires; but how ſhould he ever reflect on his end, who deſires to know no end, and lives as if all things were to laſt for ever?

There is no meditation ſo neceſſary as frequent thoughts on our latter end. The thoughts employ'd upon other ſubjects may prove vain and ſuperfluous. Is our mind prepared againſt the ſtroke of poverty? It happens not; our riches have not yet taken wing. Have we armed ourſelves ſo, as to deſpiſe all pain? The continued happineſs of a ſound and healthful body, never puts us to the trial. Have we prevailed upon ourſelves, patiently to ſuffer any loſs whatever, particularly the loſs of a dear friend or relation? Fortune hath been ſo kind to us, as ſtill to preſerve alive all whom we particularly love and reſpect. But as the day of death will certainly come, in this alone our meditation cannot be vain or uſeleſs.

Nor

Nor muſt you think, *Lucilius*, that great men only have had ſtrength enough to break the bars of human ſervitude; as if no one but a *Cato* would dare to let looſe his ſoul with his hand, when his ſword had failed him, ſeeing that men of the loweſt rank in life have with great courage and impetuoſity ſet themſelves free: and when they could not die commodiouſly, nor chuſe at pleaſure the inſtruments of death, have laid hold on any thing that came to hand, and made weapons of ſuch as ſeemed by no means capable of doing them any hurt. Not long ago a certain *German*, among thoſe who were condemned to fight with wild beaſts, when he was brought out in the morning, pretended a neceſſary call, where they were admitted without a guard; and being there alone, he took a dirty ſpunge belonging to the place, and thruſting it down his throat, put an end to his miſery. "This, you will "ſay, was putting an affront upon death: not to die more cleanly, "and decently." Be it ſo; what can be more fooliſh than to be ſqueamiſh and finical in death? Thou wert a brave man, I ſay, and worthy to have thy choice of death *(p)!* how courageouſly would ſuch a one have uſed a ſword; how freely have leaped into the deep, or thrown himſelf from a precipice! being deſtitute of means, he yet found out wherewithal to diſpatch himſelf: that you may know there is no let or hindrance, to death, but the being unwilling or afraid to die. Let what will be thought of this fellow's violent action; it is certain, the moſt naſty death is preferable to the cleaneſt ſervitude.

As I have begun to make uſe of low examples, I will go on; for it cannot but have the greater influence with every one; who ſees, that this *thing, death*, hath been contemned by the moſt contemptible of men. The *Cato's*, the *Scipio's*, and others, whom we are wont to have in great eſteem and admiration, may ſeem indeed to be placed in a ſphere above imitation; but I can ſhew you as many examples of this *virtue*, among the gladiators, as among the chieftains of civil wars. As one of them the other day, was brought out by the guard to the morning *ſport*, (as it is called), he went nodding his head, as if yet aſleep, and at laſt ſtooped it down ſo low from the carriage, that the wheel laid hold of it and broke his neck: and thus he eſcaped puniſh-

ment,

ment, by means of the vehicle that was carrying him to it. Nothing can prevent the man, who is ready and desirous to depart: nature keeps us in an open place and at large: as far as necessity will permit, the most easy death is certainly the most desirable: he that hath not an opportunity for this may take what method he can, however unheard of, however new: ingenuity in dying is never wanting, but, where courage is wanted: you see, how the vilest slaves, when the fear of being scourged impells them, are provoked to make their escape as they can, from the strictest guard: he is a great man, who not only designs his own death, but can find the means to accomplish it *(q)*.

But I promised you more examples. In the second *Naumachia (given by* Nero), there was a barbarian, who thrust into his own throat, a launce which he had received to be employed against his adversary; *why* says he *have I not long since endeavoured to escape all manner of torment, and the being made the sport of the people? Why should I wait for death with a weapon in my hand?* Now this was so much the more comely a sight, as it is the more honourable to die one's self, than to kill another man (*r*). Well then, shall they, whom frequent meditation, and reason, have instructed, and ought to have fortified against all casualties, hesitate to do, what is done by men of the lowest characters and criminals? Reason teaches us that the ways to death are various, but the end the same; and that it signifies nothing how soon it comes since it *will* come. The same reason teaches us, that if you can, it is best to die without pain; but, if this cannot be effected, to die as you may. It is injurious and base *to live* by stealth and rapine; but to lay hold on death, and *steal* one's self away is honourable (*s*).

ANNOTATIONS, &c

† *Muretus*, very justly condemning several parts of this Epistle, though, in other respects, there are many excellent things full worthy the great Author, observes, that the former are the dictates of that foolish wisdom of the *Stoics*, whereby they maintained that a man may be so circumstanced as to make *suicide* a meritorious act: and *I wish*, says he, *that* Seneca *had not been infected with this madness, or at least had more sparingly and moderately defended so great an error*.

For my own part, I am not afraid that this extraordinary Epistle should fall into the hands of such as are of a melancholy cast, or even desponding; provided they will be pleased to join the following

Annotations

Annotations with it. For, strong as this poison of *Stoicism* is, (I cannot call it *Seneca's*, as he so often contradicts himself in this point) I am persuaded that, with reason and a little sense of their own, they will find it attended with a sufficient antidote; especially if they consider its being wrote by an Heathen before the Christian æra, or the happy publication of the Gospel.

(*a*) This metaphor is in frequent use. So, *Sen.* (ad Polyb. c. 28.) In hoc tam procelloso—mari navigantibus, nullus *portus* est nisi mortis. *To all that sail in this stormy sea (of life), no other haven is to be expected than that of death.*

(*b*) So *Plutarch.* Μετρον γαρ τυ βιυ το καλόν κ. τ. λ. *The true mean or measure of life consists not in length of days but in virtue.* Consol. ad Apoll. c. 29.) And just before; *not he who hath longest professed musick, or rhetoric, or navigation, but he who hath performed best in his proper vocation is most commendable.*

(*c*) *Emittit se*; stoicum loquendi genus, *εξαγειν ἑαυτον, ευλογος εξαγωγή*.—but it is to be observed that this horrid doctrine of the *Stoics* originates from the fond persuasion that *life* and *death* are to be reckoned among the (*αδιαφορα*) *the things that are indifferent.* (Vid. *Lips.* Manud. p. 812). and what can be more ridiculous than for a man to *destroy* himself on the account of any thing that seems *indifferent!*

(*d*) And (with *Seneca's* leave) I cannot help thinking he spoke like a wise and good man. *See the* foregoing Ep. (N. d.) Ep. 24. (N. n.) The *Rhodian's* name was *Telesphorus*, who when *Lysimachus* (one of *Alexander's* successors) had cut off his ears and nose, was encaged by him as a curious new animal. *Sen.* (de irâ iii. 17.) And indeed this, *if any thing could*, would have justified him in following *Seneca's advice.*

(*e*) I think, and so ought every Christian to think, that this opinion is entirely right, not only in *some* cases, but in *all*: and for the very same reasons that are *here* mentioned by *Seneca*; *it is absurd to die for fear of death*, &c. So in Ep. 24. (see N. t.) *It is folly or rather madness to rush on death for fear of dying.* As I remember, when I was a boy at *Eton*, a silly old almswoman (Mrs. Pain) having been cut down alive, gave this reason for hanging herself, *that she was afraid of dying*: whom I think I may as well take notice of, as *Seneca* of the two poltroons mentioned in this Epistle, the *German* and the *Barbarian*; or even the blockhead *Drusus Libo*, notwithstanding his good aunt *Scribonia* pointed out the way to him. *Tacitus*, Ann. l. ii.

Concerning this ridiculous timidity, *Lucretius* (iii. 80)

Ut sæpe usque adeo, mortis formidine, vitæ
Percipit humanos odium, lucisque videndæ,
Ut sibi conciscant mærenti pectore letum;
Obliti fontem curarum hunc esse timorem.

This dread oft strikes so deep, that life they hate;
And their own hands prevent the stroke of fate:
Yet still are ignorant, that this vain fear
Breeds all their trouble, jealousy and care. Creech.

Many, says Arcesilaus, *through weakness and the calumny bestowed on death, die, for fear* of dying. Πολλοι δια ασθενειαν, και την προς τον θανατον διαβολην, αποθνησκειν, μη αποθανωσι. Plut. (Consol. ad Apollonium.

—— multos ad summa pericula misit
Venturi timor ipse mali; fortissimus ille est
Qui promptus metuenda pati.——*Lucan* vii. 103.

In war, in dangers, oft it has been known,
That fear has driv'n the headlong coward on;
Give me the man, whose cooler soul can wait
With patience for the proper hour of fate. Rowe.

4 This

This, as indeed every other extreme, is well set off by *Randolph* in his *Muses Looking-glass.*

Colax. ——— Fear you not sudden death?

Aphobus. Not I, no more than sudden sleep. Sir, I dare die.

Deilus. I dare not. Death to me is terrible.
I will not die.

Aphobus. How can you, sir, prevent it?

Deilus. Why I will kill myself.

Colax. A valiant course!
And the right way to prevent death indeed!
Your spirit is true *Roman.*——

(*f*) Whatever a Stoic may think, I can see no greater *reason* for it than in the case of *Socrates* beforementioned; whose *decent exit*, after a respite of 30 days (on account of the *Delian* Festival) is approved of by *Seneca* himself: as also his submission to the law.

(*g*) Here the *Stoic* forgets what *Seneca* has many times said in praise of *Patience*, *Fortitude*, *Constancy*, &c. *and that pain must be tolerable or soon over*, and the like; (see N. k.) But the Christian must go further, and rest satisfied, from the sure word of God, that the severer his pain, the greater trial is made of his virtue, and the more glorious will be his reward. (See N. n)

(*h*) There can be no doubt that the easiest death is the most eligible (as *Seneca* says afterwards); and it may so happen that a man under sentence of death may have his choice; as when Sir *Jeffery Elwes* for the murder of Sir *Edmundbury Godfrey*, desired to be hanged in a *silken halter*; but this is still in submission to the law: he is not at liberty to dispatch himself, at what time or in what manner he pleases; for the power of man, however free he is, is limited in this respect both by the laws of God and nature. (See N. m.)

(*i*) To me it seems *a want of spirit*
To shrink from life for fear of future ill;
'Tis to distrust the justice of the Gods,
Or else their power; and in my opinion,
Not courage, but a bold disguise for fear. *D. of Buck.* M. Brutus.

(*k*) Yes; not only *Aristotle* and the *Peripatetics*, but, among many great names of antiquity, I might mention *Homer*, *Euripides*, *Epictetus*, *Plato*, *Varro*, *Cicero*, *Curtius*, *Apuleius*, and others; of whom, perhaps, in a future Note; at present I shall be contented with adding to this good company *Seneca* himself; who, in Ep. 14, is pleased to say, *When even reason persuades us, it would be happier for us to die, we must not be rash, and hasten the fatal design.* Ep. 26. The passage *is still free and open, but there is a strong chain that binds* us down; *the love of life*; *that is not to be flung off entirely at once*;—Ep. 30. *I esteem them more who welcome death, not out of any hatred or indignation to life, but who rather receive him as a visitor, than force him to them.* Add to what is said even in this Epistle, *'Tis folly to die for fear of death*, &c. See Epp. 24, 76, 104, and particularly 107.

(*l*) So in *Sen.* Thebaid.

Ubique mors est: optime hoc cavit Deus;
Eripere vitam nemo non homini potest,
At nemo mortem.——

Death reigns throughout; such is the will of heav'n:
Life's tenure they, who please, may take away;
But Death none can prevent.——

(*m*) This is all mere declamation; for if life be such that in its nature it cannot *detain any one against their will*; yet the laws of God and man *do*; nay, life itself *does*; as *self preservation* is one of the first principles.

(*n*) *Do you love to be wretched?* No ſurely. But a man that puts any truſt in the providence of God, will ſtill chuſe *to live*; and wait his good time for the removal of all difficulties, which, when he pleaſes, he can effect in this life, or reward in the next. (See N. g.)

(*o*) I cannot help tranſcribing thoſe fine lines of *Shakeſpear*, which cannot be inculcated too often, as an antidote againſt all that *Seneca* has advanced, or any one can advance, on the ſaid topic:

> But in that ſleep of death, what dreams may come,
> When we have ſhuffled off this mortal coil,
> Muſt give a pauſe.—There's the reſpect
> That makes calamity of ſo long life:
> For who would bear the whips and ſcorns of time,—
> When he himſelf might his quietus make
> With a bare bodkin?——
> But that the dread of ſomething after death,
> The undiſcover'd country, from whoſe bourn
> No traveller returns, puzzles his will,
> And makes us rather bear thoſe ills we have,
> Than fly to others that we know not of? *Hamlet.*

(*p*) I queſtion, *Seneca*, whether any one elſe will ſay ſo, or whether this man would have done any of the great feats you mention, who was afraid to undergo his deſtin'd lot, and ſhew his courage in a brave defence of life.

The late Mr. *Donaldſon*, on reading this Epiſtle, ſent me the following remark; ſo take it as it is. "It is difficult to inveſtigate the operations of the human mind; as the machine which infolds it are ſo various, and oppoſitely conſtructed. It is generally governed by ſituations. Death occupies the mind with all its terrors in ſickneſs; in danger, it ſeems to be the *mode* of dying, and not the *fear* of death, that agonizes the mind; I will give you two inſtances to illuſtrate my poſition. In the late war, a general officer (P--rr--y) was ordered upon ſervice to *America*; as he approached the ſcene of action, he became melancholy, and the morning after he ſaw the land, Admiral *Holmes* found him in his cott, with a ſword through his body.—At the ſiege of *Martinique*, 1759, a Captain in the army *ſtole* into the arms of death, through a port-hole of the tranſport in which he took his paſſage, in the harbour of *Port-Royal*, the inſtant he was going upon dangerous ſervice; where he might have made himſelf as ſure of death, and in a manner *more honourable*, as it would have been more in the way of his profeſſion. It was pride in *Cato*; it was patriotiſm in *Curtius*."

(*q*) Surely *Seneca* was never more miſtaken in his character of a *great man*, if he thinks it an accompliſhment, for one wicked enough to deſign his own death, to find out the means for it.

(*r*) Stoiciſm hath induced *Seneca* here to advance a doctrine, than which nothing can be more abſurd and ridiculous, eſpecially among the ſoldiery.

(*s*) Rather the contrary; eſpecially in one concerned in arms; and in a Chriſtian, extremely wicked: who ought to reſt aſſured, if he believes there is a God, that he has not made any man a judge in his own caſe to determine for himſelf concerning his own life and uſefulneſs, in oppoſition to the general ſenſe both of Nature and Scripture, and the conſtant judgment of divine as well as human laws. *See* above, (N. k, m, p.)

EPISTLE

EPISTLE LXXI.

All Virtues equal.

YOU frequently consult me, *Lucilius*, on particular subjects; forgetful that we are separated from each other by a vast sea: and since it must be long before my advice can reach you; it may so happen, that, my opinion concerning some things may be received at a time, when the contrary would be preferable. For, advice and counsel must be adapted to circumstances, but circumstances are for ever fluctuating and rolling off: therefore advice should be given *the same day*: and even this may sometimes be too late: it must be given, as they say, *on the nail.* I will shew you then how it may at once be given and receiv'd.

As often as you would know, whether such a thing is to be avoided or pursued; have regard to the *Summum bonum*, or chief purpose of life: for whatever we do must be consonant with *that*. He will not act orderly in particular things, who hath not before him the summary intention of his whole life. No one, though he hath his implements ready by him, can paint a picture, without having first made a design of what he intends to draw. We are often therefore guilty of error, because we generally deliberate on the parts of life, without taking in, and reflecting upon the whole. The man, who lets fly an arrow to any purpose, must first know the mark he aims at, and accordingly direct and guide it with a skilful hand (*a*). To one, ignorant of what port he is steering to, all winds are the same; he cannot call any one his own (*or as what is for him*). Chance must necessarily have great power over our lives, because we live, as it were, by chance. Some men are not even conscious of their own knowledge: as we often enquire after those in whose presence we are standing; so for the most part, we are ignorant of the *summum bonum*, that is ever placed before us: nor need there many words, or a long circumlocution, to decypher what this *sovereign good* is: it is to be pointed at, if I may so say, with the finger.

There is no need of divifions and fubdivifions here; it confifts not of variety; you may fay, in general, whatever is *right and fit*, is the *fummum bonum:* and what you may ftill more admire, *this is the only good* (*b*): all other *good* is falfe and fpurious. If you can be perfuaded of this and are *fond* of virtue (for it is not enough barely to *love* it) whatfoever fhe is pleafed to appoint, feem it as it will to others, will certainly prove happy and profperous to *you* (*c*): even were you to be tortured; provided you fhew yourfelf fuperior to, and even lefs concern'd than the torturer himfelf; or to be grievoufly fick; provided you curfe not fortune, nor tamely furrender yourfelf to your difeafe. In fhort, all difafters, which to other men feem evils, will be attenuated, and turn to good; if your virtue rifeth eminently above them: only be affured that nothing is *good*, but what is virtuous; and all the inconveniencies attending it, will, in their own right, claim the title of *good*, when virtue hath adorned, and given them a grace.

Many may think that we promife greater things than human nature is capable of accepting, and not without reafon: they refpect only the body; let them return to the confideration of the foul, and they will take the meafure of man from *God*. Exalt thyfelf, O *Lucilius*, beft of men, and quit the trifling fchools of fuch philofophers, as are weighing the moft noble things in the world by fyllables, and by their minute inftructions rather degrade and impair the noble faculties of the mind. I had rather you fhould imitate thofe philofophers, who firft invented thefe ftudies (*d*), than thofe who teach them; and who make it their bufinefs to render philofophy rather difficult, than great: you will follow the former, if I have any authority with you. *Socrates*, who reduced all philofophy to the conduct of found morality, affirmed that the principal part of wifdom was, to diftinguifh *good and evil: would you be happy*, fays he, *be not concern'd to be thought by fome a fool:* if any one fhould reproach you contumelioufly let him do it, you can fuffer nothing, fo long as you adhere to virtue (*e*). Would you be happy, being ftrictly a good man, with an honeft heart, you need not be concerned that any one defpifeth you. But this happinefs no one can obtain, except the man who thinks all *good equal* (*f*). Becaufe there is no *good*, but virtue; and virtue is alike in all.

What

What then, is there no difference between Cato's being elected Prætor and his meeting with a repulse (*g*)? *Does it make no difference, whether* Cato *is a conqueror in the battle of* Pharſalia, *or is conquered? Would this* good, *in being unconquerable himſelf, though his party was beat, have been equal to that, which he would have obtained, had he returned victorious to his country, and given the nations peace?* Why not? It is ſtill the ſame virtue, by which bad fortune is overcome, and good aright directed. Virtue cannot be greater or leſs: ſhe is of one and the ſame ſtature. But ſuch is the inſtability of human affairs;—*Pompey* ſhall loſe an army; and that moſt glorious cauſe ſhall fail;—men of the firſt quality, and the flower of *Pompey's* party, the whole ſenate bearing arms, ſhall all be routed in one battle;—the ruin of ſo great an empire ſhall affect the whole world; it ſhall be felt in *Egypt*, in *Africa*, and in *Spain*;—nor ſhall this wretched Republic have the bleſſing to fall at once;—though all things be done, the knowledge of places ſhall be of no ſervice to *Juba*, even in his own dominions; nor the moſt ſtubborn valour of his affectionate ſubjects ſave him;—the fidelity alſo of the men of *Utica* (*the friends of* Cato) now broken with calamity, ſhall no longer ſupport them;—and the good fortune of *Scipio's* name ſhall abandon him in *Africa* (*h*):—what though a decree was made, that *Cato ſhould receive no detriment*, yet *Cato* is conquered; and you may reckon this among his diſappointments: the loſs however of victory he bore with as great magnanimity as the loſs of the prætorſhip; the day he was rejected he diverted himſelf at tennis, and the night he was about to die, he amuſed himſelf with reading; it was the ſame to him to loſe his life and the prætorſhip; he knew it was his duty (as a philoſopher) to ſuffer patiently whatever might happen; and why indeed ſhould he not ſuffer with a great and equal mind, this ſudden change of the ſtate? What is there that is excepted from the danger of a change? Not the earth, not the heavens, not the whole form and contexture of the univerſe, though God be the director and diſpoſer thereof: the preſent order of things ſhall not always continue (*i*): a day will come, that ſhall throw them out of their courſe; all things have their time: they ſpring up, they flouriſh, and are gone: the glorious orbs we ſee above us, and all things we are converſant with here below, and on which we ſtand as on a ſolid

baſe,

base, shall wear away and come to an end: there is nothing but what hath its age and declination: though Nature exhibits all these things at different times, and gives them unequal existence; whatever is, shall not be; and though it perish not, shall be dissolved into its first principles (*k*): to us dissolution is to die.—But the misfortune is, we extend not our view beyond what we see before us; the mind, dull and addicted to the care of the body, stretches not its sight to things remote and at a distance; otherwise it would suffer this our dissolution, and all things belonging thereunto, with more constancy and courage; if it did but consider that all things undergo the vicissitude of life and death; that being dissolved, they are renewed; and renewed to be again dissolved; and that in this work is employed the agency of God, who governs all things.

Cato therefore when he reflects on the life of man, and the state of things, will say, "All mankind, whoever are, or shall be, are condemned to die (*l*). All those flourishing cities that have the world at command, and all the greatness and splendour of foreign empires, in whatever part of the globe, shall one day be no more, and fall into various kinds of ruin (*m*). War proves the destruction of some; of others idleness and sloth; peace turned into listlessness and inaction consumes others; and luxury is destructive of the greatest opulency: a sudden inundation of the sea shall cover all these fruitful plains (*n*), or an earthquake swallow them up in its hideous cavity. Why then should I complain, or be grieved, that I precede the general fate of things but a few moments?"

Thus let the constant mind submit to providence, and suffer, without a murmur, whatever the universal law of Nature commands. The soul is either set free to enjoy a better life, to remain more bright, and tranquil for ever in heaven; or, at least, without any further inconvenience or annoy, will according to its nature, be blended and coincide with the *whole* of things. The noble life of *Cato* therefore is not a greater *good* than his noble death: because virtue admits not of extension or increase. *Socrates* was used to say, that truth and virtue were the same thing; as that increaseth not (in the abstract idea of it) so neither

neither doth virtue: it is ever complete and full. There is no reason therefore you should wonder at my saying, *All good is equal*; both that which ariseth from design, and that which a sudden exigency requireth. For, if you allow such an inequality, as to reckon the enduring torture with magnanimity, a *less good*, you will also account it an *evil*, and call *Socrates* an unhappy wretch while in prison; and *Cato* no less miserable, when he tore open his wounds with more spirit than he gave them; and *Regulus* the most unfortunate of men, in suffering the severest punishment for keeping his word with an enemy: but no one, even of the most effeminate, have dared to say this: they deny him indeed to be happy, yet at the same time deny him to be miserable. The antient *Academics* confess him to be happy even amidst his torture, but such happiness not to be complete and perfect; which can by no means be admitted: for if a man is happy, he hath reached the *summum bonum*, the chief, or sovereign *good*; and what is chief and sovereign admits of no degree above it, provided it still adheres to virtue, which no adversity can lessen or destroy; and remains sound, however the body be impaired and bruised in pieces; and it certainly does so remain: for, by virtue, I mean that generous and noble spirit, which is incited in the mind, against every molestation that can annoy it: and this spirit or courage will true wisdom give or infuse into the minds of such young men as are of a generous disposition, and are so smitten with the beauty of an honourable action, as to make them despise all casualties, in the steady performance of it: it will persuade them, that the one only good consists in virtue. And that this can neither be lower'd or heighten'd any more, than a ruler, by the direction of which is drawn a straight line; and which if you vary, the least bend or change will destroy the intention. The same we say of virtue: it is ever right and straight; admits of no flexure; is stubborn, and cannot be bent, or raised: it is a square, by which all other things are measured; itself its own measure. And if virtue itself cannot be more right or straight: neither can any thing effected thereby; for every thing must necessarily correspond and answer to this; and therefore they are *all equal*.

What then, you say, *is it equal to lie upon the rack, and to feast at a banquet?* And does this seem strange to you? Hear then something more

more ſtrange: I affirm, that to feaſt at a banquet is a bad thing, and to be tortured on the rack a good thing; if the former be carried on luxurioufly and fcandaloufly; and this endured fitly and honourably. It is not the ſubject matter but virtue that makes the difference: wherever this is apparent, all things are of equal meaſure and worth. This doctrine perhaps may offend the man who judgeth of another's underſtanding by his own: and methinks, I ſee him ready to fly in my face, for ſaying, that the *good* is *equal* in him, who manfully bears adverſity, and him, who carries himſelf virtuouſly in proſperity; or in him, who triumphs, and the unhappy prince, who is carried, in chains, before the triumphant car, with a ſtill unconquer'd mind. They think it impoſſible for a man to do, what they cannot do themſelves, and according to their own poor abilities, bear ſentence concerning virtue. Why do you wonder at my ſaying, that ſome rejoice in being burned, wounded, bound in chains and ſlain? Nay, that ſometimes they have made it their choice (*o*)? Frugality is a heavy puniſhment to the luxurious; as labour is to the idle; the nice and delicate pity the induſtrious; and to the indolent, ſtudy is torture: in like manner, we think thoſe things hard and intolerable, which we are too weak and infirm to bear; forgetting that it is even a torment to many, to be debarr'd their bottle, or to be diſturb'd at break of day. It is certain theſe things are not hard and ſevere in the nature of the things themſelves, but we are recreant and wavering. Great things are only to be judged of by great minds; otherwiſe the fault will ſeem to lie in the things, which is really our own; thus the ſtraighteſt ſtick, if you ſink part of it under water will appear crooked and broken. It matters not what you ſee, but how, or through what medium you ſee it. Our mind is dim in the inveſtigation of truth: give me a youth, uncorrupt, of good parts, and ſound judgment; and I make no doubt but that he will own, he thinks him an happier man, who bears up, with a ſtubborn neck, the heavieſt burden of adverſity, than the man whom a proſperous fortune hath ſatiated with all that he can deſire.

There is nothing extraordinary in a man's being firm and unſhaken in the calm of proſperity: but he is worthy our admiration, who is exalted, where others are depreſſed; and there ſtands his ground, where others crouch and lie down. What evil is there in torment, or in other accidents which we call afflictions? In my opinion, no more than this; to deſpond, to be bowed down, to be vanquiſhed; none of which can fall to the ſhare of the wiſe man: he ſtands erect under any weight whatever; nothing can make him leſs; nothing, let what will happen, diſpleaſe him: whatever affliction can befall mankind, he complains not of its being his lot: he knows his own ſtrength; he knows that he is ſubject to misfortune, and muſt bear it: not that I ſuppoſe him to be as inſenſible of pain as a rock (*p*); no; I conſider him as ſtill having his feeling; but as compoſed of two parts, the one irrational; and this indeed is wrung with grief and pain; the other rational, which in its reſolutions remains unſhaken, intrepid, invincible. In this part then is placed the *chief good* of man; which, before it is accompliſhed, is but an uncertain wavering of the mind, but when it is perfected, becomes an immovable ſteadineſs of temper. Therefore a man, when he begins this ſtudy of perfection (*q*), and ſeriouſly to follow virtue, though he draws near the *chief good*, yet not having put the laſt hand to it, is apt to ſtop, and forego ſomething of the intention of the mind; for he has not yet paſſed the bounds of uncertainty, but walketh ſtill in ſlippery places: whereas the man, whoſe wiſdom is compleat, is never better pleaſed with himſelf than when he can give ſome generous proof of his virtue: and ſuch things as others dread, provided they are conſequences of ſome juſt and honeſt duty, he not only bears, but embraces them with joy; and had rather be called ſo much *the better man*, than ſo much *the happier*.

I come now to what I know your expectation longeth for: that our virtue may not ſeem extravagant, and beyond the nature of things, I own the wiſe man will tremble, grieve and look pale; for theſe are the ſenſations of the body. From whence then ariſeth miſery? what is truly evil? It is this: when ſuch things diſtract the mind; when they reduce it to acknowledge ſervitude, and cauſe murmur and regret. A wiſe man indeed overcomes fortune by virtue; but many who profeſs wiſdom are ſometimes terrified by her ſlighteſt threats: in this reſpect

 it

it is our own fault if we require from the proficient the ſame as from the wiſe man. I am ſatisfied that what I recommend is praiſe-worthy, but I ſtill want reſolution: and was I fully reſolved to put ſuch things in practice, I ſhould ſcarce find them in ſuch order, and ſo well exerciſed as to be ſerviceable upon all occaſions.—As wool will ſometime take a certain die at once, but will not imbibe other till after being dipped and ſoaked ſeveral times; ſo, though a fit diſpoſition may receive certain doctrines at once; yet even this unleſs it deſcends and remains fixed a long while does not tinge, but only ſtains, the mind. There is need then but of little time, and few words to ſhew, that the only good is virtue; at leaſt that there is no *good* without virtue; and that virtue hath its reſidence in the better part of us, I mean the *rational*.

But after all what is virtue? A judgment true and firm; from whence comes that promptitude of mind, that will ſtrip things of their vain appearances, and will ſhew them in their proper light: and to this judgment it will be conſonant and agreeable, to think all things, that come under the hands, or are the effects of virtue, are *good*; and that all *good is equal*. *Good* belonging to the body is ſo far good, as it belongs to the body: but not upon the whole: it may have ſome value, but at the ſame time it will want *dignity:* for even among theſe bleſſings ſome will be greater, ſome leſs: as even among the followers of wiſdom, we muſt neceſſarily own, there is often a wide difference: ſome have advanced ſo far, as to dare to look up to fortune, but not with a ſteady eye; dazzled with too great ſplendour, they own themſelves vanquiſhed: others proceed ſo far, as to be able to engage her face to face, and having attained to perfection, are ſo full of confidence, as never to be caſt down. Things not carried on to perfection are never ſure; they fruſtrate themſelves, and often fall to decay and ruin. This muſt certainly be the conſequence where perſeverance is withheld. If the mind lets go her intention and purſues not her ſtudies faithfully, ſhe has done nothing; nor can what is loſt be eaſily recover'd. We muſt therefore puſh on, and ſtrenuouſly perſevere: more remains behind than we yet have encountered: the being willing however to proceed is great part of the way: for my part, I am very ſenſible of this; and therefore am willing, yes, I am willing with all my ſtrength and mind: and tis my happineſs, *Lucilius*, to ſee you alſo, ready, and eager with all your might, ſo to adapt your actions, to the fitneſs of things, as ſoon to reach the deſired goal. Let us then haſten; and life will be a bleſſing; otherwiſe it will only be lingering here, among thoſe who are doing nothing, or nothing to the purpoſe of being: and be this our care; that our time may be our own; it cannot be our own, unleſs we are maſters of ourſelves. O, when ſhall we be ſo happy, as to deſpiſe fortune, good or bad! when ſhall we be ſo happy, as having ſubdued all vile affections, and got the maſtery over our paſſions, we may joyfully cry out, *I have conquer'd*. Do you aſk, whom or what it is we have conquer'd? Not the *Perſians*, nor the far diſtant *Medes*; nor any warlike people beyond the *Dabæ:* but avarice, ambition, and, above all, the fear of death; which hath conquered the conquerors of nations.

ANNOTATIONS, &c.

(a) Ariſtotle, (Ethic. i.) Αρ' ὖν καὶ πρὸς τὸν βίον ἡ γνῶσις τῦ τέλυς μεγάλην ἔχει ῥοπὴν κ. τ. λ. *The knowledge of the end is of great conſequence in the conduct of life; as archers having fixed their aim, are more likely to obtain their purpoſe.* Cic. (de fin.) Quid eſt in vita tantopere quærendum quàm quis ſit finis, quod extremum, quod ultimum, quo ſint omnia bene vivendi, rectèque faciendi conſilia referenda! *What is there in life ſo requiſite to be enquired after, as what is the end, the laſt, and chief thing, to which all the counſels of good life and juſt actions are to be referred?*

(b) This is a principal dogma of the Stoics, to which all the reſt are to be referred. See Ep, 74. *Lipſ.* Manud. ii. 20.

Virtus omnia in ſe habet, omnia adſunt bona
Quem penes eſt virtus. *Plaut.* Amphit. ii. 2.
In virtue all things are contain'd; where'er
Dwells Virtue, *there dwells* every good.

In all ſtations of life, virtue hath or ought to have the principal command. Quæ homines arant, navigant, ædificant virtuti omnia parent. *Salluſt*—The arts *of agriculture, building, navigation, are all owing to the virtues of induſtry.*

Scriptura, inquit Ambroſius, nihil bonum niſi quod honeſtum aſſerit; virtutemque in omni rerum ſtatu beatam judicat, quæ neque corporis bonis, vel externis, augeatur, neque minuatur adverſis. The *Scripture*, ſays Ambroſe, *admits of no* good, *but what is* right and fit; *and that* virtue *renders life* happy, *in every condition; not heightened by any external good, nor lowered by adverſity.*——— Deut. xxx. 19. *I call heaven and earth to witneſs againſt you*, ſays *Moſes* to the *Hebrews*, *that I have ſet before you life and death, bleſſing and curſing; therefore chuſe life*, by your love and fear of God.— Pſ. cxix. 1. Bleſſed *are they that are undefiled in the way, and walk in the law of the Lord.* And *Solomon*, Wiſd. vii. 7. *I called upon God, and the Spirit of* Wiſdom *came upon me.*—All good things *together came to me with her, innumerable riches and honour.*

(c) Rom. viii. 28. See Epp. 31. 66. (N. k.) 118.

(d) As *Socrates*, *Zeno*, and other philosophers, in the conduct of life.

(e) *Blessed are ye when men shall revile you, and persecute you, and speak all manner of evil against you* falsely *for my sake: rejoice and be exceeding glad, for great is your reward in heaven.* Matth. v. 2. *If ye be reproached for the name of* Christ, *happy are ye, for the Spirit of Glory and of God resteth upon you.* i Pet. iv. 14. And accordingly saith St. *Paul, Being reviled, we bless; being persecuted, we suffer it; being defamed, we still intreat.* i Cor. iv. 11.

(f) See this professedly and fully treated of, Ep. 66.

(g) *Cato* was rejected by the underhand management of *Pompey* and *Crassus*; when *Vatinius* was elected prætor in his stead. (*See* his Life in *Plutarch*.)—" *Cato* lost the election of prætor and that of consul, but is any one blind enough to truth to imagine that these repulses reflected any disgrace upon him? The dignity of those two magistracies would have been encreased by his wearing them. They suffered, not *Cato*. Bolingbroke *on exile*.——However, when chosen prætor, the suffering his authority to create in him the contempt and dislike of established customs, so as to appear in public barefooted, and without his robe, and to sit in that condition to hear causes in open court, caused him to be justly reproached with having undervalued and disgraced the dignity of his office by these indecencies. It is said in the following, Omnia quæ acciderent ferenda esse persuaserat sibi. But if he knew *patience* was the duty of a philosopher, did he put it in practice when most required? surely not. If I should say, that he ought, in love to his country, to have reserved himself for a better opportunity of serving it;—that it is probable from the events which followed, that he might afterwards have been an instrument of good to it;—that he rashly, and in a passion, judged of what he could not well judge of; that it was a sullen pride of heart not to deign to live, because in one trial his cause had not been successful;—and that a true greatness of soul had been more seen in accepting his life, (if that had been necessary) at the hands of a man, in whose power *Omnipotent Providence*, or *Fate*, (which he believed irresistible) had put it. All this would be hard to refute upon the principles of any philosophy." See *Watts*, on the unlawfulness of self-murther.

(h) *Cæsar* in a great battle fought near *Thapsus*, took the camps both of *Scipio* and *Juba*, who fled only with a few of their men, and the rest were cut in pieces, *Plut.* ib.

(i) *Lipsius* thinks this to be referred to the Stoic *ἐκπύρωσιν*, *conflagration* of the world. *Consol.* ad Polyb. cxxi. *Lips.* (Physiol. ii. 22.)

(k) The cloud-capt tow'rs, the gorgeous palaces,
The solemn temples, the great globe itself,
Yea, all which it inherit, shall dissolve.—*Shakesp.* Tempest.

(l) *As by one man sin entered into the world, and death by sin; so death passed upon all men, for that all have sinned.* Rom. v. 12.——*It is appointed for all men once to die.* Heb. ix. 27.

(m) *Behold the day of the Lord cometh, when the stars shall fall from heaven, and the constellations shall not give their light, the sun shall be darkened in his going forth, and the moon shall not cause her light to shine*, &c. Is. xiii. 10. Ezek. xxxii. 7. Joel. ii. 31. Matth. xxiv. 29.

(n) This is likewise a stoical tenet—. So *Cic.* (somn. Scip.) Propter eluviones exustionesque terrarum quas accidere tempore certo necesse est, non modo non æternam, sed ne diuturnam quidem gloriam assequi possumus. *When we consider the inundations and conflagrations that must necessarily happen in the course of things, we must be sensible that all the glory we can attain to, far from being eternal, cannot be lasting.* See *Lips.* Physiol. ii. 21.

(o) *Others were tortured not accepting deliverance, that they may obtain a better resurrection*, &c. Heb. xi. 35. *Not only so, but we glory also in tribulations, knowing that tribulation worketh patience, patience experience, and experience hope.* Rom. v. 3.—*But let patience have her perfect work, that ye may be perfect and entire, wanting nothing.* Jam. i. 4.

(p) See Epp. 85. 116. *Lips.* Manud. iii. 7.

(q) Sc. The *Proficient*. *Lips.* Manud. ii. 9. See Epp. 72, 75.

EPISTLE LXXII.

On the Study of Philosophy.

THE solution of the question you proposed to me, *Lucilius,* I should have sent to you, if my memory had not failed me; but it is grown very deficient of late, for want of exercise. It is with me, as with books, that, having been laid by in some damp place, grow mouldy, and the leaves stick together: the mind must be often unfolded: and whatever is deposited therein, must be frequently canvassed; in order to have it ready for use, when called for. We must therefore defer this your request for the present; as what would demand more labour and application, than I can now spare: as soon as I can get more leisure, and can make a longer stay in the same place, I promise you I will take it in hand. For there are some things, which a man may write in his chariot; but there are some that require musing, leisure, and privacy (*a*). Nevertheless something may be done, though the whole day be taken up with business; for when will it be otherwise? As one new business generally creates another; we sow it, as it were, and from one spring many; till at length we recover ourselves; so that when I have finished the work in hand, I will give up my whole attention to your request; and, having got over this troublesome task sit down to my studies.

• But know, *Lucilius,* that philosophy admits of no delays: it is not to be deferred to leisure hours; every thing else is to be postponed that we may apply ourselves closely to this: no time can be sufficient for it. Though extended from youth, to the longest term of human life, with regard to philosophy there is very little difference between omission and intermission; for where it is interrupted, it abideth not; but as some things by being overstretched are broken; philosophy being discontinued returns to its first principles. We must resist all other engagements,

ments, not to be put off for a time only, but quite set aside. There is no time less fit than another for such salutary studies: but many study not for such ends as they ought principally to study.

Should any obstacle interfere, it concerns not the wise man, whose mind in every business is intent, yet ever chearful: such as are imperfect find continual interruptions in their mirth; but the joy of the wise man is firm and lasting (*b*): it has no connexion with chance or accidents; it is always calm and easy: for it depends not upon any thing foreign; nor waits the applause of men, or the smiles of fortune: its felicity is truly domestic and within: it might depart out of the mind, if it had entered in: but it was born there: it is sometimes indeed reminded of mortality by an external accident, but what is generally slight and only grazeth the top-skin: it may be somewhat blasted by a small annoyance, but the *chief good* is still permanent and fixed: some inconvenience, I own, may attend it from without, as in a body otherwise hale and strong, some pustules or small eruptions will break out, that strike not deep enough to do any harm within. This then I say, is the difference between a man of consummate wisdom, and one in his way thereto (*c*); the same as between a man in sound health, and one that is upon the recovery from some grievous and chronic disorder; when instead of health he enjoys only a shorter or less painful fit. Such a one without constant care and application, is now and then afflicted and in danger of a relapse: whereas the wiseman neither fears the return of any former disorder, nor the attack of a new one: to the body a good state of health is but precarious; which though the physician hath restored, he cannot insure: and is often recalled to the same patient: but the mind when healed, is healed once for all.

And I will tell you, *Lucilius*, how you shall know, when a man is thoroughly well;—if he is content and satisfied in himself, if he rests well-assured, and knows that all the desires of mortals, all the blessings that are given or pray'd for, are of no great moment with regard to an happy life. For that to which any accession can be made, is as yet imperfect; that which can lose any thing, cannot be perpetual: he whose

joy

joy is like to be perpetual, for ever triumphs in his own: whereas the things that the vulgar are gaping after, are ever upon the ebb and flow: fortune gives not the conveyance of any thing in perpetuity; yet even theſe caſual things can give delight, when reaſon hath well temper'd and blended them together: this is what alſo recommends external things, when they are not too greedily coveted, and if gained, uſed with diſcretion. *Attalus* was wont to uſe this ſimile: " you have ſometimes " ſeen a dog, catching with open mouth a bit of bread or fleſh toſſed " him by his maſter, whatever he gets, he ſtrait devours, and ſtill " gapes in expectation of more: ſo it is with us; whatever fortune is " pleaſed to throw to us, we ſwallow it down, without any taſte or " pleaſure, and are ſtill intent and eager after another morſel." This is not the caſe of a wiſe man; he is full; if any thing offers, he accepts it without any agitation, and lays it by; his joy is perfect and conſtant, becauſe it is his own: whereas the man, who, however good his diſpoſition, or whatever progreſs he hath made, hath not yet reached the ſummit of perfection, is alternately raiſed or depreſſed; one while lifted up to heaven, and now again thrown down upon the earth: nay to the ignorant and unſkilful, there is no end of their fall; down they go, as it were, into the *Epicurean* Chaos (or *Vacuum*) that knows no bounds.

There is a third ſort of men; who likewiſe pretend to wiſdom; but have not attained thereto: they keep it ſtill in ſight, and, if I may ſo expreſs it, can reach her with their hand (*d*); theſe ſtand their ground, ſo as not to make a ſlip: they are in the haven but not yet ſafe aſhore. Seeing then there is ſo great a diſparity between the higheſt and the loweſt, and even the middle ſtate is ſtill ſubject to ſtorms: and ſtill in danger of being carried out to ſea again; we muſt by no means indulge any avocation from this our ſtudy; one buſineſs will ſtill introduce another without end: we muſt therefore prevent them in their firſt riſe: it is better and eaſier not to ſuffer them to begin; than when once begun to put an end to them.

ANNO-

ANNOTATIONS, &c

(*a*) Lectum et otium] See Ep. 67. (N. c.) Plin. Ep. (4. 5.) Visus est sibi jacere in *lectulo* suo, compositus in habitum studentis. Caius Fannius *dreamt that he lay on his couch, in an undress, fit for study, with a desk as usual before him.* Orrery.

Non hæc in nostris, ut quondam scribimus, hortis;
Nec, consuete, meum, lectule, corpus habes. *Ovid.*
Not in the garden now, as erst, I write,
Nor on my usual couch these lines indite.

(*b*) Ep. 27. Aliquod potius bonum mansurum circumspice; nullum autem est nisi quod animus *ex se sibi* invenit: *sola virtus*, præstat gaudium, *perpetuum*, securum, &c. See also Epp. 23. (N. b.) 59.

(*c*) This distinction between the *complete* wise man, and the *proficient*, is frequent. See the foregoing Epistle, and Ep. 75. (N. b.) *Lips.* Manud. ii. 9.

(*d*) Sub ictu habent.] As a mark, at which an archer hath taken aim, but hath not yet let fly his arrow. Or, alluding to the gladiators when they lift up their hands over an adversary, and are ready to strike. So *Lactantius*, vii. 12. Nec vim repellere potest, quia sub aspectum *et sub ictum* venit. *Gruter.*——Be that as it will, the sense is plain from the like expression in *Sen.* (de Benef. ii. 29) nihil mortale non *sub ictu* nostro positum—Its contrary we read in l. 7. Deum *contra ictum* sua divinitas posuit. *See* also De Vit. beat. c. 12. Ad Marciam, c. 19. Lucan. v. 729.

—— Quòd nolles stare *sub ictu*
Fortunæ, quo mundus erat, Romanaque fata,
Conjux sola fuit.——
See what new passions now the hero knows,
Now first he doubts success, and fears his foes;
Rome, *and the world he hazards in the strife,*
And gives up all to Fortune, *but his wife.* Rowe.

EPISTLE LXXIII.

On Philosophers,—considered as Friends to Government.

THEY seem to me, *Lucilius*, greatly mistaken, who think that such as have given up themselves strenuously to philosophy, are stubborn and refractory, despisers of magistrates and kings, and of all that bear office in the administration of public affairs (*a*). On the contrary, none are more grateful, none more affectionate; and with good reason; for to whom can we be more obliged, than to those by whose means we live in the enjoyment of ease and tranquillity? They therefore to whom a peaceful

peaceful government gives leiſure and opportunity of deſigning to live well and happily, cannot but think themſelves obliged to the kind author of this bleſſing, and honour him as a parent; much more than ſuch as are ever reſtleſs and buſy in public life; who owe many things to their princes and governors, yet ſtill think them in their debt for more; and whom no liberality can ſo fully oblige as to ſatisfy their deſires; which are ſtill increaſing the more they are indulged: for whoever is thinking upon what he is ſtill to receive, generally forgets what he has already received; nor hath covetouſneſs any greater evil attending it, than that it is ungrateful.

Add, moreover, that none of thoſe who are converſant in public affairs, conſider whom they may ſurpaſs, but by whom they may be ſurpaſſed in dignity; nor is it pleaſant to ſee many below them, as it is grievous to ſee one above them. Ambition of every kind hath this failing, never to regard what is paſt: nor is it ambition alone that is thus unſettled; but all manner of covetouſneſs; for wherever it leaves off, it begins again: whereas the man who is upright and ſincere, who hath left the court, the forum, and all concern for public buſineſs, that he may apply himſelf to ſomething greater, cannot but have a reſpect for thoſe who permit him to do this in ſafety: he acknowledgeth the favour, and is ever ready to give ample teſtimony of gratitude, as being obliged to them for a bleſſing, which they *unknowingly* have conferred upon him. As he admires and reverenceth his predeceſſors, by whoſe inſtructions he diveſts himſelf of all vice; ſo does he thoſe, under whoſe protection he freely exerciſeth the diſcipline of virtue.

But does not a king by his great power protect others likewiſe? who denies it? But as they, who have traded for the more precious wares on the ſame ſeas, think themſelves the more obliged to *Neptune* for a ſucceſsful voyage; and as a merchant pays his vows more heartily than a paſſenger; and as among the merchants he is more profuſely thankful, or has reaſon to be ſo, who hath brought over ſpices, and cochineal, and gold, than thoſe who have freighted a veſſel with ordinary things, that only ſupply the place of ballaſt; ſo the bleſſing of peace belonging to all in general more deeply affects thoſe, who make a right uſe of it *(in cultivating the mind)*: for there are many in the retinue of the great, who find more work in peace than in war: and do you think they are under the ſame obligation for the enjoyment of peace, who are given to drunkenneſs, and riot, and other vices, which war alone can break off? unleſs perhaps you judge ſo unjuſtly of the wiſe man, as to ſuppoſe that he thinks himſelf in particular under no obligation for common bleſſings: for my part, I think myſelf indebted to the ſun and moon, though they riſe not to me alone; and I own an obligation to the ſeaſons, and the Almighty power that directs them, though they are not appointed to do me any particular honour. The fooliſh covetouſneſs of mortals makes a diſtinction between poſſeſſion and property, nor thinks any thing his own that belongs to the public: but the wiſe man judgeth nothing more his own, than what he enjoys in common with mankind (*b*): nor indeed could theſe be ſaid to be common unleſs every one partook of them: a participation of the leaſt portion whatever creates fellowſhip. Add now that what is great and truly *good*, cannot be ſo divided, as that part of it alone can be obtained by any ſingle perſon: no; the whole of it belongs to every one. A largeſs is diſtributed at ſo much a head; a treat, or dole (*c*), or whatever the hand can receive, may be divided into ſhares; but of ſuch an individual *good*, as peace or liberty, the whole belongs as much to all as to any ſingle perſon whatever: therefore the wiſe man conſiders by whoſe aſſiſtance he enjoys the benefit of theſe things, and by whoſe wiſe adminiſtration he is not compelled to bear arms, or keep watch, or guard the walls, and pay ſuch exorbitant taxes, as neceſſity requires in time of war; and therefore is thankful to his governor. For this too philoſophy eſpecially teacheth; to acknowledge favours; and duly, if poſſible, requite them; but ſometimes a bare acknowledgment ſerves for payment: he will acknowledge therefore that he is infinitely indebted to thoſe by whoſe wiſe adminiſtration and forecaſt he happens to enjoy fattening eaſe, and to be maſter of his own time, and to live undiſturbed by any public employ.

O melibæe, Deus nobis hæc otia fecit:
Namque erit ille mihi ſemper Deus.—

This

This soft retirement some kind God bestow'd,
For never can I deem him less than God.

Now if such pleasurable times owe much to their Author, the great benefit whereof consists only in this:

Ille meas errare boves, (ut cernis) et ipsum
Ludere quæ vellem, calamo permisit agresti. *Virg.* Ecl. i.

He gave my kine to graze the flowery plain,
And to my pipe renew'd the rural strain.

Of how great value must we think that tranquillity which the gods enjoy, and which of man makes a *god!* Yes, *Lucilius*, thus it is: and thus in a compendious way, I even call you to heaven.

Sextius was wont to say, Jovem plus non posse quam bonum virum, Jupiter *could not do more than a good man (d). Jupiter* indeed hath the means to be more liberal to man; but among two men that are *good*, he is not the better who is the richer; any more than among two pilots, who are equally skilful in guiding and navigating a ship, you call him the better, who is master of the larger and finer vessel. In what does *Jupiter* then excel a good man? He is *everlastingly good.* The wise man however does not think the worse of himself because his virtues are confined within a narrower space. As of two wise men he that dies an old man is not happier than he whose virtue is terminated within a few years: so the gods excel not a wise man in happiness, though they excel them in the duration of happiness. Virtue is not greater for being of long duration: *Jupiter* possesseth all things, but he obligeth others with the use of them. This one enjoyment then belongs to him, that he is the cause of enjoyment to all others: the wise man likewise is pleased to see others enjoy these things; but despiseth them with as much æquanimity as *Jupiter* himself: and in this admires himself the more, as *Jupiter* cannot use these vanities, and the wise man will not.

Let us therefore believe *Sextius* shewing us the most excellent way, and crying out, Hac itur ad astra, *this is the way to heaven*; this I say, by by frugality, by temperance, by fortitude. The gods are neither diſdainful, nor envious; they admit, and reach out their hands to, thoſe who are aſcending (*e*).—Do you wonder that men ſhould aſcend to the gods? God deſcends to men (*f*); or rather he dwells within them: there is no good man without God (*g*). The divine ſeeds are ſown in the human breaſt, which, if they meet with a good huſbandman, produce fruits like their original, and a divine crop ſprings up; but if with a bad huſbandman, they die as in a barren and marſhy ground; or bring forth cockle and weeds inſtead of corn (*h*).

ANNOTATIONS, &c.

(*a*) *Seneca* (de Clem. ii. 5.) obſerves that this behaviour is frequently laid to the charge of the *Stoics* (Scio male audire *apud imperitos* ſectam ſtoicorum tanquam *nimis duram*, et minimè principibus regibuſque daturam bonum conſilium) ſed nulla ſecta benignior, leniorque eſt, nulla amantior hominum, et communibus bonis attentior; ut cui propoſitum ſit, uſui eſſe aut auxilio, nec ſibi tantum, ſed univerſis ſinguliſque conſulere. *Whereas there is no ſect more kind and gentle; none more a friend to mankind, and attentive to the common good; none more ready to aid and aſſiſt their friends when called upon; and to conſult the happineſs, not only of themſelves* (like the Epicureans,) *but of every individual*—Lipſius *Manud.* l. 151. enters further into a defence of the Stoics in this reſpect. But our buſineſs is to obſerve the ſame of the primitive Chriſtians, whoſe behaviour and writings ſufficiently clear them of the like charge. *Eſteem all men, love the brotherhood, fear God, honour the King.* i Pet. ii. 17. *Let every ſoul be ſubject unto the higher powers. For Rulers are not a terror to the evil: Wilt thou not be afraid of the power, do that which is good, and thou ſhalt have praiſe of the ſame: for he is the miniſter of God to thee for good.* Rom. xiii. 1—8. *I exhort therefore that, firſt of all, ſupplications, prayers, interceſſions, and giving of thanks be made for all men; for Kings, and for all that are in authority: that we may lead a quiet and peaceable life, in all godlineſs and honeſty.* i Tim. ii. 1, 2.

(*b*) This is another paradox of the Stoics, Omnia ſapientis; *the wiſe man poſſeſſeth every thing.* See Epp. 9. 12. 13. 62.—Cic. Parad. vi.—*Empir.* (contr. Mathem.) Qui ea poſſidet quæ ſunt magnæ æſtimationis et pretii, eſt dives, virtus autem eſt magnæ æſtimationis et pretii, ſoluſque ſapiens eam poſſidet; ſolus ergo eſt dives: *He that poſſeſſeth what is of great eſteem and value, cannot but be rich; virtue is of great eſteem and value; and the wiſe man alone poſſeſſeth virtue; therefore the wiſe man alone is rich.* See *Lipſ.* Manud. iii. 11.——And what ſay the Scriptures to this point? *They that ſeek the Lord ſhall not want any thing that is good.* Pſ. xxxiv. 10. *Wiſdom is a treaſure to men, which never faileth.* Wiſd. vii. 14, &c. *Seek ye firſt the kingdom of God, and his righteouſneſs, and all theſe things ſhall be added to you.* Matth. vi. 33.

(*c*) Viſceratio] The ſame word is uſed in Ep. 19. (ſee N. i.) but there it relates to a private ſacrifice or entertainment; and here to a public one, given by ſome prince or magiſtrate. *See* Plut. Quæſt. Conviv. 11.

(*d*) All this is ridiculous vanity, and one of the moſt objectionable points in the whole ſyſtem of Stoiciſm. The compariſon however runs ſmoothly enough under the character of *Jupiter*, whom the

the poets and others made ſo free with even from his *birth*. But what Chriſtian can bear ſuch expreſſions as, Quæris quæ res ſapientem efficit? Quæ DEUM, (Ep. 87) and the like? See Epp. 31. (N. e) 53. (N. k.)

(*e*) *The Lord is nigh to all them that call upon him, to all that call upon him in truth.* Pſ. cxlv. 18.

(*f*) Deus ad homines venit, imo in homines.] Though the Stoic means no more here by the word Deus, *God*, than *right Reaſon*, which they held as (divinæ particula auræ) part of God: in a Chriſtian ſenſe, I think we may juſtly apply it to that of St. *John*. *The Word was made fleſh and dwelt among us, and we beheld his glory*, &c. John i. 14. See Ep. 31. (N. d, h.) and particularly the following Note.

(*g*) *Hereby we know that we dwell in God and he in us, becauſe he hath given us of his Spirit.* i John iv. 13. *We have known and believe the love that God hath to us. God is love, and he that dwelleth in love, dwelleth in God, and God in him.* Ib. 16. *Know ye not that ye are the temple of God, and that the Spirit of God dwelleth in you?* i Cor. iii. 16. vi. 19. *For it is God that worketh in you both to will and to do of his good pleaſure.* Phil. ii. 13. See Ep. 41. (N. c.)

(*h*) See the parable of the Sower, Matth. xiii. 18. Luke viii. 5. See Ep. 38. (N. a.)

EPISTLE LXXIV.

On Virtue, and the Gifts of Fortune.

YOUR Epiſtle, my *Lucilius*, gave me great delight, and rouzed my drooping ſpirits: it alſo refreſhed my memory, which now begins to fail me. Why ſhould you not think this perſuaſion to be the chief means of an happy life, that *virtue is the only good* (*a*)? He that hath this opinion engraven on his heart, is happy in himſelf: for he that thinks there is any other *good*, ſubjects himſelf to the caprice of Fortune, and the pleaſure of others, having no will of his own. Such a one gives himſelf up to ſorrow at the loſs of his children; he is troubled at their being ſick, and greatly afflicted at their diſgrace: you will ſee him tortured with the love of another man's wife, or perhaps of his own.

own (*b.*) There are thoſe who cannot bear a repulſe of any kind, and thoſe whom honour itſelf fills with vexation.

But the greateſt part among the wretched crew of mortals are thoſe whom the expectation of death keeps in perpetual dread; as every where, and from every thing, impendent. Therefore as in an enemy's country a man is obliged to look about him, and apt to be ſtartled at every the leaſt noiſe, unleſs the *fear of death* be eradicated from the mind it is impoſſible to live, but with an aching heart. Here we meet with ſuch as are baniſhed, and turned out of their poſſeſſions; in another place with (what is the moſt grievous ſort of indigence) thoſe who are poor amidſt plenty of wealth: we meet alſo with ſome that have been ſhipwreck'd; and others that have ſuffered as great afflictions; whom popular fury (*c*) or envy (that pernicious plague to the beſt of men) hath flung down from their height of grandeur, when they thought themſelves quite ſafe and ſecure; like a ſtorm, that riſeth in the ſea at the time of an aſſured calm; or like a ſudden burſt of thunder, at the ſound whereof all things around tremble: for as in this caſe, he that ſtands near where the fire falls is not leſs terrified, than if he had been ſtricken with it; ſo, in theſe forceful accidents, calamity ſtrikes one perſon, and fear many; and the poſſibility of ſuffering affects not leſs with painful ſorrow than the ſuffering itſelf: the ſudden affliction of others harraſſeth the minds of all about them: as the ſound of an uncharged ſling terrifieth the birds; ſo are we frightened, not by any ſtroke, but a mere noiſe.

No one therefore can be happy without being diveſted of this timidity: nothing can be happy but what is intrepid: it is a miſerable life to live in ſuſpenſe and fear: who gives himſelf up to the dread of accidents, creates himſelf an infinite deal of trouble, very difficult to be got rid of. The only way wherein to walk ſecurely, is to deſpiſe all external things, and be ſatisfied with doing what is right and fit (*d*). For he that thinks there is any thing that excels virtue, or that there is any other good, opens his breaſt to the caſual largeſs of Fortune, and expects it with great anxiety. Form in your mind this picture; Fortune

Fortune proclaims an holiday; and among the crowd of mortals aſſembled on this occaſion diſtributes her favours, riches and honours, ſome of which, among the hands of the ſcramblers, are torn and greatly abuſed; other favours are unfairly divided among faithleſs companions; others prove of great detriment to the receivers; among whom are ſome who were thinking of nothing leſs than ſuch favours; others by graſping at too much, get nothing; or by greedily catching at more, loſe what they have got; and even they who have happily ſucceeded, enjoy the fruits of their rapine but a little while. Therefore ſuch as are moſt prudent, as ſoon as the *play* begins, quit the theatre, well knowing that ſuch trifles often coſt a man very dear. Diſdainful of her favours, no one contends with him that retires; no one ſtrikes him who is going off; the conteſt is there only, where the prize is exhibited. Thus it is with regard to thoſe things which Fortune ſcatters at random from above. We labour, and ſweat, wretched creatures as we are; we crowd; we are torn in pieces; we wiſh Nature had given us more hands: we look with envy upon one man, and then upon another; Fortune is dilatory; her gifts ſeem too ſlowly to fall to our lot; they provoke our appetite; and though few can enjoy them, yet all expect them; we are eager to come in Fortune's way, and rejoice to have got a chance; or are grieved at being diſappointed; we ſuffer ſome great detriment to obtain a booty, which if obtained deceives us, by being of little or no value. Let us therefore retire from theſe idle ſports, and give them up to the ſcramblers; let them hanker after theſe uncertain gifts, and live for ever in ſuſpenſe. Whoever deſires to be happy, let him think that *whatever is, is right*; if he thinks otherwiſe, he by no means judgeth rightly of Providence; ſince many inconveniencies happen to juſt men, and ſince whatever is our lot, it is but of ſhort duration in compariſon of the time paſt, and to come. From this murmuring it follows, that we are very ungrateful interpreters of divine matters; we are continually complaining, that we enjoy but few things, and them not always, or at beſt they are uncertain, and of ſhort duration: and from hence it is, that we neither wiſh to live, nor wiſh to die: we grumble at life, and are afraid of death: our thoughts are ever wavering, and no felicity whatever can fill our minds with complacency and ſatisfaction. Now, the reaſon of this is, we are not come to that immenſe and ſuperlative *good*, where the *will* muſt neceſſarily ſtop; for, beyond the laſt and *chief good* there is no room for progreſſion.

Do you aſk, *Lucilius*, why virtue knows no want? It is becauſe ſhe rejoiceth in what ſhe has, nor hankereth after what ſhe has not: every thing is great to her, becauſe, be it what it will, it ſatisfies. Set aſide this opinion, and there can be no piety, no fidelity; as many things, which are called evil, muſt be endured by him who deſires to perform his duty in theſe two points; and many things of thoſe we call good, and are therefore fond of, expended: there can be no fortitude, which cannot be known but upon trial: there can be no magnanimity, but when diſplayed in contemning thoſe things which the vulgar look upon as the greateſt bleſſings; all courteſy is loſt, and the requital of a good turn accounted unneceſſary labour, if we think any thing preferable to a faithful diſcharge of duty, and the purſuit of what is beſt.

But to paſs by theſe, either ſuch things as are good, are not ſo, or man is happier than God: becauſe the things that are provided for us, God hath no need of for his own uſe; no inordinate pleaſures, no banquetings, no wealth, nor any of thoſe things that decoy and enſnare man with the vile bait of pleaſure, belong to God. Therefore either (what is incredible) God muſt want ſuch things as are *good*; or, this is an argument that ſuch things are not good, becauſe God does not want them. Add alſo, that of many things which unto man ſeem *good*, other animals enjoy a greater portion:. they eat with a better appetite; they cloy not themſelves with love; their ſtrength is greater, and more conſtantly firm; from whence it would follow, they are happier than man; foraſmuch too, as they live without malice, and diſhoneſty; and enjoy their pleaſures more abundantly and eaſier, without fear either of ſhame or repentance.

Conſider therefore, *Lucilius*, whether that can be called *good*, in which man ſurpaſſeth God: no, as the ſeat of the chief good is in the mind,

mind, it loseth all its value when transferred from the best part of us to the worst; and even to the senses, which are stronger and more alert in many brute beasts. The sum of our happiness consists not in gratifying the flesh (*e*). That only is the *true good*, which is prescribed by reason; solid, and everlasting; which cannot decrease or be diminished: other things are good merely in fancy and opinion; they may have the name of *good*, but without propriety: let them be called, if you please, *conveniencies*, or, as we say, revenues; but we must consider them as conveyed over to us for a time, not our certain portion; we may have them, but must remember at the same time they are foreign to us; even if we have them, I say, we must look upon them as too low and mean for a man to pride himself in: for what can be more foolish than to vaunt of those things which a man hath not done himself (*f*)? They may come near to us, but not cleave so close to us, as when taken away to distract and tear the man; we may use them, but not glory in them; and we must use them sparingly too, as things deposited with us, only for a season (*g*).

Whoever possesseth these worldly goods, without regard to reason, holds them on a weak tenure; even happiness becomes a burthen to itself, if it be not used with discretion: if it hath trusted in such transitory goods, it soon finds itself deserted; or if not deserted, chagrined and cast down: few men can forego their happiness calmly and gradually; the generality fall at once with all their grandeur; and the very things that exalted them, now serve only to depress them. Providence therefore, which teacheth moderation and parsimony, must be timely applied, because a disordinate liberty hurries on the destruction of its own wealth; nor can ever so great an abundance last long, unless conducted and restrained by instructive reason. This is manifest from what hath befallen many large cities, which, in their most flourishing state, have been ruined by licentiousness, and whose luxury and intemperance have destroyed all that valour and virtue had gained.

We must be guarded against these accidents: but as no wall is impregnable against the power of fortune, we must be well armed within:

 if

if this the better part be ſafe, a man indeed may be aſſaulted, but he cannot be taken. And if you deſire to know how he muſt be armed, let him not repent or repine at any thing that may befal him; and know, that thoſe things which ſeem to hurt *him*, tend however to the preſervation of the whole; and without which the order and courſe of the world would be defective. Let whatever hath pleaſed God, pleaſe man (*h*). Let him admire and reverence himſelf, and all that belongs to him on this account; that he cannot be overcome; that he is above misfortune; that he can ſubdue by reaſon (than which nothing is more powerful) chance, pain, or injury.—Love Reaſon: the love of Reaſon will arm you againſt the ſevereſt troubles. Affection for their young, drives the wild beaſts into toils; whom otherwiſe their natural ferocity and raſh vehemence render untameable. A thirſt of glory hath impelled ſome young and brave diſpoſitions to the contempt of fire and ſword; even the reſemblance or ſhadow of virtue hath forced others upon a voluntary death (*i*). Now by how much ſtronger and more conſtant than all theſe incitements Reaſon is, by ſo much the more ſtrenuouſly will it make its way through all manner of dread and danger. But you will ſay, that "we contradict ourſelves, when we deny there is any "other *good* but the *honeſtum*, (*what is right and fit*); or pretend that "this is a ſufficient protection againſt fortune: foraſmuch as we allow "a place among good things to dutiful children, affectionate parents, "and a people of good and ſound morals; and that we cannot ſee any "of theſe in danger without concern: or not be troubled if our country "is beſieged, if our children die, or our parents are carried into "ſlavery." Now, I will firſt lay down what anſwer is generally made for us, to ſuch as make theſe objections; and then I will add what further anſwer, I think, may be given them.

I. Very different is the nature of things; ſome, when taken away from us, ſubſtitute in their room what may be diſagreeable and hurtful to us; as a good ſtate of health, when impaired, turns to ſickneſs; and the ſight of the eyes, when extinguiſhed, affects us with blindneſs; or if the hamſtring be cut, not only our ſpeed is taken away, but perpetual lameneſs enſues. But there is no ſuch danger in the things before

ſpoken

ſpoken of: if I have loſt a faithful friend, there is no reaſon that perfidiouſneſs ſhould ſupply his place; or if I have buried a dutiful child, that impiety ſhould ſucceed him: neither by their deaths have I loſt either the friend or the child, but their bodies only. Good is to be loſt but one way; by being changed into evil; which is contrary to the nature of things; becauſe every virtue, and every effect of virtue, remain incorruptible. Beſides, though our friends, and dutiful children, anſwering every wiſh of a fond parent, have died; there is ſtill ſomething to ſupply their place: even *virtue*, that alſo made *them* good.

Virtue ſuffers no vacancy in the place ſhe inhabits; ſhe fills the whole ſoul; takes away the ſenſibility of any loſs, and is of herſelf ſufficient: for in *her* conſiſts the origin and ſtrength of all *good*. What matters it if a ſtream be interrupted or cut off, if the fountain from whence it flowed be ſtill alive? You will not call a man more juſt, more temperate, more prudent, more honeſt, and conſequently a better man, becauſe his children are either alive or dead; a goodly troop of friends make not a man more wiſe, nor the want of them more fooliſh; and conſequently not more happy in himſelf, nor more wretched. So long as virtue is preſerved entire, you cannot be ſenſible of any loſs. What then? is not a man the happier for being ſurrounded with friends and children? perhaps not; for the *chief good* is not to be dimniſhed or encreaſed: it ever remains in its proper ſtation; let Fortune behave herſelf as ſhe pleaſes, whether a man hath reached a good old age, or died in his prime, the meaſure of the *chief good* is ſtill the ſame, whatever difference there may be in years. Whether you deſcribe a larger circle or a leſs, the difference relates only to the ſpace, not to the form of it: though one remains a long while, and you obliterate the other, the form was ſtill the ſame in both: what is right and fit, is not meaſured by greatneſs, or number, or time; it cannot be extended or contracted. Reduce a virtuous life, as much as you pleaſe, from an hundred years to one day, it is equally a virtuous life. Virtue is, one while, expanded; and diſplays itſelf in the government of cities, kingdoms, provinces; it cultivates friendſhips; and diſpenſeth its good offices among our neighbours and children; at another time, it is contracted within the narrow bounds of poverty, banishment, solitude; without a child, without a friend; yet it is not the less, for being reduced, from grandeur to a private state; from royalty to a mean condition; or from the enjoyment of a spacious field of liberty, to the scanty boundaries of an house, or a little cell; nay, it is equally great, if, being every where extended, it retires into itself; forasmuch as it still keeps up a great and noble spirit, is strictly prudent, and inflexibly just; consequently is equally happy: for this happiness is situated in one and the same place; it is fixed in the mind, ever steady, grand, and tranquil: which cannot be effected without the knowledge of things both human and divine. But,

II. With regard to what I proposed as a further answer from my own opinion---A wise man is not afflicted at the loss of children or friends, for he bears *their* death with the same firmness of mind that he expects *his own:* he no more fears the one, than he grieves at the other. Virtue consists in the fitness of things, and all her works in their agreement and consonancy thereto: now, this concord is dissolved; if the mind, which ought to be sublime and stately, ever submits to demean itself with grief and sorrow: all manner of trepidation, anxiety or remissness in any action is unfit and dishonourable. For the *honestum (virtue)* is secure, expeditious, unterrified, and prepared against all events. What then? will not a wise man be obliged to suffer something, that looks, at least, like perturbation (*l*)? Will he not sometimes change colour; his countenance be disordered, his limbs tremble; or whatever else happens, not by command of the will, but by a certain unadvised impulse of nature? It may be so, but still he will retain the same persuasion, that none of these things are evils, nor worthy that a sound mind should grieve, much less despond on this account. All that is possible to be done, or he ought to do, will be performed with earnestness and courage.

It is consummate folly for men to do what they do, with regret, idly and frowardly; to have the body impelled one way and the mind another; and to be distracted with a variety of contrary motions. Hence it is, that where they expect admiration and honour, they meet with ſhame and contempt; nor do they undertake thoſe things willingly and with affection, wherein they glory: if any evil is apprehended, they are diſturbed with the expectation of it, as if it were really come; and what they are afraid leſt they ſhould ſuffer, they ſuffer through fear. As in our bodies certain ſymptoms precede a fit of ſickneſs, a ſudden liſtleſſneſs ſeizeth upon the nerves, we gape and yawn, and, without any toil, wearineſs and a ſhivering run through the limbs; ſo, an infirm mind, before it is oppreſſed with any evil, is ſhaken; it anticipates the evil, and ſubmits to an untimely fall. But what can be more ridiculous, than to be troubled for what is not yet come to paſs? not to reſerve, as it were, one's ſelf for it; but to provoke miſery and call it to ourſelves, when it is certainly the beſt way to put it off as long as poſſible, though it cannot be prevented? Would you know, why no one ought to torment himſelf with what is to come? Conſider, when a criminal has got a reprieve for fifty years, he is no longer troubled at the thoughts of his puniſhment; unleſs he ſkips over the intermediate ſpace, and flings himſelf upon anxiety an age beforehand; in like manner it happens, that even former ills, and ſuch as ought to have been forgotten, diſturb the minds of thoſe who are voluntarily ſick, and catch at every cauſe of grief and pain: whereas, both the evils that are paſt, and ſuch as are to come, are alike abſent; we feel neither the one nor the other; and there can be no real pain, but from what we at preſent feel.

ANNOTATIONS, &c.

(a) —— Neque ulla officii præcepta firma, ſtabilia, conjuncta naturæ tradi poſſunt, niſi aut ab iis qui *ſolam*, aut ab iis qui maximè *honeſtatem* propter ſe dicant expetendam. Cic. (de Off. l. 2.) *Neither can any firm, permanent, or natural rule of duty, be laid down, but by thoſe who eſteem virtue to be the ſole, or by thoſe, who deem her to be the chief object of deſire.* See Ep. 71. (N. b.)

(b) Like *Mecænas.* Ep. 19. But I believe examples may be found in every age.

(c) As lately in this our metropolis, ſee Ep. 8. (N. b.)

(d) *He that walketh uprightly, walketh ſecurely.* Prov. x. 9. xxviii. 18. *Who is he that will harm you, if ye be followers of that which is good?* i Pet. iii. 13.

(e) *It is the Spirit that quickeneth; the fleſh profiteth nothing.* John vi. 63. *For they that are in the fleſh cannot pleaſe God.* Rom. viii. 1, 13. *Remember that ye were in time paſt Gentiles in the fleſh, aliens from the commonwealth in Iſrael, having no hope, and without God in the world. But now ye are*

no

no more strangers and foreigners, but fellow-citizens with the saints and of the houshold of God. Ephes. ii. 11, 19. *See also* Rom. vii. 6. ix. 8. Gal. v. 16, 19. Phil. iii. 3, 11. Cor. vii. 1. i Pet. iv. 2, 6. ii John, 15, 17.

(*f*) Nam quæ non fecimus ipsi
Vix ea nostra voco. *Ovid.* Met. 13, 140.
We cannot call another's deeds our own.

(*g*) *Conveniencies*, commoda Ευχρηστα. Thus saith the Lord, *Let not the wise man* glory *in his wisdom, neither let the mighty man glory in his strength, nor let the rich man glory in his riches; but let him that gloryeth, glory in this, that he understandeth and knoweth me that I am the Lord.* Jer. ix. 23. i Cor. i. 31. ii Cor. x. 17. *But this I say, the time is short: it remaineth that they that rejoice as though they rejoiced not; and they that buy as though they possessed not; and they that use this world as not abusing it; for the fashion of this world passeth away.* i Cor. vii. 29.

(*h*) Resting assured, as before, that *whatever is, is right.* Thy will be done. Matth. vi. 10.

(*i*) I know not but that we may justly apply this to the *Decii, Curtius*, and other antient Heathens, animated with expectation of immortal fame after death; who had some excuse for thus *glorying in their shame*; but are by no means to be set up for our guides or patterns, in the ordinary situation of human life.

(*k*) Ep. 120. Magnam rem puta, unum hominem agere. *D. Ambros.* Ep. 83.—Vetus dictum est, adsuesce *unus* esse; ut vita tua quandam picturam exprimat, eandem servans imaginem, quam acceperit. *Endeavour to be always one and the same; representing a lasting picture.* See Ep. 20. (N. b.)

(*l*) See Ep. 57. (N. d.) 75. (N. e.)

EPISTLE LXXV.

Our Actions must agree with our Words.—There are certain Degrees in the Way to Perfection.

YOU are pleased, *Lucilius*, to complain, that my Epistles are not so accurate as usual: he that studies to speak accurately, generally speaks affectedly: in the same free and easy stile that I would converse with you, were we sitting or walking together, I would fain write my Epistles; without any thing forced or disguised by art. If it were possible, I should chuse to express my mind rather by signs than words. Even

Even were I disputing, I would not stamp with my feet or toſs about my hands, or raiſe my voice; I would leave ſuch geſtures and vociferation to public orators, being ſatisfied with conveying to you my meaning, without endeavouring to adorn, and explain it away: and of this one thing I ſhould be glad to convince you, that I ſpeak as I think; that whatever I advance, I not only *believe* myſelf, but *love* it alſo. Men ſalute not their children with that ardency they do their miſtreſſes, yet even in that ſacred and moderate embrace they give ſufficient teſtimony of their affection. However I would not what I write on theſe great matters ſhould be dry and jejune; nor indeed does philoſophy renounce all manner of wit and humour: yet there is no neceſſity for taking much pains in ſeeking proper words. Let this be the ſum of our intention, to ſpeak what we think, and to think what we ſpeak: let our ſpeech agree with our conduct in life. He hath fulfilled his engagements, who, both when you ſee, and when you hear, him, is the ſame man. We ſhall ſoon ſee, what, and how great a man he is, whoſe importance conſiſts in ever being one and the ſame (*a*).

Our words muſt be formed rather to inſtruct, than to pleaſe; yet, if a man is not over-anxious after eloquence, if it flows naturally, without pains or affectation, let him uſe and employ it on the moſt worthy ſubjects; yet ſo as to diſplay the thing deſigh'd, rather than his own vanity. Other arts belong wholly to ingenuity and fancy; but here the very ſoul is concerned. The ſick man enquires not after an eloquent phyſician, one that can prattle, but one that can cure him. But ſhould it ſo happen, that the ſame perſon who knows how to cure, can alſo harangue fluently and neatly upon what he is about, let it be taken in good part; there is no reaſon however the patient ſhould congratulate himſelf upon the happineſs of having ſo facetious a doctor; for this is no more a neceſſary qualification in a phyſician, than for a ſkilful pilot to be an handſome man. (I ſhould ſay, were it my caſe, " why do you tickle my ears? why do you ſtudy to delight me? " This is not our preſent buſineſs, I am to be cauterized, to be lanced, " * to be almoſt ſtarved: you are called in to preſcribe ſuch things, in " order to cure an old, ſtubborn, and grievous diſeaſe; you have as " much

"much businefs cut out for you, as for a phyfician in time of peftilence; and do you think that talking is all you have to do? it will be time enough to talk and even to rejoice, if you can perform a cure." (Or without a metaphor) When will you learn the many things that are to be learned? When will you fo fix them in the mind that they cannot be erafed? When will you put them to trial? For it is not enough to treafure up thefe like other things in the memory; they muft be called forth to action. He is not the happy man, who knoweth thefe things, but he that *doeth* them.

What then, is there no degrees below fuch a one? Is a man exalted at once to the perfection of wifdom? I think not. For though a man, who has made a beginning, may ftill be reckoned among the ignorant, yet there is a wide difference between them; as there is even among the proficients themfelves (*c*); who are divided, according to fome, into three claffes: the firft are they (*d*), who, though they have not reached wifdom, are come to the borders of it; and being only near, are ftill *without*: I mean thofe, who having laid afide all vicious paffions and affections, are come to the knowledge of what is right; but they have not put their confidence to trial, nor their good in practice: yet even now, there is no fear of their relapfing into thofe vices they have folemnly efchewed; they are arrived there, from whence they cannot go back: but this is not as yet manifeft to themfelves; or, as I have elfewhere expreffed myfelf in a former Epiftle, they *are ignorant of their own knowledge*; they are fo happy as to enjoy their *good*, but not fo happy as to confide therein. Some confider thefe proficients of whom I am fpeaking, as men who have efcaped the difeafes of the mind, but not being as yet entire mafters of their affections, they ftill walk in flippery places, becaufe no one is out of the reach of malignity, but he that hath entirely thrown it off; and no one hath entirely thrown it off, but he that hath fubftituted virtue in its room.

I have fhewn you, *Lucilius*, the difference between the difeafes of the mind and the affections (*e*); and fhall now remind you of it again. The difeafes of the mind are inveterate and ftubborn vices, fuch as avarice, and

and vain-glorious ambition: when they have infected the mind, and begin to fix a perpetual refidence therein. In a word, it is a grievous difeafe, when the judgment is fo perverted as to be pertinacious of trifles; as if thofe things that are attainable by the flighteft means were to be purfued with all our might; or thus, if you pleafe:—to defire that over-vehemently, which ought fcarcely to be wifhed for, or perhaps not at all *(f)*; and to hold *that* in great efteem, which deferves but little, or perhaps contempt. But the affections are certain motions of the mind, unaccountable, fudden, and violent, which being frequent, and for a while neglected, introduce a troublefome malady; as a fmall defluxion of rheum, not yet grown conftitutional, caufeth a cough; but by continuance and neglect brings on a confirmed afthma. Therefore, they who have made the greateft proficiency in the way we are fpeaking of, however fubject to the affections, yet being free from the difeafes of the mind, come neareft to the adepts in wifdom.

The fecond fort are they who have thrown off the greateft evils of the mind, and all untoward paffions; yet not fo as to be in full poffeffion of their fecurity; for 'tis poffible they may relapfe.

A third fort are they who have taken leave of many and great vices, but not all. They avoid covetoufnefs, but are ftill fubject to anger: they are not folicited by voluptuoufnefs, but ftill are ambitious; they are not much tortured by defire, but they ftill live in fear; but even amidft their fear, the mind is fufficiently firm againft fome things, yet yields to others; it defpifeth death, yet dreads to fuffer pain.

Let us reflect a little upon the laft order; it were well if we were admitted even here: by a particular felicity of nature, and by continual ftudy and application of the mind, a place in the fecond is attainable; yet the third has its merit. Confider what numberlefs evils are fpread around: there is no fin but what you fee exemplified: wickednefs is daily making greater progrefs both in public and private life: and you will learn from hence, that it is fomewhat commendable, not to be fo wicked as the reft of the world. But, you fay, you hope to be admitted

ted of an higher order. This indeed is what I could rather wiſh for ourſelves than promiſe: we ſeem pre-engaged: we aim at virtue, but are buſied in vice: I am aſhamed to ſay it, we follow what is good only as opportunity ſerves (*g*).

But how great will be our reward if we throw off our preſent engagements, and releaſe ourſelves from theſe bonds! So ſhall no unwarrantable deſire nor fear aſſail us; unharraſſed by terrors, uncorrupted by pleaſures, we ſhall fear neither death, nor the power of the gods; we ſhall know that death is no evil, and the gods too good to be the authors of evil (*h*): he that hurteth is as weak as he that is hurt: the beſt things have no noxious qualities. If then we diſengage ourſelves from theſe dregs, and riſe to the ſublime and noble height of wiſdom; tranquillity of mind, and abſolute liberty, all ſin and error excluded, will be our portion (*i*). And what is this, but not to fear man below, nor dread the powers above; not to will what is baſe and vile, nor covet ſuperabundance; and eſpecially to have an abſolute command over ourſelves? for believe me, *Lucilius*, to be maſter of one's ſelf, is to be in poſſeſſion of an ineſtimable treaſure.

ANNOTATIONS, &c.

I cannot but think, the former part of this Epiſtle inſtead of concluding this Volume, would have ſerved very well for a Preface to it; but ſuppoſing ſomewhat more would be required, I endeavour'd to oblige the courteous reader therewith.

(*a*) See Ep. 20. (N. b.) 35. 74. (N. k.)

* I have ſomewhere before obſerved that the *phyſicians* of old, were likewiſe *ſurgeons*. So, in *Homer*, λ. 832.

Ιητροὶ μὲν γὰρ ποδαλείριος ἠδὶ Μαχαων.——
Of two fam'd ſurgeons Podolarius *ſtands*
This hour ſurrounded by the Trojan *bands*;
And great Machaon *wounded, in his tent,*
Now wants the ſuccour, which ſo oft he lent. Pope.

Who obſerves in his Note, that *Machaon* in having cured *Philoctetes*, was an abler phyſician than *Chiron*, who could not cure himſelf of the like poiſonous wound.

They are ſtill ſo abroad; as under a print of my friend, the incomparable *Handel's* father, there is a *German* inſcription, to the following purpoſe:

This print George Handel's *pourtraiture diſplays*;
'Tis hard to ſay, which moſt demands our praiſe,
His dextrous hand, or well experienc'd art,
In the phyſician's, *or the* ſurgeon's *part.*

(*h*) See

(*b*) See Ep. 16. (N. c.) 20. (N. a.) *If ye know these things, happy are ye if ye do them.* John xiii. 17. *Not the hearers of the law are just before God, but the doers of the law shall be justified.* Rom. ii. 15. *Be ye doers of the word, not hearers only, deceiving your own selves,* &c. James i. 22. See also Matth. vii. 21.

(*c*) See Ep. 71. 72. (N. c.) *Nostrum vitium est*, qui quod dicitur de sapiente, exigimus et a proficiente. *Sen.* (de vit. beat. c. 24.) *We are much to blame if we expect from the proficient the perfection of a wise man.*

(*d*) Stobæ. 101. Ὁ δ' ἐπ' ἄκρον προκόπτων, ἅπαντα πάντως ἀποδίδωσι τὰ καθήκοντα, κ. τ. λ. *Chrysippus* asserts, *that though a proficient of the first class should do every thing, and leave nothing undone, that becomes a good man; yet his life cannot be said to be completely happy, until these ordinary actions are worked up into habit, and a peculiar firmness and constancy of mind.*

(*e*) *Cicero* often confounds them, and calls *affections* diseases.—Tuscul. iv.—Intelligatur perturbationem (*Senecæ*, affectum) jactantibus se opinionibus inconstanter et turbide, in motu esse semper; cum autem hic fervor concitatio que animi inveteraverit, et tanquam in venis medullisque insederit, tum existit et morbus. *Let us then understand* perturbation, (*called by Seneca* affection) *to imply a restlessness from the variety and confusion of contradictory opinions*; and that when *this heat or disturbance of the mind is of any standing, and has taken up its residence, as it were, in the veins and marrow, then commence diseases and sickness, and those aversions which are in opposition to them.*

(*f*) The like definition in *Laertius*; Νόσημα, ἐστὶν οἴησις σφόδρα δοκοῦντος αἱρετοῦ· *It is a disease, to set so high a value upon any thing, however desirable.*

(*g*) See Ep. 52. (N. a.)

(*h*) This reminds me of the extravagant rant in *Randolph's* Muses' Looking-glass.—

Aphobos. " What can there be
" That I should fear? The gods? If they be good,
" 'Tis sin to fear them: if not good, no gods;
" And then let them fear *me*."——Act ii. Sc. 2.

(*i*) *Who is he that will harm you, if ye be followers of that which is good? But if ye suffer for righteousness sake, happy are you; be not afraid of their terror, neither be troubled, but sanctify the Lord God in your hearts,* &c. i Pet. iii. 13.

I shall conclude this volume, with an observation from *Cicero's Lælius*, pertinent to this Epistle. " I would not be thought (says he) to adopt the sentiments of those speculative moralists, who pretend that no man can justly be deemed *virtuous*, who is not arrived at that sort of absolute perfection, which constitutes, according to their ideas, the character of genuine wisdom. This opinion may appear true, perhaps, in theory, but is altogether inapplicable to any useful purpose of society; as it supposes a degree of virtue, to which no mortal was ever capable of rising.—In my opinion, whoever restrains his passions within the bounds of reason, and uniformly acts, in all the various relations of life, upon one steady consistent principle of approved honour, justice, and beneficence, that man is, in reality, as well as in common estimation, strictly and truly *good*: inasmuch as he regulates his conduct (so far, I mean, as is compatible with human frailty) by a constant obedience to those best guides of moral rectitude, *the sacred laws of Nature*."——So far *Cicero*; and his elegant translator, as a good and grateful Christian, is pleased to add his acknowledgment of the superior excellency of divine revelation; " which not only exhorts to virtue, upon motives far more suitable to the moral constitution and circumstances of human nature, but supplies in the person of its sacred Author, that real and animating example of *consummate* perfection, which the disciples of *Zeno* could only form to themselves in *imagination*." (Remark, N. 19.)—Moreover, though it is certain, on the Christian scheme, that ever since the apostacy and rebellion in Paradise, *he that saith*

he

THE EPISTLES OF *LUCIUS ANNÆUS SENECA.*

EPISTLE LXXVI.

On Wiſdom; the chief Good.

YOU threaten, *Lucilius*, to take it ill, if I do not inform you of my daily tranſactions. Obſerve how ready I am ſincerely to anſwer your requeſt. I go to hear a certain philoſopher; and it is now the fifth day that I have attended his ſchool, and heard him diſpute from the eighth hour of the morning. *At a good age, truly!* Indeed I think ſo, *Lucilius*, (though you laugh); for what can be more ridiculous than to think, becauſe you have ſome time deſiſted from ſtudy, you need no further inſtruction? What would you have me do? mount my horſe, and act the young eſquire (*a*)? Happy would it be for me indeed, if this *(going to ſchool*, as you call it) was the only thing that diſgraced my old age!

The ſchool of philoſophy invites men of every age: here let us grow old, and ſtill follow it as earneſtly as young men (*b*). Shall I at this age frequent the theatre, and be carried into the circus, and no two gladiators be matched to fight without my presence; and at the same time shall I be ashamed to attend the lectures of a philosopher? No; a man must still be learning somewhat, as long as there is any thing to be learned; that is, according to the proverb, *as long as he lives* (*c*). Nor is this more applicable to any other purpose than to the following, *you must be learning as long as you live*, how to live. But know also, that I teach at the same time: do you ask what? why, that old age hath always somewhat still to learn: and indeed in this respect, I am ashamed of the folly of mankind. You know the way to the house of *Metronactes*, is by the *Neapolitan* theatre; this I find always full; and it is debated with great earnestness, who is the best piper. Nay, a Grecian fidler or the common cryer shall gather around them a vast concourse of people: but the place where a man is taught sound morality, very few attend *(d)*; and such as are pleased to attend, are thought by many to have no extraordinary business there; nay are even called idle blockheads. They may laugh at *me* too if they please; the opprobrious language of the rude and illiterate is easily to be borne: and their contempt to be despised by those, whose endeavours aim at what is right and fit.

Go on, my *Lucilius*, and make all the speed you can, that it may not be your case as it was mine, to be obliged to learn in your old age; and hasten so much the more; because you have undertaken that which you can scarce be master of, live you ever so long. What *improvement shall I make?* as much as you endeavour after *(e)*. *What do you expect?* wisdom is not an accidental accomplishment. Riches will sometimes come of themselves, honour will be offered you; favour and dignity, will haply be your portion; but virtue is not to be obtained but by great and incessant labour; but it is worth while so much the more to labour, as this will confer all good whatever: for this indeed is *the only good*. There is no truth, no certainty, in those things, so highly extolled by common fame. But I will now shew you, the *honestum*, or *virtue*, is the *only good:* because you seem to think that in my former epistle I have not executed the said purpose; and that I have exhibited virtue rather as recommended, than proved; and to contract all in a few words.

Know,

Know, that *all things have their proper good.* Fertility recommends the vine, as a fine flavour does the juice of the grape; the excellency in a stag is swiftness; in beasts of burthen, a strong back: an exquisite quickness of scent distinguishes the hound; speed the greyhound; fierceness and courage the bull-dog, or such as are ordained to attack wild beasts *(f)*: and what is the excellency in man? *reason.* It is this, wherein man excells the brute creation, and draws near to the gods *(g)*. Perfect reason therefore is the proper good of men. Other qualities he hath in common with plants and animals: is he strong? so are lions. Is he beautiful? so are peacocks. Is he swift? so are horses. I do not say how far he may excell, or be excelled in any of these points; for I am not enquiring after what is greatest in him, but what is *his own.* Has he a body? so has a tree. Has he internal power of self-motion! so have beasts, and even worms. Hath he a voice? some dogs have a louder; more shrill is that of the eagle, more deep that of the bull; and more sweet and voluble is the voice of the nightingale. What then is proper only to man? *reason.* This when right and perfect, completes the happiness of man. If therefore every thing that hath accomplished its own proper good, is praise-worthy, and hath reached the end of nature's designation; reason being the proper good of man, if he hath perfected the same, he is then praise worthy, and hath attained the end of being. Now, this reason when perfect, is called *virtue,* or what is *right and fit* in all circumstances. That therefore is the *one* good in man, which is his proper good: for we are not now enquiring after what is good, but what is the peculiar good of man. If there is no other good peculiar to man, then this is the *one good,* in which is comprehended all other.

Further, is any one a bad man, I doubt not but he will be condemned; and if good he will be approved of: that therefore is, the proper and only good in man, according to which he is blamed, or praised. But perhaps you doubt not whether this be a good, but whether it be the *only* good. Surely, if a man hath all other enjoyments of life, as health, riches, statues of his ancestors, and a large leveé of his own, but is confessedly a bad man, you will condemn him. Again, if a

 man

man hath none of these things, if he wants money; hath no clients, is not noble: nor can boast a long line of ancestors, yet is a good man; you cannot but commend him. Therefore that is the *only* good of man, which if he possesses, tho' destitute of all other things, he is very respectable, and praise-worthy; and he that hath it not, tho' in full possession of all other enjoyments, is condemned and despised. As the condition of other things; such is that of man. It is called a good ship, not because it is painted with the most brilliant colours; and hath its decks of silver or gold; and its prow decorated with ivory (*b*); nor because it is freighted with royal treasures; but because it is not crank, but firm and steady; well caulked, so as to admit no leak, and with such strong sides, as to defy the violence of the waves; ever obedient to the rudder; and swift and easy to tack about with every wind. You will not call a sword good for hanging at a golden belt, and having the hilt adorn'd with jewels: but because it carries a fine edge for cutting, and a point able to pierce an armour of steel. A ruler or square is not required to be beautiful, but strait and true. Every thing is excellent when adapted to its proper use *(i)*. Therefore in man also, it is of little avail, how many acres he ploughs, how much money he hath out at interest; how many salute him by the way; how rich his bed; or how transparent and costly his cup; but how *good* a man he is; now, he is a good man, whose reason is explicit and right; in all respects adapted to the will of nature. This is all called *virtue*; this is the *Honestum*, and *only* good of man. For since reason alone perfects the man; perfect reason alone hath made him happy; and that is the only good of man, by which only he is made happy.

We likewise call all those things good, which proceed from or are in contact with virtue; they are all her works. But, therefore is virtue only good, because there cannot be any good without her. And if all good be in the mind, whatever strengthens, exalts, and enlarges the mind, is good. Now virtue makes the mind stronger, nobler, more extensive. Whereas all other things, which provoke our appetites and desires, depress and weaken the mind; and when they seem to raise, they only puff it up, and delude it with much vanity. Therefore that is the only

good,

good, which improves the mind. All the actions of the whole life of man are measured by the moral ſenſe of good and evil, from whence reaſon takes her directions for doing, or not doing ſuch and ſuch things. I ſhall further explain this.

A good man will always do what is right and fit, whatever pains it coſts him. Again, he will not do any thing, that is baſe and vile, were he to gain thereby riches, or pleaſure or power. He will not abſtain from what is right, for any terror; nor, by any hopes whatever, be drawn in to a baſe action. Therefore as he will follow what is juſt and fit, he will always eſchew what is unjuſt and vile; and in every action in life, he will have theſe two principles in view; that there is no good but what is right and fit, nor any evil but what is vile and ſcandalous. If then virtue alone is pure, and ever of the ſame tenour; virtue is the only *good*; nor is it poſſible it ſhould be otherwiſe than good. Wiſdom is not ſubject to the danger of a change; as it is not to be taken from us forcibly, nor will ever revert into folly (*). I told you, if you remember, that many by a ſudden tranſport of zeal, have contemn'd and trodden under foot things ſo indiſcreetly coveted or dreaded by the vulgar: there have been found thoſe, who would thruſt their hand into the flames (*k*); whoſe ſmiles no torture could interrupt (*l*), who have not ſhed a tear at the loſs of their children: and have themſelves met death with intrepidity. Love, anger, deſire, have defied all manner of danger. And if a ſhort obſtinacy of the mind, inſpired by ſome ſudden impulſe could do this; how much more can virtue, which is ſtrong, not by fits, or on a ſudden, but with ever-equal ſteadineſs; and whoſe ſtrength never faileth? It follows then, that ſuch things, as are deſpiſed, *ſometimes* by the raſh and inconſiderate, and *always* by the wiſe, are in themſelves neither good nor evil. The only good therefore is virtue, who proudly marches between good and bad fortune, and treats them both alike with contempt. If you fancy, there is any good, but ſuch as conſiſts in what is *right and fit*, there is no virtue but what will prove defective: for none can be obtained, if it has regard to any thing without, or beyond itſelf. And were it ſo, it would be repugnant

so

to reaſon, from whence proceed all virtues; and alſo to truth, which ſubſiſts in reaſon: now whatever opinion is repugnant to truth, is falſe.

Further, you muſt grant it neceſſary for a good man to be truly pious, and to have the higheſt veneration for the gods; conſequently whatever happens to him, he will bear it with a patient and even mind, being perſuaded that it proceeds from the Divine Law, which governs the univerſe. And if ſo, that will be the only good to him, which is right and fit: foraſmuch as it conſiſts in this, to obey the gods, not to fall into ſudden paſſions, nor to bewail his lot, but patiently to abide his fate, and willingly perform what is enjoined by the powers above. Beſides, was there any other good than what is right and fit, we ſhould be perſecuted with the deſire of life, and an inſatiable hankering after all the requiſites thereto, which is intolerable, infinite, vague: therefore what is right and fit, is the only good, becauſe it hath its certain meaſure and end.

I have before ſaid, if thoſe things of which the gods make no uſe, ſuch as riches and honours, were really *good*, the life of man would be much more happy than that of the gods: add now, that if ſouls, when ſet free from the body, ſtill exiſt, they are in a much happier ſtate than when detained in the body (*m*). But if thoſe things be good, which are made uſe of while in the body, it would then be worſe for them to have been ſet free; but it is not credible that being impriſoned and confined they ſhould be happier than when at liberty to range the univerſe. I ſaid alſo, if thoſe things be good, which happen to dumb animals as well as to man, that then even dumb animals live an happy life: which by no means can be admitted. All things are to be endured for the ſake of virtue, or doing that which is right and fit; but this would be unreaſonable, if there was any other real good but virtue.

Thus, *Lucilius*, have I contracted and run through the ſeveral points, which I explained more at large in my former Epiſtle. But you will never approve of this my opinion or think it true, unleſs you raiſe your

your mind, and ask yourself this queſtion; whether, *if upon an emergency you are required to die for your country, and to redeem your fellow-citizens at the expence of your own life, you would ſtretch out your neck to the ſword, not only with a patient but a willing mind?* If you can do this, there is no other good: you poſtpone all things to this. See how great is the force of virtue. You will die for the good of the commonweal, though it be not at preſent required of you, yet whenever it ſhall ſo happen. In the mean while, from a good and beautiful action, great joy may be received in a ſhort ſpace of time; and though no benefit from the ſaid action were to accrue to the perſon defunct, and taken from the world, yet the very contemplation of the good intended gives delight; and the brave and juſt man, when he hath in view the price and conſequence of his death, ſuppoſe, the liberty of his country, and the welfare of all thoſe for whom he lays down his life, is in the higheſt glee, and enjoys his peril. Nay, even he that is deprived of the joy, which the execution of ſo great an affair would give him, as the greateſt and laſt pleaſure of his life, will yet brook no delay, but will ruſh upon death, well ſatisfied with doing what is right and fit, ſuppoſing it right and fit ſo to do.

Oppoſe to this however all that can be objected againſt it: tell him, *the favour will ſoon be loſt, and buried in oblivion: that the citizens will not make him any return of grateful eſteem.* He will readily anſwer, *all theſe things concern not my action: I conſider it in itſelf: I know it to be right and fit; therefore wherever it leads or invites me, I come.* This then is the *one good*, which not only a perfect mind, but a generous and good diſpoſition is ſenſible of. All other things are light and changeable: therefore they are poſſeſſed with anxiety, though kind fortune heaped them all upon one man: they become a heavy burden to the owners, they always oppreſs them, and ſometimes weigh them down. Not one of thoſe whom you ſee arrayed in purple, is happy; any more than thoſe whom you ſee dreſſed up for kings on the ſtage: they ſtrut in their buſkins, and look big during the time of action; but having made their exit, they are diſrobed, and ſhrink again to their own ſtature. Not one of thoſe whom wealth and honours have ſet on high

high is a great man. How comes it then that he seems so? Because you measure him base and all. A dwarf is still little though you set him upon a mountain; and a Colossus will maintain his bulk though he stands in a well. This then is the error we labour under: thus it is we impose upon ourselves: we esteem no one according to what he really is in himself; but we add to him all external advantages: but in order to make a true estimate of man, and to know what he really is, view him in himself: let him lay aside his patrimony, his honours, and all the lying ornaments of fortune. Nay, let him throw off the body; inspect the mind alone; examine what, and how great it is, and whether great in itself, or from some foreign good. If with a steady eye he can look upon the drawn sword; if he knows that it is of little concern, whether the soul depart from him naturally, or forcibly from a wound, call him happy. If he is threatened with excruciating torture of the body, either such as is casual or inflicted by the injurious treatment of those in power; if, of chains and banishment, and all the terrors that affright the mind of man, he hears without anxiety, and saith (with *Æneas* in Virg. 6. 103)

—— Non ulla laborum,
O virgo, nova mi facies inopinave surgit.
Omnia præcepi, atque animo mecum ipse peregi.

—— No terror to my view,
No frightful face of danger can be new.
Innur'd to suffer, and resolv'd to dare,
The Fates, without my pow'r, shall be without my care.

Dryden.

You but now *threaten me with these things, but I always threatened myself with them; being a man, I was always prepared against whatever man is subject to*; call him happy. The stroke of an evil preconceived, comes easy: but to fools and such as trust in fortune, every change seems new, and comes upon them with surprize; and the greatest part of evil, to the unexperienced and unprepared, is the novelty of it. This you may learn from their bearing patiently such things as they have been accustomed to. Therefore a wise man makes himself acquainted with evils ere they happen, and such as others make light by long suffering, he he makes eaſy by due reflexion. We often hear the unſkilful crying out, *I could not imagine that this would ever be my lot*. But the wiſe man knows that all things are incident to him, and therefore whatever happens he ſaith, *It is what I expected (o).*

ANNOTATIONS, &c.

(a) Troſſuli] See Ep. 87. *Lipſ.* Elect. ii. 1. Perſ. Sat. i. 81. ubi in N.—Troſſulus, vel a Troſſulo Tuſcorum oppido: vel qu. Toroſulus dim. a Toroſus, ut notentur homines delicatuli.

—— Unde iſtud dedecus in quo
Troſſulus exultat tibi per ſubſellia lævis?
Whence that diſgrace, when the aſſemblies meet,
To ſee a coxcomb ſkip from ſeat to ſeat?

(b) In hac Seneſcamus, hanc ut juvenes ſequamur. *Lipſius* doubts this expreſſion, ſcholam ſequi.—But *Gronovius* proves it juſt, from *Cicero*, when *ſequi* is uſed in the ſame ſenſe with *petere*; and adds from *Virgil*, Italiam ſequimur.—However, he is not ſatisfied with the reading, as all the MSS. want the demonſtrative pronoun *hanc*; and therefore propoſeth the conjecture of *Schrevelius*, In hanc Seneſcamus, ut juvenes ſequantur.—*Let us old men go thither, that the young men may follow us.*

(c) According to that in *Plato* (in amator) τί οὖν ἐστιν φιλοσοφῆσαι; κ. τ. λ. *what is it to philoſophize? what, but as* Solon *ſaith,*

Γηράσκω δ' αἰεὶ πολλὰ διδασκόμενος;
I ſtill learn ſomewhat as I grow in years.

Live and learn, ſays the Engliſh proverb. *Non ſi finiſce mai d' imparare.* Ital.—And very properly, as *Hippocrates* begins his aphoriſms with, Ars longa, vita brevis. *Ray*, p. 170. *Lipſ.* Manud. i. 1.

(d) According to the proverb in *Cicero*, (de Orat. ii.) Diſcum audire malunt quam philoſophum. *They will rather hear the ſound of a Coit than a philoſopher.* Which *Eraſmus* (i. v. 2. 19) thinks may be transferred to (diſcus eſcarius) *the rattling of plates for dinner.*

(e) This is according to the Stoical maxim; Velis eſſe bonus, eris. *If you have an inclination to be good, you will be ſo.*

(f) So Phocyllides. Ὅπλον ἑκάστῳ νεῖμε θεὸς, φύσιν ἐμφέρεσθαι,
Ὀρνέοις μὲν πολλὴν ταχυτῆτ', ἀλκήν τε λέουσι,
Ταύροις δ' αὐτοφυεῖς κεράεσσιν κέντρα μελίσσαις,
Ἔμφυτον ἄλκαρ ἔδωκε, λόγον δ' ἔρυμ' ἀνθρώποισι.
On every animal hath Nature's God
Its proper uſeful implement beſtow'd.
To all the feather'd their ſwiftneſs of wing,
To bulls their ſprouting horns, to bees their ſting.
Reaſon his ſtrength, and ſureſt guard, is giv'n
To man alone, the richeſt gift of heav'n. M.

Sidon. Apoll. vii. 14. Statum noſtrum ſupra pecudes—Ratiocinatio animæ intellectualis evexit, &c. *Nicetrius* Genes. i.

Unumquodque ſuo donavit munere largus
Armavitque manu, cornu, pede, dente, veneno, &c.

Boethius. iii. 8. Jam verò qui bona præ ſe corporis ferunt, quàm exiguâ, quàm fragili poſſeſſione nituntur!

nituntur! Nam etiam elephantes mole, tauros robere superare poteritis? Num tigres velocitate prœibitis, &c. *Now is it wel ysene, how litel and how brytel possession they coveten, that putten the goodes of the bodie above her own reason. For mayst thou surmounten these olifaunts in greatnesse, or in weight of bodie? or mayst thou be stronger than the bull? mayst thou be swifter than the tyger?* &c. Chaucer.

Cic. de Nat. Deor. ii. de Fin. v. Sen. Ep. ult.

(*g*) Deos sequitur] *Inferieur a un seul Dieu.* Vet. Gall.

Puteanus reads it, Diis æquatur. *He is equal to the gods,* according to the insolence of the Stoics. *See* Epp. 31, 92.

(*h*) Navis tutela] Gr. Νεως παρασημον, *Lat.* Insigne. *The image,* from whence the ship generally had its name.——Tutelæque Deum fluitant. *Sil.*

——Et pictos verberat unda Deos

Navis tutelam—*Ov.* de Trist. i.

Visa coronatæ fulgens tutela carinæ. *Val. Flacc.* i. Vid. Brodæ, Misc. i. 10. Turn. Adv. xix. 2.

(*i*) See an ingenious modern treatise, called *The Analysis of Beauty,* by Mr. *Hogarth,* p. 72.

* For according to the Stoics their wise man is ever fixed on good.

(*k*) As *Mutius Scævola,* Ep. 24.

(*l*) As the servant who in revenge of his master killed *Asdrubal.*

(*m*) This is one of those passages, wherein *Seneca* speaks in a clear and noble manner of the happiness of souls after death, when freed from the incumbrance of the body, and received into the place or region of departed souls. *Vid.* Consol. ad Polyb. c. 28. Cons. ad Marc. c. 25. But especially Epist. 102, where he has some sublime thoughts on this subject, and among the rest—Dies iste quem tanquam extremum reformidas, æterni natalis est. *The day which you dread as the last of life, is to be regarded as the birth-day of an eternal one*—though it must be owned he speaks of this elsewhere with doubt and uncertainty. *See* Leland ii. p. 287.

(*n*) They strut and fret their hour upon the stage,
And then are heard no more.—*Hamlet.*

(*o*) Dixit, sciebam.] As some of the editions want *sciebam,* I was thinking that if we might transfer the three letters S. V. B. which begin the next Epistle, and instead of *Si Vales, Bene est,* they might be allowed to stand for *Si Vult* (Deus) *Bene est,* this would make a proper ejaculation not only for a wise heathen, but a good Christian; *God's will be done.*

EPISTLE LXXVII.

Against the Fear of Death.

I (*Hope you are well;* (*a*) *and*) beg leave to inform you, *Lucilius,* that, this day, somewhat unexpectedly appeared in sight the *Alexandrian ships* (*b*), which are usually sent before to announce the approach of the

the whole fleet; they are called packet boats. Very grateful was the ſight of them to all *Campania:* The people were ſtanding on the mole of *Puteoli,* and could eaſily diſtinguiſh the *Alexandrian* from the reſt of the numerous fleet by their ſails; foraſmuch as theſe veſſels alone have the privilege of ſpreading their top-ſails, which the other never hoyſe, but when out at ſea: as nothing contributes more to ſwift ſailing, than the top-ſail by which the veſſel is chiefly carried along; therefore when the wind ariſeth, and blows too ſmart a gale; the top-yard is generally ſtruck, whereby the wind hath leſs force on the body of the ſhip. Now when they have enter'd between *Capreæ* and the promontory, from whence

Alta procelloſo ſpeculatur vertice Pallas *,
Pallas looks down upon the foamy deep.

The reſt are oblig'd to be contented with the mainſail, and the top-ſail (*c*) is left as a mark of diſtinction to the *Alexandrian.* In this great concourſe of people, that were flocking to the ſhore, I enjoyed ſome ſatisfaction in walking at my leiſure, foraſmuch as tho' I expected letters from my correſpondents; I was in no ſuch great hurry to know their contents, and how my affairs ſtood at *Alexandria*; having long ſince been indifferent either to loſs or gain. Was I not ſo old as I am, I ſhould ſtill have thought the ſame; but much more now, when, however ſmall my ſtock, I have far more proviſion left, than way to travel (*d*), eſpecially too, when on a journey, which there is no neceſſity I ſhould completely finiſh. A journey cannot be ſaid to be finiſhed if you ſtop in the midway, or before you have reached the deſtin'd place; but the journey of life is ſuch, that it is at all times complete, provided it be juſt and honorable. Whenever you finiſh it, if finiſhed well, it will be entire: nay it may ſometimes be finiſhed courageouſly even upon the ſlighteſt cauſe; for in truth there are no other that detain us here.

Tullius Marcellinus, whom you knew very well, a ſweet-temper'd youth, but of a crazy conſtitution, was ſurpriſed by a diſeaſe, not perhaps incurable, but ſuch as was tedious, and very troubleſome, and which obliged him to ſuffer much; he therefore was deliberating concerning death. He called many friends about him: when ſome of them, of a timorous diſpoſition, perſuaded him to act, as they ſhould in the like caſe; while others, more inclined to ſooth and flatter, gave him ſuch advice, as they thought would be moſt acceptable to him. But at laſt a friend of ours, a *Stoic*, a moſt excellent man, and to give him his due commendation, ſtrenuouſly brave, gave him, as I think, moſt admirable counſel, when he began as follows; *Be not overmuch concern'd, dear Marcellinus, as if you was deliberating on ſome affair of conſequence; it is no ſuch great matter to live; all your ſlaves, and all ſorts of animals live; but it is a great thing to die honorably, prudently, and courageouſly. Conſider how long you muſt ſtill be doing the ſame thing; food, ſleep, dalliance, fill up the round of life; ſo that not the prudent and brave, or the wretched, but even the moſt delicate and effeminate may well be willing to die:* this he ſaid; when *Marcellinus* ſtood in more need of an aſſiſtant than a counſellor; his ſervants loved him too well to obey him in this reſpect; the ſtoic therefore firſt endeavour'd to root out their fears; and ſhewed them, that domeſtic ſlaves were then only in danger, when it was uncertain, whether their maſter came by his death, voluntarily or not (*e*); and beſides, that they would ſet as bad an example, in preventing him, when deſirous to die, as in killing him (*f*). And then he exhorted *Marcellinus* himſelf to a kind and generous action: that, as, when ſupper is ended, what is left is divided among the ſtanders-by; ſo, at the concluſion of life, ſome legacies were due to thoſe who had waited upon him all his days. *Marcellinus* was of an eaſy and liberal diſpoſition, eſpecially in thoſe things that were properly his own; he therefore parcell'd out ſome ſmall ſums to his ſervants who ſtood weeping by; and gave them all the conſolation in his power. There was no need of the ſword, or ſhedding of blood: he entirely abſtained from food three days; and having ordered his pavilion to be placed in his bed-chamber, as alſo his bathing tub, he lay therein; and having warm water continually poured over him, he grew fainter by degrees, and as he declared, not without a ſenſation of pleaſure; ſuch as a gentle ſwooning is apt to bring, and as we have often experienced who have been ſubject to fainting.

I doubt

I doubt not but that this digreſſion will be acceptable to you; as you will learn from hence, that your friend made not either a painful or miſerable exit. For tho' indeed he brought death upon himſelf, yet it was in ſuch an eaſy manner, that he rather ſeemed to ſteal out of life. The relation likewiſe of this incident hath its uſe; as ſuch an example of conduct is ſometimes neceſſary (*g*). We have often reaſon to wiſh to die, and yet we are not willing; and when we really die, it is with regret.

No one indeed is ſo ignorant, but that he knows he muſt die; yet when the time draws near, he flinches, he trembles, he weeps. Would you not think a man ridiculouſly fooliſh, who weeps, becauſe he did not live a thouſand years ago? it is equally abſurd, for him to weep, becauſe he ſhall not live a thouſand years hence. There is no difference between, *thou ſhalt not be, and thou haſt not been*. In either of theſe times you have no concern. Your lot is fallen upon a point; which if you would prolong, how many years will you think to prolong it? why do you weep? what do you require? it is to no purpoſe.

Deſine Fata Deum flecti ſperare precando.

They are ſettled and fixed; they are conducted by a powerful and everlaſting neceſſity. You will go, where all things go. Is there any thing ſtrange in this? you was born upon theſe conditions: your parents, your anceſtors, and all poſterity are ſubject to the ſame. A chain of cauſes, invincible and invariable, binds and draws all things with it [illegible]. What numbers ſhall follow you, when you are dead! how many ſhall accompany you in death! I am perſuaded that you would be more contagious, if thouſands were to die with you: know then, that, at this very moment in which you make ſuch a difficulty in dying, thouſands of men, and other animals, are breathing their laſt by various kinds of death. And did you not think, you ſhould one day reach the place, to which you have been travelling your whole life? every journey has its end. You perhaps now expect I ſhould ſtrengthen my exhortation by the example of ſome great man; no, I ſhall only give you one of a young lad: I mean, that famous Lacedæmonian, who tho' a ſtripling, when taken priſoner cried out in the *Doric* dialect, *I*

will

will not be a ſlave; and made good his words; for at the firſt vile and mean office that he was put upon, (the emptying a cloſe-ſtool) rather than comply, he daſhed his brains out againſt the wall. When liberty is ſo near to a man, ſhall he ſubmit to ſlavery? had you not rather a ſon of yours ſhould die ſo gloriouſly, than grow old in idleneſs and diſhonour? Why then are you diſturb'd at the thoughts of death; when even a child can die ſo courageouſly? and what if you are unwilling to go, know you not, that you ſoon will be compelled! transfer this power, to yourſelf (*k*). Will you not aſſume the magnanimity of a boy, and ſay, *I will not be a ſlave?* Thou wretch, a ſlave to men, and, among other things, to life! for life if you have not courage to die, is ſervitude. Have you any thing more to wait for? you have already enjoy'd thoſe pleaſures that make you ſo dilatory, and ſtill detain you. None of them are new to you (*l*); none, but what are become diſguſtful from ſatiety. The taſte of metheglim you know; and the taſte of wine; no matter, whether an hundred or a thouſand rundlets have paſs'd through you. You are a mere ſtrainer. No one knows better the flavour of an oyſter, or of a mullet: in ſhort, your luxury hath left nothing in ſtore for you to treat your palate with a novelty. And yet theſe are the things you are ſo forcibly plucked away from. What elſe, I ſay, is there that you complain of being robbed of? your friends, and your country? but did you ever honour them ſo far as to put off your ſupper on their account? nay if you could, I believe you would extinguiſh the ſun itſelf. For what did you ever do that would bear the light! confeſs, O man, that it is not any reſpect to the ſenate, or forum, or to the nature of things that makes you ſo backward and afraid to die. No; you unwillingly bid adieu to the ſhambles, though you have left nothing there untaſted. You are afraid of death: and yet you ſeem to contemn it, in the height of your pleaſures. You would fain live; for you know what life is, but you know not what death may be; and therefore are afraid of it (*m*). But is not ſuch a life death itſelf? As *Caligula* was paſſing along the latin way, an enchained priſoner, who had a beard down to his girdle, aſked death of him: *why*, ſaid the Emperor, *do you think then you are ſtill alive?* The ſame anſwer may be made to thoſe whom death can in any

any way give relief to. Are you afraid to die? *do you think then you are ſtill alive? yes ſurely,* you will ſay, *and I would ſtill live; for I employ myſelf in many good and decent actions: I am unwilling to forego the duties of life, which I perform with fidelity and induſtry.* What then, know you not, that it is one of the duties of life, to die? You forego no duty; for the number of them being uncertain, what was incumbent upon *you* is already finiſhed (*n*). There is no life, that can be called *long*. For if you conſider the nature of things, the life of *Neſtor* or *Statilia* (*o*), was comparatively ſhort; though the latter order'd an inſcription on her monument, to ſhew that ſhe had lived ninety nine years. You ſee how an old woman can glory in her length of days. Surely her vanity would have been inſupportable could ſhe have completed her hundredth year. Life is like a play upon the ſtage; it ſignifies not how long it laſts, but how well it is acted (*p*). Die when, or where you will, think only on making a good and decent exit (*q*).

ANNOTATIONS, &c.

(*a*) S. V. B. Si vales benè. *Muret.* But *Lipſius* rejects this form, as not exhibited in the MSS. nor agreeable to the cuſtom of the times. *See* the laſt note of the foregoing Epiſtle.

(*b*) Vid. *Lipſ.* Elect. i. c. 8. de frumentatione.—*Suet.* Aug. c. 98.

* Where ſtood a temple of *Minerva*, to whom the ſailors, as there was danger in weathering the point, made libation, according to *Statius*;

Prima ſalutavit capreas, et margine dextro
Sparſit Tyrrhenæ Mareotica vina Minervæ.

(*c*) Supparum] al. ſeparum vel ſipparum.—Luc. v. 428.

Obliquat lævo pede carbaſa, ſummaque pandens
Suppara velorum perituras colligit auras.
When looſing from the ſhore the moving fleet,
All hands at once unfurl the ſpreading ſheet:
The ſlacker tacklings let the canvas flow,
To gather all the breath the winds can blow. Rowe.
—— Summis annectite ſuppara velis. *Statius.*

——Non invehet undis ſuppara. *Manilius.* Ubi communiter pro velis. *Vid.* Turn. Adverſ. xxi. 4.

(*d*) Cic. de Sen. 18. Poteſt quidquam eſſe abſurdius, quàm quo minus reſtat viæ, eo plus viatici quærere? *Can any thing be more abſurd, than the ſhorter a journey is, to lay in the more proviſion?*—*See* the Life of *Seneca*.

(*e*) Upon a debate in the ſenate, concerning the death of *Afranius Dexter*, mentioned by *Pliny*, Ep. viii. 14, Lord *Orrery* obſerves, "the plain and legal queſtion to be decided by the ſenate was, whether *Dexter* had been killed by his freedmen, from their malice, or in purſuance of his own command:

mand: if they were convicted of the former, the punishment was death; if it was proved that they killed him in obedience to his own orders, they ought to have been acquitted. The opinion of *Pliny* therefore is not to be justified. He declares that *the freedmen ought to be put to the question, and afterwards released.* If they were innocent, why should they be punished? If guilty, why released?—Throughout the whole Epistle the quibbles of the lawyers are much more conspicuous than the dignity of the Senator. *Vid.* Sidon. Ep. viii. 11.

(*f*) Invitum qui servat idem facit occidenti. Hor. A. P. 467.

For 'tis a greater cruelty to kill
Than to preserve a man against his will.

(*g*) God forbid that suicide should *ever* be thought *necessary* among heathens, much less among Christians. When Nature speaks for herself, even the *Stoics* with whom it was an avowed doctrine, speak in a softer tone. For thus *Epictetus*, l. i. c. 9. "*My friends*, saith he, *wait for God, till he shall give the signal, and dismiss you this service; then return to him. For the present be content to remain in this post, where he has placed you. Stay; depart not inconsiderately.*" And again, with an entire resignation to the divine will—*Whatever post or rank thou shalt assign me, like* Socrates, *I will die a thousand deaths rather than desert thee.* Nor can it by any means be pretended that when we meet with great adversities in life, it is a call from God to quit it; on the contrary, it is a call to the exercise of patience, resignation, and fortitude.

Rebus in adversis facile est contemnere vitam:
Fortiter ille facit qui miser esse potest.
'Tis easy to spurn life in wretchedness,
But far more brave to triumph in distress. M.

(*k*) Epp. 24. (N. p. q.) Sen. de Tranq. Animi, 2.

(*l*) Ep. 24. (N. r.)——Lucretius iii. 1095.

Nec nova vivendo procuditur ulla voluptas.
Life adds no new delight to those possess'd.

(*m*) Aye, but to die and go we know not where?——Ep. 82, (N. f.) See *also* the incomparable soliloquy in *Hamlet*.

(*n*) (Non enim certus numerus quam debeas explere, finitur.) *Pincean.* reads it with an interrogation; *num enim——Have you done all that was your duty to do?*

(*o*) She was of a noble family, the daughter of *Statilius* the Consul, in the reign of *Claudius*. *See* Plin. vii. 48 ——It may not, perhaps, be right to mention a relation of mine with this noble lady; yet out of respect to the memory of my father's grandmother, Mrs. *Combes*, of Windsor, I cannot help observing that she died of a fall (a violent death) at 107.

(*p*) All the world's a stage;
And all the men and women merely players.
They have their exits and their entrances;
And one man in his time plays many parts;
His acts being seven ages.—(incomparably described in *Shakespear's* As You Like It.
Life's but a walking shadow; a poor player,
That struts and frets his hour upon the stage,
And then is heard no more.——*Id.* Macbeth.

(*q*) Which title, the death recommended under the Note (*g*) can, by no means, lay any claim to, in any Christian or Heathen.

EPISTLE

EPISTLE LXXVIII.

On Sickneſs, Pain, and Death.

IT is the more diſagreeable to me, *Lucilius*, to hear, that you are frequently troubled with colds, and ſlight fevers, ſuch as generally attend defluxions of ſo long continuance, as to become conſtitutional; becauſe I have been ſubject to them myſelf, and have ſuffer'd not a little by neglecting them at the firſt attack. The ſtrength of youth indeed could ſupport ſuch violence, and ſtubbornly bear up againſt theſe infirmities; but at length the burden was too great for me, and I fell into a ſevere diſorder of this kind. I was quite emaciated (*a*), and began to think that life was not worth preſerving: but the old age of a moſt indulgent father check'd the daring thought: for I conſider'd not ſo much how reſolutely I could die myſelf; but that the loſs of me would neceſſarily afflict my father. I was therefore determined to ſtruggle for life. For even this is *ſometimes* a manly deſign (*b*). What at that time particularly comforted me, I will tell you, having firſt premiſed, that the things which gave me repoſe of mind, had the real effect of medicine. Juſt and pleaſant conſolations are at times the beſt of remedies; as whatever raiſeth the ſpirits is of great ſervice to the body.

Know then, I found health in ſtudy. I am indebted to philoſophy for the recovery of my ſtrength. I am indebted to her for nothing leſs than my life. My friends indeed contributed ſomewhat thereto; having ſupported and comforted me, with their good counſel, watchings, and diſcourſes. Nothing, my *Lucilius*, beſt of men, ſo revives, and helps a man in ſickneſs, as the affectionate tenders of a friend: nothing ſo much alleviates, and ſteals away the expectation and fear of death. So long as theſe ſhould live, I did not think I could die: I thought, I ſay, I ſhould ſtill live, if not in their company yet in their

 memory;

memory; and that I was not pouring out my ſpirit, but delivering it up to them. From hence I took upon me the reſolution of doing what I could for myſelf, and of enduring patiently all manner of pain. Otherwiſe, it would have been very miſerable, to have no inclination to die, and yet, make no endeavours to live. Apply therefore the remedies preſcribed. As to the reſt, your phyſician will direct you how far you are to walk, and what other exerciſe to take; he will order you likewiſe not to indulge that liſtleſſneſs which an ill ſtate of health is apt to bring upon us; to read aloud; and by exerciſe ſtrengthen the breath, that labours in its paſſage from the lungs, ſo choak'd up as not to have free play; he will ſometimes recommend ſailing to ſtir the bowels, and procure an appetite; he will inſtruct you in what food is moſt proper, and when to refreſh yourſelf with a glaſs of wine, or when to abſtain from it, for fear it ſhould provoke and heighten your cough.

But ſuch is *my* preſcription, that it will not only ſerve for this diſeaſe, but the whole life. *Contemn Death.* Nothing is diſtaſteful, when we have got over the fear of death. There are three things, which in every diſeaſe are grievous. *The fear of death, the pain of the body,* and *the intermiſſion of pleaſures.* Of death, we have ſaid enough already, I ſhall only add, that this fear proceeds not from the diſeaſe, but from nature itſelf. A diſeaſe hath often prevented death, and the very thoughts of dying have contributed to health. You will die, not becauſe you are ſick, but becauſe you live. Be you ever ſo well recovered, death ſtill expects you. You have not eſcaped death but only ſuch a fit of ſickneſs. But to return to what is properly diſagreeable and irkſome in this reſpect.

A diſeaſe is generally attended with great pains, yet ſome intervals make even theſe tolerable. And the more intenſe the pain is the ſooner it comes to an end. No one can ſuffer any torture long. Kind nature hath been ſo indulgent to us, as to make our pains either tolerable or ſhort. The moſt ſevere are felt in thoſe parts of the body that are leſs muſcular, The nerves, the joynts, and the fineſt membranes rage

moſt

moſt furiouſly, when they have contracted a vitious humour. But then theſe parts are ſoon benumb'd, and in the agony loſe the ſenſe of it; either becauſe the animal ſpirits, being hinder'd from their natural courſe, and flowing irregularly, loſe the power with which they before ſtrengthen'd and animated the body; or becauſe the corrupted humour, having met with a ſtoppage, deprives the aggrieved part of ſenſibility. So, the gout in the hand or foot, and every pain of the *vertebræ*, or nerves, finds intermiſſion, when the part they before racked, is deaden'd. The pricking and ſhooting of the firſt attack is generally moſt painful; the violence goes off in time, and ends in ſtupefaction. The pain of the teeth, eyes and ears is moſt acute upon this account, nor leſs certainly the pain of the head: but the more violent this is, the ſooner it turns into inſenſibility or a delirium. This then is our great comfort, when afflicted with any ſore diſeaſe, that, if we feel it too much, we ſhall ſoon feel it no more. But what greatly adds to the torment of the ignorant, is, that, when the body is afflicted, they have no recourſe to the ſatisfaction of a ſound mind: the body engroſſeth their whole care: therefore a great and prudent man diveſts himſelf, as it were, of the body, and converſeth much with that divine part of him, the ſoul; taking no more thought of that frail, and ever-querulous part of him, the body, than is merely neceſſary.

But it is very grievous, you ſay, to remit our wonted pleaſures, to abſtain from food, and to ſuffer hunger and thirſt. I grant, at firſt ſuch abſtinence is irkſome; but the hankering after them grows weaker by degrees: nor do the things themſelves retain the ſame incitement and provocation. Hence the ſtomach grows moroſe and ſqueamiſh, and a loathing comes on even of what we moſt greedily coveted. Deſires themſelves often die away, and we cannot think it hard to be denied that which we no longer covet. Add to this, that there is no pain, but what finds ſome intermiſſion, or certainly a remiſſion. Add likewiſe, that a diſeaſe may ſometimes be prevented, or at leaſt checked by timely medicine: for there is no diſeaſe but what hath its ſymptoms, particularly ſuch as we have been ſubject to before. In ſhort, any diſeaſe may be render'd tolerable, by deſpiſing the laſt extremity that it threatens. Make not therefore thine afflictions more grievous than they are by impatience and heavy complaints: the pain is light, when not aggravated by fancy and opinion. If you can be persuaded to comfort yourself with saying, *It is nothing, or in effect very little, let us bear it patiently*; it will be soon at an end; or this very thought will make it easy and tolerable.

All things depend upon opinion: not only ambition, but even luxury and avarice, refer to it. Pain also is proportioned to opinion. Every one is as wretched as he thinks himself to be (*b*). The complaints of former grievances, especially, I think, are to be forgotten, nor any such acclamations to be heard, as, *no one was ever worse: what afflictions, what tortures have I endured! no one could think that I should ever recover: how affectionately did my friends weep for me! when the physicians gave me over! men upon the rack were never tortur'd more.* Though all this may be true; it is now past and gone. What avails it to reflect upon the pains we have suffer'd, and to make ourselves miserable, because we were once so? Besides there is no one, but who makes some additions to his misfortunes, and often gives himself the lye. Not but that there is a certain pleasure in recounting past sufferings; and it is natural to rejoice in an escape.

There are two things therefore to be particularly renounced, *the fear of what may happen*, and *the recollection of an evil past*. The one is no concern to me now, nor need I anticipate the other. A man under present difficulties may comfort himself with saying,

—Forsan et hæc olim meminisse juvabit. Virg. i. 207.

An hour will come, with pleasure to relate
Your sorrows past———

But let him strive against them with all his might: he will certainly be overcome if he gives way; but if he bears up with patience and resolution against pain, he will overcome it: but the manner of most men, is, to draw upon themselves that destruction, which resistance might have prevented. That which presseth hard upon you, and is very urgent, if you begin to withdraw yourself, will certainly pursue you,

you, and fall the heavier; if on the contrary, you ſtand your ground, and ſeem reſolv'd upon oppoſition, you will drive it from you. How many ſtrokes do the boxers receive on the face and over the whole body! yet a thirſt of glory makes them regardleſs of pain, and patiently bear it; not only becauſe they fight, but that they may fight on. Torture to them is exerciſe. We likewiſe may overcome every thing, if we would conſider, that the reward propoſed to us is not a ſimple coronet, a palm, or the trumpet commanding ſilence at the proclamation of our honour; but virtue, ſtrength of mind, and everlaſting peace, if in any conflict we have ſubdued fortune.

But I feel, you ſay, *great pain*. And how ſhould you do otherwiſe than feel it, if you bear it like a weak woman? As an enemy is more pernicious to thoſe that fly; ſo every fortuitous evil preſſeth hardeſt upon the ſubmiſſive coward. *But indeed it is very grievous*; what then? does bravery conſiſt in the ſufferance of light things? which had you rather undergo a ſlow chronic diſeaſe, or a ſudden, violent, but ſhort, fit? the former can never be ſo long, but it will have ſome intermiſſions, and permit ſome refreſhment; at leaſt it gives time, and muſt one day come to a criſis, and go off. And a ſhort and violent ſickneſs, will ſoon, either carry *you* off, or itſelf. And where is the difference, whether that, or you, ſhall be no more? in either caſe, there is an end of pain.

It may likewiſe be of ſervice to divert the mind with other thoughts, and not ſo much as to dream of pain. Reflect upon ſuch actions, as were founded upon the principles of honour and virtue: look upon yourſelf in the beſt light you can; call to memory ſuch feats as you moſt admired in other men; and take the braveſt of thoſe, whom you know to have overcome pain, for example. There have been found thoſe who could amuſe themſelves with reading, while their ſwellings were lanced and ſcarified: others perſiſting in a contemptuous ſmile, while their executioners, the more enraged upon this account, have tried upon them the ſevereſt tortures, that cruelty could invent. And ſhall not reaſon overcome that pain, which laughter can get the better

of?

of? Tell me now what you pleafe of rheums, and the violence of a cough, throwing up part of your lungs; and of a fever burning your heart-ftrings; of the moft painful thirft; and of limbs and joints diftorted and diflocated with pain: yet how much more fevere is it, to be burned alive; to be torn in pieces on the rack; to have red hot pads of iron laid upon the body; and a preffure made upon the fwoln wounds, to renew the pain, and make it pierce the deeper? And yet there have been thofe who have endured all this without a groan: nay more, they afk'd for no remiffion: and more, no word could be extorted from them; yet more, they laughed, and earneftly from the foul. After all this, will you not fcoff at pain?

But your difeafe, you fay, *will not permit you to do any thing; it prevents all manner of bufinefs.* Be it fo; ficknefs indeed reftrains the body but *not the mind*; it fetters the feet of the running-footman and will tie up the hands of the cobler and blackfmith: but if you have learned the right ufe of the mind, you will ftill give advice, teach, hear, learn, be inquifitive, reflect, and the like. Befides, do you think you are doing nothing if you are temperate in your ficknefs? you will hereby fhew that your diftemper may be conquer'd, or at leaft fupported with patience. Believe me, *Lucilius*, virtue finds a place even in the fick-bed. Not only arms and battles give teftimony of a valiant mind, unterrified by danger; the brave man is alike feen under his coverlet. You have ftill wherewithal to employ you. Contend ftrenuoufly with your difeafe; if it can neither compel you, nor perfuade you, to do an unworthy action, you fet a rare example. O how great caufe of triumph is it, to be look'd upon with admiration on the bed of ficknefs! look upon, nor fcruple to praife, yourfelf.

Moreover there are two forts of pleafure; ficknefs indeed reftrains bodily pleafures, but does not altogether take them away: nay, if you judge rightly it rather enhanceth them: the thirfty have more pleafure in drinking; and food is the more tafteful to him that is hungry: whatever we have been commanded to abftain from we now receive more greedily. But no phyfician can debar his patient the other pleafures of of the mind, which are ſtill greater and more certain. He that follows theſe, and underſtands them well, deſpiſeth all the blandiſhments of the ſenſes. *O, how wretched is a ſick man!* and why? becauſe he dilutes not his wine with ſnow; becauſe he cools not his draught with ice, broken into it, and mixed in a great glaſs; becauſe no oyſters from the *Locrian* lake are opened at his table; becauſe the dining room does not ring with the noiſe of the cooks that are bringing in their ſtew pans and chafing diſhes. For this too hath luxury introduced; that the meat may not grow cool; that it may be hot enough for the palate, now grown callous; the whole kitchen attends at ſupper.

O how wretched is the ſick man! he muſt eat no more than he can digeſt, he ſhall not ſee a whole boar, meſſed up and ſet upon a ſide table, as coarſe commons; nor ſhall he have the breaſts of fowls (for it is not the faſhion to ſee them whole) heaped up for him in different diſhes in the larder. And what harm do you ſuffer in all this? you ſhall ſup as becometh a ſick man: nay, ſometimes, as if really in good health. But we ſhall eaſily endure theſe things, weak broths, warm water, and whatever the delicate, and luxurious, and ſuch as are rather ſick in mind than in body, think intolerable; if we once get over the horror and fear of death: and this we certainly ſhall do, if we rightly diſtinguiſhed the ends of good and evil: for by this means neither life would ſeem tedious or diſtaſteful, nor death terrible. For a life, taken up with reflecting on things ſo various, ſo great and divine, can never be cloy'd with ſatiety. Eaſe and idleneſs only are wont to give it a diſreliſh. Truth never fatigues the mind when traverſing the nature of things; it is falſehood alone that gives it a diſguſt.

Again, if death makes his approach, and calls upon us, though ſomewhat immaturely; nay, though he cuts us off in the flower of our age, yet the fruit of the longeſt life may yet have been gathered. Nature for the moſt part is open to the knowledge of the wiſe man; who plainly perceives, that virtue (or *what is right and fit*) is not enhanced by length of days. But every life muſt neceſſarily ſeem ſhort to thoſe who meaſure it by their pleaſures, vain, and therefore infinite.

Comfort:

Comfort yourself, *Lucilius*, with these reflections, and at leisure peruse my Epistles. The time will come when we may meet again and converse together: how short soever that time may be it may be lengthen'd by knowing how to use it well. For, as *Posidonius* writes, Unus dies hominum eruditorum plus patet, quam imperiti longissima ætas, *One day enjoyed by the* Literati, *is of longer duration than whole years among the ignorant and unlearned* (*d*). In the mean while adhere stedfastly to these precepts; *not to yield to affliction nor put your trust in prosperity*; *to set the whole power of fortune before your eyes*; *and to suppose that she* will *do*, *what she* can *do*. An evil that hath been long expected, gives the milder stroke when it happens.

ANNOTATIONS, &c.

(*a*) In the time of the emperor *Caius*, who dreading his eloquence, was determined upon his destruction, but he was saved by the declaration of an old woman, *that he was in so deep a consumption it was impossible for him to live long*.

(*b*) It is always so.—Pliny (Ep. l. 22.) speaking of his friend *Titus Aristo*, says, "He desired us "to inquire of his physicians into the nature of his distemper, that if it was incurable he might "chuse an immediate death: but if only stubborn, and tedious, he might stand firm and struggle, as "*he ought*; for he thought it not allowable, to frustrate the prayers of his wife, the tears of his "daughter, and the hopes of his friends, if there were any grounds for these hopes, by putting an "end to his own life. A noble determination; and always proper!—

(*c*) Si possis sanum fingere, sanus eris.
Think yourself well, and all complaint will cease.

(*d*) From this saying of *Posidonius*, *Murctus* supposes that *Cicero* took in his *Tusculan questions*, l. v. Unum bene et ex philosophiæ præceptis actum, esse pœne toti immortalitati anteponendum; *One day spent well, and agreeable to the precepts of philosophy, is preferable to an eternity of sin*. But more just and sublime is that of the royal *Psalmist*, *One day in thy courts*, O *Lord*, is better than a thousand. Ps. 84. 10.

EPISTLE.

EPISTLE LXXIX.

On Wisdom. All wise Men equal.

I Expect letters from you, *Lucilius*, with an account of what new things you obferv'd in your voyage round *Sicily*; and particulatly what you have learned of certainty concerning *Charybdis*. I know well enough that *Sylla* is a vaft rock, and confequently very terrible to failors, but I fhould be glad to be inform'd whether the ftories related of *Charybdis* have any foundation; and if you have obferv'd, (for 'tis a thing worthy to be obferved) whether it is one particular wind, that forms thefe hideous whirlpools, or whether every tempeftuous wind alike difturbs that boifterous fea: and whether it be true, that whatever is fucked in, is carried under the water many miles, and flung up again in the *Tauromenitan* bay (*a*). When you have oblig'd me herein I will make bold to defire the favour of you to afcend mount *Ætna*; which fome have fuppofed to have been fomewhat confumed and lower'd by degrees; as they were wont to fhew it formerly to paffengers at a greater diftance than they do now (*b*). Though this might happen, not becaufe the mountain's height is lowered, but becaufe the fires are weaken'd and do not blaze out with their former vehemenence: and for which reafon it is that fuch vaft clouds of fmoke are not feen in the day time. Yet neither of thefe feem incredible: for the mountain may poffibly be confumed by being daily devoured: and the fire not be fo large as formerly: fince it is not felf-generated here, but is kindled in the diftant bowels of the earth and there rages, being fed with continual fuel: not with that of the mountain, through which it only makes its paffage. In *Lycia* there is a famous territory, which the inhabitants call *Hephæftion*, where the foil is perforated in many places (*c*). From whence breaks forth a lambent flame, that is not in the leaft detrimental; the country therefore is ftill pleafant, and fertile, with good herbage, as the flame does not fcorch it,

 but

but only makes it ſhine with a faint and glimmering brightneſs. But for the preſent we ſhall wave this matter, and reſume it again when you have inform'd me how far from the orifice of *Ætna* are thoſe heaps of ſnow which the ſummer itſelf does not diſſolve: ſo little danger are they in, from the neighbouring heat.

Now, there is no reaſon you ſhould ſay that I impoſe this work upon you; for I know, you would indulge your poetical vein herein, though no one required it of you; nay, it would be in vain to pretend to bribe you, not to undertake a deſcription of *Ætna* in verſe, or not to treat on a ſubject that has been thought ſo worthy the pen of all the poets: For tho' *Virgil* had before elegantly and fully deſcribed it; this did not prevent *Ovid* from the attempt; and neither of them debarred *Cornelius Severus* from writing on the ſame ſubject. It is a ſubject moreover ſo happily copious, that they who have gone before, ſeem by no means to have exhauſted it, but to have opened matter for further explanation. There is alſo a great difference, whether you undertake a ſubject that is quite exhauſted, or ſuch a one as only exhibits a rough draught; for this daily increaſes, and ſupplies room for further invention. Add likewiſe that the laſt writer hath generally the greateſt advantage. He finds words already prepared, which, under a different arrangement, put on the ſemblance of ſomething new; nor does he uſe them as the property of another, but as things in common; and the lawyers ſay, *that what is in common no one can claim as his own property*. If I know you then, *your mouth waters, as they ſay*, at a deſcription of *Ætna*: you long to write ſomething great and ſublime, and to ſhew yourſelf at leaſt equal to thoſe who have wrote before you. For your modeſty will not permit you to hope any thing more: nay, it is ſo great, that I verily believe, you would check your genius in its career, if there was any likelihood of excelling them. Such reſpect you pay to your predeceſſors.

Be that as it will; know, that wiſdom hath this peculiar good, among many other, that not one profeſſor of it can excell another, but in the time and act of aſcending: when they once come to the ſummit of perfection, there is no room for any advantage of one above another. There is is a full ſtop to advancement. Can the ſun receive any addition to his greatneſs? or the moon make a further progreſs than uſual? the ſeas ſtill keep their bounds: and the world maintains one conſtant order and meaſure. Such things as have attained their juſt and proper magnitude, can riſe no higher.

All men that are truly wiſe, are equal and alike; though each may be endowed with a peculiar gift; as one may be more affable, another more expeditious; another more prompt in declaiming; and another more eloquent; but the particular under conſideration, *what conſtitutes the happy man*, will be equal in all. I know not whether your *Ætna* will ſink and be conſumed; or whether the fire by degrees will firſt eat away its lofty ſummit, now ſo conſpicuous many leagues at ſea: but this I know, that no flame, no ruin can ever ſubdue virtue. The majeſty of this alone is not to be depreſſed, no nor exalted nor perverted. Her magnitude is fixed like that of the heavenly bodies. To this then let us faſhion ourſelves; we have gone a great way towards it already; a great way, did I ſay? I am miſtaken. To confeſs the truth, we have advanced but a little way as yet; It is not goodneſs, to be better than the worſt: who can boaſt of thoſe eyes, that can behold and admire the brightneſs of the ſun only through a cloud; though in the mean time it is ſome ſatisfaction not to be in the dark; yet we enjoy not the pure benefit of light. Then will the mind have wherewithal to congratulate itſelf, when, ſet free from the darkneſs wherein it is now involved, it ſhall ſee things as they are; not with theſe dim viſual rays: but a full and continual day, without night, ſhall ſhine upon it; and, returning to its own heaven, it ſhall be reſtored to the happy manſion, from whence it came into the world. Its firſt original ſummons is to ſoar aloft; it may be there even before it is ſet free from this priſon of clay; when it has thrown off all vice, and ſhines out pure and ſplendid with the brightneſs of divine contemplation.

This then, deareſt *Lucilius*, is what we muſt do. To accompliſh this we muſt uſe our utmoſt endeavours: though few men know it and ſcarce any can ſee it. Glory is the ſhadow of virtue; and attends on its professors whether they will or not. But as sometimes our shadows go before, and sometimes follow us: so glory sometimes precedes, and is visible to all; at other times it stalks behind us, and is so much the larger, as it is later, ere envy is quite destroy'd. How long was *Democritus* taken for a madman? Fame scarce took any notice of *Socrates*. How long was it ere *Rome* knew the value of *Cato?* She even rejected him and knew him not, till she had lost him. The innocence and virtue of *Rutilius*, had never been known, had he not been treated injuriously; but having been wronged, his glory shone out; and he could not but thank his fortune, and enjoy his banishment. I am speaking of those, whom fortune honoured, while she persecuted them. But how many are there, whose merit was never published, till after their decease! how many, whom fame passed disrespectfully by, while living, and raised them, as it were, again, when dead! you see *Epicurus*, whom not only the better learned, but the most ignorant rabble now admire. He was scarce known at *Athens*, where he lived and died in obscurity. He survived his friend *Metrodorus* many years, and making grateful mention, in an Epistle, of their friendship, he added in the conclusion, that *as they had happily partook of manifold blessings in life, it was of very little consequence, that so renowned a country as* Greece, *should not only pretend not to know them, but scarce ever to have heard of them.* May he not therefore be said to have been found when he was no more in being? and did not his opinion and reputation still grow more famous? this is also what *Metrodorus* confesseth in a certain epistle, that *himself* and Epicurus *were not indeed as yet sufficiently known, but that the time would come when they both should be readily and highly extolled among those especially who would walk in the same steps.*

No virtue can lie unconcealed long: and even to lie concealed is no detriment thereto. The day will come that shall draw it from the obscurity, wherein through the malignity of the age it is hid and oppressed. He is born but to few, whose thoughts are taken up with those only of his own time. Many thousand years, many thousand people shall come after us. Let these have your regard. Though envy hath enjoyed silence to all your cotemporaries, another race will spring up, that

that ſhall judge you without prejudice or partiality. And if fame be any recompence for virtue, it will not ſoon die. Tis' true, what poſterity will ſay of us, will not concern, or perhaps reach us. Yet ignorant as we may be of what they are doing, it may pleaſe them to reverence our memory, and do us honour. Not that there is any man whom virtue hath not recompenſed and dignified, in life as well as in death; provided that he followed her with ſincerity and integrity; that he dreſſed not up himſelf with a painted outſide; that he was ſtill the ſame man, whether upon warning given, or ſet upon unprepared, and ſuddenly ſurpriſed. Diſſimulation profiteth nothing. A feigned countenance occaſionally and lightly put on, can impoſe upon but very few. Truth is always the ſame; turn her which way you will. But there is no ſolidity in falſehood. A lye is generally ſo thin, that it is tranſparent, and eaſily ſeen through, when narrowly inſpected.

ANNOTATIONS, &c.

(*a*) According to Salluſt—Ea (abſorpta) circa Tauromenitanum litus egerit. Vid. Strabo, l. vi.

Dextrum Sylla ſatus, lævum implacata Charybdis.
Obſidet, &c. Virg. iii. 420.
Far on the right, her dogs foul Sylla hides,
Charybdis *roaring on the left preſides:*
And in her greedy whirlpool ſinks the tides:
Then ſpouts them from below, with fury driv'n,
The waves mount up, and waſh the face of Heav'n;
But Sylla *from her den, with open jaws,*
The ſinking veſſel in her eddy draws,
Then daſhes on the rocks:——Dryden.

(*b*) Ælian. Var. Hiſt. l. ſ. c. ii.

(*c*) Plin. l. iv. c. 27.

EPISTLE.

EPISTLE LXXX.

True Felicity lies in the Mind.

I Am entirely my own maſter to-day, *Lucilius*, not only at my own re-queſt, but a great match at ball (*a*), hath withdrawn all troubleſome viſitants. No one breaks in upon me to diſturb my thoughts: which from this aſſurance now take a larger range. My door has not creaked as uſual; nor has the curtain been lifted up. I can now think as I pleaſe; which you know is agreeable to one who loves to have his own way. Do I then not follow the ancients? yes certainly, in ſome things; but I take the liberty to find out ſomething myſelf; to change or leave what I diſlike; I am not a ſlave to them, but a follower. But I ſaid too much when I promiſed myſelf an uninterrupted privacy. For lo; a great noiſe reaches me from the *Stadium*, which does not indeed take me from myſelf, but transfers all my contemplation to the ſports there going on. I conſider with myſelf, how many there are who exerciſe their bodies and how few the mind: what a concourſe of people flock to theſe ſights, vain and trifling as they are; and how deſerted are the liberal ſciences; how weak they are in underſtanding, whoſe broad ſhoulders and brawny limbs we are apt to admire.

But this I chiefly reflect upon, that if the body may be trained up to ſuch hardineſs as to bear the blows and kicks of more than one man (*b*); and a man, beſmeared with his own blood and duſt, can endure all the day long the ſcorching heat of the ſun (*c*), as reflected too from the hot ſands; how much eaſier would it be for him ſo to ſtrengthen his mind, as to be invincible againſt the ſtrokes of fortune; and though flung down and trod upon, to be able to raiſe himſelf up again, and conquer! The body wants many external things, to render it firm and ſtrong: the mind grows great of itſelf; is its own nutriture, and exerciſe: the body wants meat and drink to ſupport it; much oyl to make it lightſome;

and

and much labour to make it hardy; whereas virtue is attainable without any apparatus or expence. What can make you good, is ever in your own power. And what is that? why, *the will.*

And what can you *will* better, than to deliver yourself from the servitude, which tyranniseth over the world: and which even slaves of the meanest sort, and who were born to this vile condition, endeavour by all means to cast off? All the little stock of cattle which they can pick up, by pinching their own bellies they are ready to give up, for *liberty*. And will not you, who thinkest thyself a free-born man, desire this attainment at any rate? why do you cast a look upon your coffers? it is not to be bought. It is an idle thing therefore to set the name of *liberty* in the tables of manumission; since neither the buyer nor the seller are in possession of it. It is a good which you must bestow upon yourself; *there* apply for it. And first of all extricate yourself from the *Fear of Death*. This is what lays upon us the first and heaviest yoke (*d*).

Proceed next to discharge the *Fear of Poverty*. If you would be certain that there is no great harm in this, only compare the countenances of the rich and the poor: and you will find that the poor man laughs more frequently and more heartily. No anxiety racks his bosom: whatever befalleth him, it passeth away like a light cloud. Whereas the gayety of those we call happy, is all feigned. Sorrow lies heavy and suppurates at the bottom; and so much the heavier is it, as they cannot give it vent, and dare not discover their wretchedness; but amidst the sorrows that are preying upon their hearts, they are obliged to set a face of felicity upon discontent. I often make use of this example, nor can any other so well express this farce on the stage of life (*e*), wherein are assigned to us our several parts, which we act so aukwardly (*f*). The fellow who struts about the stage, and with his head aloft bellows out,

> En! impero Argis, regna mihi liquit Pelops,
> Quà Ponto ab Helles, atque ab Ionio mari,
> Urgetur Isthmos—(*g*)

is but a needy ſlave, that hath five buſhels of corn and five *deniers* for his pay (*b*): and he that ſo proudly boaſts his ſtrength, ſaying,

> Quòd niſi quieris, Menelae hac dextrâ occides,
> *Be ſatisfied*, Menelaus, *or this hand*
> *Shall ſtrike thee dead*—

is but a poor weak wretch, that hath his daily allowance, and lies upon a truckle bed in a garret (*i*). We may ſay the ſame of all thoſe delicate minions, who are carried on a litter above the heads of the people, and the gazing mob. Their felicity is all perſonated, you would utterly deſpiſe them were you to take off the maſk. When you would buy a horſe, you ſtrip it of the ſaddle and furniture (*k*): you likewiſe order the ſlave you would purchaſe to be turned out naked; leſt any blemiſh of the body ſhould be concealed: and do you eſtimate a man in all his trappings? nothing is more common than for jockeys and dealers of this kind to hide by ſome artful ſleight, whatever might diſcredit the thing upon ſale: therefore all external ornaments are to be ſuſpected by the buyer. Should you ſee a leg or an arm bound up, you would immediately deſire it to be unſwathed, that you may inſpect the whole body. Behold that King of *Scythia* or *Samaria*, with the royal diadem glittering on his head; would you know him thoroughly, take off his diadem, and you will find much miſchief and cruelty beneath it. But why ſpeak of others? If you would duly weigh yourſelf, throw aſide your wealth, your fine ſeat and outward dignity: conſider yourſelf within: you now truſt to others, who do not ſo well know you, and therefore cannot ſhew you, what you are.

ANNOTATIONS, &c.

(*a*) Sphæromachiam] not the common play at ball, like our *fives*, which would ſcarce have drawn a concourſe of people together, but Sphyromachiam, as *Pincian* writes it, *i. e.* calcium et talorum pugnam, *i.e.* *foot-ball*. Vid. Steph. Epiſt. ad *Dalech.* 34. P. Fab. l. 1. c. 6. *Agoniſt.* Polluc. l. 9. Præf. Stat. Silv. 4.

(*b*) They generally fought in pairs, but ſometimes a mixed battle, or what we call a battle *royal*; which is here alluded to.

(*c*) So *Cicero*, Pugiles inexercitati, etiamſi pugnos et plagas ferre poſſint, ſolem tamen ſæpe ferre non poſſunt. *Boxers, not thoroughly exercised, may endure thumps and blows, when they cannot bear the violent heat of the ſun.*

(*d*) This

(*d*) This is the true liberty; the end of all philosophy; and to which alludes that paradoxical decree, Solum sapientem liberum esse; *that the wise man only is free.*

(*e*) Augustus is said, when dying, to have asked, *Whether he was thought to have acted his part well on the stage of life.*

Σκηνὴ πᾶς ὁ βίος, καὶ παίγνιον, καὶ μάθε παίζειν,
Τὴν σπουδὴν μεταθεὶς, ἢ φέρε τὰς ὀδύνας. Anthol.
Life is a farce; hence learn to play thy part;
Be chearful; and despise a gloomy heart.

It is impossible here not to be reminded of the wretched if not wicked Epitaph, bestowed on the late Mr. Gay in *Westminster Abbey.*

Life is a farce, &c.

(*f*) Laertius in Zenone; Εἶναι γὰρ ὅμοιον τῷ ἀγαθῷ ὑποκριτῇ κ. τ. λ. *The wise man is like a good actor, who whether he represents* Thersites *or* Agamemnon, *is alike careful to play his part well.*

(*g*) Taken from the *Atreus* of *Attius.*

Of Argos *I am king:* Pelops, *my sire,*
Bequeath'd me kingdoms, whose vast bounds extend
From Hellespont *to the* Ionian *sea.*

(*h*) *Muretus* supposeth this to be the monthly pay.

(*i*) In cœnaculo] As *Jupiter* says jocosely of himself in *Plautus:*

In superiore qui habito in cœnaculo.

(*k*) Regibus hic mos est, ubi equos mercantur, apertos
Inspiciunt——Hor. f. i. 2. 86.
Our jockeys when a horse is set to sale,
Examine him, uncloth'd, from head to tail.

Sic Macrob. Saturn. i. 11. Quemadmodum stultus est, qui empturus equum, non ipsum inspicit, sed stratum ejus et frænum. Sic est Qui hominem ex veste aut conditione, quæ modo vestis nobis circumdata est, æstimandum putat. *As a man is a fool, who when he is to buy a horse examines no further than the bridle or saddle; he is no less who estimates a man by his outward appearance and condition in life.*

EPISTLE LXXXI.

Of Ingratitude.

YOU complain, *Lucilius,* that you have met with an ungrateful man. If this is the first time, you ought to thank either your good fortune, or your own care and diligence. But care and diligence can do little or nothing in this respect, unless it were to make you malevolent. For in order to ſhun this danger, you muſt never confer a benefit while you live. And ſo leſt benefits ſhould be loſt upon others, you will yourſelf loſe the ſatisfaction of conferring them. However, it would be better they were never recompenſed, than not conferred. The huſbandman muſt ſow again, though he had a bad crop laſt year. Oftentimes the plenty of one year makes up for the long unfruitfulneſs of a barren ſoil. It is worth while, to make trial of ungrateful men, in order to find one grateful. No one is ſo certain in the benefits he is pleaſed to confer, but that ſometimes he may be deceived. They muſt often miſs a mark, ere they hit it (*a*). Men venture again to ſea after a ſhipwreck. The uſurer ſtill lends his money, though he hath ſuffered loſs by a bankrupt. Life would ſoon grow dull and ſtupid in fruitleſs indolence were we to meet with no rubs in our way. But let this very accident make you kind and generous. For where the event of any thing is uncertain, frequent eſſays muſt be made if you deſire an happy iſſue.

But I have ſaid enough of this in my *treatiſe on benefits*. Our preſent enquiry, in a point not as yet, I think, ſufficiently diſcuſſed, ſeems to be this, *whether he that hath done us ſome ſervice, and afterwards injured us, hath not balanced the account between us, and releaſed us of our debt?* Suppoſe likewiſe this, if you pleaſe, *that he hath done us more prejudice than he ever did us good.*

If you apply to the judgement of one ſomewhat rigid in his diſpoſition, he will releaſe them reſpectively; and will ſay, "though the "injury done preponderates, yet what is over and above on this ſide, "muſt be given to the benefit. He hath indeed hurt you, but here-"tofore he was ſerviceable to you. The time therefore of either muſt "be brought to the account. And it is too manifeſt to need any par-"ticular admonition, that you ought to enquire, how willingly he ſerved "you, and how willingly he did any thing to your prejudice. For "both injuries and benefits are to be meaſured by the intention. You "may ſay, perhaps, I ſhould not have been ſo bountiful, but I was pre-"vail'd upon through fear of ſhame, or by the pertinacy of the im-

"portunate

" portunate fupplicant, or by hope. Every obligation arifes from " the mind with which a benefit is confer'd: nor is the greatnefs of " it confider'd, but the will of the perfon conferring it. Let all con- " jecture now be laid afide, and in the cafe before put, the benefit will " appear as fuch, and all beyond it, an injury; but a good man in " fettling the account, will condefcend to cheat himfelf, by adding to " the benefit, and fubtracting from the injury."

A more candid judge in this matter would act, as I fhould chufe to do in the like cafe; forget the injury, and be always mindful of the benefit. " It is certainly, he will fay, confonant to juftice, to " give every one their own, to repay a favour, to retaliate an affront, or at leaft to take it ill". All this will be true, where one man does an injury, and another confers a favour; but where they both come from the fame man, the ftrength of the injury is extinguifhed in the benefit. For if it is generous to forgive a man, even though he has not really deferv'd it by any paft favours, fomewhat more than pardon is due to him who hath injured us, after having confer'd a benefit upon us. I eftimate not both alike; but take more notice of a benefit than of an injury. Few know how to repay a kindnefs gratefully. Even an ignorant rude and vulgar fellow can return a favour, when he hath received one, upon the fpot, and in fome meafure recompenfe the fame; but he knows not his obligation *(b)*. It is the wife man alone, who knows what value is to be fet upon every thing: the fool I was fpeaking of, however good his will may be, either repays not as much as he owes, or does it fo awkardly or at fuch an improper time or place as lavifhly to throw away the intended recompenfe.

There is a wonderful propriety in certain words, and the ufage of the antient form of fpeech points out fome things in the moft fignificant and inftructive terms. We are wont to fay, Ille illi gratium retulit, *fuch a one* hath requited *a favour*. Now, referre, *to requite*, is to give voluntarily what you owe. We do not fay, gratiam reddidit, *he hath* reftored *a thing given*; for they may *reftore* a thing, who are demanded fo to do, or unwillingly, or juft when they pleafe, or by another hand: neither

 do

do we say, Reposuit beneficium aut solvit, *he hath* remitted or repaid *a kindness*; for no word that signifies the payment of a debt, as of money, pleaseth me in this respect. Referre, *to requite*, is gratefully to bring somewhat to him, from whom you have received: it signifies a voluntary retribution. He that hath *requited* another, hath appealed to, and summoned himself.

A wise man will weigh every circumstance with himself. He will consider what he hath received, from whence it came, when, where, and in what manner. And therefore we deny, that any one, save a wise man, knows how truly to requite a favour. As indeed no one but a wise man knows how to confer a benefit; he, in truth, who rejoyceth more in what he gives, than another does in what he receives. This some perhaps will reckon among those positions that are thought strange and extravagant, and by the *Greeks* called Παραδοξα, *Paradoxes*; and they will say, *what, does no one but a wise man know, how to requite a good turn? you may as well say, that no one but the wise man, knows how to pay a just debt; or, when he buys a thing, to pay a just price for it?* That no blame however may be laid upon us for advancing this seeming paradox, know, that *Epicurus* says the same thing; and *Metrodorus* expressly, solum sapientem *referre gratiam* scire, *that the wise man alone knows how to love (c) affectionately; and no one but a wise man can be a true friend.* But it is undoubtedly a part of love and friendship to requite a benefit. They may likewise wonder at our saying, *that fidelity is only to be found in the wise man*; as if they themselves did not say the same thing. Do you think a man can possibly be faithful, who knows not how to requite a courtesy? Let them cease therefore to defame us as if we had advanced what is not credible: and let them know that all that is great and honourable is to be found in the *wise man*; and nothing but the resemblance and appearance of it in the vulgar.

No one, I say, knows how to requite a good turn, save the wise man. A fool indeed may do the same to the best of his knowledge, and ability: when knowledge rather may be wanting than good will: for good will is natural and not acquired. The wise man will compare all things with

with themſelves; for the ſame thing is render'd greater or leſs by circumſtances, according to the time, place, or manner. It often happens that a thouſand pence, given opportunely, does more good than a maſs of treaſure would at another time. For there is a great difference between giving and ſuccouring: between having ſaved a man from ruin, or aggrandized him, by your bountiful kindneſs. A gift may be ſmall, but the conſequences of it very great. But what difference is there between a man's retaking what he before had given, or receiving a benefit in order to grant one? Not to return however to thoſe points, which have been ſufficiently diſcuſſed already, I ſhall only obſerve that a good man in comparing benefits with injuries, will judge what is moſt *right and fit*; will always have his eye upon benefits, and will be more inclined to favour them. Now, the perſon of the receiver, whether it be of an injury, or a benefit, is of the greateſt moment in this affair: for inſtance; you have done me a kindneſs indeed in my ſervant; but you have injured my father; you have preſerv'd for me a ſon, but you have deprived me of a ſire; conſequently he will purſue and examine all other circumſtances, from which every compariſon is formed; and if there ſhall appear but a ſmall difference he will overlook it; or ſhould the difference be great, he will pardon it, provided he can do it without the breach of piety and fidelity; i. e. if the whole of the injury appertains only to his own perſon *(d)*.

The ſum of the whole matter is this; he will be eaſy and gracious in commuting; he will ſuffer rather more to be ſet to his account than ought to be; he will be unwilling to diſcharge a favour upon the conſideration of a receiv'd injury; ſuch his inclination, and ſuch his endeavours that he may manifeſt his deſire not only to acknowledge a favour but to requite it. For the man judgeth wrong, who is more ſollicitous and glad to receive a benefit, than to confer one (*e*). By how much the man is happier who pays, than he that borroweth; ſo much more joyful ought the man to be who hath diſcharged a vaſt debt, incurred by benefits received, than he that lays himſelf under the greateſt obligation in receiving them. For in this alſo, the ungrateful are deceiv'd, in thinking they have done a great thing, when they have repaid a creditor

creditor ſomewhat more than his demands; and in ſuppoſing that benefits exact no intereſt. Whereas they certainly encreaſe by delay of a return: and ſo much the more is to be paid the longer the payment has been neglected. He is ungrateful who returns a benefit, without ſome addition, when it is in his power. This therefore is to be taken into the account, when we compare the things received with diſburſements.

Every thing, in ſhort, is to be done, that we may appear as grateful as poſſible. For this is our *own good:* and not, like an act of juſtice, as is thought, the concern of others. The beſt part of a benefit returns upon the benefactor. There is no one, who hath done good to another but hath done good to himſelf. I do not mean that a man having been aſſiſted will be ready to aſſiſt, or having been protected will protect, others; or becauſe a good example returns upon him, who ſets it, as bad examples generally revert upon the authors; nor does any one pity thoſe, when they ſuffer injuries, who by their actions have taught others to commit them; but becauſe the value of every virtue ſubſiſts within itſelf. They are not practiſed with a view to a reward. The reward of a good action, lies in the performance of ſuch an action. I am grateful, not in order to excite others to be more liberal to me, having ſet ſuch an example, but becauſe it is moſt agreeable, and very right. I am grateful, not becauſe it is expedient, but becauſe it gives me delight and ſatisfaction. To convince you of this I aſſure you, that could I not expreſs my gratitude, otherwiſe than by a ſeemingly ungrateful action, I ſhould have recourſe to the honeſt counſel of an upright mind, notwithſtanding in ſo doing I ſhould run the riſque of loſing a good name. No one ſeems to have a greater veneration for virtue, no one to be more devoted thereto, than the man who rather than make ſhipwreck of his conſcience is determined to hazard the reputation of a good man. Therefore, as I have before obſerv'd, thou art grateful, more for thine own good than another's. For nothing but what is ordinary and common happeneth to a man, who only receives what he had given; but to you, ſomewhat great, and flowing from the moſt happy temper of the mind, *to have been grateful.* For if the doing evil makes men miſerable,

ſerable, and virtue renders them happy; and if to be grateful is virtue; though you have done nothing extraordinary, you have attained what is ineſtimable, the conſciouſneſs of a grateful heart, which is not attainable but by a divine and happy diſpoſition.

The contrary affection is for ever attended with extreme infelicity. The ungrateful man will be always miſerable: I except not the time preſent. Let us therefore avoid being ungrateful for our own ſake, if not for the ſake of others. The leaſt and lighteſt conſequence of wickedneſs falls upon others, the worſt and heavieſt part of it ſtays behind and afflicts the doer. As our *Attalus* was wont to ſay; Malitia ipſa maximam partem veneni ſui bibit, *malignity generally drinks the greateſt part of its own poiſon* (*f*). The venom, which ſerpents throw out to deſtroy withal, and yet retain without prejudice to themſelves, is not like this: for this torments the poſſeſſor. The ungrateful man torments and racks himſelf. He hates the gift he hath accepted, for fear of the obligation of a return; and conſequently undervalues it; but exaggerates and magnifies an injury. And what can be more wretched than the man who forgets a benefit, and dwells upon an injury? On the contrary, wiſdom extolls a benefit, recommends it to herſelf, and delights in the daily commemoration of it. The pleaſure the wicked enjoy in the reception of a benefit, is but one and ſhort; whereas the pleaſure it gives a wiſe man, is large and perpetual; for he not only feels a delight in receiving, but in having received, which is continual and immortal. He contemns an injury, and forgets it; not through negligence, but wilfully. He takes not things in the worſt light: nor does he enquire on whom to lay the blame: but rather imputes the errors and miſcarriages of men to misfortune, than to malicioufneſs. He takes no exceptions either to the words, or to the look of a man. Whatever happens he extenuates by ſome kind interpretation, and is ever more mindful of a favour than of offence. As far as it is in his power, he fixeth his mind on ſome former and better object; nor changeth it againſt thoſe, who have once well deſerved: unleſs the evil far ſurpaſs the former good deeds; and the difference is palpable, though he ſhuts his eyes; and then goes no farther, than, to appear, after an injury, the

 ſame

ſame he was before he receiv'd the benefit. For when the injury is equal to the benefit, there will ſtill remain ſome ſpark of benevolence in his mind. As a culprit is acquitted when the opinion of the judges is equally divided: and in all doubtful caſes, humanity is always inclined to the merciful ſide: ſo the mind of the wiſe man, where merit is equal to demerit, ceaſeth to be really indebted, but ceaſeth not to acknowledge an obligation; as one, who after an acquittance in full, ſtill thinks himſelf in debt.

No one however can be grateful; but who deſpiſeth thoſe things that ſo greatly affect the vulgar. In order to return an extraordinary favour, you muſt defy baniſhment, ſhed your blood, endure want, and even ſuffer innocence to be traduced, and ſubject to the moſt unworthy reports. It coſts a man no ſmall matter to be grateful. But we are apt to think nothing ſo precious as a benefit when we aſk it, and nothing cheaper when we have received it. Do you aſk what it is that makes us forgetful of a benefit received? the deſire of ſtill receiving more. We reflect not upon what we have obtained, but upon what we ſtill hope to obtain. We are drawn from the right path, by riches, honours, powers and the like: which are dear and precious in our opinion, but in themſelves vile and of little value. We know not to eſtimate things rightly: concerning which we ought not to conſult fame and report, but the nature of the things themſelves. The things before mention'd have nothing really great in them, to attract our minds, but foraſmuch as it is cuſtomary to admire them. For, not becauſe they are deſireable, are they praiſed, but becauſe they are praiſed, they are coveted. And when the error of particulars hath cauſed a general blindneſs, to this at the ſame time may be refer'd any particular error. But as in ſome things we believe the vulgar, let us take this alſo upon the ſame credit, that *nothing is more juſt and honorable than a grateful mind.*

All cities and nations, in the moſt remote and barbarous regions, will join to condemn ingratitude. The good and bad all agree in this. There are ſome who prefer their pleaſures: others take more delight in labour and induſtry; ſome think pain the greateſt of all evils: others ſcarce

ſcarce look upon it as an evil; ſome think riches the moſt ſovereign good, others look upon them as the *root of all evil* in human life; and think that no one can be more happy than the man for whom fortune cannot find out an acceptable gift. Now various as the opinions of men are in theſe reſpects; yet all, with *one mouth*, as they ſay, declare, *that a grateful return is due to the well-deſerving*. In this the very rabble, however diſſentient in other matters, all agree. And yet we are apt to repay favours with injuries; and the chief reaſon that any one gives for ingratitude, is, that it was not in his power to be ſufficiently grateful. Nay, the madneſs of mankind is ſuch that it is the moſt dangerous thing in the world to confer an extraordinary benefit. For, inaſmuch as a man thinks it ſcandalous not to make ſome return, he wiſheth his benefactor out of the world. But whoſoever hath been benefited by me, let him enjoy what he hath received. I aſk it not again: I inſiſt not upon a requital. There is no hatred more pernicious than that of a man, who is aſhamed of not having repaid an obligation.

ANNOTATIONS, &c.

(*a*) Aberrent—*al.* non errent,—ut aliquando hæreant.] Hæſère omnia tela haud difficili ex propinquo in tanta corpora ictu. *Liv.* l. 27.

——Pars ad faſtigia miſſas
Exultant *haſiſſe* faces,—*Stat.* Theb. l. 10.
——non *exiſſe*.—*Græevius.*

(*b*) He may return the like favour; yet not make ample amends; for in a favour conferred, other things are to be conſidered; as *the intention of the mind*; the *propriety of time and place*, &c. as is afterwards obſerved.

(*c*) *Epictetus* likewiſe mentions this among the philoſophical paradoxes, and has beſtowed a diſſertation on the ſubject, l. 11. c. 22.—*Cic.* de Amic. Hoc primum ſentio, niſi in bonis amicitiam non eſſe; *Let me premiſe this, that no friendſhip can ſubſiſt but among the good.* Where by *good*, *Lipſius* tells us we muſt underſtand *the wiſe man.* So *Seneca*, de Benef. vii. 12. Inter ſapientes tantum amicitia eſt; cæteri non magis amici ſunt, quàm ſocii. *Friendſhip is only to be found among the wiſe; others are to be looked upon rather as companions, than friends.* Cic. ib. Eſt autem amicitia nihil aliud niſi omnium divinarum humanarumque rerum, cum benevolentiâ et caritate conſentio. *Friendſhip is nothing, but the complete harmony of all divine and human conſiderations, with kindneſs and endearment.* See Ep. 5. 9. 35. *Lipſ.* Manud. iii. 16.

(*d*) Then came *Peter* unto him, and ſaid, *Lord, how often ſhall my brother ſin againſt me, and I forgive him? 'till ſeven times?* *Jeſus* ſaith unto him, *I ſay not unto thee, until ſeven times, but until ſeventy times ſeven.* Matth. 18. 21. Luke 17. 4.

(*e*) *It is more bleſſed to give than to receive.* Act. 20. 35.

(*f*) Thus *Hierax*, the Pythagorean, Ουτω καὶ πᾶς ἄδικος, αὐτὸς τῆς κακίας πρῶτος γεύεται, πρὶν εἰς ἄλλους ἀφίκηται. *Every unjuſt man has the firſt taſte of his own malignity, before it reacheth others.*

EPISTLE LXXXII.

On the Study of Philosophy, Virtue, and the Fear of Death.

I AM no longer, my *Lucilius*, under any great concern for your welfare. What *God* then, you ſay, do I depend upon for your ſafety? Why truly on one that deceiveth no man; viz. *A mind, that purſues what is right and fit with pure affection.* Hence the better part of you is in full ſecurity. Fortune perhaps may do you ſome miſchief; but what is of much greater moment, I have no fear leſt you ſhould prove your own enemy. Go on as you have begun. Fix yourſelf in ſuch a habit of life as may ſhew complacency, not effeminate delicacy. I had rather, you ſhould live *ill*, than in ſoft idleneſs: by *ill* I mean here, an hard, rough, and laborious life. We often hear the lives of ſome men praiſed, (being much envied too) after this ſort, ſuch a one lives moſt *delicately*. Now, what is this but ſaying *He is a bad man?* For the mind is rendered effeminate by degrees, and ſoften'd down, as it were, into the likeneſs of that indolence and idleneſs wherein it lies buried. And would it not be better for a man to be quite ſtiff, and ſenſeleſs? But the delicate are afraid of death, howeverlike it they render life: though I allow there is ſome difference between repoſe and the grave. And is it not better, perhaps you will ſay, ſo to live, than be toſſed about in the whirlpools of officious buſineſs? They are indeed alike fatal, both the convulſion of the nerves and the languor of the mind. I think him as truly dead, who lies buried in his perfumes *(a)*, as he that is drawn about the ſtreets with a hook (*b*). Retirement without ſtudy is death, and the ſepulchre of a living man.

Beſides, what does it avail a man to have retired? As if the cauſes of ſollicitude and trouble would not follow him, even beyond the ſeas? What ſo ſecret place is there, excludes *the fear of death*? What place of of reſt ſo well guarded as to be raiſed above the dread of pain and grief? Whereever you hide yourſelf, human miſeries will alarm you. There are many external things which ſurround us, and either deceive us, or preſs hard upon us: there are many internal paſſions which enflame us in the midſt of ſolitude. We muſt therefore throw ourſelves into the arms of philoſophy; it is an impregnable wall (*c*), which fortune with all her engines cannot penetrate. The mind that hath once diſclaim'd all external things, and is determined to quit the field, ſtands upon an inſuperable eminence, protecting itſelf in its own citadel: while every hoſtile weapon falls beneath it. Fortune hath not ſuch long hands, as ſhe is generally ſuppos'd to have; ſhe ſeizeth on none but ſuch as willingly cleave to her. Let us leap from her as far as we can. But it is the knowledge of ſelf and nature that can enable us to do this. Let a man therefore know and conſider, from whence he came: and whither he is going; what is good for him, what the contrary: what to purſue, and what to avoid: what *that* reaſon is which can diſtinguiſh between ſuch things as are deſireable, and ſuch as are to be eſchewed: and which can aſſwage the madneſs of luſt, and ſoften the ſeverity of fear.

There are ſome indeed who think that even without philoſophy, ſuch a maſtery is to be gained over the paſſions; but their ſecurity being once put to the trial, they are forced too late to confeſs the truth. Their big words fail them, when the executioner takes them by the hand, and death ſtares them in the face. We may juſtly ſay to them; *'Twas an eaſy matter to bid defiance to abſent evils: behold the pains now threaten which you boaſted were tolerable: behold death, againſt whom you have often ſpoke ſo courageouſly: the whips yerk; the ſword glitters;*

Nunc animis opus, Ænea, nunc pectore firmo.

Now is the time firm courage to aſſume. *Virg. Ib.* 261.

And nothing but daily meditation can inſpire this conſtancy; if you exerciſe not the tongue, but the mind; if you are prepared againſt death; which you cannot be ſufficiently exhorted or ſtrengthen'd againſt; by thoſe who, with certain cavils would fain perſuade you, that, *Death is no evil.*

And here, *Lucilius*, beſt of men, I have a mind to ridicule ſome trifling argumentations among the Greeks, which, as much as you wonder at them, I have not quite diſcarded: our *Zeno*, for inſtance, thus argues ſyllogiſtically;

No evil is glorious,
But Death is glorious;
Therefore, *Death is no evil.*

You have prevailed, *Zeno*, you have deliver'd me from the fear of death. I ſhall moſt willingly ſtretch out my neck to the ſword. Will you not ſpeak more ſeriouſly, but make even a dying man to ſmile? But truly I cannot eaſily ſay which I take to be the more ſilly of the two: he who thought by this queſtion to extinguiſh the fear of death, or he who pretends to anſwer it, as if it was at all pertinent to the matter.

Nay, he himſelf, hath oppoſed thereto a contrary argument, taken from our placing death among things indifferent, which the *Greeks* call αδιαφορα:

Nothing that is indifferent is glorious:
But Death is glorious;
Therefore *Death is not an indifferent thing.*

You ſee where this queſtion halts, and would impoſe upon us. *Death in itſelf* is not *glorious*; but to die bravely is glorious. And when he ſaith, *nothing that is indifferent is glorious*, I grant it, but with this reſtriction, that nothing is glorious but what hath ſome connection with things indifferent: by *things indifferent*, I mean ſuch, as are neither good nor bad, conſider'd in themſelves, as ſickneſs, pain, poverty, puniſhment, death: and I maintain, that none of theſe things are glorious; but may be made ſo by their connexion. Poverty is not commendable; but it is commendable not to be dejected and bowed down by it: ſo neither is baniſhment; but he that is not grieved at ſuffering it, is praiſe-worthy. No man praiſeth death; but he is juſtly praiſed, who is deprived of life, before death could give him any perturbation.

All theſe things therefore are neither honourable, nor glorious in themſelves; but whenever virtue joins herſelf thereto, and hath the management

management of them, they are indeed both honourable and glorious. They are, as it were in common, and have no other difference than what they obtain by their connection with virtue or the contrary disposition. For death which in *Cato* was glorious, was soon after vile and shameful in *Brutus*: I mean *that Brutus* (*d*), who when he was about to die, sought all possible means to delay the time; nay he pretended to go aside to ease himself (*e*), and when called forth to die, and commanded to lay his head upon the block; *I will,* says he, *so I may but live.* What madness is it to fly when it is impossible to escape? *I will bow my neck,* says he, *so I may but live:* he had almost said—*even a slave to* Anthony. O worthy man to have thy life given thee! but as I was saying; from hence you may observe, that death, considered in itself, is neither good nor evil; seeing that *Cato* made a glorious use of it; and *Brutus* a most dishonourable one.

Every thing not honourable in itself is ennobled by the accession of virtue. We say such a room is light and magnificent: but how dark and dull is the same by night? It is the day that gives it all its splendour, which the night soon deprives it of: so of those things which we call common and indifferent, as riches, strength, beauty, honours, a kingdom; and on the other hand, banishment, sickness, pain, death, and the like, which we dread more or less, a virtuous or vicious behaviour under them, gives them the title of good or evil. A mass of iron, is neither hot nor cold in itself. It grows hot in the furnace, and is soon made cold by being thrown into the water. Death is honourable, through such means as are honourable, in virtue: and a mind exalting itself above the gifts of fortune. There is also, my *Lucilius*, a great difference even in these common things; for death is not so indifferent a thing, as whether our hair be cut even or not. Death is one of those things, which are not evil, but have the appearance of evil.

There is implanted in every breast a certain self-love, an innate desire of self-preservation, and a dread of dissolution; which threatens to deprive us of many good things, and the enjoyment of such as we have been long accustomed to. This also is what alienates our minds from death; we know the things we enjoy at present; but we know

not

——·—— not what we ſhall meet with, whither we are going (*f*), and always apt to dread things unknown. Beſides, nothing is more natural than the fear of darkneſs; and this is what death ſeems to threaten us with: And therefore, however indifferent a thing death may be, yet it is not to be reckon'd among thoſe which may eaſily be ſlighted and contemn'd: the mind muſt be ſtrengthen'd and harden'd by continual exerciſe againſt the ſight and approach of death; not that it ought to be dreaded ſo much as it generally is. Many ſtrange things are believ'd concerning it, and many a genius hath been employ'd in encreaſing the infamy (*g*). What a terrible deſcription is given of the infernal priſon, and the diſmal region that labours under perpetual night, where the monſtrous keeper of Hell-gates

> Oſſa ſuper recubans antro ſemeſa cruento. Virg. 8. 297.
> Æternum latrans exangues territat umbras. 6. 401.
> *The triple porter of the ſtygian ſeat,*
> *Now ſeiz'd with fear forgot his mangled meat—*
> *Still may the dog his wandring troops conſtrain,*
> *Of airy ghoſts, and vex the guilty train.* Dryden.

Nay, though you ſhould be perſuaded that theſe are mere fictions and idle ſtories; and that the dead have nothing to fear, yet very far is this perſuaſion from taking away all fear; for men are as much afraid of annihilation, as of dwelling in the infernal region. Seeing then that theſe thoughts often aſſail us, which long perſuaſion hath made habitual, to ſuffer death courageouſly, cannot but be glorious, and worthy a place amongſt the ſtrongeſt efforts of the human mind. The mind can never riſe to virtue, ſo long as it thinks death an evil: but thither it will riſe, if it looks upon death merely as an indifferent thing.

It is not in the nature of things for any one to addreſs with magnanimity what he thinks an evil; ſlothful and dilatory will be his approach thereto. Now, *that* cannot be glorious, which is done untowardly, and with an unwilling mind. Virtue does nothing by conſtraint. Add alſo that nothing can be done decently and well, to which the whole mind hath not bent its ſtrongeſt application and efforts, and is in no reſpect whatever repugnant. But when an evil is ſet before us, it often happens, that the patient ſuffering of one ſingle evil, ſhall be ſwallow'd

up,

up, either in the fear of ſomething worſe, or in the hope of ſome good, which is thought worthy of purſuit. Hence the thoughts of the agent are at variance: and there is ſomething that urgeth him on one hand, to execute his purpoſe: and on the other hand, what draws him back, and deters him from the ſuſpected peril; therefore, I ſay, he is diſtracted in his thoughts: and where this is the caſe, all glory is loſt: for virtue ever performs her reſolutions with a ſteady and conſtant mind: ſhe is never afraid to enter upon action: Tu ne cede malis, ſed contra audentior ito (*b*).

But thou ſecure of ſoul, unbent with woes,
The more thy fortune frowns, the more oppoſe. Dryden.

But you cannot go on ſo boldly, if you think them real evils. This notion therefore muſt firſt be rooted out, otherwiſe ſuſpicion will traverſe and ſtay thy courſe: or the mind will be *forced* upon that, which it ought to have undertaken willingly.

The Stoics indeed ſeem to think the queſtion, as firſt put by *Zeno*, true; but the other in oppoſition to it, falſe and vain. For my part I am not for treating theſe things *logically*; or having recourſe to the knotty quirks of idle ſophiſtry. I think all this kind of buſineſs ought to be diſcarded: wherein he, to whom the queſtion is put, is ſuſpicious of a fallacy, and being brought to confeſſion, anſwereth one thing, and thinks another. Truth is to be dealt with in a more plain and ſimple manner; and in order to root out all fear, we muſt deal more openly and manly. The things which by theſe ſophiſters are involv'd in ſuch intricacies, I had rather ſolve and explain; that I might perſuade, and not impoſe upon, the hearer. When a general is leading an army into the field, there perhaps to die for their wives and children, in what terms will he exhort them! Look upon the *Fabii* (*i*) transferring the whole war of the republic upon one family. Look upon the *Lacedæmonians* in the ſtreights of *Thermopylæ* (*k*); without any hopes of victory or a return; when that place ſeem'd their deſtin'd grave: what will you alledge in order to intice them to ſacrifice themſelves for the republic; and rather part from their lives, than their ſtand? you will ſay;

What is evil is not glorious,
But Death is glorious.
Therefore *Death is no evil.*

O moſt

O most powerful harangue! who after this, would scruple to give himself up to the drawn sword, and die upon the spot? But what a noble speech was *that* of *Leonidas*, when he said, *so dine my fellow-soldiers, as if ye were to sup in another world*(l) They snapped up their meat; scarcely staid to chew it; nor did any fall from their hands. They went cheerfully to dinner, and to supper both. And how did that brave *Roman* General address his soldiers, whom he ordered to take a certain place, which they could not come at, but by forcing their way through the vast army of their enemies? *There is a necessity, my fellow-warriors, for your going thither, but none for your coming back.* You see how plain and imperious, virtue, or true valour is. What mortal can your circumlocutions make more valiant, more firm, and steady? Such amusements are apt to break the mind, which ought by no means to be contracted and driven into difficulties, at a time, when it ought to be the more enlarged for some great enterprise.

But the fear of death ought to be rooted out not only from the minds of a few hundred, or of an army, but of all men in general. And how will you teach them, that it is not an evil? How will you overcome the prejudices of men, in every age, imbibed from their very infancy? What help will you find? What remedy will you propose for the weakness of human nature? What will you say to animate men so, as to make them rush into the midst of danger? With what harangue will you avert this universal fear? With what strength of reasoning will you dissuade mankind from a persuasion, so universal, and determined against all you can say? Will you study captious words, and form petty questions? Know that mighty monsters are not to be quelled but by mighty weapons. In vain did the *Roman* soldiers discharge their slings and quivers against that large and cruel serpent in *Africa*, which was more terrible to the *Legions* than war itself. Like the *Python* he was invulnerable, when from the vast and solid bulk of his body, the steely weapon, or whatever else was thrown by mortal hand, rebounded; but at length he was crushed by mill-stones(m) And do you now throw such petty weapons against death? Will you encounter a lion with a bodkin? They are sharp things which you advance. And what is sharper than the bearded ear of barley? But their own fineness makes some things useless, and ineffectual.

ANNO-

ANNOTATIONS, &c.

(*a*) Theognis, v. 1193. *Ασπαλαθοι δ' ἢ ταπητες ἴσον στρωμα θανόντι.*

——— *to the dead,*

To lie on thorns or tapestry, is the same.

(*b*) As they treated criminals, both before and after execution.

(*c*) So *Antisthenes* ap. Laert. Τειχη *κατασκευαστέον ἐν τοῖς ἡμῶν αναλωτοις λογισμοῖς.* For as it was said with great applause on the stage——

—— Si regnum a me Fortuna atque opes
Eripere quivit, at virtutem non quit.
Fortune may rob me of my wealth and throne;
She can no more: still Virtue is my own.

(*d*) This must be understood of *Decius Brutus*, who, as *Vellius* writes, flying for shelter to the house of one *Capenus*, a nobleman, was there slain by those whom *M. Anthony* sent in pursuit of him. For this contemptuous relation will by no means suit with the story of the famous *Marcus Brutus*, the friend and assassin of *Cæsar*. See *Valer. Max.* l. 9. c. c. 13.

(*e*) For this anecdote we must give credit to *Seneca*, as not related elsewhere. *Lipsius* gives you the like story of one *Cneius Carbo*, from *Valer. Max.* l. 19. 13. who mentions the death of *Brutus*, but without this circumstance.

(*f*) Aye, but to die, and go we know not where;
To lie in cold obstruction, and to rot;
This sensible warm motion to become
A kneaded clod, and the delighted spirit
To bathe in fiery floods, or to reside
In thrilling regions of thick-ribbed ice;
To be imprison'd in the viewless winds,
And blown, with restless violence, round about
The pendant world, or to be worse than worst
Of those, that lawless and incertain thought
Imagines howling!—'tis too horrible.
The weariest and most loathed worldly life,
That age, ach, penury, and imprisonment
Can lay on nature, is a paradise
To what we fear in death.—*Shakesp.* Measure for Measure.

(*g*) *Plato* also highly inveighs against the poets for making Death, terrible enough in itself, much more terrible by such their fictions and idle stories. *Vid.* de Republ. l. 3.

(*h*) To which some copies add that unnecessary hemistic——

Quàm tua te Fortuna sinet——not in *Virgil.*

(*i*) *Fabius* (so called from faba, a *bean*, being the first planter of beans in *Italy*) with his family and children, 300 in number, waged war with the *Veiates*, and were all slain to one man: from whom was descended this noble family down to the celebrated *Fabius Maximus*, Consul with *Julius Cæsar*, Ann. M. C. 709.

(*k*) Thermopylæ] The straits between the mountains of *Thessaly* and *Phocis*; where *Leonidas*, King of *Sparta*, opposed a vast army of the *Persians*.

(*l*) As I think it is ſomewhere ſaid by *Cæſar*, *Fight on, my brave fellow-ſoldiers, you will either conquer or ſup with* Jupiter.

(*m*) Ne Python quidem vulnerabilis----*al.* invulnerabilis---ne pilo quidem *vel* ne pnblis---*Eraſm.* ne Pythio (i. e. Apollina) *Suret.* But I am more apt to think, with *Pincian*, that the whole ſentence is not genuine. Or, if I may not be allowed the ſenſe given it in the tranſlation, I ſhould ſooner prefer *Eraſmus'* pilo, (i. e. *he was invulnerable to the pyke or ſpear*) than either *Python* or *Pythio*.

EPISTLE LXXXIII.

On Drunkenneſs.

IT ſeems you are inquiſitive, *Lucilius*, to know how I ſpend my time, even my whole time; and are pleaſed to entertain ſo good an opinion of me as to think, that I deſire not to conceal any part of it from you. Indeed we ought ſo to live, as in the ſight of man; and ſo to employ our thoughts, as if the inmoſt receſſes of our hearts were open to ſome inſpector. They certainly are ſo: for what avails it to keep any thing ſecret from man; when we can hide nothing from God! He is intimate to our ſouls (*a*); and interpoſeth himſelf in our common thoughts; ſo indeed as never abſolutely to leave us. I will oblige you therefore in your requeſt, and will tranſmit to you in writing how I paſs my time, and after what method I generally act. I will, forthwith, make ſome obſervations on myſelf; and what is truly uſeful and of conſequence, review the day paſt.

Nothing contributes more to the making men worſe, as to their morals, than their not regarding their paſt conduct. We think indeed upon what we are about to do; though this but ſeldom; and what we have done, is entirely forgotten. Good counſel however for the future depends, in a great meaſure, upon the experience of what is paſt. This, my *Lucilius*, hath been a complete day with me (*b*): not a perſon hath broke in upon a moment of it. The whole was divided between my couch and reading-deſk: very little allowed for exerciſe of the body: I am oblig'd to old age for this; it puts me to very little trouble in this reſpect; when I ſtir, I am ſoon tired. But this is the common end of exerciſe, even to the ſtrongeſt. Would you know, who are my companions (*c*) herein? One is enough for me, *Eurinus*, an amiable boy not unknown to you. But I muſt change him. He grows too robuſt for me. He ſays indeed, that we are both at the ſame criſis of age, foraſmuch as we are ſhedding our teeth; but the young rogue runs too faſt for me; I can ſcarce overtake him; and in a few days I ſhall not be able; ſo much he gains upon me by daily exerciſe. In a very ſhort time there is a great diſtance between two that are travelling different ways. As he is going up, I am going down: and you know how much ſwifter the one travels than the other. Did I ſay, I was *going* down? I was miſtaken; for my age is ſuch I am not *going*, but *falling* down. But would you know how ended this day's contention between us? why, as ſeldom it does between two racers, neither of us beat (*d*).

From this, rather a fatigue, than exerciſe, I go into the cold bath; I do not mean ſuch as is extremely cold: for I (who took ſo much delight in bathing and ſwimming that even on the *Kalends of January*, I would leap into the coldeſt pond; and as I was wont to begin the new year (*e*) with reading, writing, or dictating ſomething, as a foretoken of ſucceſs; ſo began I to bath, by plunging into ſpring water) firſt moved my tent to the river Tyber (*f*), and afterwards had recourſe to the bathing tub: which, as I am yet pretty ſtrong, and would have all things done as ſhould be, the ſun alone ſufficiently warmeth for me. I ſpend not however much time in bathing; and after that, I eat a piece of dry bread, or biſcuit, and dine without a table; nor have I any occaſion to waſh my hands after dinner. I ſleep a little while: you know my cuſtom: my ſleep was always very ſhort; I reſt, as it were a while (*g*); and think it enough not to be broad awake. Sometimes indeed I know that I have ſlept; but ſometimes I only think ſo. Lo! the noiſe of the *Circus* is continually buzzing in my ears, and ſometimes ſtrikes them with a ſudden and univerſal ſhout: however it does not chaſe away my thoughts: nor even interrupt them. I bear the clamour moſt patiently: and the many voices, that are joined together in one confuſed ſound, are no more to me than the rolling of a wave, or the ruſtling of wind through a wood; and the like inſignificant noiſes.—And what of all this? why, I will tell you now, what I was meditating upon. For I am ſtill reflecting upon the ſame to-day as yeſterday: *what thoſe wiſe men could mean, who in ſome ſerious matter, uſed the moſt trifling and perplexing arguments: which however true were to be ſuſpected of a falſity.*

Zeno, (*b*) for inſtance, that moſt extraordinary man and the founder of the braveſt and moſt religious ſect, propoſed to deter man from drunkenneſs. And you ſhall hear in what manner he proves that a good man will never be drunk.

No one truſts a ſecret to a drunken man:
But a good man is truſted with ſecrets.
Therefore, *A good man will not be drunk.* (*Ebrius.*)

But obſerve now how you may play upon him with the alike-form'd ſyllogiſm: for one of many will ſerve our preſent purpoſe:

No one commits a ſecret to one that is aſleep,
Secrets are committed to good men:
Therefore, *A good man will not ſleep.*

Poſidonius endeavours, as well as he can, to defend our *Zeno* herein: but, in my opinion, he makes but a poor defence of it. For, he ſays, that a man may be called *a drunken man* two ways; the one, when he is overcharg'd with wine, and not maſter of himſelf; the other, when he is ſubject to this vice, and only now and then gets drunk. *Zeno* here means the latter, one that is ſubject to be drunk, not one that actually is ſo; and *ſuch a one,* he ſays, *no one will truſt with a ſecret* leſt he ſhould blab in his cups. But this is falſe. For the former ſyllogyſm abſolutely includes the man that *is drunk,* not one that may be ſo: as there is a great difference between (*Ebrium* and *Ebrioſum*), *one that is drunk,* and *a drunkard.* For it may be that he who is now drunk, was never ſo before: and he that is a drunkard may often be ſober; therefore by the word, *Ebrius,* I muſt underſtand what is generally meant by the ſame, *one that is drunk;* eſpecially as the word is uſed, by a man of learning, and profeſs'd diligence in weighing well his expreſſions. Add likewiſe, that *Zeno,* if he underſtands him, hath left

room

room for a fallacy, by uſing an ambiguous word, which by no means becomes a man, who is in ſearch of truth.

Be this as it will; he could not but know that the major (firſt) propoſition is falſe, *no one truſts a ſecret to a drunken man*. For conſider how many ſoldiers, who are none of the ſobereſt people, are truſted with ſecrets by their general, the tribune or centurion. *Tullius Cimber* was truſted with the ſecret of a conſpiracy againſt the life of *Cæſar* (I mean *Caius Cæſar*, who having overcome *Pompey* ſeiſed upon the government) as well as *Caius Caſſius*. *Caſſius* had, all his life, drank nothing but water: *Tullius Cimber* was ſcarce ever ſober, and a prattler. He uſed often to jeſt upon himſelf, ſaying, *How can I carry any one, who cannot carry my wine?* Let any one now name thoſe, whom he thinks worthy to be truſted with a ſecret, but not with wine. I will give you one example, that recurs to me, before I forget it. For life is beſt inſtructed by ſome famous example; nor need we always have recourſe to antiquity. *Lucius Piſo* (*i*), The warden of the city, after he was once drunk, ſpent the greater part of the night in banqueting and riot: and then would he ſleep 'till noon the next day, which was generally his morning. Yet was he very diligent in the adminiſtration of his office, wherein depended the ſecurity and welfare of the city: even the godlike *Auguſtus* entruſted him with ſecret orders, when he gave him the government of *Thrace*, which he had ſubdued. And *Tiberius*, when he was going into *Campania*, and leaving *Rome*, in ſuſpicion and diſguſt, yet, I ſuppoſe, becauſe drunkenneſs had no worſe an effect upon *Piſo*, made *Coſſus* (*k*) governor of the city in his abſence. Now *Coſſus* was a grave and moderate man, but would ſometimes get ſo very drunk as to be carried out of the ſenate, (when he was come thither from ſome banquet) overwhelm'd with ſo ſound a ſleep, that it was impoſſible to wake him: yet to this man did *Tiberius*, with his own hand, write many things, with which he was afraid to truſt his own miniſters: and never did a ſecret, either of a public or private nature, drop from *Coſſus*.

Let us hear no more then thoſe frequent declamations,—*the mind has no command of itſelf, when fetter'd with drunkenneſs.--As barrels are burſt with*

with new wine, and the lees are thrown to the top by fermentation; so when wine boils within a man, and stupefies the brain, whatever secret is hid in the heart, it is thrown up and made public.--I own this may sometime happen, yet it also happens, that we scruple not to consult even in serious and necessary matters with those, who are given to wine. This is false therefore what is here set forth as an indisputable maxim, that *a secret is never entrusted to a man who is subject to drunkenness.* How much better is it openly and plainly to accuse, and shew forth the vice and folly of it; which even a decent man would avoid, and much more one that is wise and perfect: who is satisfied with quenching his thirst; and who, at a time of mirth, though it be carried to a great height upon some extraordinary occasion, still refrains from drunkenness.

We shall dispute hereafter, whether the mind of a wise man may be disturb'd by too large a dose, and whether he will act as drunken men generally do. In the mean while, if you would prove that a good man ought never to be drunk, what need is there of having recourse to syllogism? Rather shew, how ridiculous and vile a thing it is, for a man to pour down more than he can hold, and not to know the strength of his constitution.--How many things drunken men are apt to do, which when sober they would be ashamed of.--And that drunkenness is nothing else but a voluntary madness.--And, suppose this evil habit to grow upon a man (*l*), can you doubt of its being somewhat more than madness, even rage and fury? The fit is not less though it be shorter.--Declare how *Alexander*, King of *Macedon*, slew at a banquet *Clytus*, his dearest and most faithful friend; but being made conscious of the fact, when sober, he desired to die, and indeed he deserv'd no better (*m*).

Drunkenness heightens and displays every vice. It takes away modesty, the usual restraint upon every bad intention. For many, it is to be feared, abstain from vice, more through the dread of shame, than their own good will. When the strength of wine hath overpower'd the mind, whatever evil lay conceal'd therein, is apt to emerge. For

drunkenness

drunkenness does not so much create faults as it betrays them; for then it is, that the libidinous stay not for the privacy of a chamber, but as far as they can, indulge their desires without delay: then it is, the debauchée confesseth openly his disease: and the petulant and wanton, give a loose to their vicious inclination: the pride of the insolent, the savageness of the cruel, and the malice of the spiteful, grow stronger hereby: in short, every vice shews itself in its proper colours.

Add that stupidity and ignorance of a man's self; his stammering and unintelligible way of speaking; his eyes see double; the roof seems to shake, and the whole house to run round: the stomach is sick and painful, while the wine is fermenting therein, and preying upon the vitals: however tolerable it may be while there is any strength left in the liquor, what must it be when corrupted by sleep? and what was drunkenness before, is now become an intolerable crudity.

Think also what cruel slaughters public riot and debauch have sometimes occasion'd. This is what hath given up the most fierce and warlike nations into the hands of their enemies; hath broken down walls, that were defended with a most stubborn war for many years: this hath drove into captivity the most brave and resolute contemners of subjection; and hath conquer'd the unconquerable in battle. *Alexander*, whom I before mention'd, and who was carried safe through so many journeys, so many engagements, so many winters, in which he overcame the difficulties of both time and place, through so many rivers whose sources were unknown, and through so many dangerous seas, was at last overthrown by an intemperate draught; and that *Herculean* (*n*) and fatal cup quite buried him.

What glory is there in being able to hold a great deal? When you have gained the victory; and your fellow-sots, overcome with sleep and nauseousness shall refuse to pledge you any more; when you alone survive the whole company; when yon have conquer'd them all with most magnificient valour (*o*); and you boast that no man can carry so much wine as yourself? Lo! you yourself are overcome by (or cannot carry so much as) an hogshead.

What

What was it else but drunkenneſs, and the love of *Cleopatra*, no leſs ſtrong than wine, that deſtroy'd *Mark Anthony*, (a very great man, and of moſt noble endowments) and led him into foreign manners, and vices not his own, nor of Roman growth? It was this, that made him an enemy to his country, and his enemies an overmatch for *him*: this taught him cruelty; when he ordered the heads of the princes of the city to be brought to him at ſupper; when amidſt the moſt exquiſite dainties that luxury could invent, or royal affluence adminiſter, he took pleaſure in beholding the ſcalps and hands of the proſcribed; when full of wine, he yet thirſted for blood. It would have been intolerable in him to have done what he did, had he been ſober; but how much more intolerable was it for him to do theſe horrid things in a drunken riot? Cruelty commonly attends upon drunkenneſs. For the ſanity of the mind is hereby diſturb'd (*p*) and exaſperated. As long diſeaſes make the eyes ſo weak as not to endure the leaſt glimpſe of the ſun; ſo, an habit of drunkenneſs weakens the mind: for as men are often not maſters of themſelves, being inured to ſuch vices as are conceived by laviſh drinking, they are apt to perpetrate the ſame without the inſtigation of wine.

Declare therefore that a wiſe man ought never to be drunk; ſhow the deformity and indecency of it, not by words only, but from fact, which is very eaſy to be done. Prove that theſe which are called pleaſures, when they exceed the proper mean, become puniſhments. For if you will argue that a wiſe man may perchance be intoxicated with wine, and yet not err, or go aſtray; you may as well ſay, that a man will not die, though he hath drank poiſon;—that opium will not make him ſleep; nor *bellebore* purge him.—But when his feet trip, and his tongue faulters, why ſhould you think him only half-gone, or fuddled? *He is drunk.*

ANNO-

ANNOTATIONS, &c.

(*a*) *Epictetus* to the same purpose (l. 21. c. 8.) *What you would not do before the statue or image of a God, that you dare do, notwithstanding God certainly sees and hears every thought, word and deed. Thou wretch, ignorant of thine own nature, and hateful to the Gods!* But our business is with the holy Scriptures, where this sentiment is so frequently and particularly inculcated. 1 Sam. 16, 7. 1 Kings, 8. 39. 1 Chron. 28. 9. Job, 26. 6. 28. 24. 31. 4. 34. 21. 42. 2. Ps. 7. 9. 44. 21. 139. 4. 11. 12. Prov. 5. 21. 15. 3. Jer. 11. 20. 16. 12. 17. 10. 20. 12. 3. 19. Zeph. 1. 12. Ecclesi. 17. 19. Luk. 16. 15. Act. 1. 24. 15. 18. 3 Joh. 3. 20. Rev. 2. 25.— See Ep. 41. De Benef. l. 4. c. 8.

(*b*) Hodiernus dies solidus est. Hor. l. 1. 20. nec partem solido demere de die spernit.

Vid. Sidon. Apoll. p. 402.

(*c*) Progymnastas] *Muret.*—Which word is used by *Plato* and *Xenophon*, in the same sense with *Syngymnastas*, i. e. eos qui una cum aliquo exercentur. *Poll.*

(*d*) Hieram fecimus] We both come equally tired to the middle line of the race, which line is called *hiera*; so neither of us beat. By ἱερὰν (Subaud. δρόμον) is meant a *vehement* and most laborious race, as the mariners say, *sacram* anchoram, and the physicians *sacram dosin*, ἱερὰν πυράν. *Erasm.*

(*e*) On this day the *Romans* generally begun what they intended for the chief employ of the ensuing year, by way of *good luck*.

Quisque suas artes ob idem delibat agendo,
Nec plusquam solitum testificatur opus. *Ovid.*
Each gives this day a specimen, in part,
Wherein he's destin'd to display his art.

(*f*) As being somewhat warmer than spring water.

(*g*) Quasi interjungo, al. intervigilo. They are said, *interjungere*, when on travelling they take off their horses to give them a bait. *Horace* calls it, *iter dividere*,

Hoc iter ignavi divisimus.

So *Varro*, *Diem dividere*,

Exarsitque dies, et hora
Interjungit equos meridiana.

Quidam medio die interjunxerunt et in pomeridianas horas aliquid levioris operæ distulerunt. *Sen.* de Tranquil. l. 1.

(*h*) *Zeno* was owner of a thousand talents, when he came from *Cyprus* into *Greece*; and he used to lend money on ships at an high interest. He kept in short a kind of an insurance-office. He lost this estate perhaps when he said, Recte sane agit Fortuna, quæ nos ad philosophiam impellit, *I am greatly obliged to Fortune, for reducing me to the study of philosophy.* Afterwards he received great presents from *Antigonus*. So that his great frugality and simplicity of life was the effect of his choice, and not of necessity. *Diog. Laert.*—He rejoiced that he had been thrown by shipwreck on the *Athenian* coast, as he owed to the loss of his fortune the acquisition which he made of virtue, wisdom, and immortality.—*Bolingbroke* on Exile.

(*i*) *The Emperor* Tiberius, *at the very time he was reforming the manners of the people, sate up one night and two days drinking and feasting with* Pomponius Flaccus, *and* Lucius Piso, *to one of which he gave the province of* Syria *immediately, and to the other the government of the city.*

(*k*) *Lipsius* doubts whether this was *Cornelius Cossus*, who was consul under *Augustus*, ann. 752, or his son, consul under *Tiberius*, ann. 778—most probably the latter.

(*l*) Extende in plures dies illum ebrii habitum. MS. In some copies the word *dies* is wanting, in others it is written in plures vires.

(*m*) Facinore intellecto mori voluit, certè debuit. *Muret. al.* mori voluit. Certè eruit omne vitium ebrietas—*al.* certè delituit. And indeed *Alexander* is said to have kept himself many days within, after this fact, discovering hereby how much he was ashamed of it. *See* Quint. Curt.

(*n*) Herculeanus scyphus] *Plutarch*, in his Life of *Alexander* informs us, "that, at an enter-"talnment given by *Medius*, *Alexander* drank all that night and the next day to such excess, as put "him into a fever, which seized him, not as some write, after he had drank off *Hercules' bowl*; "nor was he taken with a sudden pain in his back, as if he had been stricken with a lance; (for "these are the inventions of some authors, who thought it became them to make the conclusion of "so great an action as tragical as they could.) *Aristobulus* tells us that in the rage of his fever "and a violent thirst, he took a draught of wine, upon which he fell into a frenzy, and died, æt. 32. The large glasses were called *Herculean*, from the use of them, by *Hercules* the *Bœotian*, always used as the *finishing glass after supper*. Και τον σκυφον ἑλχον ἀεὶ ἐπιδειπνιον του Ηρακλεου. *Nicet.*

(*o*) Hi sunt, quorum laudari audis—inter vina Victorias. *Sidon. Apoll.* l. 5. 7. Vid. Not. ubi, *D. Ambrosius*, ibi unusquisque pugnas enarrat suas, ibi fortia facta prædicet, narrat trophæa. Et, Polycrat. l. 8. c. 6. Sine mensura bibitur ad mensuram, is cæteris prævalet, qui aut gulâ, aut dolo, stravit aut vicit compotatores.

(*p*) Violatur—sanitas mentis] *al.* Vallatur. MS. Villatur, vilatur, bellatur, bullatur, unde *Pincian*, belluatur, i. e. in belluæ naturam transit, *is made a beast*. *Lipsius*, fellatur, aut biliatur. *Gronov.* libatur, i. e. vexatur, carpitur, vel vexatur, ut mentem *vexare* mariti. *Juv.* 6. 610.

(*q*) *Plato* (in Cicerone) Σωκρατης ἐν ταῖς εὐωχιαις, κ. τ. λ. Socrates *was not fond of drinking at an entertainment, and when obliged by the company, he was generally too strong for them, so that none can say*, they ever saw Socrates drunk.

Not but that, if *a wise man should be overtaken*, as it was by chance, *not by intention*, *Lipsius* thinks it excusable.

EPISTLE LXXXIV.

On Reading, and the Study of Wisdom.

I THINK, *Lucilius*, that the little excursions I make in my chariot by way of exercise, are of great service to me, both with regard to my health and studies. You plainly see wherein they are beneficial to my health, forasmuch as the love of learning and constant application there-

to, would make me ſluggiſh and careleſs of my body, I am hereby rouſed by the help of others: and I will now ſhew you wherein they are of ſervice to the ſtudious mind. I abſtain not entirely from reading. For reading is abſolutely neceſſary. Firſt, that I may not reſt only upon my own opinion; and then, that having learned what others have been in ſearch after, I may the better judge of ſuch things as have already been, or may yet be diſcover'd. Reading nouriſheth the fancy and wit of man; and even refreſheth him when fatigued with ſtudy, and yet, ſtill it may be ſtudy. For we ought not to be always reading, nor always writing: the one will weary and exhauſt the ſtrength: I mean continual writing: and the other diſſolve and diſſipate it. They are to be uſed alternately (*a*), and the one moderated with the other; that whatever hath been collected from reading, may be digeſted and reduced into form by writing. We ought, as they ſay, to imitate the bees who fly about (*b*) and cull ſuch flowers as are moſt proper for making honey; and then they depoſit their ſeveral charges in proper order, and diſtribute them throughout the comb, as our Virgil ſaith—
Liquentia mella

Stipant, et dulci diſtendunt nectare cellas. G. i. 164.
Some purge the heavn'ly nectar, ſome condenſe,
And ſome the liquid in void cells diſpenſe. Lauderdale.

It is not certain whether they extract any liquid from the flowers, which liquid immediately becomes honey; or whether by a certain mixture and peculiarity of their breath, they change what they have gather'd into this taſteful ſubſtance. For ſome think, they have not the ſkill themſelves to make honey, but only gather it; as in the Indies pure honey is found in the leaves of certain reeds (*c*), which honey is made of the dew of that climate; or of the ſweet and fatty moiſture of the reed itſelf: and that in ſome of our herbs is found the like ſubſtance, not altogether ſo manifeſt and notable, but ſuch as an inſect, made for this purpoſe, is wont to ſearch after, and collect together. Others think that by their mixing and diſpoſing of ſuch matter as they have gather'd from the tendereſt of plants and flowers, not without a ſort of leaven, if I may call it ſo, which blends things together of a different nature, it receives this quality.

But not to digreſs farther from the buſineſs in hand, I ſay, we ought to imitate bees: and whatever things we have extracted from different books, firſt, to ſeparate them; for being diſtinct they are the more eaſily remember'd; and then to apply ourſelves with the utmoſt care and ſtrength of mind, to transform theſe various dainties into one diſh; that even if it ſhould appear from whence it was taken, it may yet appear a very different thing to that from whence it was taken. This is what we daily ſee perform'd by nature in our bodies, without any aſſiſtance from us. The aliments which we receive into the ſtomach, ſo long as they retain their own qualities, and float intire therein, are a load to it; but being digeſted and changed from what they were, they paſs into our ſubſtance and blood. We muſt do the ſame, by thoſe things, with which we nouriſh and ſtrengthen the intellectual faculties: we muſt not keep them intire, as we received them; for ſo they will not be ours, but we muſt digeſt them, or elſe they will only be a charge upon the memory, without improving the underſtanding. We muſt ſincerely give our aſſent to them, and make them our own: that one certain thing may be made of many; as from ſeveral figures ariſeth one certain number; and one ſingle computation includes many leſs and different ſums.

And this likewiſe is what the mind muſt do; it muſt conceal as much as poſſible the helps it hath been oblig'd to; and only make ſhew of what it hath done itſelf. Should there ſtill remain the reſemblance of ſome one, whom admiration hath fixed deeper in your mind, and made ſo ſtrong an impreſſion, that you cannot eaſily quit it: I would have it to be ſuch a reſemblance as is that of a ſon, rather than that of a ſtupid and lifeleſs image. And what then? you will ſay: will it not be known, whoſe ſtyle you imitate; whoſe arguments, whoſe ſentiments? perhaps not; if you follow ſome great man; who in his compoſitions hath not diſtinguiſh'd what he hath taken from others, by any particular mark, ſo as to exhibit a ſameneſs (*d*).

Do you not obſerve that a choir conſiſts of many voices? yet from all ariſeth but one harmonious ſound. One voice is treble, another baſe,

baſe, another the mean or tenour; the voices of women are joined to thoſe of men: and the flutes and other inſtruments are likewiſe added: yet the tone of no voice or inſtrument is heard in particular, but they are all happily blended in one: I am ſpeaking of ſuch a choir, or muſical performance, as was known to the antient lovers of Muſic. At the repreſentation of a play we have as many ſingers as in the Theatres formerly they had ſpectators (*e*). And yet when every avenue is filled with ſingers, and the whole pit is ſurrounded with clarinets, and from above in the galleries is heard the ſound of the organs, and other wind inſtruments; even from ſuch diſſonant tones ariſeth harmony. Thus, I ſay, I would have it with our minds; there ſhould be many arts, many precepts, the examples of many ages, all lodged therein, and yet all conſpiring together to conſtitute one form, or manner of life. But how is this to be done? why, by care and the ſteady purſuit of rational principles. If we do nothing but what our reaſon directs; if we attend to the dictates of this alone; ſhe will ſay to us; leave thoſe things which you now ſo greedily purſue; give up riches,—which either endanger, or are a burthen to their owners; renounce the trifling pleaſures both of the body and mind; they ſerve to no other purpoſe but to lull you into ſoftneſs and effeminacy: forſake ambition; 'tis a quality, light, inconſtant, full of pride and vanity; it knows not where to reſt; and is alike troubled in following as in preceding others: it labours under two ſorts of envy: and you know how wretched a man muſt be who is both envied himſelf and envieth others. Behold thoſe palaces of the great! How are their doors peſter'd with the ſquabbling throng of Leveé-Hunters! what affronts muſt you ſubmit to, before you gain admittance? and how many more when you have crouded in? paſs therefore regardleſs, by the ſteps, and lofty terrace (*f*) that leads to the rich man's door; in ſuch their court-yards, you will not only be raiſed aloft, but ſtand on ſlippery ground.

Hither then chuſe to direct your courſe; even to the houſe of wiſdom aiming, at the ſame time, to enjoy both the moſt quiet ſituation and the moſt noble. Whatever things ſeem excellent, in worldly affairs, though they are really ſmall and of no account, but in compariſon with the moſt

moſt vile and abject, yet to attain them is ſtill a difficult and arduous taſk. The way to the ſummit of dignity is rough and craggy. But would you climb the Hill of Wiſdom, to which I invite you, and to which fortune ſubmits with all her treaſures, you ſhall ſee all thoſe things, which are in higheſt eſtimation lie beneath you, nor ſhall you complain of having reach'd the top, but by a ſmooth and eaſy path.

ANNOTATIONS, &c.

(*a*) See Ep. 15.

(*b*) See the following as tranſcribed by *Macrob.* Saturnal. 1.

(*c*) *Strabo* l. 15. *It is ſaid they extract honey from the reeds, where they have no bees.* But this is to be underſtood of what we call, by the ARABIC name, ſaccharum, *ſugar.*

Quique bibunt tenera dulces ab arundine ſuccos. *Luc.* 3. 237.
Who quaff rich juices from the luſcious cane.

(*d*) See Sir John Hawkins on Muſic, vol. iv. p. 272.

(*e*) In comeſſationibus noſtris] *In our feaſts.* But Lipſius thinks it ſtretching the point a little too far, to ſay, that *in their feaſts they had more fingers, than the ancient theatres had ſpectators.* He therefore reads it as here tranſlated, in comiſſionibus noſtris ſc. *ludorum.* Lipſ. Epiſt. Qu. iii. 9.

At tuba comiſſos medio canit aggere ludos.—*Virg.* iii. 113.
The trumpet's clangor then the feaſt proclaims;
And all prepare for the appointed games. Dryden.

(*f*) Magno aggeſtu ſuſpenſa veſtibula]—aggeſtu (Spoliorum ſc. quæ poſtibus affigi ſolent.) *Lipſ.* But *Gronovius* more rightly underſtands it of the ſtructure itſelf.

EPISTLE LXXXV.

Virtue alone ſufficient to make Life happy.

I HAVE hitherto ſpared you, *Lucilius,* and not troubled you, with ſuch points as ſeem'd knotty and difficult; contenting myſelf with only giving you a taſte (*a*) of the arguments, alledg'd by the *Stoics* to prove, that *virtue alone is ſufficient to procure an happy life.* But now you require

quire me to collect whatever traditionary proofs and deductions they have advanc'd, to confirm this their opinion: which, was I to undertake, I should be oblig'd to send you a book, instead of an Epistle. I again and again protest that I am no admirer of such kind of syllogistical reasoning. I am ashamed to enter the lists, in behalf of a cause that concerns both heaven and earth, armed only with a bodkin: as thus:

He that is prudent is temperate;
He that is temperate is constant;
He that is constant is undisturb'd;
He that is undisturb'd knows no sorrow;
He that knows no sorrow, is an happy man;
Therefore *The prudent man is happy; and prudence alone is sufficient to the attainment of an happy life.*

Now, this collective syllogism (*c*) is answer'd by some of the Peripatetics in this wise: they conceive, that, when we talk of a man, *undisturb'd, constant* and *sorrowless, a man is undisturb'd who is disturb'd very seldom, or in a small degree,* not one, who is never disturb'd at all: and that a man may be said *to be sorrowless, who is so circumstanc'd as in a great measure to be free from sorrow; nor is often, or in any great degree subject to this passion: for, say they, it would be to deny the nature of man, to suppose the mind of any one to be absolutely free from sorrow. They grant that though a wise man may not be overcome with grief and pain, yet it is impossible that he should not feel it.* Such are the allegations of these philosophers, and of all who espouse their sect: They take not away the affections, but only moderate them. But how little honour do we pay the wise man, if we only suppose him stronger than the weakest; merrier than the most disconsolate; more temperate than the libidinous; and greater than the meanest. What if *Ladas* (*d*) was proud of his own swiftness, when he only compared himself with the lame and weak?

Illa vel intactæ segetis per summa volaret
Gramina, nec cursu teneras læsisset aristas,
Vel mare per medium, fluctu suspensa tumenti
Ferret iter, celeres nec tingeret æquore plantas (*e*).

Last

—Last from the Volscians *fair* Camilla *came—*
Outstript the winds in speed upon the plain;
Flew o'er the fields, nor hurt the bearded grain;
And while her course she bends o'er raging waves,
Her nimble feet no saucy billow laves.—Dryden. Lauderdale.

This is swiftness indeed, consider'd in itself, and not estimated from a comparison with the slow of foot. What if you call him sound who has a slight fever? a gentle fit is by no means sound health. But says the *Peripatetic, a wise man is said to be undisturb'd; as we say, fruit is not stony, or unkernell'd, (f) not because it has no kernels but because it has only a few, and those not hard.* This is false, for in a good man, I do not suppose a diminution of evil, but an entire exemption from it; there ought, I say, to be none: not the least imaginable: for if there be any, they may possibly encrease, and give him trouble. As a large and confirm'd cataract quite blinds the eye, so a small film darkens it. If you allow passions to the wise man, it is possible that reason may not be able to master them, and he may be carried away by them, as with a torrent; especially when you suppose him struggling, not with one passion only, but with a tribe of them: be they as small as they will, the strength of a multitude can do more, than one alone, however great and violent (g). He is covetous, but in a moderate degree; he is ambitious, but not very eager: he his passionate, but soon appeased; he is inconstant, but not vague and roving; he is libidinous, but not furious; be it so, he however is more easily managed, who is subject to one vice alone, though entire and in full force, than one, who is subject to every vice, though in a light degree. But in truth, it signifies not how great or little the passion is, when it knows not how to obey, nor will admit any counsel; as no four-legg'd animal, be it wild or ever so domestic and tame, will attend to the voice of reason; it is the nature of them to be deaf to persuasion; so is it with the passions, they will not hear you, however weak they are in degree. Tygers and Lions throw not off entirely their natural fierceness, though they sometimes submit; and when you least expect it, their ferocity, however soften'd for a while, is exasperated.

Moreover

Moreover, if reaſon prevails, paſſions will never riſe; and where they riſe againſt reaſon, they will perſevere againſt it. For it is much eaſier to check their beginning than to reſtrain their courſe, when they have once ſet out. Their mediocrity therefore with regard to paſſion, is falſe and uſeleſs: it is the ſame as if we ſhould ſay a man is *moderately* mad, or *moderately* ſick.

Virtue alone is ſubject to government; and not any evils of the mind; which it is much eaſier to get rid of, than to govern. Can there be any doubt, that the inveterate, and harden'd vices of the human heart, which we call the diſeaſes of the ſoul, (*b*), ſuch as covetouſneſs, cruelty, unrulineſs, impiety, and the like, want moderation? therefore the paſſions alſo are immoderate and exceſſive, for by theſe are we led to the former. If you give any looſe to ſorrow, fear, baſe deſire, and other vicious and depraved affections, they are no longer governable. And why? becauſe the things whereby they are provoked and enflamed are without us: therefore they encreaſe more or leſs, according to the cauſes of incitement. Fear, for inſtance, encreaſeth, when it beholds the dreaded object either greater than as at firſt imagin'd, or nearer: deſire is more eager, as the object of its hope ſeems more valuable. If it be not in our power to be abſolutely free from paſſions, neither is it in our power to ſay how far they will go: if you have once ſuffer'd them to begin; they will proceed, being urged on by their cauſes, and will riſe in proportion to any degree whatever. Add then, that how ſmall ſoever you ſuppoſe them, they are liable to be made greater; deſtructive things never obſerve a mean. Though ſlight the beginning of diſeaſes, they grow upon us; and ſometimes the leaſt acceſſion of illneſs, quite ſinks the diſeaſed body. What madneſs is it to think that the ends of ſuch things are in our power, whoſe beginnings are uncertain? how is it poſſible for me to put an end to that which it was not in my power to prevent at firſt? it is much eaſier to exclude than ſuppreſs an unmanageable gueſt.

Some diſtinguiſh after this manner; *a temperate and moderate man is calm in the diſpoſition and habit of his mind, though not ſo in the event;*

 foraſmuch

forasmuch as in his natural temper he is not disturb'd with fear or sorrow; but that many things happen from without, which cannot but give him some perturbation. Which is as much as to say, that such a one is not a choleric man, though he happens sometimes to be angry; or that he is not timorous, though he is sometimes afraid; i. e. He is free from the malignity, though not from the passion of fear. Now, if this be allow'd, frequency will convert fear to vice; and anger once admitted into the breast will quite dissolve the frame of an impassionate mind. Besides, if a man despiseth not causes from without, and is at any time afraid, when he ought boldly to advance against the weapons, and fire of an enemy, for his country, his laws, and liberty, he will but faintly set forward, and play the coward in his heart. But a wise man is never so unsettled in his temper.

This too, I think, is further to be observ'd, lest we should confound two things, which ought to be proved severally. It is self-evident that *what is right and fit is the one only good*; and likewise, *that virtue is sufficient to make a man happy*. Now if that which is right and fit be the only good, it necessarily follows, that virtue is sufficient to render life happy. On the contrary, it does not follow, that, if virtue alone can make a man happy, what is right and fit, is the only good *Zenocrates* and *Spensippus* think that a man may be happy (*i*) by virtue alone; yet that, what is right and fit is not the only good. *Epicurus* likewise thinks, if a man be virtuous, he may be happy, but yet that virtue itself sufficeth not to make him so; because the *pleasure*, that ariseth from virtue, and not virtue itself, may make a man happy. An idle distinction! for *Epicurus* himself denies that virtue can ever be without *pleasure*; and if *pleasure* always attends virtue, and is inseparable from it, virtue is then sufficient of itself; for it carries pleasure with it, and without it, it cannot be virtue, though it be said to be alone.

It is also absurd to say, (*with the academics*) that *a man may be happy by virtue alone, and yet not perfectly happy*. For I cannot see how this can be possible. For an happy life contains in itself perfect and insuperable good; and if so, it must be perfectly happy. If the life of the *Gods* knows nothing greater or better, and an happy life is a divine life, there is nothing that can exalt it higher. Besides, if an happy life wants nothing; every happy life is perfect; and the same is happy, most happy. Can you doubt that an happy life is the sovereign good? if then it be the sovereign good it must be supremely happy; being supreme it will admit of no addition, (for what can be higher than the highest?) and such is an happy life, seeing that it wants not the highest good. If you suppose any one still *more* happy, you will make the degrees of *the chief good* innumerable; whereas I mean by the *chief good*, that which hath no degree above it. Or, if you suppose any one *less* happy, it follows, that he will desire the life of one who is more happy than himself; but the happy man prefers not the life of another, whatever it be, to his own. Both these things are incredible; either, that there is something which an happy man wisheth for, more than what he hath; or, that he should not wish for that which is better than what he himself enjoys. For the wiser or more prudent a man is, the more will he extend his views to that which is best; and desire by all means to obtain it. But how is he an happy man, who still desires, or indeed ought to desire, any thing more?

I will shew you from whence proceeds this error, *(in the distinction of happiness)*. Men know not that there is but *one* happy life; the quality whereof, not the greatness, constitutes it such. Therefore it is the same thing whether it be long or short *(k)*; more diffused, or narrow; distributed in many places, and many parts, or contracted in one. He that judgeth of it by number, measure, or parts, deprives it of its chief excellency. For in what consists the chief excellency of an happy life? In that it is full. The end, suppose, of eating and drinking is satiety; but one eats more, another less; what then? they both are satisfied. One man drinks more, another less; what then? they both have quenched their thirst. One man hath lived many years, another but few; and what then; if many years made the one no happier than a few years did the other? The man you call *less* happy, is not *truly* happy. This title admits no diminution.

He that is brave knows no fear;
He that is without fear, knows no sorrow;
He that knows no sorrow, is happy.

Thus

Thus argue the Stoics; to which ſome endeavour to reply, ſaying, *that it is begging the queſtion to affirm that a brave man knows no fear. For why?* ſay they, *will not a brave man be afraid of imminent danger? not to fear in ſuch a caſe is the part of a madman, and of one out of his ſenſes, not of a brave man. He indeed fears, but in a moderate degree, as it is impoſſible, in ſuch a caſe, to be abſolutely void of fear.* Now they that ſay this, fall again into the ſame abſurdity, to take the leſs flagrant vices for virtues. For he that fears indeed, however ſeldom or in a ſmall degree, is not free from paſſion, though not greatly troubled therewith. But *is he not afraid of imminent danger?* Yes, I own he is, if they are real evils that he fears; but if he knows them not to be evils, and judgeth rightly, that a baſe and vile action is the only evil he ought to fear, he will look down upon danger undauntedly, and deſpiſe ſuch things as the generality of people are apt to dread: or if it is the part of a fool or a madman not to fear evils, the wiſer and more prudent a man is, the more will he be afraid of them.

But, ſay they, *according to your opinion a wiſe man will thruſt himſelf into danger.* No; though he will not fear danger, he will avoid it. Caution becomes him, though fear does not. What then? ſay they; *ſhall he not fear death, chains, fire, and other hoſtile darts of malignant fortune?* No; for he knows that theſe are evils but in appearance only. He looks upon theſe things as the bugbears of human life. Set before him, captivity, ſtripes, chains, want; the racking of the limbs, either by diſeaſe or violence, and what elſe of this kind you are pleaſed to name; he numbers them all in the liſt of imaginary fears; to be dreaded only by a coward mind.

For can you think *that* an evil, which we muſt ſometimes ſuffer voluntarily? You aſk then *what is evil?* To yield to thoſe things that are commonly called evils; to give up our liberty itſelf rather than endure them; even that liberty for whoſe ſake we ought to endure every thing. There is an end of liberty, if we deſpiſe not thoſe things that bend us to the yoke. Theſe very men would no longer doubt what a valiant man ought to do, if they but knew what true valour is. For,

it

it is not an unadvifed rafhnefs, nor a love of danger, nor a thirft after terrible enterprizes; no; it is a fcience that diftinguifhes good from evil; it is a noble fortitude, that is ever diligent in felf-defence; and at the fame time moft patiently endureth thofe things (*l*), if neceffarily required, that carry a falfe appearance of evil. *What then? if the fword be brandifhed over the head of a brave man; or, if firft one, then another part of his body, be pierced through; if his bowels tumble out before him; if, at intervals, to encreafe his torment, he is fmitten again and again, and the blood is made to flow afrefh from the wounds, that are fcarce dry; will you fay that in fuch a cafe a man will not fear, will not feel pain?* There is no doubt but that he feels pain, for no virtue deprives a man of his feeling; but yet he fears not; while with an invincible heart he looks down, as it were, from on high, on his pains. And do you afk, *how his mind is difpofed at fuch a time?* why the fame as when they take upon them to exhort and counfel a fick friend.

What is evil hurts a man, and what hurts a man makes him worfe;
But pain and poverty make not a man worfe;
Therefore, *Pain and poverty are no evils.*

Thus, again, the Stoics. To which it is anfwered, that *the major propofition is falfe: for a thing may hurt a man, and yet not make him worfe: ftorm and tempeft hurt the pilot, or mafter of a fhip, but they make him not a worfe pilot.* And to this fome of our Stoics reply; ftorm and tempeft really make him worfe; forafmuch as he cannot effect his purpofe, nor hold on his courfe: he is not made worfe as to his fkill, but only as to the exertion of it.—To which rejoins the *Peripatetic, Therefore pain, and poverty, and the like, make a wife man the worfe; forafmuch though they take not his virtue from him, they hinder the operation of it.*

And this indeed would be faying fomething, if the ftate of a pilot, and of a wife man, were alike in all refpects. It is not in the purpofe of a wife man, to effect that infallibly which he effayeth to do, in the tranfactions of life; but it is the purpofe of a pilot to carry his fhip into the defigned haven. The Arts are fervants, and ought to perform

what

what they promiſe; but Wiſdom is a miſtreſs and governeſs. The arts adminiſter to life, but wiſdom governs it. I think it proper therefore to give a different anſwer, and affirm, that neither the ſkill of a pilot is rendered worſe by a ſtorm, nor even the adminiſtration of it. For why? The pilot did not promiſe you a proſperous voyage, but only his endeavour for it, by his ſkill in navigating the ſhip: and ſuch his ſkill is more apparent, the more any caſual force oppoſeth it. He that could ſay, O Neptune, nunquam hanc navem niſi rectam, *O Neptune, the ſhip was always right* (*m*), hath done all that was in the power of art to do. The tempeſt does not hinder the work of the pilot, though it may prevent ſucceſs. What then? you will ſay, *does not ſuch an accident hurt the pilot, which forbids him to reach the deſigned haven; which renders all his endeavours ineffectual; which carries him back, or deſpoils him of his implements?* No; it hurts him not as a pilot, any more than as a mariner, and is ſo far from hindring him, that, as before obſerved, it ſhews his ſkill. For *in a calm*, as they ſay, *every mariner is a pilot.* The perſon of a pilot muſt be conſidered in two reſpects; the one, as common with all that are aboard the ſame ſhip; and the other as peculiar to himſelf under the character of a pilot. Now, the ſtorm hurts him as a paſſenger, but not as a pilot. Beſides, the art of a pilot is an external good; it is for the ſervice of the whole crew; as the art of the phyſician is for the good of his patients. But wiſdom is a common good, of ſervice both to the wiſe man himſelf and to all that are converſant with him. A pilot therefore may be hurt, whoſe promiſed ſervice to others is hindered by a ſtorm; but a wiſe man is not hurt by poverty, by pain, or other the like ſtorms of life. For he is not prevented in all actions relating to himſelf, though he may be in ſuch as relate to others: he is always in the ſphere of action; and then ſhews himſelf greateſt, when Fortune the more oppreſſeth him; then indeed is he employed in the work of wiſdom itſelf, which we before obſerved to be good; and of conſequence both to himſelf and others.

Moreover, however he may be oppreſſed himſelf by cruel neceſſities, he is not hereby prevented from being ſerviceable to others. Poverty

(or

(or low condition) indeed may diſqualify him, for want of opportunity, from teaching what is to be done in the adminiſtration of public affairs; but it by nó means hinders him from inſtructing a man how to behave under the like ſtroke of poverty. Nay, in every part of life he can ſtill find buſineſs; ſo that no fortune, no incumbrance can exclude the action of a wiſe man: for he does that very thing which reſtrains him from doing any thing amiſs. He is prepared againſt, and exerts himſelf in both conditions of life; he moderates the good, and overcomes the bad; he is ſo diſciplined, I ſay, that he can ſhew forth his virtue, as well in proſperity as adverſity; not regarding the ſubject of virtue, but virtue itſelf: therefore neither poverty, nor pain, nor any thing elſe that uſually keeps back the ignorant and unſkilful, or drives them headlong, can hinder the progreſs of the wiſe man. Do you think him to be preſſed down by misfortunes? No; he enjoys them, and turns them to advantage. *Phidias* could make a ſtatue not only of Ivory, but of braſs; was you to give him marble, or ſome viler ſtuff, he would yet form as complete a ſtatue as could be made of it; ſo a wiſe man will diſplay himſelf, if he may, in the management of wealth; if not, in poverty; in his own country, if he can, if not in baniſhment; as a general, if ſuch his appointment; if not, as a common ſoldier; as a ſound and hale man, if ſuch his conſtitution; if not, as weak and infirm. Whatever his condition of life may be, he will do ſomething notable. There are certain men who make it a trade to tame wild beaſts, and who make fierce animals, that terrify us at the ſight of them, to bear the yoke; nor are they ſatisfied with making them throw off their ſavageneſs, they ſo tame them, as to make them ſociable: the keeper puts his hand into the mouth of lions, and kiſſeth the tyger: the *Æthiopian* ſtroller makes the elephant ſtoop upon his knees, or walk upon ropes (*n*): like theſe, the wiſe man hath the art of taming all manner of evils; pain, want, ignominy, a priſon, baniſhment, and the like horrible things; all of which become mild and ſufferable, under the management of a wiſe man.

ANNO-

ANNOTATIONS, &c.

* *Muretus* obſerves, that much is ſaid concerning this opinion of the Stoics in *Cicero's* books, de finibus, and in the fifth of his *Tuſculan Queſtions*; but there is extant a moſt learned commentary, by *Alexander* of *Aphrodiſia*, a famous Peripatetic, profeſſedly againſt this magnificent and boaſtful maxim of the Stoics.

(*a*) Guſtum tibi dare] Euripides. Γεῦμα τὴν ὠνὴν καλῶ.

(*b*) Quicquid interrogationum, i. e. ſyllogiſmorum] Whatever queſtions, i. e. ſyllogiſms. For ſuch as argued ſcientifically, as the mathematicians, (ſaith *Muretus*) laid down their premiſes in an abſolute manner, not concerning themſelves whether their antagoniſt would allow them or not; but ſuch as argued logically, put queſtions to their antagoniſt, and uſed only ſuch poſitions as were granted them, as *Socrates* frequently does in *Plato*. Hence theſe *dialectic* ſyllogiſms were called *queſtions*; wherefore *Lucian*, bantering after his manner, a certain ſophiſter, who attempting to write an hiſtory made frequent uſe of ſyllogiſms, ſaith ἐν ἀρχῇ μὲν γὰρ εὐθὺς ἐν τῇ πρώτῃ περιόδῳ συνηρώτησε τοὺς ἀναγινώσκοντας. εἶτα μετὰ μικρὸν ἄλλος συλλογισμὸς, εἶτα ἄλλος, καὶ ὅλως ἐν ἅπαντι σχήματι συνηρωτητο αὐτῷ τὸ προοίμιον.

(*c*) Cicero calls theſe ſyllogiſms, brevia et conſectaria Stoicorum, *the briefs and corollaries of the Stoics.*

(*d*) This word was firſt reſtored by *Lipſius*, Elect. i. 16. it being commonly read laudans.—— *Ladas* was the famous running footman of *Alexander*. His name became proverbial, Lada pernicior. Eraſm. 9, 8, 91.—Pauper locupletem optare podagram

Ne dubitet Ladas——Juv. 13, 96.

Would ſtarving Ladas, *had he time to chaſe,*
And were not frantic, the rich gout refuſe?

(*e*) Volſcâ de gente Camilla Virg. 7. 803. See alſo *Virg.* xi. 535, 569.

(*f*) Apyrina vel Apyrena; *Plin.* 13, 19. as a thing is ſaid to be ἄποδα, *without feet*, not becauſe it hath no feet, but only ſuch as are remarkably ſmall.

(*g*) Συμφερτὴ δ' ἀρετὴ πέλει ἀνδρῶν καὶ μάλα λυγρῶν. Il. v. 237.
Not vain the weakeſt if their force unite. Pope.
Σμικρὰ παλαιὰ σώματ' εὐνάζει ῥοπή. Soph.
Small inclination lulls old age to ſleep.

(*h*) See Ep. 75.

(*i*) Beatum, ſed non beatiſſimum; *happy, but not* moſt happy; and herein, ſays *Lipſius*, they differ from the Stoic.

(*k*) Quicunque fuerunt ſapientes, pares erunt et æquales. *All men truly wiſe are alike and equal.* Ep. 74. Summum bonum nec infringitur, nec augetur. *The chief good is neither diminiſhed nor increaſed,* &c. *Stobæ.* Πάντα τὸν καλὸν καὶ ἀγαθὸν ἄνδρα τέλειον εἶναι, κ. τ. λ. *Every good and wiſe man is perfect; becauſe he is deſtitute of no virtue; and therefore the good are altogether alike and always happy.*——Laudaudaque velle

Sit ſatis et nunquam ſucceſſu creſcit honeſtum. *Cato ap. Lucan.*

If truth and juſtice with uprightneſs dwell,
And honeſty conſiſts in meaning well;
If right be independent of ſucceſs,
And conqueſt cannot make it more or leſs. Rowe.

(*l*) This

(*l*) This principle is most admirably exemplified in the feigned history and character of *Sir Charles Grandison*, by my late friend Mr. *Richardson*.

——— 'Tis not the appetite
Of things that carry horror, makes men valiant,
But patient bearing of afflictions,
That are necessitated.——*Microsm.* Act i. Sc. 5.

(*m*) Sic in Telete; καλῶς τὸ τοῦ κυβερνήτου, Ἀλλ' οὖν γε, ὦ Πόσειδον, ὀρθήν. κ. τ. λ. *So a good man may address Fortune, saying,* Do as you will, you shall still find that I am a man, and not a poltroon. *Senec.* ad Marc. c. 6. nec gubernatoris quidem artem, tranquillum mare, et obsequens ventus ostendit, adversi aliquid occurrat oportet, quod animum probet; *A pilot cannot display his art in a calm and favourable wind; he must be tried by a storm,* which may be so violent as to overcome his art, without any detriment to his character, as a pilot.

(*n*) *The Emperor* Galba *was advanced into places of trust, before the age appointed by law; during his praetorship, amongst the solemnities and sports called* Floralia, *he introduced a new kind of entertainment, which was elephants walking upon the rope.* Sueton. in Galba, c. 6.

EPISTLE LXXXVI.

On the Luxury of the Times; and of Husbandry with regard to the Olive and Vine.

I WRITE this, *Lucilius*, from the famous villa of *Scipio Africanus* (*a*), having first paid my devotions to his memory at the altar (*b*); which I take to be the sepulchre of that great man (*c*). Nor did I in the least doubt but that his soul returned to heaven, from whence it came; not because he was the leader of great armies, (for this is no more than what was done by the furious *Cambyses*, and who was sometimes in his rage successful) but for his excellent moderation and piety, which were more admirably conspicuous when he left his country, than when he defended it. Either *Scipio* must be deprived of *Rome*, or *Rome* of liberty (*d*). *I would by no means*, says he, *derogate our laws or civil institutes. Let every citizen have an equal right; enjoy without me, O my country, the good turn I have done you; I have been the cause of your liberty; and will give you a proof of it myself; I leave you, since I am greater than is expedient for such an equality to be preserv'd, as I sincerely wish you to enjoy.* How is it possible for me not to admire such greatneſs of ſoul? He departed into voluntary baniſhment, and diſburthened the city of their apprehenſions on his account; for things were come to that paſs, that either liberty muſt injure *Scipio*, or *Scipio* liberty. Neither of which was to be done; he therefore gave place to the laws, and retired to *Linternum*, as willing to aſcribe the baniſhment of himſelf, as of *Hannibal*, to the commonwealth.

I found this his villa built of ſquare ſtone, and a wood encloſed with a wall; a turret on each ſide of the front, by way of bulwark; a large reſervoir under the buildings and green walks, ſufficient to ſupply with water a whole army; a bath narrow and ſomewhat dark after the antient cuſtom; for our anceſtors thought it could not be warm enough, unleſs it was cloſe.

It was therefore a great pleaſure to me to reflect upon the cuſtom and manners of *Scipio* compared with our own. In this little nook was that great man (the dread of *Carthage*, and to whom *Rome* was indebted for having once taken it) uſed to bathe his body, when fatigued with ruſtic labours. For he daily exerciſed himſelf in huſbandry, and tilled the ground with his own hands, as was cuſtomary among our forefathers. Under this low and ſordid roof ſtood *Scipio*. He diſdained not to tread ſo vile and mean a floor. But who is there in our time that would condeſcend to bathe in like manner? A man thinks himſelf poor and mean, unleſs the walls are decorated with large and precious emboſſments (*e*); unleſs *Alexandrian* marble (*f*) is pointed and inlaid with *Numidian* rough-caſt; unleſs a rich and curiouſly variegated plaiſtering be ſpread upon them in pictureſque (*h*); unleſs the roof is covered with glaſs-work (*i*), unleſs the *Thaſian* ſtone, once reckoned a ſcarce and rare ornament even in ſome temples, now compaſs about our ponds; where we bathe our bodies, when enfeebled (*k*) with much ſweating at ſome trifling ſport; in ſhort, unleſs the water is conveyed through a ſilver ſpout (*l*). I am ſpeaking as yet of common ſtoves; but what ſhall I ſay when I come to ſpeak of the baths of our freed-men? What noble ſtatues! what vaſt pillars ſupporting nothing; but placed there for mere ornament, and the vain oſtentation

of

of expence! What large and far-founding cafcades! We are arrived to fuch a pitch of delicacy and extravagance, that we cannot tread but upon precious ftones (*m*).

In this bath of *Scipio* there are fome chinks rather than windows, cut out of the ftone wall, to let in the light without injuring the ftrength of the building. But now we call the baths *moth-houfes* or dungeons; if they are not fo contrived as to admit the whole day's fun through the moft fpacious windows (*n*); whereby men were tanned as well as wafhed; and from the bathing veffels they have a profpect both of the meadows and of the fea. So that thofe baths, which, at their firft dedication, called together a vaft concourfe of people (*o*), and filled them with admiration, are now rejected as poor antiquated things; while luxury is daily inventing fome novelty, that muft at laft prove its own ruin. Formerly there were but few baths, and thofe not ornamented with any coftly decorations; for to what purpofe is it to adorn a common room, open to any that paid their farthing; and which were built for ufe, not for pleafure? It was not ufual to have the water fprinkled, or poured in upon us, nor did it always run frefh, as from a warm fpring; nor did they think it at all material, how clear the water was wherein they were to wafh off their filth. But, O ye gods, how delightful was it to go into the baths, dark as they were, and covered over with a common cieling of mortar, which you knew that *Cato*, when Ædile, or *Fabius*, or fome of the *Cornelian* family, had tempered with their own hands! For thefe moft glorious *Ædiles* vouchfafed to enter thefe places of public refort to examine whether they were kept clean and well aired with a wholefome and proper heat, not fuch a one as is now ufed, which is more like fire than water: fo that to punifh a flave convicted of any heinous crime, you need only to fet him therein, and boil him alive. They feem to me to make no difference between a warm and a fcalding bath.

Some would now condemn *Scipio* for not admitting the fun into his warm baths by large cafements (*r*), and becaufe he would not be fodden'd in open light; nor regarded whether his meals were fully digefted in a bath. *Poor man!* ſay they, *he knew not how to live!* He waſhed not himſelf in clarified water, but was content with ſuch as was thick, and oftentimes, after a great ſhower, muddy. Nor did he care whether he ſo bathed or no; for he came not to waſh away ointment and perfume, but ſweat. And what do you think ſome of our young gentlemen will ſay? why that *they ſhould not have envied* Scipio; *for he truly lived in baniſhment who had no taſte in bathing*. Nay, to tell you the truth, we did not uſe to bathe daily. For, as they ſay, who have written on the antient cuſtoms of the city, they daily indeed waſhed their legs and arms which were made dirty by toil and labour, but they never waſhed the whole body above once in nine days. No doubt but that hereupon ſome one will ſay, *ſurely our anceſtors muſt have been great ſlovens*. But if they ſmelled of any thing, it was of military duty, hard labour, and manlineſs. For my part I think men are more naſty, and ſmell worſe, ſince the invention of theſe fine and clean baths. For what ſays *Horace* in his deſcription of an infamous young ſpark, that was remarkable for his delicacy?

Paſtillos Rufillus olet—Rufillus *ſtinks of the waſhball.*

Take now ſome *Ruſillus*, and ſmell him: he ſtinks worſe than a *goat*, or like that *Gorgonius*, whom *Horace* in the ſame verſe ſets in oppoſition to *Ruſillus*, (*Gorgonius hircum*)—A man uſeth not ointment enough now-a-days, unleſs he be perfumed twice or thrice every day, leſt it ſhould ſoak into his ſkin, and be loſt: nay more, they glory in the ſmell as if it was natural.

If what I have ſaid, *Lucilius*, ſeems too ſevere, you will pleaſe to impute it to the villa from whence I am writing; where I have learned from *Ægialus*, a moſt excellent huſband, and who is now in poſſeſſion of this farm, that a ſhrub, be it ever ſo old, may be tranſplanted. This is neceſſary, I think, for us old men to learn, ſince there is ſcarce any one of us, but who is planting olive-grounds for the uſe of others. I have ſeen *Ægialus* in autumn tranſplant trees of three or four years growth; ſo that a tree ſhall give ſhade to you, which otherwiſe

Tarda venit, ſeris factura nepotibus umbram, ii. 57.
The plant which ſhoots from ſeed, a ſullen tree,
At leiſure grows, for late poſterity. Dryden.

As our *Virgil* ſaith in the *Georgics*, who, by the way, was more concerned to ſpeak what was elegant than what was ſtrictly true; and ſtudied more to delight the reader than inſtruct the huſbandman: for to paſs by other things, I ſhall only take notice of one, which I am this day convinced deſerves reprehenſion:

Vere fabis ſatio eſt; tunc te quoque, medica, putres
Accipiunt ſulci; et milio venit annua cura. G. i. 216.
Sow beans and clover in a rotten ſoil,
And millet, riſing from your annual toil. Dryden.

Now whether theſe things are to be ſet or ſown at the ſame time of the year, or whether the ſpring time may be the more proper (*s*), you may judge from hence; it is now about the latter-end of *June*, and this very day did I ſee men gathering in their beans, and ſowing millet. (*s*)

But to return to the olive trees. I have ſeen them tranſplanted two different ways; *Ægialus*, having cut off the branches around the trunks of the great trees, ſo as to reduce them to about a foot in length, hath tranſplanted the remainder; having alſo pared the roots, leaving only the head from whence they ſprung; and then encompaſſing this with dung, he ſet it in a trench ſufficiently deep, and not only heaped the earth upon it, but trod and preſſed it down; affirming that nothing could be more effectual than thus ramming it cloſe, as it excludes both the cold and wind: it is likewiſe hereby kept ſteady, as it permits the growing roots to burgeon and faſten in the earth, which otherwiſe being tender and having but ſlight hold, every breath of wind would be apt to tear it up. But before he covers it in, he ſcrapes the bottom of the trunk, becauſe from every part ſo bared, the new roots ſhoot more eaſily. But you muſt obſerve that the trunk above ground ought not to exceed above three or four feet; for it will be ſoon clothed from the bottom; and not have any part of it ſcorched or dried, as we ſee them in ſome of our old olive-yards. Another way of managing olive-trees was this: they cut off ſome of the larger branches, that are ſtrongeſt, yet ſuch whoſe bark was not yet harden'd, but ſoft as they generally are in young trees, and then ſet them as before deſcribed. Theſe indeed are ſlow of growth, but when once they are come a little forward, and have taken root, they are fair and pleaſant.

I have

I have often ſeen an old vine tranſplanted. They bind up as well as they can the ſmall ſtrings and threads that are about the root, and then ſpreading the vine more freely under ground, they cover it ſo, that roots may ſprout from the ſtem itſelf. And I have ſeen them not only thus ſet in *February*, but by that time *March* is over, clinging to and twiſting about elms they never knew before. Now all theſe trees, which are of a larger ſtem, are beſt water'd, he ſays, with ciſtern water: if ſo, we have, at any time, rain at our command. I think it not proper to give you any further inſtructions, leſt as *Ægialus* hath made me his rival, I ſhould make you mine.

ANNOTATIONS, &c.

(*a*) See Ep. 51. (N. i.)

(*b*) Manibus ejus, *his ſpirit or genius*, et ara; which others, with *Lipſius*, read arca, *the cheſt containing his aſhes*; on account of his being of the *Cornelian* family. *Plin.* l. 1. In gente Cornelia nemo ante Syllam Dictatorem traditur crematus, idque voluiſſe, veritum talionem, eruto C. Marii cadavere. *In the* Cornelian *family, no one is ſaid to have been burned, before* Sylla the Dictator, *who appointed this for fear of retaliation, having before dug up, and expoſed the body of* C. Marius.

(*c*) Why *Seneca* ſhould make any doubt of it, ariſes from its being ſaid by ſome, that *Scipio* died and was burnt at *Rome*, by others at *Linternum*. Liv. 38. Africanum alii Romæ, alii Linturni, et mortuum et ſepultum tradunt. Utrobique monumenta oſtenduntur et ſtatuæ; *his monuments and ſtatues were ſhewn at both places.*

(*d*) Many are the various readings here as uſual; but they all tend to the ſame purpoſe, viz. that it ſeemed as if ἰσονομία, *equity*, could not be maintained at *Rome*, while *Scipio*, by reaſon of his great actions, and noble ſpirit, was ſo adored by the people, that they would not permit him to anſwer for himſelf upon the accuſations of the Tribunes againſt him.

(*e*) Pretioſis orbibus. So *Juv.* 11, 173. Lacedæmonium—orbem.

(*f*) There were many ſorts of marble brought from *Alexandria* and *Egypt*; as the black *Lucullеum*, brought to *Rome* by *Lucullus*; the ſpotted *Ophites*; and the red *Porphyry*; or perhaps it may be a particular ſort of marble called the *Alexandrine*.

(*g*) Vid. Sidon. Epiſt. ii. 2. Plin. xxxv. 1.

(*h*) In *Moſaic* work.

(*i*) Statius Effulgent cameræ vario faſtigia vitro.
The cielings ſhine with variegated glaſs.

(*k*) Corpora exinanita] Epiſt. 108. Decoquere corpora, et ſudoribus *exinanire.*—al. *corpora exſaniata.*

(*l*) Argentea Epiſtomia; *the cocks*, through which the water was conveyed into the baths.
Statius——in balneo Etruſco.

Nil ibi plebeium nuſquam Temeſæa notabis
Æra, ſed argento felix propellitur unda,
Argentoque cadit, labriſque nitentibus inſtat.
Nothing was vulgar; nothing ſeen of braſs;
Through ſilver pipes the happy waters paſs.

(*m*) Nifi gemmas calcare] Statius *in Tibertino Manlii* calcabam nec opinus opes; *I trod regardless on a mass of wealth.* Plin. 23, 12. Strata argento balnea mulierum; *the baths for the ladies were floored with silver.* Sen. de irâ, iii. 35. Qui nolunt domi nifi auro pretiofa calcare. *Who deigned not to tread upon any thing in their houses but cloth of gold.* Ep. 16. Non tantùm habere, fed calcare divitias; *not contented with only having riches, they trod them under foot.*

(*n*) *Lucian* commends a bath, for being τὸ εὐφεγγὲς, *very luminous:* fo *Statius*, Multus ubique dies. *Plin.* Ep. i. 3. Balneum plurimus fol implet et circumit; *a bath open to the fun on every fide.* *Martial*, on *Tucca's* bath:

Lux ipfa eft ibi longior, diefque
Nullo tardior a loco recedit.
The light continues longer here; and day
Flies not fo late, from any place, away.

(*o*) They were generally dedicated and appropriated to the ufe of the public.

(*p*) Thefe were the *Curule Ædiles*, who were elected out of the nobility to infpect the public games—and befides their proper office, they were to take care of the building and reparation of temples, theatres, baths, and other notable ftructures. *Kennet.*

(*q*) Formerly, fays *Plutarch*, (Sympos. 8. 9.) *they ufed fuch mild, gentle baths, that* Alexander the Great, *being feverifh, flept in one; and the wives of the* Gauls *carry their pots of pulfe to eat with their children while they are in the bath; but our own baths now inflame, vellicate and diftrefs; and the air which we draw in is a mixture of air and water, difturbs the whole body, toffes and difplaces every atom, 'till we quench the fiery particles, and allay their heat.*

(*r*) Latis fpecularibus] *Martial.*

Hibernis objecta notis fpecularia puros
Admittunt foles et fine fæce diem.
The windows broad admit the folar ray,
Drive back the wintry winds, and give a warmer day.

(*s*) *Pliny* (18. 7.) places it among thofe things that are fown *thrice* a year, in fpring, fummer, and winter.

EPISTLE LXXXVII.

On Frugality. The Sufficiency of Virtue. Cafual Things not to be reckoned good.

I HAVE been fhipwreck'd, *Lucilius*, before I went aboard. How this could happen, I intend not to tell you, that you may place this likewife among the Stoical paradoxes (*a*): which receive as you will, I am am ready to prove, that not one of them is falſe; nor indeed ſo extraordinary, as it appears at firſt ſight; and this, when you pleaſe; nay whether you are pleaſed or no.——In the mean while let me inform you of what I have learned from this journey: what abundance of ſuperfluous things we make uſe of, and which we might moſt judiciouſly throw aſide, ſince they are ſuch, that if neceſſity ſhould at any time deprive us of them, we ſhould not be ſenſible of the loſs.

With no more ſervants than one carriage could hold, and no manner of luggage, not the leaſt thing but what was on our backs, have my friend *Maximus* (*b*) and I ſpent two moſt agreeable days. A mattreſs lies upon the ground, and I upon the mattreſs. Of two cloaks, one ſerves for an under-blanket, the other for a coverlid. Our repaſt was ſuch, that nothing could be ſpared from it, nor did it take up much time in dreſſing (*c*). I am ſatisfied with a few dried figs and dates. When I have any bread, the figs ſerve me for a dainty diſh; when I have no bread, they ſupply its place (*d*). They make me fancy it to be New-year's day (*e*); which I endeavour to render auſpicious and happy, by harbouring good thoughts, and keeping up a greatneſs of ſoul; which is never greater, than when it hath withdrawn itſelf from all external things; and hath obtained for itſelf peace, by fearing nothing, and wealth by coveting nothing. The vehicle I ride in is plain and of the country-faſhion. The mules ſhew they are alive only by their walking (*f*). The muleteer is without ſhoes, but not becauſe the weather is warm. And indeed I can ſcarce prevail upon myſelf to ſubmit to the being thought the owner of ſo mean a carriage. I have not as yet thrown off that perverſe baſhfulneſs, which is aſhamed of doing what is right. For as often as I fall into company with any one who has a more ſplendid equipage, I cannot help bluſhing againſt my will; which is a manifeſt ſign, that thoſe things which I approve and commend, have not as yet got a ſure and ſteady hold *. He that is aſhamed of a mean chariot, would be proud and vain of a rich one. I have made but a ſmall progreſs in philoſophy, ſince I dare not openly profeſs frugality, and am under a concern at the opinion of every one that paſſeth by. Whereas we ought to exclaim againſt the opinions of the whole world, ſaying, "ye play the fool; ye are miſtaken; ye doat "on vanities; ye eſteem no man for what he can call his own; when "ye come to conſider patrimony, ye are moſt diligent reckoners; and "rate every one according to their abilities, that ye may know where "to lend, and where to give: for this alſo ye ſet down in the account: "ſuch a one hath large poſſeſſions, but he is greatly in debt; and "ſuch a one indeed has a very fine houſe, but he purchaſed it with "other people's money: you will not eaſily find any one, who ſhews "ſo ſplendid a retinue; but he does not pay his debts; was he to "ſatisfy every creditor, he would not be worth a penny."

Now this is what ye ought to do with regard to other things; to examine what a man poſſeſſeth, that he can properly call his own. You think ſuch a one rich, becauſe he carries a load of plate with him, when he travels; becauſe he hath a landed property in many provinces; becauſe he hath a large rent-roll (*g*); or becauſe he is the landlord of ſo much ground in the ſuburbs, as would almoſt be envied in the deſerts of *Apulia*. And after all, he is but a poor man. Why ſo? becauſe he is in debt. What then, do ye ſay, does he owe? Why, all that he has; unleſs you think it makes a difference whether a man borrows from his neighbour, or from Fortune. What avails it, that his mules are ſo ſleek and fat, and all of one colour? or that his chariot is finely carved?

— Inſtrati oſtro alipedes, pictiſque tapetis.
Aurea pectoribus demiſſa monilia pendent;
Tecti auro fulvum mandunt ſub dentibus aurum!
The ſteeds capariſon'd with purple ſtand,
With golden trappings, curious to behold;
And champ betwixt their teeth the foaming gold. Dryden.

Theſe things make not the owner a better man, nor his mules more ſerviceable.

Marcus Cato, the Cenſor, (whoſe birth was truly of as great advantage to the *Roman* people, as that of *Scipio*; for as the one waged war againſt our profeſſed enemies, the other ſet himſelf to oppoſe the deprapravity of our morals) *Cato*, I ſay, generally rode upon a gelding, with his bags (*b*) acroſs, to carry ſuch things as were neceſſary. O how glad ſhould I have been to have ſeen him meet in the way one of our foppiſh cavaliers (*i*) with running footmen and his blacks (*k*), driving a cloud of duſt before him! Undoubtedly ſuch a one would appear more ſpruce and better attended than *Cato*; though at the ſame time amidſt this ſplendid equipage he greatly doubts whether he ſhall not let himſelf out *to engage with men or beaſts at the public ſhews* (*l*). But how did it redound to the honour of that age, that a General, who had triumphed, had been Cenſor, nay (what is above all) that a *Cato* ſhould be contented with a ſingle horſe, and indeed ſcarce that, for the bags on either ſide took up part of it? And would you not then prefer this one ſtrong gelding, which *Cato* deigned to curry and rub down with his own hands, to all thoſe plump eaſy pads, Spaniſh gennets (*m*), and ambling nags, that are of little other ſervice than for mere ſhew? But I find I ſhould not know when to end this ſubject, unleſs I reſolved with myſelf ſo to do; and ſhall therefore ſay no more of theſe things, which no doubt he foreſaw would prove juſt what they now are, who firſt called them, impedimenta, *uſeleſs incumbrances*.

I will now lay before you, *Lucilius*, a few more queſtions, as maintained by our ſect, in relation to *the ſufficiency of virtue to render life happy*. What is good in itſelf makes men good; as, what is truly good in muſic, makes a man a good muſician. Caſual things make not a good man, therefore they cannot be reckoned good. Now in anſwer to this the Peripatetics ſay, that *our firſt propoſition is falſe; foraſmuch as that which is good, does not always make men good. There is ſomething good in muſic, as the flute, the harp, or other inſtruments adapted to accompany the voice; but none of theſe things accompliſh a muſician.* Whereunto we reply, you do not rightly underſtand the queſtion, with regard to what we ſuppoſe good in muſic, for we call not that good in muſic which helpeth, or inſtructeth, but what completes, the muſician; whereas you conſider only the inſtruments belonging to the profeſſion, and not the profeſſion itſelf. Now whatever is good in the art of muſic

music itself, it is that which maketh a good musician. But I will endeavour to make this plainer. That which is good in the art of music, is said to be so in two respects; the one as promoting the effect, the other as assisting the art of the musician. Now the instruments such as the flute, the harp, the organ, belong to the effect, and not to the art itself. For without these a man may be well skilled in music, though without them he cannot display his powers. But good is not alike twofold in man; for good both of the man and of life is still the same good. What may befall the most contemptible and vilest of mankind is not good; but riches may fall to the share of a bawd, or a prize-fighter; riches therefore in themselves are not good.

Again, the Peripatetics say, *our proposition is false:* for in *Grammar, and in the art of physic or of government, we see that good befalleth even those of the lowest rank.* Be it so, these arts profess not any greatness of mind; they rise not above the common pitch; they disdain not casual things; whereas Virtue raiseth a man on high; and even exalts him above all that is dear to mortals; neither anxiously desiring those things that are called good, nor dreading those things that are called evils. *Chelidon*, one of *Cleopatra's* eunuchs (*n*), possessed a large estate. And it is not long since one *Natalis* (*o*), a man no less wicked than abominably foul-mouthed, was heir to many, and left many heirs. What then, shall we say that money made him pure, and not rather that he polluted money? which so falls upon some, as a piece of silver thrown into the common shore.

Virtue is seated far above these things; she reckons them not among her treasures; but rates every thing as herself is rated, according to its real worth; not judging any of these things good, fall they how or where they will; whereas physic and politics blend these things together, and forbid not their professors the pursuit of them. He that is not a good man, may yet be a physician, a pilot or a Grammarian, as well indeed as a cook. You will not rank him among others, who hath some quality which others have not (*p*). What any man hath in possession, such is the man. The exchequer is rich according to what it has; yet all that it hath is but adventitious: no one ſets any price upon a full bag, but upon what is contained therein. The ſame happens to the owner of a large eſtate: it is ſtill but an acceſſion or appendix to the man. Why then is a wiſe man great? Becauſe he hath a great ſoul; and not on the account of any external things. It is therefore true, that what may befall even the moſt contemptible of men, is not to be called good. Accordingly I will not allow freedom from pain and ſorrow a good thing; ſince this is no more than what a graſshopper or a gnat may enjoy. Nor will I affirm that reſt, and having nothing to trouble us, are good, ſince what can be more free from trouble than a worm? Do you aſk then what it is that conſtitutes a wiſe man? The ſame that conſtitutes *a God* (*q*); you muſt grant him ſomething divine, heavenly and truly noble. Good falls not to every one's ſhare, nor is indifferent to every poſſeſſor. Obſerve,

> Et quid quæque ferat regio, et quod quæque recuſat.
> Hîc ſegetes, illic veniunt felicius uvæ;
> Arborci fœtus alibi; atque injuſſa vireſcunt
> Gramina, nonne vides croceos ut Tmolus odores
> India mittit ebur, molles ſua tura ſabæi?
> At Chalybes nudi ferrum.—
>
> *The culture ſuiting to the ſeveral kinds*
> *Of ſeeds and plants; and what will thrive, and riſe,*
> *And what the genius of each ſoil denies:*
> *This ground with* Bacchus, *that with* Ceres *ſuits;*
> *Another loads the tree with happy fruits;*
> *A fourth with graſs, unbidden, decks the ground:*
> *Thus* Tmolus *is with yellow ſaffron crown'd:*
> India *black ebon, and white ivory bears,*
> *And* ſoft Idume *weeps her od'rous tears.*—Dryden.

Now theſe wares are diſtributed in different countries, that men might be conſtrained to traffick; as one wants what another enjoys. The chief good hath alſo its proper ſeat. It ſpringeth not where ivory or iron is found. Would you know its ſituation? It is in the mind. Unleſs this be pure and holy, it is not fit for the reſidence of God (*r*).

Good

Good cometh not of evil: riches ſpring from covetouſneſs: riches therefore are not good. But ſome one will ſay, *It is not true that good cometh not of evil; for money is got by theft or ſacrilege. However bad then theft or ſacrilege may be, it is therefore bad only as it doth more evil than good; for it procureth gain, though it be with fear, anxiety, and torment both of body and mind.* Whoever ſaith this, muſt admit, that as ſacrilege is bad, becauſe it doth many bad things; ſo likewiſe it is good, becauſe it doth ſome good: but can there be a more monſtrous opinion, than to rank ſacrilege or theft, or adultery, among good things? certainly not: yet how many are there who are not aſhamed of theft, and even glory in adultery? for ſmall ſacrileges are ſeverely puniſhed, while great procure a triumph (*s*). Add moreover, that if in any wiſe ſacrilege be good, it muſt alſo be a fit and commendable action, for it is a man's own act and deed: but ſurely this is what no mortal can admit; therefore I conclude that good cannot come of evil; for if, as you ſay, ſacrilege is only on this account evil, becauſe it bringeth much evil; if you remit the puniſhment, and promiſe ſecurity, it will be altogether good. By no means: for the greateſt puniſhment of evil deeds lies in the deeds themſelves. You err, I ſay, if you put them off to the executioner or the jailer. They are puniſhed immediately, as ſoon as they are done; nay, while they are doing. Good therefore ſpringeth not from evil, any more than a fig from an olive-tree. Every leaf and fruit anſwers its own ſeed: that which is good cannot degenerate: as what is fit and honourable cannot riſe from what is wrong and vile; ſo neither can good ſpring from evil: for fit and good is the ſame thing (*t*).

Some of the Stoics anſwer this as follows: *Suppoſe money to be good in itſelf, come how it will; it follows not that it hath ſacrilege in it, though it be taken by ſacrilege:* as thus, *in the ſame urn are both gold and a viper; if you take the gold from the urn, it follows not that the urn giveth gold, becauſe it hath a viper; but it giveth gold, though it alſo contains a viper. In like manner, gain cometh from ſacrilege, not as ſacrilege is vile and wicked, but as gain attends it; as in the urn, the viper is a bad thing, not the gold, which lies with the viper; ſo in ſacrilege, the heinouſneſs of the fact is bad, but not the gain.* To which it is replied, the caſes are by no no means ſimilar; for in the one, I can take the gold without the viper; but in the other, I cannot make gain, without committing ſacrilege: this gain is not added to, but mixed and blended with, the guilt.

Again, *if, in order to purchaſe a thing we fall into many evils, that thing cannot be good; but in the purſuit of riches we fall into many evils, therefore riches are not good.* But this propoſition *it is ſaid,* hath a twofold meaning; the one is, that in purſuit of riches we run into many evils; *but ſo we do even in the purſuit of virtue; as ſome in making a voyage, in order to get knowledge, have ſuffered ſhipwreck or been taken priſoners.* Another meaning is, *that thing whereby we fall into miſchief cannot be good* But it will not follow from this propoſition, that in purſuit of riches and pleaſures we muſt *neceſſarily* fall into miſchief; or, that, if by riches we fall into evils, therefore riches are not only not good but bad; whereas ye only ſay *they are not good.* Moreover it is ſaid, *ye cannot but grant that riches have ſome uſe; ye reckon them among the advantages of life* (*u*), but by the ſame way of reaſoning, they will not be even an advantage, ſince many inconveniencies flow from them. To this again ſome make anſwer, *ye are miſtaken if ye impute any inconveniencies to riches; they hurt no one. Every one is hurt or prejudiced, either by their own folly or the wickedneſs of others; juſt as a ſword kills no one of itſelf, but is the inſtrument in the hand of him that killeth. Riches therefore of themſelves do not hurt a man, though they may prove the cauſe of his being hurt.*

Poſidonius, I think, argues better, who ſaith that, *Riches are the cauſe of evil, not becauſe they do any thing of themſelves, but becauſe they invite others thereto* (*x*). For the *efficient* cauſe, which muſt neceſſarily and immediately do hurt, is one thing, and the *precedent* cauſe another: Now riches have in them the precedent cauſe: they puff up the mind, they contract envy, and ſo far alienate the mind, that the fame of being rich, however it may hurt, delights us. But good things ought to be free from all manner of blame: they are pure; they corrupt not the mind, nor diſturb it: they raiſe indeed and dilate it, but without puffing it up. Things that are good, create confidence, but riches bold-

 neſs;

nefs; the former caufe a greatnefs of foul, but riches infolence. Now infolence is nothing elfe but the falfe appearance of fuch greatnefs.

From hence then you will fay, it is plain that *riches are not only not good, but evil.* They would indeed be evil, if of themfelves they were hurtful; if, as I faid, they had in them the efficient caufe; but they have the precedent caufe, and fuch indeed as not only incites, but forcibly attracts the minds of men; forafmuch as they make a certain fhew of goodnefs very probable and credible to many. And even Virtue hath a precedent caufe that induceth envy; for many are envied on account of wifdom, and many on account of juftice; but then it hath not this caufe in itfelf, nor the likelihood of it; for, on the contrary, it is more likely that the form, which Virtue fets before the minds of men, fhould incite love and admiration.

Pofidonius faith, the queftion ought to be thus ftated: *Such things as give neither magnanimity, nor confidence, nor fecurity to the mind, are not good*; but riches, health and the like, have not this effect, therefore they are not good. And this argument he further amplifieth in this manner: *fuch things as give not magnanimity, nor confidence nor fecurity to the mind, but on the contrary create infolence, haughtinefs, and arrogance, are evil: but by cafual things we are drawn into thefe vices, therefore cafual things are not good.* For the fame reafon it is faid, *that fuch things are not even convenient.* But the condition of things *convenient* and of things *good*, is not the fame. A thing is convenient that hath more profit than difadvantage; but *good* ought to be entirely fo, and pure in all refpects. For that is not good which profits, but which only profits. Wherefore what is convenient may belong to brute animals, to imperfect men, and to fools. And therefore annoyance may be mixed therewith; but it is called convenient, being eftimated by its greater part; whereas good belongeth to the wife man alone, and ought to be inviolate.

Be of good courage, *Lucilius*, I fhall ftart but one difficulty more, though I muft own it is an *Herculean* one, not very eafy to be determined.

mined. *Good cometh not of evil; but from many poverties (or the poverty of many) are riches derived; therefore riches are not good.* The Stoics acknowledge not the queſtion as thus ſtated; the Peripatetics both form it in this manner, and likewiſe ſolve it. But *Poſidonius* ſaith, that this ſophiſm, which runs through all the ſchools of the logicians, is thus refuted by *Antipater*. *Poverty is ſaid to be ſuch, not from poſition* (*y*), *but from ſubtraction*, or, as the antients expreſs it, by *deprivation:* the Greeks ſay, κατὰ στέρησιν; *it is called ſuch, not from what it hath, but from what it hath not. As from many vacuums nothing can be filled; many things, not many wants, make riches.* For poverty is generally miſunderſtood. That is not poverty which poſſeſſeth a few things, but that which poſſeſſeth not many. I could expreſs what I mean was there any Latin word to anſwer the Greek ἀνυπαρξία (*z*); by which *Antipater* aſſigneth *poverty*. But for my own part, I cannot ſee that poverty is any thing elſe but the *poſſeſſion of little*. However no more at preſent; we ſhall conclude this matter when we have full leiſure to conſider what is eſſential to riches, and what to poverty; when we ſhall alſo conſider whether it be not better to alleviate poverty, and take ſuperciliouſneſs from riches, than to diſpute about words, as if we were fixed in our judgment concerning things.

Let us ſuppoſe ourſelves called to a public aſſembly; a law is propounded for aboliſhing riches. Now ſhall we either perſuade or diſſuade, from the foregoing queſtions? Shall we by theſe puzzling deductions cauſe the *Roman* people again to wiſh for and admire poverty, the ſource and foundation of their empire? to dread the conſequences of their immenſe wealth? and to reflect upon their having gained it all from conquered nations? That from hence, ambition, bribery, and tumults have crept into the moſt holy and temperate of all cities? that they make too ſplendid and luxurious a ſhew of the ſpoils of nations? that it is more eaſy for all nations to retake that from one people, which one people at different times have took from them? It is better to perſuade them of theſe things, and teach them to conquer their affections, rather than pretend to exterminate them entirely by dint of argument. If it be in our power let us ſpeak more boldly; if not, at leaſt more freely and openly.

ANNOTATIONS, &c.

(*a*) A paradox, *what is strange but true.* Cleanthes, παραδοξα μὲν ὁ παραλογα. *I have for amusement, says* Cicero (Pref. Parad.) *digested into common places those topics, which the Stoics, even in their literary retirement, and in their schools, find difficult to prove. Such topics they themselves term* paradoxes, *on account of their singularity and disagreement with the general sense of mankind. Lips.* Manud. iii. 2.

(*b*) *Cæsonius Maximus*, a particular and faithful friend, for which he suffered, as mentioned by *Tacitus*, (Annal. 15) and *Martial*, (l. 7. 43) from whom likewise we learn that he was of consular dignity.

Maximus ille tuus, Ovidi, Cæsonius hic est
  Cujus adhuc vultum vivida cera tenet.
Hunc Nero damnavit, sed tu damnare Neronem
  Ausus es, et profugi, non tua, fata sequi.
Æquora per Scyllæ magnus comes exsulis isti
  Qui modo nolueras consulis ire comes.
Si victura meis mandantur nomina chartis
  Et fas est cineri me superesse meo;
Audiet hæc præsens venturaque turba, fuisse
  Illi te, Senecæ quod fuit ille tuo.

Ib. Ep. 44. Facundi Senecæ potens amicus,
  Caro proximus, aut prior Sereno,
Hic est maximus ille quem frequenti
  Felix litera pagina salutat, &c.

(*c*) Non magis hora paratum fuit] *Muretus* knew not what to make of this expression, and as he found it in one of his books, sine magis hira, he conjectures, sine magiro, *without a cook*, using the Greek word μαγειρῳ, for a cook, because *Greek* cooks were then as fashionable among the *Romans*, as *French* cooks among the *English*.

(*d*) Plin. xv. 21. Ficus panis simul et obsonii vicem siccatæ implent; utpote cum *Cato* cibaria ruris operariis justa ceu lege sarciens, minui jubeat per fici maturitatem. *Cato* de re rust. c. 56. Familiæ cibaria, ubi vineam fodere cœperint, panis pondo v. usque adeò dum ficus esse cœperint. Deinceps ad pondo iv. redito. Cato *shortened the allowance of bread in his family one fifth as soon as figs were in season.*

(*e*) It was customary to make a present of, and to eat figs on New Year's Day, by way of *good luck* the ensuing year.

Quid vult palma sibi rugosaque carica, dixi,
  Et data subniveo condita mella cado?
Omen, ait, causa est ut res sapor ille sequatur
  Et peragat cœptum dulcis ut annus iter. Ov. Fast. 1.
What mean these dates and wrinkled figs, I said,
And, in white vessels, honey newly made?
That with like relish things, *said he*, may go,
And the whole year with equal sweetness flow.

(*f*) Mulæ vivere se ambulando testantur; i. e. vix vivæ, *scarce alive*, as lean men are said to be, malè vivi, *and* vix vivere. So *Lucretius*.

— Vivere non quit præ macie.—

And Ovid — Macie quæ malè viva sua est.

So contrary to those mules mentioned afterwards *sleek and fat and of one colour*.

* i. e. have not obtained credit with me, so as to fix my resolution.

(*g*) Magnus Calendarii liber.] *Martial.*

Superba densis arca palleat nummis
Centum explicentur paginæ kalendarum.

(*h*) Hippoperis] which *Horace* calls *Manticam*. S. l. 6. 106.

—— Nunc mihi curto ire licet mulo.——
Mantica cui lumbos onere ulceret, atque eques armos.
—— *Now on my bob-tail mule I ride;*
And with my budget press each galled side.

(*i*) Trossulis] See Ep. 76.

(*k*) Ep. 123. Omnes jam sic peregrinantur ut illos præcurrat equitatus, agmen cursorum antecedat.

(*l*) To such extremities had some young gentlemen reduced themselves by their extravagance, as to let themselves out for a *gladiator*, or a huntsman.

(*m*) Asturconibus] Martial xiv. 199.

Hic brevis ad numerum rapidos qui colligit ungues
Venit ab auriferis gentibus astur equus.
This nag, which keeps due time in every pace,
From Spain's *rich climate boasts his ambling race.*

(*n*) Ex Cleopatræ mollibus] Livy, l. 33. Prosequentibus mollibus viris, qui joci causa convivio interfuerant.

(*o*) Not that *Antonius Natalis*, who in the *Pisonian* conspiracy (Tac. Annal. 15) accused *Seneca* himself, for he says *some time ago*, (nuper,) perhaps it was his father. L.

(*p*) Cui contingit habere non quælibet, hunc non quemlibet dixeris] al. cui contigit habere rem non quamlibet, i. e. *rem minime vulgarem*, πρᾶγμα τι τῶν τυχόντων, hunc non quemlibet dixeris, i. e. *scito ipsum minime vulgarem esse*. Muret. Cui contingit habere non quælibet, hunc---- Which the old translation renders, *Thou canst not say that a man is all, who hath not the fortune to have all.*

(*q*) Ep. 31. (N. e.)

(*r*) *If ye walk in my statutes, and keep my commandments and do them, I will walk among you, and will be your God, and ye shall be my people.* Levit. 26. 3, 12. *If thou wert pure and upright, surely God would make the habitation of thy righteousness prosperous.* Job, 8. 6. *The Lord seeth not as man seeth, for man looketh on the outward appearance, but the Lord looketh on the heart.* 1 Sam. 16. 7. 1 Chron. 28. 9. *God is of purer eyes than to behold evil, and cannot look upon iniquity.* Habb. 1. 13. *Blessed are the pure in heart, for they shall see God.* Matth. 5. 8.---See Ep. 41. (N. b. c.)

(*s*) Sacrilegia minuta puniuntur, magna in triumphis feruntur] *ut alibi*, parvos fures in compedibus, magnos in purpura spectari.

For little villains must submit to fate,
That great ones may enjoy the world in state. Garth.

(*t*) *Ye shall know them by their fruit: do men gather grapes of thorns, or figs of thistles? Even so every good tree bringeth forth good fruit, but a corrupt tree bringeth forth evil fruit: a good tree cannot bring forth evil fruit, neither can a corrupt tree bring forth good fruit.* Matth. 7. 16. 18. *A good man*

man out of the good treasure of his heart bringeth forth that which is good; and an evil man out of the evil treasure of his heart bringeth forth that which is evil: for of the abundance of his heart the mouth speaketh. Luke. 6. 44. 46.

(*w*) Commoda] Ep. 92. τὰ εὐχρηστα Stoicorum. *Lipf.* Manud. ii. 22.

(*x*) So in the *Antigone* of *Sophocles*, v. 301.

Οὐδὲν γὰρ ἀνθρώποισιν οἷον ἄργυρος
Καλὸν νόμισμ' ἔβλαστε. κ. τ. λ.
— *Gold is the worst of ills*
That ever plagued mankind: this wastes our cities,
Drives forth the natives to a foreign soil,
Taints the pure heart, and turns the virtuous mind
To basest deeds; artifices of fraud
Supreme, and source of every wickedness. Franklin.

(*y*) Non per positionem] *al.* per possessionem, which *Muretus* approves of, because it follows immediately, paupertas est, non quæ pauca possidet.

(*z*) ατοφιη] al. ανευπαρσια. l. ἀνυπαρξία, which *Muretus* thinks more expressive of the sense here than ἀπορας, as this signifies *absolute want of every thing*, and that only *a deficiency*.

EPISTLE LXXXVIII. *

On the Liberal Sciences †.

YOU desire, *Lucilius*, to know my opinion concerning the *Liberal Sciences:* I cannot say that I greatly admire any one of them (*a*), nor reckon any of them among what I call *good*, especially when pursued merely for lucre (*b*). They are arts, meritorious, and useful indeed, so far as they prepare, and do not detain and cramp, the genius. For no longer are they to be indulged and dwelt upon, than while the mind is not capable of any thing greater: they are the rudiments, but not the whole exercise of man. They are called *liberal*, you know, because they become a *free* man, and are full worthy the application of a gentleman.

N 2 But

But there is only one ſtudy or ſcience that is truly *liberal*, viz. that which gives freedom indeed. And what is that, but *the ſtudy of wiſdom*, ſublime, ſtrong, and manly? All other are trifling and puerile. Can you think there is any thing good in thoſe ſtudies, the profeſſors whereof you ſometimes ſee the vileſt and moſt flagitious of men? In ſhort, they are what we ought not to be continually learning; it is enough to have learned them.

Some have made it a queſtion concerning the *liberal* arts, whether they could make a man *good*; but it is plain they promiſe no ſuch thing; neither do they at all affect ſuch knowledge. The Grammarian's principal ſtudy is to ſpeak accurately; and if he launcheth out any further, it is to have ſome knowledge in hiſtory; and his largeſt ſtretch is but a taſte in poetry. Now what is there in all theſe that leads to virtue? The weighing of ſyllables, and the propriety of words, the remembrance of ſtories, the ſcanning of verſes, and the laws of poetry? which of theſe can take away fear, can root out a fond deſire, or bridle headſtrong luſt?

Let us paſs on to Geometry, and, if you pleaſe, to Muſic, you will find nothing in either of them that forbids fear, or reſtrains deſire; which paſſions, unleſs a man knows how to govern, all other knowledge is but vain.

Let us conſider whether the profeſſors of the forementioned qualifications teach virtue, or not; if they do not teach it, they tranſmit it not; if they do teach it, they are more than what they profeſs themſelves to be; they are philoſophers. Would you know how little they are concerned in teaching virtue, only obſerve what a difference there is in their ſeveral ſtudies. But their ſtudies would be alike if they taught the ſame thing: unleſs perhaps they perſuade you that *Homer* was a philoſopher; when by the ſame arguments they would prove him a philoſopher, they deny him to be ſo (*c*). For one while they make him a *Stoic*, in purſuit of virtue alone (*d*), and flying from pleaſures, ſo as not to be drawn thereby from what is *right and fit*, even

by

by a promiſe of immortality: at another time they repreſent him as an *Epicurean* (*e*); highly extolling the happy ſtate of a peaceful city, whoſe inhabitants ſpend their time in ſongs and banquets: at another time as a *Peripatetic*, allowing three ſorts of good (*f*): at another time as an *Academic* or *Sceptic*, affirming all things to be uncertain. Now to me he ſeems to be none of theſe in particular, becauſe their ſeveral doctrines are all to be found in him; and they are all very different from each other. But let us grant then that *Homer* was a philoſopher: undoubtedly it was not the power of verſifying that made him a philoſopher; let us learn then what it was. To enquire whether *Homer* or *Heſiod* was the elder, or prior in time (*g*), is no more to the purpoſe, than to know whether *Hecuba* was younger than *Helen* (*h*); and why the former carried not her age ſo well. And do you think it of any more conſequence to know the years of *Patroclus* and *Achilles* (*i*)? Are you curious to know whether *Ulyſſes* ſo long wandered in his travels, rather than to take care that we wander not ourſelves daily in the road of life? It is all one to me, whether he was toſſed about in the ſtraights between *Sicily* and *Italy*, or in ſome unknown ſeas: though by the way it ſeems impoſſible for him to make ſo long a voyage, in ſo narrow a ſea, as is ſuppoſed (*k*).

It is certainly of more conſequence to reflect upon the tempeſts of the mind that daily toſs us, and the iniquity that drives us into all the evils that *Ulyſſes* ſuffered (*l*). There is not wanting beauty to captivate our eyes, nor an enemy to take our perſons: on this ſide are many fell monſters that delight in human blood; on that ſide, are the moſt inſidious blandiſhments to charm the ear; and all around us are ſhipwrecks, and a vaſt variety of calamities. Teach me then how to love my country, my wife, my parents: how in deſpite of danger, nay, though wrecked, I may reach this happy port by a perſeverance in well-doing. Why are you deſirous to know, whether *Penelope* was unchaſte (*m*), whether ſhe impoſed upon the men of that age; and whether ſhe ſuſpected her viſitant to be her huſband before ſhe knew him? Teach me rather what chaſtity is; and how great a good; and whether it be placed in the body or in the mind (*n*).

And

And now, as to *Mufic* (*o*). Here you teach me how the treble and bafe agree together; and how from ftrings of a different tone arifeth harmony. Teach me rather how my mind may agree with itfelf, and my thoughts be free from jarring difcord. You fhew me what notes or key are proper to exprefs forrow (*p*); fhew me rather how in adverfity I may abftain from fighs and groans, and fuch lamentable founds.

And then for *Geometry*: it teacheth me to meafure large tracts of land; but I had much rather it fhould teach me how much is fufficient for man. *Arithmetic* teaches me to caft accounts, and to practife my hands in the arts of avarice; rather let it teach me that computations of this kind belong not to the main bufinefs of life; and that he is by no means the happier man, whofe large patrimony fatigues his fteward; nay, let it teach me how many fuperfluous things he poffeffeth, whom nothing could make more unhappy, than to be obliged to keep his own accounts. What availeth it me to know how to divide a field into feveral parts, if I have not the heart to give my brother a fhare of it? Of what profit is it to me, to know with great exactnefs, how many fquare feet are contained in an acre of ground; and alfo to find out if it be not exactly meafured by the perch or pole; if fome overpowerful neighbour wrings me with forrow, having encroached upon what is mine? Do you teach me to keep my own? I had rather learn how, was I to lofe the whole, I might ftill be chearful.

Alas! I am driven, fome one will fay, from an eftate, that was my father's and grandfather's. What then? can you tell me who was in poffeffion of it before your grandfather? I do not fay what man, but what people? You entered upon it, not as the lord of it, but as a tenant. Do you afk, whofe tenant you are? Why, if things go well with you (*q*), and the inconftancy of human affairs prevent it not, you are tenant to your heir. The lawyers deny, that prefcription of ufe can be pleaded for any thing that is common; now what you poffefs, is in common; it belongs to mankind.

O the excellency of art! you know how to meafure a circle; you can reduce to a fquare any given figure; you can tell the diftances of the

the stars; in short, there is nothing that belongs to numbers or figures, but what falls within your art: if then you are so great an artist, measure me the *mind of man*; say how great it is; rather say how little? You know what is a right line; but what availeth this, if you know not what is right in the conduct of life?

I come now to the man who boasteth of his skill in *Astronomy*; who knows

> Frigida Saturni quo sese stella receptet,
> Quos ignis cœli Cyllenius erret in orbes. G. I. 337.
> *See to what house cold Saturn's beams repair,*
> *Or where Cyllenius points his erring star:* Lauderdale.

And what is there in all this, that I should be sollicitous to know when *Saturn* and *Mars* are in opposition? or when *Mercury* sets in the evening in the sight of *Saturn*? I would rather know, that, whatever aspects these planets are in, they are still propitious to me, and cannot change their course, to which they are fixed by an immutable decree of the fates: they return according to their stated seasons; they either bring on, or only point out (*r*), and denote, the effects of all things: but whether they are the cause of every thing that happens, what availeth the knowledge of a thing that is immutable; or, whether they only signify and presage such events, of what use is it to provide against what you cannot possibly escape? Whether you know these things, or know them not, they will certainly come to pass.

> Si vero solem ad rapidum *Stellasque* sequentes
> Ordine respicias, nunquam te crastina fallet
> Hora, nec insidiis noctis capière serenæ. G. l. 424.
> *Observe the daily circle of the sun,*
> *And the short year of each revolving moon:*
> *By them thou shalt foresee the following day,*
> *Nor shall a starry night thy hopes betray.* Dryden.

I am sufficiently and amply provided against any surprise. But may I not be deceived in to-morrow? certainly I may; for that deceives a man, which happens to him unknowingly. Now, I know not what will *happen*, but I know what may happen. Fortune can do nothing against

against my expectation; I expect all she can do; if any thing be remitted, I take it in good part. The hour deceives me if it favours me; yet even so, it does not altogether deceive me; for as I know all things may happen, I know likewise that they may not happen: I expect therefore good fortune, and am prepared against bad (*s*).

You must bear with me, *Lucilius*, if I am not led in these matters by prescription; if I am somewhat particular in regard to the *liberal Sciences*; for I cannot be persuaded to take painters into the number of their professors, any more than I would statuaries, masons, and other ministers to luxury: I likewise exclude wrestlers; and the whole tribe of those whose art consists in dawbing their limbs with dust and oyl; as well as perfumers, cooks, and others, who study with great ingenuity to serve us in our pleasures. For what pretence, I pray you, have those morning sots (*t*), who fatten the body, but starve the mind, to be called professors of liberal arts? Can gluttony and drunkenness be thought a liberal study fit for youth, whom our ancestors were wont to exercise always in an erect attitude, in throwing darts, tossing the pike, breaking their horses, or handling their arms? They taught their children nothing that was to be learned in an easy and lolling posture. But after all, neither these arts nor the former teach and nourish virtue. For what avails it a man to manage a horse, and break him to the bit, if still he himself is carried away by his unbridled passions? What advantageth it a man to overcome many in wrestling and boxing, if in the mean time he is overcome himself by anger? *What then, are the* liberal Sciences *of no advantage to us?* Yes, certainly, of great advantage, in all other respects, save in regard to virtue. For low as the mechanic arts are, which are wholly manual, they are most useful instruments, and of great service in life, though they belong not to virtue. *Why then do we instruct children in the* liberal Sciences? not because they instil virtue, but because they prepare the mind for the reception of it (*u*). As the first principles of literature (so called by the ancients) by which children were taught their A, B, C, teach not the liberal arts, but only prepare them for instruction therein; so the liberal arts carry not the mind directly to virtue, but only expand, and make it fit for it.

Posidonius ſaith, there are four kinds of arts; the mean and vulgar; the vain and ſportive; the puerile, and the liberal. The *vulgar* are ſuch as employ handicraftſmen in the neceſſary occupations of life; in which there is not the leaſt pretence to gentility and honour. The vain and ſportive are ſuch as tend only to the pleaſure of the eyes and ears; among theſe you may reckon thoſe ſubtle engineers, who contrive theatrical machines (x) to riſe, as it were, of themſelves; and the ſtage to widen and enlarge itſelf in all dimenſions, without the leaſt noiſe; with other ſuch curious and unexperienced entertainments; ſuch as ſeparating the parts that were joined together; or things that were far aſunder, uniting of their own accord; or ſome lofty pyramid ſinking gradually down into its baſe; all which things ſtrike the eyes of the unſkilful; and ſeem, as they know not the cauſe of them, inſtantaneous miracles. The *puerile*, but ſuch as have the appearance of *liberal*, are thoſe which the Greeks call ἐγκύκλιοι, and we *liberales*; but the only true *liberal*, or, if I may ſo ſpeak, *free* arts, are ſuch as are wholly employed in the purſuit of virtue.

It is likewiſe ſaid, that *as ſome part of philoſophy is called* Natural; *another part* Moral; *and another* Rational; *ſo this whole company of* liberal arts *claim to themſelves a place in philoſophy*. When we come to *natural queſtions*, we have recourſe to the teſtimony of geometry; but does it therefore follow that it is part of that ſcience which it aſſiſteth? Many things aſſiſt us, and yet are not part of us; nay, if they were really part of us, they would not aſſiſt us; as meat is an help to the body, yet it is no part of it. Geometry hath certainly its peculiar uſe, and is ſo far neceſſary to philoſophy as the artiſt is to that: but neither is he a part of geometry, nor geometry of philoſophy.

Moreover, each profeſſion hath its proper ſphere; the philoſopher ſtudies and knows the cauſes of natural things; the numbers and meaſures of which the geometrician is hunting after and computing. The philoſopher knows the formation of the heavenly bodies, their nature, and ſeveral powers; while the mathematician calculates their appearances, their motion direct and retrograde, their riſing and ſetting, and ſeeming ſtationary, though they are all in perpetual motion: the philoſopher knows the reaſon of the appearances of images in a glaſs; the geometrician can tell you the proper diſtance of the object from the glaſs, and what ſort of glaſs will reflect ſuch an image. The philoſopher will prove the ſun to be a very large body; the mathematician will tell you how large it is; but then he proceeds upon uſe and practice; and in order thereto, you muſt grant him certain principles and maxims: but the ſcience that depends upon ſo precarious a foundation cannot be called ſure and perfect. Philoſophy never begs the queſtion, it aſks no *foreign* aſſiſtance, but raiſeth the whole work itſelf from the foundation. Mathematics, if I may ſo ſpeak, is a ſuperficial art; the foundation on which it is built is not its own; it is obliged to other principles, whereby it proceeds to higher matters. Could it indeed reach truth of itſelf; could it comprehend the nature of the whole world; I ſhould ſay that it contributed much to the improvement of our minds; which, by being converſant in heavenly matters, grow enlarged, and are ſtill acquiring new knowledge. But there is only one thing which perfects the mind, and that is, the immutable knowledge of *good* and *evil*, which belongs to philoſophy alone; no other art concerns itſelf with this diſtinction.

To run over a few particular virtues;—*Fortitude* is a contemner of ſuch things as men are generally afraid of; it deſpiſeth, provokes, and breaks the force of ſuch terrors as are apt to enſlave the mind, And how in any wiſe is this virtue ſtrengthened and confirmed by the *liberal arts?* *Fidelity*, the moſt ſacred good of the human breaſt, cannot be compelled to deceive, by any neceſſity; cannot be corrupted by any reward, how great ſoever; *burn*, ſaith ſhe, *ſmite, kill, I will not betray my friend; the more ſeverely torture endeavours to come at any ſecret, the more cloſely will I keep it*. Do the *liberal Sciences* ever inſtill ſuch courage? *Temperance* reſtrains our pleaſures; ſome ſhe utterly deteſts and abhors; other ſome ſhe diſpenſeth with, having reduced them to a proper mean, and never purſues them merely for pleaſure's ſake. *Humanity* forbids a man to be haughty towards his companions, or covetous: in words, in deeds, in affections ſhe ſheweth herſelf gentle and condescending unto all; she judgeth not ill of any man; and delights in that as her own chief good, which is likely to promote the good of others. Do the *liberal Sciences* teach such good qualities? No; no more than they do simplicity, modesty, frugality, and good œconomy; no more than they do *clemency*; which is as sparing of another's blood as of her own; and knows that man is not to be treated by man prodigally or cruelly.

But when you affirm, it is said, *that without the* liberal Sciences *a man cannot reach virtue; how can you deny that they contribute to virtue?* Why, because neither without food can a man arrive at virtue, and yet food belongeth not to virtue. Timber of itself contributes nothing to a ship, though without timber a ship cannot be built. There is no reason, I say, to think, that a thing should be made by that, without which it cannot be made. It may indeed be said, that without *the liberal Arts* a man may arrive at virtue: for though virtue be a thing to be learned, yet it is not learned merely by these sciences. And why should I not think that a man may become a wise man, though he knows not his letters; since wisdom consists not in the knowledge of letters? It is conversant about things, not about words; and I know not whether that may not prove the more faithful memory, which depends upon its own intrinsic strength (*y*).

Wisdom is very powerful and extensive; it requires a large space to range in; it must study all things both divine and human; things past, and to come; transitory, and eternal; and even Time itself: concerning which alone, consider how many questions may be started; as first, *whether any thing be self-existent*; and next, *whether any thing was before Time; if Time began with the world*; or *whether before the world had being, because there must have been something, there was not also Time* (*z*). Innumerable are also the questions concerning the soul; as, *whence it is*(*aa*); *of what quality; when it begins to be; and how long it shall continue in being; whether it be subject to transmigration; and, still changing its habitation, passeth from one form of living creatures into another; whether it performs no more than one service, and being set free wanders about the universe; whether it be a body, or not; what it will be employed upon when it ceaseth* *to to act in conjunction with the body; how it will use its liberty when it hath escaped from this prison; whether it will forget all that is past, and there begin to know herself, when, dislodged from this body, she seats herself on high.* Thus, how great part soever of things, or human or divine, you at present comprehend, you will still find matter enough to employ and fatigue the mind in the search of farther truths.

That things therefore so many and of so great consequence may find place for their reception, it is necessary that all that are superfluous should be removed from the mind. Virtue cannot endure to be straiten'd; she is so great as to require boundless room: let all things therefore be expell'd; and the whole mind laid open for the reception of her alone. But forasmuch as there is a certain delight in the knowledge of many arts; let so much of them be retained as may be thought necessary. If you think a man worthy of reproof who spends his money in superfluities, and is proud of adorning his house with the most pompous furniture; will you not also think him blameable, who is busied in filling his head with a lumber of useless knowledge? To desire to know more than is requisite for a man to know, is a sort of intemperance.

Besides this eager pursuit of the liberal arts is apt to make a man troublesome, verbose, impertinent, self-conceited, and therefore disdaining to learn things necessary, being already overstocked with superfluities. *Didymus* the Grammarian is said to have wrote 4000 books (*bb*); how wretched must a man have been only to have read so many trifling things? for, in these books, great enquiry is made after the country of *Homer*; who was the true mother of *Æneas* (*cc*); whether *Anacreon* was more sottish than amorous; whether *Sappho* was a prostitute; and other the like trifles; which, if a man knew them, he would not be sorry to forget. Go now, O man, and deny, that *life is long*.

But to come to our own sect: I will shew you, *Lucilius*, that even here many things are to be rooted out; many to be cut down as it were with an axe. With how great loss of time, with how much impertinence, and plague to the ears of other men, have some laboured to obtain

obtain that empty commendation, *O what a learned man!* We ought rather to be content with that more ſimple and plain one, *O what a good man!* If ſuch then our duty, ſhall I peruſe the annals of all nations, in ſearch of the man who firſt wrote verſes? Shall I pretend to reckon up, though I have no records, the time between *Orpheus* and *Homer*? Shall I review the critical remarks of *Ariſtarchus* wherein he takes upon him to cenſure the verſes of others? and wear out an age in counting ſyllables? Shall I for ever be poring over the duſt of Geometricians (*dd*)? Shall I be ſo regardleſs of that wholeſome precept, *Tempori parce, huſband well your time?* Muſt I know all theſe things? What then can I pardonably be ignorant of (*ee*)?

Appian, the Grammarian, who in the time of *Caius Cæſar*, was carried about all *Greece*, and was every where honoured with the title of a *ſecond Homer*, ſaid, that *Homer*, after he had compoſed the *Odyſſes* and *Iliad*, added to the latter, which treats of the *Trojan* war, the beginning, as it now ſtands; and in order to prove this, he alledged, that *Homer* had deſignedly began the firſt line with two letters that pointed out the number of both books (*ff*). Such then are the trifles which a man muſt know, who is ambitious of knowing many things.

But think now, my friend, how much time you may be deprived of by a bad ſtate of health; how mnch muſt be taken up with neceſſary buſineſs, public, private, daily; and how much by ſleep; meaſure the days of man; they are not ſufficient for ſo many things; I am ſpeaking of the *liberal ſtudies*; but among the philoſophers themſelves how many things are ſuperfluous! and how great is their idle waſte of time! for they alſo have condeſcended to the weighing of ſyllables, and to the peculiar uſes of conjunctions and prepoſitions, ſo as even to envy both the Grammarians and Geometricians: and whatever they found ſuperfluous in the ſchools of theſe they have tranſplanted into their own. Hence it is they knew better how to ſpeak than to live. Learn now, O *Lucilius*, what great miſchief may accrue from too much ſubtlety; and how great an enemy it is to truth!

Protagoras

Protagoras (*gg*) ſaith, that *upon every ſubject men may argue indifferently pro and con*; *even though the ſubject be, whether every thing is diſputable on each ſide of the queſtion*. *Nauſiphanes* (*hh*) ſaith that *nothing can be ſaid more* to be, *than* not to be. *Parmenides* (*ii*) ſaith, that *all we ſee, is nothing upon the whole*. *Zeno* of *Elea* cuts ſhort the queſtion, and affirms, that *nothing is*. Of much the ſame opinion are the *Megarenſians* (*kk*), the *Eretricians* (*ll*), and *Academics*, who have introduced a new ſort of knowledge, *to know nothing* (*mm*): now you may fling all theſe into the common ſtock of thoſe who profeſs the *liberal arts*; as thoſe profeſſors teach me a knowledge of little or no profit to me; theſe philoſophers rob me of the hopes of knowing any thing at all: it is better however I think to know what is ſuperfluous, than to know nothing. The former holds out no light to direct me in the way to truth, but theſe quite put out my eyes. If I believe *Protagoras*, there is nothing in the nature of things but *what is doubtful*; if *Nauſiphanes*, this one thing only is certain, that *nothing is certain*: if *Parmenides*, *there is but one thing*: if *Zenon*, *there is not even one*. What then are we? and what are all things that ſurround, nouriſh, and ſuſtain us? The whole nature of things is but a ſhadow, vain and deceitful. Indeed I cannot eaſily ſay, whether I am more angry at thoſe, who would have us to know nothing; or thoſe, who have not left us ſo much as this, *to know nothing*.

ANNOTATIONS, &c.

* In ſome books this Epiſtle is ſtyled, L. Annæi Senecæ *Liber* de ſeptem artibus Liberalibus, as if it was a ſeparate treatiſe; but long as it is (and indeed there are ſome longer) *Lipſius* perſiſts in ranging it among the Epiſtles.

† The Romans called thoſe the *liberal* ſtudies, or ſciences, which the Greeks called εγκυκλια μαθηματα, i. e. *certain exerciſes*, which almoſt all gentlemen of birth and fortune were uſed to employ themſelves in, not in order to make themſelves thorough maſters therein, but only to acquire ſuch a ſmattering and taſte in them, as might become their gentility, and without which they would make but a poor figure in life.. They therefore were firſt taught *Grammar*, in order to form a juſt expreſſion and propriety in ſpeech. From hence they paſſed on to the reading the Hiſtorians and Poets: nor was it thought leſs neceſſary to inſtruct them in *Arithmetic*, *Geometry*, *Muſic*: ſome were likewiſe taught *Painting*; they had alſo their ſeveral (*Angelo's* or) maſters, to teach them to wreſtle, to ride, and to perform other manly exerciſes of the body. Concerning theſe ſtudies

therefore

therefore *Seneca*, in this most excellent Epistle, pronounceth in general, that not one of them is to be pursued merely upon its own account; and they are only useful forasmuch as they are subservient to qualify and prepare the minds of young men, as yet not capable of more weighty or solid matters for the study and acquisition of *wisdom*; which, and only which, among them all, deserves to be called *liberal*; as being that alone which is of sufficient force to deliver man, from the vilest of all slavery, even that of sin and lust. M.

Fundamenta, quibus nixatur vita salusque.
——— *Such the foundation, such the end*
On which the life and health of man depend.

(*a*) Nullum suspicio.] This he speaks as a Stoic. So *Zeno*, (which many object to him) *τὴν ἐγκύκλιον παιδείαν ἄχρηστον ἀποφαίνει*, *declares the cycle of literature useless.* And principally the *Cynics*, according to *Laertes*, decried the same, *παραιτοῦνται τὰ ἐγκύκλια μαθήματα*. This however is speaking comparatively; *letters* indeed considered in themselves are little more than mere amusement, *for*, says *Seneca* (De Brev. Vit. c. 14.) cujus errores minuent! cujus cupiditates premunt, quem fortiorem, quem justiorem, quem liberaliorem facient, *whose errors will they lessen, whose passions will they check, whom will they make more brave, more just, more liberal?* Sed

— Non animum metu,
Non mortis laqueis expedient caput. *Hor.* Od. iii. 24. 8.
— *Not all thy wealth shall save*
Thy mind from fear, or body from the grave. Creech.

But after all, says *Clemens*, *unless wisdom is protected by the fence of philosophy, and erudition, it will be exposed to the snares and insults of sophistry.* And *Justin*, *Philosophy is a truly great and noble possession, venerable in the sight of God, forasmuch as it leadeth us to him, and fixeth the mind there. Happy and blessed are they whose minds are so fixed!*

(*b*) Quod in aes exit] *Muretus* says he knows not what to make of this expression: and as to what follows, *meritoria* artificia, he reads *militaria*. He might as well, I think, read *mercatoria*, as being somewhat nearer the original.

(*c*) Many of the ancients had such a veneration for *Homer*, that they would have it thought, *all philosophy, and every tenet of the philosophers flowed originally from him.* But *Seneca* maintains that this very argument proves *Homer* to be *no philosopher*, because the first seeds of opinions so widely different in themselves, are found scattered in his works. *Muret.*

Certainly a Philosopher, says *Lipsius*, *if there ever was one*, Basil. Πᾶσα μὲν ἡ ποίησις τῷ Ὁμήρῳ ἀρετῆς ἐστιν ἔπαινος, κ. τ. λ. *The whole poetry of* Homer *is in praise of virtue, unless what is added for the sake of grace and ornament.* Vid. *Lips.* Manud. l. 7.

(*d*) For, because *Ulysses* sets so high a value upon his own country, rocky and barren as it was, as not to be diverted from the desire and love of it, by the promise of immortality from *Circe* and *Calypso*; this they interpret, as that by the name of *Ithaca* you are to understand *Virtue*, for whose sake alone all other things are to be despised by a wise man. *Muret.*

But *Homer* goes still farther, as if the possession of virtue was nothing, unless it was brought forth into action, as when *Patroclus* chiding *Achilles*, calls him Αἰναρέτην.

Μὴ ἐμέ γ' οὖν οὗτός γε λάβοι χόλος, ὃν σὺ φυλάσσεις,
Αἰναρέτη·---Il. 16. 30.
May never rage like thine my soul enslave,
O great in vain! unprofitably brave!
Thy country slighted in her last distress,
What friend, what man, from thee shall hope redress? Pope.

Vid. Plutarch. de Homero, 6. 76.

(*e*) As when he introduced *Ulysses* saying,

Ου γαρ εγωγε τι φημι τελος χαριεστερον ειναι. κ. τ. λ. Οδ. 9. 5.
How sweet the products of a peaceful reign!
The heaven-taught poet and enchanting strain!
The well fill'd palace, the perpetual feast,
A land rejoicing, and a people blest!
How goodly seems it ever to employ
Man's social days in union and in joy!
The plenteous board high-heap'd with cakes divine,
And o'er the foaming bowl the laughing wine! Pope.

But particularly the description of one of the cities on the shield of *Achilles*. Il. 18.

Here sacred pomp and genial feast delight,
And solemn dance, and Hymeneal rite,---
Along the streets the new-made brides are led,
With torches flaming to the nuptial bed:
The youthful dancers, in a circle bound
To the soft flute, and cittern's silver sound, &c.

(*f*) Allowing *three* sorts of good, as comprized in the description of *Mercury*---

Οἷος δὴ σὺ δέμας καὶ εἶδος αγητὸς,
Πεπνυσαί τε νοον, μακαρων δ' εξ εσσι τοκηων. Il. ω. 377.
A beauteous youth, majestic and divine,
He seem'd; fair offspring of some princely line. Pope.

But as the word *tria* is wanting in some copies, it may be understood of wealth, prosperity, and other good things of life of which *Homer* says the Gods are the *givers*, δωτῆρας εαων. *See* Ep. 66.

(*g*) Some suppose *Homer* to be the elder, as *Philochorus*, *Xenophanes*, and *Plutarch*. (Consol. ad Apoll.) Others give the seniority to *Hesiod*, as *Accius*, the poet, and *Ephorus*, the historian. But *Varro* seems to determine it, saying, non esse dubium quin aliquo tempore eodem vixerint; vel Homerum aliquanto antiquiorem, *that they lived much about the same time*, (A. M. 3000), *or that Homer was somewhat the elder of the two*. Agell. iii. 11. xvii. 21.

(*h*) *Muretus* supposeth, that *Helen* was much older than *Hecuba*, but that she carried her age better, because she was the daughter of *Jupiter*.

(*i*) *Patroclus* is generally thought to have been the younger; but *see Politian*. Miscell. c. 45.

(*k*) Some therefore have fancied that he wandered in the *Atlantic* Ocean. But certainly there is no need to be scrupulously inquisitive concerning such things as are manifestly fabulous. *Agellius* alludes to this question, (l. 14. c. 6.) where he introduces one of his servants disputing, whether Ulysses *wandered*, εν τῃ εσω θαλασσῃ κ. τ. λ. *in the Mediterranean, according to* Aristarchus, *or in the Ocean, according to* Crates.

(*l*) In like manner *Diogenes* is said to have reproved the Grammarians; forasmuch as they were sollicitous to know what evils *Ulysses* suffered, but were negligent of their own.

(*m*) Sunt enim qui dicant, eam omnibus porcis fecisse copiam sui, atque ex illo promiscuo coitu natum *Pana*. At alii hunc ipsum capripedem Deum natum ex *Penelopa* et *Mercurio* in hircum converso, egregiam mulieris pudicitiam! quæ cum se a virorum consortio puram integramque servaret, ad hirci, belli videlicet et suaveolentis animalis concubitu non abhorruerit. *Muret.*

(*n*) Undoubtedly in the mind, nec oppresso corpore amittitur, August. (de civ. Dei. l. 17. Vis aliena pudicitiam non excutit, etsi pudorem incutit.

(*o*) *Diogenes* saith of musicians, τὰς μουσικὰς μὲν ἐν τῇ λυρᾳ χορδὰς ἁρμοττεσθαι, αναρμοστα δὲ ἔχειν τὰ τῆς ψυχῆς ηθη. *That they kept the strings of their harps in tune, but neglected to tune their souls to good morals.*

(*p*) Modi flebiles] *Softly sweet in Lydian measure.* Dryden's Ode.

(*q*) i. e. if you are happy in having an heir to your mind.

(*r*) Effectus rerum omnium aut movent aut notant] Vid. *Lips.* Philol. ii. 13.

(*s*) In Anthologia.

Εἰ μὲν ἦν μαθεῖν, ἃ δεῖ παθεῖν,
Καὶ μὴ παθεῖν, καλὸν ἦν τὸ μαθεῖν·
Εἰ δὲ δεῖ παθεῖν, ἃ δ' ἦν μαθεῖν
Τί δεῖ μαθεῖν; χρὴ γὰρ παθεῖν.
It avails nothing, or to know,
Or not, what we must undergo;
Since, for whate'er we must endure,
Sweet patience is the only cure.

(*t*) Jejuni vomitoris] See Epist. 122.

(*u*) Philo, Ὥσπερ ἐν οἰκίαις αὔλειοι πρόκεινται; *As the vestibule to a house, and suburbs to a city, such are the liberal arts to virtue; they are the way that leads to it.*

(*x*) Pegmata per se surgentia] Augustin de Civ. Dei, c. 24. Ad quàm stupenda opera industria humana pervenit? quæ in theatro mirabilia spectantibus audientibus incredibilia facienda et exhibenda molita est! Crescebant in sublima *Pegmata*,

Et crescunt mediâ pegmata celsa viâ. *Martial.*

Subsidebant eadem. *Claudian.*

Mobile ponderibus descendat Pegma reductis.
Inque chori speciem spargentes ardua flammas
Scena rotet, vanos effingat mulciber orbes
Per tabulas impunè vagus: pictæque citato
Ludant igne trabes, et non permissâ moræri
Fida per innocuos errent incendia turres.

Apuleius l. x. Jamque totâ suave fragrante caveâ montem illum ligneum terræ vorago decepit. Machinatores fabricarum astutiâ unius conversionis, multa et varia pariter administrant. *Id.* Vid. *Lips.* de Amphitheatro, c. 22. *Philand.* in Vitruv. l. 9. *Sueton.* in Nero.

(*y*) It was thought by many of the antients that *letters* rather hurt than profit the memory; forasmuch as trusting to these, men are less diligent in fixing in their minds such things as they learn; as *Dictionaries*, &c. are apt to make schoolboys more careless and idle. Whereupon *Thamas*, king of *Egypt*, when *Theuth* the inventor of letters called them *an help and sure remedy for the memory*, thus refutes him, Καὶ νῦν σὺ πατὴρ ὢν γραμμάτων,----οὔκουν μνήμης, ἀλλ' ὑπομνήσεως φάρμακον εὗρες---ας. Plato in Phædr. *The inventor of letters hath found out an help or remedy, not of* memory, *but of* reminiscence. And, Cæs. de Bell. Gallico, l. 6. c. 8. Cæsar *tells us that the* Druids *instructed their pupils in the* Greek *tongue; for two reasons*, first, that *their learning might not become common and vulgar*; and, 2dly, *that scholars might not trust so much to their writings as to their memory; as it happeneth for the most part, that men rely upon the trust of books and papers, and in the mean time omit the benefit of good remembrance.*

(*z*) Negamus, ubi sola principia sunt, tempus esse. Non habet tempus æternitas, omne enim tempus ipsa est. *Tertullian.* See Epp. i. 49. 117. *Lips.* Physiol. ii. 24.

(*aa*) *Whence it is*, the soul was held by most of the antient philosophers, especially by the *Pythagoreans* and the *Stoics*, to be a discerped part of the *divine essence*. *Cicero* represents it, as acknowledged by the best and wisest men, that our souls are emanations from *the universal mind*; and consequently immortal; and *this conviction*, says he, *arises within me, from reflecting, that considering the mighty quickness with which the human soul is endowed, its vast collection of past, and provision for future events; the variety of the Arts, and the importance of the Sciences, with all its numerous inventions*; I say, *considering all this, it is impossible for that nature, that is the receptacle of so many different properties, to be mortal.* Cic. de Sen. c. 21. *Subject to transmigration.* See Epist. 65. (N. k) *Ovid* introduces *Pythagoras* as delivering his doctrine to the people of *Crotona.*

Morte carent animæ, semperque priore relictâ
Sede novis domibus vivunt, habitentque receptæ. Met. xv. 156.
—— *Our souls their antient houses leave,*
To live in new, which them, as guests, receive.

—— *She seats herself on high.* *Socrates*, in *Plato*, says many excellent things concerning the happiness to be enjoyed in a future state; he talks of its going, after its departure hence, *into a place like itself, noble, pure, invisible, to a wise and good God, whither*, says he, *if it pleases God, I shall soon go.* And particularly, that *the soul which gives itself up to the* study of wisdom and philosophy, and lives abstracted from the body, *goes at death to that which is like itself, divine, immortal, wise, to which when it arrives it shall be happy, freed from error, ignorance, fears, disorderly love, and other human evils, and lives, as it is said of the initiated, the rest of its life with the Gods.—Blessed are the pure of heart*, for they *shall see God.* Matth. v. 8. *The righteous shall shine forth as the sun in the kingdom of the Father.* xiii. 43.

(*bb*) *Suidas* says 3500, and that on account of his laborious works he was called χαλκέντερος, *Ironsides.* He lived in the time of *Cicero* and *Augustus.*

(*cc*) *Venus* being generally supposed his mother.

(*dd*) In geometriæ pulvere] So pulvis eruditus, in *Cicero*; i. e. the dust wherein the geometricians were used to draw their figures.

(*ee*) Ep. i. Hæc sciam? et quid ignorem? i. e. as it is impossible for a man to know all things, there must be some things, which if I am obliged to know, I cannot conceive what those things be; which it is pardonable not to know.—*Muretus*, Hæc sciam, ut quid—*Erasmus* et quid si—*Stephanus*, et quid sim.—So the old translation, *shall I know these things, and be ignorant of myself?* *Lipsius*, et quid ignorem? *Juretus*, without an interrogation, nec sciam quid ignorem, i. e. *I am not concerned at not knowing many things which it is better to be ignorant of than to know.*

(*ff*) MΗνη—M. 40. H. 8. i. e. 48.

(*gg*) *Protagoras*, a scholar of *Democritus*, and the son of *Menander*, the richest man in *Thrace*, who entertained *Xerxes* in his expedition against *Greece*; for which bounty the magi or wise men that were with *Xerxes*, instructed his son, *Protagoras*, in all their learning, which they could not have done but by permission of the King.

(*hh*) *Nausiphanes*, a follower of *Democritus*; abused by *Epicurus* with all manner of contumely. Cic. de Nat. Deor. I. 26.

(*ii*) *Parmenides*, a philosopher of *Elis*, scholar and friend of *Xenophon*. He is mentioned by *Plato*, who hath also wrote a dialogue (*concerning ideas*) in his name. He is supposed to be the first who took notice of *Lucifer* and *Hesperus*, the Morning and Evening Star being the same.

(*kk*) The people of *Megara*, a city of *Achaia*, between *Athens* and the isthmus of *Corinth*. The birth-place of *Euclid*. It still retains the name.

(*ll*) Eretrici] So called from *Eretria*, a city in the isle *Eubœa*, the birth-place of *Menedemus*, their founder.---*al.* Cretici. *Pincian.* ridiculously enough; *Critici*, i. e. judiciales.

(*mm*) A sect of philosophers, who followed the doctrine of *Socrates* and *Plato*, as to the uncertainty of knowledge, and the incomprehensibility of truth. Among the antients they were called Academici; but since the restoration of learning they have assumed the denomination of *Platonists*.

EPISTLE

EPISTLE LXXXIX.

The Distinction between Wisdom and Philosophy.

YOU desire, *Lucilius*, to have philosophy rightly distinguished, and its vast body disposed into members: this is certainly of consequence, and very necessary for a man who aspires after wisdom; for by the parts we are more easily led to a knowledge of the whole. I could wish therefore the whole of philosophy was presented to our view in like manner as the face of the universe, exhibiting a sight like that of the world; it would surely transport mankind with admiration of its beauty; and draw them off from those things which they now think great, merely through ignorance of what is really so. But because this is not to be expected, we must rest satisfied with beholding her under the same obscurity as we do the mysteries of the world.

The mind indeed of a philosopher comprehends the whole frame thereof, and passeth over it not less swiftly, than the eye over the visible heavens. But to us, who have as yet great darkness to break through, and whose sight faileth even in things that are near at hand, as we are not capable of receiving the whole, the parts separately considered are much more intelligible. I will endeavour therefore to grant your request; and will divide philosophy into parts, not into scraps; for it will be more proper to divide, than to hack it; since it is as difficult to comprehend the smallest things as the largest. It is usual therefore to divide a people into tribes, and an army into companies; whatever is very extraordinary, either in size or quantity, is much better known, I say, when divided into parts; provided they are not too numerous, or too small. Divisions too minute render a thing as intricate, as if no division had been made at all: subdivisions, as it were, to the least particle of dust, only create confusion.

First then I will ſhew you, *Lucilius*, according to your deſire, the diſtinction that is to be made between *Wiſdom* and *Philoſophy* (*a*). Wiſdom is the perfect good of the human mind; Philoſophy is the love and affectation of Wiſdom; ſhe points out the way thereto: the word *Philoſophy* diſcovers plainly enough what it is, and from whence it has its name; Wiſdom is by ſome defined, *the knowledge of things divine and human*; by others, *the knowledge of things divine and human, with their cauſes:* but this addition ſeems to me ſuperfluous, foraſmuch as the *cauſes* are parts of things human and divine. Philoſophy likewiſe hath been defined different ways; ſome have called it, *the ſtudy of virtue* (*b*); others, *the ſtudy of the mind's improvement*; and others ſtill, *an earneſt deſire of, or an inclination to, right reaſon.*

From whence it is plain there is a difference between Philoſophy and Wiſdom; for it is impoſſible the thing affecting ſhould be the ſame with the thing affected. As then there is a great difference between avarice and wealth; inaſmuch as that covets, and this is coveted; ſo is there between Philoſophy and Wiſdom; as this is the effect and reward of the other; the one is the road, the other the end of the journey. Wiſdom is what the Greeks call Σοφια, *Sophia*; the Romans likewiſe adopted the ſame word; and ſtill make uſe of it in *Philoſophia*. This is manifeſt from ſome antient comedies, and the inſcription on the monument of *Doſſennus* (*c*).

Hoſpes reſiſte, et *ſophiam* Doſſenni lege.
Stay, ſtranger, and learn the wiſdom of Doſſennus.

Some indeed of our ſect have thought, that though Philoſophy be *the ſtudy of virtue*, and *this* the thing ſought after, and *that* what ſeeks, yet they are ſo cloſely connected, as not to be divided; ſince neither is Philoſophy without virtue, nor virtue without Philoſophy. Philoſophy is the ſtudy of virtue, but by the means of Virtue itſelf; as there cannot be virtue but what delights in itſelf, nor a deſire of virtue but by virtue itſelf: for, it is not here, as when any thing is aimed at from afar, the perſon who takes aim is in one place, and the thing aimed at in another; nor as the ways that lead to a city, and are without; ſince the way to virtue is in and through itſelf; Philoſophy and virtue therefore coincide.

Again;

Again; many and very principal authors have divided Philoſophy into three parts (*d*), *moral*, *natural* and *rational*, or diſcourſive. The *firſt* frames and ſets in order the mind: the *ſecond* ſearches into the nature of things; and the *third* ſtudies the propriety of words, the ſtructure and manner of reaſoning, ſo as not to be impoſed upon by falſehood for truth. But there are thoſe who are pleaſed to divide Philoſophy, ſome into fewer, and ſome into more parts; ſome (for inſtance the *Ariſtotelians*) have added a fourth branch, the *civil*, or public; becauſe it is engaged in a peculiar exerciſe, and employed upon a different ſubject: and ſome have added to theſe another diviſion, which the Greeks call Οικονομικην, *œconomical*, or the art of managing family affairs. Some have likewiſe aſſigned a place to the different kinds and occupations of life: but there are none of all theſe but what come under the firſt diviſion, *Moral Philoſophy*.

On the other hand the *Epicureans* rejected the third branch (*e*), and only retained the two former, *Moral* and *Natural*; and being conſtrained in the examination of things to diſcern antiquities, and to diſcover the falſities, that are often concealed under the appearance of truth, they have given another name to the *rational*, and aſſigned it a place under the title of *judicial* and *regular* (*f*), but they ſtill look upon it only as an appendix to *natural* Philoſophy. The *Cyrenaics* take away both *natural* and *rational*; contenting themſelves with *moral* only; but they introduce, what they before rejected, in another way: for, they divide *moral* Philoſophy into five parts; one relating to things to be purſued or avoided; a ſecond, concerning the paſſions and affections; a third, concerning actions; a fourth, concerning cauſes; and a fifth concerning arguments: but the cauſes of things belong to *natural*; arguments to *rational*; and actions to *moral* Philoſophy. *Ariſto* of *Chios* (*g*) maintained that *natural* and *rational* Philoſophy were not only ſuperfluous but contrary; (Sc. *to Wiſdom and Virtue*) and the *moral*, which was the only one he allowed, he greatly maimed; foraſmuch as he aboliſhed that part which relates to *admonitions* (*h*), ſaying, that *this belonged rather to the Pedagogue than to the Philoſopher*; as if the wiſe man was any thing elſe than the *inſtructer* of mankind.

Concluding

Concluding therefore *Philosophy* to be rightly divided into three parts, we will begin with the *moral*. Now, *moral* Philosophy may likewise be divided into three parts; the first relates to diligence in giving suum cuique, every *one their own*; and estimating every thing according to its true worth. A very useful part indeed! For what can be more necessary than to set a due value upon things? The second regards power, or a desire to act; the third actions. By the first, you are taught to judge of things according to quantity or quality; by the second, to direct the affections, and moderate their impulse: and by the third, to suit your endeavours to the action; that in all things you may be consistent. Whatever is wanting of these three, the loss of it will disorder the rest. For what signifies it to be able to estimate all things rightly, if you have no command of yourself? Or what avails it to restrain the vehemence of desire, and to have the affections under command, if, as things may require, you know not the proper time, when, or what, or where, or how to act? For it is one thing to know the dignity and value of things, and another, to know times and seasons; and another, to restrain the vehemence of desire, so as to go calmly, and not rush precipitately, upon action. Life therefore is then consistent with itself, when the effort and the action agree together. An effort proceedeth from the dignity of things, and is either remiss or more earnest, according to the worthiness of the object pursued.

2. *Natural* Philosophy is twofold; as it relates to things corporeal, or incorporeal; and these again are divided, as I may so speak, into their several degrees. The part that relates to body, first considers the things that make or engender; and next the things that are made or engendered. Now, the elements are supposed to be made, or to receive being from another. Element is considered by some as a single topic; by others, as a subject divided into matter, and a *cause* moving all things, even the elements themselves (*i*).

3. And now as to the division of *rational* Philosophy. Every speech is either a continued one, or divided into question and answer: this they

they call διαλεκτικὴ, *dialectic*, or the art of logic; and the other, ῥητορικὴ, *rhetorical*. Rhetoric is concerned about the ſenſe and conſtruction of words; logic, or the dialectic, is divided into two parts, *viz.* words, and their ſignifications; i. e. into things which are ſpoken of, and the expreſſion in which they are delivered. And then follows too great a deſcription to be diſcuſſed at preſent; ſo here I ſhall conclude the ſubject,

——— Et ſumma ſequar faſtigia rerum,
And treat on things of higher conſequence;

Otherwiſe was I to enter on all the diviſions and ſubdiviſions it would ſwell this Epiſtle into a large volume of queſtions (*k*). I would not however deter you, *Lucilius*, from reading thoſe things, provided you immediately refer whatever you read to the improvement of *morals*. Study principally to correct theſe: ſtir up in you whatever ſeems languid; bind up the looſe; check the ſtubborn; and thwart, as much as you can, your own irregular deſires, and thoſe of the public; and ſhould the world ſay, *Will you be always in the ſame ſtrain of reproof?* make anſwer, *It is for me rather to ſay, Will ye be always giving the ſame offence? ye would have the remedies ceaſe, while the malady ſtill continues: it behoves me ſo much the more to ſpeak; and, becauſe ye are obſtinate, to perſevere in my reproof. A medicine begins to take effect, when a diſtempered body is ſenſible of pain, at being touched: refractory as ye are, I will ſtill utter ſuch things as, I think, will profit you; with words perhaps that may ſometimes prove not very ſmooth and agreeable: and, becauſe ye do not chuſe to hear them ſeverally, and in private, I thus exhort you publickly, and in general.*

" How far will ye extend the bounds of your poſſeſſions? A large " tract of land, ſufficient heretofore for a whole nation, is ſcarce wide " enough now for a ſingle Lord! How far will ye enlarge your " arable, not content with the tillage of whole provinces, which ye " hold only as a ſingle farm? Famous ſtreams running through pri- " vate grounds, and great rivers, the boundaries formerly of great " nations, from their fountain head to their mouth are yours: and " even this is not enough, unleſs you gird the ſeas within your eſtates;

" unleſs

" unleſs your bailiff extends his authority beyond the *Adriatic*, the " *Ionian*, and *Ægean* ſeas. Nay, unleſs the iſlands, the ſeat of ſome " great generals, be reckoned as inſignificant trifles. But go on; " extend your poſſeſſions as far as ye pleaſe; call it only a country " farm, which was once an empire; make all you can get your own; " there will ſtill be ſomething left for others."

A word or two now with you, whoſe luxury is as extenſive as the avarice of the former. I aſk you, " whether you intend to leave no " lake, but what the tops of your villas hang over? No river, whoſe " banks are not covered with your magnificent buildings? Shall " wherever any vein of warm water ſprings up, new baths be erected " to indulge you in luxury? Wherever the winding ſhore forms itſelf " into a bay will ye lay a foundation for building; and not content " with the firm ground, unleſs it be of your own making, drive the " ſeas before you, by flinging into it numberleſs loads of rubbiſh (*l*)? " But know, that ſplendid and pompous as your houſes are, in various " places; ſome raiſed on mountains, for a wide proſpect over ſea and " land; and others on the plain, to the height of mountains; build, " I ſay, as many as ye will, and as great; ye are ſtill, ſeverally conſi- " dered, but as a ſingle perſon, and a little, a very little, body. Of " what uſe are many ſtately bedchambers? you yourſelf can lie but in " one; and where you are not, that cannot be called *your's*."

Laſtly, I addreſs myſelf to you, whoſe throat is ſo deep and inſatiable, that every ſea and every land muſt be ranſacked for your proviſion. " Hence, with great toil and trouble, hooks, and ſnares, and va- " rious kinds of nets, are continually made uſe of in purſuit of prey. " No living animal can have peace, but ſuch as ye are already glutted " with. How little can you reliſh of thoſe banquets, prepared as they " are by ſo many hands, and at ſo great an expence, when ye ſit down " to them, with a mouth already palled with the like dainties? How " little of that wild boar, which was taken with ſo much hazard, can " the maſter eat, with a queaſy and loathing ſtomach? How few of " thoſe ſhell-fiſh, brought from afar, can the mouth that never thinks

" it has enough, devour? How wretched are ye not to know, that " *your eye*, as they ſay, *is bigger than your belly!*"

Let ſuch be your diſcourſe to others; and while you ſpeak, *Lucilius*, attend to what you ſay: and ſo write, that what you have wrote, you may read with pleaſure. Refer all to *Morality*, and to calming the rage of the headſtrong paſſions. Study not ſtill to know more, but, from what you know, to be a better man.

ANNOTATIONS, &c.

(*a*) They are generally confounded by the philoſophers; as when *Plato* ſays, Ἡ δέ γε φιλοσοφία, κτῆσις ἐπιστήμης, Philoſophy *is the acquiſition of* Wiſdom: and *Ariſtotle*, ἐπιστήμη τῆς ἀληθείας, *the knowledge of Truth.*—*Clemens Alexandrinus*, more agreeable to our author, *As the Liberal Sciences refer to* Philoſophy, *which is their miſtreſs, ſo does* Philoſophy *herſelf to* Wiſdom. And he adds, ὅτι γὰρ ἡ μὲν φιλοσοφία, ἐπιτήδευσις, ἡ σοφία δὲ, ἐπιστήμη θείων καὶ ἀνθρωπίνων, Philoſophy *is ſtudy and meditation; but* Wiſdom *the knowledge of things divine and human; and their cauſes.* Plutarch, Οἱ μὲν Στωικοὶ ἔφασαν, σοφίαν εἶναι θείων καὶ ἀνθρωπίνων ἐπιστήμην, *The Stoics ſaid, that* Wiſdom *was the knowledge of things divine and human.* Where we may obſerve, he with *Seneca* omits the *cauſes.* See other definitions, *Lipſ.* Phyſiol. p. 698.

(*b*) Many excellent paſſages, to this purpoſe, we meet with in *Cicero's Tuſculan* Diſputations: Philoſophy *is the culture of the mind, and plucketh up vice by the roots; it is the medicine of the ſoul, and healeth the minds of man; that from thence, if we would be good and happy, we may draw all proper helps and aſſiſtances for leading virtuous and happy lives.*—O Philoſophy, *thou guide of life! the ſearcher out of virtue, and expeller of vice! what ſhould we be, nay, what would human life be without thee! Thou calledſt us together into ſocial life; to thee we owe the invention of laws! thou teacher of manners and diſcipline! From thee we beg aſſiſtance: and one day ſpent according to thy precepts is preferable to an immortality ſpent in ſin.*—Some of the moderns have come little behind the antients, in the admiration they have expreſſed for the Heathen *moral Philoſophy*. See *Leland*, vol. ii. p. 72.

(*c*) *Fabius Doſſennus*, al. *Dorſennus*, a writer of comedies, (Atellanarum ſc. fabularum)

> Quantus ſit Dorſennus edacibus in paraſitis. Hor. Ep. ii. 1. 173.
> *How great is* Dorſenn *when he writes*
> *Of all-devouring paraſites!*

See *Plin.* xiv. 13. where you will find ſome quotations from him.

(*d*) There is the ſame diviſion in *Macrobius*, (Somn. Scip.) but differently explained: *Moralis*, quæ docet morum elimatam perfectionem; *Naturalis*, quæ de divinis corporibus diſputat; *Rationalis*, cùm de incorporibus ſermo eſt, quæ mens ſola complectitur, &c. l. ii. Moral, *which teacheth the perfection of moral behaviour;* Natural, *which treats of the heavenly bodies; and* Rational, *concerning things incorporeal, which the mind only can comprehend.*

(*e*) As ſuperfluous] *Laertius*, τὴν διαλεκτικὴν ὡς παρέλκουσαν ἀποδοκιμάζουσι.

(*f*) *Al.* τὸ κανονικὸν, *canonical.*] And this, as it forms, and prepares the mind, is said to be, περὶ κριτηρίου, καὶ ἀρχῆς, καὶ στοιχειώτατον, *Of the criterion, beginning and elementary.* Vid. *Laert.* in Epicurus.

(*g*) He was cotemporary with *Zeno*, and one of the disciples of the founder of the Stoical sect. He published several philosophical treatises, by which he acquired the reputation of an agreeable and elegant, rather than of a solid and judicious writer. See *Melmoth*, on *Cicero's* Cato, N. 5.

Laertius says of him, τόν τε φυσικὸν τόπον καὶ τὸν λογικὸν ἀνῄρει, λέγων τὸν μὲν εἶναι ὑπὲρ ἡμᾶς, τὸν δὲ οὐδὲν πρὸς ἡμᾶς. He took away from the common division, *both the* natural *and the* rational *part, saying*, this *was far above us, and* that *nothing to us.*

(*h*) Sc. τὸν παραινετικόν. See Ep. 94.

(*i*) i. e. God; or, as the *Stoics* speak sometimes, *His Reason*, or Wisdom: and by *elements*, we understand, the first and constituent principles of things, as derived from him.

(*k*) *Lipsius* observes that in some books, this is the beginning of another Epistle.

(*l*) Hor. Carm. iii. 1. 34.

Contracta pisces æquora sentiunt
Iactis in altum molibus. Huc frequens
Cæmenta remittit redemptor
Cum famulis, dominusque terræ
Fastidiosus.

The fish that in the ocean rang'd
Perceive their territories chang'd.
The moles thrown in extend the shore;
The Lord grown weary of the land,
New builds upon the settled sand,
And scorns the bounds that Nature fix'd before.

Sallust. Bell. Cat. Quid ea memorem, quæ nisi his qui vidêre, nemini credibilia sunt? A privatis compluribus subversos montes, maria constrata, &c. *What need I mention other things, that will hardly meet with credit from those who have been eyewitnesses of their truth? such as levelling hills and mountains, and raising palaces in the sea itself by private men for the purposes of pleasure*, &c. See also *Suetonius in Caligula*, c. 37.

Petronius, l. ii. ——— Aspice latè
Luxuriam spoliorum, et censum in damna furentem.
Ædificant auro sedesque ad sidera mittunt.
Expelluntur aquæ saxis; mare nascitur arvis;
Et permutatâ rerum statione rebellant.

See, all around luxurious trophies lie,
And their decreasing wealth new ills supply.
Here golden piles the azure skies invade,
There in the sea incroaching moles are made —
Inverted Nature's injur'd laws they wrong——

Hor. Carm. ii. 18. 20. Marisque Baiis obstrepentis urges
Summovere littora,
Parum locuples continente ripâ.

The moles and thy encroaching mounds
Remove the floods to straiter bounds;
For greedy you would seem but poor,
Confin'd by Nature's narrow shore. Creech.

But as some read in *Seneca*, *arva*, instead of *maria*, we may apply the words that follow in *Horace*:

Quid quod usque proximos
Revellis agri terminos, et ultra
Limites clientium
Salis avarus?—
Nay more, you pass the sacred bounds,
And seize your meaner client's grounds;
No fence too high, no ditch too deep,
For wealthy injury to leap. Id.

EPISTLE XC.

On Philosophy, and the Invention of Arts.

WHO can doubt, my *Lucilius*, but that it is from the blessing and gift of the immortal Gods that we live; but from *Philosophy* that we live well (*a*)? that consequently we owe more to this than to the Gods; inasmuch as a good life is better than mere existence. Undoubtedly we ought to think so, unless Philosophy itself might be also thought the gift of the Gods (*b*), the knowledge whereof they have given to no one, but the ability of acquirement to all. For if they had vouchsafed this as a common good, and we had been all born good, wisdom would have lost what is of greatest account therein, *that it is not to be reckoned among casual things*: for it hath this most precious and noble quality, that it comes not accidentally; that every one owes it to himself, an acquisition not to be sought for elsewhere *. What would there be in Philosophy worthy admiration, if it was holden of the donor? One of her principal offices is to search out truth, in things both divine and human: justice, piety, religion, and the whole train of virtues, that are in perfect union with one another, are all attendant upon her: she teacheth us to worship God, and to love our neighbour (*c*); that government is the prerogative of heaven †; and the social virtues necessary upon earth; which for some time remained

 pure

pure and inviolate, before covetousness distracted society; and introduced poverty even among those whom she had most enriched: for they ceased to possess all things, when they began to call any thing their own.

But the first men and their immediate descendants followed Nature; pure and uncorrupt; and held the same both for their leader and the law; by an orderly submission of the worse to the better: for this was ever the rule of simple Nature. In the brute creation the strongest and most fierce generally preside; nor does a bull of a cowardly spirit ever lead the herd; but he that is master over the rest by his strength and magnitude; as among elephants the tallest; so among men the best was chief: according to the endowments of the mind a ruler was chosen. Exquisitely happy then must the people have been, among whom none could obtain power but he that was a good man: for he may do whatever he pleases, who thinks he can do no more than what he ought to do. *Posidonius* therefore judgeth, that wise men only ruled in the age that was called *the golden*. These tied down the hands of the populace to good behaviour; and even defended the weak from the more strong. They persuaded to good, and dissuaded from evil (*d*); shewing what things were useful and profitable, and what the contrary. By their prudence they took care that nothing should be wanting to their subjects: by their fortitude they encreased and enriched their people: to rule was not looked upon as a lordship, but as an office; not to tyrannize, but to be the ministers of God (*e*). No one therefore was ambitious to try his power over those who had raised him to that power; nor was there any inclination to do an injury; nor any cause for it; while the due administration of government challenged due obedience; and a King could threaten nothing more grievous to the disobedient than that he would leave the kingdom.

But when, vices having crept in, Kings were obliged to shew their authority, then was there a necessity for making penal laws, which the wise men were at first the authors of: as *Solon*, who founded the *Athenian* state on the laws of equity, was numbered among the seven sages,

ſages, remarkable for their wiſdom in that age (*f*). And had *Lycurgus* been then living, he had juſtly been reputed the eighth in that ſacred order. The laws alſo of *Zaleneus* and of *Charondas* (*g*) are highly commended: and theſe men learned the ſtatutes, (which they publiſhed and eſtabliſhed throughout *Sicily*, then in a flouriſhing ſtate, and which through *Italy* paſſed into *Greece*) not at the bar, nor in the courts of law, but in the ſilent and ſacred ſchool of *Pythagoras*.

Hitherto then I agree with *Poſidonius* (*h*), but I deny that thoſe arts which are in daily uſe for the neceſſaries of life, were the invention of Philoſophy; nor will I give ſo great an honour to the workſhop. He ſaith indeed that Philoſophy taught men when they were ſcattered up and down, and lived in cottages, and in hollow rocks, and in the trunks of decayed trees, to build houſes: but I can no more think that Philoſophy taught them to build houſes upon houſes, and turrets upon turrets, than that it inſtructed them in making ſtews and fiſhponds; to the intent that the gormandizing throat might not run any hazard in ſtormy weather; and that, let the ſea rage as it will, luxury might ſtill have its quiet waters, wherein to fatten fiſh of every kind.

And what do you ſay, that Philoſophy taught the uſe of locks and keys! Pray what can be a greater ſign of timid avarice? Or was it Philoſophy that formed theſe lofty geometrical roofs to the great danger of the inhabitants? as if it was not ſufficient to meet with a chance covering; and natural for man, without any art or difficulty, to find reſt for himſelf in ſome proper habitation? Believe me, *Lucilius*, the happy age before mentioned, knew not either maſons or carpenters; whoſe art in ſquaring and ſawing timber by the line, ſo as to make a beam of juſt proportion, ſprung up with the luxury of after-ages.

(Nam primis cuneis ſciendebant fiſſile lignum.) Virg. G. i. 146.
Then ſaws were tooth'd and ſounding axes made,
(For wedges firſt did yielding wood invade.) Dryden.

For they had no banqueting-houſes for the entertainment of numerous gueſts (*i*); nor to this uſe were whole pines and fir-trees dragged along the trembling ſtreets (*k*) in a long train of carriages, in order to form therewith large cielings, decorated with maffey gold; two forked ſticks at ſome little diſtance, with poles acroſs, ſupported the roofs of their little tenements; which being covered with dry ſticks and leaves plaiſtered together, and laid ſloping, proved ſufficient to throw off a ſhower of rain, was it ever ſo great; and under theſe roofs they lived in peace and ſecurity. Thatch covered men that were free, but ſlavery now dwells under marble and gold.

I likewiſe differ from *Poſidonius*, in that he thought all working tools made of iron the invention of wiſe men: for he might as well call them wiſe by whoſe invention men firſt began:

> Tum lequeis captare feros, et fallere viſco
> Inventum, et magnis canibus circumdare ſaltus. Virg. G. i. 140.
> *Thus toils for beaſts, and lime for birds were found;*
> *While deep-mouth'd dogs the foreſt-walks ſurround.* Dryden.

For it was the cunning and ſagacity, not the wiſdom of man, that firſt found out theſe things. I alſo diſſent from him in ſuppoſing they were wiſe men, who found out the ſeveral metals, iron and braſs: when the earth being accidentally heated with fires enkindled in the woods, melted the ore, and by pouring it forth, diſcovered the veins of thoſe metals that lay neareſt the ſurface: ſuch men as honour theſe things, generally find them out.

Nor does that ſeem ſo ſubtle a queſtion to me as to *Poſidonius*;—*whether the hammer or the pincers were firſt in uſe.* Some one no doubt of ingenuity and acute parts, though not very great and ſublime, found out theſe things, and whatever elſe was to be ſought for, with a body bowed to the ground, and a groveling mind. A wiſe man took not ſo much pains to live: no wonder, ſince even in this age he deſires to be as eaſy as poſſible. How, I pray you, is it conſiſtent, to admire both *Diogenes* and *Talus* (*l*)? which of them, think ye, was the wiſer man? He that invented the ſaw; or he that, upon ſeeing a boy drink out of the hollow of his hand, immediately took his cup out of his pouch and brake it, thus reproving himſelf; *How long, fooliſh man as I was,*

have

have I carried about me a ſuperfluous burthen? I am ſpeaking of that *Diogenes*, who, folding himſelf double, lived in a tub.

And which, at this day, do you think the wiſer man; him, who contrived to raiſe to a great height, and ſprinkle around ſaffron or roſe-water from hidden pipes (*m*), and to fill the canals with a ſudden flow of water, and again to empty them; and ſo to couch together the changeable roofs of our banqueting houſes (*n*), that one ſcene may ſucceed another; and a new cieling appear upon every change of the diſhes: or him, who can demonſtrate to himſelf and others, that Nature requires nothing of us that is hard and difficult; that we can very well live without maſons, and be clothed without trafficking with the Indians for ſilk; and have every thing that is neceſſary for the uſes of life, were we content with ſuch things as the earth produceth on its ſurface? which things, if mankind would give their attention to, we ſhould find there would be no more need of cooks than of a ſtanding army.

They were certainly wiſe men, or ſomething like it, who were not over-anxious with regard to the care and protection of the body. Neceſſary things coſt but little trouble; men muſt labour for dainties; you will not want artificers if you follow Nature: ſhe would not have us embarraſſed: ſhe can eaſily equip us with every thing we want. Wintry cold is certainly intolerable to our naked body: what then? cannot the ſkins of wild beaſts or other animals defend us from it? do not ſome nations cover their bodies with the inner barks of trees, and others dreſs themſelves with the feathers of birds (*o*), ſown together? Do not great part of the *Scythians* cloath themſelves with the ſkins of foxes and ermins (*p*), ſoft to the touch, and impenetrable to the winds? And what if there is need of a thicker ſhade to repel the heat of the ſummer's ſun; has not length of time or other accidents ſcooped out caves and places fit for a cool retirement? And have not men wove hurdles of twigs, and plaiſtered them with vile clay; and alſo with ſtraw and reeds made coverings for their cottages, wherein they have paſſed their winters dry and ſecure? Do not the *Syrtic* people (*q*) live in holes dug under ground, where nothing elſe could defend them

from

from the exceſſive heat of the ſun? Nature was never ſo cruel to man, that, ſeeing ſhe had provided an eaſy means of life for all other creatures, man alone ſhould not be able to live, were it not for the invention of ſo many arts as are now in uſe; none of which ſhe abſolutely demands of us; nor in order to prolong life need there any thing be ſought, with care and difficulty. Neceſſaries are provided for us at our birth; all difficulties ariſe from a diſdain of things every-where to be obtained. Houſes, clothing, medicine, food, and what are now thought a weighty concern, were obvious, freely given, or procured with little pains. For what neceſſity required, was the meaſure of all things. We ourſelves made them rare and precious, and not to be obtained but by extraordinary arts. Nature is ſufficient for her own demands. Luxury is a revolt from Nature. She is daily provoking herſelf with new temptations; and in ſo many ages hath been ſtill encreaſing, and aſſiſting every vice with her ingenious fancies. At firſt ſhe began to deſire ſuperfluities, and then contraries; and at laſt hath entirely devoted the mind (*r*) to the body, and commanded it to ſerve the luſts thereof.

All thoſe arts wherein cities are exerciſed, and ſo buſily employed, carry on the affairs of the body; which formerly was treated only as a ſervant; but now is waited on as an imperious Lord (*s*). Hence the many ſhops of weavers and ſmiths; hence your perfumers; and a tribe of dancing-maſters to teach the body a ſoft and delicate motion; and of ſinging-maſters to modulate the voice into quavers and looſe airs. The natural mean, which bounded all deſires with a ſupply of neceſſaries, is quite forſaken. It is now thought clowniſhneſs and miſerable, to wiſh for no more than is enough. It is incredible, *Lucilius*, to think eaſily how a few ſoft and ſweet words can draw even great men from the truth of things. Behold *Poſidonius*, who, it muſt be owned, hath contributed much to Philoſophy, yet how does he trifle when he is deſcribing, firſt, how ſome threads may be hard-ſpun, and other ſome drawn out fine from the ſoft and looſened tow; and then how a web of cloth may be ſtretched in the loom by hanging weights thereon; and how the woof is woven in to take off the roughneſs of the threads uſed

in

in the shuttle, and then with the slay to make them unite and thicken the cloth! He was pleased also to say, that the whole art of weaving was the invention of *wise men*, forgetting that more subtile way, which was afterwards found out, wherein

> Tela jugo juncta est, stamen secernit arundo:
> Inseritur medium radiis subtemen acutis,
> Quod lato feriunt insecti pectine dentes (*t*).
> *The web inwraps the beam, the reed divides,*
> *While through the widening space the shuttle glides;*
> *Which the swift hand receives; then pois'd with lead*
> *The swinging weight strikes close th' inserted thread.* Sewell.

What if he had seen the weaving of our days; whereby they make our apparel so very fine that it conceals nothing beneath it. I do not say that it is no covering to the body, but it does not even hide our shame (*u*).

He then passeth on to the husbandman; nor less elegantly describes the soil, as torn up, and renewed by the plough (*x*), that the loosen'd earth may the more easily permit the roots to shoot out; and then he describes the manner of sowing several sorts of seeds, and of plucking up the weeds by hand, that no casual and wild plants may choak the corn. This he likewise attributes to the invention of the wise men; as if in our days there are not many things invented by our farmers to render the ground more fertile.

And not contented with these arts alone, he thrusts the wise man into the bakehouse; and tells you that from an imitation of Nature, he first began to make bread. For observing, says he, that whenever grain is put into the mouth, by joining the hard teeth together, it is broken in pieces, and what escapes this pressure is gathered and put under it again by the tongue; and then it is mingled with spittle, to pass the more glibly down the throat; and when it comes into the stomach it is there digested, by the natural heat of the maw; and at last is converted into nutriment, and the substance of the body. The wise man, he saith, observing this operation of Nature, first placed one rough ſtone upon another, to reſemble teeth, the upper part of which, being immoveable, expects the motion of the other, and then, by theſe rubbing together, the grain between them is broken, and well pounded, 'till it is reduced to meal; this he then ſprinkled with water, and by kneading it into dough, made bread thereof: which at firſt they baked under warm aſhes, or upon a hot tile or ſtone; and after this ovens were invented, and other kinds of ſtoves, to be heated, as would beſt ſerve the turn.

It is a wonder he did not tell us that the ſhoemaker's art was alſo owing to the *wiſe men* (*y*); all theſe things indeed were the invention of Reaſon, but not of philoſophic Reaſon: they are the invention of man, but not of a *wiſe man*, any more than ſhips: in which men paſs over great rivers, and even the ſea itſelf; the ſails being fitted to receive the force of the winds, and rudders being joined to the ſtern of the ſhip, which turn it either one way or the other. And this was learned from obſerving how fiſh guide themſelves by their tails, and by the leaſt motion thereof give a direction to their ſwiftneſs.

All theſe things, ſaith *Poſidonius*, were invented by ſome *wiſe man*, but being too low for himſelf to be concerned with, he left the working part to meaner heads. But in truth theſe things were invented by none other men than ſuch as are living at this day, and who buſy themſelves therein. We know that in our time many inventions have been firſt publiſhed; for inſtance, the windows made of fine tranſparent tiles (*z*); alſo hanging baths (*aa*); and pipes, of ſtoves, ſo concealed in the walls as to ſpread an equal heat through every part of the room: not to mention ſeveral works in marble, by which our temples, and even our houſes are ſo finely decorated: or the huge piles of ſtone (pillars) which being made round and ſmooth form our portico's, and ſupport ſuch ſpacious buildings as will contain a multitude of people: nor need I mention the cyphers and characters (*bb*) whereby a man can take down a whole oration, be it ever ſo ſwiftly pronounced, and with his hand keep pace with the ſpeaker's tongue. Theſe are, or may be, the invention of the meaneſt ſlaves.

True

True wiſdom ſitteth aloft, and inſtructeth not the hand, but the mind. Would you know what is of her invention, and what her work? Not the unſeemly motions of the body in dancing; not the flute or the trumpet, through which the breath paſſing or held, gives the tone of a voice; not weapons, nor walls, or the art of war; ſhe contrives things of more uſe and conſequence; ſhe loves peace, and invites mankind to amity; ſhe is not, I ſay, the author of inſtruments even for neceſſary uſes; ſhe forms the life and manners; and hath indeed all the other arts in ſubjection. For as life, ſo all the ornaments of life are ſubſervient to her: but her chief end is *bleſſedneſs*; thither ſhe leads; thither ſhe opens to us the way. She ſheweth us what is truly evil, and what only ſeems ſo; ſhe roots out vanity from the mind, and implanteth ſolid greatneſs: all that is arrogant and pompous without foundation, ſhe entirely ſuppreſſeth; nor ſuffers men to be ignorant of the difference between grandeur and a proud appearance; ſhe giveth the knowledge of all Nature, and particularly of herſelf: ſhe alſo teacheth who, and what the gods are, the infernal, the houſehold, the guardian (*cc*): and what thoſe ever-living ſouls, that are admitted in the ſecond rank of deities (*dd*); where they dwell (*ee*); how employed (*ff*); what their power, and their will.

Theſe are the firſt principles, or grounds, wherein ſhe inſtructs her pupils; and by which no private hallowed place, but this univerſe, the great temple of all the gods (*gg*), is open to them; the true images whereof, and true repreſentations, ſhe diſcovers to the eyes of the underſtanding; thoſe of the body being too dull to diſcern ſuch a great and noble object. She then goes back to the beginning of things, and ſheweth eternal wiſdom diffuſed throughout the whole; and the power of every ſeed forming its own particular body (*hh*). She next enquires into the nature of the ſoul; from whence it was derived, where it ſubſiſts, how long, and into how many parts to be diſtinguiſhed (*ii*). And thus ſhe paſſeth on from things corporeal, to things incorporeal, examining the truth and all the arguments relating thereto. After this ſhe points out the ambiguities concerning life and death (*kk*); for on both these topics many false things are often blended with truth.

But to return: it was not, as *Posidonius* thinks, that the *wise man* withdrew himself from the forementioned arts: he was never in the least concerned with them; for he would not think any thing worthy his invention, that he did not think worthy of perpetual use; he would never admit what was to be dismissed. *Anacharsis*, he tells us, invented the potters wheel (*ll*), by the turning whereof vessels were differently fashioned: and because mention is made in *Homer* of the potter's wheel, he had rather the verses should be thought spurious, than his story. I will not contend whether *Anacharsis* was the author of this wheel or not: but supposing he was, a wise man then invented it, but not as being a *wise man*; since wise men do many things as men, not as being wise. Suppose a *wise man* could outrun all his cotemporaries; this would not be owing to his wisdom but to his agility, and swiftness of foot. I could wish *Posidonius* was now to see some of our glass-makers, who with their breath alone fashion glass into diverse shapes, which is more than an artist could do with the most industrious and careful hand. And these things were found out, long since a wise man was to be found among us.

Democritus, he saith, is reported to be the inventor of an arch, or vaulted roof; when two stones inclining gradually to one another, are pinned together by another stone between them, that binds upon them both. But this I take to be false, as there must have been bridges and gateways, whose upper part generally forms an arch, long before the time of *Democritus*. It must be remembered too, that the same *Democritus* is said to have found the way of softening ivory (*mm*); and by a certain degree of heat, to change a pebble into an emerald; which art is made use of in colouring bricks and stones to this day. But however I say a *wise man* may find out these things, the invention is not owing to him merely as a *wise man*; for a wise man does many things, which a blockhead may perform as well, or better, and with more expedition.

Do

Do you aſk me then, what I take to be the inveſtigation of a wiſe man, and what accordingly he hath publiſhed to the world? *Firſt*, the true nature of things; which he looked not upon, as other animals do, with eyes too weak and dull for divine matters: *next*, the law of life, which he directed to the good of the whole; and not only taught us to know, but to imitate *the Gods* (*nn*); and to receive all accidents with as much æquanimity as if they were ordered by the will of heaven (*oo*). He forbade us to be carried away with falſe opinions (*pp*): he hath weighed every thing in the balance, and eſtimates them truly according to their worth. He hath condemned all pleaſures that are bought with repentance; he hath recommended what is good (*qq*), as what will always pleaſe; and made it manifeſt, that he is the happieſt man who is happy in himſelf alone; and he the moſt powerful, who hath power over, and can command, himſelf.

I am not ſpeaking of that philoſophy (*the Epicurean*) which looked upon a man, as a citizen, ſuppoſe, of the world, unconcerned for his own country; and who diſcharged the Gods of any concern with human affairs, and who made pleaſure a virtue; but of that philoſophy (ſc. the *Stoic*) which thinks nothing good but what is fit and honourable; which is not to be corrupted by the gifts of man or fortune; and whoſe principal value conſiſts in not being to be bought by any thing how valuable ſoever. Now, I do not think this Philoſophy was extant in the firſt rude age of the world, when as yet all arts were wanting, and men were continually learning the uſefulneſs of things from the uſe itſelf; as, before thoſe happy times, when the benefits of Nature lay in common, and were uſed promiſcuouſly; nor had avarice and luxury diſunited mortals, and made them prey upon one another, there were no *wiſe men*, though in many reſpects they acted as ſuch. The ſtate however of mankind was ſuch, that I know of none to be more admired: nor, if God permitted man to form, as he would, terreſtrial things, and to eſtabliſh ſuch manners, as he pleaſed, among the nations, would he approve of any thing more than what is ſaid to be found among thoſe, with whom

—— Nulli

—— Nulli ſubigebant arva coloni
Nec ſignare quidem, aut partiri limite campum,
Fas erat; in medium quærebant, ipſaque tellus
Omnia liberius, nullo poſcente, ferebat.
Ere this no peaſant vex'd the peaceful ground,
Which only turf and greens for altars found;
No fences parted fields, nor marks nor bounds
Diſtinguiſh'd acres of litigious grounds;
But all was common, and the fruitful earth
Was free to give her unexpected birth. Dryden.

What could be happier than the race of man? They enjoyed all Nature in common; ſhe as a kind parent was the protectreſs of all men; and gave them ſecure poſſeſſion of the public wealth. Why ſhould not I think them the richeſt of all people, among whom there was not to be found one poor man? But avarice ſoon broke in upon the world under this happy diſpoſition; and while ſhe endeavoured to appropriate ſomething to her own uſe, ſhe hereby made every thing the property of others; and being reduced into narrow ſtraights, from unmeaſurable grandeur ſhe introduced poverty; and, from coveting many things, loſt all. Though now therefore ſhe would fain recover her pretended rights (*ss*), and repair her loſſes;—though ſhe is ſtill adding field to field, and continually driving her neighbours from their poſſeſſions, either by force or purchaſe;—though ſhe extends her lands to an equality with provinces;—and though it requires a long journey to go over all that ſhe can call her own; yet no enlargement of our bounds whatever, can bring us back to the ſtate we were in before: having done all we can, we ſhall indeed poſſeſs much, but then we were in poſſeſſion of all.

The earth itſelf was the more fruitful without any laborious tillage; and bountiful enough for the uſe of a people not given to plunder. Whatever Nature brought forth, they took not more pleaſure in enjoying, than in ſhewing it to their brethren: nor could any one have either too much or too little, when every one was ſatisfied with their own ſhare. The ſtronger man had not yet laid his hands upon the weak and feeble; nor had the covetous man, by hoarding treaſure, excluded others even from neceſſaries: every one had the ſame concern for his neighbour as for himſelf: war was not heard of; nor were any hands ſtained with human blood: all hatred and animoſity was exerciſed on wild beaſts alone. The peaſants whom ſome thick wood protected from the ſcorching rays of the ſun, and who lived ſafe from the inclemency of ſhowers and wintry ſtorms under the covering of their homely cottages, paſſed their nights in tranquillity without a ſigh or groan; while anxiety and trouble diſturb *us* under a purple covering, and keep us waking with the ſharpeſt ſtings; the hard ground lulled *them* in ſoft repoſe (*tt*). They had no carved roofs hanging over their heads; but often lying in the open air they were canopied by the ſtars; and ſaw (what a glorious ſight in the night-time!) the heavens rolling along, and carrying on their great work in ſilence.

Nor did the proſpect of this their large and moſt beautiful manſion leſs entertain them by day than by night. What a pleaſure muſt it have been to ſee the *ſigns*, ſome declining from the middle part of the heavens, and others riſing from their ſecret places! How could it but delight them to wander among miracles ſcattered every where ſo thick! whereas *ye* now tremble at the leaſt crack or noiſe in the houſe; and fly away aſtoniſhed at an accidental ſound behind your pictures. They had no houſes as large as a city (*uu*); but lived in the free and open air; the ſhade of ſome rock or tree, clear fountains, and rivers, not made with labour, or conveyed through pipes, but gently flowing, of themſelves, through meadows not adorned with artificial beauty, and amidſt theſe a little tenement built by ſome ruſtic hand; theſe were the ſweet bleſſings they enjoyed; this the dwelling-place aſſigned by Nature, the inhabitants whereof were in no fear, either from it, or for it; whereas great part of our fear now ariſeth merely from our houſes.

But excellent as their life was and void of all deceit, they were not however *the wiſe men* (*xx*); becauſe this title relates to a perfect work: nevertheleſs I would not deny they were men of a noble ſpirit; and, if I may

I may ſo ſpeak, the immediate offspring of the gods *(yy)*. Nor is there any doubt but that the world, as yet under no decay, produced better things than now. But however they might have ſtronger natural parts, and were better made and diſpoſed for labour; yet their judgment was not complete and perfect in all things: for Virtue is not the gift of Nature; it is really an art or ſcience to become *good*. They indeed ſought not gold, or ſilver, or precious ſtones in the bowels of the earth; they likewiſe ſpared many animals (*zz*); ſo far were they from ſeeing one man kill another in cool blood, without fear, and by way of paſtime. Their garments were not as yet dyed with any colour, nor embroidered with gold; for gold in thoſe days was not ſeen above the earth. What then? they were innocent through ignorance; and there is a great difference between a man's being unwilling to ſin, and being a ſtranger to it. They really wanted juſtice, prudence, temperance and fortitude; 'tis true there was ſome things in this rude ſtate of Nature that reſembled theſe Virtues; but Virtue belongeth not to a mind, that hath not been taught, and inſtructed, and brought to perfection by continual exerciſe. To this indeed we are born, but born without it: and in the beſt of men without ſtudy and application, there is a capacity for Virtue, but not Virtue itſelf.

ANNOTATIONS, &c.

(*a*) And for this reaſon *Ariſtotle* ſays we owe more to the philoſophers, than to our parents, τὺς μὲν γὰρ τῦ ζῆν, τὺς δὲ τῦ καλῶς ζῆν παρασχέσθαι.—The Chriſtian acknowledgeth an higher obligation, viz. The *grace of God*. i. Cor. 15, 10. But *by the grace of God I am what I am. And his grace which was beſtowed upon me was not in vain: but I laboured more abundantly than they all; yet not I, but the grace of God that was with me.*

(*b*) Philoſophia verò, omnium mater artium, quid eſt aliud niſi ut *Plato* ait, *donum*, ut ego inventum, deorum? *What is philoſophy, but as* Plato *calls it the gift; and I, ſays* Cicero, the invention *of the Gods?* (Tuſc. Diſp. i. 26.) The ſame, (de leg. i. 22.) Nihil a Diis immortalibus uberius, nihil florentius, nihil præſtabilius hominum vitæ datum eſt. *Nothing more excellent, more beautiful, more uſeful, more profitable was ever given by the immortal Gods for the benefit of human life.* Plato (*in his* Timæus) carries it farther, for he ſays not only that *no greater good ever was given, but ever will be given by the favour and bounty of the Gods to the human race*; thus tranſlated by *Cicero*—Quo bono nullum optabilius nullum præſtantius, neque datum eſt immortalium Deorum conceſſu atque munere, neque dabitur. (Fragm. de Univ. c. 14.) See Leland, i. p. 231,

• See (N. 2.)

(*c*) This

(*c*) This is likewise a summary of Christian Philosophy; for *on the love of God and our neighbour hang all the law and the Prophets.* Matth. 22. 40. And it is the principal command of the Apostles, *to fear God, and to love our brethren.* i. Pet. 2. 17. *The Lord shall reign for ever and ever.* Ex. 15. 18. Pf. x. 16. cxlv. 13.

(*d*) So the Prophet *Isaiah*, *Cease to do evil, learn to do well.* i. 16. *Abhor that which is evil, cleave to that which is good.* Rom. 12. 9. And the Apostle *St. Peter*, *Eschew evil, and do good.* i. 3. 11.

(*e*) Officium erat imperare non regnum] *For he* (a ruler) *is the Minister of God to thee for good.* Rom. xiv. 4.

(*f*) About the time of *Josias*, K. of *Judah*, A. M. 3310.—Their names, *Thales*, *Solon*, *Periander*, *Cleobulus*, *Chilo*, *Bias*, *Pittacus*.

(*g*) *Many learned and good men* (καλοὺς καὶ ἀγαθοὺς) *hath* Italy *produced, particularly the lawgivers,* Zaleucus *and* Charondas. They are likewise mentioned together in *Cic.* de Leg. 1. 22. For part of their history, see *Val. Max.* 6. 5.

Zaleucus, (the *Locrian*, who may be regarded as having been a wise philosopher as well as a lawgiver, in his celebrated proœmium or preface to his laws) saith, that *all men ought first to be persuaded of the existence of the Gods, especially when they look up to heaven, and contemplate the world, and the orderly and beautiful disposition of things—And that they ought to worship and honour them as the authors of all the real good things that befall us.* See *Leland*, i. p. 78.

(*h*) What *Cicero* saith of philosophy he took from *Posidonius*: Tu eas inter se primò domiciliis, deinde conjugiis, tum literarum et vocum communione junxisti. *It was philosophy that first taught mankind to provide themselves with proper habitations and to unite in the bonds of wedlock and freedom of conversation.*

Sed nemora atque cavos montes, sylvasque colebant,
Verbera ventorum vitare, imbresque coacti.
Nec commune bonum poterant spectare, nec ullis
Moribus inter se scibant nec legibus uti.——
Inde casas, postquam ac pelles, ignemque parârunt
Et mulier conjuncta viro concessit in unum.——
Tum genus humanum primùm mollescere cœpit. *Lucret.* 5. 953.

They knew no use of fire to dress their food,
No clothes, but wander'd naked in the wood;
They liv'd, to shady groves and caves confin'd;
Mean shelter from the cold, the heat, the wind.
No fix'd society, no steady laws,
No public good was sought, no common cause:——
But when they built their huts, and fire began,
And skins of murther'd beasts gave clothes to man;
When male with female join'd in chaste embrace,
Enjoy'd sweet love, and saw a num'rous race,
Then man grew soft, the temper of his mind
Was chang'd from rough to mild, from fierce to kind. Creech.

(*i*) Cænationi epulum] *Lipsius* conjectures *populum*; so, *Seneca*; Ep. 115. Capacem populi cœnationem.

(*k*) Viais intrementibus] So *Juvenal*, iii. 254.

——— modo longa coruscat
Sarraco veniente abies, atque altera pinum
Plaustra vehunt, nutant altè, populoque minantur.
Unwieldy timber-trees in waggons born,
Stretch'd at their length beyond their carriage lie;
That nod, and threaten ruin from on high. Dryden.

(*l*) The invention of the *saw* is given by some to *Dædalus*, *Plin*. 7. 57. Fabricam materiariam Dædalus (invenit) et in eâ serram, asciam, *the saw, the ax*, &c. Others give it *Talus*, as *Isidor*. 19. Origen. 19, *Hyginus*, Fab. 174, and particularly *Diodorus Sic*. l. 4. So *Ovid*, but without naming him,

Ille etiam medio spinas in pisce notatas
Traxit in exemplum: ferroque incidit acuto
Perpetuos dentes, et serræ repperit usum.———
Dædalus invidit sacrâque ex arce Minervæ
Præcipitem mittit, lapsum mentitus.———
He marks the bones which in the fish he spies,
Where rows of dents appear of equal size.
Then dents, like those, in harden'd steel he makes,
And hence the saw *its first foundation takes.*
But Dædalus *his skill with envy views,*
And with inhuman rage his death pursues;
From off Minerva's *tow'r he threw the youth,*
And with a lye conceal'd the fatal truth.

Not so the master of the youth, who built the beautiful tower of *Bray* (in *Berkshire*) who (by tradition) through envy, flung himself from the top of the said tower.

(*m*) *Quest. Nat*. l. ii. Nunquid dubitas quin sparsio illa, quæ ex fundamentis mediæ arenæ crescens, in summam altitudinem Amphitheatri pervenit, cum intentione aquæ fiat?—That this extravagant sprinkling, or *sweet-scented shower* was made of wine, wherein *saffron* was particularly infused, and other perfumes, we learn from *Apuleius*, l. x. Tunc de summo montis cacumine *per quandam latentem fistulam* in excelsum prorumpit *vino crocus diluto*, sparsimque defluens pascentes circa capellas odorato perpluit imbre.—*Martial*, v. 26.

Hoc rogo, non melius, quam rubro pulpita nimbo
Spargere, et effuso permaduisse croco?
Is not this better in a trifling age,
Than with sweet water to perfume the stage?

And not only from pipes but from the statues themselves oozed this sort of perfume.

Utque solet pariter totis effundere signis
Corycii pressura croci: sic omnia membra
Emisere simul rutilum pro sanguine virus. Lucan. 9. 808.
And as when mighty Rome's *spectators meet,*
In the full Theatre's capacious seat,
At once by secret pipes and channels fed,
Rich tinctures gush from ev'ry antique head;

At once ten thousand saffron currents flow,
And rain their odours on the crowd below.—Rowe.

Vid Lipſ. de Amphitheat. p. 1034.

(*n*) Which (ſays *Suetonius*, in his life of *Nero*, c. 31.) were whirled round, vice mundi, *like the world*. *Lampridius* makes mention of the ſame in his life of *Heliogabalus*, *who ſtifled ſome of his paraſites with violets and roſes, before they could get up again*. Oppreſſit in *tricliniis verſatilibus* paraſitos ſuos violis et floribus, ſic ut animam aliqui efflaverint, cum eripi ad ſummam non poſſent. *Fulv. Urſin.* in Append. Ciacconii de Triclinio.

(*o*) As *Philoctetes* ſays (in Attio, ap. Cic.)

Configo tardus celeres, ſtans, volatiles,
Pro veſte pennis membra textis contegens.
The winged tribe fall wounded at my feet,
Whoſe painted feathers my warm veſt complete.

As we hear and read of the wild *Indians*.

(*p*) Tergis vulpium ac murium] The antients underſtood by the word Mus, not only that little domeſtic animals we call *a mouſe*, but all the wild ones of a ſmall kind, as *ferret*, *weaſel*, *ermin*, and the like. See Turneb. Adv. 15. 23.

So *Juſtin*. l. 2. ſpeaking likewiſe of *Scythians*, ſays, *not knowing the uſe of wool, they were clothed with the like ſkins*; Lanæque uſus, ac veſtium, ignotus; et quanquam continuis frigoribus urentur, pellibus tamen ferinis aut murinis veſtiuntur. Of old, the heroes were clothed in ſkins, as *Diomede*, in Homer, Il. κ. 177.

Ὣς φάθ' ὁ δ' ἀμφ' ὤμοισιν ἑέσσατο δέρμα λέοντος
Αἴθωνος μεγάλοιο ποδηνεκές.——
This ſaid, the hero o'er his ſhoulders flung
A lion's ſpoils that to his ankles hung. Pope.
—— Ad Scythiæ proceres regeſque Getarum
Reſpice, queis oſtro contempto et vellere ſerum,
Eximius decor eſt tergis horrere ferarum.——Proſper. de Provid.
The Scythian kings deſpis'd their golden veſts,
More nobly clad in ſkins of frightful beaſts.

(*q*) Syrticæ gentes, a people of *Africa*.

(*r*) What *Seneca* here calls the *mind*, the Apoſtle calls the *Spirit*.

(*s*) *Let not ſin reign in your mortal body that ye ſhould ſerve the luſts thereof.* Rom. vi. 12. *Know ye not, that to whom ye yield yourſelves to obey, his ſervants ye are whom ye obey.* Ib. 16. See Ep. 92.

(*t*) In *Ovid*. (Met. 6. 55.)

Quod *digiti expediunt, atque inter ſtamina ductum*
Percuſſæ feriunt inſecti pectine dentes.
Quod lato *feriunt*, al. *feriunt*, unde etiam *pariunt*. Lipſ.

(*u*) *Sen.* de Benef. 7. 9. video ſericas veſtes, ſi veſtes vocandæ ſunt, in quibus nihil eſt quo defendi aut corpus, aut denique pudor poſſit; quibus ſumptis mulier parum liquida, nudam ſe non eſſe jurabit;—*et pater ejus*. Controv. 7. 2. Ut adultera tenui veſte perſpicua ſit; et nihil in corpore uxoris ſuæ plus maritus quàm quilibet alienus agnoverit.

(*x*) i. e. ploughed a ſecond time, and ſometimes a third.—*Columella*. Arationem iteratio ſequitur ut vervactum reſolvatur in pulverem.

(*y*) And why not? says *Lipsius*. Si dives sapiens est

Et sutor bonus, et—non nostri quid pater ille
Chrysippus dicat? Sapiens crepidas sibi nunquam,
Nec soleas fecit: sutor tamen est sapiens. Quo?
Ut quamvis tacet Hermogenes, cantor tamen atque
Optimus est modulator.——
—— Sapiens operis sic optimus omnis
Est opifex.——Hor. Sat. l. iii. 125.

But what *Chrysippus* said thou dost not know;
No wise man yet did ever make a shoe:
And yet the cobler's a wise man. *How so?*
Why, as *Hermogenes*, though he hold his tongue,
Is skill'd in music, and can set a song. *Creech.*

But in *Apuleius*, l. 11. it is said of one *Hippias*, that *every thing he had was of his own manufacture.* Omnia quæ secum habebat nihil eorum emerat, sed suis sibi manibus confecerat. And indeed I had a neighbour, Mr. *Eldridge*, of the same taste and ingenuity; nay, and who even bound his own books; the whole *apparatus* for this I purchased at his death; but never found time or thought it worth while to make use of them.

(*z*) Ut speculariorum usum,—perlucente testâ] *Plin.* Epist. ii. 17. Nam specularibus—muniuntur.——The *specularia* of the ancients answered the effects of our glass windows. The *lapis specularis* was a transparent stone which *Pliny* the elder tells us was originally found in the farthest parts of *Spain*. The nature of the stone, according to that historian, was remarkable. Humorem hunc terræ quidam autumant crystalli modo glaciari: *some philosophers are of opinion that the* lapis specularis *is a certain juice of the earth, which congeals after the manner of crystal.* Orrery.

(*aa*) Plin. ix. 59. Sergius Orata primus invenit pensiles balneas;—Sergius Orata *first invented hanging baths, which soon grew into vogue.* Pensilium balnearum usu ad infinitum blandiente, ib. xxvi. 3.

(*bb*) The writing of short-hand. See Lips. Epist. ad Belg. 27. Cent. 1.

(*cc*) Lares et Genii] Ghosts, or souls divested of the human body, were in the old Latin called *Lemures*; Ex his Lamuribus, inquit *Apuleius*, qui posteriorum suorum curam sortitus, pacato et quieto numine domum possidet, *Lar* dicitur familiaris. And *of these* (Lemures) *the one, who out of regard to posterity, takes upon him to order the family in peace and quietness, with divine authority, is called* Lar familiaris, *and in the plural* Lares.

Et vigilant nostrâ semper in æde Lares. Ovid.

Supposed of so great power as to drive *Hannibal* from *Rome.*

Hannibalemque Lares Romanâ sede fugantes. Prop. 33.

The *Genii*, supposed the protecting power of men; also of places and things. With regard to man, says *Menander*,

Ἅπαντι δαίμων ἀνδρὶ συμπαραστατεῖ
Εὐθὺς γινομένῳ μυσταγωγὸς τοῦ βίου.
A genius thus attends on every man,
His kind instructor, soon as life began.

Hesiod.

Τοὶ μὲν δαίμονές εἰσι Διὸς μεγάλου διὰ βουλὰς
Ἐσθλοὶ, ἐπιχθόνιοι, φύλακες θνητῶν ἀνθρώπων.

To man, these Genii ministers of heav'n
As faithful guardians here on earth are giv'n.

Homer Od. ρ. 486.

Καί τε θεοὶ ξείνοισιν ἐοικότες ἀλλοδαποῖσιν,
Παντοῖοι τελέθοντες ἐπιστρωφῶσι πόληας,
Ἀνθρώπων ὕβριν τε καὶ εὐνομίην ἐφορῶντες.
—— *In this low disguise,*
Wanders, perhaps, some inmate of the skies.
They (curious oft of mortal actions) deign
In forms like these to round the earth and main,
Just and unjust recording in their mind,
And with sure eyes inspecting all mankind. Pope.

There is none but he
Whose being I do fear: and under him
My *Genius* is rebuked; as it is said
Antony's was by *Cæsar's*.——*Shakespear*.

See the foregoing Note; and *Lips.* Physiol. p. 886.

(*dd*) In secundam numinum formam——*al.* nominum, *al.* hominum. *Erasmus* reads it secundum numinum formam, i. e. more numinum, without the preposition, *in*. As when the body perisheth, the better part remains, or a nobler form is given:) understanding it of human souls, as possessing a lower degree of immortality than the Deity: because they began *to be*, though they never cease to be.

(*ee*) Ubi consistant] sc. circa imum ætherem, et lunæ cœlum. *Lips.*—So Lucan ix.

Quodque patet terras inter cælique meatus,
Semidei manes habitant: quos ignea virtus
Innocuos vitâ patientes *ætheris imi*
Fecit, et æternos animam collegit in orbes.

Beyond our orb, and nearer to that bright
Where Cynthia *drives around her silver light,*
Their happy seats the demigods possess,
Refin'd by virtue, and prepar'd for bliss:
Of life unblam'd, a pure and pious race,
Worthy that lower heaven, and stars to grace, Rowe.
Divine, and equal to the glorious place.

Which Stoical opinion *Cicero* has more fully expressed, in *Tusc.* Disp. i. Necesse est animus, quo nihil velocius, &c. *The soul, than which nothing is swifter, should it remain uncorrupt, and without alteration, must necessarily be carried with that velocity, as to penetrate and divide all the region, where clouds, and rain, and wind, are formed; and having passed this region, it falls in with, and perceives, a nature like its own—where it rests, and endeavours no higher flight.*

(*ff*) *Sen.* ad Polyb. 38.——nunc liberè vagatur, et omnia rerum naturæ bona, cum, summa voluptate perspicit——*ad Marc.* c. 25. In arcana naturæ penetrat, et scrutatur cœlestium causas, et in profunda terrarum permittere aciem juvat: *It extends its view through all nature, from the skies to the deep below.*

(*gg*) *Sen.* (de Benef. 7. 7.) Totum mundum deorum *templum*, solum quidem amplitudine illorum ac magnificentia dignum. *Cic.* Somn. Scip.——Homines tuentur illum globum quem in *templo*

templo hoc medium, qui terra dicitur. *The condition of man's existence is, that he garrison that globe which you see in the middle of this* temple, *and which is called the earth.* Upon this *Macrobius* observes, *that every one who is admitted into this* temple, (i. e. every mortal) *ought to live as righteous, as if he were a priest, in the said temple.* Quidquid humano aspectui subjicitur templum ejus vocavit, qui sola mente concipitur, ut qui hæc veneratur ut templa, cultum tamen maximum debeat conditori: sciatque quisquis in usum templi hujus inducitur, ritu sibi vivendum sacerdotis. *Philo Judæus,*——ἱερὸν Θεῦ νομίζειν τὸν σύμπαντα χρὴ κόσμον εἶναι, κ. τ. λ. That *every one ought to think* the universe *the Temple of God*; *forasmuch as it has a sextry,* i. e. *the purest part of the nature of things,* Heaven: *its ornaments,* the stars; *its priests,* the Angels, and ministers of his power. For, says *Cicero* (Stoically speaking, De Nat. Dear. ii.) Nihil omnium rerum melius est mundo, nihil præstabilius, nihil pulchrius: nec solum nihil est sed ne cogitari quidem quidquam melius potest. *Certainly there is nothing better, more excellent, or more beautiful than the world, nor can we conceive any thing to excel it.*

(*bb*) There are seven different ways of accounting for the origin of mankind. 1. By *Prometheus,* with clay, and fire stole from heaven; and after a deluge repaired by his son *Deucalion,* poetical and merely fabulous. 2. According to *Anaximander* the *Milesian,* they were formed of *water* and *mud,* but were only fish at first, and afterwards turned into men. 3. *Empedocles* supposes them born of the earth, but only part at a time, and to grow as a *blite* or beat. 4. *Democritus* supposes *they rise in and from the ground, like worms, entirely of themselves.* Democritus ait homines vermiculorum modo, effusos de terrâ, nullo autore, nullâque ratione. *Lactant.* vii. 7.——5. Epicurus,

Haud, ut opinor, enim mortalia secla supernè
Aurea de cœlo demisit funis in arva.
Sed genuit tellus eadem, quæ nunc alit ex se. *Lucret.* ii. 1153.

For who can think these pygmies fram'd above,
The little business of some meddling Jove?
And thence to people this inferior ball,
By Homer's *golden chain let gently fall?*
Nor did they rise from the rough seas, but earth,
To what she now supports, at first gave birth. Creech.

Crescebant uteri terræ radicibus apti
Quos ubi tempore maturo patefecerat ætas
Infantum, &c. V. Gob.

Next beasts, and thoughtful man receiv'd their birth:
For then much rural heat in mother earth,
Much moisture lay; and where fit place was found
There wombs were form'd and fasten'd to the ground.
In these the yet imperfect embryos lay,
Through these when grown mature they forc'd their way,
Broke forth from night, and saw the chearful day.

The sixth opinion was that of the Stoics, (so very near the truth) that *they were born of God.* Cic. (de Leg. 1.)

Hoc animal providum, sagax, multiplex, quem vocamus
Hominem, præclarâ quadam conditione generatum esse
Summo Deo.——So *Ovid.* Met. i. 76.
Sanctius his animal mentisque capacius altæ
Deerat adhuc, et quod dominari in cætera posset

Natus homo eſt, ſive hunc *divino ſemine* fecit
Ille opifex rerum, mundi melioris origo,
Sive recens tellus, ſeductaque nuper ab alto
Æthere, cognati retinebat ſemina cœli.

A nobler creature yet was undeſign'd,
Of higher pow'rs, and more exalted mind;
Of thought capacious, whoſe imperial ſway
The lower mute creation muſt obey:
Then man was made, whoſe animated frame
Or God inform'd with a celeſtial flame,
Or earth from purer heaven but lately freed,
Retains ſome particles of kindred ſeed;
And on the noble work was then impreſs'd,
The Godhead's image in the ſoul expreſs'd. Sewell.

The laſt opinion was that of the vulgar, that men ſprung out of the ground, like muſhrooms, firſt in *Arcadia*, and elſewhere. All which ſerve to enhance the value of *divine revelation*; and to make us the more thankful to God, for the advantages we enjoy by the Goſpel, both for religious and moral improvement.

(*ii.*) *Tertullian* (de Anima, c. 14.) ſays, *The ſoul is divided by* Plato *and* Pythagoras *into two parts*; *the* rational, *and* irrational; or, more accurately, *into three*, by dividing the latter into the *iraſcible* and *concupiſcible*: Ariſtotle into *five*, Panætius into *ſix*; Soranus into *ſeven*; Chryſippus, *and moſt of the Stoics into* eight: by adding to the five ſenſes, ſays *Varro*, (ſextam quâ cogitamus, ſeptimam quâ progeneramus, octavam, quâ vocem emittimus) the powers, *cogitative*, *procreative*, and *vocal*. The Stoics (ap. *Stobæ.*) make one, the *principal*, (τὸ ἡγεμονικὸν) the *governing power*, the reſt *miniſterial*. See Ep. 92. *Lipſ.* Phyſiol. iii. 17.

(*kk*) Nam vita videtur nobis quod mors eſt, et contra. *Lipſ.*———As in a violent fit of ſickneſs at *Eton*, in 1720, I deſigned the following for part of my epitaph.——

March 18, 1702.

Ut morior fuit illa dies mihi janua vitæ,
Ut vivam, *hæcce (cùm Deus voluerit.)* Dies janua mortis erat.

(*ll*) *Anacharſis*, a philoſopher of *Scythia*, which being looked upon as ſomewhat extraordinary, it became proverbial. Anacharſis inter Scythas. *Cicero* gives him a great character for *ſobriety and temperance*. Sobrius, continens, abſtinens, et temperans, (Tuſc. 5.) Being aſked whether there were any muſicians in *Scythia?* *No*, ſaid he; *neither have they any vines*. Being aſked likewiſe, whether they had any Gods? *yes*, ſaid he; *and they underſtand the ſpeech of mortals*.——Endeavouring to introduce the *Athenian laws*, he was ordered to be ſhot with an arrow, by his brother, then king of the place.

Strabo reproves *Ephorus* for giving the invention of the *potters wheel* to *Anacharſis*, as mention is made of it in *Homer*. Il. Σ. 600.

——Ὡς ὅτε τις τροχὸν ἄρμενον ἐν παλάμῃσιν
Ἑζόμενος κεραμεὺς πειρήσεται αἴ κε θέῃσιν.
As when the potter ſitting on the ground,
Forms a new veſſel as the wheel whirls round.

(*mm*) This likewiſe, as *Lipſius* obſerves, is a miſtake, as ivory by way of ornament is mentioned more than once by *Homer*. Il. δ. 141.

Bu

'Ως δ' ὅτε τίς τ' ἐλέφαντα γυνὴ φοίνικι μιήνῃ.——
As when some stately trappings are decreed
To grace a monarch on his bounding steed,
A nymph, in Caira, *or* Mæonia *bred,*
Stains the pure ivory with a lively red.
Δινωτὴν (κλισίην) ἐλέφαντι καὶ ἀργύρῳ,——Od. τ. 56.
An ivory seat with silver ringlets grac'd. Pope.

(*nn*) Nec nosse tantum sed sequi docuit Deos] So our Saviour, *Be ye perfect even as your heavenly Father is perfect.* Matth. v. 48.

(*oo*) Et accidentia non aliter excipere, quàm impetrata] Perhaps it may be rendered, *to perform all occasional duties, as if they were positive commands.*

(*pp*) So the *Apostle* to the *Galatians*; *That ye henceforth be no more children tossed to and fro, and carried about with every wind of false doctrine, by the sleight of men and cunning craftiness, whereby they lie in wait to deceive.* 4. 14. And to the *Hebrews*, *Be not carried about with divers and strange doctrines.*——13. 9.

(*qq*) *Prove all things, hold fast that which is good.* 1. Thess. 5. 21.

(*rr*) For *Epicurus* discharged his followers from having any thing to do with the Republic: they were to live to themselves alone.

(*ss*) Licet itaque velit nunc *concurrere*, et reparare quod perdidit] al. occurrere, f. convertere. *Lips.* f. conquirere. *Gronov.* But I take *concurrere* here in the law-sense, *to pretend a right to the same thing as another doth.*

(*tt*) Mollem somnum illis dura tellus dabat] ad aquam. *Lips.* at quàm mallem. *Gronov.*
—— Certior somnus premit
Secura duro membra versantem toro.——*Sen.* in Hippolyto.
In a hard bed a sounder sleep invades
The tired limbs.

(*uu*) Vid. *Lips.* in admirandis.

(*xx*) Vid. *Lips.* Manud. ii. 8. 5.

(*yy*) *For we are also his offspring.* Act. xvii. 28. Omnes si ad primam originem revocentur, a Diis sunt. *Sen.* Ep. 44. Denique cœlesti sumus omnes semine nati. Lucr. ii. 989.
Lastly we all from seed celestial rise,
Which heaven, our common parent, still supplies. Creech.

(*zz*) Parabantque adhuc mutis animalibus] By the word *mutis*, *Lipsius* understands *fish*, and saith, *that the first slaughter of living creatures for food was made of fish.* But *Gronovius* justly wonders at this mistake, and asketh, *whether* Seneca *can possibly mean* fish, by the word *mutis* in Ep. 92. excedit ex hoc animalium numero, pulcherrimo, ac diis secundo, mutis aggregetur animal pabulo lætum? But not only *Seneca* but the most approved authors use the word *mutum* for *brutum*. And here it is undoubtedly to be understood of all *animals* whatever, in opposition to men. *al.* multis animalibus. MSS.

EPISTLE

EPISTLE XCI.

Of natural Evils; and the Uncertainty of human Affairs.

OUR friend *Liberalis (a)* is at present full of grief, having heard of the terrible fire that hath destroyed our colony at *Lyons (b)*. This is an accident which would move any one, and much more a man, than whom no one better loves his country. He had recourse therefore to that firmness of mind, which he hath always exercised with regard to any thing that was to be feared: but I do not wonder that he was in no fear of this unexpected, I might say unheard-of evil. For I know not where to find an example of the like. Fire indeed hath damaged many cities, but not, as I can remember, utterly destroyed one: for even where an enemy hath set fire to a town, some houses have been left standing; and though it may rekindle in different places, it seldom hath made such an entire devastation as to leave nothing to the weapons of war.

In the most dreadful and destructive earthquakes it seldom happens that whole towns are swallowed up; nor did I ever hear of such a malicious fire as to leave nothing for a second to prey upon. But it hath so happened here, that in one night have been destroyed many beautiful and stately buildings, and other works; any one of which alone might have served as a sufficient ornament for a city; and more mischief hath been done in the time of peace, than could have been dreaded in the day of battle. Who could believe it, that at a time when war had every where ceased, and the blessing of security was spread throughout the earth, *Lyons*, the glory of *Gaul*, should be lost in ruin? Fortune hath generally reminded those, whom she intended publickly to afflict, to dread their danger: every great event hath given time for ruin: but here there was the space only of one night, between its being one of the noblest cities, and not so much as the appearance of a city; in short,

 it

it was ſcarce ſo long in periſhing, as I have been in relating the dreadful accident.

Now theſe things greatly afflict the generous mind of *Liberalis*, firm and ſteady as it is againſt any accident that may befall himſelf. And indeed there is reaſon for it. Unexpected accidents are apt to ſtrike deepeſt. Novelty adds weight to calamity; nor is there any mortal but who is more afflicted at what falls upon him by ſurprize. Nothing therefore ſhould come upon us unexpectedly: The mind ought to be prepared not only againſt what uſually happens, but againſt whatever may happen. What is there that *Fortune* cannot throw down when ſhe pleaſes, from its moſt flouriſhing ſtate? and which ſhe will not more readily attack and more violently ſhake, the more ſpecious and ſplendid it is in appearance? What is arduous or difficult to her? ſhe does not aſſault us always in the ſame manner; nor exert all her ſtrength at once. Sometimes ſhe ſets us to oppoſe ourſelves: at another time depending upon her own ſtrength, ſhe finds out dangers for us which we cannot account for: all times are alike to her. We are never ſafe. Even in the midſt of our pleaſures ſhe giveth cauſe to mourn. War is ſtirred up in the calm of peace; and the means of ſecurity converted into fear. Our friend becomes a foe; and our companion a cruel adverſary *. The ſerenity of ſummer is often changed into ſudden tempeſts, and more violent than wintry ſtorms. Without an enemy we ſuffer hoſtilities; and too great proſperity hath proved its own ruin, when other cauſes have been wanting. Diſeaſes fall upon the moſt temperate; a conſumption ſeizeth upon the moſt robuſt conſtitution. The innocent ſuffer puniſhment; and uproar diſturbs the moſt retired. Chance is continually making choice of ſome new evil to remind us of her power, as if we had forgot it. Whatever by a long continuance of much labour, and the kind favour of Providence, hath been ſcraped together and raiſed on high, is ſcattered and demoliſhed in one day: nay, he that ſaith a day (*c*) and not rather an hour, a moment, ſufficeth for the overthrow of empires, aſſigneth too long a time to the more ſpeedy progreſs of human calamities.

It

It would be ſome comfort to us, in our infirm and uncertain ſtate of things, if they could be repaired as eaſily, and ſoon, as they are deſtroyed. But now, alas! improvements are ſlowly made (*d*), while deſtruction comes on amain. Not any thing, either public or private, is firm and ſtable. Men and cities are alike the ſport of fate. Amidſt the moſt pleaſing ſcenes terror breaks in; and when there is no cauſe of trouble and confuſion from without, evils ruſh in upon us from whence we leaſt expected them. Kingdoms that have ſtood the brunt both of foreign and civil wars, have without any oppoſition fell to ruin. What commonwealth could ever ſupport its own happineſs?

All things therefore are to be reflected on, and the mind ſtrengthened againſt whatever accident may poſſibly happen. Think upon exile, war, torture, diſeaſes, ſhipwrecks (*e*). Chance may ſnatch you from your country, or your country from you. She may throw you into ſolitude, or make deſolate this very place where the multitude is ſtifled with thronging. The whole ſtate of human affairs muſt be placed before our eyes; and we muſt conceive in our minds not only what frequently happens, but what may happen extraordinarily, if we would not be ſurpriſed, and ſtupefied with any unuſual accident, as being new and ſtrange. Fortune muſt be conſidered in all her miſchiefs. How often have the cities of *Achaia* and *Aſia* been thrown down by earthquakes? how many towns in *Syria*? how many have been ſwallowed up in *Macedonia*! How often hath deſtruction been ſpread through the iſland *Cyprus*? how often hath *Paphos* been buried in its ruins? how often do we hear of the deſtruction of whole cities; and how ſmall a part of the world are we among whom theſe rumours are ſpread?

Let us riſe up therefore, and ſtand firm againſt all caſualties: and whatever happens, let us think that rumour hath exaggerated the evil. A city is burned, that was very rich and the ornament of all the neighbouring provinces, though built upon one hill (*f*), and that none of the higheſt: and time ſhall eraſe the very marks of all thoſe cities that are now called magnificent and noble. See you not that the very foun-

 dations

dations of the moſt famous cities in *Greece* are quite deſtroyed, and that nothing is left whereby to conjecture there ever were ſuch cities? Time not only overthrows the works of mens hands, and the wonders of human art and induſtry; even the tops of mountains have mouldered away, and whole regions became a deſert. Places that were far diſtant from the ſea have been overwhelmed with a ſudden inundation; and fire hath quite conſumed the hills, from whence it before gave only a ſplendid flame; and in times paſt hath eaten away the loftieſt promontories, once a joyful ſight to the fatigued mariners; and reduced the higheſt landmarks to a bank of ſand.

Seeing then that the works of Nature herſelf are often thus deſtroyed, we ought to bear with æquanimity the ruin of a city. All things are frail and periſhable, and muſt one day come to decay: whether it be that the winds, pent up beneath the earth, have by a ſudden blaſt, or their own internal ſtrength, thrown off the weight that before preſſed them down; or the force of the waters in ſecret places hath made its way through all oppoſition; or the violence of flames have rent the cloſures of the earth; or age, againſt which nothing is ſafe, hath gradually wore it away; or whether the unwholeſomeneſs of the air hath driven away the people, and infection even poiſoned a deſert, it would be endleſs to recount the many ways whereby Fate haſtens on deſtruction. But this one thing I know, that all the works of mortals are ſubject to, and condemned by, mortality; and that we live in a ſtate wherein all things around us muſt one day inevitably periſh.

Theſe then and the like reflections I often advance, in order to comfort our friend *Liberalis*, whoſe breaſt, I ſay, is inflamed with inexpreſſible love of his country, and of this city in particular; which perhaps is now deſtroyed, that it may be rebuilt in a nobler taſte. Injuries have often made way for better fortune; and many things have fallen only to riſe higher and greater. *Timagenes* (g) no well-wiſher to the proſperity of the city, was wont to ſay, *that he ſhould be ſorry if* Rome *was deſtroyed by fire, for he well knew that it would riſe again in greater ſplendour than before.* And with regard to the city now loſt, it it is probable that all men will endeavour, that greater and more laſting buildings may be erected, than those they have loſt. May they be laſting indeed, and built under more happy auſpices! For, ſcarce an hundred years have paſſed, ſince this colony was firſt founded; (which is not the extremeſt age of man himſelf) under the conduct of *Plancus (h)*, and by reaſon of its agreeable ſituation, it ſoon grew very populous; and yet hath ſuffered the moſt grievous calamaties within the age of man.

Let the mind therefore be taught to underſtand, and patiently to bear, whatever may be its lot; and let it know, there is nothing beyond the daring of Fortune. That ſhe hath the ſame power over kingdoms themſelves, as over the rulers thereof. We are to repine at none of theſe things; we have entered upon a world, where we live ſubject to theſe conditions. Are you not pleaſed with it? *Regret not the being taken out of it (i).* You might well be angry, was any thing to happen *particularly* to you. But if the ſame neceſſity binds both high and low, you have nothing to do but to reconcile yourſelf to *Fate*, by whom all things are determined *(to their proper end.)* There is no need to meaſure man by his tomb, or by thoſe monuments that are ſpread on each ſide the road of an unequal ſize. The grave ſets all men upon this level. We are born unequal, but we die equal.

The ſame I ſay of cities, as of the inhabitants thereof. *Ardea (k)* hath been taken as well as *Rome*. The ſupreme Author of mankind hath not diſtinguiſhed us in our birth and nobility, but during life. When we come to the end of all mortal things, *Be gone*, ſaith he, *Ambition; and let there be the ſame law to all things that tread the earth.* We are alike born to variety of ſuffering: no one is more frail than another; no one more ſure of ſeeing to-morrow's ſun.

Alexander, king of *Macedonia*, wretch as he was, begun to learn geometry, that he might know how little the earth was, of which he poſſeſſed ſo ſmall a part: I call him wretched, becauſe he ought to have known from hence, that he had no title to the ſurname of *Great*; for

for what can be called *Great* in so small a space? The things taught him were subtle, and not to be learned but by close attention, and constant application, not such as a madman could well comprehend; whose thoughts were intent upon plunder, and roving beyond the ocean. *Teach me*, saith he, *easy things*. To which his tutor replied, *These things are the same to all: every one finds in them the like difficulty.* Suppose now, *Lucilius*, Nature to say the same thing to you. The things whereof you complain are the same to all men: she admits no one on easier terms: but every one that pleases may make them easier. Do you ask how? by *æquanimity*.

You must necessarily feel pain, be hungry, and thirst, and grow old; and though a longer time be given you among men, you must one day be sick, and die. Yet there is no necessity for believing all that is said by those who are continually buzzing about you with complaints. None of these things are properly evils; none intolerable, or even hard to be borne. They became dreadful by prejudice and common consent. Ye are as afraid of death, as of a false report. But what can be more ridiculous than to be afraid of mere words? Our *Demetrius* used pleasantly to say, *that the reports of the ignorant were to him like breaking wind. What is it to me*, he said, *whether the sound comes from above or below?* (*l*) How absurd is it to be afraid of infamy from infamous men? And as you are causelessly afraid of what fame says of you, so are ye of those things which ye would never have feared, had not fame or report commanded ye so to do. What detriment can a good man receive from being scandalized by malicious tongues? for even Death is alike scandalized. No one of those who accuse him, speaks from experience. In the mean time we should not condemn what we do not know. But this you know, that it hath proved a great benefit to many in delivering them from tortures, from want, from complaints, from punishment, from anxiety. We are subject to the power of no one, when it is in the power of death to deliver us (*m*).

ANNO-

4

ANNOTATIONS, &c.

(*a*) *Æbutius Liberalis*, to whom *Seneca* inscribed his book (de beneficiis) *of benefits*.

(*b*) Tacit. Ann. l. 16. *To the inhabitants of* Lyons, *as a relief for their late calamity by fire, the Emperor presented* 100,000 *crowns, to repair the damages of the city*.

• As in *David's* complaint——*Yea, my own familiar friend in whom I trusted, which did eat of my bread, hath lift up his heel against me*. Ps. xli. 9.

(*c*) *Euripides* Phœn. 561. Ὁ δ' ὄλβος οὐ βέβαιος ἀλλ' ἐφήμερος

Wealth is the unstable blessing of a day.

So *Diphilus* (ap. Stobæ.) Ἀπροσδόκητον οὐδὲν ἀνθρώποις πάθος.

Ἐφήμερος γὰρ τὰς τύχας κεκτήμεθα.

There is no evil, while we sojourn here,
But what poor mortals daily have to fear.

——— Καὶ μί' ἡμέρα ———

Τὸν μὲν καθεῖλεν ὑψόθεν, τὸν δ' ἦρ' ἄνω.

——— *one day serves*
Some to depress, and others to exalt.

(*d*) Incrementa lente.] Tacitus (in Agricola) Naturâ infirmitatis humanæ, tardiora sunt remedia quam mala; et ut corpora lentè augescunt, cito extinguuntur: sic ingenia facilius oppresseris, quàm recreaveris. *Such is the frailty of man, and its effects, that much more slow is the progress of the remedies than of the evils, and as human bodies attain their growth by degrees, and are subject to be destroyed in an instant; so it is much easier to suppress than to revive the efforts of genius and study*. Gordon.

(*e*) War, famine, pest, volcano, storm, and fire,
Intestine broils, oppression, with her heart
Wrapt up in triple brass, besiege mankind.
Want and incurable disease, (fell pair!)
On hapless multitudes remorseless seize,
At once, and make a refuge of the grave. *Young*.

(*f*) Alluding to the seven hills, on which *Rome* was built.

(*g*) A Rhetorician and Historian of *Alexandria*. He was brought captive to *Rome* by *Gabinius*, under *Pompey* the Great, and redeemed by *Faustus*, the son of *Sylla*; but was expelled the city on account of his malevolent tongue; though *Ammian* speaks well of him. He died in his exile.

Rapit Hiarbitam Timagenis æmula lingua.

But *Pincian* supposes that *Seneca* meant this of the Emperor *Caligula*, who, as *Suetonius* reports, was most inveterate against the prosperity of *Rome*.

(*h*) A *Planco* deducta] So *Lipsius*; which from among the various readings seems to be right. For, according to *Eusebius*, *Munatius Plancus* Ciceronis discipulus, orator habetur insignis; qui cum Galliam comatam regeret, Lugdunum condidit; *Munatius Plancus, a disciple of Cicero, was esteemed an excellent orator; who when he commanded in* Gaul *(beyond the* Alps*) founded the city* Lyons. An. U. C. 811.

(*i*). Non placet ? quacunque vis exi.] This also is an expression which I thought myself obliged not to translate literally; it being a doctrine totally repugnant to the Christian; and indeed to what

Seneca

Seneca hath advanced elsewhere, and particularly in the foregoing sentence; where he says, *the mind ought to be made sensible of the infirmities of human nature, and the unsteady course of things, that so it might patiently endure whatever may be its lot.*

(*k*) Once a city in *Italy*, where *Turnus*, king of the *Rutilians*, kept his court.

(*l*) And our facetious *Tom Brown*, in the same strain speaks of death itself; which, however false the logic, or impolite the terms, is so much to our purpose, that the reader, I hope, will excuse my transcribing it, as it is not every one that has read, or will read, *Tom Brown*.

If man must die as oft as breath departs,
Then he must often die, who often ——— :
And if to die, is but to lose one's breath,
Then Death's a ———, and so a ——— for Death.

(*m*) That is (not I own what *Seneca* means by, *cùm mors in nostrâ potestate sit*, but) as I would understand it; *No power on earth can hurt us, but for a short time; seeing that Death* must *come, which, when Providence thinks proper, will deliver us out of all our trouble.*

EPISTLE XCII.

The Difference between exhortatory and dogmatical Philosophy.

THAT part of philosophy, *Lucilius*, which adapts proper precepts to particular persons, and forms not the man in general, but directs the husband how he ought to behave himself towards his wife; the father how he ought to educate his children; the mother how to govern his servants, and the like; some are so very fond of, as to reject all other parts as useless and extravagant, as if any one could teach particulars, who was not master of the whole Duty of Man in the conduct of life.

But *Aristo*, the Stoic, on the contrary, thinks this but a trivial part of philosophy, as not reaching the heart of man: and affirms *that* part (*the dogmatical*) to be the more profitable; and that the axioms or decrees of philosophy are what constitute the *chief good*; which part of philosophy when a man hath sufficiently learned and understood, he needs nothing more, by way of instruction, throughout the whole business of life. As he that learns to throw a dart, takes a fit stand for aim,

aim, and forms his hand to a proper direction of whatever he throws from it; and when by instruction and practice he hath made himself a master in this art, he useth it as he pleases; for he hath learned not to hit this or that thing in particular, but whatever he thinks proper to hit; so he that instructeth himself in the whole duty of life, needs no particular admonition; being taught in general, not how to live, with regard to his wife or his children, but *to live well*, which includes every relative obligation. *Cleanthes* likewise allows the *Parænetic* Philosophy, or knowledge of particulars to be in some measure profitable; but weak and defective; unless as it flows from the universal understanding of the principles, and decrees of philosophy.

Here then is started a question or two; whether this *preceptive* philosophy be useful, or not useful; whether alone it can make a good man; i. e. whether it be superfluous itself, or so important as to render all other parts of philosophy superfluous? They who maintain it to be superfluous, argue thus; If any thing placed before the eyes obstructs the sight, the impediment must be removed, or else it is to no purpose *to bid a man walk to such a place, or to reach such a thing with his hand.* In like manner, when any thing so darkens the mind as to prevent an insight into the whole order of duty, it is in vain to direct a man, saying, *thus you shall live with your father, or thus with your wife*; for precepts avail nothing, so long as ignorance and error cloud the understanding; these must be removed, and every requisition of duty will be manifest. Otherwise, you teach him what a sensible man ought to do, but do not make him so; you shew one that is poor how to act the rich man, which it is impossible for him to do so long as he continues poor; you bid the hungry man behave himself as with a full stomach; whereas you ought first to satisfy the painful cravings within (*a*).

Now I will maintain the same concerning all manner of vice: these must be removed, or, so long as these remain, precepts will have no effect: unless all such false opinions, as we generally labour under, are expelled, the covetous man will not hear how he may put his money to a right uſe; nor the timorous, how he may contemn danger. You muſt make the one underſtand that money is neither good nor bad in itſelf; and that rich men are ſometimes miſerable, and perſuade the other, that ſuch things as men are moſt apt to dread, are by no means ſo terrible as common fame reports them; no, not even pain and death: that oftentimes in death, which by the law of Nature we muſt one day undergo, is to be found great comfort, *that it comes but once.* And as for pain, reſolution of mind, which makes every burthen the lighter, the more ſtubbornly and contemptuouſly it is endured, will prove a certain remedy: that, one excellent quality of pain is, it muſt not be very great, if yet it may be encreaſed;—and if it be great indeed, it cannot laſt much longer *:—that all things therefore, which the neceſſity of the world brings upon us, are to be endured with courage and patience.

When by theſe and the like axioms a man is brought to a thorough ſenſe of his condition, and is perfectly aſſured that the happineſs of life conſiſts not in being pleaſurable, but in its correſpondency with nature; when he ſhall be enamoured with virtue, as the chief good of man; and fly from turpitude, as the only evil; looking upon all other things, as riches, honour, health, ſtrength, power and dominion, with indifference, as being neither good nor bad in themſelves: he will no longer want a monitor to inſtruct him in particulars, ſaying, *thus you muſt walk; thus you muſt ſup; ſuch a behaviour becomes a man; and ſuch is proper for the fair ſex; thus ſhould a married man act, and thus a batchelor:* for they who moſt induſtriouſly offer their preſcriptions, follow them not always themſelves: they are nothing more than what the pedagogue teacheth his ſcholar, and the grandmother her darling: and you ſhall often hear the moſt choleric man in the world proving that it is not a right thing to be paſſionate; nay, were you to go into any of our ſchools, you would find that the lofty precepts of the philoſophers, pronounced with a ſupercilious air, are nothing more than the uſual leſſons given to children.

And, after all, are the precepts given manifeſt or doubtful? if manifeſt, they need no teacher; if doubtful, they can gain the philoſopher but

but little credit from his audience. The giving therefore ſuch particular precepts is ſuperfluous. Or, *take it thus*; if what you propoſe to teach or adviſe be ambiguous or obſcure, you muſt explain, and prove it, by dint of argument; and if you prevail, ſuch proofs and arguments are what do the buſineſs, and are ſufficient of themſelves, without the particular precept: *thus uſe your friend*; *thus a fellow-citizen*; *thus a companion*: but why? becauſe *it is juſt*. Common-place then, relating to juſtice, will teach me all theſe things. Hence I find that equity is to be purſued upon its own account; that we are not to be compelled thereto by fear; nor bribed by reward: that he is not a juſt man who approves of any particular in this virtue, but the virtue itſelf. When I am perſuaded, and have imbibed this principle, what ſignify thoſe particular precepts towards the edification of one thoroughly inſtructed before? To give precepts to the knowing, is ſuperfluous, and too much; to give them to thoſe who know nothing, is by no means enough; for they are not only to be told what they are to do, but why they are to do ſo.

Again; are theſe precepts neceſſary for one who hath true notions of good and evil; or for one who hath them not? He that hath them not, will never be moved by any thing you can ſay to him; having his ears prejudiced with ſuch common notions, as militate againſt your admonitions; and he that forms a right judgment of what he ought to avoid, and what to purſue, knows already how to act under every circumſtance, without further inſtructions from you. All this part of philoſophy therefore may well be ſpared.

There are two errors, to which is owing the commiſſion of evil; either the mind hath contracted a malignity from falſe opinions; or, if not already infected, it hath a propenſity thereto; and by this wrong bias, under ſome ſpecious reſemblance of truth, is ſoon corrupted: it behoveth us therefore to cure the ſick mind, and purge it from every vicious principle; or, if it be free, and as yet only prone to evil, to pre-engage it as ſoon as poſſible before it comes to an ill habit. Now in both theſe caſes the ſolemn decrees of philoſophy will ſufficiently enable us; when the manner of giving precept upon precept would avail nothing.

Beſides, were we to give precepts to every individual, the labour would be infinite: for we muſt give one ſort to the uſurer; another to the huſbandman; another to the merchant; another to ſuch as dangle after the favour of princes, or of great men; another to thoſe who make their court to their equals; and another to thoſe who are obſequious to their ſuperiors: in matrimony you muſt teach a man how to behave to his wife, whom he married a virgin; and how to a widow; how to one who brought him a large fortune; and to one whom *he thought ſufficiently portioned with virtue and good ſenſe*. And think you not ſome difference is to be made between a barren and a fruitful woman; between one advanced in years and a mere girl; between a mother and a ſtep-dame? the different ſorts are inconceivable; yet every individual requires a particular charge. But the laws or decrees of philoſophy are brief, and contain every obligation.

Add now, that the precepts of a wiſe man ought to be limited and certain; if infinite, they pertain not to wiſdom; for wiſdom knoweth the bounds of all things: therefore is this preceptive part of philoſophy to be rejected; becauſe what it promiſeth to few it cannot make good to all; but wiſdom extends to all.

All the difference between the common madneſs of the world (*b*) and of ſuch as are delivered into the hands of the phyſician, is, the one ſort labours under a diſeaſe, the other under falſe opinions. The one hath drawn the cauſes of his frenzy from an indiſpoſition of the body, the other is the ſickneſs of the mind. Should any one pretend to preſcribe to the madman, *how he ought to ſpeak, how to walk, how to behave himſelf in public, and how in private*, ſuch a doctor would be thought not leſs mad than his patient. No; the black bilious humour muſt firſt be purged off, and the very cauſe of the diſeaſe removed; and in like manner muſt we proceed with any other frenzy of the mind;

this must first be discussed and driven away; or otherwise all manner of precepts and admonitions will at present have no effect.—So far *Aristo*, whom we propose to answer in every particular.

And first, in regard *to the eye*, it is said, *if any thing obstructs the sight, it must be removed.* I own that in this case there is no need of precepts to make a man see; but of medicines proper to clear the sight, by removing the film or suffusion, or whatever else obstructs it: for by nature we see; and whoever removes any obstacle, restores the eye to its proper use. But nature points not out the obligation of every duty. Besides, he that is cured of a suffusion in the eye, though he immediately recovers sight himself, cannot give it to others; whereas he that is cured of any malignity of mind, may possibly cure others. There is no need of any exhortation or advice to understand the qualities of colours: the eye will customarily distinguish white from black without a teacher; but the mind wants many precepts before it can see the fitness of every action in life. Howbeit, the physician not only cures the diseased eye, but also gives his advice, saying to his patient, *you must not expose the eye as yet to too glaring a light, but must proceed from darkness to a gloomy shade; and then venture further, 'till by degrees you accustom it to endure broad day-light: you must not study immediately after dinner, nor impose a duty upon the eye when swoln or watery* (*c*). *Keep also the wind or wintery cold from beating on your face*; with the like admonitions, that are as requisite and useful as medicine itself. Thus I say physicians think it necessary to add good advice to their prescriptions.

But *error* is said *to be the cause of sin*; and that *precepts are of little avail, either in removing this, or in conquering false opinions concerning good and evil.* I grant that precepts are not effectual of themselves to drive a perverse opinion from the understanding; yet it does not follow but that in some measure they may prove useful: for first, they undoubtedly refresh the memory; and, secondly, as they bring us to a distinct view of the parts, which we saw but confusedly in the whole.

Your

You might as well ſay, that all manner of conſolation and exhortation are ſuperfluous: but as theſe are not ſuperfluous, ſo neither are admonitions.

It is ridiculous, ſaith *Ariſto, to preſcribe to a ſick man what to do as if he was well; you muſt firſt reſtore him to health, without which all precepts are to no purpoſe.* But are not ſome things alike common both to the ſick and well, of which they ought to be reminded; as, *not to eat voraciouſly; not to uſe immoderate exerciſe?* So the poor and the rich have alike ſome common precepts: *cure men of avarice,* he ſaith, *and you will have no reaſon to admoniſh either the rich or poor, when once the deſires ſubſide:* but it is one thing not to covet money, and another to know how to uſe it. The covetous know no meaſure in their deſires of it; and ſuch as are not covetous, may not know the right uſe of it.

Take away error, ſaith he, *and all precepts are ſuperfluous.* This is falſe; for ſuppoſe avarice relaxed, luxury reſtrained, raſhneſs curbed, and idleneſs ſpurred on; nay even all vices removed; yet have we ſtill to learn what we ought to do, and in what manner.

Admonitions, he ſaith, *will have no effect when applied to enormous vices.* Medicines indeed heal not incurable diſeaſes; yet are they to be applied, if not by way of remedy, at leaſt in order to mitigate and aſſuage the pain. Not all the power of philoſophy, applied to this one purpoſe, can totally eradicate from the mind an inveterate and ſtubborn evil; yet it will not follow that ſuch application does good in no reſpect, becauſe not in all.

Of what advantage is it, ſays he, *to point out things already manifeſt?* It may be of very great advantage; for ſometimes, though we know a thing, yet for want of due attention we regard it not. Admonition perhaps availeth not in its deſign; yet it makes the mind more intent, excites diligence, refreſhes the memory, and ſuffers not a thing to be loſt. We paſs regardleſs by many things that are before our eyes. To admoniſh, is a kind of exhortation; the mind alſo ſometimes pretends

not

not to comprehend things that are evident: it is neceſſary therefore ſometimes to inculcate the knowledge even of ſuch things as are beſt known.

It will not be amiſs here to take notice of the reproof of *Calvus* to *Vatinius*, factum eſſe ambitum, ſcitis; et hoc vos ſcire, omnes ſciunt, *you know there has been bribery in the caſe; and all men know that you know it.* You know that the duties of friendſhip are ever to be religiouſly obſerved; but you obſerve them not. You know that it is unfair for a man to require chaſtity in his wiſe; when he himſelf is continually hunting after, and corrupting the wives of other men; and you know, that as ſhe ought to have nothing to do with an adulterer, ſo ought you to have nothing to do with a ſtrumpet (*d*): but you regard it not. Therefore it is neceſſary that you ſometimes ſhould have your memory refreſhed; for it ought not to be lulled aſleep, but kept awake and of uſe. Whatever is ſalutary and requiſite muſt frequently be brought before and impreſſed upon it. That what is proper may not only be known to us, but worked into an habit. Add alſo, that things, how plain and manifeſt ſoever, may yet be made ſtill plainer and more manifeſt.

If things, ſaith he, *are doubtful, there is a neceſſity for proofs and arguments; conſequently theſe are what do the buſineſs, and not precepts.* Now beſides that even without proofs the very authority of the adviſer goes a great way in the credit of the advice, as the opinions of men learned in the law are accepted, without their giving a reaſon for them, the preſcriptions themſelves, and the manner wherein they are delivered, are ſometimes of great weight: as when intermixed with poetry, or contracted into a ſhort and ſolid ſentence in proſe, like thoſe of *Cato:* Emas non quod opus eſt, ſed quod neceſſe eſt; *buy not every thing you want, but only what is neceſſary.* Quod non opus eſt, aſſe carum eſt; *what you really do not want, is dear at a farthing* (*e*), or, thoſe admirable ſentences, delivered by ſome oracle, or of like autho-

rity;

rity; χρόνου φείδου, *husband well your time* (*f*); γνῶθι σεαυτόν, *know thyself* (*g*). Will you insist upon a reason, when any one reminds you of the following?

Injuriarum remedium est oblivio.
Forgetfulness is injury's best cure (*h*).
Fortes fortuna adjuvat.
Fortune promotes the brave (*i*).
Piger ipse sibi obstat.
The idle stand in their own way (*k*).

Such sentences as these want no advocate. They touch the passions; and let Nature exert her own power they cannot but do good. Our minds carry in them the seeds of what is *right and fit*, which are stirred up by admonition, as a spark of fire, being assisted by an agreeable blast, bursts forth into a flame. Virtue rouseth herself, when touched or shaken. Besides, many things lie dormant in our minds, and quite disregarded, 'till being quickened by admonitions, they begin to shew their worth: and there are other scattered here and there, which the understanding, not properly exercised, cannot recollect; and therefore are they to be got together, and set in one view, that they may be more effectual, and ease the burthened mind. Or, if precepts are of no use, all discipline and instruction are to be exterminated, and we must be content with rude Nature alone: but they who say this seem not to know that some men have quick and lively parts, and others are dull and stupid; as one man is much more ingenious than another. But the natural powers of the mind are nourished, and grow stronger by precepts; from whence he adds new opinions to such as were innate, and learns to correct every vicious principle.

If any one, it is said, *knows not the decrees of philosophy, how will admonitions profit him, when tied and bound by his sins?* Why, in this; to loose him from them. Forasmuch as his natural disposition towards goodness is not totally extinguished, but only obscured and oppressed, it sometime endeavours to raise and exert itself against evil; and being so happy as to meet with a guide, and to be assisted with good counsel, soon grows stronger, and recovers itself; provided it be not so thoroughly infected with the contagion of sin, as to be quite mortified (*l*).

For

For in such a case, I own, that not even discipline, supported by all the powers of philosophy, would be able to restore it. Besides, what difference is there between the decrees and the precepts of philosophy, except that the former are general and the latter special? they both give directions, but the former in the gross, and these in particulars.

If any one, it is said, *knows what is fit and right from the decrees, all admonition is superfluous.* By no means; for learned as you suppose a man therein, there are many things which he ought to do, for which he does not thoroughly perceive the obligation; as we are not only hindered by the passions from doing those things, which we approve, and know to be good; but by not being able to find out what every exigency may require of us as a duty; our minds are sometimes so very sedate and composed, as not to exert themselves in looking after the way of duty, which admonition points out to us.

Expel, saith he, *all false opinions concerning good and evil; and in their stead place such as are true and just; and admonition will have nothing left to do.* The mind undoubtedly is governed, and rightly ordered by these means, but not by these only. For though what is good and what is evil may be gathered from arguments; yet precepts have their several provinces, and prudence and justice consist of particular offices; and all offices are directed by precepts. Besides the judgment itself concerning good and evil is confirmed by the execution of offices, to which we are induced by precepts. For they agree with each other; neither can general precepts go before, but the particular will follow them, and still keep their rank; which shews that the general will always take the lead.

Precepts, saith he, *are infinite.* This is likewise false: for they are not infinite concerning the greatest and most momentous affairs; though there is some small difference made in them by the different exigencies of circumstance, time and place.

No one, he faith, *pretends to cure madneſs by precepts; and therefore not the malignity of the mind.* The caſe is not the ſame; for if you take away madneſs the patient is reſtored to health; but if we have excluded ſome falſe opinions, it does not follow all the *agenda (things not to be omitted)* are clearly ſeen: or, if this did follow, yet admonition will ſtrengthen and confirm the moral ſenſe of good and evil. It is likewiſe falſe, that *precepts have no effect with madmen:* for though of themſelves they cannot cure, yet they aid and aſſiſt therein; as menaces and chaſtiſement have been of uſe in reſtraining the ſallies of ſome madmen. I am ſpeaking only of thoſe madmen, whoſe ſenſes are ſhattered, but not entirely loſt.

But *laws,* it is rejoined, *make not men do always what is right, and what are theſe but precepts, mixed with threatenings?* Yes; there is this difference between them: firſt, laws do not always perſuade, becauſe they threaten; but precepts pretend not to compel any one, they only intreat. And 2dly, laws deter us from doing evil, but precepts exhort us to do what is right. Add hereunto, that laws alſo promote good morals: foraſmuch as they do not only command, but inſtruct. Herein then I differ from *Poſidonius;* I approve not of the Prefaces to *Plato's* book of laws (*m*); for a law ought to be very ſhort, that it may be the more eaſily comprehended and received by the unſkilful: it ſhould bear the reſemblance of a divine oracle. It ſhould command, and not diſpute. Nothing ſeems to me more inſipid and impertinent than a long preamble to a law. Adviſe me, tell me at once, what you would have me do. I liſten, not in order to learn, but to obey. Laws then have their uſe; ſince it is obſervable that in governments where there are bad ordnances there are worſe morals.

Laws however, it will be ſaid, *prevail not with every one.* True; neither doth philoſophy itſelf; yet it is not upon this account uſeleſs and ineffectual in forming aright the minds of men. And what alſo is philoſophy, but the law of life? But were we to ſuppoſe the laws of no uſe or profit, it does not follow that admonitions are likewiſe uſeleſs: you might as well deny that there is any uſe in conſolations, exhortations, diſſuaſion, reproof, and commendation: for all theſe are different kinds of admonition, by which we attain to a perfect ſtate of mind. Nothing is more apt to inveſt the mind with virtue; to fix the wavering; to ſtrengthen the weak; to recall the viciouſly-inclined, and confirm them in all goodneſs than the converſation of good men: for it deſcends by degrees into the heart; and to be often ſeen, and often heard, hath the ſame effect as precepts. Nay, the bare meeting with a wiſe man hath its uſe; there is ſomething to be learned from a great and a good man, even though he were ſilent. I cannot indeed ſo well expreſs the particular good to be found therein, as that I have really found it from experience. There are ſome alimalcules, as *Phædon* obſerves, that are ſcarcely perceptible when they bite you; and ſo very fine and ſharp their ſting, that you ſcarce can feel it; a ſwelling however ſhews that you have been ſtung, though no wound appear therein. The like will happen to you in the converſation of wiſe men; you will not perhaps be apprehenſive how, or in what manner they have done you good, but you will certainly find they have done you good.

But what is all this, it will be ſaid, *to the purpoſe?* I will tell you: good precepts, if well attended to, will, in all probability, have the like effect with good examples. *Pythagoras* ſaith (*n*) that the mind and thoughts of thoſe who enter the temple and ſee before them the aweful images of the Gods, are differently affected from thoſe who attend the voice of ſome oracle at the door. But who will deny, that even the moſt illiterate are powerfully ſmitten with certain precepts, of few words indeed, but of great weight; as

Nihil nimis. (*o*)
Nothing too much.
Avarus animus nullo ſatiatur lucro.
No gain can ſatisfy the covetous (p).
Ab alio expectes alteri quod feceris.
Do as you would have others do unto you (q).

When we hear ſuch ſentences as theſe, we are immediately ſtruck with their force and propriety, without being permitted in the leaſt to doubt or diſpute their authority. And why? becauſe truth is perſuaſive with-

X 2 out

out any further argument. If reverence then to either perſons or things can reſtrain the mind, and check us in our vicious courſes, why ſhould not admonition do the ſame, though we make uſe only of bare precepts? But it muſt be owned, that ſuch admonition is more prevalent, and ſtrikes deeper, which adds a reaſon for what it commands, and ſhews for what, and wherefore ſuch a thing is to be done, and alſo what profit will accrue to the doer from a ready and dutiful obedience. If authority can prevail, ſo will admonition: but authority oftentimes prevails, and conſequently admonition.

Virtue is divided into two parts (*r*), the contemplation of truth and action: good inſtitution teacheth contemplation, admonition action; and upright actions exerciſe and diſplay virtue. If a man can do good by perſuaſion, he can alſo by giving good advice; therefore if acting uprightly be neceſſary to virtue, and admonition points out the fitneſs of action, then is admonition alſo neceſſary. Two things greatly contribute to ſtrengthen the mind; aſſurance of the truth, and confidence therein; both which are greatly owing to admonition: for we truſt to it; and when we do ſo, the mind is elevated, and full of confidence: admonition therefore is not ſuperfluous.

Marcus Agrippa, a man of great underſtanding, who alone was happy, for the public good, among all thoſe whom the civil wars had rendered famous and powerful, was wont to ſay, that he was much indebted to that ſentence, Concordiâ parvæ res creſcunt, diſcordiâ maximæ dîlabuntur; *by concord ſmall things increaſe, and by diſcord the greateſt fall into ruin*; and that from hence he became an affectionate brother, and a faithful friend. If then ſuch ſentences, familiarly entertained in the mind, form it aright; why ſhould not this part of philoſophy, conſiſting of the like ſentences, have the ſame effect? Part of virtue conſiſts in diſcipline, or theory, and part in the exerciſe or practice of it. A man muſt firſt learn, and then confirm what he hath learned, by actions: and if ſo, not only the general decrees of philoſophy are profitable, but alſo the particular precepts, which reſtrain and bind our affections, as by a ſolemn edict (*s*).

Philoſophy,

Philosophy, it is said, *is divided into two things*; knowledge, *and an* habit of the mind (*t*): *for he that hath learned it, and perceives what is to be done and what to be avoided*, is not *completely a wise man, until his mind be transformed, as it were, into those things which he hath learned: the third part therefore which consists of precepts, being composed of the former two, is superfluous; because the other two suffice to accomplish virtue*. On this account then all consolation would be superfluous; for this likewise consists of the two things before mentioned; as also exhortation, persuasion, and even argumentation, for this also proceeds from the habit of a mind well composed, and established in goodness. But notwithstanding these proceed from a habit of mind, yet the best habit of mind is formed from the other (precepts) as well as from these.

Besides, all that hath been hitherto advanced relates to a man completely perfect, and who hath reached the summit of human felicity: but to this men generally make but slow advances: in the mean time the way of righteousness is to be shewn to the man, who is as yet imperfect, but who is continually making some further progress: wisdom perhaps may present herself at last to such a one without the help of admonition, when she hath brought him to such a pass, that he cannot be moved to do any thing but what is right. It is necessary however that some one should conduct weaker minds, saying, *you must avoid this; you must do that*.

Moreover, was a man to wait the time, when of himself he may know his duty, he may chance to wander, and by wandering in error be hindered from arriving at such a state as can possibly give him complacency and content. He must therefore be governed, until he is capable of governing himself. Children are taught by rule; their fingers are held and directed by another hand, and carried through the several figures and proportions of letters; then they are ordered to imitate some copy, and from thence learn to settle their hand or manner of writing. In like manner our mind is assisted, while led and instructed by by rule and precept.—And thus have I endeavoured to prove that the preceptive part of philoſophy is by no means ſuperfluous.

But it is further aſk'd, whether *this alone is ſufficient to make a man truly wiſe?* We ſhall anſwer this queſtion another day: in the mean while, omitting other arguments, is it not evident that we ſtand in need of ſome advocate or tutor, at leaſt to countermand the common precepts of the world? Scarce any word comes to our ears but what is prejudicial to us: they hurt us, who bleſs and wiſh us well; and they hurt us, who malign and curſe us: for the imprecations of theſe ſtrike us into a panic; and the affection of the other prompts us to ill, by wiſhing us all worldly proſperity; foraſmuch as it drives us to a diſtant good, uncertain and erroneous; when we may enjoy happineſs at home.

It is almoſt impoſſible to walk uprightly; our parents nay our ſervants entice us to ill: nor does any one err to his own prejudice alone; but ſpreads folly among his neighbours, and catcheth it likewiſe in his turn from them: from whence the vices of the common people become general; for they communicate them from one to another, and in making others worſe they become ſo themſelves; they learn all manner of evil, and then teach it; from whence comes that monſtrous pile of iniquity, whereby every one becomes as wiſe as his neighbour in the knowledge and practice of ſin.

It is neceſſary therefore we ſhould have ſome tutor to check us now and then; to chaſe away idle rumours (*u*), and gainſay the flatteries of the common people. For it is a miſtake to think that vices are born with us (*x*); they ſteal upon us, and are engrafted into us as we grow up. Therefore by frequent admonitions we muſt repel thoſe falſe opinions that are for ever ringing in our ears. Nature obligeth us to no ſin whatever; ſhe brought us forth ſound and free; nothing that might incite our avarice hath ſhe placed in open ſight; gold and ſilver ſhe hath put under our feet, that we might preſs and trample upon them; and whatever elſe there may be, for which we are preſſed and trampled upon

upon ourſelves: ſhe hath given us a countenance erect towards heaven *(y)*, that we might look up and behold her great and wonderful works: as, the riſing and ſetting of the ſun, the ſwift motion of the voluble world, that by day gives a delightful view of the things on earth, and by night diſplays the glittering ſplendour of the heavens; the progreſſion of the ſtars, ſeeming ſlow, when compared with the rapid courſe of other bodies; and yet exceeding ſwift, if we conſider the vaſt ſpaces they travel over with inceſſant velocity; the eclipſes alſo of the ſun and moon, when in oppoſition; theſe and many other the like wonderful phænomena, whether they proceed in a regular courſe, or break forth ſuddenly from ſome hidden cauſe, as the nightly ſtreams of fire, and the flaſhes of lightning *(meteors)* from the opening heavens, without any ſtroke or ſound of thunder; the beams alſo, and pillars, and other various appearances of flames: theſe, I ſay, Nature hath placed viſibly above our heads; but gold and ſilver, and iron (z), (which on their account knows no reſt) hath ſhe hid in the earth, as being dangerous things for us to be truſted withal: we brought them to light, only to ſcramble and fight for them: we ourſelves took the pains to dig up from the very bowels of the earth, both the cauſes and inſtruments of our dangers: we have truſted our miſery to fortune; and are not aſhamed to hold thoſe things in the higheſt eſtimation, which lie buried in the loweſt depth of the earth. Would you know how falſe a glare it is, which dazzleth your eyes? Believe me, nothing can be more abject and vile than theſe things are, while ſunk and involved in their native ſoil. For why? when they are firſt drawn from the mines in the ore, nothing can be more ill-favoured, 'till they are worked into form, and purged from the droſs: only behold the workman, by whoſe hands this ſteril and ſhapeleſs kind of earth is refined: you ſee how they are beſmeared with dirt and ſmoke; but theſe things rather defile the mind than the body; and there is more ſordid baſeneſs in the poſſeſſor of them, than in the refiner.

It is neceſſary therefore that men ſhould be admoniſhed, and have ſome counſellors of a good underſtanding and ſound judgment, that they may hear the voice of truth amidſt ſo great confuſion, and ſuch a jargon

jargon of falsities: and what shall that voice utter? Why, such good and wholesome counsel as may open your ears, when deafened by so many vain and ambitious clamours, that are every where poured forth around you. Let it inform you, that *there is no reason for you to envy those whom the vulgar call great and happy*; or, that *vain applause should shake and disturb the sweet composure of a sound mind*; or, that *a man clothed in purple, and stalking along with the ensigns of authority carried before him, should make you disdain your tranquillity of soul*; or *that you should think him a greater and more happy man, to whom every one gives way, than yourself, whom the beadle drives out of the way before him.* If you likewise would exercise a power, that may be profitable to yourself, and hurtful to no one, drive vice from thee.

There are many who set fire to cities, and throw down towns that have stood safe and impregnable many ages; who raise platforms as high as castles, and overturn walls of an immense height, with battering rams and other engines of war; there are many who have drove armies before them, and pressing hard upon the flying enemies, and covered with the blood of nations, have made their way to the great ocean; and yet these mighty conquerors have been conquered by loose desires. No one could withstand them, when rushing on in full career; neither could they themselves withstand the temptations of ambition and cruelty: while they seemed to be driving others, they were driven themselves.

A strange madness drove unhappy *Alexander* upon plundering divers countries; and still ranging into unknown regions. For can you think the man in his senses, who first began upon the destruction of *Greece*, and seized upon every thing that was valuable therein: he enslaved *Sparta*, and made *Athens* silent: and not contented with the spoils of many cities, which his father *Philip* had either conquered or bought, he fell upon other unprovoked, and and carried his arms throughout the known world; nor was he ever tired with acts of cruelty; imitating herein the wild beasts, who generally tear more than they can devour. He had now contracted many cities into one; both

4 the

the *Greeks* and *Perſians* dread his power, and the nations that were free under *Darius* ſubmit to his yoke; yet he ſtill puſheth on, and would fain extend his conqueſt beyond the riſing or ſetting ſun; he cannot bear to be confined by the pillars of *Bacchus* (in the eaſt), or of *Hercules* (in the weſt). He endeavours to force Nature herſelf; he hath no mind to march; yet will not ſtay in any place; as reſtleſs as an heavy weight, which thrown down an hill, will not reſt 'till it comes to the bottom.

So neither did reaſon or virtue inſtigate *Cneius Pompey* to wage either foreign or domeſtic wars; but mad with the love of falſe greatneſs at one time, he marched his army into *Spain*, and againſt *Sertorius*; at another time he took upon him to humble the pirates, and ſcour the ſeas: ſuch were his pretexts to keep up an army, and maintain his power. What drew him into *Africa*, what into the North, what againſt *Mithridates*, and into *Armenia*, and every corner of *Aſia*? What, but an inſatiable thirſt of greatneſs, when no one but himſelf thought he could be greater?

And what provoked *Caius Cæſar* to ruin himſelf and the commonwealth? Glory, ambition, and an unmeaſurable deſire of pre-eminence. He could not endure to have one maſter; though the Republic was contentedly ſubject to the dominion of two (Conſuls.) Or, think you, that it was a virtuous principle, that puſhed on *Caius Marius*, who was *once* Conſul (for he was *once* duly elected, the other ſix times he gained his point by bribes or force of arms †) to undergo ſo many perils, when he ſlaughtered the *Cimbrians* and *Germans*; and purſued *Jugurtha* through the deſerts of *Africa*? No; *Marius* led an army; but ambition led *Marius*.

Theſe men when they ſhook all things, were themſelves miſerably ſhaken; like whirlwinds that invelope the things they ſeize upon, but are themſelves toſſed about, and ruſh with the greater force, being under no command. And therefore when theſe heroes have cruelly injured many, they themſelves feel the pernicious violence wherewith they inflicted others. There is no reafon you fhould think any one happy in the unhappinefs of his fellow-creatures.

All thefe examples, which we daily fee, and hear of, are to be kept in memory; and our hearts, full of evil furmifes, are to be cleanfed. Virtue muft difengage us from our prefent employ, and take its due place in the mind, in order to extirpate all pleafing lyes againft the truth; to feparate us from the common people, (to whom we give too much credit) and to confirm us in fincere and juft opinions. For this is wifdom; to return to Nature, and to be reftored to the happy ftate from whence public errors had drove us.

It is a great ftep toward health and foundnefs, to have forfaken the counfellors of folly, and to have fled from the common people, who are daily corrupting one another. That you may know this to be true, behold how differently men live in public and in private: yet it is not folitude that teacheth fimplicity and innocence; nor does a country-life of itfelf make us more frugal and temperate; but it is the having no witnefs or fpectator which makes many vices, that have no other aim but to be feen and admired, fubfide of themfelves. Who would be cloathed in purple was there no one to gaze upon him? who in private would have dainties ferved up to him in a golden difh? who, when lying under the fhade of a green tree in fome rural fpot, would difplay the pomp of luxury? No man is very fpruce and fumptuous when by himfelf, or even in the prefence of two or three fervants or familiars, but according to the number and quality of his vifitants, makes he a fhew of his coftly vanities. So that the chief inftigation to all thofe things we are fo foolifhly mad after, is, the teftimony of fuch as know and admire us: take away the witnefs, and you will abolifh thofe fond defires. Ambition, luxury and pride, require a public ftage: you will certainly cure them, if you will but conceal them.

And therefore, if we refide in a noify populous city, it would be requifite to have always a monitor at our elbow; who, in oppofition to flatterers, and fuch as commend a large eftate, fhould rather praife the

3 man

man who is contented with a little, and who meaſures his wealth by the good uſes he makes of it: againſt thoſe, who extol favour and power, let him recommend retirement, when devoted to the ſtudy of literature; and a mind withdrawn from external things, to reflect upon its own real and proper good. Let him ſhew how theſe great men, who in vulgar eſtimation are accounted happy, tremble and are aſtoniſhed at their envied height; and have a very different opinion of themſelves, from what others entertain of them: that what ſeems a lofty ſeat to others, ſeems to them but a ſteep and broken rock: therefore are they ſpiritleſs, and ſhudder with fear when they look down from this dangerous precipice of greatneſs: they ſuſpect a thouſand accidents to which their ſlippery ſituation is ſubject: then they dread what they ſo greatly courted: and the proſperity which hath made them troubleſome and injurious to others, lays an heavier burthen upon themſelves: then they extol a calm retirement, and the ſweet liberty of being their own maſters: ſplendour grows diſtaſteful to them, and they gladly ſeek a diſcharge from their high offices: then at length you ſhall ſee them play the philoſophers through fear, and take good counſel from their wretched ſituation: for theſe two things ſeem inconſiſtent with each other, *a good fortune,* and *a ſound mind:* as we are generally more wiſe in adverſity; but proſperity is apt to blind the judgment, and warp us in our duty.

ANNOTATIONS, &c.

* *Muretus* in his preamble to this Epiſtle obſerves that as *Ariſto* maintained the *decretal* or dogmatical philoſophy; *Seneca* defends the *exhortatory* or preceptive: but particularly, that from a diligent peruſal of this Epiſtle may be learned what is the true meaning of that obſcure ſentence in the firſt book of *Tully's* Offices, Omnis de officio duplex eſt, quæſtio; *every queſtion relating to duty is twofold,* i. e. either particular or general: which none of the expoſitors or commentators ſeem to have hit upon before.

(*a*) This is ſomewhat like what St. *James* ſaith; *If a brother or ſiſter be naked, and deſtitute of daily food; and one of you ſay unto him,* depart in peace, be ye warmed and filled, *notwithſtanding ye give them not thoſe things which are needful for the body, what doth it profit?* ii. 5. 6.

† See Epp. 24. 30. 78.

(*b*) The Stoics ſuppoſed all men to be mad except their wiſe man, though they drank not ellebore nor applied themſelves to a phyſician. Of which ſort of madneſs *Horace* ſpeaketh, when he ſaith,

Inſanire putas ſolennia me; neque rides;
Nec medici credis, nec curatoris egere. Ep. i. 1. 101.

You count me mad in fashion, you forbear
To laugh, nor think I want a doctor's care,
Or guardian from the Prætor.——Creech.

See the fourth Paradox of *Tully*, (omnes stultos insanire, *that every fool is a madman*) which is supposed to be addressed to *Clodius*, who had driven *Tully* into exile.

(c) Non est quod plenis ac tumentibus imperc.] *Suetonius* (in Tiberio;) contentis ac tumentibus oculis prosequi. *To fix or strain the eyes*, says *Lipsius*, *as in love or devotion.*

(d) Lactant. l. 6. c. 23. Servando igitur ab utroque fides alteri est, imò exemplo continentiæ docenda uxor, ut se castè gerat, iniquum est enim ut ipse exigas quod præstare ipse non possis. *Fidelity therefore in the married state is respectively required from both parties:* without which the rational and moral human species could be retained with no rules of *order*, becoming their nature; no decency; but a variable, unsettled, roving appetite, would soon gain the transcendency over *reason*, and introduce universal confusion. Marriage was therefore rendered *holy* and *honourable* by a particular sanction of the all-wise, omnipotent Creator.

Marriage, thou easiest, safest, happiest state!
Let debauchees and drunkards thee prophane:——

(What follows I cannot recollect, nor whose lines they are.)

(e) By not observing these two precepts of *Cato*, I believe many have been imposed upon under the specious pretence of *buying bargains*. Our English proverbs are—*Good cheap is dear. A good bargain is a pickpurse.* The French say, *Bon marchè tire l' argent hors de bourse.* As I saw an old gentlewoman buy a parcel of *shalots* which she would not taste, and even abominated; because they were offered at a penny cheaper than the usual price.

(f) This precept *Clemens* of *Alexandria* interprets two ways; either, *because life is short, and therefore ought not to be spent in vain or idle amusements*; or, *that we ought to be careful in our daily expences*, lest we should live so long as to want necessaries. See Ep. i. (N. a.)

Take Time while Time is, for Time will away. Scotch Proverb.

(g) 'Tis true, as *Seneca* says, *such sentences as these want no advocate:* yet, as the different usage and application of them may be acceptable to some sort of readers, I shall further observe, that *this* is the first of the three sentences which *Plato* saith were fixed upon the doors of the *Delphic* Oracle, as seeming worthy to have come from God. Among the proverbial sentences is this verse:

Τὸ γνῶθι σαυτὸν πανταχοῦ ἐστι χρήσιμον.

Nonnus Marcellus quotes a satire by *Varro* under this title;

γνῶθι σεαυτὸν——Famâ celebrata per orbem
Littera, cognosci quæ sibi quemque jubet.

Juvenal saith it came down from heaven,——e cœlo descendit. But *Ovid* gives it to *Pythagoras*; *Socrates* the Platonic, to *Apollo*. *Diogenes* gives it to *Thales*; *Antisthenes* to *Phenomöe* the Sybil; but that *Chilo* made use of it. *Thales* being asked, τί ἐστι δύσκολον; *what is a difficult thing?* answered, *to know one's self.* τί εὔκολον; *what an easy thing?* ἄλλῳ ὑποτίθεσθαι, *to give advice to another.* *Cicero*, (Tusc. Qu. l. 26.) Nimirum hanc habet vim præceptum *Apollonis*, quo monet, ut *se quisque noscat*, &c. *This, doubtless, is the meaning of the precept of* Apollo, *which advises every one to know himself. I do not apprehend his intention to have been, that we should inform ourselves of our stature and make; nor do I address myself to your body; when therefore he saith* know yourself, he saith this, inform yourself of the nature of your soul, *for the body is but a kind of vessel or receptacle of the soul. Whatever your soul doth, is your own act.* To know the soul *then, unless it had been divine, would not have been a precept of that excellent wisdom, as to be attributed to a God.* And elsewhere, *we must not think this precept given only to lessen our pride, but also to make us understand our own good.*

Tecum habita, et nôris quàm sit tibi curta supellex. Perf. iv. 57.
Survey thy soul, not what thou dost appear,
But what thou art, and find the beggar there. Dryden.
Teipsum concute.———Hor. S. l. 3. 35.
Examine then thyself with strictest care.

Macrobius tells us of one, who consulting the oracle, asked, *by what means he might attain happiness?* it was answered, *Know thyself.* But this answer was supposed to have been given to *Crœsus.* Somhthing like it is that of *Antiphanes.*

Εἰ θνητὸς εἶ, βέλτιστε, θνητὰ τὰ φρόνει.
As thou art mortal, think of mortal things.

Some give it to *Homer* as the grand source of all wisdom and learning. From *Hector's* declining to fight with *Ajax*, knowing him to be a better man,

Αἴαντος δ' ἀλέεινε μάχην Τελαμωνιάδαο.
Ajax *he shuns thro' all the dire debate,*
And fears that arm, whose force he felt so late. Pope.

This admirable sentence however is bantered by the comic poet *Menander;*

Κατὰ πολλ' ἄρ' ἐστὶν οὐ καλῶς εἰρημένον,
Τὸ, γνῶθι σαυτὸν, χρησιμώτερον γὰρ ἦν
Τὸ γνῶθι τοὺς ἄλλους.
Talk not of that fam'd sentence, Know thyself,
'Twere better far a man should know the world.

(*b*) Magni est animi injurias oblivisci. *Cic.* (de Orat.) *It shews greatness of mind to forget an injury.* Delle ingiurie il remedio a lui scordarsi. *Ital.*

Semper et infirmi est animi exiguique voluptas
Ultio———Juv. xiii. 191.
Revenge betrays a weak and little mind.

(*i*) Fortes enim non modo fortuna adjuvat, ut est in veteri proverbio, sed multo magis ratio. *Cic.* (Tusc. Q. ii.) *It is not Fortune alone that assists and advanceth the brave, but Reason; which, by certain precepts, as it were, confirms even courage itself.*

Audentes fortesque Deus juvat. *Ovid.*
—— Audaces adjuvat ipsa Venus. Id.
A faint heart never won fair lady. Prov.

Or as the French say, *Le coüard n' aura belle amie.*

'Αλλ' οἱ μὲν ἀθυμῶντες ἄνδρες οὔποτε τροπαῖον ἐστήσαντο.
—— Timidi nunquam statuére tropæa.
No trophies ever grac'd a coward's name.
Πρὸς σοφίαν μὲν ἔχειν τολμὰν μάλα σύμφορόν ἐστι,
Χωρὶς δὲ, βλαβερὴ, καὶ κακότητα φέρει.
Unless to wisdom fortitude is join'd,
Losses ensue, and fortune proves unkind.

(*k*) So *Gronovius*, that it may seem an Hemistic.

al. piger sibi——ipse obstat.
Idle folks have the most labour. Prov.
Idleness is the key of beggary.
Idleness turns the edge of wit.
Idle folks want no excuse.

Desuetudo omnibus pigritiam, pigritia veternum parit. *Apul.*
Disuse begets idleness, and idleness a lethargy.

(l) Si tamen illam diutina pestis non infecit, nec enecuit—*(sic ferè omn.)* but *Muretus* from *Pincian* reads it, si tamen illam diutina pestis infecit nec enecuit, *provided the contagion of sin, which hath so long infected it, had not quite destroyed it.* *Gronovius* prefers the former, because *Seneca* useth the word *infici*, in a stronger sense, than merely a slight and easily-curable disorder. Ep. 59. Diu in istis vitiis jacuimus; elui difficile est; non enim inquinati sumus sed *infecti*. Ep. 71. Animum non coloravit sed *infecit*.

(*m*) But as *Seneca*, saith *Muretus*, differs from *Posidonius*, so I must beg leave to differ from *Seneca*: for I think the prefaces to the laws of *Plato* are admirable; first, on account of the love of virtue, which is so eminently displayed therein: and, secondly, that where this prevails not, the minds of men are to be drawn off from sin and wickedness by the fear of punishments, under the sanctions subjoined to those prefaces. Be this as it will, nothing, I think, can be more just than what *Seneca* here saith, with regard to the brevity of laws; and nothing more applicable to our due observance of the positive laws of God, in the Christian scheme, than his; mone, dic quid me velis fecisse: non disco, sed pareo. *Tell me what you would have me do; I am all obedience.* God hath told us what we ought to do, and what to believe; and if through the weakness of our understandings we cannot in some cases see the reason of such a law; or, where the sublimity of the subject will admit of no greater clearness, give a reason of the things we believe; yet we may give a good reason for our belief in those things: *It is the word and will of God, therefore we believe; we believe, and therefore we obey.* M.

(*n*) Cicero, (ii. de leg.) Et illud bené dictum est a Pythagora, doctissimo viro, tum maximi et pietatem et religionem versari in animis, cum rebus divinis operam daremus. *That the time when men are most honest, is, when they present themselves before the Gods.* This is mentioned likewise by *Plutarch*. De Superst. p. 169. De Def. Orac. p. 447.

(*o*) *Gr.* μηδὲν ἄγαν. *Gall.* Assez y a si trop n' y a. *Ital.* L'abondanza delle cose ingenera fastidio. And our English proverb, *Too much of one thing is good for nothing.*

Diogenes ascribes it to *Pythagoras*; *Aristotle* to *Bias*; others to *Thales*, and others to *Solon*; and some ascribe it, as the *nosce teipsum*, to *Homer* from *Od.* ο. 69.

——νεμεσσῶμαι δὲ καὶ ἄλλῳ
Ἀνδρὶ ξεινοδόκῳ, ὅς κ' ἔξοχα μὲν φιλέησιν,
Ἔξοχα δ' ἐχθαίρησιν· ἀμείνω δ' αἴσιμα πάντα.
For oft in others freely I reprove
The ill-tim'd efforts of officious love:
Who love too much, hate in the like extreme,
And both the golden mean alike condemn. Pope.
Παντων μὲν κορος ἐστὶ, καὶ ὕπνου καὶ φιλότητος
Μολπῆς τε γλυκερῆς, καὶ ἀμύμονος ὀρχηθμοῖο. Il. ν. 637.
The best of things beyond their measure cloy;
Sleep's balmy blessing, love's endearing joy;
The feast, the dance; whate'er mankind desire;
Ev'n the sweet charms of sacred numbers tire. Pope.
Τυδείδη, μήτ' ἄρ με μάλ' αἴνεε, μήτε τι νείκει. Il. κ. 249.
Be not too lavish, or in praise or blame.

But I had rather saith *Erasmus* give it to *Hesiod*.

Μέτρα φυλάσσεσθαι· καιρὸς δ' ἐπὶ πᾶσιν ἄριστος.

Pindar in imitation of the foregoing lines from *Homer*;

> Κόροι δ᾽ ἔχει καὶ μελι, καὶ
> Τὰ τερπν᾽ ἄνθ᾽ ἀφροδίσια.

Pindar in *Plutarch*, σοφοι δὲ καὶ τὸ, μηδὲν ἄγαν, ἔπος περισσως ἄινεσαν.——*As if the wise men had extolled above measure that saying*, too much of nothing.

> Παντων μέτριον ἄριστον——Phocylides.
> *The mean of every thing is best.*

Sophocles in Electra. Μηθ᾽ οἷς εχθαιρεις

> ὑπεράχθεο μήτ᾽ ἐπιλάθου.
> —— *Patient submit; nor let thy rage*
> *Too far transport thee, nor oblivion drown*
> *The just remembrance of thy matchless woes.* Franklin.

Euripides *Hippol.* 264.

> οὕτω τὸ λιαν γ᾽ ἧσσον ἐπαινῶ
> Τοῦ μηδὲν ἄγαν---
> Και ξυμφησουσι σοφοι μοι.
> Too much *of any thing is sure amiss;*
> *Since all philosophers agree in this.*

Alpheus, Anthol, l. 1. c. 12. τὸ μηδὲν γὰρ ἄγαν, ἄγαν με τερπει·

Athenæus, l. 1. Πασας δ᾽ εκκραδιας ἀνιας ἀνδρων ἀλαπαζει

> Πινόμενος κατὰ μετρον ὑπὲρ μετρον δὲ χερείων.
> *A chearful glass revives the drooping soul;*
> *Not so, o'ercharg'd, with the unmeasur'd bowl.*

Plin. l. 11. Perniciosissimum autem est in omni quidem vita quod nimium est.——*In every circumstance of life too much of any thing is dangerous.*

Quintilian (l. 12. c. 6.) writes, modum in pronunciatione regnare, quemadmodum in cæteris omnibus, *that a mean is to be observed in pronunciation as in all other things.*

Plautus, in *Pænulo*, Modus omnibus in rebus,---est optimus.

> Est modus in rebus sunt certi denique fines,
> Quos ultra citraque nequit consistere rectum. *Hor.* S. 1. 1.
> *In every thing observe the golden mean,*
> *Virtue within fix'd bounds is only seen.* Shard.
> Virtus est medium vitiorum utrinque redactum. Id. Ep. i. 18.
> *On each extreme a different vice is seen,*
> *For virtue's throne is seated in the mean.* Id.

Lastly *Plutarch*, in the life of *Camillus* teacheth, that true piety consists in the *mean between Atheism and Superstition.*

(*p*) The same with *Horace*; Semper avarus eget.——Ep. i. 2. 5.

> *See the pale miser, (who intensely pries*
> *On untouch'd bags with ever watchful eyes,*
> *Nor dares to use the wealth his labour won,)*
> *Create the very want he means to shun.* Anon.

(*q*) *With what measure you mete it shall be measured to you.* Therefore, *whatsoever you would that men should do to you, do you also to them, for this is the Law and the Prophets.* Matth. vi. 2. 12.

(*r*) The contemplative and the active. So Philosophy; Ep. 95. See *Lips.* Manud. Diss. ii. 5.

(*s*) Alluding

(*s*) Alluding to the customs of the times when the Princes or Governors published the edicts, for the admonition, correction, and compulsion of the people. See *Lips.* ad *Tacit.* Ann. l. 3.

(*t*) i. e. knowledge of what is contained in the decrees; and an habit obtained, by that means, of doing what is right.

(*u*) Abigatque rumores] The edition of *Muretus* reads it *tumores*, perhaps by the error of the press; though it hath its meaning; *to pluck down our pride*.

(*x*) This is what the *Stoics* absolutely deny, and maintain *that men are all naturally born good, but that from our communication with a corrupt world the innate sparks of virtue are extinguished, and the contrary vices arise, and are confirmed.* Cicero (de Leg. i.) Justos quidem Naturâ nos esse factos, tantum autem esse corruptelam malæ consuetudinis, ut ab eâ tanquam igniculi extinguantur a Naturâ dati, exorianturque et confirmentur vitia contraria.

Not so the *Academics*, who maintain, with *Apuleius*, in a Platonic sense, Hominem ob stirpe ipsa neque absolutè bonum, nec malum nasci, sed ad utrumque proclive ingenium esse. Habere quidem semina quædam utrarumque rerum, cum nascendi origine copulata, quæ educationis disciplina in alteram debeant partem emicare. *That man is not born absolutely either good or bad; that he has certain innate qualities, which from discipline and instruction, or the want of it, are inclined to either side. If virtue,* says Galen, *comes by nature, and depravity from sentiment and example; tell me who corrupted the first man, when as yet, it is supposed, there was no malignity in the world?* They could not but have it from themselves. It is said that this argument converted *Posidonius* from Stoicism, and inclined him to think with the *Academics*.

Horace speaks more agreeably with the *Christian* scheme, when he says, Nemo vitiis sine nascitur. So *Demosthenes*, μόνον ἀναμάρτητοι οἱ Θεοί, *the Gods alone are free from all sin*. And *Propertius*,

> Unicuique dedit vitium Natura creato.
> *Nature in every breast implanted vice.*

Undoubtedly, let some affected disputants argue as they please. Every man is sensible of that depravity, or proneness to evil, which deviating from original righteousness, and being repugnant to the law of God, *hath of itself the nature of sin*; and is therefore by *Divines* called *original sin*.

(*y*)

> Os homini sublime dedit, cœlumque videre
> Jussit et erectos ad sidera tollere vultus. Ov. Met. i. 88.
> *Hence, while his fellow-creatures of the earth,*
> *Prone to the ground their sight, betray their birth:*
> *Man of erected frame looks up on high,*
> *Heav'nward he casts his elevated eye,*
> *And grows familiar with his native sky.*

Cicero (de Leg. i. 9.] Cum cætera animalia abjecisset ad pastum, solum hominem erexit ad cœli cognitionem. *Id.* (de Nat. Deor.) Qui Deus) constituit eos (homines) humo excitatos, celsos, et erectos constituit ut Deorum cognitionem cœlum intuentes capere possint. Sunt enim ex terra homines, non ut incolæ et habitatores, sed quasi spectatores superarum rerum atque cœlestium, quorum spectaculum ad nullum aliud genus animantium pertinet. *He* (the God of Nature) *hath made us of a stature tall and upright, that beholding the heavens we might arrive to the knowledge of the Gods; for we are not simply to dwell here as inhabitants of the earth, but to contemplate the heavens, and the stars; a privilege not granted to any other kind of animated beings.*—*Xenophon* has used the same argument to shew the wisdom of the Deity in the constitution of man, as he hath other arguments similar to what are used by the *Stoic*, soon after in his Examination into the Senses. (N.)

(*z*) *Seneca* (de Benef. vii. 10.) Video ferrum ex iisdem tenebris esse prolatum, quibus aurum et argentum; ne aut instrumentum in cædes mutuas deesset, aut pretium: *I observe that iron is produced from the same seat of darkness as are gold and silver, that there may not be wanting an instrument for murder, or a reward for the same.*

—— nec

——nec bella fuerunt
Faginus adstabat cùm scyphus ante dapes.
——*Then wars began,*
When the gold cup expell'd the beechen can.

So *Romeo* to the Apothecary:

There is thy gold; worse poison to men's soul,
Than these poor compounds, which thou dar'st not sell.
I sell thee *poyson*; thou hast sold *me* none.

† This *Lipsius* does not allow, if you except the two last; as the foregoing honours were conferred upon him in his absence.

EPISTLE XCIII.

Of Examples, or Characters. *

YOU desire, *Lucilius*, that I would consider of what I told you in my last, should be deferred to another day (*a*); and to let you know whether I thought that part of philosophy, which the *Greeks* call παραινετικη, and we (præceptiva) *preceptive*, or exhortatory, sufficient to make a man perfectly wise. I know you would not take it amiss should I refuse you. I therefore renew my promise, notwithstanding that proverbial form of speech—postea noli rogare, quod impetrare nolueris—*Ask not again for what you wish not to obtain.* For it is no uncommon thing to ask with earnestness, what if offered we should refuse: now, whether this is owing to levity, or sauciness, the best way of punishing it is by a ready compliance.

We would fain seem, I say, to desire many things, which, in reality, we are averse to. A certain Author produced a large history, wrote in small characters and closely folded up, which when he had read great part of, *I will give over*, said he, *if you please. No, no; read on, read on*; cry the audience, who had much rather he should hold his tongue. Thus we often wish for one thing and pray for another; and speak not the truth to the Gods themselves: but the

Gods either hear us not, or have mercy upon us! But, for my part, I ſhall have no mercy on you, *Lucilius*, intending to diſcharge my duty, and to trouble you with another long Epiſtle; which if you read and cannot reliſh it, ſay, Ego mihi hoc contraxi, *I have brought this upon myſelf*; and reckon yourſelf among thoſe whom a coſtly wife, gained by aſſiduous courtſhip, is continually tormenting; among thoſe who enjoy not the wealth, amaſſed with great toil and labour—among thoſe, whom honours, obtained by all that art or induſtry can do, rack with diſquiet—or other coiners of their own wretchedneſs. But omitting any further preamble, I now come to the point in hand.

An happy life, they ſay, *conſiſts in fit and juſt actions*; therefore *precepts are ſufficient to make life happy*. I deny the *minor* propoſition: precepts do not always incite fit actions; unleſs attended to with an obſequious diſpoſition of the mind. Sometimes they are applied in vain; when the underſtanding is prejudiced by falſe opinions. And again, if men happen to do right, they do not always know it (*b*): for it is not every one, unleſs they are tutored from the beginning, and faſhioned in all points of reaſon, that can be perfect in every rule of decency; knowing what they ought to do, how much, in what relation, and in what manner; wherefore they cannot in every action purſue virtue, at leaſt not conſtantly, nor deſignedly: they will often look back and heſitate.

If fit and juſt actions, it is ſaid, *ſpring from precepts, then are precepts ſufficient to make life happy: but the one is true, conſequently the other*. To this we anſwer, juſt and fit actions ariſe from maxims and general rules, and not from precepts only.

Again it is ſaid, *if other arts are contented with precepts, ſo is wiſdom*, or the art of life. But a man is made a pilot, by ſuch inſtructions as theſe: *thus you muſt ſteer; thus ſtrike ſail; thus uſe a favourable wind; thus a contrary one; thus make a doubtful or croſs wind ſerve your turn: and ſo in other arts are men tutored by precepts; cannot then ſuch as teach the art of living, purſue the ſame method with the like effect?* No; all

theſe

these arts are employed in, or relate only to, the means of life, and not to the whole life: and therefore many things from without may restrain and impede them, as hope, desire, fear, and the like: but wisdom, which professeth the art of life, cannot be prevented from exercising herself at all times: for she shakes off all impediments, and manageth all opposition.

Would you know wherein the condition of this differs from all other arts (c)? Know, that in these it is more excuseable to err by choice than accidentally; but in this there cannot be a greater crime than to sin voluntarily. I will explain what I mean: a grammarian is not ashamed of a solecism, when he commits it knowingly; but would blush at one committed through ignorance, or carelessness: a physician, if he perceives not that his patient grows worse, is more in fault with regard to his art, than one who perceives the defect, yet pretends not to know it. But in that art of life a wilful error is the more criminal.

Add now, that most of these arts, I might say all that are truly liberal, have their general maxims, and not precepts only. As in physic, for instance, there is one sect that follows *Hippocrates*, another sect *Asclepeiades*, another *Themison*. Besides, there is no contemplative art but what hath its decrees, which the Greeks call δογματα, and we *decrees*, *maxims*, or *axioms*; such as you will find in geometry or astronomy. But philosophy is both contemplative and active. She meditates, and also sets her hand to work. You are mistaken, if you think she is only engaged in terrestrial affairs. She aspireth much higher. *I range*, saith she, *the universe; nor am satisfied with the conversation of mortals, in order either to persuade or dissuade them; sublime matters, far above your reach, invite me:*

Nam tibi de summa tali ratione Deumque,
Differere incipiam, et rerum primordia pandem
Unde omnis natura creet res, auctet, alatque,
Quoque eadem rursus natura perempta resolvat. Lucr. l. 50.

I treat of things abstruse, the Deity,
The vast and steady motions of the sky;

The rise of things; how curious Nature joins
The various seeds, and in one mass combines
The jarring principles; what new supplies
Bring nourishment and strength; how she unties
The Gordian knot, and the poor compound dies. Creech.

As saith *Lucretius:* it follows therefore that being contemplative, she hath also her maxims and decrees. Besides that no one can do what he ought to do, unless a reason be pointed out to him, whereby he may punctually discharge every office in life; which it is impossible for him to do, who hath received nothing but mere precepts; the precepts being distributed in parcels are but weak in themselves, and if I may so speak, without root, and a solid foundation: decrees and certain maxims are what must protect us, and maintain our security and peace; and which comprehend all life, and all nature. There is the same difference between the *decrees* and *precepts* of philosophy, as there is between letters and whole sentences; these depend upon the former which gave rise both to them, and to every thing of the like kind.

The antient wisdom, it is said, *taught by precept nothing more than what was to be done and what was to be avoided; and yet men were far better in those days than they are now: as soon as learning began to flourish, good men grew scarce. For that simple and open virtue is now turned into obscure and subtle science. We learn rather to dispute, than to live.* Undoubtedly, as you say, that antient wisdom was in the beginning rude and single, no less than other arts, that in process of time grew more refined and polished. But there was no need of such choice remedies as are now presented: wickedness was not grown to such a height, nor had it spread so wide: simple remedies were applied to simple vices. But now there is a necessity for stronger battlements, and more laboured fortifications, as the mischiefs that assault us are grown so much stronger and more powerful.

Physic formerly was nothing more than skill in the virtues of some few herbs whereby the flowing blood might be staunched, and wounds closed by degrees; but now it is become an extensive study, and consists in in a ſurpriſing multiplicity of preſcriptions. No wonder it had ſo little to do in thoſe antient times, when the bodies of men were hale and robuſt, and their diet plain and eaſy, uncorrupted by art and delicacies; which in aftertimes began to be ſought for, not in order to ſatisfy hunger, but to provoke it; and a thouſand high-ſeaſoned ſauces were invented to raiſe an appetite; ſo that meats which before ſuſtained, and proved wholeſome nouriſhment to thoſe who wanted them, ſerve now only to overload the full ſtomach. Hence proceed paleneſs, and trembling of the nerves relaxed by wine; and a more miſerable leanneſs, cauſed rather by crudities than hunger; hence ſuch a tottering gait, and perpetual ſtumbling, as if men were always drunk; hence the ſmall veſſels of the cuticle are filled with water, and the belly diſtended, being accuſtomed to be crammed with more than it can well hold; hence the black jaundice; the wan countenance of ſuch as are in a deep conſumption; the crooked fingers from the ſtiffneſs of the joints; the unfeeling apoplexy, and the everſhaking palſy. What need I mention the ſwimming of the head; the torment both of the eyes and ears; the acute pains of the raging brain; the paſſages of the body afflicted with ulcers; beſides numberleſs ſorts of fevers, ſome high and violent, others creeping on by ſlow degrees; others ſeizing us with horror and great ſhaking of the limbs; with a thouſand other diſtempers, the juſt plagues of luxury and intemperance?

The antients were free from theſe dreadful evils; who had not as yet debauched themſelves with the moſt delicate viands; who were their own maſters, and their own ſervants: they harden'd their bodies with toil and uſeful labour; and when tired with running, or hunting, or tilling the ground, they ſate down to ſuch a repaſt, as would not have been reliſhed, had they not been hungry. There was no need therefore in thoſe days of ſhops full of drugs, nor of ſo many inſtruments, gallipots and boxes. Simple was their health, from a ſimple cauſe; but variety of diſhes introduced a variety of diſeaſes *(d)*. Only obſerve what a ſtrange mixture of things, luxury, having ravaged both the land and ſea, hath provided for the ſwallow of one gormandizing throat. Things of ſuch different qualities can never agree, in, or with the

the ſtomach: it is impoſſible they ſhould digeſt, as one thing prevents another. No wonder then that uncertain and various diſeaſes ſhould ariſe from ſuch diſcordant meats; and that humours, collected from ſuch oppoſite parts of nature, and now conjoined in one, ſhould redound as they do; for as we live by no rule, we ſicken by none.

The greateſt phyſician, and founder of the profeſſion, obſerved, that *women never ſhed their hair, nor were ever lame with the gout:* but now are they both gouty and bald. The nature of women however is not changed, but the manner of life: for by taking the ſame liberties with men, they have ſubjected themſelves to the ſame diſorders; they keep as bad hours (*e*); they drink as deep; and challenge them as well in the uſe of oyl, as of ſtrong wine; they alike eat without an appetite; and are not aſhamed of diſcharging an overloaded ſtomach by the mouth (*f*); they likewiſe make their teeth chatter with ice, by way of cooling and refreſhing the overheated liver; nor in any luſtful action will they ſuffer men to ſurpaſs them; may all the Gods and Goddeſſes confound them for their abominable practices! What wonder is it then that the greateſt phyſician and moſt experienced naturaliſt, ſhould be liable to a miſtake, ſince we now ſee women afflicted both with the gout and baldneſs? They have loſt the privilege of their ſex by their vices, and, having thrown aſide the woman, ſubjected themſelves to the diſeaſes of debauchees.

The antient phyſicians knew not to preſcribe frequent eating, or to drench the flagging veins with wine; they knew not the art of cupping or ſcarifying; or to eaſe a chronic diſorder by bathing or ſweating; they knew not, by binding the legs and arms to recall the vital heat from the central parts to the extreme. There was no need of conſultations, or to hunt after various kinds of remedies, when the dangers of their patients were few, and in a narrow compaſs. But now, alas! to what a degree are diſorders multiplied! Such is the intereſt we pay for the irrational and inordinate pleaſures that we indulge ourſelves in!

But

But do you wonder that diſeaſes multiply? Count the cooks. All ſtudy is given over; the profeſſors of the liberal arts ſit in ſome lonely corner without an audience; the ſchools of rhetoric and philoſophy are quite deſerted; while the taverns and cook-ſhops are full: what a crowd of young fellows ſurround the hearth of ſome ſpendthrift? I paſs by the troops of poor boys, natives or foreign, diſtinguiſhed by their nation, and complexions, and ranged according to their ſize, their age, and even their hair, thoſe who have lank and ſtraight locks not being admitted among the curled: I omit likewiſe the crew of bakers and confectioners, and other ſerving men whoſe buſineſs it is, at a ſign given *(g)*, to bring in the ſupper. Good gods! what a number of men does one belly employ!

But can you think thoſe muſhrooms (a taſteful poyſon) do not ſecretly and gradually operate, though no bad effect is immediately perceived from them? Do you think that the ſummer-ice does not chill, and by degrees make the liver callous? or that thoſe oyſters, a moſt inert kind of fleſh in itſelf, being fattened with mud, engender not viſcous and muddy humours? or that ſoy (*h*), or the pickle made of the gravy of unwholeſome fiſh, does not burn up the entrails with its ſaline and poyſonous particles? or that thoſe ſtrong ſoups which are ſwallowed down hot from the fire, can without doing any prejudice, be extinguiſhed in the bowels? How filthy and peſtilent are their belches! How do they loth themſelves, while diſgorging their laſt furfeit! Know, that ſuch eatables as the luxurious are now fond of, may putrefy, but digeſt not.

I remember to have heard of a famous diſh (*i*), into which a lickeriſh glutton, haſtening his own deſtruction, was wont to gather all the dainties that were uſed to be ſerved up at the tables of great men; all kinds of ſhell-fiſh, cockels, muſcles, and oyſters with their beards cut off, are intermixed with ſea-urchins (*k*), and poulets crimped and boned; no one can now eat of a ſingle diſh *(l)*, they muſt all be mingled together, and ſuch an hotch-potch prepared for ſupper, as we may ſuppoſe made in the belly after a full meal. For my part, I expect

4 ſoon

ſoon that the victuals will be ſerved up already chewed: for there is but little difference in having things ſo mangled and maſhed together, and having a cook perform the office of our teeth.

It is thought tedious to indulge the taſte with one thing after another; all things muſt be ſet on together and diſguiſed with one flavour: it would be too much trouble to reach out the hand for any particular thing; every thing muſt come on at once: the garniſhing of many diſhes muſt unite, and be blended together; and let thoſe, who ſay that all this is by way of grandeur and oſtentation, know, that the ſame exceſſes are committed not only in public but in private. Tho' a man ſups alone, upon one meſs of ſoup, it is compounded of various ingredients, that uſed to ſerve for ſo many diſhes; but now there muſt be no difference between oyſters and muſcles; and ſea-crabs muſt be mixed, and cooked up with mullets; ſo that the ſight of it, if thrown up again, could not be more confuſed, *(as I before obſerved)*. Now, as theſe viands are thus mixed and confounded, no ſingle diſorder can be ſuppoſed to ariſe therefrom, but ſeveral, unaccountable, different, and multiplied diſeaſes, againſt which phyſic hath begun to arm herſelf, with many remedies founded on obſervations and experiments.

The ſame I ſay of philoſophy—it was once of a more ſimple nature, among thoſe whoſe ſins were not ſo enormous, but curable with ſlight and eaſy remedies. Againſt ſuch a degeneracy and corruption of manners as now reigns, every thing is to be tried; and I wiſh that even ſo, this dreadful malady may be overcome. We play the madmen not only in private, but in public: we forbid homicide, and ſingle ſlaughters; but wars, and the ſlaughter of nations, ſeem moſt glorious miſchief. Neither avarice nor cruelty know any bounds; theſe however when exerciſed by ſtealth, as it were, and by ſingle perſons, are leſs hurtful and leſs monſtrous: but what ſhall we ſay when by the decrees of the ſenate, and edicts of the Government, thoſe heinous offences are committed and publickly commanded, which are condemned in the practice of a private man? as ſuch things when committed by the ſoldiery are applauded, for which other men would ſuffer death? Ought not

 men,

men, the mildeſt of animals by nature, to be aſhamed of rejoicing in the blood of one another; and not only in waging *unneceſſary* wars, but delivering them down for poſterity to carry on; when dumb and ſavage beaſts have peace among themſelves? Againſt ſo potent and general a madneſs philoſophy is obliged to take more pains, and to aſſume to herſelf ſtrength in proportion to the ſtrength of thoſe againſt whom it is applied.

It was an eaſy matter in former days to chide an accidental ſot, and reprove ſuch as luxuriouſly coveted mere dainty food; the mind was eaſily brought back to frugality, that had wandered but a little way therefrom:

Nunc manibus rapidis opus eſt, nunc arte magiſtrâ.

Virg. E. 442.

——— *But now there's need*
Of forceful ſtrength, and well-experienced art.

Pleaſure is ſought out in every quarter: no vice keeps within its own ſphere. Luxury runs headlong into avarice; juſtice and honeſty are quite forgot; nothing is thought baſe and ſcandalous where the gain is ſweet: man, that ſacred animal, (*m*), *man*, I ſay is killed in mere jeſt and ſport; and whom it was thought impiety to inſtruct in the ſcience of defence, is now expoſed naked and unarmed, as if it was a pleaſing ſpectacle only to ſee him butchered (*n*).

In this perverſity therefore of manners, ſomething ſtronger than uſual is required to throw off the inveterate evil; we muſt apply decrees and maxims; that the received perſuaſion of falſe opinions may firſt be rooted out: to theſe if we add precepts, conſolations, and exhortations, they will probably prevail; they are ineffectual of themſelves; if we would ſet men free from their bonds, and deliver them from the entanglement of evil; we muſt inform them what is evil, and what is good; they muſt be taught that all things, except virtue, are liable to a change of appellation, being ſometimes good and ſometimes bad: as the firſt bond of a ſoldier is the military oath, to follow his ſtandard, and to think it a ſin to deſert; every thing elſe is eaſily obtained, and the word of command readily obeyed, by all ſuch as know themſelves bound by this obligation; ſo among thoſe whom you would conduct to an happy life, the firſt foundation muſt be laid in virtue. Let rhem reverence her to a degree of ſuperſtition; let them love her, and reſolve rather to die than live without her.

But have not ſome without ſuch diſcipline, and curious inſtructions proved good men, and made great proficiency in the ſchool of virtue, while obedient only to bare precepts? No doubt of it; but this hath been owing to an happy diſpoſition and good natural parts, which in a moment apprehended their duty in the ſalutary purſuit of what is right and fit. For, as the immortal Gods never learned virtue, nor had any need to learn it, being by nature perfectly good; ſo, ſome men, being endowed with an excellent genius, give due attention to the lectures of morality, and as ſoon as they hear of virtue, readily embrace her. From whence ſome naturally catch at every thing that is good, and without culture bring forth fruit: whereas it requires great pains to rub off the ruſt from the minds of thoſe who are dull of apprehenſion, or have long laboured under ſome evil habit: but how neceſſary the *maxims* of philoſophy are, as well in bringing to perfection ſuch as are prone to good, as in aſſiſting the weaker, and diſpoſſeſſing them of prejudice, and falſe opinions, you will learn from what follows.

There are certain inclinations within, which make us ſlow and lazy in ſome affairs, and light and raſh in other: nor can this raſhneſs be reſtrained, nor this ſluggiſhneſs enlivened, unleſs the cauſes of them are firſt cut off, viz. *falſe admiration* and *falſe fear:* ſo long as theſe poſſeſs the mind, you may tell a man what duty he owes his father, what to his children, what to friends and what to ſtrangers; but avarice will turn his endeavours another way: he will know, that he ought to fight for his country, but fear will diſſuade him: he will know, that without grudging, he muſt do all he can, to ſerve a friend, but eaſe and pleaſure will forbid him: he will know, that it is a moſt grievous injury to a wife, to keep a miſtreſs, but heedleſs luſt will incite him. It will avail nothing therefore to give precepts, unleſs every

every bar to ſuch precepts be firſt removed; no more than it will to lay arms before a ſoldier, or to put them into his hands, ſo long as his hands are tied, and he cannot, or will not, uſe them.

That the mind may duly attend to the *precepts* given, it muſt firſt be free. Suppoſe any one to do a right thing, he will not do ſo continually, nor act uniformly; becauſe he knows not a reaſon for it. Some things may happen to be right, either by chance or cuſtom, but he ſtill wants a rule whereby to ſquare his actions, and to have aſſurance that they are right: you can never depend upon a man, from his being caſually good, that he will always continue ſo. Beſides, *precepts* perhaps will inform you what you ought to do, but not the manner of doing it; and without this, they will not bend to virtue.

But a man that follows good advice, will certainly do what he ought to do. I grant it; but this is not enough, becauſe a deed is praiſeworthy not merely in itſelf; but in the manner how, or why, it is done. What can be more ſcandalous than to ſpend at one ſupper a knight's yearly revenue (2000*ls. Sterling!)* what more worthy cenſorial reprehenſion, than for a man thus to treat, or, in the language of a debauchee, joyouſly indulge himſelf? Yet there have been men, otherwiſe of a frugal temper, who, on ſome extraordinary occaſion, have made an entertainment which coſt 30000 ſeſterces. Now if ſuch a ſum was expended merely by way of feaſting and gluttony, nothing could be more ſcandalous; but if it was in honour of ſome great perſonage, and a noble aſſembly, it may well eſcape cenſure; for then it it is not extravagant luxury, but a grand and ſolemn treat.

Tiberius Cæſar ordered that a mullet of an extraordinary ſize, (why ſhould I not mention the weight, to make gluttons gape? it weighed four pounds and an half,) which was ſent him for a preſent, to be carried into the market, and ſold, ſaying, *I ſhould be much miſtaken, my friends, if either* Appius *or* P. Octavius *buy not this fiſh.* The thing fell out beyond his expectation: theſe very two men bid upon one another for it: *Octavius* got it, and not only the fiſh, but great glory

 among

(2.) among his companions, for having bought a fish for 5000 sesterces, which *Cæsar* had sold, and *Apicius* could not buy: now it was shameful in *Octavius* to buy it at such a price; but not in the person who bought it for a present to *Tiberius*, whatever it cost him; though I do not think it altogether excusable; it was vanity that made him admire a thing which he thought worthy *Cæsar*.

Again; a man, suppose, is sitting by a sick friend; this is certainly a kind office; but if he sits there, in order to be appointed his heir, he is then a mere vulture, waiting for carrion (*o*). Thus the same thing may be both vile and honest, according to circumstances; it is of great moment therefore, why, or in what manner a thing is done: but all things will be done decently, if we abide by the fitness of action; and judge this principle, and what flows therefrom to be the *only good* in human affairs; all other things being good only for a time, and with regard to circumstances. Therefore some firm persuasion concerning the *whole of life*, must be implanted in the mind; and this is what I call *a philosophical* decree. Such as this persuasion is, such will our thoughts and actions be; and on our thoughts and actions depends the just conduct of life.

It is not enough, for one who intends to form the whole aright, to give direction in particulars. *Marcus Brutus* in his book Περὶ Καθήκοντος, *of offices (p)*, gives many precepts, to parents, to children, to brethren; but no one can follow these as he ought, unless there be some rule to go by; some foundation to build upon: we must propose some end, as *the principal good*, at which we must aim strenuously, by addressing generally, every thought, word, and action thereto, as the mariner steers his course by a certain star. Life without a fixed view is loose and vague. If then such a view or principle is to be fixed, *decrees* will soon discover how necessary they are. I think you will grant this, that nothing can be more shameful, than to see a man doubtful, irresolute, timorous; now setting his foot backward, and now forward; and this must be our case continually, unless those impediments are rooted

rooted out, which tie down, and cramp the underſtanding, not ſuffering us to exert the whole man.

We are uſually told, how the Gods are to be worſhipped: we are forbid to light our lamps on the Sabbath-day (*q*), becauſe the Gods want no light, nor are men themſelves delighted with ſmoke. Let us likewiſe forbid the morning ſalutations (*r*), and ſitting at the Temple (before the doors are opened) to receive ceremonial compliments. Theſe are vain allurements, that pleaſe human ambition. He who knows God, ſerveth and honoureth *him*. Let us forbid the bringing linnen, and fleſh-bruſhes and combs to *Jupiter*, or the holding out a mirror to *Juno* (*s*). God wants not ſuch ſervices, nor requires at his altars ſuch idle miniſters. For why? He himſelf miniſtreth to man; he is every where preſent and eaſy of acceſs to all (*t*); a man may be taught how to behave himſelf at ſacrifices and in public worſhip, without any curious and troubleſome ſuperſtition; but he will never be perfect in religious duty, 'till he hath conceived in his mind a right notion of God; as the poſſeſſor, and giver, of all things, and who freely and graciouſly beſtows ineſtimable benefits upon us (*u*). And from whence ariſeth this affection for man? What induceth the Almighty thus to pour his benefits upon us? Nature, (or *his own goodneſs*.) The man is miſtaken who thinks the Gods afflict any one willingly (*x*). They cannot; they neither can *do*, nor receive an injury. (For there is a connection between doing and ſuffering harm.) That ſupreme and moſt excellent Nature which hath exempted them from danger, hath likewiſe rendered them not dangerous to their creature, man.

Now the firſt ſtep to the right worſhipping of God, is, to believe *there is a God* (*y*). And next, to aſcribe unto him all Majeſty and all Goodneſs (*z*), without which true Majeſty cannot ſubſiſt; to know likewiſe, that it is he who governs the world, and preſides over the univerſe as his own, who hath taken mankind in general under his protection; and on ſome is pleaſed to beſtow particular favour (*aa*). *He* can neither *do*, nor ſuffer evil. God however is ſometimes pleaſed to

4 chaſtiſe,

chaſtiſe, and lay heavy penalties upon ſome perſons under the appearance of ſome good *(bb)*. But would you be happy in his favour? be a good man *(cc)*. To be a good man, and to honour God as you ought, is to endeavour as much as poſſible to imitate him in all things.

Another queſtion is, how we muſt behave ourſelves towards man? And how do we behave? What precepts do we give in this reſpect? To abſtain from ſhedding human blood? But what a ſmall thing is it not to hurt him, to whom we ought to do all the good that lies in our power? It is indeed praiſe-worthy for men to be kindly affectioned, one towards another *(dd)*. Shall we then direct a man to reach out his hand to the ſhipwreck'd; to ſhew the wandering traveller his way; and to divide our bread with the hungry (*ee*)? Yes, certainly. But every thing that he ought to do, or avoid doing, may be comprehended in a few words; when, *to follow Nature*, may be looked upon as a complete direction and rule of human duty: all that you ſee, (the heavens and the earth wherein are contained all things, both human and divine) is *one*. We are members of this great body *(ff)*: we are all akin by Nature, who hath formed us of the ſame elements, and placed us here together for the ſame end: ſhe hath implanted in us mutual affection, and made us ſociable (*gg*); ſhe hath commanded juſtice and equity; by her appointment it is more wretched to do an injury than to ſuffer one (*hh*); and by her command the hand is ever ready to aſſiſt our brother. That excellent verſe (of *Terence*) ſhould ever be in our breaſt and in our mouth;

Homo ſum, humani nihil a me alienum puto (*ii*):
I am a man, and, as ſuch, concern'd
In every buſineſs that relates to man.

We muſt conſider that we are born, for the good of the whole: human ſociety reſembles a vaulted roof of ſtone, which would ſoon fall, unleſs prevented by one ſtone ſupporting another (*kk*).

Having thus conſidered our duty with regard both to God and man, let us ſee how we are to act with regard to things. *Precepts* would be entirely ſuperfluous, unleſs it were premiſed what opinion we ought to have of every thing, as of poverty, riches, glory, ignominy, our own country, and banishment. We must weigh each particular severally, without any regard to common report, and duly examine what they really are, and not what they are called.

To pass on to the consideration of virtues. Some one perhaps will direct us, highly to esteem Providence; cordially to embrace friendship; to love temperance, and that, if possible, we should more strictly adhere to justice than to any of the rest. But all this would be to little purpose, if we knew not what *virtue* is; whether there be one or more; whether they are separable, or indissolubly connected together (*ll*); whether he that hath one virtue, hath all the rest, or what is the difference between them. There is no need for a smith to be inquisitive after the origin of his art, or of what use it is, any more than for a player of pantomimes to make the like enquiries concerning the art of dancing. Such occupations are fully comprehended in the knowledge of the art itself; they need nothing more, for they appertain not to the whole of life. But *virtue* is the knowledge of other things as well as of herself: we must learn from her what the *will* is, or ought to be. An action can never be fit and right where the will is not so; for on the will depends the action.

Again, the will can never be right, unless the habit or disposition of the mind be so; for from this proceeds the will; the disposition of the mind cannot be in its best state unless it perceives the whole duty of life, knows how to judge of things, and can reduce them all to truth. None but such as have a steady and immutable judgment can enjoy true tranquillity: other men fall now and then, and again recover themselves; and are continually fluctuating between desire and aversion. Now the reason of this is, that, being led by common report, that most uncertain guide, they are confident in nothing. Would you always will the same thing? you must always will that which is right and according to the truth of things (*mm*.) But no one can come at truth without certain maxims and decrees which comprehend the whole of life.

Good

Good and evil, honourable and base, just and unjust, pious and impious, all virtues and their uses, the possession of all conveniencies (*nn*), esteem, dignity, health, strength, beauty, sagacity, and wit, all these things require such a one as can truly judge of them, and rate them according to their merit, or demerit. For you are often mistaken, and estimate things at more than their real value; nay, you are so far deceived that those things, which are generally esteemed at the highest rate, as riches, favour, power, are intrinsically of little or no worth at all. Now this you cannot know unless you inspect the nature of things, and observe the decree itself, whereby all things are comparatively valuable: as the leaves of trees cannot live of themselves, but require a branch whereon to stick, and receive therefrom their proper sap and nutriment; so precepts while single, wither away and die; they require to be fixed and supported by the mother-root (*oo*).

Besides, they who would discard *decrees*, seem not to know, that they confirm them by the very reasons they give for discarding them. For they say, that *life being sufficiently displayed and tutored by precepts, the decrees or maxims of wisdom are therefore superfluous:* but even this assertion is itself a *decree*; just as were I to say, *that we ought to give over precepts, and apply ourselves only to decrees*; in the very article by which I deny the use of precepts, I should offer a precept myself.

There are some things which require only the simple admonition of philosophy; other things require proof; and there are some so very intricate and confused, that with the greatest subtilty, diligence and application, a man can scarce come at the true sense and meaning of them. If proofs then are necessary, so are decrees, which are founded upon truth collected from arguments. Some things are clear and manifest; other things dark and obscure; the former are such as are comprehended by the senses and memory; the latter such as lie beyond their reach: but reason is not satisfied with the things that are manifest; the greater and more beautiful part thereof is employed on things that are hidden: now hidden things require proof, and proof cannot be without decrees; decrees therefore are necessary.

Again,

Again, *the persuasion or apprehension of certain things, without which persuasion the mind would be ever wavering and unsteady, is what forms common sense, and perfects the same*. Decrees are therefore necessary; inasmuch as they endow the mind with a steady, and inflexible judgment. Lastly, when we exhort a man to hold his friend as dear to him as his ownself; and to think that it is possible to make a friend of an enemy (*pp*); that he may encrease the affections of the former, and moderate the aversion of the latter, we add hereunto, that *this is just, and fit, and honourable*. But in the reason of our decrees are this justice and honesty comprised; therefore is reason necessary, and consequently the decrees.

But let us join both *precepts* and *decrees* together; for without the root the branches are fruitless; and even the roots are aided and assisted by the branches they themselves produced. No one can be ignorant of the usefulness of the hands; they do their work openly; but the heart, whereby they live, from whence they receive both power and motion, lies hidden in secret: I may say the same of precepts, they are open, and plain to view; but the decrees of wisdom are hidden. As in sacreds none know the mysterious parts but such as have been initiated; so in philosophy, her mysteries are unfolded to none but to such as are admitted into her sanctuary (*qq*).

But precepts, and the like, are also known to the vulgar and profane. *Posidonius* not only judgeth *preception* (for I know not why I should not use the word) but also persuasion, consolation, and exhortation necessary. To these he adds *an enquiry into causes*, which I see not why I may not call (ætiologiam), *ætiology*, since the Grammarians, the professed guardians of the Latin tongue, make use of it in their own right. *Posidonius*, I say, affirms that profit may be received from *the description of every virtue*, and this he calls *ætiology*; others call it [illegible], *characteristics*, that give the signs or marks of every vice and virtue, whereby such things as seem alike are distinguishable.

This then hath the ſame force as precepts; for he that gives precepts, ſaith, *you muſt do ſo and ſo, if you would be temperate*; and he that draws a character, ſaith, *he is a temperate man, who takes care to do, or to avoid ſuch and ſuch things*. Nor is there any other difference between them, than that one gives the precepts, the other the example, of virtue. Now, theſe deſcriptions, or to uſe the term of the publicans) (*rr*) εἰκονισμοὶ, *ſignatures*, (or ſamples) I own are borrowed from uſe and experience. Let us propoſe what is commendable, and we ſhall find thoſe who will follow it. You think it requiſite when you would buy an horſe, that ſome one ſhould acquaint you with the marks that promiſe a good one, leſt you ſhould be bit, and put off with an arrant jade; how much more uſeful is it to know the ſigns of an excellent underſtanding, which are transferable from one man to another?

Continuo pecoris generoſi pullus in arvis
Altius ingreditur, et mollia crura reponit.
Primus *inire* viam, et fluvios tentare minaces
Audet, et ignoto ſeſe committere ponto.
Nec vanos horret ſtrepitus; illi ardua cervix,
Argutumque caput, brevis alvus, obeſaque terga,
Luxuriatque toris animoſum pectus.——
——— tum ſi qua ſonum procul arma dedére
Stare loco neſcit, micat auribus, et tremit artus,
Collectumque premens volvit ſub naribus ignem. G. iii. 75.

The colt that for the field of battle is deſign'd,
By ſure preſages ſhews his generous kind,
Of able body, ſound of limb and wind;
Upright he walks, on paſterns firm and ſtraight,
His motions eaſy, prancing in his gait;
The firſt to lead the way to tempt the flood,
To paſs the bridge unknown, nor fear the trembling wood;
Dauntleſs at empty noiſes, lofty neck'd,
Sharp-headed, barrel-belly'd, broadly back'd;
——— *when he hears from far*
The ſprightly trumpet, and the ſhouts of war,

Pricks

Pricks up his ears, and trembling with delight,
Shifts place, and paws, and hopes the promis'd fight. Dryden.

While our *Virgil* is here describing an horse, he gives you an excellent description of a brave man; at least for my part I should desire no better: was I to draw *Cato* fearless and intrepid amid the clashing noise of civil discord, and marching foremost to invade an army that had took possession of the *Alps*, and opposing himself to all the dangers of a civil war; I should paint him in the same colours, with such a fierceness of look, and in such an attitude. Surely no man could do more than he did, when he made head at the same time both against *Cæsar* and *Pompey*; and while some espoused *Cæsar's* party, and others *Pompey's*, he challenged them both, and shewed them, that the poor commonwealth had yet one party left. But it is too little to say of *Cato*,

——— nec vanos horret strepitus;
——— *nor trembles at empty noises:*

for why? he was not afraid of true alarms, nor the real approach of his enemy: when in defiance of ten legions, besides the auxiliaries from *Gaul*, and other nations, intermixed with the *Romans*, he spake freely, and aloud exhorted his countrymen to maintain their *liberty*; and to try all means, even to the death itself, rather than to lose it; at least that it was more honourable to fall into slavery by constraint, and the chance of war, than calmly and voluntarily to receive the yoke. What vigour! what a noble spirit! what confidence in the midst of such hurry and public confusion! He knew himself to be but one, and of too little consequence to be concerned for; and that the question was not, *whether* Cato *should be free, but whether he should live among a free people.* From hence sprang that contempt of danger and of death. While I am admiring this great man's invincible constancy, which he still preserved, though his country was ruin'd, I cannot help saying with *Virgil*,—

Luxuriatque toris animosum pectus.
His big-swoln muscles shew his lofty spirit.

It will be of use not only to declare who are usually good men, their shape and lineaments, but who have been such, and to describe their actions, or whatever else rendered them famous in their generation; as that laſt and glorious wound of *Cato's*, through which in the arms of liberty he diſmiſſed his indignant ſoul. The wiſdom of *Lælius*, and his cordial amity with *Scipio*; the excellent deeds of *Cato* the Cenſor, both at home and abroad; the couches of *Tubero* (*tt*), made of plain wood, and ſet in open view, and covered with goat-ſkins inſtead of an embroidered counterpane; and the earthen veſſels ſet before the gueſts, at a ſolemn banquet in *Jupiter's* chapel; what was this but to conſecrate poverty in the *capitol?* Had we no other great action of this man, to rank him with the *Catos*, was not this enough? This was a cenſure, a tacit reproof, not a banquet. O how little do theſe men of our times, who are ſo fond of *glory*, know what it means, and how to be attained? The people in *Tubero's* days ſaw the furniture of many noblemen, but admired only *his:* all *their* gold and ſilver hath been broken and melted down a thouſand times, but theſe earthen veſſels of *Tubero* ſhall laſt for ever.

ANNOTATIONS, &c.

* This Epiſtle is an appendix to the foregoing, ſetting forth, that neither the preceptive nor dogmatical philoſophy are ſufficient of themſelves; but that examples or characters after the manner of *Theophraſtus* have their uſe, and conſequently lay claim to recommendation.

It will be proper to obſerve here, that, in determining characters among the ancients, it is neither juſt nor candid to examine them by thoſe rules of moral conduct which if known were at leaſt not admitted, with the ſame purity and extent, to which they have ſince been refined and enlarged, by the clearer diſcoveries and ſtronger authority of divine Revelation. *Melmoth* Lælius, p. 173.

(*a*) Ut id quod in diem ſuum dixeram debere referri repræſentem.] *Lipſius* (Elect. c. 26) reads it, quod in diem dixeram debere repræſentem; the reſt he rejects as being injudiciouſly inſerted. *In diem debere*, and *repræſentare*, are oppoſite terms, borrowed from the law, relating to pecuniary matters; as if *Seneca* ſhould ſay, metaphorically, *You deſire*, Lucilius, *that I would make my appearance, and pay the money down, and not ſet another day.*

(*b*) At leaſt they do not know the reaſon of the fitneſs and propriety of the action; and herein, ſaith *Muretus*, the Stoics ſeem to judge rightly: but it is very abſurd to ſay as ſome of them do, that a man from being very miſerable may become happy, and yet not in the leaſt be ſenſible of the change.

(*c*) See Ariſtotle's Ethic. l. 2.

(*d*) *Plutarch*, (Sympoſ. viii. 9. *'Tis rational to conclude that all diſeaſes that riſe from want, heat or cold, bear the ſame date with our bodies; but afterward, over-eating, luxury, and ſurfeiting encouraged by eaſe and plenty, raiſed bad and ſuperfluous juices, and theſe brought various new diſeaſes, and their perpetual complications and mixtures ſtill create more.*

(*e*) Non

(*e*) Non minus pervigilant] Some copies read, *pervigilantur*, from whence *Pincian*. conjectures *pugillantur*, as *Juvenal* makes mention of women-boxers—

Endromidas Tyrias, et femineum ceroma
Quis neſcit? vel quis non vidit vulnera pali? Juv. vi. 245.
They turn virages too, the wreſtlers toil
They try, and ſmear their naked limbs with oil. Dryden.

And *Terence* alludes to them when he ſays, ſi qua eſt paulo habitior, pugilem eſſe aiunt; and *if ſhe is a little plumper than ordinarily, they ſay ſhe is a* bruiſer.

(*f*) Et vinum omne vomitu remetiuntur] So *Martial*, Data vina remenſus.

Nec cœnat prius aut recumbit ante
Quàm ſeptem vomuit meri deunces.

Juv. 6. 424.——tandem illa venit rubicundula, totum
Oenophorum ſitiens, plenâ quod tenditur urnâ
Admotum pedibus, de quo ſextarius alter
Ducitur ante cibum, rabidam facturus orexim,
Dum redit, et terram loto ferit inteſtino,
Marmoribus rivi properant aut lata falernum
Pelvis olet. Nam ſic tanquam alta in dolia longus
Deciderit ſerpens, bibit, et vomit. Ergo maritus
Nauſeat, atque oculis bilem ſubſtringit opertis.
At length ſhe comes, all fluſh'd, but ere ſhe ſup,
Swallows a ſwinging preparation cup,
And then to clear the ſtomach ſpews it up.
The deluge vomit all the floor o'erflows,
And the ſour ſavour nauſeates every noſe.
She drinks again; again ſhe ſpews a lake:
Her wretched huſband ſees, and dares not ſpeak;
But mutters many a curſe againſt his wiſe,
And damns himſelf for chuſing ſuch a life. Dryden.

And theſe preparatory doſes are what *Plutarch* reckons among the cauſes of ſo many new and ſtrange diſeaſes. This abominable cuſtom, as *Lipſius* obſerves, began and came into faſhion in the time of *Pompey*; when *Aſclepiades*, the phyſician was living, who very juſtly condemned it. *Plin.* c. xxvi. c. 3. Damavit merito et vomitiones, tunc ſupra modum frequentes. As does *Celſus*, (l. 1. c. 3.) Qui iſtud luxuriæ causâ fieri non oportere confitetur; interdum valetudinis causâ rectè fieri experimentis credit.

(*g*) *De brevit. Vit.* c. 12. Quanta celeritate, ſigno dato, glabri ad miniſteria diſcurrant.

With what ſpeed, at a ſign given, do they attend their ſeveral offices bareheaded?

(*h*) Sociorum garum, pretioſam malorum piſcium saniem] N. *Lipſius* rejects the word, *malorum*. Plin. l. 31. ſ. 43. Garum conficiebatur ex piſce, quem Græci *Garon* vocabant,——nunc ſcombro piſce laudatiſſimum, et quamvis nunc ex infinito genere piſcium fiat, nomen tamen priſtinum retinet, a quo initium ſumpſit.—— *Sociorum* dict. quòd a ſociis P. R. nempe Hiſpani Romam deſerretur; vel a ſocietate publicanorum qui vectigal *garo* impoſitum exigerent: (N. in loc.) vel quia in ſodalitatibus et conviviis eo uterentur. (*Voſſ.*)

Pliny ſays it was made of (Scombri, ad nihil aliud utiles) *Tunny fiſh, good for nothing elſe.* Be that as it will, it was in high vogue, as we learn from *Martial*:

Sed

Sed coquus ingentem piperis consumit acervum,
Addit et arcano mixta Falerna *garo*. l. 7. Ep. 26.
Exspirantis adhuc scombri de sanguine primo
Accipe fæcosum, munera cara, *garum*. l. 13. Ep. 102.
al. fastosum, munera rara, *garum*.

Hor. s. ii. 8. 46.——Garo de succis piscis iberi.
Wine five years old, and Caviare *I join.*

See Hadr. Jun. Animadv. l. 6. c. 17. Rhodig. Ant. Lect. l. 30. c. 25.

(*i*) Some refer this to a dish of *Æsop's*, and indeed *Pincian.* inserts his name, Quondam *Æsopi* nobilem patinam, but this *Lipsius* does not approve of; for the dish here spoken of consists of fish, but *Æsop's* was of *fowl*. (Plin. x. 51.) This *Æsop* was an excellent player of tragedies, cotemporary with *Cicero*, and very rich, but a most extravagant glutton. And he had as extravagant a son, taken notice of by *Horace*, s. ii. 3. 239. *Seneca* therefore alludes to some one else. And I will venture to say that my neighbour, the late Mr. Quin, the comedian, did not deserve all that is said of him on this account.

(*k*) Veneriæ, sphondylique] Plin. ix. 52. Navigant ex his veneriæ præbentesque concavam sui partem, et auræ oppomentes per summa æquorum velificant.

Plin. l. 32. s. 53. Spondylus. N. Gr. σφόνδυλος. Athenæ. l. 3. p. 87. *Macrobius*, l. 2. c. 9. makes mention of them in a *pontifical* feast. *Martial.* l. 7. Ep. 19.

Rosos tepenti spondylos sinu condit.

See *Kendelit.* de Test. l. 1. c. 40.

(*l*) I have chiefly followed *Gronovius* in order to give the words another turn from what follows, as *piget esse singula*, would be much the same with *grave est luxuriari per singula*, though I must own that *Seneca* frequently repeats the same meaning under different expressions; so that one would often think, as here, that some gloss had crept into the text.

(*m*) Homo sacra res.] Alluding to that proverbial saying, Homo homini Deus. Gr. ἄνθρωπος ἀνθρώπῳ δαιμόνιον, applicable in many cases of beneficence, but never more justly than to the honest, intelligent, and consequently successful physician. Was I to mention the names of *Heberden* and *Baker*, I am sure every one would accept it but themselves.

(*n*) See Ep. 7. s. Tricies H. S.] which if only *millia* be understood, it is about 214l. 2s. 6d. if centena millia 21412l. 10s. the old English translation renders it 75000 crowns. *infr.* Quinque mill. H. S. which is about 35l. 13s. 9d. the old English translation about 200 crowns.

(*o*) *Catullus.* Suscitata cano vulturium capite.
Martial. Cujus vulturis hoc erit cadaver.

(*p*) Which *Cicero* entitles, de virtute; *Pincian.* de officio.

(*q*) It was usual to light up lamps not only in honour of the gods, but of some great personage, or on some extraordinary occurrence.

Herodis venere dies, unctâque fenestrâ
Dispositæ pinguem nebulam, vomûere lucernæ.——Pers. N. 181.
When flow'rs are strew'd, and lamps in order plac'd,
And windows with illuminations grac'd,
On Herod's *day*:—Dryden.
Cuncta nitent; longos erexit janua ramos.
Et matutinis operitur festa lucernis. Juv. xii. 91.
All's right; my portal shines with verdant bays,
And consecrated tapers early blaze. Power.

(*r*) Apul.

(r) Apul. Met. l. 11. Rebus ritè consummatis inchoatæ lucis salutationibus religiosi primam nunciantes horam perstrepunt. *Arnob.* l. 7.

Quid sibi volunt excitationes illæ quas canitis matutinis
Ad tibiam vocibus? *Prudentius.*
Mane salutatum concurritur, omnis adorat
Pubes.——

Vid. *Scal.* ad Tibull. i. 1. *Brisson.* de Form. l. 6.

It will not, I hope, be taken amiss if I apply this prohibition and censure from *Seneca* to the absurd, not to say impious, salutations that we frequently see in our churches, even in the midst of the most solemn parts of divine worship. Deum colit, qui novit, *He who knoweth, and considereth what God is, will worship him aright,* will have more respect to the solemn business he is engaged in, than to be guilty of such fashionable foibles.

(s) Apul. xi. De pompa *Isidis*, Alicæ, quæ nitentibus speculis pone tergum reversis fienienti deæ obvium commonstrarent obsequium. *August.* de Cic. Dei, sunt quæ Junoni ac Minervæ capillos disponant, non tantum simulacro, stantes, digitos movent ornantium modo. Sunt quæ speculum teneant. *Tertull.* de Jejun. Qui in idolis comendis et ornandis, et ad singulas horas salutandis adulantur, *Curationem* facere dicuntur.

(t) Omnibus inque locis ades omni tempore, præsens
Deditus in partes omnes; tamen omnis ubique
Integer usque manes.——Vida. H. Deo. 204.
Since in all parts of the unbounded space,
Thy presence dwells; for God fills every place.
And what beyond those worlds hath its abode,
Is all but the immensity of God:
Thy nature still, howe'er diffus'd it be,
Is ever uniform, entire and free. M.

For where two or three are gathered together in my name, there am I in the midst of them. Matth. 8. 20. Gen. 28. 16. Job. 9. 11, Is. 139.

(u) *Thine, O Lord,* saith David, *is the greatness, the power and the victory, and the majesty, for all that is in the heaven and in the earth is thine: thine is the kingdom, O Lord, and thou art exalted as head above all. Both riches and honour come of thee; and thou reignest over all; and in thine hand is power and might; and in thine hand it is to make great and to give strength to all,* i. Chron. xxix. 11, 12.

(x) *He doth not afflict willingly, nor grieve the children of men.* Sam. 3, 33.——*The Lord is long-suffering, not willing that any should perish, but that all should come to repentance.* ii. Pet. 3. 9.—*As I live, saith the Lord God, I have no pleasure in the death of the wicked, but that the wicked turns from his way and live: Turn ye, turn ye from your evil ways; for why will ye die, O house of Israel?* Ezek. 33, 11.

(y) Primus est deorum cultus, Deos credere.] I have generally kept to *Seneca's* use of the singular or plural number when speaking of the Deity; but here, I think, I might be allowed to change the plural to the singular as he had just before used the singular, in saying almost the same thing, Deum colit, qui novit.

So the Apostle: *Without faith it is impossible to please him: for he that cometh to God must believe that he is, and that he is a rewarder of all them that diligently seek him.* Heb. 11. 6. Doubtless, it is an indisputable condition to the serving God, to believe there is a God to be served: and none are more zealous for his service than those who are most persuaded of his existence. M.

(z) *The earth is full of the goodness of the Lord.* Ps. 33. 5. *And the Lord passed by before him and*

and proclaimed, The Lord, the Lord God, merciful and gracious, long-suffering, and abundant in goodness and truth. Exod. 34. 6. i. Chron. 16. 34. Nahum, 1. 7. Matth. 20. 15.

(*aa*) *Seneca* here among other requisites towards the right worshipping of God, makes this one, *to believe a Providence,* and that the Providence of God is as general as his creation, governing all things by the same infinite power by which they were made: which is consonant to the whole tenour of Scripture. *See* Deut. 11. 14. Prov. 16. 33. Matth. 6. 28. 10. 30.

Cicero was a strenuous advocate for *Providence*; *I assert,* says he, (de Nat. Deer. l. 2.) *that the universe, with all its parts, was originally constituted, and hath without any discontinuance been ever governed by* the Providence of the Gods. "This argument the Stoics generally divide into three parts: 1st, The existence of the Gods being once known, it must follow that the world is governed by their wisdom. 2dly, As every thing is under an intelligent nature which hath produced that beautiful order in the world, it is evident that it is formed of animating principles. The 3d is deduced from those glorious works which we behold in the heavens and the earth." But the notion of a *Providence* seems first to have been entertained by the *Ægyptians,* whom, (as I have observed in my notes on *Vida's* hymns) *Arnobius* makes to reason thus: *Providence is so essential to a Prince, that he cannot be ever called a Prince without it,* (as *Seneca* says above, sine bonitate nulla majestas est,) *and the more august a prince is, the more perfect ought his providential care to be: God therefore being the greatest and most august of all Princes, to him must belong the most perfect providence.* But we must observe that *Seneca* likewise requires a belief in a special or singular providence; as when *Job* says of himself, *Thou hast granted me life and favour: and thy visitation hath preserved my spirit.* Job, 10. 12. Or as God himself saith unto *Moses*, *I will have mercy on whom I will have mercy; and I will have compassion on whom I will have compassion. So that it is not of him that willeth, nor of him that runneth, but of God that sheweth mercy.* Rom. 9, 15.

(*bb*) Hi nec dant malum, nec habent——ceterum castigant,——et aliquando *specie boni* puniunt. *al.* spe boni.---*al.* specie mali.] If *hi* in the foregoing sentence relates to the immediate antecedent, as I have rendered it, I should prefer *specie boni*; but if it agrees with *Dii*, I should rather have read it *specie mali*, in this sense, Hi nec dant malum, nec habent, *The Gods neither afflict with evil nor have any themselves*; (but this is much the same with what is said before, nec accipere injuriam queunt, nec faciunt) *though the punishment which they sometimes inflict on man, hath the appearance of evil.*

Behold, happy is the man whom God correcteth; therefore despise not thou the chastening of the Almighty. Job, 5, 17. *For whom the Lord loveth he chasteneth, and scourgeth every son whom he receiveth.* Heb. 12, 6. Prov. 3, 11. Rev. 3, 19.

(*cc*) Satis Deos coluit quisquis imitatus est.] That all worship, all religion, consists *in the imitation of God,* is an extraordinary sentence in the mouth of an Heathen; among whom the Gods were supposed to act such things which a wise man would abhor to think. But *Seneca* had higher notions of the Deity, and here affirms little less than what is consonant to the sound doctrine of Christianity. That the person who does his best endeavour to *imitate God,* and who has a firm trust in the Supreme Being, is powerful in his power, wise by his wisdom, happy by his happiness; he reaps the benefit of every divine attribute; and loses his own sufficiency in the fulness of infinite perfection. *Be ye therefore perfect,* saith our Lord, *even as your father which is in heaven is perfect.* Matth. 5. 48. See Ep. 90.

(*dd*) *Ye have heard that it was said of old time, Thou shalt not kill, and whosoever shall kill, shall be in danger of the judgment; but I say unto you, that whosoever is angry with his brother without a cause, shall be in danger of the judgment.* Matth. 5. 21. And the Apostle exhorts us, *to be kindly affectioned one to another: Recompense,* saith he, *no man evil for evil: if it be possible, as much as lieth in you, live peaceably with all men.* Rom. 12. 10.--20.

(*ee*) Thus the prophet *Isaiah*, in the name of the Lord, *Is not this the fast that I have chosen, to loose the bands of wickedness, to undo the heavy burdens, and to let the oppressed go free? Is it not* to deal thy bread to the hungry; *and that thou bring the poor to thine house; when thou seest the naked, that thou cover him; and that thou hide not thyself from thine own flesh? And if thou draw out thy soul to the hungry, and satisfy the afflicted, then shall thy light rise in obscurity, and thy darkness be as noon-day*. Is. 58. 6---10. Deut. 15. 7. Ezek. 18. 7. Matth. 25. 35.

(*ff*) And thus argues St. *Paul*. *As we have many members in one body, and all members have not the same office; so we being many are one body, and every one members one of another*. Rom. 12. 5. And again more fully, *As in the body natural the eye cannot say to the hand*, I have no need of thee; *nor again the hand to the feet*, I have no need of you; *so in the great body of mankind, all the members, even the parts that seem more feeble, are necessary, and have their office, that there should be no schism in the body, but that the members should have the same care one for another; and whether one member suffer, all the members suffer with it; or one member be honoured, all the members rejoice with it*. i. Cor. 12, 12.---26.

(*gg*) *Put ye on, therefore*, saith the Apostle, *bowels of mercy, kindness, humbleness of mind, meekness, long-suffering——but above all these things, put on charity, which is the bond of perfectness*. Col. 3. 12—14.

(*hh*) *It is better*, saith St. *Peter*, *if the will of God be so, that ye suffer for well doing than evil doing*. i. Pet. 3. 17. And *Blessed are ye*, saith our Lord, *when men shall revile you, and persecute you, and say all manner of evil against you falsely for my sake: rejoice and be exceeding glad, for great is your reward in heaven*. Matth. 5. 11. 12.

(*ii*) Terence, *Heauton*. Act. 1. sc. 1.) *Cicero* applies this excellent sentence, as the *voice of nature*, to the practice of all social virtues, saying, est enim difficilis cura rerum alienarum quanquam Terentianus ille Chremes, *humani nihil a se alienum putet*.

And yet this very *Chremes*, this man of universal benevolence, is the same person who commands his wife to expose his new-born daughter, and flies into a passion with her, for having committed that hard task to another, by which means the infant escaped death: si meum imperium exequi voluisses, interemptum oportuit: and he likewise characterises such who had any remains of this natural instinct as persons, qui neque jus, neque bonum, atque æquum sciunt, *who know not either justice or equity*: such were the sentiments published with applause on the *Roman* theatre. And it appears from our Author so late as his own time, that it was usual to destroy weak and deformed children. Portentosos fœtus extinguimus. *Sen*. de Ira, l. 1. c. 15.

(*kk*) The Apostle makes use of much the same metaphor, Ephes. 2. 19 --22. *Know therefore ye are no more strangers and foreigners, but fellow-citizens with the saints, and of the houshold of God, and are built upon the foundation of the Apostles and Prophets, Jesus Christ himself being the chief Corner Stone: in whom all the building fitly framed together groweth unto an holy Temple in the Lord. From whom* (saith he in another place) *the whole body fitly joined together, and compacted by that which every joint supplieth, according to the effectual working of the measure in every part, maketh increase of the body unto the edifying itself in love*. Ephes. 4. 16.

(*ll*) *Ambros*. Virtutes individuas esse, sed opinione vulgi sejunctas.——Connexæ sibi sunt concatenatæque virtutes ut qui unam habet, plures habere videatur. *Gregor*, Una virtus sine aliis, aut omnino nulla est aut imperfecta. *Apuleius* imperfectas virtutes semet comitari negat, eas vero quæ perfectæ sunt, individuas sibi, et inter se connexas esse. The reason given is, that *where there is any one perfect virtue*, (and of such the *Stoics* always speak) *there is reason also perfect; which cannot be, unless it extends its force and influence to all other virtues*. So *Cicero* (de Fin. 5. cum sic copulatæ connexæque sint virtutes, ut *omnes* omnium participes sint, nec alia ab alia possit separari, tam proprium suum cujusque munus est; ut fortitudo in laboribus periculisque cernatur; temperantia in voluptatibus, prudentia in dilectis. *The union and blending of the virtues, however is distinguished by a certain philosophical way of reasoning; for when they are so joined and connected that they all partake of one another, and are inseparable, yet each of them has its proper function. Thus courage discovers itself in toils and dangers*; Temperance *in neglecting pleasures*; Prudence, *in distinguishing things good and evil*: Justice, *in giving every one his own*. See Ep. 67.

(*mm*) The Apostle to the same purpose, *Let us walk worthy of the vocation wherewith we are called. 'Till we all come in the unity of the faith, and of the knowledge of the Son of God unto a perfect man: that we henceforth be no more children tossed to and fro and carried about with every wind f doctrine, by the sleight of men, and cunning craftiness whereby they lie in wait to deceive: but, speaking the truth in love, may in all things grow up into him, which is the head, even Christ*. Ephes. 4. 1---15.

And again, *Be not carried about with divers and strange doctrines; for it is a good thing to have the heart established with grace*. Heb. 13. 9.

(*nn*) So the Stoics call all external, otherwise *good* things.

(*oo*) So our Lord to his Disciples, *As the branch cannot bear fruit of itself except it abide in the vine, no more can ye, except ye abide in me. I am the vine, ye are the branches; he that abideth in me, and I in him, the same bringeth forth much fruit; but severed from me, ye can do nothing: if a man abide not in me, he is cast forth as a branch and is withered*. John, 15. 1---6.

(*pp*) *If thine enemy hunger*, saith St. *Paul*, *feed him; if he thirst, give him drink; for in so doing thou shalt heap coals of fire on his head*. Rom. xii. 20. from Prov. 25. 21. compared with ii. Kings, 6. 22.

(*qq*) Like this is what St. *Paul* saith to the *Corinthians*, *We speak wisdom among them that are perfect, yet not the wisdom of this world, nor of the princes of this world, who come to nought; but we speak the wisdom of God in a mystery, even the hidden wisdom, which God had ordained before the world unto our glory*. i. Cor. 2. 6.

(*rr*) The Receivers or Farmers of the customs or public revenues.

(*ss*) Per quod *liber* amisit animum] al. *Libertas*. So the old translation, *Through the which Liberty herself lost her existence*.

(*tt*) *Tubero*. Vid. Ep. 98.

EPISTLE XCIV.

On Contentment and Magnanimity.

STILL, *Lucilius*, are you forgetful, and still complaining; and seem not to understand, that there is nothing evil in these worldly affairs, but what you make so yourself; by being thus displeased and ever querulous. For my part, I think there is nothing that can be called miserable

miſerable in man, unleſs he thinks there is ſomething miſerable in the *nature of things*. I would quarrel with myſelf, if I thought there was any thing that I could not endure. Am I ſick? It is part of my deſtiny. Is my family afflicted? am I hard preſſed by the uſurer? does my houſe crack? loſſes, wounds, difficulties, fears, do they all aſſault me? It is nothing more than what is common in the world: nay, further, *it muſt be ſo*. Theſe things therefore cannot be ſaid to *happen*, they are *decreed*.

If you will believe me, *Lucilius*, I will lay open to you my inmoſt thoughts and affections. Thus then, when any thing ſeems adverſe or hard to me, do I behave myſelf: I obey not God forcibly, but willingly; I follow him, not from neceſſity, but with all my mind and all my ſoul (*a*). Nothing can befall me that I will receive, either with an heavy heart, or a ſorrowful countenance. There is no kind of tribute but what I will pay readily; conſidering that all we either mourn or fear is but the tribute we owe to Nature for our exiſtence. It is in vain either to expect an exemption from theſe things, or to aſk it (*b*). Are you racked with pains in the bladder? have you had continual loſſes?—I will go further: are you in fear of your life? And did you not know that you wiſhed for theſe things when you wiſhed for old age (*c*)? All theſe things as neceſſarily attend a long life, as in a long journey we muſt expect duſt, and dirt, and ſhowers.

But you would fain live, you ſay, *and yet be free from all theſe inconveniencies*. Such an effeminate declaration by no means become a man. I would fain ſee how you would take this wiſh of mine; which I proteſt I make, not only with a great, but good, intention; *may neither Gods nor Goddeſſes permit Fortune to indulge you in eaſe and pleaſure*. Put to yourſelf this queſtion, whether, if God was pleaſed to favour you with your choice, you had rather live in the ſhambles than in a camp. Know, *Lucilius*, that life is a warfare (*d*): ſuch men therefore who are ordered from place to place; who undergo all manner of difficulties in the execution of the moſt dangerous commiſſions; theſe are your brave men, and chiefs in an army: while they who enjoy public eaſe at the expence of others labours, are mere poltrons (*e*) who buy their ſafety with diſgrace.

ANNOTATIONS, &c.

(*a*) This is true wiſdom, the principal doctrine of the Stoics, and confirmed throughout the whole tenour of the Goſpel. "He is but a bad ſoldier, who ſighs and marches on with reluctancy; we muſt receive the orders with ſpirit and chearfulneſs, and not endeavour to ſlink out of the part aſſigned us in this beautiful diſpoſition of things; whereof even our ſufferings make a neceſſary part. Let us addreſs ourſelves to God who governs all; as *Cleanthes* did in thoſe excellent lines which are going to loſe part of their grace and energy by my tranſlation of them. *Bolingbroke.* (See the original Epiſtle, 107, N. f.)

Parent of Nature, maſter of the world,
Where'er thy providence directs, behold
My ſteps with chearful reſignation turn.
Fate leads the willing, drags the backward on.
Why ſhould I grieve, when grieving I muſt bear,
Or take with guilt, what guiltleſs I might ſhare?

——— Thus let us ſpeak, thus let us act. Reſignation to the will of God is true magnanimity. But the ſure mark of a puſillanimous and baſe ſpirit, is to ſtruggle againſt, to cenſure, the order of Providence; and inſtead of mending our own conduct, to ſet up for that of correcting our Maker. *Id.*——See alſo *Adams* on Suicide, p. 176.

(*b*) "This eſtabliſhed courſe of things it is not in our power to change: but it is in our power to aſſume ſuch a greatneſs of mind as becomes wiſe and virtuous men; as may enable us to encounter the accidents of life with fortitude; and to conform ourſelves to the order of Nature; who governs her great kingdom, the world, by continual mutations. Let us ſubmit to this order: let us be perſuaded that whatever does happen ought to happen; (or, as Mr. *Pope* expreſſes it, *whatever is, is right*;) and never to be ſo fooliſh as to expoſtulate with Nature."

The beſt reſolution we can take, is to ſuffer what we cannot alter; and to purſue, without repining, the road which Providence, who directs every thing, has marked out to us. *Id.*

(*c*) Γῆρας ἐπὰν μὲν ἀπῇ, πᾶς εὔχεται, ἢν δὲ ποτ᾽ ἔλθῃ,
Μέμφεται· ἔστι δ᾽ ἀεὶ χρεῖσσον ὀφειλόμενον.
All wiſh for age, but when it comes, they cry,
They have enough, and rather wiſh to die.
Εἴ τις γηράσας ζῆν εὔχεται, ἄξιος ἐστι
Γηράσκειν πολλῶν εἰς ἐτέων δεκάδας.

(*d*) This alluſion is common in ſcripture. *I have fought a good fight*, ſaith St. *Paul*; *I have finiſhed my courſe; I have kept the faith; henceforth is laid up for me a crown of righteouſneſs.* ii. Tim. 4. 7. *This charge I commit with thee, ſon Timothy, that thou mayeſt war a good warfare.* i. Tim. 1. 18.

(*e*) Turdilli ſunt, tuti contumeliæ cauſa.---*Al.* Turburilla ſunt. *Pincian.* Tubilinæ, the name of a Goddeſs amongſt the ancients. *Lipſ.* Turdi ſunt. From one *Turdus*, a man of ſo infamous a character, that his name became a proverb.---*Seneca*, the father, makes mention of him, in l. 9. *Controv.* 4.---Turdilli, *Ouſels*; or ſome ſuch birds, that are ſafe in being deſpicable.

EPISTLE XCV.

The Wicked never ſecure.

YOU are miſtaken, *Lucilius,* if you think luxury, diſorderly behaviour, and other indecencies, which men are apt to lay to the charge of their own times, the peculiar vices of this age (*a*). There is no age exempt from them: but it is man that is in fault, not the age. And if once we begin to examine into the licentiouſneſs of certain times, I am aſhamed to ſay, that nothing could be more notorious, than the crimes that were committed in the face of *Cato.*

Would any one think that money ſhould be employed in that ſolemn trial, when *Clodius* was accuſed of adultery, committed in diſguiſe with the wife of *Cæſar*; and of violating the holy rites, inſtituted for the good of the people (*b*); at what time men are ſo far from being admitted, that the very pictures of any male animal were covered (*c*)? But the Judges took money; nay, what is much worſe, they exacted, by way of fees, the violation of matrons and young noblemen. There was leſs heinouſneſs in the crime, than in the abſolution of it. The accuſed of adultery divided with his Judges his ſinful ſport; nor was he ſecure until he had involved his Judges in the ſame guilt with himſelf.

Such were the tranſactions in the trial of *Clodius,* wherein *Cato,* if nothing more, was ſummoned to give evidence. But becauſe the thing exceeds all belief, I will give you the very words of *Cicero*; Accerſivit ad ſe, promiſit, interceſſit, dedit, jam verò, (O Dii boni, rem perditam!) etiam noctes certarum mulierum, atque adoleſcentulorum nobilium perductiones, nonnullis *judicibus pro mercedis* cumulo fuerunt. *Calvus,* the manager for *Clodius, called the Judges to him: he made them large promiſes, he entreated, he gave them money; but now, (O ye Gods,) what abominable wickedneſs! ſome of the Judges, by way of*

3 *a bleſſing,*

a blessing, above their fee, were to be introduced by night to the enjoyment of certain women of quality and young noblemen. There was no room to complain of the fee, be it what it will, since it was attended with such *a blessing*, as, *would you have the wife of that severe old fellow,* (*Cato,* suppose?) *I will procure her for you. Or do you prefer the wife of that rich man* (*Crassus?*) *you shall enjoy her.* And when you yourself have committed adultery, condemn it, *if you can.* Yes, that beautiful lady, if you desire her, shall be at your service; I promise you a night with her, when you please; you shall be sure to have her during the adjournment of the trials. It is more to procure and distribute adulteries, than to commit them: the former consists in summoning the matrons, and artfully taking them off their guard; the latter in freely abusing them. These Judges however of *Clodius,* demanded of the senate protection and a guard, which they had no need of, as they had no design to condemn him; but they obtained it: whereupon when they had acquitted him, *Catulus* said smartly to one of them, Quid vos præsidium a nobis petebatis? *To what intent do you ask a guard? was you afraid any one should take* the bribe *from you, which you had just received?*

Amidst all these jokes the adulterer was acquitted, even before the trial; and his pimp taken no notice of during the process; who indeed escaped sentence, which he more deserved than the other. Can you think then any age more corrupt in morals than this; when lust could not be restrained by holy ceremonies, nor public justice? when in that very enquiry, which was extraordinarily debated in the senate, greater villainy was committed than in the matter in question? The enquiry was, whether a man, after committing adultery, could live safe in *Rome?* and it appeared, that *without committing adultery* he could not be safe.

Such were the transactions in the time of *Cæsar* and *Pompey*; nay, in the time of *Cicero* and *Cato,* even that *Cato,* in whose presence the people dared not to demand the celebration of the sports called *Floralia* (*d*). Think you, then, men were more severe with regard to what they saw, than in the courts of judicature? No; such excesses have happened,

and

and will happen. The licentiousness of critics is sometimes restrained by fear and discipline, but never subsides of itself. There is no reason therefore you should think, that in our time *only*, the laws have little credit, and licentiousness the fashion. For my part, I think our youth are not so profligate as at the time when the person accused of adultery denied the fact to his judges, and the judges confessed, or exposed their guilt to him. When whoredoms were committed in order to qualify such as were to try the cause; and when *Clodius*, (becoming gracious by those very crimes that rendered him guilty) instead of proper allegations, and proving his innocence, turned procurer for his judges. Would any one believe this, that he who was accused of one criminal fact, should get acquitted by committing more? Every age will have a *Clodius*, but not every age a *Cato*.

We are all prone to evil, because herein we seldom want either a leader or a companion: not but that the business goes on without either a companion or a leader. Men are not only prone, but run headlong into evil: and what renders many incurable is, that artificers are ashamed of any errors in their professions, but men delight in the errors of life. A pilot rejoiceth not in the wreck of his ship, nor a physician in the death of his patient, nor an orator in losing his client's cause: but, on the contrary, men take pleasure and even glory in their sins. One man, for instance, triumphs in committing adultery, especially if with great difficulty he obtained the favour; another, in overreaching, and pilfering from, his neighbour: nor does the sin ever displease them, provided they have the good fortune to escape punishment.

Now this is owing to the prevalency of bad custom. For, observe, that you may know, there is still a sense of good, left even in minds that are most corrupt; and that men, however negligent, are not quite void of shame; almost all dissemble their crimes: and, when they have succeeded, they enjoy the fruits of their actions, but at the same time endeavour to conceal the actions themselves. Whereas a good conscience desires to appear openly, and *to be seen of men*; nay wickedness is afraid of darkneſs itſelf. I think it therefore elegantly ſaid by *Epicurus*, Poteſt nocenti contingere ut lateat, latendi fides non poteſt; *a guilty perſon may poſſibly lie concealed, but he cannot truſt to it*; or perhaps you may think it better expreſſed in this manner: Ideo non prodeſt latere peccantibus, quia latendi etiam ſi felicitatem habent, fiduciam non habent: *it is of little avail for a ſinner to hide himſelf, for let him hide himſelf as he will, he can never be aſſured of peace and ſecurity.*

Thus it is; *wickedneſs may be ſafe, but it never can be ſecure.* And I cannot think this aſſertion anywiſe repugnant to the doctrine of our ſect (*e.*) And why? becauſe the firſt and greateſt puniſhment of offenders is in the offence itſelf: nor does any wickedneſs, though fortune may adorn it with her choiceſt gifts, nay, though ſhe may defend and protect it, go unpuniſhed. Becauſe the puniſhment, I ſay, of wickedneſs is in wickedneſs itſelf: nevertheleſs both the one and the other are ſtill preſſed upon and followed with this ſecondary chaſtiſement, a continual dread, and diffidence of ſecurity.

And why ſhould I deſire to deliver wickedneſs from this certain puniſhment? why ſhould I not leave a mind ſo engaged ſtill in ſuſpenſe? We muſt diſſent indeed from *Epicurus*, when he ſaith (*f*), *nothing is juſt* by nature; *and that crimes are avoided, becauſe fear is not to be avoided:* but herein we muſt agree with him, that *evil deeds are ſcourged by conſcience, and the greateſt part of her torture conſiſts in that anxiety which preſſeth upon and wrings her, becauſe ſhe can put no confidence in any thing that promiſeth her ſecurity.* For thus *Epicurus* argues, we naturally abhor villainy, becauſe no one is ſo ſafe as to be out of the reach of fear; good fortune delivers many from puniſhment, but no one from the fear of it; becauſe there is implanted in us an averſion to whatever is condemned by nature: therefore there can be no ſurety of concealment, even to thoſe who endeavour to conceal themſelves; ſince conſcience accuſeth them, and betrayeth them to themſelves. It is the property of guilt to tremble. It would be bad for us indeed, foraſmuch as many crimes eſcape the law, the Judge, and penal ſtatutes, if theſe natural and grievous puniſhments were not immediately inflicted; and fear ſupplied not the place of a beadle.

A N-

ANNOTATIONS, &c.

(a) Et alia quæ objecit fuis quifque temporibus.] So *Hefiod*, the moft antient author of that fiction, relating to the four ages of the world, complains of his being born in the *iron* age, the worft of the four.

> Μηκέτ' ἔπειτ' ὤφελλον ἐγὼ πέμπτοισι μετεῖναι
> Ἀνδράσιν, ἀλλ' ἢ πρόσθε θανεῖν, ἢ ἔπειτα γενέσθαι,
> Νῦν γὰρ δὴ γένος ἐστὶ σιδήρεον· Hef. 1. 172.
> *Of public vice now reigns fuch ample ftore,*
> *Would I had ne'er been born, or born before!*
> *This furely is the iron age.*———

(b) "This feaft, or facrifice, was made to *her* whom the Romans called Bona Dea, *the good Goddefs*, the Greeks *Gynæcæa*; and it being celebrated only by women, *Clodius*, being a handfome young man, took on him the difguife of a finging girl, in order to carry on an intrigue with *Pompeia Cæfar's* wife; but being difcovered, he was brought to trial, when *Cæfar* himfelf appeared, and to the furprize of every one declared, *he had nothing to charge him with. Why then*, faid the accufers, *have you divorced your wife? Becaufe*, fays he, *it is enough for Cæfar's wife to be fufpected*. So *Clodius* got clear of the judgment, moft of the judges giving their opinion in a confufed manner, upon feveral caufes at the fame time, that they might not be in danger from the people in condemning him; (for in oppofition to the nobility they all took his part) nor in difgrace with the nobility by acquitting him." So far *Plutarch* in his Life of *Cæfar*.

And *Cicero* in his Epiftle to *Atticus*, (l. 1. Ep. 15.) concerning this affair, fays, "Our illuftrious *Areopagites* called out that they would not affemble, unlefs a guard was appointed them. This matter was debated, and only one member was found who did not defire the guard. The affair was then carried before the Senate, where it was granted in a moft formal, honourable manner: the judges were commended, the providing a guard was committed to the magiftrates, nor was there a man found who imagined that *Clodius* would ftand his trial. Twenty-one of the judges were determined againft him, though they were threatened with the greateft dangers. But thirty-one of them obeyed the calls of hunger rather than of honour."

(c) So *Juvenal* fpeaking of this very affair, f. 6. 336.

> ——— ubi velari pictura jubetur
> Quæcunque alterius fexus imitata figuram eft.
> *And ev'n male pictures modeftly are veil'd.*

(d) At what time the more celebrated courtefans dance naked. The learned are agreed that the vulgar notion of *Flora* the ftrumpet, is purely a fiction of *Lactantius*; from whom it was taken. *Flora* appears to have been a *Sabine* goddefs, and the *Ludi Florales* to have been inftituted A. U. C. 613. The main part of the ceremony was managed by a company of lewd ftrumpets, who ran up and down naked. However the wifeft and graveft *Romans* were not for difcontinuing this cuftom, though the moft indecent imaginable. For *Cato* when he was prefent at thefe games, and faw the people afhamed to let the maids ftrip while he was there, immediately went out of the theatre, to let the ceremony have its courfe. *Liv.* xxv. *Kennet.*

(e) i. e. Stoicifm. The Stoics maintained that virtue and vice were to be followed or efchewed, merely upon their own account; whereas the *Epicureans* had refpect to reward and punifhment.

(*f*) *Epicurus* adds, τὴν ἀδικίαν ȣ̓ καθ' ἑαυτὴν κακόν, κ. τ. λ. *Injustice is not an evil in itself, but in the fear and suspicion of being discovered.* On the contrary the *Stoics* (Cic. de Fin. l. 3.) minimè vero probatur huic disciplinæ (*Stoicæ*) aut amicitiam aut justitiam, ob utilitates adscisci aut probari, jus autem, quod ita dici appellarique possit, id esse natura, alienumque a sapiente, non modo injuriam cuiquam facere verùm etiam nocere.

There absolutely could be no such things as justice *or* friendship, *unless they were cultivated for themselves. As to what is termed* right, *the* Stoics *hold it to be Nature itself; and that it is inconsistent with the character of a wise man to do an injury, nay, the least prejudice to any person.*

EPISTLE XCVI.

All Happiness from within; in this transitory State of Things.

NEVER think a man happy, *Lucilius*, whose happiness is in suspense. He depends on frailty, who rejoiceth in an adventitious good. Such joy will pass away as lightly as it came: but the joy that ariseth from within, is faithful, is firm; it continually grows stronger, and holds out to the last *. Other things which the vulgar admire are only good for a time. What then is there no pleasure or profit in them? who denies it (*a*)? but it must be when they depend upon *us*, and not we upon *them*. All things within the power of fortune may thus be made fruitful and pleasant to us; if he that possesseth them is master also of himself; and subjects not himself to his possessions.

For they are mistaken, my *Lucilius*, who think that what fortune can give us is either good or bad. She gives us indeed the material part of good and evil; and to her we owe the beginning of those incidents, which in the issue may prove either happy or unhappy for us. But the mind is stronger than any fortune; it conducteth its own affairs, right or wrong; and is itself the cause of its own happiness or misery. A bad mind turns every thing to bad; even such things as have the appearance of good: but the man of an upright and pure mind corrects the depravity of fortune; and softens, by the art of patience, every hard and disagreeable condition. The same likewise receives prosperity with gratitude and moderation; and adversity with constancy and courage. Who although he is prudent, although he is so judicious in his transactions, as never to engage in any enterprize beyond his ſtrength; yet never can attain that entire good, which is placed beyond the threats of fortune, unleſs he is fixed, and ſteady againſt all uncertainties.

Whether, *Lucilius*, you will be pleaſed to obſerve other men, (for in ſuch a caſe we are apt to judge more freely) or to conſider yourſelf, without prejudice or partiality; you will perceive, and confeſs, that none of theſe things, which are eſteemed ſo precious and deſirable, are truly uſeful; unleſs you will arm yourſelf againſt the levity of chance, and the uncertainty of things depending thereon; unleſs you frequently, and without murmuring and repining at any loſs, can ſay, Diis aliter viſum eſt,—(*I might think perhaps I deſerved better fortune, but) the Gods thought otherwiſe* (*b*). Or to give you a verſe of a more ſtrong and juſt expreſſion; ſay this, when any thing happens contrary to expectation, Dii melius (*c*). *The Gods know better*, (what is good for us than we do ourſelves). A mind thus compoſed no accident can injure; and thus will a mind be compoſed, if a man reflects upon the variety of contingencies in human affairs, before he is made ſenſible of them; if he enjoys his children, his wife, his eſtate, as if he was not always to enjoy them; and if he could not be made more wretched upon this account, was he obliged to part from them. *That* mind alone is wretched, which is ever anxious concerning what may happen; which is miſerable before real miſery reacheth it, and in continual dread leſt thoſe things which it now delights in ſhould not continue to the end of life: for ſuch a one can never be at reſt; and, in expectation of ſome future evil, will loſe the enjoyment of the preſent good.

There is but little difference between grieving for a thing loſt, and the fear of loſing any thing. Not that I hereby, *Lucilius*, recommend negligence or careleſſneſs: no; do your endeavour to avoid ſuch things as are to be dreaded; do all that can be done by prudence and forecaſt (*d*); conſider well what may hurt you: nothing can be more ſerviceable to this purpoſe than a reaſonable confidence, and a mind reſolutely ſteeled with patience. The man is ſecure againſt the power of fortune, who is determined to be ſubmiſſive. Tranquillity excludes all manner of

 tumult.

tumult. Besides, nothing can be more miserable, nothing more ridiculous, than to be always in fear: what madness is it for a man to anticipate his misfortunes!

Lastly, to include in a few words my sentiments on this subject, and to describe these over-busy-bodies, and self-tormentors, let me observe, they are as impatient and intemperate, when what they expected comes upon them, as they were before. He certainly grieves more than is necessary, who grieves before it is necessary: for, by the same infirmity, that he does not expect sorrow, he knows not how to consider it rightly; and by the same unreasonableness, he not only fancies that his felicity will be lasting, but that whatever good hath befallen him, it must necessarily encrease: and forgetful of the grand machine *(f)*, whereby all things are tossed and scattered about, he promiseth to himself alone stability in casual things. *Metrodorus* therefore seems to speak excellently well in that Epistle where he comforts his sister upon the death of her son, a child of a charming disposition, saying,

Mortale est omne mortalium bonum (*g*).

Mortal is every good of mortal men.

He is speaking of those goods which men so greatly affect and readily pursue: for the *true good* never dies: it is sure, and everlasting, *wisdom and virtue* (*h*). This is the only good to mortals; but so unreasonable are they, so forgetful of what they are; and whither they are going; nay, whither every day pusheth them on; that they wonder and are amazed at losing any thing, though it is certain they must one day lose all.

Whatever it is that you call yourself master of, you may have it indeed, but it is not thine. Nothing can be firm to an infirm creature; nothing eternal and unperishable to frail mortals on this side the grave. It is as necessary that all worldly goods should perish, as at any time be lost. And this, if rightly understood, would prove a comfortable inducement to us to part, with a steady mind, from what we knew we must necessarily lose.

What remedy then ſhall we find out againſt theſe loſſes? Why, this; that we ſtill keep in memory the things that are loſt, and ſuffer not the fruits we received from them to periſh with them. *To have*, may be taken from us; but *to have had*, never. He is very ungrateful, who when he hath loſt any thing, ſuppoſeth that he owes no thanks for the enjoyment of it. Chance may rob us of a thing, yet leave us the benefit of it; unleſs we loſe this too by an unreaſonable deſire and longing after it.

Say moreover to thyſelf; there are none of all theſe things that ſeem ſo terrible, but what are conquerable. There are many who have overcome each particular, as, *Mucius*, fire; *Regulus*, torture; *Socrates*, poyſon; *Cato*, death, by his own ſword. Let *us* alſo endeavour at ſome glorious victory. Again,—thoſe things which under a ſpecious ſhew of happineſs allure the vulgar, have been often, and by many deſpiſed. *Fabricius (i)*, when general in chief, deſpiſed riches; and, when cenſor, condemned them. *Tubero* (*k*) adjudged poverty worthy of himſelf and the capitol; when, at a ſolemn feaſt, uſing earthen veſſels, he ſhewed that men ought to be contented with theſe things wherewith the Gods themſelves diſdained not to be ſerved. *Sextius* the elder, a man every way qualified for a ſtateſman, when offered the ſenatorial robe by *Julius Cæſar*, would not accept it, for he well knew that what was given him, might be taken from him. Let *us* likewiſe aſſume this noble ſpirit, and prove as exemplary to others, as theſe have been to us. Why do we draw back? Why do we deſpair? What has been may be. Let us only make pure the mind, and *follow nature*; (*m*) for whoever ſwerves from following her, muſt fear, muſt deſire, and be a ſlave to caſualties. We may return to the right way, we may recover ourſelves, if we pleaſe. Let us then endeavour it, that we may patiently bear whatever may afflict the body, and ſay to Fortune, Cum viro tibi negotium eſt, quære quem vincas; *you have now got a man to deal with; look out elſewhere for one whom you may conquer* (*n*).

By theſe and the like ſpeeches, is aſſuaged the virulence of that ulcer, which I heartily wiſh eaſed, and if not cured, made ſupportable,

able, that I may grow old under it. Not that I am greatly affected in this matter: our present question is concerning our loss of a most excellent *old* man (*o*); for he truly may be said to be full of days, who desires no more should be added to his life, for his own sake, but for theirs to whom he may be serviceable. He acts generously in that he still lives. Some men would not so long have endured their pains, but he thinks it as scandalous to fly to death as to fly from it. *But supposing him otherwise persuaded, shall he not go?* Why not; if he can be no longer of service to any one; if he can do nothing more than attend upon his pain? But this, my *Lucilius, is to put philosophy into practice, and to be exercised* in the truth; to shew how a prudent man can fortify his mind against death, and against pain, when either that approacheth, or this oppresseth him. What is to be done, must be learned from the doer of it.

Thus far then we have argued, whether it be possible to resist pain; and whether death, how near soever, can make a great mind stoop and tremble. And what need is there of many words? The thing speaks itself. Let us observe this, that neither death makes such a one more courageous and strong against pain, nor pain against death: he arms himself against both, and puts his confidence therein. Neither thro' hopes of death, does he more patiently endure pain; nor does the irksomeness of pain make him die more willingly: he bears the one, and waits the other *(p)*.

ANNOTATIONS, &c.

* Those indeed who have no internal resource of happiness will find themselves uneasy in every stage of human life: but to him who is accustomed to derive all his felicity from within himself, no state will appear as a real evil into which we are conducted by the common and regular course of Nature. *Melm.*

(*a*) See Ep. 23.——*For every creature of God is good, and not to be refused, if it be received with thanksgiving.* i. Tim. 44.

(*b*) This is spoken of *Ripheus*, a just and good man, whose hard fate *Æneas* is lamenting; and thinking that he deserved much better, he checks himself with this excellent reflection, *that it was the will of the Gods that he should suffer with the rest.* Cato, p. 8.

" Vain men! how seldom do we know what to wish, or pray for! When we pray against misfortunes, and when we fear them most, we want them most. It was for this reason *Pythagoras* forbade

bade his disciples to ask any thing particular of God; the shortest and the best prayer we can make to him, who knows our wants, and our ignorance in asking, is this, *Thy will be done.* Bolingbroke on Exile.

The Christian on the like occasion is taught and commanded, by our Lord himself to say, *O Father of Heaven, thy will be done.* Matth. 6. 10. Luke, 11. 2.

(*c*) *Ovid.* Met. ix. 496.——Dii melius—*The Gods forbid.*——Sewell.

(*d*) So the charge of our Lord to his Disciples, *Be ye as wise as serpents, and innocent as doves.* Matth. 10. 16.

(*e*) *Take therefore no thought for the morrow, for the morrow shall take thought for the things of itself: sufficient unto the day is the evil thereof.* Matth. 6. 34.

And St. Paul, *I would have you without carefulness.* i. Cor. 7. 32.

(*f*) Obliti hujus petauri, quo humana jactantur. *Pincian al.* hujus peccati,—*al.* obliti fati quo——

An magis oblectant animum jactata *petauro*
Corpora——*Mart.*
Ad numeros etiam ille ciet cognata per artem
Corpora, quæ valido saliunt excussa *petauro*,
Alternosque cient motus: elatus et ille
Nunc jacet, atque hujus casu suspenditur ille.
To these join those, who from an engine tost,
Pierce through the air, and in the clouds are lost;
Or poise on timber, where by turns they rise,
And sink, and mount each other to the skies.

(*g*) *Muret.* observes that *Metrodorus* borrowed this sentence from *Euripides*——Θνητῶν δ' ὀυδεὶς ὄλβιος.

(*h*) Like the Christian charity, *it never faileth.* i. Cor. 13. 8. Or, like the word of God; *Heaven and earth shall pass away, but my words shall not pass away.* Matth. 24. 25.

(*i*) *Fabricius* was in the highest veneration among the *Romans*, as a man of virtue, and a good soldier, but extremely poor. Being sent embassador to *Pyrrhus*, *Pyrrhus* received him with great kindness, and pressed him in private to accept of a handsome present in gold, not to engage him in any thing dishonourable, but as a pledge of friendship and hospitality. *Fabricius* however would not accept it upon any terms. See *Plutarch.* Life of *Pyrrhus*.

(*k*) *Elius Tubero*, the very best of men, and who above all the *Romans* knew how to support his poverty with magnificence. *Id.* in the Life of *Emilius*. See Ep. 95.

(*l*) See Ep. 59.

(*m*) The nature of man as it now is cannot justly be set up as a proper rule or standard of virtue, but must itself be regulated by an higher cause, by which we are to judge of its rectitude, and of its corruptions and defects; and therefore the ablest of the Stoics in judging of what is according to nature, were for considering the nature of man as in a conformity to the law of reason and the nature of the whole. But this way of talking seems not well fitted to furnish us with clear notions; and only serves to enhance our obligation to the Almighty for the further discovery of his will in his holy word.

(*n*) In order to which great end, it is necessary we should stand watchful as centinels, to discover the secret wiles and open attacks of this capricious goddess, before they reach us. When she falls upon us unexpected, it is hard to resist, but those who wait for her will repel her with ease.

" I learned this important lesson long ago, and never trusted to Fortune, even while she seemed to be at peace with me. The riches, the honours, the reputation, and all the advantages which her treacherous

treacherous indulgence poured upon me, I placed them fo that fhe might fnatch them away, but fhe could not *tear* them from me. No man fuffers by bad fortune, but he that hath been deceived by good.——If we do not fuffer ourfelves to be tranfported by profperity, neither fhall we be reduced by adverfity. Our fouls will be of proof againft the dangers of both thefe ftates; and having explored our ftrength we fhall be fure of it. For in the midft of felicity, we fhall have tried how we can bear misfortune." *Bolingbroke* on Exile.

(*o*) There being no mention made before of any perfon to whom thefe words are referable, *Muret.* concludes that this Epiftle is imperfect, (as certainly it is) and that much is wanting at the beginning. *Lipfius* thinks the fame; but makes a doubt whether the perfon here alluded to may not be the *Marullus* mentioned in the next Epiftle.

(*p*) Hunc fert, illam expectat] Whatever *Seneca* may have faid elfewhere feemingly in favour of fuicide, is fufficiently confuted by the example here recommended, which breathes the pure and found doctrine of Chriftianity.

EPISTLE XCVII.

Confolatory, on the Death of a Son.

I HAVE fent you, *Lucilius*, the Epiftle I wrote to *Marullus* on the death of his young fon; for whom I was told he indulged an unmanly forrow; and therefore I have fwerved from my ufual ftyle as not thinking that he ought to be treated gently, when more worthy of reproof than confolation. To one indeed afflicted with a deeper wound than he knows how to bear, it is proper to give way a little: let him fatiate himfelf; at leaft let him give vent to the figh, and gufhing tear: but let fuch as take upon them to weep at every trifling accident, be chaftifed, and taught to know, that even tears have their folly.

— Do you expect comfort? No: I fhall rather reprove you. Are you fo effeminately moved at the death of your fon; what would you have done if you had loft a *friend?* Your fon is departed, a child, an infant, in whom you could place no certain hope: nothing then is loft but a little time. We are too apt to feek occafions of forrow, and unjuftly to complain of Fortune; as if fhe would not give us, at fome time or other, juft caufes of complaint. Truly I thought your mind ftrong enough

enough to ſupport real afflictions, and conſequently would deſpiſe ſuch ſhadows of evil, at which men grieve merely for cuſtom ſake (*a*). Had you even loſt a friend, (which ſurely is the greateſt of all loſſes) you ought rather to rejoice in having had ſuch a friend, than to mourn for having loſt him. But few, alas! take any account of what courteſies they have received, or what favours they have formerly enjoyed. This evil then, among many other, attends upon ſorrow; it is not only ſuperfluous, but ungrateful.

And is it then all in vain, that you once had a friend? Is it nothing that you lived ſo many years in ſtrict amity; and a ſocial communication of improvements in ſtudy? Haſt thou buried friendſhip too with thy friend? Or, if he was not ſerviceable to you, while living, why ſhould you grieve at having loſt him? Believe me, great part of thoſe whom we loved, though chance hath taken them from us, ſtill remains with us. The time paſſed is all our own; nor can any thing be more ſafe and ſurely ours, than what hath been. But we are indeed ungrateful for what is paſt, through the hopes of what is to come; as if this too, were we to ſucceed herein, would not ſoon come under the ſame predicament. He ſets too narrow bounds on the enjoyment of life, who only rejoiceth in the preſent. Both the things that are to come, and the things that are paſt have their endearments; the former from expectation, the latter from memory: but thoſe are ſtill depending, and may not happen, whereas theſe cannot but have been. What madneſs is it therefore to forego that which is moſt certain! Let us acquieſce in thoſe things which we have taſted; unleſs we entruſted them to ſo leaky a boſom as tranſmits every thing that it receives.

There are innumerable inſtances of thoſe who have loſt their young children without a tear: who returned from the funeral rites to the ſenate-houſe, or ſome public office, and were taken up with their proper regards; and that wiſely too: for, 1ſt, it is in vain to grieve where grief can do no good: 2dly, it is unjuſt to complain of that happening to one, which happens unto all; and, laſtly, it is a folly to lament and mourn, when there is ſo little difference between the perſon loſt and

 the

the ſriend that loſeth him. We ought therefore to be of a more equal and ſteady mind, becauſe we muſt certainly follow thoſe we have loſt.

Conſider the celerity of moſt rapid Time: think on the ſhort race we ſo ſwiftly run: obſerve the whole aſſembly of mankind, all going the ſame way; and ſeparated by the ſhorteſt intervals, however long they ſeem. He whom we thought dead, is only gone before us: what then can be greater folly, than to bewail him who hath juſt ſtepped before you, when you yourſelf are travelling the ſame road? It is ridiculous to mourn, that an accident hath happened, which a man could not but know muſt one day happen: or, he muſt be very ignorant indeed, and impoſe upon himſelf, who knows not that man carries the ſeeds of death about him. It is to mourn a thing, which he allows could not be otherwiſe than as it is. Whoever complains at the death of any one, complains of his having been born. The ſame conditions bind all men. Every one that is born muſt die. We are diſtinguiſhed I ſay by ſmall intervals, but are all equal in death. The ſpace between our firſt and our laſt day is various and uncertain: if you conſider the *troubles* of life; even the life of a boy is long: if the *velocity* of it, the life of an old man is ſhort. There is nothing that is not uncertain, deceitful, and variable as the weather. All things are toſſed to and fro, and are transferable to their contraries, at the command of fortune. And in ſuch a rotation of human affairs, there is nothing certain, I ſay, but death: and yet all men complain of that in which alone no one is deceived.

But *he died a child!* Perhaps it may be the better for him. But I am not as yet ſpeaking of an early death. Let us conſider the old man; and how little hath he exceeded the infant! Set before your view the ample round of Time; reflect upon the ages paſt and to come; and then compare with Time's immenſity the ſpace we call *the age of man*, ſo ſhall you ſee how little a thing it is that we ſo earneſtly covet, and would fain extend. Conſider likewiſe how much of this little is taken up with tears, with troubles, with the wiſhing for death before it comes: how much is tortured with a bad ſtate of health, and with fear; how

how many years are ſpent in childhood, in ignorance, and unprofitable ſtudies! almoſt half of it is loſt in ſleep. Add hereunto labour, ſorrows, perils, and the like; and you will find that in the longeſt life, little of it can properly be called *living*. And who will not grant it better, *ſoon* to return from whence we came, and to end our journey without fatigue?

Life in itſelf is neither good nor evil; though both good and evil dwell therein; ſo that your child hath loſt nothing but the chance of falling into evil. He might indeed have proved decent and prudent; he might poſſibly, under your inſpection, have been formed to good; yet, (what is more juſtly to be feared) notwithſtanding all your care, he might have proved as bad as many other. Behold thoſe young rakes, whom, though born of a noble family, luxury and intemperance have reduced to the conſtitution of a prize-fighter! Look upon thoſe, who contaminate themſelves with abominable luſts for hire! who ſcarce paſs a day without being drunk, or committing ſome flagitious crime; and you will think it evident that more was to be feared than hoped for. You ought not therefore to provoke ſorrow; and, by repining at ſmall inconveniencies, accumulate real grief.

Do I then exhort you to ſtrive and exert yourſelf? No, my friend, I ſhould be aſhamed to have ſo mean an opinion of you, as to think there was any neceſſity for ſummoning all your virtue to your aid in ſo trifling an affair. This is no cauſe of grief, it is only a ſlight ſting, which you yourſelf have made painful. Philoſophy *truly* hath been of great ſervice to you, if you ſtrenuouſly bewail the loſs of a child, who was better known to his nurſe than to his father!

But do I then recommend a flinty heart? would I have you look up chearfully at the funeral of your ſon? nor ſuffer your mind to ſhrink at ſo great a loſs? No; this would be inhumanity, not virtue, to behold the dead, with the ſame delighted eye we do the living, relation; or not to be moved at the firſt forcible ſeparation in a family. And what if I was to forbid lamentation? There are ſome things not in our power; tears will flow from the moſt ſtubborn eyes; and thus, tears plentifully

 ſhed,

ſhed, often eaſe the heart. What muſt we then do?—why, permit them, but force them not. Let them drop as long as they ſpring from affection; but not ſo long as cuſtom or imitation may require. Let us not add to our ſorrow, nor increaſe it by the example of others. An oſtentation of grief demands more than grief itſelf. Who is it that indulgeth ſorrow, while alone? The deep groan is utterd, to be heard. In private your mourners are calm and eaſy; but at the ſight of any one, they burſt into tears (*k*). Then it is they tear the hair, and beat the breaſt, which they might have done much more freely, when there was no one to forbid them. Then they wiſh for death themſelves; and flounce upon the couch: but let the company depart, and their grief is over.

In this as well as in other exceſſes, we are wont to follow bad examples; and regard not what beſt becomes us, but what is cuſtomary on the like occaſion. We loſe ſight of nature, and addict ourſelves to the faſhion of the vulgar; no proper guide in any reſpect, but in this, of all other, the moſt inconſtant. Do they ſee any one bearing themſelves up againſt affliction, they call him impious and cruel-hearted; do they ſee him dejected and overcome with ſorrow, while hanging over the deceaſed, they call him weak and effeminate. We muſt reduce then all things to the ſtandard of reaſon; but nothing can be more ridiculous than to make a parade of ſorrow; and to ſeek approbation from a flood of tears; which I conſider, with regard to a wiſe man in two reſpects, ſometimes as iſſuing forcibly, and ſometimes as flowing by permiſſion. I will ſhew you the difference.

When ſome menger ſtrikes us with the diſagreeable news of a departed friend; or, when a body is torn from our embrace to be laid on the funeral pile, a natural neceſſity excites our tears: the ſpirit of man, being ſmitten by a ſudden impulſe, as it ſhakes the whole frame, ſo it ſpareth not the eyes, preſſing out and extorting the ever-ready fluid. Such tears as theſe ſtart involuntarily. There are other, to which we willingly give vent, when put in mind of ſome dear friend we have loſt; and there is indeed ſomething ſweet in ſuch an indulgence of ſorrow:

when

when we reflect upon their affability, chearful converſation, kind affection, and duteous piety, ſo that the eyes diſcharge as it were a flood of joy. Theſe we indulge, and by the other we are overcome.

There is no manner of reaſon then, that you ſhould either reſtrain, or pour forth tears, on account of viſiters with their compliments of condolance. They flow not, nor ceaſe to flow diſgracefully, provided there is no feigning nor affectation in the caſe. Let them ſtart if they will; it is no more than what may happen to men moſt moderate and compoſed. Nay, they have flowed, even whilſt reaſon hath kept up her authority; with ſuch moderation however, that both humanity and dignity were preſerved. We may obey nature, I ſay, herein, and ſtill maintain ſedateneſs and gravity. I have ſeen thoſe who looked venerable at the funeral of a relation: while in their countenance love ſat enthroned; without exhibiting the leaſt oſtentation of mourning. There was nothing but what aroſe from pure affection. Such a decency is there in ſorrow, which is always to be obſerved and kept up by a wiſe man: and as in other things, ſo in tears, there is a proper boundary: whereas among the imprudent, as their joy, ſo their grief, generally knows no bounds.

Receive then ſuch things as neceſſarily happen with an equal temper. What is there incredible? what is there that is new and ſtrange, in this affair? How many yet daily find employ for the undertakers? How many are the diſſections (*c*)? How many will grieve upon the ſame account with you? As often then as you think on your deceaſed child, think him alſo to have been born a mortal creature; to whom as nothing certain was promiſed, fortune did not think herſelf obliged to carry him on to old age, but diſmiſſed him at her pleaſure. Speak of him however as often as you pleaſe; and celebrate his memory (*d*) as long as it is agreeable; for no one delights to converſe with a ſorrowful perſon, much leſs with ſorrow itſelf. Do you recollect any witty ſayings, any jeſts which you once heard with pleaſure, repeat them often, and conſtantly affirm, that you doubt not, but he would have fulfilled the hopes your fatherly affection entertained of him. To forget a relation; to to bury the memory of him in his grave, to weep moſt profuſely, and yet be ſparingly mindful of him, is the part of a ridiculous and inhuman diſpoſition. Thus the birds and beaſts love their young, with a ſtrong, and almoſt outrageous affection for a time; but being loſt, or parted from them, all affection is extinguiſhed. This becomes not a wiſe man. Let him perſevere in the remembrance of a departed friend, but ceaſe to mourn.

I can by no means approve of what *Metrodorus* ſaith;—eſſe aliquam cognatam triſtitiæ voluptatem; hanc ipſam captendam in ejus modi tempore; *there is a certain pleaſure allied to grief, which, at ſuch a time, is to be covetted and embraced.* I have ſubſcribed the words of *Metrodorus (f),* and doubt not the cenſure you will paſs upon them. For, what can be more baſe, than to affect a pleaſure in grief itſelf? nay, to ſeek delight in tears and mourning? Theſe are the men who object againſt us, as being too rigid, and defame our precepts as hard and cruel, in that we affirm, that grief is not to be admitted into the mind, or ſoon expelled. But which do you think the more incredible, or the more inhuman, for a man not to be ſenſible of grief at the loſs of a friend, or to expect pleaſure in the depth of ſorrow? What we preſcribe is juſt and right; when affection hath poured forth ſome tears, and hath, as I may ſay, eaſed the eye of its load, the mind is no longer to be given up to ſorrow. And what ſay you? Why, that *there is a pleaſure mixed with grief itſelf*; as when we dry up a boy's tears with a cake, and ſtop the crying of infants with the milky treat. Nor even when the child is on the funeral pile, or this friend is expiring, will you permit pleaſure to ceaſe; but would fain tickle and flatter ſorrow itſelf. But which of the two is more fit and decent; either that ſorrow ſhould be removed from the mind; or pleaſure admitted thereto? admitted, did I ſay? nay, it is expected, and ſought after even in grief itſelf.

There is a certain pleaſure, ſaith *Metrodorus, allied to ſorrow.* We (*Stoics*) indeed might ſay this; but not you, (an Epicurean). For as you acknowledge but one good, which is pleaſure; and but one evil,

 which

which is pain and ſorrow, what affinity can there be between good and evil *(g)*? or if there was, we ſhould now eſpecially find it out; and now ſee, if ever, whether in grief itſelf there is any thing pleaſing and delightful. Certain remedies there are, which are ſalutary and of good effect to ſome parts of the body; but being lothſome, and not very decent, cannot fitly be applied to other parts; and what might prove of ſervice at one time without putting modeſty to the bluſh, may at another time, in caſe of a wound, be not ſo fit or decent. Are you not aſhamed to think of healing or aſſuaging grief by the pleaſure that is ſuppoſed to attend it? It is a wound, that requires the application of a ſeverer remedy. Rather apply this reflection thereto; that no ſenſe of pain can reach the dead; if it can, the perſon is not dead. Nothing, I ſay, can hurt him who is no where, who is nothing: if he can be hurt, he is ſtill living. And which do you think the worſe either that he is no more, or that he is ſtill in being? Certainly in that he is no more, no torment can affect him: for what feeling can he have, who is not? nor yet in that he ſtill is; for he hath got over the greateſt danger, which is death, by being no more.

This likewiſe we may urge to one who mourns and repines at the death of a young child. We are all, with reſpect to the ſhortneſs of life, compared with the immenſe circle of Time, both old and young upon the ſame level. So ſmall a portion of the many ages paſt is ours; that we cannot but call it the leaſt imaginable; though however little it be, it is ſtill ſomething. The time we live, I ſay, is next to nothing; though ſuch is our folly, to enlarge and ſtretch it out, as a matter of great conſequence.

Thus have I wrote to you, not as if you had expected from me ſo late conſolation; for I doubt not but that you have reflected before upon all that you have read; but in order to reprove you for that delay, ſhort as it was, in which you ſeemed to depart from your uſual judgment; and in concluſion exhort you, to buoy up your mind againſt any ſtroke of fortune, and prevent by forecaſt all her darts; not as what may poſſibly be aimed at you, but as what you certainly will one day feel.

ANNO-

ANNOTATIONS, &c.

(*a*) Moris causâ] al. amoris And ſo the old French tranſlation, *a cauſe de l'amour, qui eſt la plus grande playe de toutes.*

(*b*) Clarius cum audiuntur, gemunt] So, *Martial*;

Amiſſum non ſtet, cum ſola eſt, Gallia patrem,
Si quis adeſt, juſſæ proſiliunt lacrymæ.
Thus Gallia mourns; the ever ready tear
Starts from the eye when any friend is near;
But when alone, ſad as ſhe was before,
Sorrow ſubſides, and grief is heard no more. M.

Quam multis vitalia cruuntur, (for the improvement, ſuppoſe, of the young ſurgeon.) So *Eraſmus*, *al.* emuntur, al. emittunt.——*Gruter.* ſuſpects ſome defect here, but deſpairs of curing it. *Lipſius* ſays, he ſhould not have diſapproved of *cruuntur*, in the ſenſe *Eraſmus* received it, (ut poſſint condiri) if *Seneca* had wrote in *Egypt*, where it was uſual to embalm the dead, and not at *Rome*, where there was no ſuch cuſtom. He therefore conjectures——Quam multi vitam alii emittunt——but waving all theſe, ſays *Gronovius*, *I think the reading according to* Eraſmus *is right:* but he takes it in another ſenſe, not as relating to embalming, but to ſome violent operation in phyſic or ſurgery; as *Seneca* writes elſewhere——Lacerationes medicorum eſſe vivis legentium, et totas in viſcera manus demittentium. *Sen.* Conſol. ad Marc. 22. I have taken them in another ſenſe, which I think the words will bear; but after all ſhould chuſe the reading of *Lipſius*, becauſe the plaineſt, Quam multi vitam alii amittunt; *we daily ſee funeral after funeral.*

(*d*) Ὀφείλεται δὲ τοῖς ἀφῃρημένοις, ἡ διὰ τῆς ἀγαθῆς μνήμης τιμὴ, κ. τ. λ. *Plutarch.* Conſol. ad Apoll. *'Tis the duty we owe a deceaſed friend to keep him in pious memory. No good man requires hideous groans, but hymns and praiſes; not grief, but a commendable remembrance.* Fœminis lugere honeſtum eſt, viris meminiſſe. *Tacitus.* *It is for women to weep and bewail a deceaſed friend; it better becomes men to keep a reſpectful memory of him.*

(*e*) Vid. Ariſtot. Rhet. i. 11.——

Fleque meos caſus, eſt quædam, flere, voluptas. *Ovid.*
Bewail my lot; 'twill give you ſome relief;
A certain pleaſure oft attends on grief.
——— Tunc flere, et ſcindere veſtes
Fataque, et injuſtos rabidis pulſare querelis
Cœlicolas, ſolamen erat.——*Statius,* in Priſcillam.
It was a conſolation, to complain
Of unjuſt heav'n, and mourn a rabid ſtrain.

Apul. l. 6. inextricabilis periculi mole obruta, lacrymarum etiam extremo ſolatio carebat. *Pacat.* in Paneg. Theodoſii.——Eſt aliquid calamitatum delinimentum, dediſſe lacrymas malis, et pectus laxaſſe ſuſpiriis. *D. Ambros*, de obitu *Valentiniani*, paſcunt frequenter lacrymæ, et mentem allevant, fletus refrigerant pectus, et mœſtum ſolantur affectum.——Eſt enim piis affectibus quædam etiam flendi voluptas, et plerumque gravis evaporat dolor.

Nam miſeris nec flere quidem aut lenire dolorem
Colloquiis impunè licet. *Claud.* in Ruffin, l. 1.

Me

No harder lot can misery attend,
Than not to weep, or not enjoy a friend.

But how great is *Shakespear* in this respect, when he describes *Constance lamenting* her princely son *Arthur !*

" Grief fills the room up of my absent child;
" Lies in his bed, walks up and down with me;
" Puts on his pretty looks, repeats his words,
" Remembers me of all his gracious parts,
" Stuffs out his vacant garments with his form;
" Then have I reason to be fond of grief——
" O my dear boy, my Arthur, my fair son!
" My life, my joy, my food, my all the world!
" My widow's comfort, and my sorrow's cure!"

(f) The words are wanted in all the copies but two, which *Erasmus* says he saw; but the letters or characters were such that he could not read or make any sense of them, worth transcribing.

(g) For what communion hath righteousness with unrighteousness, and what communion hath light with darkness? ii. Cor. 6. 14.

EPISTLE C.

On the Writings of Fabian *.

YOU are pleased to inform me, *Lucilius*, that you have read with eagerness the books of *Caius Fabian*, which are entitled, *Civilium (a) of Politics*, and that they did not answer your expectation; and then, as if you had forgot you was talking of a *Philosopher*, you censure his composition. Suppose it to be as you say, and that he pours forth his words, unweighed *(b)*, there is sometimes a grace in this manner, and a peculiar excellency in an easy flowing style. For I think there is a great difference between *rushing* and *flowing*. So in the works I am speaking of, *Fabian* seems not lavishly to waste his words, but to pour them forth with fluency. He is prolix indeed, but without disorder and confusion. This he himself confesseth and declares, that his style is by no means affected, or laboured, but such however as might be known to be his. He pretended not to compose words, but to reform manners. He wrote not to please the ear, but to instruct the heart.

Besides, in his manner of writing, you have not time to examine particulars, but are smitten at once with the whole: though seldom such things as please at the first stroke will bear retailing, and the being scanned at the fingers ends. It is however of no little consequence to take the eye at first sight; though a diligent examination may possibly find out some things to be carped at, and disputed. If you ask my opinion, I think he is a greater man who hath seized upon our approbation, than one that hath merely deserved it: and I know too that he is more secure, and may more boldly promise his writings perpetuity. A laboured discourse becomes not a philosopher. When will he prove resolute and constant; or when make trial of his abilities, who is timorously concerned for the accuracy of expression?

Fabian was not negligent in his discourse, but sure: you will therefore find nothing in him low and mean: his words though chosen, are not affected; and though brilliant, yet are not unnatural, or inverted, as the manner of some is in this age. Nay, where they are common, not to say vulgar, they have an honest and noble meaning; not forced upon the sentence, but gravely and judiciously introduced. We shall see how little is pared too close; how little is too stiff; and how little wants polishing according to the present taste. When you take a view, I say, of the whole building at once, you will find it nowhere narrow or slight; though I must own there is no variegated marble, nor are the roofs interwoven with curious fretwork (*c*), nor is there a butler's hall; (*d*); or whatever else luxury, not contented with any simple decorations, hath invented and jumbled together in building. It is what is commonly called *a good house* (*e*).

Add this likewise, that all men are not agreed with regard to composition. Some would have the rough style made smoother, and others are so fond of the harsh and rugged, that if by chance they meet with a clause of a smooth and easy cast, they purposely strike it out; or make it break off abruptly, so as not to answer expectation. Read *Cicero*. His style is uniform: he keeps due measure: it is neatly worked up: soft and delicate, without trifling and effeminacy. On the other hand, the ſtyle of *Aſinius Pollio* is uneven, ever ſkipping, and ſtarting, leaving his reader in the lurch, when he leaſt expected it. In a word, every ſentence of *Cicero* is complete; but *Pollio* drops us at once; except in a few ſentences which are cloſed exactly in the ſame manner and form of expreſſion.

Moreover, *Lucilius*, you are pleaſed to ſay, that *Fabian* appears to you every where low and groveling; whereas I think he by no means deſerves this cenſure. What you object to, is not low and mean, but eaſy and pleaſing; adapted to the tenor of a calm and compoſed mind; not rugged or waving, but every where ſmooth and plain. Though I grant he wants the ſpirit and fire of an orator, and thoſe points and ſmart ſtrokes that you require. But view, I ſay, the whole body, and you will find, if it be not very ſpruce, it is decent.

But you likewiſe ſay, *it wants dignity*. Pray tell me, whom you will prefer to *Fabian*? *Cicero*? who has wrote almoſt as many books on philoſophical ſubjects as *Fabian*? If you do, I yield. But he is no little man, who is not much leſs than the greateſt. Or, do you prefer to him *Aſinius Pollio*? Again I yield: but in anſwer, beg leave to ſay, that a man muſt be allowed excellency, who, in ſo great a point as eloquence, hath but two before him. Or do you name *Livy*? for he not only wrote dialogues, which might be called philoſophical, as well as hiſtorical, but ſeveral books that profeſſedly treat of philoſophy. And to him too I give place. But conſider how many he muſt excel, who is excelled himſelf but by *three*, and theſe three the moſt eloquent.

But ſtill there is ſomething wanting in him. However elate his diſcourſe it is not ſtrong: and though abundantly flowing, it is never violent or rapid; and however pure, not ſufficiently clear. You deſire, you ſay, ſomething ſharp and ſevere againſt vice; ſomething high-ſpirited and bold againſt dangers; ſomething proud and haughty againſt fortune; a ſtrong invective againſt ambition. You would have luxury reprimanded, luſt diſgraced, impatience bridled in: *I would have ſomething*, ſay you, *rhetorically ſmart, tragically ſublime, and ſomething plain and familiar as comely*. Would you then have him fit down to fo trifling an affair as the ftudy of words? He devoted himfelf to the greatnefs of things, and draws eloquence after him as a fhadow, being intent on more weighty affairs. I do not pretend to fay that every fentence is exactly turned, and clofely connected; nor will every word ftrike and rouze the reader. This I confefs; that many periods run on without exhibiting any thing remarkably ftriking; and fometime will flip away unnoticed; but depend upon it you will every where find fome new light; and however long he detains you, you will not think him tedious.

Laftly, he hath this further excellency; that he will convince you he wrote as he thought, and believed himfelf what he affirmed; you will find that his chief intent was, to let you know what pleafed *him*, not what might pleafe and flatter *you*. All that he fays leads to perfection, and a good underftanding. He feeks not applaufe. And fuch I may venture to fay are his writings; though I truft more herein to my memory, than to reading what I have by me; and the chief tenor of it remains with me; not from any late converfation particularly, but fummarily, as is ufual, from an old acquaintance. When I had the pleafure of hearing him, fuch at leaft feemed his difcourfe, if not fwelling it was full, and fuch as was proper to incite the minds of well-difpofed youth, and allure them to walk in his fteps; not without hopes of bringing them to perfection. And this I take to be the moft effectual method of inftruction. For a mafter rather frightens his pupils, who hath only infpired them with a defire of imitation, but gave them no hopes of fuccefs. In fhort, *Fabian* perhaps might abound in words, and is not to be commended for every particular; yet upon the whole he is very magnificent.

3

ANNO-

ANNOTATIONS, &c.

* Caius Fabianus Papinius, an eloquent *Roman* orator, mentioned by *Pliny*. 36. 15.

(*a*) Civilium] *al.* artium civilium, *al.* artium et vilium. *al.* artium culium. *al.* archinilium. From which *Lipſius* ſuſpects ſome Greek word, f. αἰτιῶν φυσικῶν, as it is cited under this title by *Chariſius*, Cauſarum naturalium, *of natural cauſes*.

(*b*) Et effundi verba, non fingi] *al.* figi.---inſ. non effundere, ſed fundere. *Pincian*, non fundere ſed effundere---becauſe it follows, *adeò larga eſt*; and ſoon after, nec torrens, quamvis effuſa ſit.--- From theſe expreſſions, *non effundere ſed* fundere.---Electa verba, ſed non captata,---nec contra naturam ſuam poſita, ſplendida tamen.---Nec depreſſa, ſed plana,---effuſa ſed non rapida, &c. One would think that Sir *John Denham* had this Epiſtle in view, when he wrote thoſe celebrated lines, wiſhing his ſtyle to flow, as it certainly does, like the river he is deſcribing.

Tho' deep, yet clear; tho' gentle, yet not dull;
Strong without rage; without o'erflowing full.

(*c*) Nec conciſura laquearium cubiculis interfluentium. *Lipſ.* Elect. i. 15. *al.* nec conciſura aquarum a cuniculis---*al.* a cubiculis---*Eraſmus* only leaves out the prepoſition. If ſo, the luxury here pointed at, is their having ſmall reſervoirs of water under the table in their ſummer-houſes, wherein you may ſee the fiſh playing, ſuppoſe like our *gold fiſh*.

(*d*) Nec pauperis cella] *Eraſmus* will not allow *pauperis* to be the genuine word; but he offers no other. *Muret.* thinks the ſame, and leaves, as he found it. But *Opſopæus* affirms the common reading to be right from the like expreſſion in Ep. 18. Nec *pauperis cellas*, et quicquid aliud eſt, per quod luxuria divitiarum tædio ludit. So *Sen.* Rhetor. Ex cella migrabit in cubiculum dominæ ſuæ. *Controv.* vi. 7. The meaning then is, in carrying on the metaphor, that it was not ſo grand a houſe, as to have peculiar offices, or halls, for the ſervants.

(*e*) Quod dici ſolet, domus recta eſt.] *al.* tecta. Recta domus a Seneca dicitur, quæ nimio luxu corrupta non eſt, neque laquearibus et marmoribus pellucet, neque eleganti tectorio, aut lacunari perpolita eſt: ſed laudabilem quandam mediocritatem oſtendit. *Turneb.* Adv. l. 26. c. 12. Sic *rectus* apparatus, Ep. 111. *recto* vivere, Ep. 123. Hor. S. l. 2. de parabili ſuo venere, *candida rectaque* ſit. Plin. Ep. 9. 26. Dixi de quodam oratore ſeculi noſtri *recto* quidem et ſano, ſed parum grandi, et ornato, ut opinor, aptè; nihil peccat, niſi quod nihil peccat. In my opinion *I judged right of a certain orator of our times, who is juſt and exact, but not elevated and graceful, when I declared, he has but one error,* he never errs. Orrery.

EPISTLE

EPISTLE CI.

Reflections on the Uncertainty of human Affairs; occasioned by the Death of Cornelius Senecio.

EVERY day, every hour, *Lucilius*, certifies us that we are nothing; and, by some new argument, admonisheth us, while forgetful of our frailty; and then sets us upon thinking on death and eternity. Would you know what I mean by this preface, I will tell you.

You knew *Cornelius Senecio*, a Roman knight, eminent and courteous, who had raised himself from a small beginning to an ample fortune; and was now in a fair way to be what he pleased. For dignity is more easily advanced, than raised at first. Money also meets with many difficulties and impediments ere it can reach the poor man (*a*). *Senecio* as he aspired to wealth, took the two most effectual methods to obtain it; being industrious to get, and prudent to save; either of which are sufficient to enrich a man. This good man wonderfully frugal, and as careful of his constitution as of his estate, after a visit to me, as usual, in the morning, went and sat the whole day by a friend who lay desperately sick; and in the evening, having made a chearful supper, was seized with a violent disorder, the quinsey, which strangled him, and narrow as the passage was, set his soul at liberty.

And so within a few hours after having performed all the duties of a sound and able man, he died; even he, who was transacting money-affairs both by sea and land; who applying himself to public business, left no kind of profit unpursued, in the very height of his success, and when money came pouring in from every quarter, was unhappily snatched away.—

Insere nunc, melibæe, pyros; pone ordine vites. Virg.E. 1. 74.
Now graft your trees, my friend, and prune your vines.

How

How ridiculous is it to promiſe ourſelves a long life, when we are not certain of to-morrow? O! what folly is it, to ſtretch out and enlarge our diſtant hopes! ſaying, *I will buy; I will build (b); I will give credit; I will call in my debts; I will ſue for honours; and when I have had enough of public buſineſs, I will retire, and indulge my weary age, in repoſe and quiet.* Believe me, all things are doubtful and uncertain, even to the moſt happy. No one ought to promiſe himſelf any thing that is to come. Nay, ſometimes what we have got, ſlips through our hands (*c*), and caſualty cuts the cord that was our ſureſt hold.

Time rolls on indeed by a ſtated law, and makes many revolutions by a determined ordinance; but it is dark and obſcure to us. And when a thing is certain to nature, but uncertain to me, what am I the better for it? We propoſe long voyages and a tour through many diſtant nations, and after that to return to our own country: or, we deſign ourſelves for the field, and dream on the ſlow-coming rewards of the laborious camp *(d)*, gradual commiſſions, and the paſſing through many poſts of honour, 'till we reach the higheſt: while in the mean time death is waiting at our elbow, which, becauſe it is ſeldom thought on, but when happening to another, we are now and then to be reminded of mortality by ſuch examples; notwithſtanding they ſtick by us no longer than while we are wondering at them.

But what can be more abſurd than to wonder at ſuch a thing happening to-day, which might happen every day? Our life is limited by the inexorable neceſſity of fate, though none of us know how near we are to our end. Let us therefore ſo diſpoſe our minds, as if this day were to be our laſt. Let us defer nothing. Let us daily make even with life. The greateſt and moſt common default in life is that it is imperfect; and yet amendment is ſtill put off from one day to another. He that daily ſets his laſt hand to the duties of life, ſtands in no need of further time.

But

But from this indigence, this want of time, ariſeth fear; and an earneſt deſire of longer life ſtill preys upon the mind. Whereas nothing can be more miſerable than to live in continual doubt of what may happen (*e*). The mind that is continually reflecting upon how great, or what, our future fortune may be, is racked with inexplicable fear. By what method then ſhall we avoid this perplexity? Why, by this only, *if our life be not prolonged in fancy, but ſtands collected in itſelf*. For he can have no dependence on the time to come, who makes not a good uſe of the preſent. But when I have once diſcharged the debt I owe myſelf, the mind becomes eaſy, and aſſuredly knows that there is little or no difference between a day and an age: and then, as from on high, looks down with contempt on the days or things to come; and with great complacency reflects on the courſe of time.

For why ſhould the variety of accidents, or the inconſtancy of fortune, give him any diſturbance, who is conſtant and fixed againſt all contingencies? Therefore, my *Lucilius*, make haſte to live; and think every day a life. He that forms himſelf upon this plan, and who hath looked upon every day as his whole life, is always ſecure. They who live upon diſtant hopes not only loſe the time preſent, but undergo the anxiety of deſire, and the miſerable apprehenſion of death, which makes every thing miſerable. Hence ſprung that ridiculous wiſh of *Mecænas*, wherein he is contented to be weak, deformed, or to ſuffer the moſt acute pains that life can ſuffer, provided it were prolonged amidſt theſe evils;

Debilem facito manu;
Debilem pede, coxa;
Tuber adſtrue gibberum;
Lubricos quate dentes;
Vita dum ſupereſt, bene eſt:
Hanc mihi, vel acutam,
Si das, ſuſtineo crucem.

Did

Did Nature me unkindly treat;
Distorted both my hands and feet;
A bump unnatural on my back;
My loosen'd teeth of jetty black;
Or was I tortur'd with sharp pain,
In every muscle, every vein;
All this, and more, I would endure,
Of life's enjoyment still secure. M.

What would have been extreme misery, should it have seized upon him, is here wished for; and a lingering punishment desired, as if it were life. But how contemptible must we think a man, who would wish to live, though he were tied to a gibbet? *Yes,* saith he, *render me as weak as you please, so long as life remains in my broken and helpless body; disfigure me, provided this monstrous and deformed body may lengthen my life a few days; nay nail me to the cross, and torture me with the sharpest pains, provided I can feel them.* Such a desire has he to enrage his wound, and to hang stretched out on the cross, so long as he can defer that, which is the remedy of all evils, and the end of his punishment; and to have breath, so as to be ever dying, yet not die. Now, what can we wish worse for such a man, than that the Gods would hear his prayer? What could *Mecænas* mean by that his shameful and effeminate poetry? What by such a scandalous covenant with senseless fear? What by such a cowardly begging of life? Do you think *Virgil* ever recited that verse to him—

Usque adeone mori miserum est?
Is it then so hard to die?

He wisheth for the worst of evils; and desires such pains, as are most grievous to be endured, may be prolonged: and what the recompence? a longer life. But what sort of life would this be? only to be long in dying.

Can it be possible there should be found a man, who had rather pine away in torment, die piecemeal, and pour out his soul, as it were, drop by drop, than breathe it out at once? who being brought to the fatal

 tree,

tree, already weak, deformed, diſtorted and afflicted with many other infirmities no leſs mortal than the croſs itſelf, would wiſh to drag on a life loaded with ſo many pains? Deny now, if you can, that we owe Nature any thanks for this, among other her benefits, *that we muſt neceſſarily die.*

Many however are ſtill ready to make worſe covenants than this: they will betray a friend, ſo that they might preſerve their own wretched lives, and proſtitute their own children, for the poor benefit of ſeeing the light; which ſerves but to diſcloſe their heinous crimes. We muſt ſhake off this fond deſire of life, and learn that it is of little or no conſequence, *when* we ſuffer, what we muſt *one day* ſuffer; that it is of greater moment *to live well,* than to live long; and that oftentimes it is living well, not to live long.

ANNOTATIONS, &c.

(*a*) Pecunia circa paupertatem plurimam moram habet, dum ex illa ereptat—*al.* plurimum amorum—which will not admit, I think, of any meaning except it be, that *the money is ſweeter, and better loved which is got by a poor man.* *Pincian* reads it, plurimam molem—no doubt the ſenſe is the ſame with that in Juv. 3. 164.

Haud facile emergunt, quorum virtutibus obſtat
Res anguſta domi.——
Rarely they riſe by virtue's aid, who lie
Plung'd in the depths of helpleſs poverty. Dryden.

So when *Lampis,* a rich merchant, was aſked how he got his vaſt fortune, he anſwered, *the greateſt part of my wealth I got ſoon, and with eaſe, but ſlowly and with great pains the ſmall part I begun upon.* See *Plut.* Mor. in the diſſertation, *Whether aged men are fit for public offices.*

(*b*) *And he ſaid, This will I do, I will pull down my barns, and build greater, and there will I beſtow all my fruits, and my goods; and I will ſay to my ſoul, thou haſt much goods, laid up for many years, take thine eaſe, eat, drink, and be merry. But God ſaid unto him, Thou fool, this night thy ſoul ſhall be required of thee, then whoſe will theſe things be?* Luke, 12. 20.

(*c*) Id quoque quod tenetur per manus exit] So. *Curt.* vii. 8. Fortunam tuam preſſis manibus tene, lubrica eſt, nec invita teneri poteſt. *Having got Fortune in your hands, hold her faſt, ſhe is ſlippery, and not eaſily detained againſt her will.*

(*d*) Ut locupletem aquilam tibi ſexageſimus annus
Adferat——
That ev'n the ſixtieth year to you may bring
The eagle, and rich enſigns of a King.

(*e*) Nihil

(*e*) Nihil est miserius dubitatione venientium—*al.* vehementer irruentium—*Pincian.* f. volventium five volutantium, *as it follows,* Quomodo effugiemus hanc volutationem.—Quantum fit quod restat, aut quale collecta mens inexplicabili formidine agitatur.—*Pincian.* non collecta, *vel* incollecta.—*Lipsius,* aut quale collectu, mens.—*Gronov.* aut quale conjectantes.—*Seneca* in Thyeste,

Anxius sceptrum tenet, et moventes
Cuncta divinat, matuitque casus.
With great anxiety he rules the state,
And all the ills forebodes of adverse fate. M.

(*f*) On this great theme kind nature keeps her school;
To teach her sons herself: each night we die,
Each day are born anew: *each day a life;*
And shall we kill each day?——*Young.*

(*g*) So, *Achilles* to *Ulysses* in *Homer.* Od. λ. 490.

Βυλόιμην κ' ἐπάρυρος ἐὼν θητέυέμεν ἄλλῳ
Ανδρὶ παρ' ἀκλήρῳ ᾧ μὴ βίοτος πολὺς εἴη
'Η πᾶσιν νεκύεσσι καταφθιμένοισιν ἀνάσσειν.
Rather I chuse laboriously to bear
A weight of woes, and breathe the vital air;
A slave to some poor hind who toils for bread,
Than reign the scepter'd monarch of the dead. Pope.

And *Euripides* in *Iphigenia,*

Τὸ φῶς τὸ δ' ἀνθρώποισιν ἥδιστον βλέπειν·
Life is sweet.
Τὰ νέρθε δ' ὐδὲις μαίνεται δ' ὃς ἐυχεται
Θανειν· κακῶς ζῆν κρεῖσσον ἢ θανεῖν καλῶς.
Below we're nothing; better 'tis to breathe
A wretched life, than lie renown'd in death. M.

Epicurus in *Laertius*—τὸν σόφον καὶ πηρωθέντα τὰς ὄψεις, μεθέξειν τῦ βίυ. *The wise man, though he were blind, would still wish to live;* which *Lipsius* supposes *Seneca* to have had in view.

'The foregoing lines were thus parodied in a newspaper, *March* 14, 1782.

Aye, tye my hands up if *you* will,
Pass vote on vote, and bill on bill,
 Expose me to the worst disgraces;
Though all my slippery friends grow slack,
And *Charles F.* ride upon my back,
 I care not, so I keep my *places.*

EPISTLE CII.

On Renown after Death; and the Immortality of the Soul.

As a man seems troublesome who wakes another out of an agreeable dream; for he deprives him of a pleasure, which however false it may be, yet it hath the effect of truth: so your Epistle, *Lucilius*, did me an injury, in that it took me off from a very proper meditation, wherein I was engaged, and should have gone further, had I not been prevented thereby.

I was delighting myself with an enquiry into *the Immortality of the soul*; nay more, with a firm belief of it. For I was easily induced to give credit to the opinions of some great men; though I must own they seemed rather to promise this great truth, than to prove it (*a*). However I gave myself up to this so great hope: I began to disdain myself, and despise the concerns of life; even the remains of my yet unbroken age, being about to launch into that immeasurable time, and take possession of eternity; when I was suddenly awakened by the receipt of your Epistle, and so lost the sweet reverie, which I will try to recover, and redeem, as soon as I have dispatched this my present engagement to you.

You deny, it seems, that I was explicit enough with regard to the whole question in my former Epistle, wherein I endeavoured to prove, what most of our sect (the *Stoics*) agree in, that *the praise wherewith a man is honoured after death, is a real good.* For you say I have not fully answered this objection, *No good can arise from things distant; but praise is distant.* What you require, *Lucilius*, is indeed part of the question, but more properly to be debated in another place; and therefore I not only deferred this, but other things appertaining thereto. For, as you know, there are rational or logical questions intermixed with *moral*, I thought proper to treat only of the latter, as, *whether it was foolish and vain to transport our thoughts beyond the grave; whether all good dies with us; and nothing of the man remaineth, who is himself nothing! or whether we can receive any fruits from those things (whatever they be) which we shall be partakers of hereafter, before we actually enjoy them* (*c*)? Now as all these questions relate to *morals*, they are therefore ranged in their proper place. But what logicians object against the foregoing opinion is to be distinguished from these, and therefore is set apart. At your request however I will examine into all that they affirm to the purpose, and then answer their objections. Yet unless I premise a few things, my refutations will not so easily be understood.

Know then that some bodies are continuous *(d)* and uniform, as man; other bodies are compounded, as a ship, an house, and every thing, the different parts whereof are joined, and united in one body: others again consist of things distinct from each other, and whose several members still remain separate, as an army, a people, a senate. For however the individuals, which constitute these bodies, are conjoined, either by law or duty, yet are they, in nature, distinct; and each a several body. Well then, to come to the point.

We suppose, *it cannot be a* good, *which depends upon things distinct*: for one *good* must be ruled and governed by one and the same spirit (*e*); there can be but one principal of one good *(f)*. This is self-evident; as you will find upon reflection, if you at any time desire a proof of it. In the mean while, we lay down certain positions, whereon to fix the thread of our discourse *(g)*.

You say then, that " *nothing can be* good, *which consists of or depends* " *on things* distinct. Now this praise or *renown*, that we are speaking " of, is the favourable opinion of good men. For as fame is not the " esteem of one man; nor infamy the malignant report of one; so " *renown* consists not in the approbation of *one* good man (*h*). Many " men, famous and excellent in themselves, must agree therein, before " it can be called *renown*. This therefore consisting in and depending " upon the judgment of divers persons (i. e. such as are distinct) can- " not be a good."

Renown

" *Renown* (it is further ſaid) *is praiſe of good men given to good men.* " Praiſe is a ſpeech, and ſpeech is a voice, ſignifying ſomething; but " mere voice, though it be that of a good man, is not *good*; nor is " every thing that a good man does, alike good; for he ſometimes " applauds, and ſometimes condemns. But no one can ſay, that either " his clapping his hands, or hiſſing, though he may approve and ad- " mire all that is done, is of any more real conſequence than if he had " ſneezed or coughed; therefore his praiſe or *renown* is not a good. In " a word tell us, if you pleaſe, whether it be the good of the perſon " who praiſeth, or of him who is praiſed? If you ſay it belongs to " the latter, it is no leſs ridiculous than to ſay, that another man's " health is mine. But to praiſe a worthy man is a juſt action; ſo that " it is the good of the former, or the perſon who praiſeth, and not of " the perſon who is praiſed." Now this is begging the queſtion; but I will curſorily anſwer the particulars.

Firſt, it is ſtill made a queſtion *whether any good can ariſe from things* diſtinct; and each ſide of the queſtion hath its party, and reaſons to ſupport it. Secondly, this praiſe or *renown* requires not the ſuffrages of many; it may reſt ſatisfied with the judgment of one great and good man: for one good man is a competent judge of all other good men. *What then* (it is urged) *ſhall fame be the eſteem of one man, and infamy the malicious report of one only? Glory* (ſay they) *we underſtand to be more widely diffuſed, as it requires the conſent of many (i).* But the condition is not the ſame in both caſes. Becauſe, if a good man thinks well of me, I am as happy therein, as if all men were to think the ſame. A right judgment is the ſame in all, as in one, and as they judge alike, they cannot diſagree in their opinions concerning my deſerts. Therefore what one hath ſaid, imports as much as if they all had ſpoke, as they cannot but think the ſame thing. But then as to *glory* and *fame*, the opinion of one is not ſufficient. In the former caſe, the opinion of one would be the opinion of all, becauſe if all were aſked it would be the ſame; but in the latter, divers men have divers judgments, and their affections alſo are different. When all things in this world are doubtful, light, and to be ſuſpected, do you think that all men can be of one mind?

mind? The opinion of one man is not always the ſame. Truth indeed is always pleaſing to good men; and the force and colour of truth is always the ſame. But there are thoſe who delight in, and give their aſſent to, falſities; and in falſities there can be no conſtancy, they are ever varying, and diſcordant.

But *praiſe* (they ſay) *is nothing more than voice, and mere voice cannot be a good.* When men ſay that *renown* is the praiſe that is given to good men, by ſuch as are good themſelves, they allude not to the mere ſound of words, but to the ſenſe and meaning. For though a good man ſhould hold his peace, and yet ſhould think any one worthy praiſe, ſuch a one is praiſed thereby.

Beſides, *praiſe* is one thing, and *praiſing* another: this indeed requires the voice. In ſpeaking of a funeral oration we ſay not (funebris *laus) praiſe*, but (laudatio) *praiſing*: the buſineſs whereof conſiſts in elocution. But when we ſay ſuch a one is worthy praiſe, we do not promiſe him the favourable report of men, but their judgment. Therefore praiſe is the approbation of one who thinks rightly, and who, though he be ſilent, yet praiſeth the good man in his heart. For praiſe (as I ſaid) is referred to the heart, not to the words, which expreſs the praiſe conceived, and uſher it into public notice. He ſufficiently praiſes a man, who thinks him praiſeworthy. When our tragic poet (*k*) ſaith

Magnificum eſſe laudari a laudato viro;
'Tis great by the praiſeworthy to be prais'd.

And when as antient a poet ſays

Laus alit artes, *Praiſe cheriſheth the arts (l).*

He does not ſay *praiſing* which is a ſort of flattery, that rather ſpoils and corrupts them. For nothing hath done more prejudice to eloquence, and the like arts adapted to the ear, than popular applauſe. Fame requires the public voice; renown doth not: for it repeats not words, being ſatisfied with the judgments of men. It is accompliſhed, not only among thoſe who are ſilent, but even thoſe who oppoſe it. I will ſhew the difference between *renown* and glory. Glory conſiſts in the

the judgment of many, but true praiſe or *renown* in the judgment of good men only.

But whoſe good, it is aſked, is *renown*, i. e. *the praiſe given to good men, by good men themſelves? Is it the good of him that is praiſed, or of him that praiſeth?* Of both; it is mine who am praiſed; foraſmuch as nature hath created me a lover and a friend to all mankind: I both rejoice in having done good myſelf, and in having met with grateful interpreters of ſuch my actions, as tend to virtue. It is indeed the good of many in that they are grateful, but it is mine alſo: for I am of ſuch an happy diſpoſition as to look upon the good of others as my own; eſpecially the good of thoſe to which I have in anywiſe been inſtrumental. And it is the good of him that praiſeth me, becauſe it is an act of virtue; and every act of virtue is good. But this good he could not have enjoyed, were I not what I am. Therefore worthy praiſe is the good both of the giver and of the receiver, as the paſſing a juſt ſentence is the good of the judge, and of the party in whoſe favour the ſentence is given. Or can you doubt but that juſtice is the good both of the creditor and debtor, in the payment of a debt? Now to praiſe a worthy man is juſtice: praiſe therefore is the common good, both of him that praiſeth, and of him that is praiſed.

And thus, I think, I have ſufficiently anſwered theſe cavillers. But we ought not deſignedly to ſow ſubtleties, and draw down philoſophy from the extenſive throne of her majeſty into narrow ſtraights. How much better is it to walk in the plain and direct way, than to pretend to find out bye-paths, 'till we loſe ourſelves therein, and are conſtrained to return back again, after much pain and labour? neither indeed are theſe ſcholaſtic diſputations any thing more, than the ſport of men artfully endeavouring to beguile one another. Say rather how natural it is, and much more commendable in a man to ſtretch out his mind, as far as it can reach, into immenſity.

The ſoul of man is great, and generous, admitting no other bounds to be ſet to her, than what are common with God. *Firſt*, ſhe acknowledgeth

ledgeth not any terreſtrial city, as *Epheſus*, or *Alexandria*, or if there be any more populous, and whoſe buildings are more beautiful and of larger extent. No; ſhe claims for her country the univerſe; the whole convex, wherein are included the lands and the ſeas; wherein the air expending itſelf between the earth and the heavens, conjoins them both; and wherein are placed the inferior deities, intentive to execute their commiſſions. Nor, *ſecondly*, does ſhe ſuffer herſelf to be confined to any number of years. *All years*, ſays ſhe, *are mine*. No age is locked up from the penetration of learned men; no time ſo diſtant, or dark, that is not pervious to thought.

When the day ſhall come that will ſeparate this compoſition, human and divine, I will leave this body here, where I found it, and return to the Gods (*m*); not that I am altogether abſent from them even now; though detained from ſuperior happineſs, by this heavy earthly clog (*n*). This ſhort ſtay in mortal life, is but the prelude to a better, and more laſting life above (*o*). As we are detained nine months in our mother's womb, which prepares us not for itſelf, to dwell always therein, but for that place whereunto we are ſent, as ſoon as we are fit to breathe the vital air, and ſtrong enough to bear the light; ſo, in that ſpace of time, which reacheth from infancy to old age incluſive, we aſpire after another birth as from the womb of Nature; another beginning, another ſtate of things expects us. We cannot as yet reach heaven, 'till duly qualified by this interval.

Look then with an intrepid eye upon that determined happy hour. It is not the laſt to the ſoul, if it be to the body. Whatever things are ſpread around thee, look upon them only as the furniture of an inn. We muſt leave them and go on. Nature throws us out of the world, as ſhe threw us into it. We can carry nothing away with us, as we brought with us nothing into it (*p*). Nay even great part of that which attended us when we came into the world, muſt be thrown off. This ſkin, which Nature threw over us as a veil, muſt be ſtripped off: our fleſh, and our blood, that ſo wonderfully circulates through every part of it, muſt be diſperſed; as alſo the ſolids, the bones and nerves,

 which

which ſupported the fluids and weaker parts. This day, which men are apt to dread as their laſt, is but the birth-day of an eternity (*q*).

Be reſigned then, and willingly lay your burthen down. Why do you delay, as if this was the firſt time that you departed from a body, wherein you were encloſed? Still you heſitate, and are reluctant; and it was not without great pain and labour your mother was delivered of thee. You ſigh and cry; thus didſt thou weep (as it is uſual) when a little infant *: at ſuch a time excuſable indeed, when you came into the world a mere novice, ignorant of every thing, and when taken out of a warm and ſoft bed, a freer air blew freſh upon you; and when you was as yet ſo tender as not to bear the touch of the hard hand, and ſo great a ſtranger as to be amazed at every thing you ſaw around, and knew them not. But now, it can be no new thing to you, to be ſeparated from that, which was a part of you before: throw off then willingly this ſuperfluous part; and patiently quit the body, which you have ſo long inhabited: why are you ſo ſorrowful? was it to be torn in pieces, or drowned, or burned, there is nothing in all this but what is common.

The cawl, or covering of new-born infants ſoon waſteth away and periſheth: ſo will thoſe worldly goods with which you are ſo enamoured: they are but the outward coverings wherein you are enwrapped. The day will come that ſhall unfold them and give you liberty, delivering you from this filthy apartment wherein you are now quartered. Even now deſert it as much as poſſible, and ſoar aloft; eſtrang'd even from thoſe things, which ſeem moſt neceſſary and dear to you. Meditate ſomething more noble and ſublime (*r*); that bleſſed day, ſuppoſe, when the myſteries of Nature ſhall be revealed to you; this darkneſs be diſperſed; and the light ſhall break in upon you on every ſide. Imagine with yourſelf how great that brightneſs is, where ſo many ſtars intermingle their glorious beams; a light ſo ſerene and clear, that not the leaſt ſhadow of darkneſs ſhall reſt upon it (*s*); all heaven ſhines out with equal ſplendor; day and night have their turns only on this earthly globe, and the airy regions round about.

You will then ſay, you lived in darkneſs before: when you ſhall behold the full glories of that light, which now thou ſeeſt dimly (*t*), through the narrow circles of the eyes, and yet at ſo great a diſtance as to fill the mind with admiration and aſtoniſhment. How then will it amaze you, when, I ſay, you ſhall behold that divine light in its full ſpread of glory in heaven? Such a reflection as this cannot but raiſe the mind above every mean thought, and deter us from every vile and cruel practice. It informs us the Gods are witneſſes of all our actions: (*u*) it commands us, to make ourſelves acceptable to them; to prepare ourſelves for communion with them; and have always eternity in view; (*x*) which whoever hath any conception of, he dreads no enemies; he hears the trumpet's ſound undiſmayed; nor can all the threats in the world terrify his manly ſoul: for why ſhould he be afraid of any thing (*y*)? What can deter him from the punctual diſcharge of every duty, who dies in this hope? When even the man, who thinks that the ſoul ſubſiſts no longer than while it is impriſoned in the body, and at its departure hence is entirely diſſipated and diſſolved, yet ceaſeth not to endeavour to make himſelf uſeful, and to live in ſome meaſure after death? For though he be taken from our ſight (*z*), yet

Multa viri virtus animo multuſque recurſat
Gentis honos.—*Virg*. iv. 3.
The heroe's valour, acts, and birth, occur
To the attentive mind——

Think how profitable good examples are; and you will find, that the remembrance of great perſonages is no leſs ſerviceable, and uſeful, than their preſence.

ANNOTATIONS, &c.

* I know not where *Seneca*, in all his writings, has a better claim to the title given him, by Pope *Linus*, *Augustin*, and others of *almost a Christian*, than in this excellent epistle.

(*a*) *Seneca* (as Dr. *Leland* observes) seems to have been strangely unsettled in his notions with regard to the immortality of the soul, and a future state. Sometimes however he speaks in a clear and noble manner of the happiness of souls after death, when freed from the incumbrance of the body, and received into the place or region of departed souls. *Consol.* al. Ep. 6. c. 28. ad Marc. c. 25. *See* also Epp. 63. 76. And in this epistle it cannot but be acknowledged that he has some sublime thoughts on this subject. *See* Lips. Physiol. iii. 11.

(*b*) As *Solomon* saith, *I hated life, because the work that is wrought under the sun is grievous to me; for all is vanity and vexation of spirit.* Eccles. ii. 17.

(*c*) An ex eo, quodcunque erit, sensuri sumus aliquid fructus antequam percepi possit. *al.* antequam aliquis fructus percipi, aut peti possit. *al.* an ex eo quod cum erit sensuri non sumus antequam——*Pincian.* an ex eo, quod cum erit sensuri non sumus, aliquis fructus, percipi possit, i. e. *whether any profit can accrue to us, from that, be it what it will, which we shall not be sensible of.* *Gruter.* antequam sit, aliquis—i. e. *whether we can receive any profit from a posthumous fame, which when we shall have, we shall not be sensible of, being dead, before such fame can be.* *Gronovius* only omits the particle *quam*, and understands it thus, *whether such things* as shall be said *of us when we are not sensible of them, being thought upon while we are here, can be of any service to us.*——*Lipsius* reads it, quod tum erit, aut ecquando aliquid fructus, i. e. *immediately*, or after (what has since been called) purgatory.

(*d*) So *Plutarch* (in præcept. connub. 31.) Τῶν σωμάτων φιλόσοφοι τὰ μὲν ἐκ διεστώτων λέγουσιν εἶναι, κ. τ. λ. *Philosophers assert that of bodies which consist of several parts, some are composed of parts distinct and separate as a fleet, an army: others of contiguous parts as a house, as a ship; and others of parts united at the first conception, equally partaking of life and motion, and growing together as are the bodies of all living creatures.* Vid. *Sen.* Nat. Qu. ii. 2.

(*e*) *Now there are diversities of gifts, but the same spirit; for by one spirit are we baptized into one body.* i. Cor. 4. 13. *I beseech you,* saith St. *Paul*, *that ye walk worthy the vocation wherewith ye are called—endeavouring to keep the unity of the Spirit in the bond of peace: there is one God, and one Spirit, even as ye are called, in one hope of your calling. One God, and father of us all.* Ephes. iv. 1. 6.

(*f*) Τὸ ἡγεμονικόν.

(*g*) Quo nostra tela nitatur. *Muret.* Cui nostra tela innitatur. Sentit enim assumendum aliquid per se notum, ad fulturam argumentationis; quemadmodum tela substernitur stamen. *Erasm.* *al.* in nostra tela mittuntur. From whence *Pincian* reads it, quia in nos tela mittuntur, in this sense, which, I think, is not to be rejected, *In the mean while we must give you the objections that are thrown out against us.*

(*h*) Sidon. Carm. 24. Hic si te probat, omnibus placebis.

(*i*) *Philo Judæus*, on the words, *Evigilavit Noë*, ὁ ἀστεῖος οὐκ ἔνδοξος, ἀλλὰ εὐκλεής, κ. τ. λ. *The wise man is not glorious, but renowned, and enjoys praise, not adulterated by flattery, but established in truth.*

(*k*) *Lipsius* gives this verse to *Nævius*, who in Cicero (Ep. Fam. xv. 6.) Lætus sum laudari me (inquit Hector) abs te, pater, laudato viro. See the *Spectator*, No. 108.

(*l*) So, *Erasmus.* *al.* Laus alterius. *al.* laus a literis. From *Cicero.* Honor alit artes,—and *Ovid*, Laudataque virtus crescit, *The more 'tis prais'd, the more will virtue thrive.*

(*m*) *Then shall the dust return to the earth as it was, and the spirit shall return unto God, who gave it.* Eccles. xii. 7.—iii. 20. 21.

(*n*) *We are always confident, knowing that while we are at home in the body we are absent from the Lord; (for we walk by faith, not by sight) we are confident I say, and willing to be absent from the body, and to be present with the Lord; wherefore we labour, that whether present, or absent, we may be accepted of him.* ii. Cor. v. 6—9. See Ep. 65.

(*o*) Some notion and belief of the immortality of the soul and a future state obtained among mankind from the most antient time, and spread generally among the nations: not originally as the mere effect of human wisdom and reasoning, but as derived by a most antient tradition from the earliest ages, and probably made a part of the primitive religion, communicated by divine revelation to the first parents of the human race. The belief of it was countenanced and encouraged by the wisest legislators; but was much weakened by the disputes of the philosophers; and the general corruption of manners: from whence is justly inferred *the necessity of a divine revelation*, to assure mankind of the truth of this important article. Ita quicquid est illud quod sentit, quod sapit, quod vivit, quod viget, cæleste ac divinum est, ob eamque rem æternum sit necesse est. *Whatsoever thing is in us, which perceives, which understands, which lives, which has a force and vigour of its own, is celestial and divine; and for that reason must necessarily be eternal.* See N. q.

(*p*) *Be not then afraid, when one is made rich, when the glory of his house is increased; for when he dieth, he shall carry nothing away with him; his glory shall not descend after him.* Ps. xlix. 16. *Naked came I out of my mother's womb, and naked shall I return.* Job. 1. 21. *For we brought nothing into this world, and it is certain we can carry nothing out.* i. Tim. 6. 7.

(*q*) Dies iste quem tanquam extremum reformidas æterni natalis est. I have observed in N. o, that the belief of the immortality of the soul was much weakened by the disputes of the philosophers; when they who professed to believe it, often spoke of it with great doubt and uncertainty, or argued for it upon insufficient grounds. Thus *Seneca*, notwithstanding the clear and sublime sentence before us, yet in this very Epistle represents it as a kind of pleasing dream, and as an opinion embraced by great men, very agreeable indeed, but which they *promised rather than proved.* See also Epp. 69. 76. *Lips.* Physiol. iii. 11. *Leland*, vol. ii. p. 3. c. 3.

* *I myself am a mortal man, like to all, and the offspring of him that was first made of the earth.—And when I was born, I drew in the common air and fell upon the earth, which is of like nature; and the first voice that I uttered was crying, as all others do; I was nursed in swadling clothes, and that with cares. For there is no king that had any other beginning of birth.* Wisd. viii. 1—5.

(*r*) Aliquid altius sublimiusque meditare] *Set your affections on things above.* Col. 3. 2. See Epp. 58. 65.

(*s*) So St. *John*, speaking of the new *Jerusalem*, *And the city had no need of the sun, neither of the moon, to shine in it, for the glory of God did lighten it: and the nations of them that are saved shall walk in the light of it; and the kings of the earth do bring their glory into it: and the gates of it shall not be shut at all by day; for there shall be no night there.* Rev. 21. 23. 25.

(*t*) *For now we shall see as through a glass darkly, but then face to face; now I know in part, but then shall I know even as also I am known.* i. Cor. 13. 12. See Epp. 79. 93.

(*u*) The almighty Agent that created the universe must necessarily know all things that are, and all the powers and faculties of them, and consequently all that they can or ever will produce. He must thoroughly comprehend what is best and properest in every one of the infinitely possible cases, and methods of disposing things; how to order and direct the respective means, to bring about what is best and fittest to be done; and this is what we call *infinite knowledge*, or *omniscience*.

—What

—— What can 'ſcape the eye
Of God all-ſeeing, or deceive his heart
Omniſcient? Milton, x. 5.

(*x*) *Set your affections on things above.* Col. 3. 2. See Ep. 79. 93. *Ye were ſome time darkneſs, but now are ye light in the Lord: walk as the children of light*; proving what is acceptable to the Lord: *and have no fellowſhip with the unfruitful works of darkneſs.* Epheſ. v. 8. 11. *I beſeech you, brethren, for the mercies of the Lord, that you preſerve your bodies a living ſacrifice, holy,* acceptable unto God, *which is your reaſonable ſervice*; *and be not conformed to this world, but be ye transformed by the renewing of your mind, that ye may prove what is the good, and acceptable and perfect will of God.* Rom. xii. 1. 2.

(*y*) *Be not afraid of them that kill the body, and after that have no more that they can do. But I will forewarn you whom ye ſhall fear. Fear him which after he hath killed hath power to caſt into hell.* Luk. 12. 5. Matth. 10. 28.

(*z*) *In the ſight of the unwiſe they ſeemed to die, and their departure is taken for miſery; and their going from us to be utter deſtruction; but they are in peace. For though they be periſhed in the ſight of men, yet is their hope full of immortality.* Wiſd. iii. 2.

EPISTLE CIII.*

The Duty of Man, with regard to Caution, and a Knowledge of the World.

WHY, *Lucilius*, with fear and trembling, do you regard thoſe things, that may poſſibly happen, and perhaps may never happen; I mean, fire, the fall of a houſe, and the like caſualties, which are incident to us, but await us not? Rather inſpect, and avoid, if poſſible, ſuch things as lie upon the catch, and ſeize us unawares. Caſualties are rare, though ſometimes grievous indeed; ſuch as ſhipwreck, or the being overturned in a chariot: but man is every day in danger from man his fellow-creature (*a*). Be prepared againſt this, and contemplate with open eyes; for no evil is more frequent, none more pertinacious, none more ſoothing: the tempeſt lours before it riſeth; our houſes crack before they fall; and ſmoke bewrays the kindling flame. But deſtruction from man comes on a ſudden, and is the more cloſely and diligently concealed, the nearer it approacheth. You will be deceived,

ceived, if you truſt to the countenances of all you meet: ſome have the appearance indeed of men, but the hearts of wild beaſts (*b*). Except that the onſet of theſe is more violent, and pernicious, being made without diſtinction on the firſt they meet, whom nature ſuffers them not to paſs by: for 'tis neceſſity alone that ſets them upon doing miſchief. They are compelled to fight, either through hunger or fear: whereas man, unprovoked, takes a pleaſure in deſtroying man.

But at the ſame time that you reflect upon what danger is to be expected from man, think alſo upon what is *the duty of man.* Conſider the former to avoid being hurt, and the latter that you may do no hurt. Rejoice at the ſucceſs of every one, and be grieved at their misfortunes: ever mindful of what you ought to do, and what to leave undone (*c*). And what will be the conſequence of living in this manner? Why, it will not indeed certainly prevent you from being injured, but it will certainly prevent you from being deceived. Make your retreat however as ſoon as poſſible into the courts of Philoſophy. She will protect you in her boſom. In her ſanctuary you will be ſafe; at leaſt much ſafer than at preſent. Men joſtle one another, only when walking together; and as to philoſophy, pride not yourſelf thereon: many have ſuffered from their inſolent and diſdainful behaviour in this reſpect. Let it expel your own vices, and not upbraid thoſe of other men. Nor be ſingularly averſe to the manners and faſhions of the public (*d*); nor ſo act as to ſeem to condemn every thing but what comes from yourſelf. A man may be wiſe without ſuch pomp and ſhew as to raiſe jealouſy and envy in others.

ANNOTATIONS, &c.

* Some have thought this epiſtle nothing more than an appendix to the foregoing: but *Lipſius* approves not of this opinion.

(*b*) Homo homini lupus. *Plaut.* *Anacharſis*, the *Scythian*, being aſked, τί ἐστι τὸ πολέμιον ἀνθρώποις, *what is hoſtile to man?* anſwered, Αὐτοὶ ἑαυτοῖς, *man himſelf.*

(*b*) As *David* ſaith, *they gather themſelves together, they hide themſelves and mark my ſteps, when they lay wait for my ſoul.* Pſ. 56. 6. *My ſoul is among lions, and I lie even among them that are ſet on fire, even among the ſons of men, whoſe teeth are ſpears and arrows, and their tongue a ſharp ſword.* Pſ. 57. 4. *Preſerve me, O Lord, from the violent man, who imagine miſchief in their hearts; they have*

have sharpened their tongues like a serpent; adders poison is under their lips. Ps. 140. 1. *There is no faithfulness in their mouth; their inward part is very wickedness, their throat is an open sepulchre, they flatter with their tongues.* Ps. 59. *They come to you in sheeps cloathing, but inwardly they are ravening wolves.* Matth. vii. 15.

Hominum effigies habent, animos ferarum, nisi quod *illarum* perniciosior est *primus* incursus, quos transire non queunt. *Lipsius* (Elect. l. c. 16.) reads it, *primis.*—*Pincian.* quos transiere non querunt. *i. e. only the first assault of wild beasts is dangerous and destructive; they return not upon whom they have passed by. Gronovius,* nisi quod *illorum,* sc. hominum, i. e. *men differ from wild beasts but in this, that their first onset is generally more dangerous and destructive,* because it is made on those, who are not upon their guard, and who seek not to avoid them the first time, as they do the attack of wild beasts. Quos transire non quærunt, *nempe illi, qui obvios sunt habituri.* This defect of a nominative case, he shews to be frequent in his note on *Sen.* de ira l. 2. 12. Mentior nisi adhuc quærit ascendere. *Ovid.* Met. xi. 754. Et si descendere ad ipsum ordine perpetuo quæris. So that according to *Gronovius* we may render it thus; *except that the first attack of man is the more pernicious in that we seek not to avoid them.* But I have followed *Lipsius,* as I think the reading more plain and natural.

Epictetus Diss. i. c. 3. observes that *some men are like wolves, false, treacherous, hurtful; others like lions, wild, fierce, cruel: and most men like foxes, sly and fraudulent.*

Lycurgus, an antient poet, says,

Φεῦ πῶς πονηρόν ἐστιν ἀνθρώπων φύσις
Τὸ συνολοι· ὐ γὰρ ἂν ποτ᾽ ἐδεήθη νόμων
Οἶοι τὶ τῶν ἄλλων διαφέρειν θηρίων
Ἄνθρωπον, ὐδὲ μικρὸν ἀλλὰ σχήματι·
Πλάγι᾽ ἐστὶ τἄλλα, τῦτο δ᾽ ὀρθὸν θηρίον:
How great the sinfulness of man! the cause
Of such a vast variety of laws!
The difference 'tween man and beast; no more,
Than, that on two legs walks, and this on four.

(c) *He that will love life, and see good days, let him eschew evil, and do good, let him seek peace, and ensue it. Who is he that will harm you if ye be followers of that which is good? But if you suffer for righteousness sake, happy are ye.* i. Pet. 3. 8—17.

It is remarkable that the precepts here given by *Seneca* are the very same with those of St. *Paul* to the *Romans,* and follow almost in the same order: *Rejoice with them that do rejoice, and weep with them that weep. Be of the same mind one towards another. Mind not high things, but condescend to men of low estate. Be not wise in your own conceits. Recompense to no man evil for evil. Provide things honest in the sight of all men. If it be possible, as much as lieth in you live peaceably with all men.* Rom. xii. 15—18. See also Prov. iii. 7. xx. 22. If. xii. 21. i. Thess. v. 15. Heb. xii. 14. which seems, in some measure, to confirm what I have elsewhere observed, that they were in some sort known to each other.

(d) So in a fragment of *Cicero's*; Philosophiæ quidem præcepta noscenda, vivendum autem civiliter. *'Tis necessary indeed to know the precepts of philosophy, though a man lives in the common way.*

(e) He that, &c.

EPISTLE

EPISTLE CIV.

On Travelling.

I HAVE fled, *Lucilius*, to my feat at *Nomentum (a)*: from what, think you? from the city? No; from a fever, that I found creeping upon me, nay that had actually laid hold upon me, as I thought; I therefore ordered my chariot to be got ready immediately, though my wife, *Paulina*, was againft my moving. But the phyficians affuring me that the fymptoms were ftrong upon me, as my pulfe kept not its due motion in the arteries, but was high and irregular, I infifted upon going, and repeated the words of my Lord *Gallio*; who being in *Achaia*, and finding a fhivering come upon him, immediately took fhip, faying, *it was not a natural difeafe of the body, but accid.ntal from the bad air of the place.*

This I told my *Paulina*, who always wifhes me to take care of my health; and as I know her life is wrapt up in mine, it is for her good I confult my own. And though old age hath hardened and fortified me in many refpects, I put it not to the trial: remembering that in this old perfon of mine there lives a much younger in participation of it, or for whom it is indulged; and therefore, as I cannot require or expect from her that fhe fhould love me, if poffible, better than fhe does (*b*); fhe may well require this from me, that I fhould love, and take better care of myfelf than ufual. It is reafonable to indulge all juft and pure affections: and fometimes, if urgent caufes require it, our breath, in honour to, and for the fervice of our friends, muft be retained, and kept in, as it were, with the teeth; becaufe a good man is bound to live, not only fo long as it liketh him, but fo long as he ought, and can poffibly live, for the fervice of others (*c*).

The man who thinks that his wife or his friend is not of fuch confequence that he fhould wifh to continue in life for their fakes, and not rather die when he pleaſes, is a coxcomb. Let the ſoul have ſo much command over herſelf, when the ſervice of a friend or relation requires it, as not only to be unwilling to depart, but, even when it is upon the wing, to return, if poſſible, to their aſſiſtance. It ſhews a nobleneſs of ſoul, thus to return again, as it were, to life, for the benefit of our relations; as many great men have done.

And this alſo I think a point of great humanity, for a man more induſtriouſly to keep up his old age; (the chief benefit whereof is the more prudent care of a man's ſelf, and a more orderly and manly uſe of life;) particularly if he knows it can be agreeable, uſeful, and deſirable to thoſe about him. This affair alſo carries with it no ſmall joy or recompence; for what can be more delightful than for a man to be ſo dear to his wife, as to make him more dear to himſelf? My *Paulina* therefore may think herſelf obliged not only to *her* fear and concern, but to mine alſo.—But to return:

Would you know what ſucceſs my determination of going into the country met with? No ſooner had I got out of the foggy air of the city, (and the ſtink of the ſmoke from ſo many kitchen fires, which being ſtirred ſend forth whatever poiſonous vapours were contained therein, ſo as almoſt to choak us,) than I found an alteration for the better: how much more then muſt you think my health reſtored, when I reached my delightful vineyards *(d)*? As let looſe into good paſture, I ruſhed upon my food with an eager appetite; and am perfectly recovered: the liſtleſſneſs that attends a weak and crazy conſtitution is gone off; and my whole mind is again intent upon ſtudy.

The place however that a man is in, contributes very little to the ſtudy of philoſophy, unleſs the mind aſſiſts itſelf; which can even give itſelf privacy in the midſt of buſineſs and company. But he that chuſeth his country-ſeat, only by way of idle retirement, will every where find enough to perplex and diſturb him. For it is ſaid that *Socrates*, when a perſon was complaining to him that he had received very little benefit from travelling, made this reply: *I do not wonder at it,* *it, ſince you travelled with yourſelf* *. O how happy would many a man be, if they could but throw off themſelves! The chief adverſaries that trouble, corrupt, and terrify them, are themſelves. What avails it to travel over the ſeas, or to travel from city to city? If you would avoid that which moſt torments you, it is not your going to another place that will do it, but your being another man. Suppoſe you were to come to *Athens* or to *Rhodes*; it is nothing to the purpoſe what the manners are of the inhabitants, you bring your own thither.

You will think riches the only thing that can make a man happy. Poverty then will be ſure to rack you, and (what is moſt miſerable) even falſe poverty. For though your poſſeſs much, yet becauſe another hath more, you will think you want at leaſt as much as that wherein he exceeds you. Or do you think that happineſs conſiſts in honours? How will it torment you to ſee ſuch a one made *Conſul*; and much more to ſee another rechoſen! It will ſting you to ſee another's name oftener than your own in the *faſti*, or *public regiſter*. Nay, ſo blind and mad will be your ambition, that if there is any one before you, you will think no one behind you. You will fancy death to be the greateſt of all evils, when it has no other evil in it than to be feared before it comes; not only danger will affright you, but even the ſuſpicion of danger. Vain ſhadows will ſcare thee.

For what will it profit you,

——— Evaſiſſe tot urbes
Argolicas, medioſque fugam tenuiſſe per hoſtes;
Pleas'd to have ſail'd ſo long before the wind,
And left ſo many Grecian towns behind; Dryden—

when peace itſelf, inſtead of comfort ſhall adminiſter fear? You will give no credit to, nor put your truſt in, things moſt ſafe and ſure; when once the mind is diſturbed, and having got an habit of heedleſs timidity, you are no longer able to provide for your own ſafety; for you will not ſhun, but fly from the ſtroke: and we are always moſt expoſed to danger, when we have turned our backs.

If you think it a moſt grievous affliction to loſe any one you love; know, that this is as ridiculous as to weep, that the leaves of fine ſhadowing trees that adorn your houſes are fallen. Whatever elſe you delight in, hath its time to flouriſh, and alike decays (*c.*) Time and Death ſhake off one thing after another. But as the loſs of the leaves is eaſy to be borne, becauſe they ſhall one day bud forth again; ſo likewiſe is the loſs even of thoſe whom you loved, and thought the delight of your life. Becauſe, though they themſelves return not again, yet the loſs of them may be repaired by aſſociating, ſuppoſe, with others. *But theſe are not the ſame.* True; neither will *you* be the ſame. Every day, every hour makes a change in you: but in others the alteration is more viſible: here indeed it is not perceivable, becauſe not ſo public and open: others are ſnatched away from us, but we ſteal as it were from ourſelves. You will not reflect on theſe things, nor apply a remedy to theſe wounds in time; but are continually ſowing the ſeeds of perplexity and trouble, by hoping ſome things, and deſpairing of others: If you are wiſe you will join theſe two together; and never hope, ſo as to think you cannot be diſappointed; nor ſo deſpair, as to leave no room for hope. But to return:

Wherein can travelling be of any ſervice merely as travelling! It will not of itſelf moderate pleaſures, refrain deſires, pacify anger, break the untameable power of love, root out any evil habit from the mind, endow it with ſound judgment, and diſpel error. In ſhort, men that go out fools, will return the ſame, if not worſe; on whom travelling hath no other effect, than for a while to amuſe them with ſome novelty; as children are apt to admire every thing which they never ſaw before. And as to inconſtancy of mind, this roving from place to place rather encreaſes it, which was bad enough before; and renders it more light and wavering. Hence you often ſee men paſſing from a place, at which they before moſt earneſtly deſired to arrive; and like birds of paſſage flock away faſter than they came.

But travel, you will ſay, furniſhes a man with the knowledge of nations; ſhews him mountains of different forms, deſert plains, valleys watered with everlaſting rills; rivers of an extraordinary nature, full worthy obſervation; as the *Nile* in *Egypt*, which flows higheſt in the

ſummer

ſummer ſeaſon; or the *Tigris* in *Aſia*, which at certain places is loſt, and running far under ground, appears again, in its full magnitude; or the *Meander*, the ſportful theme of all the poets, with all its turnings and windings; when, ſeeming to leave its own channel, it approaches the bed of ſome neighbouring flood, but before it has joined it, returns back, forming as it were a circle.—It may be ſo: but how ſeldom does all this make a traveller the better or a wiſer man? We muſt be employed in ſtudy, and converſe with ſuch authors as are the maſters of wiſdom; that we may not only learn ſuch things as have been already found out, but find out other ourſelves of the like importance.

This it is that will raiſe our minds from miſerable ſervitude to a moſt happy ſtate of liberty. So long as you know not what is to be avoided, and what purſued; what is neceſſary, what ſuperfluous; and what is juſt, fit and decent; it will not be travelling, but wandering. Such an excurſion will prove but of little advantage to you; ſince you travel with the ſame affections attending you, and your vices conſequently follow you. Did I ſay *follow*? I wiſh they did, or that they were further from you. You do not lead, but carry them. Hence it is that go where you will they weigh you down, and wring you with the ſame diſtreſſes.

Medicine is requiſite for a ſick man, not a journey. Hath any one broke his leg, or put out his ſhoulder, he does not enquire after his chariot, or a ſhip, but looks out for a ſkilful ſurgeon, to ſet the broken bone, or reduce the diſlocated joint. Why then ſhould you think a mind, put out of frame, and ſo miſerably ſhattered, can be cured merely by change of place? No; this is too great an evil to be repaired by an airing.

Travelling, of itſelf, makes not either a phyſician, or an orator. No art is to be learned from the place only. How then can wiſdom, the chief of all, be picked up in travelling? Believe me, was there any ſort of journey that could ſet a man out of the reach of deſire, anger, fear;

fear; all mankind would travel, and flock to the happy place. So long will evils preſs upon and tear you, though wandering both by ſea and land, as you carry about you the cauſes of ſuch evils. Are you ſurprized then at finding no benefit? How can you find benefit, when thoſe very affections ſtill attend you, which you ſeek to fly from?—Firſt, amend thyſelf; throw off your burthen: at leaſt reduce your fond deſires within moderate bounds; root out all wickedneſs from thine heart; and if you would have a pleaſant journey, heal your inſeparable companion, Avarice will certainly not leave you, ſo long as you cohabit with an avaritious and ſordid temper: pride will not forſake you, ſo long as you converſe with one that is proud; nor will you lay aſide cruelty, while accompanied by an executioner; as fellowſhip with adulterers will blow up the luſtful flame. If you would be free from vice, depart as far as poſſible from all vicious examples.

The covetous, the debauchée, the cruel, the knaviſh, (enemies that will certainly wound you grievouſly, whenever they make their attack) are even now much nearer than you imagine, they are within thee. Addreſs yourſelf therefore to better examples *(f)*. Live with the *Cato's*, with *Lælius*, with *Tubero*; or if you chuſe to converſe with *Greeks*, live with *Socrates* or *Zeno*; the one will teach you how to die when neceſſity requires it; the other, before neceſſity compels you *(g)*: or live with *Chryſippus*, or *Poſidonius*; theſe will inſtruct you in affairs both human and divine. Theſe will command you to put this knowledge in practice, and not only to talk elegantly, and with a delicate flow of words pleaſe the ears of an audience, but ſtrengthen the mind, and fortify it againſt the frowns of the world. For the only quiet haven in this fluctuating and ſtormy life, is, for a man to contemn caſualties, to ſtand reſolutely fixed, to receive the arrows of fortune with an open breaſt, and not cowardly to hide himſelf, or turn his back.

Nature hath formed us great, and valiant. And as to ſome animals ſhe hath given a fierce and cruel diſpoſition; and to other, ſubtlety and cunning; and to other, cautious timidity; ſo hath ſhe given to man a glorious

glorious and lofty ſpirit, that puts him upon ſearching where he may live moſt juſtly and decently, not where moſt ſafely; reſembling the great world; which he follows, and emulates, as far as human ability will permit. He diſplays himſelf at all times; he offers himſelf as in a theatre, to be gazed at and applauded (*b*). He is lord of all, and above all, earthly things; and therefore he ſcorns to yield to any incident tamely; or to think it too heavy for him to bear; nor can any thing make him ſtoop, or give up the dignity of man; not even

Terribiles viſu formæ, letumque laboſque. Virg. 6. 277.

Things dreadful to behold, turmoil and death;

if he can but look on them with a ſteady eye, and pierce the gloomy darkneſs that ſurrounds them. Many things that ſtrike a terror by night, prove trifles, and a mere jeſt by day; even the before-mentioned

Terribiles viſu formæ, letumque, laboſque.

Thus excellently wrote our *Virgil:* he does not aſſert theſe to be dreadful *(re)* in reality, but *(viſu)* in aſpect, i. e. (videri) *to ſeem* (non eſſe) *not to be ſo* in fact. For what is there in theſe things ſo terrible as vulgar report makes them? What is there, I pray you, *Lucilius*, that ſhould make a hero dread *labour*, or a mortal man *death?*

'Tis true, I often meet with thoſe who think every thing impoſſible which they cannot do; and complain of our talking big, and requiring more than human nature can do: but I have a better opinion of them than they have of themſelves; I think they *can* do what is required, but they *will* not. In ſhort, who hath ever failed in his endeavours? Every thing is found much eaſier upon trial. Not becauſe they are difficult, we dare not attempt them; but becauſe we dare not attempt them they are ſo difficult; and if you deſire an example, I will give you one.

Look on *Socrates*, the moſt patient man in the world (*i*), amidſt a variety of ſufferings, and heavy laden with all manner of affliction; invincible by poverty, which was rendered much more grievous by domeſtic ills; invincible by the laborious taſk of the field, while a ſoldier; as well as by the many evils that exercifed him at home;

whether

whether you regard the ſavage temper, or petulant tongue of his wife; or his intractable children, who took after their mother, without the leaſt ſpice of the father in them.

Thus was he either engaged in war, or under the dominion of a tyrant; or if at liberty at home, it proved more ſevere than either war or tyrants. Twenty-ſeven years (*k*) he bore arms, and no ſooner were they laid down but the government became ſubject to thirty tyrants, moſt of whom were his profeſſed enemies. At laſt an accuſation is brought againſt him, of the moſt heinous crimes, (being indicted of the violation of the religious rites, and the corruption of youth) (*l*), committed againſt the Gods, the Magiſtrates, and his Country: and the iſſue of this was, a priſon and poiſon. All theſe trials however moved not the firm mind of *Socrates*, ſo much as to make him change his countenance. This ſingular, wonderful, and moſt laudable ſpirit, did he keep up to the very laſt; nor could any one ſay that they ever ſaw him either more chearful, or more melancholy; ſuch an equal temper did he preſerve in all this inequality of fortune.

Would you have another example? Conſider the late *Marcus Cato*, whom fortune harraſſed, if poſſible, with more inveterate and ſtubborn rancour. He oppoſed her however in all places, and at all times, particularly in death: ſhewing, that a brave man can either live or die, in ſpite of fortune. His whole life was ſpent either in the actual broils of civil war, or in ſuch troublous times as are uſual before it breaks out. And therefore you may ſay, that *Cato* lived in a ſtate of ſervitude, as well as *Socrates*; unleſs you think *Pompey* and *Cæſar*, and *Craſſus*, were friends to, and confederates in the maintenance of, Liberty. No one ever ſaw any change in *Cato*, whatever change was in the government: in every ſtation and in all occurrences, he continued ſtill the ſame; in the prætorſhip; in a repulſe; under an accuſation; in the province; in the ſenate; in the army; in death.

Laſtly, in that tottering condition of the commonwealth; when there ſtood on one ſide *Cæſar*, ſupported with ten legions of the braveſt veterans; and depending on his alliances with many foreign nations: *Pompey* on the other ſide, alone, and ſufficient to withſtand the oppoſition. And while ſome volunteers followed *Cæſar*, and others *Pompey*; *Cato* alone raiſed a party for the commonwealth. If you form in your mind a right conception of thoſe times, you will find on the one hand (for *Cæſar*) the buſy mob, and plebeians, always fond of novelty, and a change of government; and on the other (for *Pompey*) the Nobles and Knights, or whoever bore office ſacred or civil, in the ſtate; while between them, only two were left deſtitute, the *Commonwealth* and *Cato*. You will be amazed, I ſay, when you obſerve

> Atridem, Priamumque, et ſævum ambobus Achillem,
> Atrides, Priam, *and againſt them both,*
> *The fierce* Achilles—

For he condemns them both; he diſarms them both; affirming this to be his determination, If *Cæſar* prevailed, he would die; if *Pompey*, he would depart, ſelf-baniſhed from *Rome*. What now had he to fear, who, whether he conquered, or was conqueror, had decreed to himſelf *that*, which the moſt exaſperated enemy could but inflict upon him? and accordingly he died by his own decree.

Hence you ſee, *what fatigue it is poſſible for man to bear: Cato* led his army on foot through the deſerts of *Africa*: *that he can endure thirſt*; when *Cato*, on the barren and ſun-burnt hills, (dragging along the remains of a conquered army, that had no need of any baggage to load them, nor indeed had they any) ſuffered the want of water, though ſweating in armour; and when by chance they met with a ſmall current, he was the laſt who drank (*m*). Or, *that honours and infamy are to be alike contemned*, when, on the ſame day that *Cato* was denied the conſulſhip, he diverted himſelf at tennis (*n*), in the *campus Martius (the field of* Mars). Or, *that the power of ſuperiors is not always to be dreaded. He* oppoſed and provoked at the ſame time both *Cæſar* and *Pompey*; when no one dared to offend the one, unleſs it were to ingratiate himſelf with the other. Or, *that death may as well be deſpiſed as baniſhment*; when he pronounced againſt himſelf baniſhment, and death, and was never diſengaged from war. It is poſſible therefore for a man to attain ſuch ſtrength of mind, as to bear up againſt theſe and the like evils, ſo that it be free, and not voluntarily ſubmiſſive to the yoke.

But *firſt*, for this great purpoſe, all pleaſures muſt be renounced; they weaken and effeminate the mind; are always importunate, and ſo mean as to ſue to Fortune. *2dly*, Riches are likewiſe to be contemned; they are the chief inſtruments of ſlavery. Gold and ſilver, and whatever elſe adorns or loads the houſes of the happy great, is to be rejected. Mortifications muſt be undergone for the attainment of liberty; it is not to be purchaſed for nothing: if you have any real value for it, you will eſteem very thing elſe but in a low degree (*o*).

ANNOTATIONS, &c.

(*a*) Where he had a country-ſeat and vineyard. See Ep. cx. Columella, iii. 3.

(*b*) Ut me fortius amet—*Pincian*, ut ſe fortius amet, *becauſe otherwiſe*, ſays he, *the ſenſe would be deficient*. I cannot think ſo.

Seneca argues that becauſe *Paulina* cannot love him, better than ſhe does, he ought in juſtice to her, to love himſelf better. Beſides, ſhe ſhewed much greater love for *Seneca* than for herſelf, when ſome time after ſhe voluntarily ſubmitted to undergo the ſame fate with her huſband; and accordingly had her veins opened at the ſame inſtant that his were; but her death was prevented by an order from *Nero*. See Pref. *Tacit.* annal. 15.

(*c*) *Lipſius* here refers the reader to *Cicero* (de fin. iii.) Sæpe officium eſt ſapientis, deſciſcere a vita, cum ſit beatiſſimus, ſi id *opportunè* facere poſſit.—(Which is thus rendered by *Guthrie*)—*It is often the duty of a wiſe man to leave life, though poſſeſſed of perfect happineſs*, if it is proper for him to do it, *which propriety is to be meaſured by the opportunity he has of living agreeably to nature.* But what ſays *Seneca*?—Cùm bono viro vivendum ſit non quamdiu juvat, ſed quamdiu oportet.] This, I think, is another very remarkable paſſage againſt whatever *Seneca* hath elſewhere advanced in favour of ſuicide. *A good man*, ſays he, *thinks not his life at his own diſpoſal, but will live*; quamdiu oportet; i. e. *'till it pleaſe God to call him hence.*

(*d*) Which he took ſo much delight in as to manage them himſelf, and even to dig. *Natural Queſt.* iii. 7.

(*e*) Quicquid te delectat, æquè viget, ut videras, dum vireret. Utique aliud alio die caſus excutiet. *Lipſius.*—Which he thus explains: *As the trees though ſtripped of their foliage ſtill live, as much as when they were green and flouriſhing; ſo our friends, when abſent and inviſible to us, are ſtill alive.*—This *Gronovius* abſolutely rejects, and inſiſts upon, Quicquid te delectavit ac tenuit, ut videras, dum vireat, ubique aliud——*ut* i. e. *ſimul*, vel *ſimul atque*; (*ut* vidi, ut perii. Virg.) i. e. *Whatever hath delighted, as ſoon as you have ſeen it, in its flouriſhing ſtate, ſome accident or other will deprive you of it.*—*Pincian:* Æque viret. Vivunt dum virent. Utique alium—much in the ſame ſenſe that I have tranſlated it.—al. Æquè videt, (al. vide) ut videras,——which it is impoſſible,

ble, I think, to make ſenſe of.——*Eraſmus,* Æquè viget, dum ut videras, dum viveret. *Sentit enim nobis virere quiquid delectat.* At *delectat etiam memoria rerum bonarum.*——Tout ce qui te plaiſoit, eſt encore en la meme vigeur, qu' il eſtoit quand tu le voyois verdir. *Vet. Gall.*

(f) Muret. obſerves that this precept is taken from that when *Zeno* enquired of the oracle what were the means of living moſt worthily and happily, he received for anſwer, *εἰ συγχρωτίζοιτο τοῖς νεκροῖς. By converſing with the dead.* Whereupon he ſpent the reſt of his life in ſtudy, and reading antient authors.

(g) Zeno was ninety-eight years old, when, coming from the public ſchools, he ſtruck his foot againſt a ſtone, and tripping, fell upon the ground with one hand; whereupon he repeated theſe words of *Euripides,* ἔρχομαι τί μ' αὔεις; *I am coming, why in ſuch haſte to call me?* and went home and deſtroyed himſelf.——May we not ſay, notwithſtanding the great encomiums beſtowed upon him, that he was in his dotage? See Ep. 107. and the Index.

(h) Laudari et aſpici *credit.*——*Pincian. geſtit.*——*Lipſius* and *Gruter.* quærit. Gronovius approves of *credit,* which he thus explains: *He acts as they do, who are animated by the preſence of thoſe whom they revere, and ſtudy to pleaſe. He thinks himſelf upon a ſtage, where the eyes of every one are upon him.* So *Cæſar,* (de Gall. l. 3.) reliquum erat certamen poſitum in virtute, qua noſtri milites facile ſuperſunt, atque eo magis, quod in conſpectu Cæſaris, atque omnis exercitus res gerebatur.——*The reſt of the engagement was carried on with great valour, in which our troops have eaſily the pre-eminence, and the more ſo, as the affair was tranſacted in the ſight of* Cæſar *and the whole army.* Curt. l. 9. Ubicumque pugnabo, in theatro terrarum orbis eſſe me credam. *I will behave myſelf as upon the theatre of the world.*

(i) Perpeſſicium ſenem; the ſame word is uſed in Ep. 53.

(k) And ſome months. For ſo long laſted the *Peloponeſian* war.

(l) So in *Tertullian's* Apology. Lego partem ſententiæ Atticæ in *Socratem* corruptorem adoleſcentium pronunciatam. *Sen.* de Tranquill. c. 15. Cum pueris ludere Seneca non erubeſcebat. Vid. Sidon. l. 3. Ep. 3.

(m) Noviſſimus bibit] So *Lucan.* 9. 595.

Ultimus hauſtor aquæ, cùm tandem fonte reporto
Indiga conatur latices potare juventus,
Stat, dum lixa bibat.
Sparing of ſleep ſtill for the reſt he wakes,
And at the fountain, laſt, his thirſt he ſlakes:
Whene'er by chance ſome living ſpring is found,
He ſtands, and ſees the cooling draught go round.
Stays 'till the laſt and meaneſt drudge is paſt,
And 'till his ſlaves have drunk, diſdains to taſte. Rowe.

" Where ſhall we find the man that bears affliction,
Great and majeſtic in his griefs like *Cato?*
Heav'ns! with what ſtrength, what ſteadineſs of mind,
He triumphs in the midſt of all his ſufferings!
How does he riſe againſt a load of woes,
And thank the Gods that throw the weight upon him!——
Coarſe are his meals, the fortune of the chace;
Amidſt the running ſtream he ſlakes his thirſt,
Toils all the day, and at th' approach of night
On the firſt friendly bank he throws him down,

Or rests his head upon a rock 'till morn:
And if the following day he chance to find
A new repast, or an untasted spring,
Blesses his stars, and thinks it luxury. *Cato.*

(*n*) See Ep. 71.

(*o*) And let me perish but in *Cato's* judgment,
A day, an hour of virtuous liberty,
Is worth a whole eternity of bondage. *Cato.*

EPISTLE CV.

Certain Precepts, with regard to Happiness and Security, in the Conduct of Life.

GIVE me leave, *Lucilius*, to point out a few things which, if duly observed, will render your life more secure, and I am sure you will give the same attention, at least to these precepts, as if I had directed you what to do, in order to preserve your health in the bad air about *Ardea.*

Consider what those things are, which generally incite and provoke men to ruin one another; and you will find them to be, *Hope, Envy, Hatred, Fear, Contempt.* Of all these *contempt* is so much the lightest, that many have skulked beneath it by way of safeguard (*a*); for whom a man contemneth, he may kick at perhaps, but passeth him by. No man hurts a contemptible person frowardly, or purposely. In a battle, the man that is prostrate is passed over; he only is attacked who stands his ground.

You will frustrate the *hope* of the wicked, if you have nothing to provoke their greedy and lawless appetite; if you have nothing, I say, that is very remarkable: for whatever is extraordinary, however little known, is mostly coveted.

And

And thus may you prevent *envy*; if you live without pomp and parade; if you talk not of your wealth and endowments, but can enjoy them with ſelf-complacency.

You will prevent *batred*, by giving no offence, by provoking no one deſignedly, or wantonly, and living peaceably with all men, as common ſenſe ſhall direct you. Many have been in great danger from *batred*; though ſome have experienced it without a profeſt enemy.

Not to be feared, a moderate fortune and mildneſs of temper will prove the ſureſt means: when men ſhall know you to be one, when they may in ſome meaſure offend with impunity, being eaſily pacified, and moſt aſſuredly reconciled. But *to be feared*, is as dangerous and troubleſome at home as abroad; whether it be by ſervants or children. There is no one but who hath ſufficient power, if they pleaſe, to hurt you. Add therefore, that he who is *feared*, hath reaſon alſo to *fear*. No one who is dreaded can aſſure himſelf of ſecurity.

Laſtly, as to *contempt*, he hath the management of it in his own power, who hath brought it upon himſelf; who is deſpiſed becauſe he regarded it not, rather than becauſe he deſerved it. To prevent the inconvenience whereof, let a man ſtudy the *liberal ſciences*, and procure friendſhip with thoſe who have an intereſt with men in power: to whom it will be proper to make application; though not ſo to involve and engage yourſelf, as to make the remedy worſe than the diſeaſe. Yet nothing will be of more ſervice herein, than not to be over-buſy and talkative, converſing chiefly with yourſelf.

There is a certain pleaſure in talking, which ſteals upon a man, and flatters him; and often, like a cup too much, or love, is apt to diſcloſe the ſecrets of the heart. There is ſcarce any one but will tell again, what he hath heard, though but ſeldom the whole of what he heard. And who relates the matter, will likewiſe declare his author. All men have ſome one or other, whom they think they can truſt with what they themſelves have been entruſted. Hence pretending to ſet a watch upon

upon their lips, and to be contented with the attention of one only, they make the people privy to all they know (*b*); ſo that what before was a ſecret, is made a common report.

The beſt means however of ſecurity is to do no ill. Paſſionate men lead a confuſed and troubleſome ſort of life. They neceſſarily fear a return of what miſchief they do, and are at no time free therefrom. They tremble as ſoon as they have done it, and are ever after in ſuſpenſe (*c*). Conſcience will not ſuffer them to reſt; and often ſets them upon an enquiry into themſelves (*d*). He is puniſhed who only expects puniſhment; and he who hath deſerved puniſhment, expects it. An evil conſcience may ſometimes think itſelf ſafe, but never ſecure (*e*). For a criminal, though not immediately apprehended, muſt think himſelf liable thereto. Even his dreams diſturb him: and when he hears the crime mentioned accidentally, his own guilt ſtares him in the face: he never ſuppoſes it ſufficiently obliterated, or cloſely enough concealed from the world. Let the guilty then eſcape as they will for the preſent, they can put no confidence therein.

ANNOTATIONS, &c.

(*a*) As *Brutus* (in Livy) Neque in animo ſuo quidquam regi timendum, neque in fortuna concupiſcendum relinquere ſtatuit, contemptuque tutus eſſe, ubi in jure parum præſidii eſſet. *He was determined to leave nothing upon his mind that could affect the ſtate, or was ſubject to the caprice of fortune, chooſing to be ſafe, from contempt, where there was no dependence upon legal right*

(*b*) *Or, being contented to tell his ſtory but to one perſon, he will make the people that one.* Or, Ut garrulilatem ſuam cuſtodiat, et contentus ſit unius auribus, populum faciet. *He will ſuppoſe the people can help their prattling, and be contented with telling their ſtory, each to one perſon.* I know not what elſe to make of this paſſage, for I think *Pincian's* reading ſcarce admiſſible; *poculum*, inſtead of *populum*, i. e. *A man will prattle to one or more according to what he has drunk.*

(*c*) *The wicked are like the troubled ſea, when it cannot reſt, whoſe waters caſt up mire and dirt. There is no peace, ſaith my God, to the wicked.* Pſ. 57. 20.—The Heathens were ſenſible of theſe horrors of conſcience as well as Chriſtians. Dii deæque! quam malè eſt extra legem viventibus! quod ſemel meruerunt, ſemper expectant. *Petron.* in Claud. Ruffin. ii. *Good God! how miſerable it is to live uninfluenced by law! The puniſhment which they have deſerved they always dread.*

Quid demens manifeſta negas? en pectus inuſtæ
Deformant maculæ vitiiſque inolevit imago
Nec ſeſe commiſſa tegunt. *Claud.* ii. 504.
Wouldſt thou deny what is ſo manifeſt?
Thy guilty ſtains are openly impreſt,
And every ſecret vice ſtands full confeſt. Melampus, p. 197.

EPISTLE

EPISTLE CVI.

* *Whether* Good *be a Body* *.

I HAVE been more tardy, I confeſs, than uſual, *Lucilius*, in not anſwering your Epiſtle; not becauſe I was too buſily employed: I ſcorn ſuch an excuſe, for I have leiſure enough; as every one may have if they pleaſe. A man is not always engaged in buſineſs; but ſome create it to themſelves: nay, and place great part of their happineſs therein. Why then, you will ſay, did I not anſwer your requeſt ſooner (*a*)? Why to tell you the truth, it has ſome connexion with my preſent purpoſe; as you know I am determined to comprize the whole of *moral philoſophy*, and to explain every queſtion relating thereto. (*b*) Therefore I was ſome time in doubt, whether I ſhould put you off for the preſent, 'till this ſubject would have its proper place, or in the mean time give you ſomething extraordinary for your ſatisfaction. But it ſeemed more kind and humane not to detain one longer, who came ſo far. Therefore I have ſelected the following from the ſeries of thoſe queſtions, which depend upon one another, and will ſend you ſome other, of my own accord, to prevent your requeſt. Do you aſk what theſe queſtions are? Why, truly, ſuch as there is more pleaſure and curioſity in knowing, than profit, as in this before us—*Whether* Good *be a body*.

Now I affirm it to be a *body*; becauſe it acts. *Good* acts upon the mind or ſoul; and in ſome meaſure forms and governs it, which are the properties of *body*. Even the good of the body, is a body, and therefore ſo is that of the ſoul: for this likewiſe is a body. The good of man muſt neceſſarily be a body, foraſmuch as man is bodily, or hath a body. I am greatly miſtaken, if thoſe things which nouriſh the body, and either preſerve or reſtore health, are not alſo bodies, and therefore every *good* that is his, is body. I cannot think that you will doubt,

doubt, whether the *affections* (to throw in here another thing not contained in the queſtion) are bodies; ſuch as *anger*, *love*, *ſorrow*. If you doubt it, conſider whether they do not alter our countenances, contract and dilate the brow, raiſe a bluſh, or make us look pale. And do you think that ſuch viſible marks can be impreſſed upon the body by what is not a *body* itſelf? If the *affections* then are body, ſo are alſo the diſeaſes of the mind, as *avarice*, *cruelty*, *habitual vices*, or ſuch as are grown quite incurable; and alſo malice, or a wicked heart, with the ſeveral ſpecies of it, as malignity, envy, pride. As theſe then are bodies, ſo is *good*. Firſt, becauſe it is contrary to theſe; and, ſecondly, becauſe it exhibits the like ſigns, and has the ſame effect. See you not what fierceneſs fortitude gives the eye? How intent is prudence! how modeſt and ſtill is reverence and devotion! how ſerene is joy! how rigorous is ſeverity! how careleſs and remiſs is mirth (*c*)! Therefore they are bodies, I ſay, which alter the colour and habit of bodies, and exerciſe dominion over them.

Now all theſe virtues I have mentioned are good, and whatever proceedeth from them. Can you doubt, whether that, by which a thing is touched, is body?

Tangere enim, et tangi, niſi corpus, nulla poteſt res.
—— *now whatſoe'er does touch,*
Or tend to touch, is body,——

as *Lucretius* ſaith. But all theſe things could not have ſuch an effect upon the body, did they not touch it; therefore they are bodies.

Further, what hath power of compelling, of forcing, of reſtraining, of commanding, is body. And doth not fear reſtrain? boldneſs impell? fortitude incite, and give vehemence? Does not moderation recall, and curb in? Does not joy elate, and ſorrow caſt down? In ſhort, whatever we do, we do by command of virtue or vice. And what commands the body, muſt be a *body*; ſo likewiſe what gives ſtrength and force to body, muſt be *body*. Good of the body is bodily, or hath a body; the good of man is alſo the good of a body, therefore it hath a body.

Thus far then in anſwer to your queſtion. And now I will ſay to myſelf what I ſuppoſe will be your reply: this is mere playing at tables; our ſubtlety is ſpent in mere trifles. Theſe things make not a man good, however learned they may make him. Wiſdom is more plain and open; nay, more ſimple:. There needs not much learning, to form a good underſtanding and a ſound conſcience. But as we waſte other things, in vanities and ſuperfluities, ſo do we philoſophy itſelf. There is exceſs and intemperance in literature, as well as in other articles. We learn not what belongs to life, but what belongs to the ſchools.

ANNOTATIONS, &c.

* Many opinions of the Stoics, as *Eraſmus* obſerves, were ſolid and of great moment, (as is manifeſt from theſe Epiſtles) but ſome remarkably vain and ridiculous. Of the latter ſort is the queſtion before us, which *Seneca* touches, as they ſay, *with a light finger*. From this queſtion however, as from falſe premiſes follow falſe concluſions, they proceed ſo far as to affirm, that not only virtues and vices, and all the affections of the mind were *bodies*; but that they were *living animals*, and reverenced as ſuch. Of which folly and abſurdity, ſee more in Ep. 113.

(*a*) Quare non reſcriberem *tibi*, de quo quærebas] *Muret*. al. *ei*, de quo—which *Gronovius* abides by, ſaying he ſees no reaſon why we ſhould not as well ſay, reſcribere *rei*, as *ad rem*. Sen. Pref. 3 Excerpt.—Illius orationes non legunt, niſi eas *quibus Ceſtius* reſcripſerit.

(*b*) *Lactantius* mentions theſe books, but alas! they are not extant—an irreparable loſs!

(*c*) What vigour is given to the eye by fortitude? what ſteadineſs by wiſdom? What modeſty, what ſtillneſs, it puts on in the expreſſion of aweful reſpect! How is it brightened by joy! how fixed by ſeverity! how relaxed by mirth! *Webb* on painting, p. 136.

EPISTLE CVII.

On Patience in all the Accidents of Life.

WHY, *Lucilius*, what is become of your prudence? where is your wonted ſubtlety of diſcernment? where thy magnanimity? Can ſuch trifles move thee? Your ſervants, it ſeems, took the opportunity while you was buſy, to run away. If theſe your *friends* (for ſo our *Epicurus* was

was pleaſed to call them) have deceived you, the damage is but ſmall. They are gone, who often interrupted you in your buſineſs; and being troubleſome to *you*, made *you* ſo to others. Nothing of this kind is unuſual, or not to be expected. It is as ridiculous to be offended and troubled at ſuch an accident, as it would be to complain of being beſprinkled, or beſpattered with dirt as you walk the ſtreets.

The condition of life is the ſame with being in a public bath, in a crowd, or on a journey. Some one will intrude upon us, and accidents will happen. To *live*, a man muſt not be over-nice or delicate. You are entered upon a long journey; you muſt neceſſarily ſometimes ſlip, joſtle, fall, be weary, 'till you cry out, *O death!* that is, you muſt finiſh your journey (*b*). In ſome place perhaps you will leave a companion, bury another, and be afraid of another: ſuch continual inconveniences will you meet with in the road of life. But the mind muſt be prepared againſt theſe things; it ſhould know, that it is come to a place where

Luctus, et ultrices poſuêre cubilia curæ,
Pallenteſque habitant morbi, triſtiſque ſenectus. *Virg.* 6. 275.
Revengeful cares and ſullen ſorrows dwell
And pale diſeaſes, and repining age,
Want, fear, and famine unreſiſted rage. Dryden.

Theſe are the attendants on life: you cannot eſcape them, though you may deſpiſe them: you certainly will deſpiſe them, if you often reflect upon them, and preſuppoſe their certain attack. There is no one but who receives, more courageouſly, ſuch things, to which he hath long reconciled his mind; and who oppoſeth more boldly thoſe adverſities which he made familiar to him by reflection. But on the contrary, when a man is unprepared the lighteſt accidents ſurpriſe and terrify him: we muſt therefore take care that none may happen to us unexpectedly; and as all things are the more grievous on the account of novelty, the ſerious meditation here recommended, will cauſe that nothing ſhall happen to you, as to a mere novice.

Have

Have your ſervants left you? and is that all? Some have robbed their maſter; others have vilified him; others have betrayed him; others have trampled upon him; ſome have made an attempt on their maſter's life by poiſon; others by a falſe accuſation; others have murdered him. Theſe, and all other miſchiefs you can imagine, have happened to many, and will happen again. Many and various are the arrows that are aimed at us; ſome are ſticking in us; others, upon the wing, will ſoon reach us; others, about to pierce our neighbours, will lay us under ſome uneaſineſs, as if they were levelled at ourſelves; yet let us not wonder at theſe things, to which we were born incident; and of which no one therefore has reaſon to complain: becauſe all men have their ſhare; yes, I ſay, an equal ſhare: for what a man hath eſcaped, he was as liable to ſuffer, as they that ſuffered. A law is equal and juſt that is made for all, though all meet not with the ſame treatment.

Let equity then be the ruling principles of our mind; and let us pay the tribute of mortality without murmur and complaint. Winter brings on the cold, and we ſhiver: ſummer reſtores the heat, and we ſweat. The inclemency of the weather, and a bad air try the conſtitution; and we are ſick. A wild beaſt by chance may meet us; or man, more dangerous than wild beaſts, fall upon us. Some are loſt by water; ſome by fire: and this ſtate of things it is not in the power of man to alter.

But this we can do; we can aſſume a mind that is great and good, which will enable us patiently to bear all caſualties, and go hand in hand with Nature; by whoſe command it is that ſo many changes and revolutions happen in this her kingdom. Clear weather ſucceeds the clouds; and when the ſeas have awhile been calm, freſh ſtorms ariſe: different winds blow in their turns: day ſucceeds night: part of the heavens riſe above, and part ſink beneath the horizon (*c*). The eternity of things is made up of contraries. Let us apply our mind to their law (*d*). Let us for ever follow and obey it; concluding, that *whatever is, is right* (*e*). So that we ought by no means to cenſure and chide Nature.

The beſt way is to endure what we cannot prevent, or amend; and without murmuring hold communion with God; by whoſe providence all things are directed. He is but a bad ſoldier who follows his captain grumbling and ſighing. Wherefore let us receive his commands with earneſtneſs and alacrity; nor think of deſerting our courſe in this beautiful round of things, the work of God; though whatever we ſuffer be interwoven in it. And thus let us addreſs the Almighty, *who guides and directs this vaſt machine*; as our *Cleanthes* teacheth us in thoſe elegant verſes, which, after the manner of the moſt eloquent *Cicero*, I have endeavoured to tranſlate, in the Latin language: if they pleaſe you, well; if not, let it ſuffice for me to have followed the great *Cicero*.

Duc me, parens, celſique dominator poli,
Quocunque placuit: nulla parendi mora eſt.
Aſſum integer: fac nolle: comitabor gemens.
Ducunt volentem fata, nolentem trahunt.
Maluſque patiar, quod pati licuit bono *(f)*.

Father of heav'n, and ruler of the ſkies!
(Thy works all glorious, and thy thoughts all wiſe!)
Lead me where'er you pleaſe; without delay,
Prompt, and alert, thy ſummons I obey.
Were I unwilling, ſtill I muſt go on,
And follow thee, with many a ſigh and groan.
With gentle hand Fate leads the willing mind,
But drags along the ſtubborn, and the blind.
Thus more ſeverely ſhall I feel the load,
That preſſeth lightly on the juſt and good.

Thus let us live; thus let us pray, that death may ever find us willing and alert to go. This is true magnanimity, which reſigns itſelf to God. On the contrary, he is of a low and degenerate mind, who is reluctant, who is ſo vain, as to find fault with the diſpenſations of Providence; and preſumes rather to cenſure and amend the *Gods*, than himſelf.

ANNO.

ANNOTATIONS, &c.

* See *Bolingbroke* on Exile, ad fin —*Melmoth's* Cato, p. 263.

(*a*) The Stoics did not allow any one qualified to be a *friend* but their wiſe man: the reſt were only *companions*, united for advantage ſake: ſicut et terram ſerimus ob fructus, *as we ſow land for the ſake of the crop*. See Epp. ix. lxxxi. II. *Our* Epicurus, becauſe *Lucilius* was an Epicurean.

(*b*) Iter metiaris] *Pincian*, emetiaris, *al.* idem mentiaris, *al.* id eſt, mentiaris: *that is, you muſt lie*; in what? in calling upon death, yet not deſiring his preſence.—The word, *mentiri*, here puts me in mind of *Sir Henry Wotton's* definition of an ambaſſador: *He is one who is ſent* ad mentiendum foris, to *lie* abroad.

(*c*) This is according to the *Ptolemaic* ſyſtem, but we, who more juſtly follow the *Copernican*, know it to be in appearance only.

(*d*) This is a capital dogma of the Stoics, ſequi naturam, i. e. Deum; *to follow Nature*; that is, *God*. Ep. 4, &c. *Lipſ.* Manud. iii. 19.

(*e*) Et quæcunque fiunt debuiſſe fieri putet.] *Shall not the Judge of all the earth do right?* Gen. xviii. 25.

(*f*) These verſes are from the *Greek* in the *Enchiridion* of *Epictetus*. *Lipſius* therefore rejects the fourth of the *Latin* as ſpurious, or taken from ſome other place.

Ἄγε δέ με ὦ Ζεῦ, καὶ σύ γ' ἡ πεπρωμένη,
Ὅποι ποθ' ὑμῖν εἰμὶ διατεταγμένος
Ὡς ἕψομαί γ' ἄοκνος. ἢν δὲ μὴ θέλω,
Κακὸς γενόμενος οὐδὲν ἧττον ἕψομαι.

See Ep. 96. (N. a.)

EPISTLE CVIII.

The right Uſe of reading or hearing the Philoſophers *.

WHAT you enquire after, *Lucilius*, is one of thoſe things which it is requiſite to know, merely for knowledge-ſake: and ſince it is ſo requiſite, and you ſeem ſo earneſtly to inſiſt upon it, nor will wait a little while, 'till I have finiſhed thoſe books which will contain the whole of moral philoſophy regularly digeſted, I will oblige you; but give me leave firſt to premiſe a few things, in order to inform you, after what manner the commendable thirſt of learning, with which you ſeem

thus

thus transported, may be so ordered, as not to hinder you in your respective progress.

All sciences are not to be received at random, nor rushed upon at once. From particulars we must learn the whole. Every-one must suit their burthen to their strength †: nor must we involve ourselves in more business than we know how to go through with. You must not drink of this stream as much as you please, but as much as you can hold. Yet never fear; you shall hold as much as you can desire. The more the mind receives, the more it expands itself. This is what our master *Attalus* taught us, when we besieged, as it were, his school, coming first, and going away the last: nay, teasing and provoking him to some dispute, as we walked along, when he was not prepared for us, but met us accidentally. *Both he that teacheth*, saith he, *and he that learneth should have the same point in view*, ut ille prodesse velit, hic proficere: *they must both intend profit; the one by giving good instruction, the other by receiving it.*

He that attends the schools of philosophers should daily carry away with him some improvement. He should return home more wise, or better disposed to wisdom. And so indeed will he return; for such is the power of philosophy, that she not only improves the student, but the conversant. He that walketh in the sun will be tanned, though he did not walk there for that purpose. A man who hath set some time in a perfumer's shop, will carry away with him the scent of the place; so they who attend philosophers, must certainly reap some benefit, let them be as negligent as they please: but observe, I say negligent, not repugnant. What then? have we not known some who for many years attended on philosophy, without being in the least tinged therewith? Certainly; and even such as seemed so very constant and industrious, that we might call them not the disciples, but the inmates, of philosophy. But the misfortune is, some come only to *hear*, not to learn, as they attend the theatre for pleasure's sake; to delight the ear with some speech, or a sweet tone of voice, or a diverting story, exhibited in comedy. Such you will find great part of an audience, who make the philosophical schools but a place of idle resort: they come not thither in order to diſpoſſeſs themſelves of any vice, or to receive any law for the better regulation of manners, or better conduct of life: but to pleaſe the ear with the twang of eloquence. Some too bring their tables with them, not to ſet down and remark *things*, but *words*; which they may deliver again occaſionally with as little profit to their hearers, as they had received from them themſelves. Others are rouſed at the ſound of ſome big words, and ſeem as much affected as the ſpeaker himſelf; alert both in mind and countenance; throwing themſelves into ſuch attitudes as the eunuchs, and thoſe who were mad by command, were wont to do, at the ſound of the *Phrygian* pipe (*b*).

Theſe however are ſmitten with the beauty of things, and not with the empty ſound of words. If any thing is ſmartly ſaid againſt death, or fortune is boldly inſulted, they immediately reſolve to act upon theſe principles: they are really affected, and would be all you could wiſh them, were the ſame impreſſions to remain upon their minds; and if the people, ever diſſuaſive of what is right, were not immediately to check this remarkable impulſe. Few have been able to carry home the reſolutions they at firſt conceived (*c*). It is no difficult matter to ſtir up an audience to a deſire at leaſt of what is right and good. Nature hath laid the foundation in our ſouls, having ſowed therein the ſeeds of virtue (*d*). We are all of us born with theſe endowments and to this purpoſe. When a proper perſon inſtructs or teacheth, then are thoſe good qualities rouſed that before lay dormant.

Hear you not how the theatres reſound, when a ſentence is uttered, which we cannot but acknowledge to be juſt, and give teſtimony to the truth of it by our applauſe! as,

> Deſunt inopiæ multa, avaritiæ omnia.
> *Poverty wants many things, avarice all.*
> In nullum avarus bonus eſt, in ſe peſſimus.
> *Worſt to themſelves are miſers, good to none.*

Even the moſt ſordid and avaritious perſon applauds theſe lines, and rejoiceth in his own conviction. How much more effectually do ſuch ſentiments come from the mouth of a philoſopher? When ſalutary precepts

precepts are thus agreeably expreſſed in verſe, they deſcend the readier into the hearts even of the unſkilful. For (according to *Cleanthes)* as our breath gives a more clear and ſhrill ſound when driven through the paſſage of a trumpet, it finds a large vent at the end: ſo our underſtandings are rendered more clear, when confined to the ſtrict laws of a verſe. The ſame things are heard with leſs attention, and affect us leſs, when delivered in proſe or common diſcourſe, than when decorated with poetical numbers; and good ſenſe, pointed, and contracted within certain feet or meaſure, is darted, as it were an arrow from a ſtrong arm.

Many things have been ſaid with regard to the contempt of money, and in long harangues are we taught, that men ſhould think true riches to conſiſt in the virtues of the mind, not in patrimony;—that he is wealthy who adapts his diſpoſition to his circumſtances; and with a little makes himſelf rich by content:—yet our minds, I ſay, are more affected when we hear ſuch admonitions in verſe, as,

Is minimo eget mortalis, qui minimum cupit.
He wants but little, who but little covets.
Quod vult habet, qui velle quod ſatis eſt poteſt. *Publ. Syrus.*
He hath his wiſh, who wiſheth but enough.

When we hear theſe and the like ſentences we are brought to the confeſſion of truth. For they who think nothing enough, admire them, and will even exclaim againſt money.

Now, whenever you perceive this affection, urge it, preſs it home; perſecute your audience with this topic; laying aſide all ambiguities and ſyllogiſms, and cavils, and other whimſies of an idle brain (*e*). Speak boldly againſt avarice, againſt luxury: and when you perceive that you have in ſome meaſure prevailed, and moved their hearts, proſecute the ſubject with more vehemence: it is almoſt incredible what good effect ſuch a diſcourſe will have, being intended as a remedy, and wholly deſigned for the good of the hearers. For, tender minds are ſoon worked up to a ſenſe, and the love, of what is good and right.

Truth

Truth lays her hand upon the docil, and ſuch as are but ſlightly corrupted, when ſhe meets with an able advocate.

For my own part, when I have heard *Attalus*, inveighing againſt the vices, the errors and the evils of life, I could not help pitying the errors of mankind, and looking upon *Attalus* as a man ſublime, and far exalted above the common pitch of mortals. He ſaid indeed of himſelf *that he was a king (f)*. But to me he ſeemed ſomewhat more, who dared, and juſtly too, even cenſure kings. But when he began to recommend poverty, and to ſhew, whatever exceeded neceſſary uſe, was all a mere ſuperfluous load, and an heavy weight upon the bearer; I many times wiſhed to depart from the ſchools a poor man. When he began to traduce our pleaſures, to praiſe chaſtity of body, a ſober table, a pure mind, untainted, not only by unlawful pleaſures, but by unneceſſary and vain amuſements, I required nothing more to ſet bounds to gluttony and every irregular appetite. Some of theſe inſtructions made a deep impreſſion upon me, for I aimed at every thing with great earneſtneſs: but being drawn off from theſe lectures, to lead the life of a citizen, rather than a philoſopher's, I preſerved but a few extracts from ſo fair and good a beginning.

From hence however I took my leave of oyſters and muſhrooms; for theſe are not food, but only ſerve to provoke the appetite of thoſe, who are full, to eat more; they are things which ſlip down eaſily and are as eaſily returned; which is an acceptable pleaſure to gluttony, and ſuch as love to cram themſelves with more than they can hold. Hence too I abſtained from all manner of ointments and perfumes, becauſe the beſt ſmell of the body is none at all *(g)*. And hence my ſtomach is never indulged with wine; and all my life-time I have diſdained warm bathing, ſuppoſing it to be a too delicate and uſeleſs cuſtom to ſeeth the body, and weaken the ſolids by extravagant ſweating. Some other reſolutions indeed I have been obliged to break; yet ſo as ſtill to preſerve moderation in thoſe things wherein I propoſed abſtinence; and indeed ſuch moderation as is next to abſtinence, if not more difficult:

 becauſe

becauſe ſome things are more eaſily expelled totally from the inclination, than kept in due meaſure.

But ſince I have begun to tell you with how much more earneſtneſs I applied myſelf to philoſophy, when a young man, than now when I am old, I ſhall not be aſhamed to confeſs to you, what affection for *Pythagoras Sotion* (*h*) inſpired me with. He taught me, why *Pythagoras* abſtained from animal food (*i*), and why after him *Sextius*: their reaſons were different, but, of both, very great. *Sextius* thought, that there was food enough for man in the world without ſhedding blood; and that the taking pleaſure in butchering helpleſs animals, only inſpired men with cruelty: he added hereunto, that luxury was not to be encouraged; and ſuppoſed that variety of meats, and particularly ſuch as are foreign to our conſtitutions, are by no means a preſervative of health, but the contrary. Whereas *Pythagoras* held that there was a ſort of relationſhip among all animals, and a certain intercourſe, whereby they paſſed out of one form into another. No ſoul either of man or beaſt (if you believe him) periſheth; nor indeed ceaſeth any longer than while it is tranſmigrating into another body. And that after many revolutions and changes from one ſort of body to another, it returns again to man. In the mean while this opinion had no ſmall effect, in making men dread wickedneſs, and eſpecially parricide: ſince it is poſſible they might unknowingly light upon the ſoul of a parent, and with knife and teeth violate the body wherein was lodged ſome kindred ſpirit.

When *Sotion* had explained to me theſe things, and confirmed them by his arguments; *Do you not think*, ſaid he, *that ſouls are diſtributed from one body to another; and that it is only this tranſmigration which we call* death? *Do you not believe that in thoſe animals, wild or tame, or that dwell in the great deep, the ſouls, that were once in man, ſtill ſurvive? Do you not believe, that nothing in this world periſheth, but only changeth its place and form? and that not only the celeſtial bodies make their ſeveral circuits, but that animals, and their ſouls likewiſe, have their revolutions? Many great men have believed theſe things. Suſpend therefore for a while your judgment; and weigh every thing diligently. If these things be true, to abstain from shedding of blood is innocence; if false, frugality. And as some check to cruelty, I only ask you to abstain from what is the food of lions and vultures.*—Prevailed upon by these instructions, I began to abstain from eating flesh, and at the year's end, such abstinence became not only easy to me, but pleasant (*k*): I fancied my spirit more alert and free than it was before; nor to this day can I pretend either to affirm or deny it.

But you will ask, perhaps, how I came to discontinue this way of life? My youth fell out in the reign of *Tiberius Cæsar*, at what time the sacreds of some foreign nations were banished *Rome (l)*; and among other superstitions, this was alledged as one, *the abstaining from the flesh of certain animals* (*m*). At request therefore of my father, who was no great admirer of philosophy (*n*), but hated reproach, I returned to the eating flesh as usual: nor had he much difficulty in persuading me to eat better suppers. And as *Attalus* was wont to recommend a hard bed, which sunk not with the weight of the body, such I use to this day; in which, when I rise you cannot see the least impression.

These things I have related to you, *Lucilius*, to shew you, how readily and earnestly youth attend to the knowledge and practice of what is good; if there is any one to instruct them, any one to push them on: but on the one hand, there is generally a great defect or fault in the instructor, who teaches them rather how to dispute, than how to live; (*o*) and, on the other, in the scholars, who bring with them to their master the design of having their tongue or wit polished, and not the mind. From whence, what before was philosophy, is now become philology.

Now, it is of great moment to examine what end we pursue, or with what design we engage in any business. He that sets up for a Grammarian, and examines *Virgil*, does not read that excellent hemistich,——fugit irreparabile tempus. G. iii. 284.

Time flies irrevocable,

with

with an intention to make the following reflection; *we must watch (p), unless we mend our speed we shall be left behind: the swift day drives us on, and is driven itself: we are imperceptibly hurried away (q): we postpone every thing, and are slow and lazy, while every thing about us is posting away with great rapidity:* but that he may observe, when *Virgil* is speaking of the swiftness of time he always useth the word, fugit, *he flies*; so

Optima quæque dies miseris mortalibus ævi
Prima *fugit*; subeunt morbi, *tristisque* senectus,
Et labor, et duræ rapit inclementia mortis.
In youth alone unhappy mortals live;
But, ah! the best of days *are fugitive:*
Discolour'd sickness, anxious labours come,
Disconsolate age, and death's inexorable doom.

He who applies himself to philosophy, makes such remarks too on these words, as best suit his profession. *Virgil*, he observes, never saith, dies ire, *the day passeth*, but, fugere, *it flies*; which is the swiftest kind of speed: *and that our best days* (or prime of life) *are first torn from us. Why cease we then to incite and spur ourselves on, that if possible we may equal the velocity of the swiftest thing in the world (r)?* Our better days fly off, the worse succeed. As the contents of a vessel, when poured out, flow purest at first, while the more heavy and turbid particles subside, and thicken at the bottom; so is it in our life; the best of it comes first; and this we generally permit others to draw off, while we reserve the dregs for our own use ‡. But let this be fixed in our mind, and received with as much satisfaction as if it came from an oracle,

Optima quæque dies miseris mortalibus ævi
Prima fugit.——

Why the best (of days?) because the remainder is uncertain. *Why the best?* because, when young, we are more apt to learn; we can apply the easy, and as yet tractable, mind, to the knowledge of good: and because this time of life is fittest for labour, to exercise either the faculties of the soul in study, or the strength of the body in useful toil. The remainder is more sluggish and feeble, as being nearer the end. We must therefore bend our whole mind thereto; and, omiting *almost* all diversion, labour this one point: lest, too late, to our confusion, we come to un-

derstand

derſtand the celerity of fleeting time, which it is not in the power of man to keep back.

Let every firſt, as undoubtedly the beſt, day, give us ſatisfaction and be made our own. Let us ſeize it as it flies (*s*). This is what he does not think of, who reads theſe lines of *Virgil* with a Grammarian's eye, that therefore every firſt day is the beſt, becauſe *diſeaſes ſucceed*, becauſe *old age preſſeth hard upon us*, and percheth over the head of ſuch as ſtill think themſelves young (*t*). He only obſerves, *that* Virgil *always joins together diſeaſes and old age*; and well he may; for old age is itſelf an incurable diſeaſe. Moreover, he obſerves, that *Virgil* gives old age the epithet, triſtis, *diſconſolate*,

—— Subeunt morbi, triſtiſque ſenectus.

Nor need you wonder, that every one collects from the ſame materials what is moſt ſuitable to his particular inclination. In the ſame meadow the ox ſeeks graſs, the dog a hare, and the ſtork a lizard. When the Philologiſt, the Grammarian, and the Philoſopher take in hand the books of *Cicero*, de Republica, *of a Republic*, each one hath a different purſuit. The Philoſopher wonders that ſo much could be ſaid *againſt ſtrict juſtice*. The Philologiſt remarks, that among the *Roman* kings, there were two, for the one of whom there is no father to be found, nor for the other any mother. For it is ſtill doubted who was the mother of *Servius*; nor is there any mention made of the father of *Ancus*, who is always ſtyled *Numa's* grandſon (*u*). He likewiſe obſerves that the perſon we call *Dictator*, and read of him in hiſtory under this title, was antiently called Magiſter Populi, *the People's Magiſtrate*; as it ſtands at this day in the books of the *Augurs*; and as a further proof, he obſerves, that from hence comes the title of Magiſter Equitum, *the Maſter of the Horſe*, (or, *Premier Knight*). With the like ſagacity he obſerves that at the death of *Romulus*, there was an eclipſe (*x*): and that an appeal even from Kings has been made to the people *(y)*: and this ſome think may be proved from the *pontifical* books, and the hiſtorian *Feneſtella*. The Grammarian in explaining the ſame books obſerves, in his Commentaries, that *Cicero* firſt uſed the word *reapſe*, i. e. reipſa; and alſo *ſepſe*, i. e. ſe ipſe. And then he paſſeth on to thoſe things, wherein

wherein the custom of the age hath made any alteration; as when *Cicero* saith, Quoniam sumus ab ipsa *calce* ejus interpellatione revocati, *(because by his importunity we are called back again from the very goal)* what the antients called, *calcem*, in the *Circus*, we now call *cretam* (*z*), (*the chalk*). And then he collects some verses from old *Ennius*, and particularly those relating to *Africanus*,

—— Cui nemo civis neque hostis
Quivit pro factis reddere opræpretium (*aa*).

Wherein he remarks that *Ennius* useth the word *opera* for *auxilium*, saying, *that neither friend nor enemy could give any* assistance *to* Scipio. And he thinks himself extremely happy in having found out from whence *Virgil* took——Quem super ingens

Porta tonat cœli. G. iii. 261.
When o'er his head the rattling thunder roll'd.

This, saith he, *Virgil* stole from *Ennius*, and *Ennius* from *Homer* (*bb*): for this epigram is preserved in the same books of *Cicero*:

Si fas endo plagas cœlestum ascendere cuiquam,
Mi soli *cœli* maxima *porta* patet;
If to ascend the skies to me were giv'n,
I might expect the widest gate of heav'n.

But lest I should fall myself into pedantry, or prattling philosophy, while I have greater things in view, let me conclude with this caution, that both the reading and the hearing philosophers must be made subservient to the purposes of an happy life; that we are not to catch at old or new-coined words, or extravagant metaphors, and rhetorical flourishes of speech; but to observe such precepts as may prove of use, and remark such noble and manly sentences as may be afterwards transferred to things. Let us so learn, that words may become works.

But I think none deserve worse at the hands of all mankind, than those who teach philosophy merely as a venal trade (*cc*): who live not, as they instruct other people to live, but exhibit sad examples of the unprofitableness of their doctrine, being guilty themselves of every vice, they so severely inveigh against in others. Such a preceptor seems to me me of no greater uſe to mankind, than a pilot, who is ſea-ſick or drunk in a ſtorm. The rudder muſt be held with a ſtrict hand, the waves beating ſo ſtrongly againſt it; we muſt hale in the ſail, and wreſtle, as it were, with the ſea itſelf. Of what ſervice can a pilot be at ſuch a time, who is ſo ſick, as ſcarce to be in his ſenſes? With how much ſtronger a tempeſt, alas! is our life toſſed, than any ſhip can be! there is no time to prattle, but to direct and manage wiſely.

Beſides, all that theſe men can pretend to ſay, and proudly boaſt among their *profound* audience, the people, is not their own. *Plato, Zeno, Chryſippus, Poſidonius,* and many other the like learned men, have ſaid and reſaid the ſame things before. But I will ſhew you how they prove what they ſay to be their own: *let them live up to what they preach (dd).*

Having now ſaid all that I intended, I ſhould apply myſelf, *Lucilius,* to anſwer your requeſt, but that I think proper to refer you to another Epiſtle, wherein you may expect the diſcuſſion of all you aſk; leſt at preſent you ſhould apply an ear already tired, to what will require the moſt curious and attentive.

ANNOTATIONS, &c.

* Vid. *Plutarch.* Mor. *Fol.* p. 22. Epp. 51. 83.

† Sumite materiam, veſtris, qui ſcribitis, æquam
Viribus, et verſate diu, quid ferre recuſent
Quid valeant humeri—Hor. A. P. 39.
Ye writers, try the vigour of your muſe,
And what her ſtrength will bear, and what refuſe,
And after that, an equal ſubject chuſe——Creech.

(*a*) *They ſpeak one to another, every one to his brother, ſaying, Come, I pray, and hear the Prophet. And they come unto thee, according to the coming of the people, and they hear thy words, but they will not do them. For with their mouth they ſhew much love, but their heart goeth after their covetouſneſs. And lo! they are to them as a very lovely ſong of one that hath a pleaſant voice, and can play well on an inſtrument; for they hear thy words, but do them not.* Ezek. xxxi. 11. 30.

(*b*) The ſtatue of *Rhea* called likewiſe *Ops, Cybele, the mother of the Gods,* &c. was brought from *Peſſinus,* on the borders of *Phrygia,* to *Rome,* by *Scipio Naſica*; and was there highly honoured, and worſhipped, with the ſound of the drum, pipe, and cymbals; at what time, the prieſts, and others hired

hired for the purpose, threw themselves into all manner of antic postures. Ὥσπερ γὰρ εἰ τῷ φρυγίῳ αὐλῷ αὐλοῦντες κ. τ. λ. *Lucian* in Nigrino. Vid. Brodæ, Miscell. l. v. c. 13.

(*c*) See the parable of the Sower, Matth. 13.

(*d*) Ep. 95. Omnibus Natura dedit fundamenta semenque virtutum, &c. *Cic.* de Fin. v. 15. Est enim natura sic generata vis hominis, ut ad omnem virtutem percipiendam facta videatur, &c. *The strength of reason in man is so formed, as to be fitted for* the perception of every virtue; *therefore young children, without any instruction, are affected by the resemblance of those virtues,* which they had the seeds of within themselves, *because these are* the elements of their nature; *and as they increase, virtue proceeds to its perfection.* Vid. Lips. Manud. ii. 10.

(*e*) So St. Paul to *Timothy*, *Preach the word, be instant, in season and out of season, reprove, rebuke, and exhort, with all long-suffering, and doctrine. For the time will come when they will not endure sound doctrine, but after their own lusts, shall they heap to themselves teachers, having itching ears: and they shall turn away their ears from the truth, and shall be turned unto fables.* ii. Tim. iv. 2—5.

(*f*) This is a noted paradox of the Stoics. *Cic.* de Fin. l. 3. Quam magnifica, quam constans conficitur persona sapientis! &c. *How magnificent, how uniform, is the whole character of a wise man! who after reason has told him, that what is* virtuous *can alone be* good, *is necessarily happy, and in reality possesses all those qualifications which are scoffed by the foolish: such a one has a better right to the title of* king, *than* Tarquin *had, who could neither govern himself nor others.* And thus *Seneca* the tragedian of one, that is free from vice, nor subject to the dread of casualties, or of death itself.

> Rex est qui posuit metus,
> Et diri mala pectoris;
> Qui tuto positus loco
> Infra se videt omnia;
> Occurritque suo libens
> Fato, nec queritur mori.
>
> *He is a King, whose mind is clear*
> *From every ill, and knows not fear;*
> *Who seated high, as on a throne,*
> *Upon the busy world looks down;*
> *Nor dreads a change of mortal state,*
> *But willingly submits to fate.* M.

Which however does not escape the ridicule of *Horace*, as an *Epicurean*.

> Ad summam sapiens uno minor est Jove, dives,
> Liber, honoratus, pulcher, *rex* denique *regum*,
> Præcipue sanus, nisi cum pituita molesta est. Ep. i. i. 106.
>
> *In fine, the sage, we see, is far above*
> *All earthly Kings, and only less than* Jove;
> *Is blest with honour, freedom, beauty, wealth,*
> *And (from the* phthysic *free) with perfect health.* Shard.

Vid. *Lips.* Manud. iii. 13.

(*g*) Ecastor, mulier rectè olet ubi nihil olet. *Plaut.* Mostell.

> Esse quid hoc dicam, quòd olent tua Basia Myrrham,
> Quodque tibi est nunquam non alienus odor:
> Hoc mihi suspectum est, quod oles bene, posthume, semper,
> Posthume, non bene olet, qui bene semper olet. *Mart.* ii. 12.

—— Rides nos, Coracine, nil olentes,

Malo quàm bene olere, nil olere. Ib. vi. 55.

(*h*) *Sotion*, *Seneca's* preceptor. Ep. 49. *Lipſ.* Manud. i. 12.

(*i*) "It is plain from *Revelation*, that *animal food* was *permitted*, and fermented liquors not *forbidden*; and conſequently that there is neither *virtue* nor *vice* in the uſe of them abſolutely, but in the order, time, quantity, and other circumſtances of their uſage. Alſo, that in our preſent ſituation, and under our preſent circumſtances, for ſome perſons and for ſome purpoſes a reaſonable quantity of *animal food*, and fermented liquors, may be abſolutely neceſſary, &c." *Cheyne's* Philoſophical Conjectures, p. 87. See *Oſborne's* Paradoxes, p. 535.

(*k*) *Lipſius* freely joins with *Seneca* herein; and condemns the *Europeans* for indulging themſelves ſo groſsly in *animal food*.

(*l*) "Meaſures were alſo taken for exterminating the ſolemnities of the *Jews* and *Egyptians*, and by decree of ſenate, four thouſand deſcendants of franchiſed ſlaves, all defiled with that ſuperſtition, but of proper ſtrength and age, were to be tranſported to *Sardinia*, to reſtrain the *Sardinian* robbers; and if through the malignity of the climate they periſhed, deſpicable would be the loſs: the reſt were doomed to depart *Italy*, unleſs by a ſtated day they renounced their profane rites." *Tacit.* Ann. ii.

Hence it is manifeſt, as *Muret.* obſerves, that it was not the ſame *Seneca*, who wrote theſe Epiſtles and the Declamations, ſince he who wrote the Declamations ſays of himſelf, *that he might have heard* Cicero; and is therefore concluded to be the father of our Author.

(*m*) Particularly, *ſwine's* fleſh. And as to the doctrine of *Pythagoras* in general, he taught that the human ſoul is a part of the divine ſubſtance, and therefore it is immortal. And that after its departure from the body it is reſolved into the univerſal ſoul. Yet he maintained the doctrine of the tranſmigration of ſouls, which he learned from the *Egyptians*. He ſuppoſed it to be phyſical, and neceſſary, but endeavoured to apply it to moral purpoſes. He excepted ſome eminent ſouls, which he ſuppoſed to go immediately to the Gods. The doctrine however of the immortality of ſouls, as he taught it, was of little advantage to mankind. He held periodical revolutions of the world, and that the ſame courſe of things ſhall return, and come over again. But, *Leland* obſerves that we cannot be ſure of his real ſentiments, as he made no ſcruple to impoſe upon his hearers. Vol. ii. p. 305.

(*n*) Qui non calumniam timebat, ſed philoſophiam oderat] But *Lipſius* thinks it not quite ſo decent in *Seneca* to ſpeak thus of his father. (Though he ſeems to ſpeak much in the ſame ſtrain, *Conſol.* ad Helv. c. 16.) and therefore reads, Qui non philoſophiam oderat, ſed calumniam timebat. And indeed his father, (*in Controv.* l. ii.) exhorts his ſon *Mela*, *Seneca's* brother, to the ſtudy of philoſophy, and likewiſe recommends retirement.

(*o*) Qu. Whether this may not be laid to the charge of moſt ſchools to this day? I would fain except *Eton*.

(*p*) Vigilandum eſt] So our Lord to his Diſciples, *And what I ſay unto you I ſay unto all*, watch. Mark, xiii. 37. Matth. xxiv. 12. xxv. 13. Luk. xxiv. 36. Act. xx. 31. i. Cor. xvi. 13. ii. Tim. iv. 5.

(*q*) Inſcii rapimur] "The cunning fugitive is ſwift by ſtealth,
"Too ſubtle is the moment to be ſeen:
"Yet ſoon man's hour is up, and we are gone. *Young*.

(*r*) "So prone our hearts to whiſper what we wiſh,
"Tis later with the wiſe than he's aware;
"*Prudence itſelf* goes ſlower than the ſun;
"And all mankind miſtake their time of day;
"Ev'n in old age.

"Thus at life's lateſt eve we keep in ſtore
"One diſappointment ſure, to crown the reſt,
"The diſappointment of a promis'd hour." *Young.*

‡ See Ep. i.

(*s*) "To-day is yeſterday return'd; return'd
"Full power'd to cancel, expiate, raiſe, adorn;
"And reinſtate us on the rock of peace.
"Let it not ſhare its predeceſſor's fate. *Id.*

(*t*) "——— Freſh hopes are hourly ſown
"In furrow'd brows. So gentle life's deſcent,
"We ſhut our eyes, and think it is a plain.
"We take fair days in winter for the ſpring;
"And turn our bleſſings into bane.—Since oft
"Man muſt compute that age he cannot feel,
"He ſcarce believes he's older for his years. *Id.*

(*u*) The ſon of *Numa* was ſo eclipſed in the *ſplendor* of his father, that his name is loſt.

(*x*) Olim deficere ſol hominibus extinguique viſus eſt, cum Romuli animus, &c. *Cic.* Fragm. vid. Patric. p. 19.

(*y*) As *M. Fabius* ſaid to his ſon, videro, ceſſuruſne provocationi ſis, cui rex Romanus Tullus Hoſtilius ceſſit; *I ſhall then ſee whether you ſubmit to an appeal from the people, as did the Roman king* Tullus Hoſtilius. Liv. viii. 33.

(*z*) Cretam] So *Muret.* Eſt et viliſſima, (de *Creta* loquitur) qua circum prædacere ad victoria notam, pedeſque venalium trans mare advectorum denotare inſtituerunt majores. *Plin.* xxxv. 17. *al.* Metam. *Vid.* Patric. in Fragm. *Cic.* p. 14. Septem ſtadia quadrigæ currunt quorum finis eſt creta. *Iſidor.* 18. 34.

(*aa*) Sic f. *Ennius.* Hic eſt ille ſitus, cui nemo civis nec hoſtis——*Scipio* ſays of himſelf,

Ab ſole exoriente ſupra Mæotis paludes
Nemo eſt, qui factis me exuperare queat.
Si fas cædendo cœleſtia ſcandere cuiquam eſt,
Mi ſoli———

Vid. *Lactant.* i. i. Patric. in Fragm. Cic. Turneb. in *Cic.* de Leg. ii. 22. Ib. Opræpretium, i. e. operæ. Opera, for auxilium, as is frequent in the comedies. Da mihi hanc operam. *Do me this favour.*

(*bb*) Πρωτησιν δ' ἐν πυλῃσι πολυπτυχου Ουλυμποιο. Θ. 411.

Through the firſt gates of the wide-ſpreading heav'ns.

(*cc*) Hear ye this, ye Chriſtian preachers! yes, let us hear it and bluſh at this too juſt reproof from an Heathen. Ever mindful of *our Homer's* deſcription of a *good parſon.*

But Chryſtys love, and his Apoſtles twelve,
He taught, but firſt he follow'd it himſelve. Chaucer.

EPISTLE

EPISTLE CIX.

No one ſo wiſe but he may be improved.

YOU deſire to know, *Lucilius, whether the wiſdom of a wiſe man is improveable:* we ſay, a wiſe man is replete with all good, and hath attained to fullneſs of perfection: *how then,* it is aſked, *can any one be ſerviceable to him, who hath already attained every good?* I will tell you. Good men edify one another in the exerciſe of their virtues, and in maintaining the dignity of wiſdom. And herein one man requires the aſſiſtance of another, with whom he may converſe in friendly debate. As practice improves the ſtrength and ſkill of the wreſtler, and keeps in the hand of the muſician, who is maſter of the chords; ſo muſt the wiſe man be exerciſed in the practice of virtues: and after the ſame manner that he excites himſelf to action, is he excited by another wiſe man. But

Wherein, you ſay, *can a wiſe man profit a wiſe man?* Why, he will animate him, and give him an opportunity of diſplaying his virtues. Beſides, he will expreſs his own thoughts, and probably inform him of ſome new diſcoveries; for there will be always ſomething remaining for a wiſe man to find out, and in the ſearching whereof he may employ his mind. A bad man generally hurts his companion; in that he makes him worſe, by raiſing his paſſions, inſtilling falſe fears, flattering his chagrin, and commending his pleaſures. And *then* take evil men moſt pains, when they communicate their vices to one another, and enter into combinations of miſchief. On the contrary, the good will ever benefit the good, in that his converſation will inſpire joy, and ſtrengthen his confidence; and from the ſight of mutual complacency the pleaſure of both will be heightened. Moreover, as before obſerved, he will ſtill communicate the knowledge of ſomething new; for a wiſe man is not ſuppoſed to know all things; and though he knew them, yet perhaps ſome one may find out a ſhorter way, and point out a more compendious method of compaſſing the whole work.

A wife man will be of fervice to a wife man, not only by his own ftrength and powers, but even by thofe of him whom he affifts. He indeed being left to himfelf is able to maintain his own part, and difcharge his duty: he will exert his own fpeed: yet neverthelefs he that only encourageth another in running, affifts him. Nor does a wife man only benefit another, but likewife himfelf. You will fay perhaps, *let a man fufpend his own natural powers, and he does nothing.* You might as well fay there is no fweetnefs in honey. For he that eateth it, muft be fo qualified in tongue and palate, as to relifh, and not be offended at, the tafte of it. For to the fick, fuch may be the nature of the difeafe, as to make honey feem bitter. Each of them therefore muft be fuch, as that the one is qualified to inftruct, and the other to receive inftruction.

But you reply, *As it is in vain to heat a thing that is extremely hot, fo is it to pretend to add goodnefs to one who is fuperlatively good. Does the hufbandman who thoroughly underftands his bufinefs go to another for inftruction? Or does a foldier, when fufficiently equipped for battle, require more arms? Therefore neither does the wife man afk any thing, for he is already fufficiently inftructed, and fufficiently armed againft the perils of life. He that is exceffively hot, need not any thing more to warm him: the heat is fufficient for itfelf.* Now to this I anfwer,

Firft, the things here compared by no means agree. For heat is fimply one thing; but there are various ways of benefiting one another. And then heat, as heat, is not neceffarily affifted by any acceffion of heat: but the wife man cannot maintain and keep up the fpirit of his mind, unlefs he admits fome friends like himfelf, with whom he may communicate his virtues. Add now, that there is a certain friendfhip and connection between all virtues; he therefore is of fervice, who loves the virtues of other men that are like his own; and in his turn exhibits his own to be efteemed and beloved by them. Like things give delight; efpecially if they are juft; and men know how both to approve and be approved. None but a wife man can fkilfully move the mind of a wife man; as nothing but man can rationally move man.

As

As there is need therefore of reason to move and incite reason, so is there of perfect reason to incite perfect reason.

They are said to profit a man, who give or procure for him money, favour, safety, and the like things, that are estimable and necessary for the uses of life; and herein even a fool may profit a wise man: but to be of real benefit, is for a man to move the mind of another according to the nature and fitness of things; either by his own virtue, or by the virtue of the person moved; and this cannot be done without the good even of the person who confers the benefit; for it is necessary that in exercising another's virtue, he must exercise his own.

But waving these things which are undoubtedly the *chief good*, or efficients of the same, a wise man may nevertheless profit a wise man in other respects; for only to meet with a wise man is of itself a desirable thing to another; because good naturally delighteth itself in good (*a*), and consequently every good man is as pleased with a good man as with himself.

But I must necessarily, for argument's sake, pass from this to another question; for it is asked, *whether a wise man will deliberate upon asking the opinion of another concerning his duty in civil and domestic* (if I may so say) *mortal affairs?* Undoubtedly, as, in this respect, there is as much need of the counsel of another, as there is occasionally of a physician, of a pilot, of an advocate or proctor: therefore a wise man may be of service to a wise man, in that he will counsel and persuade him; but it is in those great and divine things before spoken of, wherein he will particularly assist him, by conferring on the *reason of things*, and by communicating their minds and thoughts to each other.

Moreover, it is agreeable to Nature or the fitness of things, to embrace our friends with sincerity, and to rejoice as much in *their* good actions as in our own; or else we should be wanting in that virtue, which in exercising itself grows splendid by use. Now, virtue persuades us to settle and dispose well of things present; to consult and provide for the future; to deliberate and apply the mind to ſtudy, with care and diligence: but much eaſier will a man do all this, and unfold his faculties, who hath taken to himſelf a proper friend: he therefore looks out for one that is perfect; or at leaſt who hath made ſuch proficiency as to be almoſt perfect; and herein will ſuch a one aſſiſt him, by the rules of common prudence.

It is ſaid, that *men generally ſee more in other men's affairs than in their own*; and this certainly happens to thoſe who are blinded by *ſelf-love*, and who, through a ſuſpicion of danger, ſee not their own intereſt: when a man is more ſecure and fearleſs he will become wiſer. But yet there are ſome things, which even wiſe men can ſee better in others than in themſelves. Beſides, a wiſe man will cauſe another to will, or not will the ſame thing (*b*), which is ever of the greateſt conſequence, moſt delightful, juſt and proper. In the diſcharge of duty an excellent work! they will always draw together.

Thus then, I hope, I have fully anſwered your requeſt, though this matter is diſcuſſed in its proper place; and comprized in thoſe books wherein I have conſidered the whole of moral philoſophy. But after all, *Lucilius*, think upon what I have often ſaid to you, that in theſe matters we do nothing more than exerciſe our ingenuity. For I muſt repeat it again, and ſuppoſe you here to ſay, " Of what real ſervice are " theſe dry ſubjects? Will they make a man ſtronger, more juſt, or " more temperate? I am not at leiſure to be exerciſed in theſe ſuper- " ficial matters; I as yet want a phyſician. Why do you teach me " an unprofitable ſcience? You promiſed me great things, but enter- " tain me with trifles. You undertook to make me intrepid, though " ſwords were flouriſhed over my head; nay, though a dagger was " pointed to my throat. You ſaid I ſhould be ſecure, though fire " raged around me; and my little bark were by a ſudden whirlwind " hurried into the wide and boiſterous ocean: make good your pro- " miſe; teach me to contemn pleaſure, to deſpiſe glory; and then, " afterwards, if you pleaſe, inſtruct me, to ſolve the moſt intricate " queſtions; to diſtinguiſh ambiguities, to inveſtigate things dark and " obſcure; at preſent, I ſhall be content with learning what is neceſſary."

ANNO-

ANNOTATIONS, &c.

(a) Ὡς αἰεὶ τὸν ὁμοῖον ἄγει θεὸς ὡς τὸν ὁμοῖον. Od. ρ. 218.
Heav'n with a secret principle endu'd
Mankind to seek their own similitude. Pope.
Τέττιξ μὲν τέττιγι φίλος, μύρμακι δὲ μύρμαξ. Theocr. 9.
To grasshoppers the grasshoppers are friends,
And ant on ant for mutual aid depends.
Αἰεὶ κολοιὸς πρὸς κολοιὸν ἱζάνει. Prov.
Γέρων γέροντι γλῶτταν ἡδίστην ἔχει
Παῖς παιδί, καὶ γυναικὶ πρόσφορον γυνή,
Νοσῶν τ' ἀνὴρ νοσοῦντι. κ. τ. λ. ap. Plut.

Lat. Pares cum paribus. Æqualis æqualem delectat. *Erasm.* l. ii. 20. Simile gaudet simili. Ib. 21. Cæcus cæcum ducit, &c.
Indica Tigris agit rabida cum tygride pacem
Perpetuam. Sævis inter se convenit ursis. Juv. xv. 163.
Tyger with tyger, bear with bear you'll find,
In leagues offensive and defensive join'd. Tate.

And yet, says *Martial*,
Uxor pessima pessimus maritus!
Miror non bene convenire vobis.
Bad husband and bad wife! 'tis strange to me,
That two, so much alike, cannot agree.

The *Italians* say, Ogni simile appetisce il suo simile. The *French*, Chescun cherche son semblable, *or*, demande sa sorte. The *English*, Like will to like, (as the devil said to the collier.)—King *Harry* (V.) loved a man, &c.

(b) *Minutius* in Octavio, ut et in ludicris et seriis pari mecum voluntate concineret, *eadem velle et nolle* crederes unam mentem in duobus fuisse divisam. Vid. *Sidon. Apoll.* v. 9.

EPISTLE CX.

On the Contempt of Riches.

I SALUTE thee, *Lucilius,* from my country-seat at *Nomentum*; and charge thee to keep thy mind ever pure; i. e. to have the Gods propitious to you; as they are ever kind to those, who are kind to themselves.

ſelves. Set aſide however that opinion at preſent, which many are ſo fond of, *that every one hath his guardian God attending him (a)*, not indeed any principal God, but one of inferior note, from among thoſe, whom *Ovid* ſtyles de plebe Deos, *plebeian Gods*. But nevertheleſs remember, that our anceſtors, who were of this opinion, were *Stoics*. For to every perſon, male and female, they allotted (his) *Genius* or (her) *Juno*. We ſhall hereafter ſee, whether the Gods are ſo much at leiſure as to attend on the affairs of every individual; in the mean time, know, that whether we are aſſigned to a ſeveral *Genius*, or quite neglected and given up to *Fortune*, you can wiſh no one a greater miſchief than for him to be his own enemy: nor is there any need of execrating a man, whom you juſtly think deſerving a puniſhment; or wiſhing the Gods incenſed againſt him; for they certainly are ſo, though he ſeems promoted by their favour.

Apply your uſual diligence, and conſider well what things *really* are, and not what they are called; and you will find that more evils come upon us to which we have been acceſſary ourſelves (*b*), than what happen merely by accident. For how often hath that which was called a calamity proved the cauſe and ſource of happineſs *? How often hath what hath been received with congratulation and joy, built its ſeat on a precipice! and hath raiſed one, who was eminent before, ſtill higher, as if he was to abide there, from whence he need dread no fall? But ſuppoſe he were to fall; ſuch fall, if you conſider the end, beyond which Nature hath no further power to caſt us down, hath no evil in it. The end of all things is at hand (*c*): the time, I ſay, is near; even that which ſhall eject the happy, and deliver the wretched. And both theſe we are apt to ſtretch in fancy, and lengthen out, either through hope or fear. But if you are wiſe, *Lucilius*, meaſure all things by the condition of human life. Contract into a narrow ſphere, both that which gives you joy and that which creates fear (*d*). It is of conſequence to rejoice in nothing long, that you may fear nothing long.

But why do I throw out ſuch hard ſtrictures on this evil? There is no reaſon you ſhould think any thing to be feared; they are all vain things that move and ſurprize us; none of us have examined into what is truth. But we teach one another to fear. No one has the courage to ſet about a thing that gives him perturbation; or to examine well into the grounds of his fear. Therefore things falſe and vain, gain credit; becauſe they are not diſproved, nor their vanity diſcovered. Whereas were we to open our eyes, and take a diligent view of things, we ſhould ſee how tranſitory, how uncertain, how harmleſs, thoſe are, we are ſo much afraid of. Such is the confuſion of our minds, as is deſcribed by *Lucretius*:

Nam veluti pueri trepidant, atque omnia cæcis
In tenebris metuunt, ſic nos in luce timenus. II. 53.
—— *as children are ſurpriz'd with dread,*
And tremble in the dark; ſo riper years
Ev'n in broad day-light are ſurpriz'd with fears;
And ſhake at ſhadows, fanciful and vain,
As thoſe that in the breaſt of children reign. Dryden.

Well then, are we not more fooliſh than children, *we, who are afraid even in the light?* But it is falſe, *Lucilius*, we are not afraid in the light; we have ourſelves ſpread darkneſs around us (*e*); we can ſee nothing; either what is hurtful or what is expedient for us. All our life-time we are continually ſtumbling; ye we ſtop not for this, nor walk more circumſpectly (*f*). Now, you ſee what a mad thing it is to run headlong in the dark; yet truly this is what we do, that we may be ſtill further off when we are recalled: and know not whither we are carried; yet we perſevere with ſpeed in our reſpective journey.

However, if we pleaſe, we may obtain light; and there is but one way to be happy in this bleſſing: which is, by the ſtudy of philoſophy, i. e. *of things human and divine*;—ſo that a man be not ſprinkled only therewith, but is dipped in and ſeaſoned;—and if, knowing theſe things, he reflects often upon them, and reminds himſelf of them;—if he enquires into, and can rightly diſtinguiſh, good and evil; to which often is aſcribed a falſe title;—if he ſeeks to know what is right and fit, and what the contrary;—but particularly, what is *providence*. Not that the ſagacity of human underſtanding reſts here: it is deſirous to look beyond this world; to know its ſeveral motions; from whence it firſt ſprung, and to what period this vaſt velocity is haſtening. But alas! we have drawn off our minds from this divine contemplation; to ſet them upon things low and mean; to be ſlaves to avarice; and having thrown aſide all uſeful reflections on the works of creation, their boundaries, and the almighty rulers and governors of the univerſe; we pry into the bowels of the earth, to learn what evils we may dig from thence, not contented with ſuch things as are offered to our view. For whatever was for our good, our God and Father hath graciouſly ſet before us (*b*). He hath not expected our laborious ſearch after it; having been pleaſed to offer it freely: but what might hurt us, he hath buried very deep. We cannot complain therefore of any thing but ourſelves. Thoſe things, which Nature had hid from us and forbidden, as tending to our deſtruction, we have brought into light ourſelves. We have devoted the mind to pleaſure: the indulgence whereof is the foundation and ſource of all evils. We have given ourſelves up to ambition, and fame, and other affections as vain and fruitleſs.

What then do I exhort you to do? nothing new or ſtrange. Our evils are not ſo new as to require new remedies. All that I aſk of you, is, that you would conſider, and weigh well what is neceſſary and what is ſuperfluous: neceſſary things are every where obvious (*i*); but ſuperfluities require the conſtant labours of our whole mind and body. *But you deſire not*, you ſay, *rich beds trimmed with gold, or furniture adorned with jewels.* It may be ſo; there is no reaſon you ſhould commend yourſelf for this: for what virtue is there in contemning ſuch things as are not neceſſary? Then it is that you may command yourſelf, when you can deſpiſe even neceſſaries: it is no great thing that you can live contented without a noble and royal equipage; that you deſire no wild boars of a thouſand weight on the ſide-table; nor a diſh of the tongues of redwings, and other prodigies of luxury, that diſdains whole animals, and only ſelects the nicer bits.

Then it is I ſhall admire you, when you diſdain not the coarſeſt bread; when you are perſuaded, that herbs and vegetables, in caſe of neceſſity,

neceſſity, were not provided only for the beaſts of the field, but for the nouriſhment of man; when you ſhall know, that the young ſhoots, or top twigs of trees can fill the belly; which we now ſtore with ſo many precious things, as if it were a treaſure-houſe to preſerve them. Whereas we need not be over-nice in filling it, it being nothing to the purpoſe what it receives, ſince whatever it be, it cannot long keep it. And yet you take pleaſure in ſeeing a courſe of many diſhes, to ſupply which both ſea and land have been ranſacked: ſome animals are the more grateful, if brought young and freſh to the table; others that have been long fed and crammed, ſo as to melt as it were in their own fat; nay, the artificial ſavour of them delights thee. But verily theſe meats, ſo anxiouſly ſought after, and ſo variouſly and highly ſeaſoned, when ſwallowed down, turn all to the ſame filth. Would you deſpiſe the pleaſure of dainty eating, only view it in its laſt ſtage.

I remember to have heard my tutor, *Attalus*, make the following harangue with great applauſe: " Riches, ſaid he, have a long while " impoſed upon me. I was amazed, when, in one place, or another, " I ſaw their glittering ſplendor. I concluded, what I did not ſee " was alike rich and beautiful with what was exhibited to view. But " in a late pageant I ſaw the whole wealth of the city, gold and ſilver, " finely emboſſed; jewels of various dies and of an exquiſite water; " and the richeſt apparel, brought not only from beyond our own " territories, but from beyond the confines of our moſt diſtant enemies. " On one hand, a tribe of boys, fair and comely, both in ſhape and " dreſs; on the other, a range of beautiful women; with many other " things, which the fortune of the greateſt empire diſplayed, as recon- " noitring at once all her treaſures. *And what is all this,* ſaid I to " myſelf, *but to provoke the ſenſual appetites of man, forward enough of* " *themſelves? What means all this pomp of money? We are ſurely* " *aſſembled here to learn covetouſneſs.* But, in truth, I carried away " with me leſs deſire for it, than I had entertained before. I deſpiſed " riches, not becauſe they are ſuperfluous; but becauſe they are trifles. " Saw you not, that in a few hours time, the whole train, though " marching ſlow and in orderly ranks, paſſed by? And ſhall that

" take up our whole life, which we ſhould have thought long and te-
" dious if it had taken up the whole day?"——*He likewiſe added,*
" Riches really ſeem to me as ſuperfluous to the poſſeſſors as to the
" ſpectators. This then is what I ſay to myſelf, whenever ſuch a
" gaudy ſcene dazzles mine eyes; when I behold a fine houſe, a ſpruce
" train of ſervants, or a litter ſupported by handſome ſtrong-back'd
" lacqueys (*l*): *what do you wonder at? why are you amazed? it is all*
" *pomp: theſe things are made a ſhew of, they are not poſſeſſed, they pleaſe*
" *a moment, and paſs by.* Turn yourſelf rather to true riches; learn
" to be content with a little, and with a truly great and noble ſpirit
" cry out, *Give me water, give me a barley cake, and I will not envy*
" Jupiter *his happineſs.* No; even if theſe things are wanting. It is
" ſcandalous to place the happineſs of life in gold and ſilver; it is no
" leſs ſo to place it in water and barley-bread. *But what ſhall I do if*
" *I have not theſe? Is there any remedy againſt extreme want and*
" *penury?* Yes, hunger will ſoon put an end to hunger (*m*). Other-
" wiſe where would be the difference between being a ſlave to great or
" little things? It is no matter how great the thing is, that fortune
" hath denied us; if we muſt depend upon the pleaſure of another for
" even this our water and barley-bread (*n*). He only is free; not over
" whom Fortune hath the leaſt power, but over whom ſhe hath no
" power at all. Thus it is then: you muſt covet nothing, if you
" would rival *Jupiter*, who hath nothing to aſk."

Thus ſpake *Attalus* to us; and Nature ſaith the ſame to all mankind. Which words if you frequently revolve in your mind, you will certainly make yourſelf not ſeemingly, but really, happy: and in effect you will think yourſelf ſo; let others think as they pleaſe,

ANNO-

ANNOTATIONS, &c.

(*a*) See Epp. 25. 93. The antients called them *δεύτεροι δαίμονες, Gods of an inferior claſs*; nay, they even ſuppoſed them mortal. But the general opinion was, that the beings they called *Genii* or *Dæmons* were certain ſpirits that adminiſtered, under the Supreme Being, the affairs of men, taking care of the virtuous, and puniſhing the bad, and ſometimes communicating with the beſt; as particularly, the genius of *Socrates* always warned him of approaching dangers, and taught him to avoid them. *Plutarch.*

> Scit Genius, natale comes qui temperat aſtrum
> Naturæ Deus humanæ mortalis in unum——
> Quodque caput, vultu mutabilis, albus et ater.
> *That Genius only knows, who's pleas'd to wait*
> *On each man's natal ſtar, and guide his fate:*
> *An arbitrary God, whoſe ſmile or frown*
> *Makes This a Gentleman, and That a Clown.*

They rather, ſays *Muret.* aſſigned a *Genius* to a man, and a *Juno* to a woman; as in *Tibullus* one ſwears to her lover,

> Perque tuos oculos, per *Geniumque* rogo.

And he again to her;

> Hæc per ſancta tuæ *Junonis* numina juro.

As in *Petronius*—*Quirtilla* curſing herſelf, ſays,

> Junonem meam iratam habeam.
> " And the tame demon that ſhould guard my throne,
> " Shrinks at a *Genius* greater than his own." *Shakeſpear.*

So *Macbeth*, ſpeaking of *Macduff*,

> —— There is none but he
> Whoſe being I do fear: and under him
> My *Genius* is rebuk'd; as it is ſaid
> *Antony's* was by *Cæſar*. Id.

Vid. *Eraſm.* Adagi i. 1. 72. *Lipſ.* Manud. 11. 19.

(*b*) This reminds me of an epitaph which I wrote many years ago upon a young gentleman; but it was thought too true for an epitaph, and therefore not accepted.

> *Here lies friend ——, whoſe death this truth confeſs'd,*
> *That mortals ſeldom know when they are bleſs'd;*
> *Becauſe he had no enemies, he tried*
> *To be his own: ſo drank, fell ſick, and died.*

This likewiſe puts me in mind of what I have heard or read of a poor man, who, in Queen *Mary's* days, as he was drawn upon a ſledge to execution on account of his religion, the ſledge broke and fractured his leg; upon which he was compaſſionately carried into an houſe, and within a few days Queen *Mary* died, and his life was ſaved.

(*c*) *The end of all things is at hand, be ye ſober therefore, and watch unto prayer.* i. Pet. 4. 7.

(*d*) Let us turn our endeavours towards ſuch remedies, as prudence and philoſophy are found

to

to preserve to us. And according to their advice, *pack up our hopes and fears into as narrow a room as we can possibly, by which we shall render the last more portable, and the first less tedious.*

Osborne. Advice to his Son.

(*e*) Omnia nobis tenebras fecimus.] Nothing is more frequent than the use of this metaphor in Scripture, but full to our purpose is, *Ye were some time darkness, but now are ye light in the Lord. All things that are reproved are made manifest by the light; for whatsoever doth make manifest, is light. Wherefore he saith (Is. 60. 1.) Awake thou that sleepeth, and arise from the dead, and Christ shall give thee light.* Ephes. v. 8. 14. *I send thee,* (Paul) *to the Gentiles, to open their eyes, and to turn them from darkness to light.* Act. 26. 18. Rom. 13. 12. i. Tim. 5. 5. i. John, 2. 8.

(*f*) Nec circumspectius pedem ponimus] *See then that ye walk more circumspectly, not as fools, but as wise, redeeming the time.* Ephes. v. 15. *Walk in wisdom toward them that are without, redeeming the time.* Col. iv. 5.

(*g*) See *Fitzosborne*, Letter 48.

(*h*) So *Moses*, in the name of the Lord, *I have set before thee this day life and good. It is not hidden from thee; neither is it far off. It is not in heaven, that thou shouldst say, who shall go up for us into heaven, and bring it us? Neither is it beyond the sea, that thou shouldst say, who shall go over the sea, and bring it unto us? But the word is very nigh thee, in thy mouth, and in thy heart, that thou mayest do it.* Deut. 30. 11---15. See also *Rom.* x. 6---8.

(*i*) See Ep. 18.

(*k*) Linguas phænicopterorum] Whatever bird it was, *Muret.* observes, that *Apicius* (that master of gluttony and dissoluteness) recommended the tongue of it as a most dainty morsel. *Sueton.* in *Vitell.* c. 13.

Dat mihi penna rubens nomen: sed lingua gulosis
Nostra sapit, quid si garrula lingua foret!
Gluttons have borrow'd this my name from Greek;
My tongue a dainty bit! oh, could I speak!

(*l*) It is observable that litters were not used by way of state, before the time of *Julius Cæsar*, but only for travelling. *Suetonius* mentions it as a particular privilege granted to one *Harpocras*, the being carried about the city in a litter, in the time of *Claudius Cæsar*: he also observes that they were not allowed to ladies *of an easy fame*, in the time of *Domitian*. See *Lips.* Flect. i 19.

(*m*) This, with *Attalus'* leave, seems a very hard lesson, and somewhat like what the old nurse said to her child: *lie still, child, you will die presently.* But his argument is, that we should not be over-anxious even for necessaries; and much less purchase them at the expence of liberty.

(*n*) See Ep. xxv. (N. d. e.) *Ælian* Var. Hist. iv. 13.

EPISTLE

EPISTLE CXI.

On idle Cavils.

YOU desire to know, *Lucilius*, by what word we express in *Latin*, what the *Greeks* called σοφίσματα, *sophisms*. I know of none who have expressed it properly, though some have attempted it; and the reason of this is, being averse to, and not using the thing itself, we made no account of the name. Yet that seems to me the most expressive which is made by *Cicero (a)*. He calls them cavillationes, *cavils*; which whoever applies himself to, he forgeth indeed subtle questions; but makes no advance in the better conduct of life: nor is made thereby more strong, more temperate, or more elate. Whereas he, who hath sought his remedy against the evils of life in philosophy, becomes magnanimous, full of confidence, insuperable; and seems the greater, the nearer you approach him: like a mountain, the height whereof is not very apparent when viewed at a distance, but when you come near it seems to reach the skies.

Such, my *Lucilius*, is a philosopher, when a philosopher indeed; according to the truth of things, and not a counterfeit by art. He stands on an eminence, is admirable, upright and truly great. He does not strut, and walk on tiptoe, like those who help their height by some shift, and would fain seem taller than they are; but is contented with his natural stature. And why should he not be content; since he is too tall for Fortune to lay her hand upon him; and is therefore above all worldly affairs? In every state or condition he is consistent with himself, and the same man; whether his life runs smoothly on with a prosperous gale, or whether it be tossed by the boisterous waves of adversity.

Now such constancy can never be procured by the *cavils* beforementioned. The mind plays with these things, without receiving any benefit from them. It is to dethrone philosophy, and reduce her to the common level. However you may sometimes amuse yourself with them, but it must be, when you intend to trifle and do nothing. But let me give you this caution; they have one bad quality attending them; they are too apt to allure the mind with a certain delight, and induce it, by a specious appearance of subtlety, to fix itself upon them; when we have so much business of the greatest importance upon our hands; when scarce our whole life is sufficient to learn this one thing, *a contempt of life*. But *what of governing it*, you say? This, *Lucilius*, is the second work we have to do; for no one can manage, or govern it well, who hath not first despised it.

ANNOTATIONS, &c.

(*a*) *Cavillationes*, the word indeed is used by *Cicero*, but not in this sense, rather signifying *quirps*, *witticisms*, and the like.

EPISTLE CXII.

Old Sinners very difficult to be reformed.

INDEED, *Lucilius*, I desire, as much as you, to instruct our old friend. But he is too tough and stubborn for me, or rather, I should say, what is more troublesome, he is too tender and delicate, his constitution having been broke by a constant and evil habit. I will give you an example from my own experience. Every vine is not fit for grafting: if it be old and worm-eaten; or if it be weak and slender, it will not receive the scyon, or not nourish it; it will not take with it, and communicate its nature and quality. We are used therefore to cut it off just above ground, in order that if it fails, a second experiment may

may be made by ſetting it again in the earth. The perſon you write about, and are concerned for, hath not ſtrength; he hath ſo long indulged himſelf in vice, that at the ſame time he both withers away, and hardens. He cannot cloſe with reaſon, nor indeed give it entertainment.

But he is deſirous, you ſay. Do not think ſo. I will not ſay that he tells you a lie; he only thinks he is deſirous. He is at preſent ſick of luxury; but he will ſoon return to it again. He ſays indeed *he is offended at his own life*. I do not deny it; for who is not offended at it? There are men, who have both hated and loved their life at the ſame time *(a)*. We will therefore *then* give you our opinion, *when* he hath given us full aſſurance, that he really deteſts luxury and all manner of exceſs; at preſent we are not clear in this point.

ANNOTATIONS, &c.

(a) Dr. *Young* hath beautifully expreſſed this but on another occaſion.

" Life we think long and ſhort; Death ſeek and ſhun;
Body and ſoul, like peeviſh man and wife,
United jar, and yet are loth to part." N. T. 11.

EPISTLE CXIII.

A trifling Queſtion, Whether Virtues and Vices are Animals *.

YOU deſire me, *Lucilius*, to give you my opinion of that queſtion, ſo bandied about among the Stoics: *whether juſtice, fortitude, prudence, and other virtues, are animals*. It is from ſuch queſtions as theſe, my dear friend, that we are thought to exerciſe our wits to very little purpoſe; and to waſte our time in idle and uſeleſs diſquiſitions. However, I will endeavour to oblige you with an anſwer, and explain what ſome among the *Greeks* (*a*) have underftood of this affair; though I muft own myfelf not of their opinion. The reafons that induced the antients to receive it, are the following:

It is manifeft, fay they, that (animus) *the foul* is an animal, feeing that it is the efficient caufe of life in us; and that animals borrow their name from it (*b*). And virtue is nothing elfe but the *foul*, under fuch a modification, and therefore it is an animal. Befides virtue acts, but nothing can act without impulfe or motion; and if it hath motion, which indeed properly belongs to animals, it is therefore an animal. If virtue, it is likewife faid, is an animal, it is an animal through virtue; for why? it contains itfelf. As a wife man does all things by, or thro' virtue; fo does virtue all things by itfelf: and therefore it is urged, that all arts are animals, all the objects of thought, and whatever is comprehended in the mind. From whence it follows, that millions of animals dwell in the narrow compafs of the human breaft; and all of us are fo many animals, or contain fo many animals.

In anfwer to this, let me obferve, *though every one of the things alledged be an animal, they are not many animals*. And this I will explain to you, if you will hear me, with your ufual attention and acutenefs.

Every particular animal muft have a particular fubftance: but all thefe fuppofed animals have one foul, or are contained in one foul, therefore they can be but one; they cannot be many. I am an animal; I am alfo a man; yet you will not fay that I am *two*. And why? becaufe they muft be feparable: the one, I fay, muft be deducible from the other, or elfe they cannot be two. *Every unit, however multiplied in itfelf, hath ftill but one nature, and is therefore one (c)*. My foul is an animal, and I am an animal; yet we are not two; becaufe, my foul is a part of myfelf. A thing is to be numbered by itfelf, when it fubfifts by itfelf; but when it is part of another, it cannot feem a different thing from that: becaufe a different, or another thing, muft be what is, properly, wholly and abfolutely within itfelf.

I told

I told you, that I professed myself of a different opinion from those who held this question in the affirmative. My reason is, because, according to this opinion, not only all *virtues* will be animals, but all other affections, and even the *vices* of the mind, as *anger*, *fear*, *grief*, *jealousy*; nay, further, all *opinions* and all *thoughts* will be animals: which by no means is to be admitted. For, not every thing that is done by, or belongs to, man, is a man.

What is justice? they say. *It is the soul, considered in such a respect, and if the soul is an animal, so is justice.* No; for justice is but a mode, or certain power of the soul. One and the same soul is convertible into various forms; but it is not so often another animal, as it was pleased to act differently; nor is whatever it does, an animal. If *justice* be an animal; if *fortitude*, and the other virtues be animals; do they sometimes cease to be animals that they may begin again? or are they always animals? They can never cease to be virtues; therefore there are many: nay, numberless animals in the one soul. *No*, say they, *they are not many, because they are connected in one; and are parts or members of one. We suppose therefore the soul to resemble the* hydra, *that hath many heads, each of which fights, and does mischief of itself.* What then? none of these heads is of itself an animal: but the *hydra* itself is one animal. No one will say that the lion in the *chimæra* † is an animal; nor the dragon an animal: these are but parts of her, and parts are not animals.

But from whence do you conclude *justice* to be an animal? *Because it acts and does good; and what acts and does good, must have power and motion, and what hath power and motion is an animal.* True, if this was its own power and motion, but it is not its own; it is the power and motion of tho soul. Every animal, 'till it dies, is what it was at first; man, 'till he dies, is man; so an horse or a dog; for these cannot be any thing else than what they are. Let us then, for argument sake, suppose *justice*, i. e. the *soul* under such a modification, to be an animal; *fortitude* then is likewise an animal, it being the soul under such a modification. *But what soul?* That which before was *justice*: it is contained in the former animal: it cannot paſs into, or belong to, another: it muſt continue there where it began firſt to be.

Moreover, it cannot be one ſoul of two animals, much leſs of more than two. If then juſtice, fortitude, temperance, and other virtues, are all animals, how will they have but one ſoul? They muſt each have a ſeparate ſoul or they will not be animals. One body cannot be the body of many animals: this they themſelves allow. Let us aſk then, what is the body of juſtice? *The ſoul.* And what is the body of fortitude? the ſame ſoul. But two bodies cannot have the ſame ſoul. *But the ſame ſoul,* they ſay, *puts on the habit of juſtice, or of fortitude or of temperance.* This might be, if at the time it was juſtice, it was not fortitude; or when fortitude, not temperance: but all the virtues happen to dwell together: yet how ſhould theſe be different animals, when there is but one ſoul, which can conſtitute but one animal?

Moreover, no animal can be part of another animal; but juſtice is part of the ſoul, therefore it is not an animal. But, methinks, I am waſting time and labour, in proving a thing ſo manifeſt to all. We ought rather to be angry, than diſpute with a man who will not allow, that *no part of an animal can be part of another.* Look around; view the ſeveral bodies of men; there is not one of them but hath its own peculiar colour, form, and proportion. And this among other things always ſtrikes me with admiration, at the infinite wiſdom of our great Creator, that in ſuch a vaſt variety of beings, he hath made no two exactly alike (*d*). Even in thoſe things which ſeem moſt alike, when compared, and curiouſly inſpected, there will be found a difference. What a great and beautiful variety is there in leaves and flowers, every one diſtinguiſhed by its own marks and qualities! So likewiſe in the different ſorts of animals, in none of which there is an exact likeneſs, not even in thoſe of the ſame kind. So hath the great Maker of all things ordered it, that, as being different beings, they ſhould be diſſimilar in form and proportion.

But

But the virtues, you ſay, *are alike*. Yes; and therefore they are not animals. Every animal acts of itſelf; but virtue does nothing of itſelf, but in communion with man. Again, all animals are either rational, as man, and the Gods; or irrational, as the beaſts: ſuppoſe then the virtues were rational, yet they are neither men nor gods; therefore they are not animals. Every rational animal does nothing but when incited by ſome ſpecious view; from this impulſe it contracts a power; and this power is confirmed by *aſſent*: (I will explain what I mean by *aſſent*. It behoves me to walk; accordingly I walk; having firſt conſulted with myſelf, and approved my own opinion: or it behoves me to ſit, accordingly I ſit.) But this *aſſent* or ſelf-will is not in virtue. For take prudence by way of example (*e*); it behoves me, I ſay, to walk; now this belongs not to its nature: for prudence looks not out for itſelf, but for him whoſe it is: it can neither walk nor ſit; therefore hath not in itſelf the power of aſſent; and what hath not aſſent is not an animal.

If virtue be an animal, it is a rational animal, but it is not rational, therefore not an animal. If every virtue be an animal and every virtue is good, then every good is an animal. This our Stoics avow. To ſave a father is good; to ſpeak wiſely in the ſenate is good, and to decree juſtly, is good: therefore to ſave a father, is an animal; a wiſe ſpeech is an animal; and ſo far will this matter go, that it is impoſſible to refrain from laughing. Prudently to be ſilent, and to ſup well, is good; therefore to be ſilent, or to eat a good ſupper, is an animal.

I muſt divert myſelf a little more with theſe fooleries, theſe ſubtle triflings. If juſtice and fortitude be animals, they are certainly terreſtrial. Now every terreſtrial animal is ſubject to cold, hunger, thirſt; therefore juſtice is cold, fortitude is hungry, and clemency thirſteth. Why ſhould I not aſk them further, what is the ſhape of theſe animals? Is it that of a man, or of an horſe, or of a wild beaſt? If they ſuppoſe it *round*, as they ſuppoſe God (*f*), I would aſk whether avarice, luxury, and madneſs, are equally round? for theſe likewiſe they ſuppoſe to be animals. Having given them this rotundity, I would further aſk them whether

whether prudent walking be an animal or not; but on their principle they cannot deny it: they muſt acknowledge that walking is an animal, and indeed round and complete *(g)*.

But that you may not think me a deſerter, and here ſpeak without book and authority, know, that there was a diſpute between *Cleanthes* and *Chryſippus* upon this very point of walking: they could by no means agree. *Cleanthes* ſaith, that there is a ſpirit that acts from the *principal*, or ſuperior and governing part of the ſoul, quite down to the feet. *Chryſippus*, that it is this very principal itſelf that acts (*h*). Why may not every one therefore after the example of *Chryſippus* maintain his own opinion, and laugh, if he pleaſes, at the ſuppoſed infinity of animals, which the whole world could not contain?

But the virtues, they ſay, *are not many animals, but yet are animals; for as a man may be both an orator and a poet and yet be but one man; ſo theſe virtues are animals though not many animals: the ſame mind is juſt, and prudent, and brave, as it reſpectively bears itſelf with regard to each virtue.* Here then let us end the diſpute: I join iſſue with them; for at preſent I allow the ſoul to be an animal, referring what I have to ſay on this matter to another opportunity: but I deny that every *action of it is an animal:* for otherwiſe all words will be animals, and all verſes; for if a prudent ſpeech be good, and every good an animal, then is ſpeech an animal. So a prudent verſe is good: but every good is an animal, therefore every verſe is an animal: therefore

Arna virumque cano Trojæ qui primus ab oris (Virg. l. 1.)

is an animal, which they cannot ſay is round; becauſe it hath ſix feet. Really this is ſuch fine ſpinning, that the more I conſider it the more I laugh: eſpecially when I fancy a ſolœciſm, a barbariſm, and a ſyllogiſm, are animals; and, painter like, aſſign to each of them a ſeveral face, which I think beſt ſuits them. Yet theſe are the things, *Lucilius*, which we ſo earneſtly diſpute upon with knitted brows, and a wrinkled forehead. I cannot here ſay with *Cæcilius*, O triſtes ineptiæ (*i*), *wretched trifling!* ridiculæ ſunt; *it is rather ridiculous.*

Let

Let us therefore treat of ſomething uſeful and ſalutary, and inveſtigate the way that leads to virtue: teach me not that fortitude is an animal, but that no animal (at leaſt man) can be happy without fortitude; i. e. unleſs he be ſtrong and reſolute againſt all caſualties, and by ſerious meditation hath, in ſome meaſure, quelled all accidents, before they reach him. What is *fortitude?* the impregnable fortreſs of human imbecility: ſo that whoſoever is ſurrounded by it, he ſtands ſecure in the ſiege of life: for he makes uſe of, and depends upon, his own ſtrength and weapons. I will here tranſcribe an excellent ſentence from our *Poſidonius*; Non eſt quod unquam fortunæ armis putes te eſſe tutum, tuis pugna contra ipſam, fortuita non arment; *Never truſt to, or think yourſelf ſafe, in the defenſive arms of Fortune, but oppoſe her with your own; Chance provides us none.* Therefore, however armed we may be againſt our enemies, we are ſtill unarmed againſt Fortune.

Alexander indeed ſpoiled and put to flight the *Perſians*, the *Hyrcanians*, the *Indians*, and every nation eaſtward to the great ocean. But he himſelf having ſlain one friend *(Clitus)* and loſt another *(Hephæſtion)* lay in darkneſs; at one time deteſting his cruel and wicked action, at another time his loſs. The conqueror of many nations was overcome himſelf by anger, and ſorrow. For ſuch was his ambition, he had rather have all things under his command than his paſſions. O, how blind, how erroneous are men, who deſire to extend their dominion beyond the ſeas, and think themſelves happy, if, by the aſſiſtance of their ſoldiery, they can be maſters of many provinces; and add continually thereto; ignorant at the ſame time of what is truly a great and godlike kingdom. *To command ourſelves*, is the greateſt empire in the world.

Teach me, what a ſacred thing is *juſtice*; which always regards the good of another, aſking nothing for herſelf, but ſelf-exerciſe. She muſt have no connection with ambition and glory; but reſt ſatisfied with ſelf-complacency. Let a man perſuade himſelf above all things, that it behoves him to be juſt, without hope or deſire of a recompence. Nor is this enough; let him further perſuade himſelf, that he muſt

 voluntarily

voluntarily incline to this the fairest of all virtues; so that all his thoughts be as averse as possible, from any private advantage (*k*). You must not think that the reward of any just action is greater than the action itself. This too, be sure to fix in your mind, what I before hinted, that it is nothing to the purpose, how many are privy to, or witnesses of, your just and righteous dealing. They who are desirous to have their virtues blazoned abroad, labour not for virtue, but *fame*. You would fain have the honour of being thought a just man; but indeed it may so happen, that justice may be attended with infamy; and then, if you are wise, you will take delight in triumphing over unjust disgrace.

ANNOTATIONS, &c.

* Unless we had manifest testimonies of it, (as *Muret.* observes) we could scarce think it credible, that any so ridiculous an opinion should have been started as that which here *Seneca* laughs at, and confutes. For what can be more absurd than to suppose that not only the *soul* is an *animal*; (if so, it must then have another soul to animate it, and that another, and so on for ever) but that all virtues, vices, thoughts, and affections, are *animals*. Yet this opinion, ridiculous and absurd as it is, was held and maintained for truth, by the principal masters among the *Stoics*, those severe censors, those long-bearded doctors, those props and supporters of wisdom. Nor did they stop here, but supposed that *quality*, *quantity*, *figure*, and the like were all *animals*. This then is the folly which *Seneca* endeavours to confute in this Epistle: and concludes admirably in praise of *justice*; and with cautioning his reader against wasting his time in the foregoing trifles. There is also extant a short commentary among the νοθευόμενα of *Galen*, wherein this very opinion is ridiculed and condemned. The title of it is, Ὅτι αἱ ποιότητες ἀσώματοι.

(*a*) Phæcasiatum palliatumque; *wearing white shoes and a cloak*, particularly the *Greek* philosophers, as distinguished from the *Roman* sandals and gown. Phæcasianorum vetera ornamenta deorum. Juv. iii. 218.

(*b*) The word *animalis* comes from *anima*; and that from *animus*; as *agna* from *agnus*. The difference between *animus* and *anima*, though not always observed, seems to be that by *anima* they understood that power of the soul which giveth *life* and *sensibility*: and by *animus*, that which giveth *understanding*, *wisdom*, and the like.

(*c*) This, I think, may, in some measure, be applied to the great mystery that *faith* requires us to believe in the Christian scheme, *I and my father are one.* John, x. 30.

† The *Hydra* and *Chimæra*, two poetical monsters; the former, a serpent in the garden of the Hesperides:

Mighty in bulk, and terrible in look:
That arm'd with scales, and in a dreadful fold,
Twin'd round the tree, and watch'd the growing gold. Creech *Lucretius*, 5. 35.

The

The latter was ſuppoſed to have,

> —— *A lion's head, a ſerpent's tail,*
> *A goat, the middle of the fancied frame,*
> *And ſtill with ſcorching noſtrils breathing flame.* Ib. 5. 960.

(d) This indeed is (as *Lipſius* obſerves, mirandum, ſtupendum, divinum) *wonderful, amazing, divine.* The late ingenious Mr. *Hogarth*, in his *Analyſis of Beauty* hath applied the like obſervation to the *human face*; which he calls *a compoſed variety*; for a variety uncompoſed and without deſign is confuſion and deformity. p. 17.

(*e*) Puta enim prudentiam animal eſſe. *Muret.* Puta animal prudentiam eſſe; but this is to ſuppoſe the thing in queſtion: *Gronovius* therefore reads with the MSS. puta prudentiam eſſe, i. e. faciamus periculum in prudentia.

(f) *Seneca* here ſeems to be witty upon his brethren the *Stoics*, with whom the *world* was both an *animal* and *God*. Concerning which *Varro* ſaith, Quomodo poteſt *rotundus* eſſe, ſine capite, ſine præputio. But *Plato* likewiſe was of this opinion; yet in *Timæus* he writes, *that it wants ears and eyes and feet, becauſe God wanteth not any inſtruments of this kind, as compelling and continuing all things in himſelf.* And to this both *Varro* and *Seneca* ſeem to allude. *Gentil.* l. 2. Parerg.

(g) In the ſenſe of *Horace*; totus, teres, atque *rotundus.* S. II. 7.

(*h*) This *principal* or governing part of the ſoul, ſome *(Ariſtotle, Plato, Pythagoras, Hippocratus)* place, ἐν τῇ ἡμετέρᾳ σφαιροειδεῖ κεφαλῇ, *in the head*; but the Stoics *(Empedocles, Parmenides,* and *Democritus)* place it *in the heart.*—Thus *Auſonius*;

> Mens quæ cœleſti ſenſu rigat emeritum cor:
> Cor vegetum, mundi inſtar habens, animæ vigor ac vis.

So the *Epicureans*, Lucret. iii. 139.

> Sed caput eſſe quaſi et dominari in corpore toto
> Conſilium quod nos *animum* mentemque vocamus;
> Idque ſitum mediâ regione in pectoris hæret.
> —— *I muſt affirm the* ſoul *and* mind
> *Make up one ſingle nature cloſely join'd:*
> *But yet the* mind's *the head, and ruling part,*
> *Call'd* Reaſon, *and 'tis ſeated in the heart.* Creech.

(*i*) O triſtes ineptias] Turpe eſt difficiles habere nugas,
Et ſtultus labor eſt ineptiarum. *Martial.*

(*k*) Like the ſummary of all Chriſtian virtues, *Charity, it ſeeketh not her own.* 1. Cor. 13.

EPISTLE CXIV.

On Language, Style, and Compoſition.

YOU are pleaſed to aſk me, *Lucilius*, how it comes to paſs that at certain times the public language becomes corrupt; and whence it is that the minds of men are ſo fickle, and inclined to error; as at one time

time to delight in pompous, ſwelling expreſſions, and at another, the ſpeech is ſo frittered into quavers, that when they talk, you would rather think they were ſinging: why, at one time, bold and extravagant periods have been in vogue; and, at another, broken ſentences, ſo very conciſe, that much more is underſtood than expreſſed; and why, in another age the uſe of metaphors, and other figures of ſpeech, by too frequent uſe, have been moſt immoderately abuſed. The reaſon is this, which you have often heard, and which is become proverbial among the *Greeks*, Talis hominibus fuit oratio, qualis vita, *as is the life of a man, ſuch is his diſcourſe* (*a*). As then the behaviour and actions of a man are, for the moſt part, anſwerable to their diſcourſe, ſo the common dialect is oftentimes an imitation, or the reſult of public manners. ——When a government hath loſt all regard to diſcipline, and given itſelf up to delicacies, it betrays its luxurious diſpoſition by ribaldry and wantonneſs of ſpeech; I mean not of one or two particulars, but as it is received and approved in general.

The ſoul and the underſtanding are ſeldom of two different colours: if that be ſound, ſedate, grave, and temperate; this likewiſe will be moderate and ſober: but where that is corrupt and vitiated, this alſo is affected. See you not, when the ſoul languiſheth, how liſtleſs the body is? the limbs become feeble, and the feet drag heavily along: that, if it be effeminate, the little mincing ſtep diſcovers the infirmity; whereas when it is vigorous and active, the ſtep is more free and bold: or, if it be mad, or what is akin to madneſs, if it be paſſionate, how turbulent is every motion! Men in ſuch a ſtate, never walk, but are hurried along; ſo affected is the underſtanding by the diſpoſition of the ſoul: nor can it be otherwiſe; ſince it wholly depends upon, and is blended with it; it is entirely formed by this, ever obeys it, and ſeeks no other law of action, but what this commands.

The manner of *Mecænas'* living is too notorious than, at this time, to need a deſcription. How prettily he walk'd! how delicate he was! how deſirous to be gaped upon! how unwilling to conceal any of his foibles! Well then; and was not his diſcourſe as diſſolute as his life? Yes;

Yes; he had as much affectation and vanity in his ſpeech, as in his dreſs, his equipage, his houſe, and his wife. He was indeed a man of great abilities (*b*), had he properly applied them; had he not ſtudied an obſcurity of ſtyle, though at the ſame time it ſeemed to flow with an air of elocution. You will find him therefore talking like a drunken man, intricate, and roving from one idea to another, and taking amazing liberties. I will give you a ſpecimen, (from his book *de cultu ſuo.)*

—— Quid purius (*c*)
Amne, ſylviſque ripa comantibus,
Vides ut alveum lintribus arent (*d*)
Verſoque vado remi iciant hortos!
Quid ſi quis fœminæ cirro criſpatæ
Labris columbatur incipitque
Suſpirans, cervice et lapſæ ſanatur.——
More tyranni irremediabilis
Rimantur factio, epulis lagenâque
Tentant domos, et ſæpe mortem exigunt,
Geniumque feſto vix ſuo teſtem.
Tenuis cerei fila et crepacem molam
Focum mater aut uxor inveſtiunt.

What can be purer than the running ſtream
Whoſe banks with a leafy coverture are ſkreen'd?
See how they plough the channel with their ſkiffs,
And row o'er the reflected gardens!——
What if ſome pretty damſel, twiſts and curls
Her jetty locks, and with her pouting lips
Bills like a dove, and now begins to ſigh,
That none are ſmitten with her beauteous bloom!—
Tyrants implacable, and their fell faction
Pry into ev'ry corner of the houſe,
For ſome rich flaggon, or ſuch delicates
As they can find; and oftentimes exact
Death of the owners——
The Genius *ſcarce is witneſs to his own feaſt,*

 When

When by the glimmering of a ſlender taper,
The mother, or the wiſe, inveſt the hearth,
Loud-cracking with the ſalt-beſprinkled meal.—

When you read ſuch affected and hyperbolical ſtuff, do you not immediately conclude, that it muſt come *from one,* who always goes about the city in a looſe robe (*e*)? For even when he was *Regent* in the abſence of *Auguſtus,* he gave orders in a diſhabille: *from one,* who in the palace, in the forum, in the tribunal, and in every public aſſembly, appeared with his face muffled, ſo that nothing could be ſeen but his ears. Like a runaway, as repreſented in a comedy *(f)*: *from one,* who, (during the tumult of a civil war, when the whole city was alarmed, and even in arms) walked careleſsly about the ſtreets, attended with only two eunuchs, better men however than himſelf: from one, who a thouſand times married his wife (*g*).—The foregoing expreſſions, ſo wretchedly conſtructed, ſo ungrammatical, and negligently thrown out, repugnant to every manner of writing, ſhew that his morals were not leſs ſtrange, depraved, and ſingular.

He was remarkable indeed and highly commended for his tenderneſs and good-nature. He made no uſe of the ſword, and abſtained from ſhedding blood: nor in any other reſpect did he take an unpermitted liberty. And yet this eſteem and praiſe he himſelf entirely ſpoiled by that monſtrous affectation of delicacy in his diſcourſe. For he appeared from hence to be a meer *Fribble,* rather than mild. Such obſcurities in expreſſion, ſuch uncouth words; the meaning of them ſometimes great and ſublime, but quite enervated in the delivery, plainly ſhew to any one that obſerves them, that the man's head was certainly turned by too great a flow of happineſs; which indeed is ſometimes the fault of the man, and not ſeldom of the times.

Where the happineſs of a ſtate hath univerſally ſpread around the principles of luxury; men firſt begin to be more curious in dreſs and outward ornament; next, extravagant expence and care are beſtowed upon their houſes, in order to make them as airy as their country-ſeats;

ſeats; that their walls may ſhine with the richeſt marble from foreign countries; that the roofs may be embelliſhed with gold; and the ſplendor of the pavement be anſwerable to that of their ceilings: after this they are exceeding nice in their furniture. From hence they proceed to ſet out their tables magnificently with the moſt coſtly diſhes; and commendation is ſought from novelties, and the changing of antient cuſtoms, that ſuch things as were uſed to be ſerved up firſt, ſhould now come in the laſt courſe (*b*): and ſuch as were preſented to the gueſts at coming in, are now reſerved for their going away.

When the mind has got an habit of diſdaining things in common uſe, and looking upon them as mean and vile, it then ſeeks out for new language alſo; and brings into play again ſuch words as are antique and obſolete; or coining new ones, introduceth ſtrange uncouth terms, or wreſt ſuch as are known, to another meaning. Any word newly come in vogue is eſteemed elegant, and metaphors every day grow more bold and frequent. Some are very conciſe in their expreſſions, and expect to be admired for leaving the hearer in ſuſpenſe: others are as much too prolix, ſpinning out their meaning to an intolerable length. Some men are cautious of falling into vice, (as they generally do, who intend any thing great) but at the ſame time love the vice itſelf. Whenever therefore you find men delight in looſe diſcourſe, you may be aſſured they are not ſound in their morals. As the luxury of entertainment, and expenſive dreſs, are a certain ſign that the ſtate is decaying; ſo a licentiouſneſs of ſpeech, if frequent, ſhews alſo, that the minds of the people, that delight in ſuch converſation, are in a bad way.

You ought not to wonder, that this corruption of language is received as well by the great vulgar as the ſmall; for they differ not in judgment but in dreſs and fortune. This is rather what you ſhould wonder at, that they not only praiſe what is vicious, but the vices themſelves. For this is uſual: there was no wit paſſing, however looſe and ſarcaſtical, but what eaſily obtained pardon (*i*). Point me out any man you pleaſe, of note and reputation, and I will tell you, wherein, the age he lived in, winked at his foibles, or knowingly diſſembled them. I will give you

you ſome, I ſay, of the greateſt renown, who have been reputed moſt excellent men, and propoſed as admirable examples; whom yet if a man preſumes to examine and cenſure, he will quite demoliſh them; for ſo many vices are blended with their virtues, that it will be difficult to ſeparate them.

Add now, that *language hath no certain criterion:* the cuſtom and faſhions of the place, which are perpetually changing, make likewiſe a change in the language: many affect to borrow words from another age; they ſpeak in the antient ſtyle of the *twelve tables.* *Gracchus*, and *Craſſus*, and *Curio* of a later date, are too polite and modern for them. They go back as far as *Appius* and *Coruncanus* (*k*). Some, on the other hand, while they approve of nothing but what is trivial and in common uſe, fall into meanneſs: both of them faulty, in a different way; as much indeed as if they were to uſe in their diſcourſe, the moſt pompous, high-ſounding, and poetical expreſſions, in order to avoid the more neceſſary and common words; the one I ſay is as faulty as the other. The one dreſſeth himſelf like a coxcomb; the other like a ſlave: the one picks the hair from the legs; the other not ſo much as from the arm-pits.

Let us paſs on now to compoſition. What a number of faults could I here point out to you? Some approve of a rough and crabbed ſtyle; whatever ſentence flows in a ſmooth and more pleaſing ſtrain, they purpoſely fling it out. They would have no period without its ruggedneſs. They think it manly and ſtrong, when it ſtrikes the ear with an unequal ſound. Of others, it cannot be called compoſition but modulation, ſo ſoft and ſoothing is the ſtrain. Ah! why need I mention that ſort of compoſition, in which ſome principal words are poſtponed, and come creeping in at the end of a ſentence? Or that which is ſmooth throughout, and clear in the cloſe, like *Cicero's* ending with a gentle cadence, and anſwering his uſual manner and meaſure? Sentences in general are not only faulty, when they are either weak and puerile, or ſo bold and luſcious as not to preſerve decency and modeſty; but if they are too florid,

florid, or too ſoft and ſweet, without any point or deſign, they are nothing more than mere ſound.

Now theſe are the faults which are introduced by ſome one who is reputed eloquent: whereupon others imitate him, and ſo on, from one to another. Hence, *Salluſt* being in vogue, curt ſentences, unexpected cadences, and obſcure brevity, were reckoned beauties. *Arruntius*, a man of uncommon frugality, who wrote the hiſtory of the *Punic* wars, was a follower of *Salluſt*, and became eminent in that mode of writing. *Salluſt* hath ſomewhere this expreſſion, exercitum argento facit, *by ſilver* he made *an army*, i. e. he raiſed an army by bounty-money. *Arruntius* began to be fond of this expreſſion; and therefore uſed it in almoſt every page. He ſays in one place, Fugam noſtri *fecere*, *Our men* made *a flight*: in another, Hiero rex Syracuſanorum bellum *fecit*, Hiero, *king of* Syracuſe, *made war*. In another, Quæ audita Panormitanos dedere Romanis *fecere*, *Which things being heard*, made *the* Panormitans *ſurrender to the* Romans. I had a mind to give you this taſte of him; but his whole book is compoſed in this manner.

Such words as are very rare in *Salluſt* are frequent in *Arruntius*, and uſed perpetually, even when there is not the leaſt occaſion for them. *Salluſt* fell upon them accidentally, but *Arruntius* ſought them. And you ſee the conſequence, when any one takes an error for his model. *Salluſt* had ſaid, Aquis hiemantibus, *the waters* being wintry; upon this, *Arrunteus*, in his firſt book of the *Punic* war, is pleaſed to ſay, Repente tempeſtas hiemavit, *on a ſudden the ſtorm* wintered: and in another place when he would tell you that it was a cold year, he ſaith, totus *hiemavit* annus, *the whole year* was winter. And again, Inde ſexaginta onerararias, leves præter militem, et neceſſarios nautarum, *hiemante* Aquilone, miſit, *From thence, beſide the ſoldiery, and neceſſary mariners, he ſent away ſixty merchantmen*, during the winter *of the north wind*. In ſhort, he thruſts this word in, where-ever he has an opportunity. *Salluſt* ſomewhere ſays, Inter arma civilia æqui boni *famas* petit, *Even amid civil broils he ſeeks* the glories *of a good and juſt man*. *Arruntius* could not refrain from laying hold of theſe words, and forthwith inſerts in his firſt book, ingentes eſſe *famas* de Regulo, *great were the* glories *of* Regulus.

Theſe however and the like quaint expreſſions, that are picked up by imitation, are not ſigns of a luxurious fancy, or a corrupt mind; for they muſt be proper, and naturally his own, from whence to judge of an author's affections. The ſpeech of a paſſionate man is paſſionate, and the more violent according as he is irritated: as the ſpeech of a fribble is delicate and flowing: as you may obſerve in thoſe, who pluck out what beard they have with knippers, or here and there a hair; or who ſhave the lip cloſe, and let the reſt grow as it can; who chuſe their cloaks of ſome odd colour, and are very conſpicuous for the richneſs of their gowns; and who deſire that nothing they do ſhould paſs unſeen; they invite and provoke every one to turn their eyes upon them, and care not how much you cenſure or laugh at them, if you vouchſafe to ſee them.

Such then is *Mecænas*, and ſuch his ſtyle, as it is of all thoſe who err not accidentally, but knowingly and willingly. Now this ariſes from a great defect of the mind. As in drunkenneſs the tongue falters not, 'till ſuch time as the mind is overpowered by its load, and reaſon is overſet or quite loſt: ſo this manner of ſpeech (what is it elſe but drunkenneſs?) is never impertinent, 'till the mind fails. This therefore muſt firſt be cured; as it is from this that ſenſe and words flow; and from this the habit, the countenance, the gait: ſo long as the mind continues ſound, the ſpeech is robuſt, ſtrong, and manly; if this be dejected, all its dependents ſink at once.

——— Rege incolumi mens omnibus una eſt,
Amiſſo rupêre fidem.—*Virg*. G. iv. 212. (Speaking of bees)
While he (the King) *ſurvives, in concord and content,*
The commons live, by no diviſions rent;
But the great monarch, Death, diſſolves the government. Dryden.

The mind, or ſoul, is our king within, while he is ſafe and well, the reſt continue dutiful: they ſubmit, and obey: when he wavers ever ſo little, the reſt fluctuate in doubt; and when he gives himſelf up to pleaſure,

pleaſure, his every art and action are enfeebled, and all his efforts looſe and languid.

To go on with the metaphor——Our ſoul is ſometimes a king, and ſometimes a tyrant: a king, when he obſerves what is right and fit; takes due care of the body committed to his charge, and commands nothing that is baſe, nothing that is mean: but when he is paſſionate, covetous, or over-nice, he aſſumes a dire and deteſtable name, even that of tyrant. Then do the unruly paſſions ſeize him, and ſollicit him inceſſantly; rejoicing at firſt in their triumph; as a people are apt to do, when they think themſelves happy in ſome largeſs from a tyrant, deſigning to enſlave them; and, being already full, accept of more than they can digeſt. But when the diſeaſe hath more and more conſumed his ſtrength, and a reliſh for pleaſure hath ſunk deep into his marrow and nerves; elevated at the ſight of thoſe things, which his over-eagerneſs, and too fond deſires render him unfit for, inſtead of enjoying them himſelf, he is contented with ſeeing others enjoy them; he ſtands pimp to the luſt of others; and is only a witneſs of thoſe delights, amid which he is ſtarved by too great plenty. Nor is it ſo grateful to abound in worldly pleaſure, as irkſome, that he is not able to ſwallow down ſo great a preparation of dainties, or wallow with his troop of bawds and harlots: it grieves him to be deprived of the greateſt part of his ſuppoſed felicity by the narrow receptacle of the body.

But is not this madneſs, my *Lucilius*, that not a man of us thinks himſelf mortal, or reflects on his infirmities. Nay, that he does not know, he is but *one*. Behold our ſmoking kitchens, and the ſweating cooks running from fire to fire: could you imagine that it was for one belly, that proviſions are making with ſo great a buſtle? Behold our cellars and ſtore-houſes, full of the vintages of many years! Would you think that it was for one paunch that the wines of ſo many conſuls reigns, and of ſo many different climates, are ſtored up for the ſame purpoſe? Behold in how many places the earth is broken up! how many thouſand huſbandmen are employed in digging and ploughing! Would you think that it is for one belly that men ſow both in *Africa*

and

and *Syria*? Believe me, we ſhould be more healthful, and keep our deſires within proper bounds, were each of us to reckon himſelf but *one*; and at the ſame time to take dimenſions of his body; and learn that it cannot receive much, or retain it long. Nothing however can contribute more to temperance and moderation in all things, than frequent reflection on the brevity and uncertainty of life. Whatſoever you do, think on mortality.

ANNOTATIONS, &c.

(*a*) So, *Plato*, Οἷος ὁ λογος τοιῦτος ὁ τροπος. And *Solon*, τὸν λογον εἴδωλον εἶναι τῶν ἔργων. And yet *Eraſmus* ſays he knows not what this proverb is in *Greek*, unleſs it be

Ἀνδρὸς χαρακτὴρ ἐκ λόγου γνωρίζεται

Euripides, much to the ſame purpoſe, μωρὰ γὰρ μωρὸς λέγει. *Solomon* frequently, *the tongue of the wiſe uſeth knowledge aright, but the mouth of fools poureth out fooliſhneſs.* Prov. 15. 2. *The heart of fools proclaimeth fooliſhneſs.* xii. 23.

(*b*) Sen. Ep. 19. *Fitzoſborne's* Lett.

(*c*) I have given you the words as they ſtand in *Muretus's* edition; but to extract a ſeeming meaning from ſuch nonſenſe, I have tranſlated them from conjecture and the various readings—al. quid turpius.—Remittant hortos, al. remigant.—Colubratur—laxâ feratur al. ferantur.—Nemo tyranni al. nemore, ne more.——They are ſuppoſed to be (imperfect) hendecaſyllables: and the ſenſe, relating to ſome tyrant's behaviour.——

(*d*) As in *Virgil*, viii. 96.——Virideſque ſecat placido æquore ſilvas,

—— *and cut reflected foreſts on the waves.* Lauderdale.

Alike bold, Ἀλίμενον αἰθέρος αὔλακα τέμνων. *Ariſtoph.* Av. 1400.

Cutting the ſhoreleſs furrows *of the air.*

(*e*) Improbe, quid tandem tunicæ nocuere ſolutæ?

Aut tibi ventoſi quid nocuêre ſinus?

(*f*) As it was uſual for the ſcribbles of that age to cover their heads with their gown to keep off the ſun.

Ut iſti Græci palliati capite operto qui ambulant. *Plaut*. Curc.

And *Plutarch* cenſuring the freed man of *Pompey*, ſays, Domino ſtante accumbebat ἔχων δ' αὐτὸν κατὰ τῆς κεφαλῆς τὸ ἱμάτιον. And *Petronius* deſcribing *Trimalchio*; Pallio coccino adraſum incluſerat caput, *we could not refrain from laughing, when we ſaw his bald pate peeping out of a ſcarlet mantle.* See *Lipſ.* Amphitheat. xx.

(*g*) *Terentia*—Somewhat hyperbolical; from their perpetual quarrels and divorces.

(*h*) This *Martial* obſerves with regard to lettice, or a ſalad:

Claudere quæ menſas lactuca ſolebat avorum,
Dic mihi, cur noſtras inchoat illa dapes?
The ſallad now comes firſt; in ages paſt,
Our anceſtors reſerv'd it to the laſt.

Plutarch, (Sympol. viii. 9.) recounting the cauſes of new diſeaſes alledges this as one; the cuſ-

toms

toms of the antients being more wholefome. Τὴν τάξιν κ. τ. λ. *The change of order in our feeding has a great influence on the alteration of our bodies; the cold courfes, as they were called, formerly confifting of oyfters, lobfters, fallad, and the like, now make the firft courfe, whereas they were formerly the laft.* I know not but that I may obferve the reverfe of our Englifh pudding.

(*i*) See *Webb*, on painting, p. 66.

(*k*) *Appius Claudius*, Conful. U. C. 489.——*Coruncanus*, the firft who from a Plebeian was made *Pontifex Max*. U. C. 489. Liv. Id.

Si tibi vetuftatis tantus eft amor, pari ftudio in verba prifca redeamus, quibus *Salii* canunt, et auguras aves confulunt, et Decemviri tabulas condiderunt. Jamdudum his renuntiatum eft, et fucceffio temporum placita priora mutavit. Symmach. iii. 44. *If you have fuch an affection for antiquity, let us return to the old language, in which the* Salii *fung their hymns, the Augurs confulted the birds, and the* Decemviri *formed the twelve tables. Thefe have long fince been renounced; and a fucceffion of ages hath changed the old decrees.*

(*l*) Atque ita hircum olet, *Lipfius.*

EPISTLE CXV.

On the fame. And the Beauty of Virtue.

I WOULD not have you, my *Lucilius*, too curious and follicitous concerning ftyle and compofition. Many things of much greater importance call for your attention. Confider rather the *matter* than the manner of your writing. I could wifh that you were more employed in thinking than in fcribbling; efpecially if you fo think, that you may apply your thoughts more and more to your own good; and feal, as it were, the fubftance of them on your heart (*a*).

Know that when you fee or hear a laboured and over-nice difcourfe, that the mind of the author is taken up with trifles and vanity. The truly great man is more remifs and free; in whatever he is pleafed to utter you will find more of confidence and folidity, than careful curiofity. You have feen and you know, many fmart fellows, whofe beards and locks are dreffed with the niceft art, as if juft taken out of a bandbox (*b*). From fuch, you can expect nothing that is manly, nothing folid. Speech is the image of the mind (*c*): if it be clipped and trimmed (*d*) very ſpruce, depend upon it the mind is not ſincere and ſound. Spruceneſs and affectation are not manly accompliſhments. Could we inſpect the ſoul of a good man, how fair, how beautiful, holy, magnificent, and pleaſing would it appear! Juſtice ſhining here, and there Fortitude! here Temperance, and there Prudence! Beſides theſe, Frugality, Continence, Forbearance, and Liberty, and Courteouſneſs, and (who would think it?) Humanity, *that* ſo rare and the choiceſt good in man, would then ſhine in their full luſtre. And then, O ye Gods! what grace, what weight and authority, would diſcretion and elegance, that moſt eminent qualification! add unto the reſt? No one would think him amiable, but who at the ſame time thought him venerable.

And was any one to view this image, in yet an higher and more brilliant light than all worldly glories can give, would he not ſtand aghaſt and ſurprized, as at the ſight of ſome deity, and tacitly pray, that he might behold him with impunity (*e*)? And then invited by the benignity of her *(virtue's)* aſpect, kneel down and adore her; and having contemplated, and for ſome time conſidered the ſame, as riſing far above the meaſure of ſuch things as the ſight of mortals is uſed to; her eyes ſparkling with a mild indeed, but yet a living flame, would he not with awe and reverence break out, in thoſe words of *Virgil*.

O quàm te memorem, Virgo! namque haud tibi vultus
Mortalis, nec vox hominem ſonat.——
Sis felix, noſtrumque leves quæcunque laborem.——
O virgin, or what other name you bear
Above that ſtyle; O more than mortal fair!
Your voice and mien celeſtial birth betray!—
Let not in vain an humble ſuppliant pray.—

She will be propitious and aſſiſt us, if we duly honour her. But ſhe is not honoured by the ſlaughtering of bulls *(f)*, nor by the richeſt offering of gold and ſilver, or by gifts caſts into the treaſury; but by a pious will, and integrity of heart. Every one I ſay would be tranſported with the love of her, were they to behold her in her genuine beauty. But alas! many things now ſtand in our way, and either

dazzle

dazzle our eyes with too great ſplendor, or retain them ſtill in darkneſs. But as the ſight is wont to be cleared and ſharpened by certain medicines; ſo were we to clear from the ſight of the mind all impediments, we ſhould be able to behold *naked virtue* in all her charms; though tabernacled in the body; nay, though poverty, meanneſs of condition, and even infamy, ſtood between us: we ſhould behold, I ſay, her incomparable beauty, though cloathed in rags. As on the contrary, we ſhould ſee iniquity, and the foul ruſt of a cankered mind *(g)*; though beaming around with the ſplendid rays of wealth, and though our eyes are dazzled with the falſe light of power and honours.

Then ſhall we underſtand on what contemptible things we beſtow our admiration; like children, who think glaring trifles of great value, and prefer their penny bracelets and toys to the love of either fathers or brothers. What difference is there, as *Ariſto* ſays, between them and us, unleſs that we are more expenſively ſilly, in being mad after pictures and ſtatues? *They* are pleaſed with the ſhells and little ſtones of various colours that are found on the ſea-ſhore; and *we* with the variegated marble pillars, whether brought from *Sandy Egypt* or the deſerts of *Africa*, they form a grand portico, or ſupport a capacious room for banqueting. But herein ſurely we are the more ridiculous; ſince when we ſo greatly admire the walls inlaid with plates of marble, we know what is behind them, and what they ſerve to hide; and thus it is that we impoſe upon our eyes: for when we ſpread the leafy gold upon our houſes, what is it but a mere counterfeit that ſo delights us; ſince we know that beneath this ſhew of gold is concealed vile and worm-eaten wood? Nor are our walls and cielings only thus thinly ornamented; but all that ſtate in which you ſee the great and noble ſo proudly ſtrut, is nothing more than *gilded happineſs* (*h*). Look within, and you will learn that miſery and vileneſs lie concealed beneath this gawdy ſhew of dignity (*i*).

It is this very thing, gold, that firſt raiſed ſo many judges and magiſtrates; and ſtill governs them with its bewitching charms: this, which from the time it firſt grew into requeſt, hath baniſhed all true worth

and

and honour. Both as buyers and ſellers, we regard not how good a thing is, but what it will fetch upon ſale. Profit is all; incited by this we are both pious and impious; we follow what is right and fit, ſo long as there are any hopes of gaining thereby, but are eaſily drawn into vice, when it promiſeth a greater advantage. Our parents originally inſtilled into us a veneration for gold and ſilver. And this principle, being ſowed in our minds when young, ſtrikes a deep root, and grows up with us: and then, all the world, in other reſpects of different opinions, agree herein: this they are ever gaping after themſelves; this they wiſh for to all their relatives; and this, as the greateſt of all human things, when they would appear grateful, they conſecrate and offer up to the Gods. In ſhort, the manners of men are ſuch, that poverty is a curſed diſgrace, and conſequently deſpiſed by the rich, and hateful to the poor.

To this beſides are added the ingenious labours of the poets, who are for ever inflaming this affection in us, by recommending riches as the only ornament and honour of life. According to them it ſeems, that the immortal Gods cannot beſtow greater bleſſings, nor have greater themſelves:

Regia ſolis erat ſublimibus alta columnis
Clara micante auro.---(*Ov. Met.* ii. 1.)
The ſun's bright palace on high columns rais'd,
With burniſh'd gold, and flaming rubies blaz'd.

And behold his chariot,

Aureus axis erat, temo aureus, aurea ſummæ
Curvatura rotæ, radiorum argenteus ordo. (107.)
A golden axle did the work uphold,
Gold was the beam, the wheels were orb'd with gold:
The ſpokes in rows of ſilver.---Sewell.

Laſtly, the age they would have thought to be the beſt and happieſt, is ſtyled *the Golden*. Nor are there wanting thoſe among the tragic poets, who barter innocence, health and reputation, for gold.

(*k*) Sine me vocari peſſimum, ut dives vocer.
An dives omnes quærimus; nemo an bonus.

Non

Non quare, et unde; quid habeat, tantum rogant.
Ubique tanti quisque, quantum habuit, fuit.
Quid habere nobis turpe sit, quæris? nihil.
Aut dives opto vivere, aut pauper mori.
Bene moritur, qui dum moritur, lucrum facit.
Pecunia ingens generis humani bonum.
Cui non voluptas matris, aut blandæ potest
Par esse prolis, non sacer meritis parens.
Tam dulce si quid Veneris in vultu micat
Meritò illa amores cœlitum atque hominum movet.
Let me be rich, and call me what you please.——
But is he rich? all cry. Not, is he good?
They ask not, why? or whence? but what *he has.*
Esteem in all, is measur'd by the purse.
Say, what 'tis scandalous to have? why, nothing.
If rich, I wish to live; if poor, to die.
'Tis he dies well, who can enrich his heir.
Money's the greatest blessing man can have.
Not the sweet pleasure that a mother feels,
Or children give, or a deserving sire;
Nor ev'n the sparkling beauty of the fair,
Can rival this delight of gods and men.

When the latter part of these verses were recited in a tragedy of *Euripides*, the whole audience rose up tumultuously; and with great resentment condemned the actor, author, and poetry. But *Euripides* sprung upon the stage, and humbly begged their patience, 'till they should see the catastrophe of the wretch who had made this extraordinary speech. It was *Bellerophons* (V.) (*l*), who here, from poetical justice, met with that condign punishment, which every guilty wretch feels in his own breast. For avarice never escapes with impunity.———O what floods of tears, what incessant toil does she exact from her devotees! How miserable does she make those who only live in expectation! How much more miserable those, who have obtained their fondest wishes? For behold! what anxieties and daily cares attend on men, according to their several possessions! Money is often possessed with greater torment than that by which it was acquired, What bitter ſighs do their loſſes create? which heavy as they fell upon them, ſtill feel heavier. Laſtly, though fortune ſhould take nothing from them, whatever ſhe denies them further, is deemed a loſs.

But all men think ſuch a one happy, they call him rich, and wiſh themſelves in his condition. It may be ſo. What then? Do you think any one can be in a worſe condition, than the man who is envied by others, and wretched in himſelf? I only wiſh that all who are greedy of wealth, would ſeriouſly and honeſtly confer with the rich themſelves. I wiſh that all who gape after titles and honours would conſult the ambitious; and ſuch as have reached the firſt ſtate of dignity! Truly, I believe, they would change their minds; as the great themſelves do, who are ſtill hunting after ſomething, and condemning what they before admired. For no one is contented with his own happineſs, tho' it flows in upon him to his wiſh. Still do they complain of their wrong deſigns, and unhappy ſucceſs; and had much rather be what they were before.

Therefore it is philoſophy alone that can give this truly valuable bleſſing; *to do nothing that requires repentance.* And this ſolid happineſs, which no tempeſt can ſhake, is not to be conferred, by the ſtudy of apt and well-choſen words, or a ſweet fluency of diſcourſe: let it flow as it will, ſo that the mind be calm and compoſed; ſo long as this continues truly great, and firm in its own conſequence, neglectful of the opinion of others; and enjoys complacency in thoſe very things, that to others are diſpleaſing. Such a one eſtimates his proficiency in life by his conduct; and rightly judgeth that his knowledge is to be valued according to his not knowing, either how to covet, or how to fear.

ANNO-

ANNOTATIONS, &c.

(*a*) Et veluti figues] So the Greeks, ἐνσημαίνειν.—τὰ μαθήματα δι' ἁπλότητα τῶν ψυχῶν ὡς ζῷδος ἐνσημαινόμενα. *Basil.* The *Latins* say *ponere signa*.

—— Non est mihi tempus aventi
Ponere signa novis præceptis.—*Hor.* S. ii. 4. 1.
I have not leisure now, to mark new rules.

(*b*) De capsulâ totos] *Lipsius.* al. tortos. *Scaliger* reads it, Descapulatos, and applies it to those who affect a loose robe, or *undress*.

Effluit effuso queis toga laxa sinu. *Tibull.* 1.
Malthinus tunicis demissis ambulat. Hor. S. i. 2. 25.
—— *Walks with his gown below his heels.*

(*c*) Oratio vultus est animi.] Much the same with what he had said in the foregoing Epistle, Talis est oratio, qualis vita. So *Democritus* ap. Laert. calls, *speech*, εἴδωλον τοῦ βίου, than which says *Erasmus* nothing can be more just. *Man is known by his speech as brazen vessels by their ringing.* And to this *Persius* alludes,

—— Sonat vitium percussa malignè
Respondet viridi non cocta fidelia limo. iii. 21.
A flaw is in thy ill-bak'd vessel found,
'Tis hollow, and returns a jarring sound. Dryden.

There is another sentence in *Latin* to the same purpose.

Tale ingenium, qualis oratio. *See* Erasm. p. 1456.

To which *Terence* alludes.—Nam mihi quale ingenium habeas, fuit indicium oratio. *Heauton.* We say in English, *speech is the picture of the mind.*

(*d*) Si circumtonsa est] *Varro* in Fragm. Alii sunt circumtonsi et torti atque unctuli, ut mangonis videantur esse servi; *others are so trimmed and curled, that you would take them for the slaves upon sale.*

(*e*) Ut fas sit vidisse] So in *Livy*, l. 1. *Proculus*, at the sight of *Romulus*, (supposed to have been made a God) venerebundus adstitit, precibus petens, ut contra intueri fas esset. It was the general opinion of all nations that no one can see God; according to that of the Evangelist—*No man hath seen God at any time.*

In a Note (in my translation) of *Vida's* hymns, (published in 1725) I have observed, That when the *Shechinah*, or divine glory filled the tabernacle, *Moses* could not enter therein but upon peril of his life. *Exod.* xl. 35. Nor could the Priests afterwards enter the temple that was built by *Solomon*, *when the glory of the Lord had filled that house.* ii. Chron. vii. 1. We understand therefore by his appearance to *Jacob*, *Moses*, &c. *Gen.* xxxii. 30. *Exod.* xxiv. 20, &c. that somewhat was obvious to their senses that plainly discovered the more immediate presence of God; so that they could no more doubt of it, than of one talking with them *face to face*; not that there was any similitude, whereby idolatry might pretend to represent him. Deut. iv. 15. Job, iv. 16. i. John, iv. 12.

(*f*) So the Prophet *Isaiah*, *To what purpose is the multitude of your sacrifices unto me?* saith the Lord; *I am full of the burnt-offerings of rams, and the fat of fed beasts; I delight not in the blood of bullocks or of lambs, or of he goats, &c. Wash ye, make ye clean, put away the evil of your doings from before mine eyes; cease to do evil; learn to do well; seek judgment, relieve the oppressed; judge the*

 fatherless,

fatherless, plead for the widow.—Come now, let us reason together, saith the Lord; though your sins be as scarlet, they shall be white as snow; though they be red like crimson, they shall be as wool. Is. i. 11—20. In burnt-offerings and sacrifices thou hast had no pleasure. Heb. x. 6. See i. Sam. xv. 22. Ps. xl. 6. li. 16. Is. lxvi. 3. Heb. xv. 6. Matth. xii. 7.

(g) Æruginosi animi veternum] al. ærumnosi. But *Gronovius* asks what connection there can be between malitiam, and ærumnosi, *iniquity*, and *the being unfortunate?* They are ærumnosi, who undergo great hardships, which they did not deserve, as *Hercules, Ulysses, Regulus*; let the paradoxical *Stoics* dispute what they please, concerning the last. This word, *ærumnosus*, belongs to Fortune, not to any fault or vice in the man. He therefore reads *æruginosi*, and supports it from the following:

—— Hic nigræ succus loliginis, hæc est
Ærugo mera.——Hor. S. l. 4. 100.
——— *Envy's weed*
Thus shoots unseen, and choaks fair friendship's seed. Duncomb.
—— Hæc animos ærugo——
Cum semel imbuerit——Hor. A. P. 331.
When this base rust hath crusted o'er their souls. Creech.
——— miseràque ærugine captus
Adlatras nomen———*Mart.* ii. 61.

(*h*) Bracteata felicitas] *Vett. Gloss.* Bratteam, *seu* Bracteam, tenuem auri argentique laminam; *a thin plate of gold or silver.* Bracteatum lacunar. *Sidon.* i. 10. Mentis aureæ dictum bracteatum. *Plin.* Paneg —Vid. Juret, ad Symm. l. i. Ep. 16.

(*i*) Alluding to what King *Antigonus* said to a certain woman admiring his felicity, O mulier si scias quantum mali sub fascia ista *(diademate)* lateat, nec humi jacentem tollas: *O woman, if thou didst know what afflictions lie under this diadem, you would not stoop to take it off the ground.*

(*k*) Sine me vocari.]———*Gronovius* reads it, *sine me*, as

— Populus me sibilat, at mihi plaudo
Ipse domi. Hor. S. i. 1. 66.
Let the poor fools hiss me, where'er I come,
I bless myself, to see my bags at home. Creech.

These verses are said to be taken from different places, the latter from the Greek of *Euripides* ap. Stob. Serm. 89.

——'Ω χρυσὲ, δεξίωμα κάλλιστον βροτοῖς,
Ὡς οὐδὲ μήτηρ ἡδονὰς τοίας ἔχει
Οὐ παῖδες ἀνθρώποισιν, ὁ φίλος πατήρ.
Εἰ δ' ἡ Κύπρις τοιοῦτον ὀφθαλμοῖς ὁρᾷ
Οὐ θαῦμ' ἔρωτας μυρίους αὐτὴν τρέφειν.
Pecunia, &c.

(*l*) *Lipsius* observes, that if *Seneca* means here the poet's *Bellerophon*, (Hor. Od. iii. 7. 15.) he cannot see what *gold* has to do in the case. *Bellerophon* was punished for his pride and ambition.

EPISTLE

EPISTLE CXVI.

On the Affections and Passions.

IT hath often been disputed, whether it were better to have moderate affections, or none at all. We *Stoics* are for discarding them entirely: the *Peripatetics* are satisfied with moderating or governing them. But for my part I cannot conceive how any degree of a disease can be thought healthful or beneficial. Be not afraid, *Lucilius*, I am not for depriving you of any of those things you are unwilling to be denied. I will grant, nay, indulge you in those which you seek after and think necessary to life, as being both profitable and pleasant. I will detract only the vicious part. For when I forbid you to *covet*, I permit you to *will (a)*: that you may make the same efforts with better courage and resolution, and better relish such pleasures. Why not? they will sooner attend you when you command, than when you serve them.

But it is natural, you say, *to be troubled at the loss of a friend: forgive a while the tears tha. so justly flow.* It is natural *to be concerned at the opinion of mankind; and be made sorrowful by adversity. Why will you not allow so just a dread, as is that of men's having a bad opinion of you?* There is no vice but what meets with an advocate; and which in the beginning is not softened and palliated by some excuse or other: but on this very account it spreads the more. You will find it difficult to put an end to it, when once you have permitted a beginning. Every affection is but weak and feeble in its first rise: but self-instigated it gathers strength as it proceeds. It is much easier therefore excluded at first than expelled afterwards.

Who can deny but that every affection flows as it were (b) from a certain natural principle? Nature hath committed us to the care and charge of ourselves. True; but when we are too indulgent herein, we become faulty. Nature hath annexed pleasure even to things necessary; not

 that

that we ſhould affect the ſame for pleaſure's ſake, but only that this acceſſion might render ſuch things as we cannot poſſibly live without, more grateful and acceptable to us. But when pleaſure challengeth reception in her own right (*c*), it is then luxury. Therefore let us reſiſt the affections at their firſt intruſion (*d*); for, as I before obſerved, they are much eaſier rejected at firſt than when left to themſelves to depart. *Permit me*, you ſay, *to grieve in ſome meaſure, and in ſome meaſure* to fear. But ſuch meaſure ſoon becomes unreaſonable: nor can you check it when you pleaſe. It may be ſafe indeed for a *wiſe* man not to ſet a guard upon himſelf: he can reſtrain both his tears and his joy when he pleaſes: but becauſe it is not ſo eaſy for us to return when we will, it is much better not to ſet forward.

Panætius (*e*), I think, gave an elegant and juſt anſwer to a young man, who enquired of him, *whether it was proper for a wiſe man* to be in love. "As concerning a wiſe man, ſaid he, we will conſider that " another time; but as for you and me, who are very far from deſerv- " ing that title, I think it would be better for us, as yet, not to ven- " ture upon an affair ſo turbulent, ſo unmanageable, ſo liable to enſlave " us to the will of another, and deſpicable to itſelf. If the beloved " object ſhews us a particular regard, we are immediately more in- " flamed with her tenderneſs and good-nature; if ſhe deſpiſes us, we " are fired with indignation and pride. The love that is too gracious " is as hurtful as that which is too rigid and ſevere. We are entangled " by favour; and muſt have a ſtrong contention with diſdain. Con- " ſcious therefore of our own weakneſs, let us deſiſt a while, and be " quiet, nor truſt our infirm mind to wine, or beauty, or flattery, or " any the like attractive charm." What *Panætius* here ſaith with regard to *love*, I think applicable to all other affections. Let us avoid, as much as we can, walking on ſlippery ground: we ſtand not over-ſteady on the more firm and dry.

I know, *Lucilius*, you will here again retort upon us the common outcry againſt the *Stoics*. *You promiſe us too great things which are unattainable: you command impoſſibilities. We are at beſt but poor and infirm mortals.*

mortals. This ſelf-denial therefore is too hard a leſſon for us (f). We will, we muſt, grieve a little: we muſt covet, but it ſhall be moderately: we muſt be ſometime angry, but we will be appeaſed again. But do you know why the things commanded ſeem impoſſible? I will tell you. It is becauſe we think them ſo: but truly, they are not ſo in fact. We defend our vices, becauſe we love them. And we had rather find out ſome excuſe for them than ſhake them off. Nature hath given us ſufficient ſtrength, if we would exert ourſelves in the uſe of it (g): if we would collect our forces, and employ them wholly *for* ourſelves, at leaſt not, as uſual, *againſt* ourſelves. We pretend *we cannot*, but the truth is, *we will not.*

ANNOTATIONS, &c.

(a) *The will,* according to the *Stoics,* is good, and reckoned among their εὐπάθειαι, *pleaſurable habits.*

(b) *Quaſi* naturali principio] *Seneca* ſays, quaſi, *as it were,* for if it was *truly* natural, it would be *good.*

(c) Not as acceſſary, but principal; not as a ſervant, but as miſtreſs.

(d) Intrantibus reſiſtamus] Sen. de Ira. i. 7. 8. Optimum itaque quidam putant temperare iram, non tollere. Optimum eſt primum irritamentum protinus ſpernere, ipſiſque repugnare ſeminibus, et dare operam ne incidamus in iram, nam ſi cœperit ferre tranſverſos difficilis ad ſalutem recurſus eſt.—In primis, inquam, finibus hoſtis arcendus eſt, nam cum intravit et portis ſe intulit, modum a captivis non accipit. *An enemy is to be driven from the gates as ſoon as poſſible, for when they are once entered, they will make their own terms with the captives.* Vid. Stobæ. Serm. i. Agell. xix. 12. Ariſtot. Ethic. ii. iii.

(e) A moſt eminent and reſpectable profeſſor of Stoiciſm at *Athens,* to whoſe writings *Cicero* acknowledges himſelf much indebted, in compoſing his admirable treatiſe of *Moral Duties.* Melm. *Lel.* p. 107. See Ep. 33. N. a.

(f) Hard as it is, this undoubtedly is the Chriſtian's leſſon. *Then ſaid* Jeſus *to his diſciples, if any man will come after me, let him deny himſelf, and take up his croſs and follow me.* Matt. xvi. 24. Mark viii, 34. Luke ix. 23.

(g) *Not that we are ſufficient of ourſelves to think any thing as of ourſelves, but our ſufficiency is of God. Who is able to make all grace abound towards you; that ye always having a ſufficiency in all things, may abound in every good work.* ii. Cor. iii. 5. ix. 8. *And the Lord ſaid unto me,* ſaith the ſame Apoſtle, *my grace is ſufficient for thee: for my ſtrength is made perfect in weakneſs.* ii. Cor. xii. 9.

EPISTLE CXVII.

A trifling Queſtion; whether, ſince Wiſdom is good, it is good to be wiſe?

YOU certainly, *Lucilius*, will create much trouble both to yourſelf and me; and, while you do not intend it, draw me into ſtrife and debate; by poſing me with ſuch queſtions, as I cannot anſwer in the negative, without diſobliging ſome of our own ſect; nor in the affirmative with a ſafe conſcience.

You deſire to know my opinion concerning that decree of the *Stoics*, *that* wiſdom *is a good, but* to be wiſe *is not.* I will firſt explain to you what the Stoics mean by this aſſertion, and then freely give you my opinion. It is maintained by ſome of us, that *good* is a *body*; becauſe what is good, muſt act in ſome ſort; and what acts is a *body*. Good profiteth, but in order to profit, ſomething muſt be done, and conſequently whatever doth it is ſomewhat, i. e. a *body*. Now wiſdom they ſay is good; it neceſſarily follows therefore that we muſt alſo call it *bodily*, or ſuch thing as hath a *body*. But *to be wiſe*, they range not under the ſame predicament. It is incorporeal, and merely accidental to ſomething elſe, i. e. to wiſdom; therefore of itſelf it doth nothing, nor profiteth. *Why then*, ſay they, *do we not affirm, that it is good* to be wiſe? We do affirm as much, only we refer it to that whereon it depends, i. e. to wiſdom itſelf.

Hear then what is ſaid by ſome in anſwer to this; before I begin to ſecede (*a*), and enliſt myſelf in the oppoſite party. *By the ſame means*, ſay they, *neither to live happily is good*; for whether they will or no, they muſt anſwer upon their own principles, *that an happy life* is good, *but to live happily, is not*, It is further urged by ſome in this manner. *Would you be wiſe? if ſo, to be wiſe is a deſirable thing, and nothing can be deſirable but what is good.* Here then they are obliged to change their terms, and to fling in a ſyllable which our language will not admit:

what

what is good, ſay they, *is deſirable, but what is only contingent to good, is* to deſirable; *which, when we have attained good, is not required merely as good, but as an acceſſion to the good required.* I am not of the ſame opinion, and cannot but think the abettors of it in the wrong; foraſmuch as they are tied down to their firſt point, and it is not lawful in diſputations to change the terms.

It is uſual to allow a *preſumptive argument*, and to look upon that as truth, which ſeems ſo to all men: as for inſtance; *that there are gods.* (b) This we eſteem as ſuch; as it is a general opinion, implanted in the minds of all men; nor is there any nation ſo abandoned, as not to believe it. When we diſpute likewiſe concerning *the immortality of the ſoul*; it is no ſmall argument with us, that all men agree in fearing, or reverencing the *infernal deities.* Here then I make uſe of the ſame common perſuaſion; you will find no one who does not think that *both wiſdom and to be wiſe are good.* I will not however do, as the cuſtom is of thoſe gladiators, who being overcome, in their laſt extremity appeal to the people. We will begin again to fight with our own weapons.

What is accidental to man is *without* the man, to whom it is accidental, or *within*: if within him, it is then a body, as much as that is, to which it is accidental; for nothing can happen to a man without touching him, and what toucheth, is body. If what happens be *without*, after it hath happened, it retires, and what retires, hath motion; and what hath motion, is body. You perhaps may expect me to ſay, that the courſe is not one thing, and the running another; nor heat one thing, and to be hot another: nor light one thing, and to be illumined another. I grant that theſe things are not ſtrictly the ſame; yet neither are they of a different claſs. If health be a thing indifferent, ſo is likewiſe to be well: if beauty be indifferent, ſo is it to be beautiful. If juſtice be good, it is alſo good to be juſt. If villainy be bad, it is alſo bad to be villainous; as truly, as if blear eyes are a misfortune, it is alſo a misfortune to be blear-eyed. This is plain, foraſmuch as the one thing cannot be without the other. To be wiſe, is is wiſdom; and wiſdom is, to be wiſe. So that it is ſo far from being doubted, whether as one is, ſuch is the other, that moſt men think them one and the ſame thing.

But this I would aſk further. Since all things are, good or bad, or indifferent, among which do you rank *the being wiſe?* They (the *Stoics)* deny it to be good: but it cannot be bad; it follows then that it muſt be indifferent. But we call thoſe things mean or indifferent, which may happen as well to a bad as to a good man; as money, beauty, nobility. Whereas this, the *being wiſe*, cannot happen, or be aſſigned, but to a good man: therefore it is not indifferent: and it cannot indeed be bad, becauſe it cannot happen, or be aſſigned, to a bad man: therefore it is good. *But it is nothing more*, they ſay, *than an* accident *to wiſdom*. Is this then which you call *being wiſe*, what makes, or is made, wiſdom? Be it either active or paſſive, it is ſtill a body: for that which makes, and that which is made, is a body; and if it be a body it is good; for this was all that you ſuppoſe wanting to it, to prevent its being a good; that it was not a body.

The *Peripatetics* hold, that there is no difference between *wiſdom* and *being wiſe*; becauſe the one is included in the other. For do you think that any one can *be wiſe*, but he that *hath wiſdom?* or that any one can have wiſdom, without being wiſe? The antient Logicians firſt made a diſtinction between them; and were followed herein by the *Stoics*. What this is I will now inform you.

A field is one thing, and to *have* a field, another. For why? to *have* a field relates to the poſſeſſor, and not to the field: ſo *wiſdom* is one thing, and *to be wiſe* another. I ſuppoſe you will grant theſe to be two things, the poſſeſſor, and the thing poſſeſſed. Wiſdom is poſſeſſed; he that is wiſe poſſeſſeth it. *Wiſdom* is, a perfect mind, or what contains the higheſt and chief good, it being the whole art of life. What then is *to be wiſe?* We cannot ſay that it is a perfect mind, but that it is contingent to ſome one having a perfect mind; ſo that the one is is itſelf an upright mind; the other, as it were, the *having* an upright mind.

There are, it is likewiſe ſaid, *different natures of bodies*: as this is a man, and this a horſe: and theſe natures are attended with motions of minds declarative of bodies: and theſe motions have ſeverally ſomething proper, and diſtinguiſhable from the bodies themſelves: as, *I ſee* Cato *walking*. This the ſenſe of ſeeing diſcovers to me, and my mind believes it. It is a body that I ſee, on which both mine eye and my mind are fixed. I ſay afterwards, Cato *walketh*. I am not ſpeaking now of body, but of ſomething relative thereto; which ſome call a *dialectical*, ſome a *declarative*, and ſome a *dogmatical* propoſition. So, when I mention *wiſdom*, I underſtand thereby a body; but when I ſay, *he is wiſe*, I mean ſomething *relative* to body. Now there is a great difference between the one and the other. Let us ſuppoſe then, for the preſent, theſe are two things; (for as yet I do not declare my own opinion) what hinders that a thing, though it may be different, may yet be good? I before obſerved, that a field is one thing, and to have a field, another. For the poſſeſſor, and the thing poſſeſſed, are different in nature: thie is land, that is man. But in the two things we are diſputing about, there is no ſuch difference, as they are both of the ſame nature; he that poſſeſſeth wiſdom, and the wiſdom poſſeſſed.

Beſides, in the former caſe, what is had, and he that hath it, are different; but in this, what is had, and what hath it, are the ſame. The field is poſſeſſed by right, wiſdom by nature; that may be alienated, and delivered up to another; but this departs not from its owner. It is not therefore conſonant to reaſon, to compare things that are diſparate. I was ſaying, they might be two things, and yet either of them good; and you grant that wiſdom and a wiſe man are two things, and either of them good. As then *wiſdom* is good, and alſo *the having wiſdom*; nothing hinders but that *wiſdom* is the ſame, and alſo *to have wiſdom*, i. e. to be wiſe. For to this end I would be a wiſe man, *that I may be wiſe*. What then? Is not *this* good, without which neither is *that* good? You moſt aſſuredly ſay, that wiſdom, if not given for

 uſe,

uſe, is by no means acceptable. What then is the uſe of wiſdom? *To be wiſe:* this is what is moſt precious and eſtimable herein: take away this, and you will render it a vain, ſuperfluous thing. If torment be an evil, to be tormented alſo muſt be an evil; inſomuch that if that were no evil, neither would the conſequence of it be ſo.

Wiſdom is the habit of a perfect mind; *to be wiſe* is the uſe and application of ſuch an habit. How then can the uſe of it not be good, when without the uſe it cannot be good itſelf? I aſk again, *is wiſdom deſirable?* You grant it. And is *the uſe of it deſirable?* It is likewiſe granted; for you ſay, you would not accept it, if denied the uſe of it. What is deſirable is good; to be wiſe, is the uſe of wiſdom; as the uſe of elocution is to ſpeak, and of the eye to ſee; ſo, I ſay, to be wiſe, is the uſe of wiſdom; but the uſe of wiſdom is deſirable, therefore to be wiſe is deſirable; and if deſirable, it is good.

I have more than once condemned myſelf for imitating thoſe I cenſure, and waſting words upon what is ſelf-evident. Who can doubt but that if extreme heat be an evil, to be extremely hot is the ſame; and that if cold be an evil, ſo is it, to be cold; and if life be good, to live is alſo good. All theſe trifling queſtions about wiſdom are certainly not comprehended in wiſdom's ſelf. But it is ſtill our duty to abide with her; or if we have a mind to make an excurſion, ſhe hath a large and copious field for us to rove in. Let us enquire into the nature of the Gods; what feeds the ſtars, and gives divers motions to the planets; and whether our bodies are affected according to theſe their motions; or whether they have an influence on the minds and bodies of all; whether the things we call caſual, are linked together in a certain chain of cauſes; or that nothing happens in this world inſtantaneous, or without the direction of Providence. Theſe things however tend but little to the reformation of manners, yet they raiſe the mind; and lift it up to the greatneſs of thoſe things it is employed about; whereas the foregoing diſpute, and the like, leſſen and depreſs the mind; and are ſo far from ſharpening it, as you ſuppoſe, that they rather dull and debaſe it.

Why,

Why, I pray you, do we ſpend our care and diligence, ſo neceſſarily required and due to affairs of greater conſequence, on what, for any thing we know, may be falſe, and certainly is uſeleſs? What will it profit me to know, whether *wiſdom* is one thing, and *to be wiſe* another? At all adventures I will ſtand the chance of this my wiſh—may *wiſdom* be *your* lot, and *to be wiſe, mine*; and I doubt not but we ſhall fare alike. Or rather, ſhew me the way to attain knowledge in the following particulars:—tell me what I am to avoid, and what to purſue—by what ſtudies I may ſtrengthen, and fix the, as yet, wavering mind—and how I may diſengage myſelf from thoſe vices that turn and drive me from the right way—and how I may relieve thoſe calamities that have broken in upon me, or thoſe that I have unwarily ruſhed upon myſelf.—Inſtruct me how I may bear adverſity without ſighing; or proſperity without making others ſigh.—How not to live in anxiety, concerning the laſt and neceſſary end of life, but to fly to it, when *proper*, as to a ſure refuge. Nothing, in my mind, ſeems more abſurd and mean, than *to wiſh* for death. For if you would live, why do you wiſh to die? if you would not live, why do you aſk the Gods for what they gave you at your birth? As it was then decreed that you ſhould one day die, whether you will or no; *(to be willing)* to die is always in your own power; the one is impoſed upon you by neceſſity, the other is left to your approbation.

In my reading I have met with a principle, ridiculous enough in theſe days, though wrote by a man, otherwiſe very learned and eloquent; Ita, inquit, moriar quamprimum, *Let me*, ſays he, *die as ſoon may be.* (*e*). Fond man! you deſire what is your own. *Let me die as ſoon as may be.* Perhaps when you ſay this, you are grown old and fooliſh; otherwiſe what ſhould prevent you? No one detains thee. Go off as you pleaſe. Chuſe ſome proper inſtrument of nature for this purpoſe. Now theſe are the elements whereby this lower world is maintained, water, earth, air, and theſe are not more the means of life than they are the ways of death. *Let me die as ſoon as may be.* How *ſoon* would you have it be? What day do you aſſign to this word *ſoon?* it may poſſibly happen ſooner than you deſire. Theſe then are the words of a weak

 mind

mind catching at mercy and a longer life, in this ſeeming deteſtation of it. He hath no mind to die, who wiſheth for it. Aſk of the Gods, if you pleaſe, life, and health: but if you had rather die, the fruit or effect of death is to ceaſe from wiſhing.

Let theſe things, my *Lucilius*, employ our meditations, in order to form our minds thereto. This is *wiſdom*; this is *to be wiſe*; *to meditate on life and death*; not to debate on ſubtle trifles with idle diſputations. So many queſtions of great importance hath Fortune propoſed to you, which remain as yet unreſolved. At preſent you only cavil. But how ridiculous is it to ſtand flouriſhing your ſword, when the trumpet calls you to battle? Throw aſide theſe ſportive weapons, theſe daggers of lath. There is need of the ſword, and to engage in earneſt. Tell me by what means no ſorrow ſhall afflict, no fear diſturb, the mind—by what means I may diſcharge my breaſt of this heavy load of ſecret deſires. Something muſt be done.

What ſay you? *Wiſdom* is good; *to be wiſe* is not good? Be it ſo, if you pleaſe. Let us deny, *that to be wiſe is good*; to the end that we may draw into contempt this whole ſtudy, as being a vain and ſuperfluous employ. And what if you ſhould know, that *this* likewiſe is made a queſtion; *Whether* future *wiſdom be a good?* But what doubt, I pray you, can there be, that the barns feel not the load of a *future* crop; and that childhood is not ſenſible of the ſtrength and vigour of youth? Health *to come* profits not the man who is ſick at preſent, any more than the reſt, that is to follow many hard and painful labours, refreſheth a man at the time of his running or wreſtling. Who knows not that *what is to come*, is not good upon this very account, becauſe it *is yet to come?* What is good alſo profiteth; but nothing profiteth that is not preſent; and if it profiteth not, neither is it good; and if it profiteth, it profiteth inſtantly. *I ſhall hereafter be wiſe*; this then will be good when it ſhall come to paſs; in the mean while it is nothing.

A thing muſt firſt be, before it acts: for how, I beſeech you, can that be good, which is as yet nothing? And how can I better prove to you, that

that a thing is not yet, than by ſaying, *it is to come?* For 'tis manifeſt, that what is ſtill coming, is not yet come. The ſpring is coming on, I know it therefore to be as yet winter. Summer will follow; it is not therefore yet ſummer. In ſhort, I ſay, the beſt argument to prove that a thing is not preſent, is, that it is yet to come.

I ſhall be wiſe, I hope; but in the mean time, I am not wiſe. The time is to come when I ſhall be wiſe, from whence you may eaſily underſtand, that as yet I am not wiſe. I cannot have that good and this misfortune at the ſame time. Theſe two things do not coincide, nor can good and evil dwell together.

But let us give over theſe imaginary trifles, and haſten to what may turn to our advantage. No parent who is going under great concern to fetch a midwife for his daughter, will ſtop by the way to read the play-bills *(f)*. No one who is informed that his houſe is on fire, will ſtand ſtudying, in a game at cheſs, how to deliver his king out of check. But from all parts news is continually flying about that one's houſe is in flames; one's children in danger, our city beſieged, and our goods plundered: add to theſe, ſhipwrecks, earthquakes, and whatever elſe is terrible to man. Diſtracted among all theſe calamities, are you at leiſure to attend to ſuch things only that amuſe the mind? Are you ſolicitous to enquire what is the difference between *wiſdom* and *the being wiſe?* Do you employ yourſelf in continually making and ſolving riddles, while matters of ſo great weight are impendent? Nature hath not ſo liberally and prodigally beſtowed the gift of *Time* upon us, as to have given us any to throw away. And yet you ſee how much of it is loſt, even by the moſt careful and diligent. Sickneſs, either our own, or of ſome friend, robs us of a great part: another part is taken up with neceſſary affairs; and another with the demands of the public: and ſleep divides with us almoſt the whole of life.

Of the time then, at beſt, ſo very ſhort and rapid, carrying us away with it, ſhall we delight in loſing the greater part, and throwing it away idly? Add hereunto, that the mind is too apt rather to [illegible] than to heal itſelf; and that philoſophy is made uſe of as paſtime, rather than as a remedy. I know not what difference there may be, between *wiſdom*, and *the being wiſe*; but this I know, that it is of no conſequence to me, whether I know theſe things or not. Tell me, when I have learned the difference between *wiſdom* and *being wiſe*, whether I ſhall be wiſe myſelf. Why elſe do you detain me upon the words rather than the works of wiſdom? Make me more brave, more ſecure; make me a match for Fortune, or rather her ſuperior. I may be ſuperior to her if I put in practice all I learn.

ANNOTATIONS, &c.

(*a*) Secedere. Figuratively, from their changing their places in the Senate by permiſſion of the Conſul.

(*b*) Expetendum, inquiunt, quod bonum eſt; *ad*expetendum quod bono contingit. Expectandum vocat αἱρετὸν, adexpectandum nova voce προσαιρετὸν, i. e. quandam quaſi προσθήκην τοῦ αἱρετοῦ. And many ſuch words, ſaith *Muret*. have the Stoics coined without any neceſſity for them. It is obſervable, that in our ancient language the ſyllable is often uſed by way of augment. as, *to-partid*, Chaucer's Knight's Tale. v. 763. *to-broſtin*, ib. 1833.

(*c*) *Cicero* in the very period wherein he gives us the names of ſeveral ancient Atheiſts, makes the belief of a God natural to all men. Quo omnes, ſays he, naturâ duce vehimur. But ſee *Locke's* eſſay, l. 1. c. 4. where this argument for the being of a God, from the univerſal conſent of mankind, is fully diſproved. See Cic. Tuſc. Qu. i. 16.

(*d*) Quomodo ultimum et neceſſarium vitæ terminum non expectem, ſed ipſemet, cum viſum fuerit, profugiam. Theſe words, like ſome other before taken notice of, required ſoftening; in order to adapt them to a Chriſtian ear: which never can be reconciled to ſuch horrid doctrine as is here exhibited in the uſual rant of Stoiciſm: and which *Seneca* himſelf never vouchſafed to follow, but by compulſion of the cruel tyrant *Nero*. This benefit however we receive from it, that it enhanceth the value of the Goſpel, and ſerves as a foyl to ſet off the purer light, which by the bleſſing of God we Chriſtians enjoy.——Ut quandoque moriaris etiam invito poſitum eſt, ut cum voles, in tua manu eſt. *Ib.* *It is appointed for all men once to die*, therefore ſaith *Seneca*, *die when you pleaſe*. No; let us remember what follows in the like ſentence in *Paul's* Epiſtle to the *Hebrews*, (9. 2.) *and after this the judgment*. So ſhall we be ſafe from giving attention to ſo raſh a precept from an Heathen; or from one much worſe, and more contemptible, a renegado Chriſtian.

(*e*) We know not whoſe words they are, but they ſeem ſpoken by one, who on the bed of ſickneſs had reſigned himſelf to patience; yet, as it is very natural, *wiſhed to die*: and however they may be condemned by a Stoic, there was wanting but a word or two more (*God willing*) to render them truly Chriſtian.

The moſt deſirable manner of yielding up our lives is,—when Nature thinks proper to deſtroy the work of her own hand, as the artiſt who conſtructed the machine is beſt qualified to take it to pieces. In ſhort, an old man ſhould neither be anxious to preſerve the final portion of life which

remains

remains to him; nor forward to resign it without a just cause. It was one of the prohibitions of *Pythagoras*, *not to quit our post of life*, without being authorised by the Commander who placed us in it, i. e. without the permission of the Supreme Being. *Cato.* Melm. 109.

(*f*) Dictum et ludorum ordinem perlegit. It was customary among the *Romans* to give out bills, shewing what day the gladiators were to fight, and how they were matched; and this they called *pronuntiare munus.* Munus populi pronunciavit in filiæ memeriam. *Sueton.* in Jul. Vid. *Lips.* I. c. 18. Saturn. Serm.

EPISTLE CXVIII.

An Enquiry into what is the true Good.

YOU require me, *Lucilius*, to write oftener. Were we to reckon, I believe, you would find yourself in my debt. It was our agreement indeed, that you should write first, and expect an answer from me: but I will not insist upon it: I know you are to be trusted, and therefore will pay you beforehand (*a*). Nor yet will I do as the most eloquent *Cicero* desires his friend *Atticus* to do; that *if nothing material occurred, he would write any thing that came uppermost.* I shall never want matter, though I pass over those things with which *Cicero* fills his Epistles; as, *what candidate was hard drove; who engageth with his own or with foreign forces—who stands for the consulship, upon the favour and authority of* Cæsar *or of* Pompey; *or upon his own art and strength:—and how hard an usurer is* Cecilius, *of whom a neighbour cannot borrow money under* cent. per cent. No; it is better for us to treat of our own failures than those of other men; to examine ourselves; and consider how many things we are candidates for without having a single vote.

This, my *Lucilius*, is excellent; this the way to live secure and free; to sue neither for place nor pension; and to let Fortune keep her court-days to herself. How pleasant is it, think you, when the tribes are assembled,

ſembled, and the candidates for an office are buſily employed in paying court to their well-wiſhers; while one promiſeth money; another ſues by his agent; another ſqueezes and kiſſes the hands of thoſe, whom, when he is choſe, he ſcorns to touch; and all ſtand in ſuſpenſe, expecting the voice of the cryer, or returning-officer! How pleaſant is it, I ſay, at ſuch a time to be entirely diſengaged, and unconcerned, as a ſpectator of the *fair*, without buying or ſelling! How much greater pleaſure does ſuch a one enjoy, who, without care or concern, beholds not only theſe mobbing elections of prætors, and conſuls, but thoſe great aſſemblies (*b*) in which ſome are canvaſſing for anniverſary honours; others perpetual power: ſome are praying for happy ſucceſs in war, and a triumph; others are intent upon riches: others on matrimony and children: others on the welfare of themſelves and their relations! How great is the mind that can prevail upon itſelf to aſk *nothing?* to ſue and cringe to no man; and to ſay to Fortune, *Begone, I have no buſineſs with you; I ſhall not put myſelf into your power; I know by your means* Cato *is rejected, and* Vatinius *choſen; I have nothing to aſk of you*. This is to humble Fortune indeed, by depriving her of all authority.

Let us then entertain each other with theſe reflections, and perpetually dwell upon this ſubject, while we ſee ſo many thouſands involve themſelves in difficulties and diſquietude; who, in the purſuit of ruin, are ſtill running from one miſchief into another; and now ſeek that which they ſoon will fly from and deteſt. For where is the man, who thinks even *that* enough, when he hath obtained it, which before ſeemed too much for him to aſk or wiſh for? Felicity is not, as men are apt to think, covetous, but mean; and therefore ſatisfieth not. You fancy perhaps ſome things great, becauſe you are not acquainted with them, but the man who hath attained them is of a contrary opinion: I belie him, if he does not yet ſtudy to riſe. What you ſuppoſe the ſummit, is but a degree or ſtep towards it. And the reaſon why men run into this error, is, they know not *truth:* being deceived by common opinion, they are carried away with the *appearance* of good; and at laſt find, when, after much toil and labour, they

have

have gained their end, that what they purſued is evil or vain, or greatly ſhort of what they expected: and the greater part admire ſuch things as certainly deceive them at one time or another, and commonly take what is *great* to be *good*. Leſt therefore we ſhould fall into the like miſtake, let us enquire what is *good*.

Various have been the interpretations hereof: ſome have defined it one way, ſome another, under different expreſſions. As, ſome define it thus, *Good is that which invites and attracts the mind of man.* But to this it is immediately objected, *And what if that which invites a man, invites him to his ruin?* You know that many evils are very attractive. Truth and veriſimilitude differ in this: what is good is annexed to truth; for it is not good, unleſs it be true. But what invites and engages by its appearance, is veriſimilar, wheedles, ſollicits, attracts.——Or, ſome thus define it; *Good* is *that which incites a longing after it, or influenceth the mind with a tendency thereto.* But to this is made the ſame objection: for many things influence the mind, which things are purſued, to the great detriment of the purſuer.——They define it better therefore, who ſay, *Good is that which influenceth the mind according to the nature and fitneſs of things*; and is then to be ſought after, when it becomes worthy our ſearch, and is truly decent and honourable. For this is by all means deſirable. And here I am called upon to ſhew the difference between bonum and honeſtum, *what is good*, and what is *fit and decent*.

They ſeem indeed inſeparable, for nothing can be good, but what in ſome meaſure is right and fit: and what is right and fit muſt alſo be good. What then, you will aſk, is the difference between them? Why, the honeſtum *(what is right and fit)* is that perfect good which completes the happineſs of life, and by communion therewith other things become good. This is what I mean: ſome things are neither good nor evil in themſelves, as *warfare, embaſſage, juriſdiction*; but when theſe offices are juſtly executed they begin to be good, and become really ſo from being indifferent. Bonum, *good*, therefore ariſeth from a communion with fitneſs. But honeſtum, *fit and right*, is good on its own account.

account. Good floweth from the fitneſs of things, but the fitneſs of things is good of itſelf. What is good might have been bad, and what is right and fit cannot be otherwiſe than good.

Others again define it thus: *Good is that which is according to Nature.* Obſerve what I ſay, what is good is alſo according to nature. But it does not follow that what is according to nature is alſo good. Many things are agreeable to nature, and yet of ſo little conſequence as not to deſerve the name of *good*; for they are light and contemptible: whereas not the leaſt good is contemptible. So long as there is any littleneſs in it, it is not good; and when it begins to be good, it is no longer little. *How then ſhall we know when a thing is good?* when it is perfectly agreeable and conſonant to nature. *You own,* you ſay, *that what is good is according to Nature: this is a neceſſary property: yet you affirm that ſome things may be accord ing to Nature; and yet not be good. How then can the former be good, and theſe not ſo? How do they attain another property or quality, when the ſame excellence, the being agreeable to Nature, is common to both?* Why, from their magnitude or greatneſs. Nor is it new or ſtrange, that things ſhould alter their properties by increaſe or growth. One that was an infant, is now a young man: and hath other inclinations. He was before irrational, but now is rational. Some things grow not only greater by increaſe, but are totally changed.

But, it is ſaid, *A thing is ſtill what it was, notwithſtanding any increaſe. Whether you fill a pitcher or a tub with wine, it makes no difference; the wine is ſtill the ſame. A ſmall or a large quantity of honey have both the ſame taſte.* Theſe examples ſuit not the purpoſe. For in theſe the ſame quality, however they are encreaſed in quantity, ſtill remains: but as ſome things, though amplified in kind, ſtill keep the ſame property; there are other, which after many additions, the laſt quite alters, and impreſſeth thereon a new and different condition from that wherein it was before. Thus one ſtone will make an arch; I mean that which is wedged in between the reclining ſides, and binds them together. Now why is this laſt addition, though a ſmall one, of ſo great conſequence? not becauſe it increaſeth, but becauſe it fills, or completes the work.

Some things alſo in their proceſs throw off their priſtine form, and take a new one. As, when the mind hath long been muſing upon and purſuing a ſubject till it is quite wearied with the greatneſs of it; that now begins to be thought another thing, and is called *infinite*, which at firſt appeared, though great, yet *finite*. In like manner when we have found a difficulty in cutting a thing, this difficulty increaſing upon us, we pronounce it impoſſible to be cut: and ſo from a thing which is hard to be moved, we paſs on to what is immovable. In the ſame way of reaſoning, ſomething that was agreeable to nature, is by an additional greatneſs transferred into another property or quality, and becomes thereby *truly good*.

ANNOTATIONS, &c.

(*a*) In anteceſſum dabo. A *forenſic* term, or what is uſed by the bankers and ſcriveners. Ep. vii. In anteceſſum accipe. *Quinctilian*. Quod apud mercatores ſolet, in anteceſſum dedi. *I gave earneſt*.

(*b*) Throughout the world, wherein Fortune preſides.

EPISTLE CXIX.

On Riches and Contentment.

AS often as I find any thing, I ſtay not 'till you cry, *half is mine (a)*, I offer it myſelf. Do you aſk what I have found? Hold up your lap: 'tis all ſolid gain. I will tell you how to grow rich at once, which I know you would be glad to learn: and you are in the right. I will ſhew you then a moſt compendious way to attain great affluence; yet you muſt be obliged to ſome creditor, with whom you may negotiate this affair; I ſay you muſt neceſſarily run in debt. Yet I would not have you borrow by your ſollicitor, or any interceſſor, nor ſhall your name ſtand in any broker's books. I have got a creditor for you. According to the recommendation of *Cato (b)*, you ſhall borrow of yourſelf. Quantumcumque eſt, ſatis erit, ſi quidquid deerit, id a nobis petierimus. *Whatever little we have 'twill be enough, if what is ſtill wanting we can borrow of ourſelves.*

For there is little or no difference, *Lucilius*, between not wanting a thing, and having it. The effect is the ſame in both; you will no longer be in pain. Not that I command you to deny Nature any thing ſhe properly aſks. She is ſtubborn, and not eaſily to be overcome. She demands her own. But I would have you know, that what exceeds the call of nature is precarious, and unneceſſary. I am hungry; and muſt therefore eat; but whether it be the common ſort of bread, or made of the fineſt wheat-flour, is of no concern to Nature; ſhe does not deſire any otherwiſe to pleaſe the belly, than by filling it. I am thirſty, and whether I drink of the next pool (*c*), or of ſuch water as is mixed with ſnow, in order to give it a coolneſs not its own, it is the ſame to nature. She deſires nothing more than to quench her thirſt; it matters not whether it be out of a cup made of gold, or of cryſtal, or of the *Chalcedonian* pebble, or a plain earthen mug (*d*), or from the hollow of the hand. Fix thine eye upon the end or deſign of all things, and you will diſdain ſuperfluities. Hunger calls upon me; I therefore reach out my hand to the next thing I meet with that is eatable. Hunger will make me reliſh it, be it what it will; an hungry ſtomach diſdains not any thing.

If you aſk now what it is that hath ſo delighted me; it is this, which I think an excellent ſentence, ſapiens, divitiarum naturalium eſt quæſitor acerrimus, *the wiſe man is a moſt diligent ſearcher after natural riches*. But *this*, you ſay, is *ſetting before me an empty platter. What can this mean? I was preparing my bags, and conſidering in what ſea I ſhould firſt make my trading voyage, what public buſineſs I ſhould take in hand, or what wares I ſhould ſend for. This is deceiving me; to teach me to be poor, when you promiſed me riches.* Do you then think the man poor, who wants nothing? *But this*, you ſay, *he owes to himſelf, and the benefit of his patience, not to Fortune.* Well; and do you therefore think him not rich, becauſe his riches, ſuch as they are, can never forſake him? Tell me, which you had rather have? much, or a ſufficient competency? He that hath much deſireth more; which is an argument that he hath not enough: he that thinks he hath enough, hath attained what the rich man never can, the end of his wiſhes (*).

Or

Or do you think them no riches, for which a man is in no danger of being profcribed? or becaufe they are not enough to tempt a bad fon or wife to prepare poifon for their father or hufband? becaufe they are fafe in time of war, or in peace at their own difpofal? Becaufe it is neither dangerous to enjoy them, nor does it require much labour to difpofe of them?

Or do you think a man hath but little, who hath juft enough to keep him from being cold, or hungry, or thirfty? *Jupiter* himfelf hath not more. It is never little, which is enough. *Alexander* of *Macedon*, after he had conquered *Darius* and the *Indians*, was ftill poor. He was ftill feeking fomewhat more, which he might call his own: he fearcheth out unknown feas: he fends a frefh fleet into the ocean: and, if I may fay it, he breaks through the barriers of the known world. What Nature is fatisfied with, fatisfieth not man. There are thofe who ftill defire fomething, when they have got every thing. So great is the blindnefs of our minds; and fo forgetful is every one of their beginning, when they fee themfelves advanced; that he, who was but now mafter of a little nook in *Greece*, and that controvertible, is foon after grieved, that, being checked in his career by the far diftant end of the world, he muft now return through that world he has made his own. Money never made any one rich. On the contrary, it only makes the poffeffor more covetous and needy. Do you afk the caufe of this? The more a man hath, the more he thinks it poffible to have.

Upon the whole, fet before me one of thofe whofe name may be joined with that of *Craffus*, or *Licinus (e)*; and let him fet down his revenues, and take into the account not only what he hath, but what he hopes to have. Yet even fuch a one, if you will believe *me*, is poor; or, if you will believe *yourfelf*, he may be fo. Whereas the man who hath fo compofed and formed himfelf to that which Nature alone requires of him, is not only out of the reach, or fenfe of poverty, but alfo exempt from the dread of it. But that you may know how difficult a thing it is for a man to ftraiten himfelf within the meafure of Nature, even he, whom we fuppofed to live according to Nature, and whom you.

you call poor, hath ſtill ſomething that is ſuperfluous. But riches attract and blind the common people; when they ſee large ſums of money expended in any houſe; or the houſe adorned with gold; or if the family be comely in body, and ſplendid in apparel; the happineſs of ſuch a family exiſts in oſtentation and outward ſhew; but the man whom we have withdrawn, both from the eye of the people, and the reach of fortune, is happy within himſelf. For as to thoſe, whom poverty hath ſeized upon, under the falſe name of riches, they have riches, as we are ſaid to *have* an ague, when the ague *hath* us. As we ought therefore to ſay, an ague hath hold of ſuch a one, in like manner we ſhould ſay, riches hath hold of him.

There is nothing therefore I would ſooner remind you of than this, which but few or none ſufficiently obſerve: *that you meaſure all things by pure natural deſires, which are eaſily ſatisfied, or with very little.* Only be careful to keep your deſires clear from vice. You enquire perhaps, what ſort of table I would keep, what plate, and how many ſpruce ſervants in livery I would have attend dinner? Know then, that Nature requireth nothing more than meat and drink;

Nam tibi cùm fauces urit ſitis, aurea quæris
Pocula? num eſuriens faſtidis omnia, præter
Pavonem rhombumque?—*Hor.* S. i. 2. 115.
When thirſty is the throat, and calls for eaſe,
Will nothing but a golden goblet pleaſe?
Or when, with hunger pinch'd, you fain would eat,
Will nothing ſatisfy but dainty meat,
An ortelan, or turbot?——

Hunger is not ambitious. It is well content when ſatisfied; nor regardeth much by what means. Such torments belong to wretched luxury: which though glutted, is continually ſeeking to get an appetite; not to fill the belly, but to ſtuff it: and how to recover the thirſt that hath been quenched by the firſt draught. *Horace* therefore hath elegantly denied that it at all concerns the thirſty, in what glaſs, or with what delicate hand they are ſerved with water. For if you think it of any

any conſequence, how frizzled and curled the page is *(f)*, and how clear the glaſs, you are not dry.

Among other favours, this particular one is beſtowed on us by Nature, that ſhe hath removed all diſdain from neceſſity. Superfluities alone require choice. *Such a thing does not become me, this is not elegant, and that offends the eyes.* The will of the Creator of the world, who hath preſcribed to us the rules of life, is, that we ſtudy to preſerve ourſelves, and not to be over-nice and delicate. All things that tend to our health and preſervation are ready and at hand. Delicacies are not provided but with care and trouble. Let us then make uſe of, and thankfully enjoy, this eſtimable bounty of Nature; and think, that in nothing ſhe hath more obliged us, than, in that whatever is neceſſarily wanted, or deſired, it is accepted without diſdain.

ANNOTATIONS, &c.

(*a*) In commune] It was proverbial among the *Greeks*, when any one found a thing, for another who was preſent, to ſay κοινὸς Ἑρμῆς, *communis Mercurius:* foraſmuch as *Mercury* was ſuppoſed to preſide over the highway or common road, and the thing ſo found was called Ἑρμαῖον, *Mercurial*, ——as we ſay, *halves*.

(*b*) Catonianum illud] *Lipſius* and *Pincian* read it, *Hecatonianum*; as frequent mention is made by *Seneca* of *Hecaton*, the philoſopher.

(*c*) So *Propertius*,

Ipſa petita lacu nunc mihi dulcis aqua eſt.
Ev'n from a pool the water now ſeems ſweet.

(*d*) Tiburtinus calix.

(*e*) Content, thou beſt of friends! for thou
In our neceſſities art ſo.
'Midſt all our ills a bleſſing ſtill in ſtore,
Joy to the rich, and riches to the poor.——
Content, the good and golden mean,
The ſafe eſtate that ſits between
The ſordid poor, and miſerable great,
The humble tenant of a rural ſeat.
In vain we wealth and treaſure heap;
He 'midſt his thouſand kingdoms ſtill is poor,
That for another crown does weep:
'Tis only he is rich who wiſhes for no more. Dryd. Miſc. ii. p. 83.

(*f*) Theſe

(e) These two names are likewise mentioned together in *Persius*, ii. 36.

Tunc manibus quatit, et spem macram supplice voto
Nunc Licini in campos nunc Crassi mittit in ædes.
Then dandles him with many a mutter'd pray'r,
That heav'n would make him some rich miser's heir,
Of Licinus, *or* Crassus.——
Dispositis prædives hamis vigilare cohortem
Servorum noctu Licinus jubet——Juv. xiv. 305.
Rich Licinus's *servants ready stand,*
Each with a water-bucket in his hand,
Keeping a guard for fear of fire all night—Dryden.

In Sidonius, Ep. v. 7. we have his Epitaph:

Marmoreo hoc tumulo *Licinus* jacet; at *Cato* nullo.
Pompeius parvo. Credimus esse Deos?

He is also mentioned in the following Epistle.

(f) *Such a one as* Horace *described*, Od. ii. 5. 23.

Discrimen obscurum, solutis
Crinibus, ambiguoque vultu.
So smooth his doubtful cheeks appear,
So loose, so girlish flows his hair.

EPISTLE CXX.

From whence we learn the Knowledge of Good.

I FIND, my *Lucilius*, that your Epistle, after wandering through many petty questions, at last fixed upon one, which you desire me to explain: *from whence do we receive the first notices, or ideas, of* Good and Right? These two things, in the opinion of some, are very different; but we *Stoics* only suppose them subject to a slight distinction. What I mean is this: some think a thing *good* from its being useful; they give this title therefore to *riches, an horse, wine, shoes*, &c. So low do they degrade the name of *good*, making it applicable to servile uses. And they suppose *that* to be *right*, which consists in the discharge of any just duty: as, in the pious care of an aged father; assisting a friend in adversity; a brave and bold expedition; or in passing a prudent

dent and merciful ſentence. Now we (Stoics) ſuppoſe *good* and *right* to be two things indeed, but of the ſame import. *Nothing is* good *but what is* right; *and what is* right, *is alſo* good. I think it unneceſſary to add the difference between them, having ſo often taken notice of it. I ſhall only obſerve, that nothing ſeems *good* to us, which may be made a bad uſe of. And you ſee how many make a bad uſe of riches, nobility, ſtrength, and the like. I therefore now return to the queſtion propoſed, *How we come to the firſt knowledge of* Good *and* Right?

Nature could not teach us this. She hath ſown in our minds the ſeeds of knowledge, but not implanted knowledge itſelf. Some affirm that we fall upon this knowledge accidentally; but it is incredible that any one ſhould have met by chance with the idea or image of virtue. We rather think it gathered from obſervation and reflection; and that from comparing ſuch things with themſelves as have been well experienced, the underſtanding formed from hence its judgment of what is *good* and right, by *analogy* *. For ſince the Latins have adopted this word, and made it a free denizen of *Rome*, I think it by no means to be rejected, or returned to its native country, *Greece*; it is to be accepted therefore, not as a ſtranger and newly-received word, but as if it were in common uſe.

To explain then what is meant by the word *(analogy)*. We know that ſanity or health is a quality belonging to the body; from hence we infer a like quality belonging to the ſoul: we know that ſtrength and vigour are properties of the body: from whence we preſume the ſoul to be endowed with the like properties. We have been amazed at ſome generous, humane, brave actions; hence we began to admire them, as ſo many perfections: but theſe however have been traverſed with many failings, which the glare and ſplendor of ſome notable action concealed from us; we therefore pretended not to ſee them. Nature commands us to magnify deeds that are praiſe-worthy; whereupon glory is generally carried beyond truth. From hence we took the idea of ſome extraordinary *good*.

Fabricius refused the gold of King *Pyrrhus*, and judged it greater than a kingdom, that he was able to contemn the riches of a King (*a*). The same hero, when a physician made him an offer to poison *Pyrrhus*, advised the King to be upon his guard against treachery. Now it was the same greatness of soul, that scorned to be overcome with gold, or to overcome his adversary by poison. We therefore justly admired this great man, who was not to be prevailed upon by the promises of a King, nor by any that were treacherously made against a King. So resolutely fixed was he on setting a good example: and what is most difficult, he preserved his innocence, in war. He thought a man might be guilty of baseness even towards his profest enemies; and in the extreme poverty, wherein he gloried, detested riches no less than poison. *Live*, said he, Pyrrhus, *by my courtesy, and rejoice at what you was so much displeased before, that* Fabricius *was not to be corrupted.*

Horatius Cocles, with his single arm, kept the narrow pass of the bridge, and ordered it to be pulled down behind to prevent the passage of the enemy: and so long did he maintain his post against the assailants, 'till he heard the downfall of the props and timbers; and looking behind and seeing his purpose affected, so as at his own peril to stop the peril of his country, *Now follow*, said he, *who will; this is the way I go.* And thereupon immediately flung himself into the river; and being not less sollicitous in the rapid stream to preserve his arms than his life, with this honourable and victorious load upon him, he got to land as safe as if he had returned by the bridge (*b*). These and the like actions give us an idea of valour and magnanimity.

I will add what perhaps may seem strange to you. Evil things have sometimes given us the idea of good. And what is most *right and fit* hath appeared from the contrary. For there are you know certain vices, which border upon, or have the resemblance of, virtues, so that even in the most vile and base men, there is sometimes the appearance of goodness. Thus the prodigal man counterfeits the liberal; whereas there is a great difference between a man's knowing how to give, and not knowing how to keep, his money. There are many, I say, *Lucilius*, who

who do not give, but throw it away. I do not call him a liberal man, who is angry, as it were, with his money. In like manner, carelessness assumes the air of ease and freedom; and rashness, of fortitude. Now this resemblance hath obliged us to examine things carefully, and to distinguish such as resemble one another indeed in appearance, but in fact are widely different. While we respect those whom some noble exploit hath rendered famous, we begin to remark that such a one hath executed an enterprize with nobleness of spirit and great resolution; yet it was but once. We see him brave in war, in the forum a coward: bearing poverty with manliness and courage; but scandal and infamy with a poor and abject mind. We have therefore praised the particular deed, but despised the man.

We have seen another person courteous to his friends; moderate towards his enemies; and both in public and private life, behaving himself soberly and righteously; not wanting patience, in what he was bound to suffer; nor prudence in what he was to perform: we have seen him, when it was a time to give, distributing his bounty with a full hand; and when labour was required of him, how resolute! industrious, subject to command, relieving the weariness of his body with constancy, and firmness of mind. He was moreover always the same, consistent with himself in every action; and not only good by intention and design, but happily arrived to such an habit, as not only to do what was right, but to be capable of doing nothing but what was right.

From whence then we learn that in such a one virtue is perfect; and this we divide into several parts: seeing that desires are to be restrained; fear to be repressed; requisite actions to be foreseen; and their several duties paid to every one (*c*): from hence we learned temperance, fortitude, prudence, justice, and gave to each their particular office. And from whence did we learn virtue? It was displayed in the order, decency, constancy and uniformity, that such a one observed in all his actions; and particularly in that greatness of soul which exalted itself above all the rest. Hence appeared that blessed state of life, which ever flows in a profperous and happy courfe *(d)*, dependent entirely upon itfelf. And what we further collect from hence is, that this perfect man, this adept in virtue, never curfed Fortune; was never caft down by any accident, and looking upon himfelf as a foldier and citizen of the world, underwent all labours as patiently as if they were enjoined him by the command of his fuperiors. Whatever happened to him he received it, not with difcontent, as an accidental evil, but as his deftined lot in life. *This*, faith he, be it what it will, *is my portion. It is hard: it is indeed fevere; but we muft bear it, and do the beft we can.*

He neceffarily appeared therefore, in all refpects, a great man; from whom no difafters could ever diftort a figh or groan; who never complained of his fate: he gave to many a tafte of his goodnefs, which fhone as a light in a dark place (*e*); turning the inclinations and affections of every one towards him, being mild and gracious, and alike juft in all affairs both human and divine. His mind was perfect, being advanced to that height, above which there is nothing but the mind of God. A part whereof condefcended to dwell even in this mortal breaft *(f)*; which is never more divine, than when it reflects upon its own mortality; and knows that man was born to this end; that he muft one day part with life; and that this body is not a fixed habitation, but an inn; and indeed an inn, where we muft make but a fhort ftay; and muft certainly leave it, at the pleafure or difpleafure of our hoft.

It is a very ftrong argument with me, dear *Lucilius*, that the foul is derived from fome higher fource, when it looks upon all earthly things, wherewith at prefent it is converfant, as mean and vile; and is under no dread to leave them. For he knows whither he is going, who recollects from whence he came. See we not how many things incommode and trouble us; and how irkfome this body is to us? Sometimes we complain of the bowels, fometimes of the head, fometimes of the breaft and throat; at one time the nerves, at another our feet rack us; to-day a lownefs of fpirit; to-morrow a violent cold; fometimes too much blood; fometimes too little; thus are we toffed about, and at laft obliged

to

to go off. This is what generally happens to thoſe who live in a tenement not their own. And yet though ſuch a weak and putrid body be our portion, we nevertheleſs lay ſchemes for eternity; and as far as human life can poſſibly be extended, ſo far do we ſtretch our hopes; never ſatisfied with riches or power. But what can be more ridiculous? What more ſhameful? Nothing contenteth *us*, who muſt die ſoon, nay, who *die every day*; for we daily draw near our end; and every hour drives us to the precipice from whence we ſhall ſurely fall.

Obſerve then in what a ſtate of blindneſs our minds are involved! That which I ſaid muſt come, is now come, and great part of it already gone: for the time we have lived, is there, where it was before we lived (*g*). We greatly err in fearing our laſt day; ſince each of the foregoing contributes as much unto death, as this. It is not this laſt ſtep that hath tired us when we drop; it only makes us know and confeſs that we are tired. The laſt day reacheth death, the former advanced towards it. Death cuts us not off at once, but only crops us continually (*h*). A great ſoul therefore, conſcious of a better ſtate in reverſion, and a more exalted condition, endeavours indeed, in the ſtation wherein it is placed, to demean itſelf induſtriouſly and honeſtly; but it looks upon none of thoſe things that ſurround it, as its own property; but as things lent us for a while, and uſeth them accordingly, as a ſtranger, and one that is haſtening to another abode (*i*).

Now when we ſee a man acting with ſuch conſtancy and integrity, it cannot but preſent us with the diſtinguiſhing marks of an uncommon underſtanding; ſomething, I ſay, above the common ſtandard of human nature; eſpecially, if as I before obſerved, this greatneſs is attended with the manifeſtation of truth. Truth ever keeps the ſame ſteady courſe. Things falſe and counterfeit laſt not, being ever ſubject to change. Thus ſome men are at one time *Vatinius*', at another time *Cato*'s; one while they think *Curius* not ſevere; nor *Fabricius* poor enough: they will ſcarcely allow *Tubero* to be frugal, and ſufficiently content with his little: and at another time they challenge *Licinius* in wealth, *Apicius* in luxury, and *Mecænas* in the moſt elegant delights.

Nothing

Nothing can be a greater ſign of a bad diſordered mind, than this reſtleſſneſs, this continual agitation, between the diſſimulation of virtue, and the love of vice :

—— habebat ſæpe ducentos
Sæpe decem ſervos; modò reges atque tetrarchas,
Omnia magna loquens; modò ſit mihi menſa tripes, et
Concha ſalis puri; et toga quæ defendere frigus
Quamvis craſſa, queat; decies centena dediſſes
Huic parco paucis contento : quinque diebus,
Nil erat in loculo.—Hor. Sat. i. 3. 11.

Sometimes two hundred ſlaves compoſe his train,
And ſometimes ten. Now, in a pompous ſtrain,
Of kings and heroes he would brag; and ſoon
Lower his ſtyle to a more humble boon;
A three-legg'd table, and of ſalt one ſhell,
And a coarſe gown the weather to repell;
Yet in five days, ſo frugally content,
Had he a million, it would all be ſpent. Duncomb.

There are many ſuch as *Horace* hath here deſcribed; ſo wavering, ſo unlike to, and inconſiſtent with themſelves. Did I ſay many? nay, almoſt all men have this foible. There is ſcarce any one but who changeth his opinion, and his wiſhes: at one time he thinks himſelf happy in a wife; at another time he prefers a miſtreſs: he will now be maſter, and ſoon after ſtoop to be an officious humble ſervant; at one time he ſhews away in the greateſt ſplendour, ſo as to create envy; at another time he ſubſides, and lowers himſelf beneath the moſt abject of mortals: at one time he is profuſely generous; at another time he ſcrapes together all he can get. Nothing ſure can diſcover a weak and imprudent mind more than ſuch demeanor; where one action is perpetually thwarting another, and (than which I think nothing can be more vile) the man is altogether inconſiſtent with himſelf.

Think it a great virtue, my *Lucilius*, to act uniformly. Now none but a wiſe man appears always one and the ſame. The reſt are daily putting

putting on new ſhapes. One while you would think us very frugal and grave; at another time, prodigal and vain. We frequently change our maſques, and put on a very different one from that we pulled off. Exact this therefore of thyſelf, having fixed upon a certain rule of life, maintain it to thy laſt breath. Endeavour to deſerve praiſe, at leaſt to make it known who you are, by an uniformity of action: for it may ſometimes be ſaid of the man you ſaw yeſterday, *who is this man?* ſo great an alteration hath one day made in him.

ANNOTATIONS, &c.

(*) Things that come not within the ſcrutiny of human ſenſes, as the virtue of the loadſtone, &c. cannot be examined by them, or be atteſted by any body; and therefore can appear more or leſs probable only as they more or leſs agree to truths that are eſtabliſhed in our minds; and as they hold proportion to other parts of our knowledge and approbation. *Analogy* in theſe matters is the only help we have, and 'tis from that alone we draw all our grounds of probability. See *Locke*, p. 285.

(*a*) See *Plutarch*. in the Life of *Pyrrhus*.

(*b*) Id. in the Life of *Poplicola*.

(*c*) The like charge is given us by St. Paul, *To render to all their dues, tribute to whom tribute is due, cuſtom to whom cuſtom, fear to whom fear, honour to whom honour*. Rom. xiii. 7. And here I cannot but recommend to the Reader's notice that moſt excellent ſermon of my good and ever-memorable maſter Dr. *Snape* on this text.

(*d*) i. e. the Εὔροια of the Stoics.

(*e*) As St. Peter ſaith of *the moſt ſure word of prophecy, whereewith ye do well that ye take heed as unto a light that ſhineth in a dark place*. ii. Pet. 1. 19. And St. *John* of our Saviour—*In him was life, and this life was the light of men, and the light ſhineth in darkneſs and the darkneſs comprehended it not*. John, i. 45.

(*f*) *For who hath known*, ſaith St. *Paul*, *the mind of the Lord, that he may inſtruct him? But we have the mind of Chriſt. Let this mind be in you, which was alſo in* Chriſt Jeſus. Phil. ii. 5. *Know you not yourſelves, how that* Jeſus Chriſt *is in you, except ye be reprobates?* ii. Cor. 13. 5. *And of his fulneſs have we all received*. John i. 16.

(*g*) The bell ſtrikes one.——If heard aright,
It is the knell of my departed hours.
Where are they? With the years beyond the Flood. *Young*. N. T.

(*h*) Carpit nos illa non corripit] The old tranſlation renders it, *Death ſwallows us indeed, but doth not devour us*. Cellu nous avalle, mais ne nous devore pas.

Is Death at diſtance? No: he has been on thee;
And giv'n ſure earneſt of his final blow. *Id*.
Each *moment* has its ſickle, emulous
Of *Time's* enormous ſcythe, whoſe ample ſweep

Strikes empires from the root: each *moment* plays
His little weapon in the narrower sphere
Of sweet domestic comfort, and cuts down
The fairest bloom of sublunary bliss. *Id.*

(*i*) *These all died in faith, not having received the promises, but having seen them afar off, and were persuaded of them, and embraced them, and confessed they were* strangers and pilgrims on the earth. *For they that say such things, declare plainly they seek a country: and truly if they had been mindful of that country from whence they came, they might have had opportunity to have returned. But now they desire a better country,* i. e. *an heavenly. Wherefore God is not ashamed to be called their God, for he hath prepared for them a city.* Heb. ii. 13. 6. *Dearly beloved,* saith St. Peter, *I beseech you, as* strangers and pilgrims, *to abstain from fleshly lusts, that war against the soul.* i. Pet. ii. 11. And St. Paul, This I say, brethren, *the time is short, it remaineth that ye use this world as not abusing it; for the fashion of this world passeth away.* i. Cor. 7. 31. See Epp. 58, 74, 98.

" The *Ægyptians* in general, according to *Deodorus*, held the present life to be of small account; but the glory of a life to come hereafter, acquired by virtue, to be the highest object of their ambition. They looked upon our houses here but as *inns*, where we are to bait but a little while." Nay, *Macrobius* assures us, Animarum originem manare de cœlo inter rectè philosophantes indubitatæ constat esse sententiæ. *Somn. Scip.* l. 1. *It was the undoubted opinion of the best philosophers, that our souls were derived to us from heaven.*

EPISTLE CXXI.

Whether every Creature is sensible of his own Constitution.

I KNOW you will chide me, *Lucilius*, when I explain to you the petty question, which I have been so long musing upon this very day. And again you will cry out, *what avails this towards reforming our morals?* But exclaim as you please, when I have called to my assistance those eminent Stoics, *Posidonius* and *Archidemus* (*a*); let them argue the point with you: what I would ask is, *whether any thing that relates to morality does not tend to create good manners?* When we consider the different engagements and pursuits of man, we find that one thing tends to his nourishment, another to exercise, another to dress, another to instruction, another to pleasure and delight. All these, I say, belong to him, yet not all of them make him a better man. So with regard

3 to

to morals; ſome things affect him in one way, ſome in another; ſome correct and regulate mankind; other things point out their nature and origin.

And when I am enquiring after the reaſon why *Nature* firſt made man, and gave him the pre-eminence over all other animals; do you think that ſuch an enquiry bears no relation to *manners?* if you do, you are miſtaken; for how will you know what manners beſt ſuit a man, unleſs you firſt find out what path it is beſt for man to purſue? unleſs you inſpect his very nature. Then indeed you will underſtand what you are to do, and what to avoid; when you have thoroughly learned what you owe to your nature and conſtitution as man.

I would fain learn, you ſay, *how to covet leſs, and leſs to fear: root out all ſuperſtition from me; teach me, that what is called* felicity, *is light and vain; and that by the acceſſion of one ſyllable, it becomes the reverſe*, *in*felicity. Know then, I will ſome day gratify your requeſt, by exhorting to the practice of virtue and ſcorning vice: and though ſome perhaps may think me too ſevere in this reſpect, I will ſteadily perſiſt in perſecuting iniquity, bridling in the moſt refractory affections, reſtraining ſuch pleaſures as neceſſarily end in pain and ſorrow, and in thwarting every idle wiſh. For why? we have often wiſhed for the greateſt of evils; and have received that with joy and congratulation, againſt which we afterwards ſo bitterly exclaim (*b*). In the mean while permit me to diſcuſs a few things, however wide they may ſeem from this purpoſe.

The queſtion was, *whether all animals have a certain ſenſe of their condition or conſtitution (c)*. And that they have ſuch a ſenſe, is chiefly manifeſt from their ſo aptly and expeditiouſly moving their limbs, as if they had been particularly inſtructed and bred up therein. There is a certain agility in all their different parts; as the artiſt uſeth his tools with eaſe and readineſs; and the pilot knows to ſteer his ſhip: and the painter, having ſet before him many various colours picks out, or forms, that which he thinks will give the beſt likeneſs; and with a quick eye and ready hand paſſeth between the pallet and the image represented. So ready and nimble is an animal in the uſe of each ſeveral motion. We are apt to admire juſt actors, in that their hand is expreſſive of every affection; and a proper attitude and geſticulation attend on the different flow of words; what theſe do by art, animals do by nature. None of them find any difficulty in moving their limbs; nor heſitate in the uſe of them. They come into life with this knowledge; and are born, as it were, with ſuch particular inſtructions.

But it is ſaid, *that animals move their limbs in ſuch an apt manner, becauſe if they were to move them otherwiſe it would give them pain.* According to this opinion then they act by compulſion; 'tis not the *will*, but *fear* that directs them to a proper motion. But this is falſe; they are ſlow upon compulſion: agility is a voluntary motion; and ſo far is the fear of pain from inciting thereto, that they will endeavour at their motion, though they ſuffer pain by it. Thus an infant, who is learning to uſe his feet and to ſtand upright, as ſoon as he begins to try his ſtrength, falls down, and not without tears riſeth again as often, 'till by frequent exerciſe and much pain he hath attained the habit Nature deſigned him. Some animals of a very hard back being turned thereon, will twiſt themſelves, and throw out their feet and ſcramble with them, 'till they are replaced in their proper poſition. The tortoiſe, for inſtance, when laid upon his back, is not ſuppoſed to feel much pain, yet through deſire of his natural poſture, he is reſtleſs, and ſtruggles, nor will ceaſe his endeavours 'till he hath recovered his feet. There is in every animal therefore a ſenſe of their conſtitution; and from hence proceeds the prompt uſe of their limbs; nor can we have any greater ſign that they came into life with this knowledge, than that no animal is ignorant in the uſe of his body.

Conſtitution, it is ſaid, as you define it, *is the governing principle of the mind, under ſuch a modification with regard to the body. But as this is ſo perplexed and ſubtle, and what you yourſelves ſcarce know how to expreſs; how ſhall an infant underſtand it! All animals ſhould have been logicians, that they might comprehend this definition, which is obſcure and unintelligible*

unintelligible to a great part of the better learned among yourselves. There would be some force in this objection, if we should allow that the animals themselves understand this definition of constitution. But constitution itself is much easier understood from Nature than it can be from any definition or expression (*d*). The infant knows not what is meant by the word *constitution*, but he well knows his own; neither does he know what an animal is, but he perceives himself to be an animal; and also understands in the gross, summarily, and obscurely, his own constitution.

We likewise know that we have a *soul:* but what the soul is, where it is, of what quality, and from whence it is, we know not (*e*). The same sense that we have of the soul, though we know not its nature and situation; such a sense have all animals of their constitution. For they must necessarily be sensible of that, by which they are sensible of other things; they must needs be sensible of that, which they obey; and by which they are governed: there is not one of us, but who knows there is somewhat within him, that stirs up his powers to action; but what it is he knows not. As infants, so likewise other animals, have a certain sense of their principal part, though it be not clear enough, nor so express, as to form a just notion of it.

You say, it is objected again, *that every animal is at first reconciled to his constitution; but that the constitution of man is rational; and therefore is man reconciled to himself, not as merely to an animal, but as to a rational animal; for in that is man dear to himself, as being man; how then can an infant be reconciled to a rational constitution, when as yet he is not rational?* Every age of life hath its own constitution. There is one constitution to infants, another to youth, and another to old age, and all are reconciled to their present condition. An infant hath no teeth, he does well without them: he cuts his teeth: this condition agreeth likewise with his age: as that herb, which in a little time will become bread-corn, hath one state, when tender and scarce rising above the furrow; another when it is grown up; and though the stalk indeed be slender, yet it is strong enough to bear its weight; another when it begins to change colour,

colour, and ripen for the barn; in whatever ſtate it is, it maintains the ſame, and in all reſpects is accommodated thereto. Thus I ſay there is an age peculiar to infants, another to children, another to youth, and another to maturity; yet I am ſtill the ſame perſon I was, when a boy, when a young man. So though the conſtitution of every man is continually changing, there is the ſame reſpect and agreeableneſs in every change: for it is not the boy, nor the young, nor the old man, that Nature recommends to my care, but myſelf (*f*). Therefore the infant is reconciled to that conſtitution which he then hath as an infant, not to that which he ſhall hereafter have when a young man. Neither, though ſome greater and better ſtate may remain, into which he ſhall one day paſs, is not this alſo in which he was born ſuitable to Nature.

At firſt, every animal is reconciled and a friend to *ſelf.* For there muſt be ſome quality to which other qualities may be referred. I ſeek pleaſure. For whom? Myſelf. Therefore I take care of myſelf. I fly from danger? For whoſe ſake? My own. Therefore am I cautious. If then I am directed by ſelf-preſervation; ſelf-preſervation muſt be before all things. And this we ſee in all living creatures; nor is it ingrafted in, but born with us. Nature bringeth forth her young, and would preſerve them: and, becauſe the nearer our defence is the more ſafe we are, ſhe hath committed the charge of every one to himſelf; and therefore, as I have ſaid elſewhere, young animals as ſoon as they come from their dam, or ſee the light, know immediately what is hurtful to them; and fly from thoſe things that threaten death. Nay ſuch as are in danger from birds of prey, are afraid even of the ſhadow of thoſe birds when flying over them. No animal comes into life without the fear of death.

It is aſked indeed, *how an animal, juſt brought forth, can underſtand what is either ſalutary or deſtructive?* But firſt the queſtion is, whether he does underſtand this, not how he underſtands it? And that they have ſuch underſtanding is manifeſt from this, *they will do nothing more than what they ſo underſtand.* Why does not the hen fly from the peacock or the gooſe, when ſhe flies from the hawk with all ſpeed, a much leſs lefs bird, and not known to her before? Why are chickens afraid of a cat, but not of a dog? It is plain they know what will hurt them, without having learned this from experience: for they are afraid before they have made any trial of their danger. And then that you may not think this happens by chance, they neither are afraid of other things than what they have caufe to fear, nor do they ever forget that fuch are their enemies. Their flight from what is pernicious is ever anfwerable to this their defenfive care and diligence.

Befides, the longer they live, they are not lefs afraid; from whence it is apparent that this comes not by cuftom, but from the natural love of their own welfare. What cuftom teacheth is learned flowly, by degrees, and in various ways: but whatever Nature propofes comes alike to all, and at once. If you defire to know, I will tell you, how every living creature comes to the knowledge of what will prove deftructive to him. He perceives himfelf to confift of flefh, and confequently knows whereby flefh may be cut, or burned, or bruifed. Such animals then as are armed for mifchief, he concludes to be his enemies, and of an hoftile difpofition. There is a connexion between thefe things. For as every animal is at once endowed with the fenfe of felf-prefervation, fuch things as tend thereto they readily perceive, and dread what is like to be hurtful.

Now this dread of, and rejecting, contraries is natural; and what Nature directs, is done, without forecaft, without deliberation. See you not with what art and fubtlety the bees form their little cells (*g*)? what amazing concord there is between them in dividing the labours of the day! See you not that no art of man can imitate the curious texture of the fpider's web (*h*)! What pains does fhe take in the juft difpofition of the threads! fome are woven in a ftrait line by way of foundation; others are entwifted circularly, and growing ftill finer but clofer fpread, are a net to catch flies, her deftined prey. Now this art is innate, not taught her, and therefore none of thefe animals are more learned than others of the fame kind. Every fpider of the kind fpins a like

like web; and every cell in the honeycomb is formed with the like angles.

Whatever is taught by art is uncertain and unequal: but what Nature teacheth is always uniform; and nothing hath ſhe taught more certainly than ſelf-defence, and ſkill in ſelf-preſervation. Animals begin to live and to learn at the ſame time; nor is it any wonder that, that inſtruction ſhould be born with them, without which they would have been born in vain. Nature hath given them this knowledge, as the firſt means of preſerving in them a conſtant agreement with, and love of their own condition. They could not poſſibly be ſafe, unleſs they had an inclination ſo to be: nor would this alone have been of ſervice to them, but without this nothing elſe could.

Laſtly therefore let me obſerve that you will find in none of them a contempt, nor even a diſregard, of *ſelf*. For even ſuch as are dumb, and brutes indeed, though in other things they are quite ſtupid, are cunning enough to get their living: and you will ſee even thoſe, which are altogether uſeleſs and unprofitable to others, are yet never wanting to themſelves.

ANNOTATIONS, &c.

(*a*) *Archidemus*, an eminent leader among the Stoics. *Cicero* likewiſe mentions him with *Antipater*. Vid. Lipſ. Manud. l. 12.

(*b*) Nos plerumque id votis expetimus, quod non impetraſſe melius foret, &c. Val. Max. vii. 2.

——— Quid enim ratione timemus,
Aut cupimus? Quid tam dextro pede concipis, ut te
Conatûs non pœniteat, votique peracti?
Evertêre domos totas optantibus ipſis
Dii faciles.——Juv. x. 6.

How void of reaſon are our hopes and fears!
What in the conduct of our life appears
So well diſpos'd, ſo luckily begun,
But when we have our wiſh, we wiſh undone?
Whole houſes of their whole deſires poſſeſt,
Are often ruin'd at their own requeſt. Dryden.

(*c*) Τὴν δὴ πρώτην ὁρμήν, φασι, τὸ ζῶον ἴσχειν ἐπὶ τὸ τηρεῖν ἑαυτόν.—*Laert.*—Placet iis quorum ratio mihi probatur, ſimul atque natum ſit animal, ipſum ſibi conciliari et commendari ad ſe conſervandum et ad ſuum ſtatum, et ad ea quæ ſunt conſervantia ejus ſtatus diligenda.—alienari autem ab interitu, iiſque rebus quæ interitum videantur afferre. *Cic.* de Fin. 3. 5. *The philoſophers, whoſe ſyſtem I approve of, are of opinion, that as ſoon as any creature is born, (for here we muſt commence our diſputation) it has an affection for itſelf; it endeavours its own preſervation and well-being; and is impelled to the love of every thing that can contribute thereto. At the ſame time it abhors diſſolution, and whatever may ſeem to threaten the ſame.*

(*d*) *We ſhould know very little indeed,* ſaith Galen, *did we know no more than what we could give a juſt definition of.*

(*e*) There was a ſtrange diverſity of opinions among the antient philoſophers about the nature of the human ſoul. The moſt eminent of them however, from the time of *Pythagoras*, maintained, that it is *a portion of the divine eſſence.* See *Leland* ii. 1. 280.

(*f*) *Self*, is that conſcious thinking thing, (whatever ſubſtance made up of, whether ſpiritual or material, ſimple or compounded it matters not) which is ſenſible, or conſcious of pleaſure and pain, capable of happineſs or miſery, and ſo is concerned for *itſelf* as far as that conſciouſneſs extends. *Locke*, p. 292.

(*g*) " See what bright ſtrokes of architecture ſhine
Through the whole frame, what beauty, what deſign!
Each odorif'rous cell, and waxen tow'r,
The yellow pillage of the rifled flow'r,
Has twice three ſides, the only figure fit
To which the lab'rers may their ſtores commit
Without the loſs of matter, or of room,
In all the wondrous ſtructure of the comb." *Anon.*

(*h*) I cannot here but pay my reſpects to the memory of Dr. *Littleton*, my late moſt worthy friend, whoſe elegant poem on a *ſpider*, is in the hands of every one.

Inſidious, reſtleſs, watchful, ſpider, &c.

EPISTLE CXXII.

On Extravagance, and irregular Living.

THE days, *Lucilius*, are now upon the decline: they are grown indeed ſomewhat ſhorter, yet are ſtill long enough to give a man ſufficient time for buſineſs; if he would riſe, as I may ſay, with the day itſelf, but to ſome other purpoſe, than merely to give the uſual ſalutation. But it is ſcandalous to lie dozing when the ſun is riſen, and not to be

thoroughly

thoroughly awake 'till noon: and yet this is what some call rising early. For there are those who invert the order of night and day, and who never open their eyes, still heavy with yesternight's debauch, 'till night returns again. They seem to be in the state of those, whom Nature, as *Virgil* saith, hath placed opposite to us, with their feet to our feet.

Nosque ubi primus equis oriens effulsit anhelis,
Illic sera rubens accendit lumina vesper. G. i. 250.
Or when Aurora *leaves our northern sphere,*
She lights the downward heav'n, and rises there;
And when on us she breathes the living light,
Red Vesper *kindles there the tapers of the night.* Dryden.

It is not that their region or country is opposite and contrary to that of other men, but their life. There are oftentimes *antipodes* in the same city; who, as *Marcus Cato (a)* observes, *never saw the sun, either rising or setting.*

Think you that those men know how to live, who know not when they live? And yet they fear death, though they bury themselves alive, and are as ominous, if you chance to meet them, as the night-raven. Although they spend their darkness in wine and perfume; although they spin out the whole time of their intemperate vigils in banqueting, and variety of luxurious dishes; they *feast* not, but are solemnizing their own funerals (*b*). The obsequies of the dead indeed are wont to be celebrated in the day-time, and are soon over: but no day is long enough for him that liveth, and worketh as he ought. We must stretch out the narrow span of life; the duty and sign whereof consist in action. We must even contract the night, and transfer part of it to the day. Birds that are cooped up for a feast, that by sitting still they may grow fat, are generally kept in the dark: so of those men, who lie all day long without any exercise, a swelling is apt to invade the sluggish body; a lazy fatness seizeth all their limbs; and having dedicated themselves to darkness, they grow filthy and ill-favoured. Their sodden countenance looks as suspicious as of those who labour under some disease; they are of an ashy colour, languid and faint; and tho' still active, their flesh seems already corrupted. This however, I may fay, is but the leaft of evils that attends fuch irregularities, fince a far greater darknefs involves the mind; it is quite ftupid; it is fo very dark, it envies the blind. Who but fuch men as thefe could ever think that the eyes were given us to be ufed in darknefs!

Do you afk whence proceeds this depravity of mind, that loaths the day, and is for turning the whole of life into night? Know that all vices are repugnant and contrary to Nature: they all defert the order and fitnefs of things. It is the very defign of luxury to rejoice in perverfenefs; and not only to depart from what is right, but to fly from it as far as poffible. Do they not feem to live contrary to Nature, who drink fafting (*c*), who pour down wine into their empty veins, and go drunk to dinner? yet fuch is the common excefs of youth, who affect in this way to try their ftrength. Upon the very threfhold of the bath they ftrip and drink; nay, they quaff down bumpers, and every now and then wipe off the fweat occafioned by their frequent and hot draughts. To drink only after meals is too vulgar a thing for men of tafte; let your country-folk, and men who know not true pleafure, follow rules; our gallants delight not in that wine which fwims harmlefs upon their food, and has a free and eafy accefs to the nerves: no drunkennefs is fo agreeable, as that which is got upon an empty ftomach.

Do they not feem to live contrary to Nature, who change habits with women, and ftudy to preferve a young bloom on a wrinkled forehead? What can be more horrid, or more wretched? They would fain never be man, that they may not leave off their boyifh tricks: and when their fex ought to refcue them from contumely and difgrace, not age itfelf can difcharge them.

Live they not contrary to Nature who covet a rofe in winter? and who by the nourifhment of warm water and a proper heat of air, force the lily and other fpring flowers, to bloom in the depth of winter?

Live they not contrary to Nature, who plant orchards on their turrets, (*d*), fo that trees may wave over the tops of their houfes; and ftrike their roots in those places, which it would have been presumption to pretend to reach with their highest boughs?

Live they not contrary to Nature, who lay the foundation of their baths in the sea; nor think they can swim delicately unless the warm water likewise be ruffled with billows?

Thus having resolved to will nothing but what is contrary to the custom of Nature, they at last entirely revolt from her. "*Is it day-*" *light?* It is time then to go to sleep (*e*). *Is it night?* Let us now "take our usual exercise: let us get into our chariots, pay our visits, "and so to dinner. But lo! the morning approaches; it is now sup-"per-time. It is not for us to act as the common people do. It is "mean to live in the ordinary and vulgar way. Let the poor wretches "enjoy the whole day to themselves; so we have but an early hour in "the morning to go to bed."

For my part I cannot but rank such extravagant fops among the dead. For how like a funeral is it, and a sorrowful one too, to live thus by the light of torches and flambeaux? I remember not long ago, there were many who lived such a sort of life, among whom was *Atticus Buta*, a Prætorian, who after he had spent a large estate, and was complaining of his poverty to *Tiberius*, received this answer, *you are too late awakened. Montanus Julius (f)*, a tolerable poet, but well known, by having been a favourite, though afterwards in disgrace, with *Tiberius*, was one day reciting his poetry; and as he was fond of using the words ortus and occasus, (*east* and *west*, or *morning* and *evening*) when a friend of his complained that he had detained him a whole day, and that it was very unreasonable to expect a man should attend so long to hear his compositions; one *Natta Pinarius (g)* said pleasantly enough, *For my part, I think a man cannot use him more courteously than I do; for I am willing to hear him*, ab ortu ad occasum (alluding to the *words* only.) But when he was reciting these verses,

Incipit ardentes Phœbus producere flammas,
Spergere se rubicunda dies, jam tristis hirundo

Argutis

Argutis reditura cibos immittere nidis
Incipit, et molli partitos ore miniſtrat.
Phœbus begins to ſhew his ſultry flame,
And ruddy morn to ſpread around the ſame;
With various food the ſwallow treats her young,
And lulls them with her melancholy ſong.

Varus a Roman knight, a companion of *Lucius Vicinius*, and an excellent ſmell-feaſt, making himſelf every where welcome by his witty, and often bitter jeſts, cried out,

And Buta *now prepares for ſleep.*

And when he repeated theſe lines,

Jam ſua paſtores ſtabulis armenta locarunt,
Jam dare ſopitis nox nigra ſilentia terris
Incipit.——
The ſhepherds to the fold their flocks had led,
And ſilent darkneſs o'er the world was ſpread:

cried the ſame *Varus, what does* Montanus *ſay? It is now night; I will go then, and give good-morrow to* Buta. Nothing was more notorious than this life which *Buta* led, ſo contrary to all rule; and in which many, as I ſaid, indulged themſelves at that time.

Now the reaſon of men's living in this prepoſterous manner, is, not becauſe they think the night itſelf hath any thing more pleaſing in it; but becauſe nothing delights them that is obvious and common; and becauſe light is generally burthenſome to a bad conſcience; and becauſe they who value every thing, according to the price it bears, be it great or ſmall, diſdain the light, which coſts them nothing.

Moreover theſe luxurious gentlemen deſire to be talked of as long as they live; if nothing is ſaid of them, they think they loſe their labour, and live to no purpoſe; accordingly they are angry with themſelves, if they have done nothing to raiſe a report. Many *devour* all their goods; others waſte them upon harlots. To gain any credit among them, a man muſt not only commit ſome laſcivious, but ſome notable folly. In a city ſo buſily employed as this, a common ſin will not be thought a ſtory worth telling.

I have heard *Albinovanus*, (an excellent ſtory-teller) (*h*) ſay, that he lived but a few doors from *Spurius Papinius*, who was one of theſe night-owls. Sometimes, ſaid he, about the third hour of the night I have heard the twang of whips (*i*). I aſk what is the matter? and I am told, *that* Papinius *is calling his ſervants to account*. About the ſixth hour of the night, I hear a loud bawling: *what is this for?* I ſay. *Why*, Papinius *is only exerciſing his voice*. About the eighth hour of the night, I hear the rattling of wheels; and, when I aſk what it means, am told, that *Papinius* is going to take the air. Towards break of day the whole houſe is in an uproar; the pages are called, and the butlers and the cooks are running up and down; *what now?* ſays I. *Papinius* is juſt come out of the bath, and calls for ſome broth and mulled wine. *What? and did his ſuppers exceed the expences of the day?* No; for notwithſtanding all this he lived very frugally: *he ſpent nothing*, but the night. Therefore to ſome who called *Papinius* a ſordid and covetous wretch, ſaid *Albinovanus*, you may as well call him *lychnobius*, a lamplighter.

You muſt not wonder, *Lucilius*, that you find ſo many peculiarities in vice. Vice hath various and innumerable appearances; the ſeveral kinds of it cannot be comprehended. The obſervance of what is *right* is ſimple and uniform; but *wrong* is manifold, and puts on whatever ſhape you pleaſe. The ſame may be ſaid of the manners of thoſe who follow Nature: they are always free and eaſy, and ſcarce ever know any difference: but the depraved, and ſuch as turn aſide therefrom, not only differ from other mortals, but even among themſelves.

The principal cauſe however of this diſeaſe, ſeems to be the diſdain of common life; as they diſtinguiſh themſelves from others by their dreſs, by the elegance of their entertainments, and by the ſmartneſs of their equipage; ſo would they likewiſe differ from them in the obſervation and diſpoſal of time. They ſcorn to ſin in a low and cuſtomary manner, who expect *infamy* for their reward (*k*). And this is what they all ambitiouſly covet; who live, as I may ſay, *retrograde*. But let *us*, my *Lucilius*, maintain the life which *Nature* preſcribes, nor ever decline

decline from it: to thoſe who follow her all things are eaſy, and readily provided; but to thoſe who are continually thwarting her, life is nothing elſe but *rowing againſt the ſtream.*

ANNOTATIONS, &c.

(*a*) *Lipſius* does not recollect this to be ſaid any where by *Cato*, but that *Cicero* makes mention of ſuch ſots; qui ſolem, ut aiunt, nec occidentem unquam viderint, nec orientem, &c. *who are carried away from their meals, and cram themſelves next day, over yeſterday's crudities, who boaſt of never having ſeen the ſun riſing or ſetting, and who are beggars, having ſpent their patrimony.* Cic. de Fin. U. 8.

(*b*) Juſta ſibi faciunt] See Ep. xii. *Pincian* reads it *buſta*. *They are digging their own graves.*

(*c*) Plutarch. Quæſ. Conviv. 8. 9.

(*d*) Seneca Frag. in Thyeſte,—nulla culminibus meis
Impoſita nutat ſylva.
Nor on my houſetop nods a ſylvan ſcene.

Sen. Controv. v. 5. Aiunt in ſummis culminibus mentita nemora et navigalium piſcinarum freta. *They have not only groves on the top of their houſes but even fiſhponds.*

(*e*) So *Tacitus* ſpeaking of *Petronius*—Illi dies per ſomnum, nox officiis et oblectamentis vitæ tranſigebatur. *He paſſed his days in ſleep, and his nights in the duties and recreations of life.* And *Lampridius* of *Heliogabalus*, Trajecit et dierum actus noctibus et nocturnos diebus, eſtimans hoc inter inſtrumenta luxuriæ; ita ut ſero de ſomno ſurgeret, et ſalutari inciperet, mane autem dormire inceptaret. *He transferred the proper actions of the day to night, and of the night to day, looking upon this as an inſtance of luxury; ſo that he would riſe from ſleep expecting a ſalutation, and in the morning fall aſleep.* So *Horace* ſpeaking of one *Tegellius*,

—— Noctes vigilabat ad ipſum
Mane, diem totum ſtertebat.——S. i. 3. 17.
All night he drank, and then all day would ſnore,
No mortal from himſelf could differ more. Duncomb.

(*f*) *Seneca*, the father, likewiſe mentions him, Controv. i. 7. *Montanus Julius*, qui comes fuit, quique egregius poeta) *as an agreeable companion and an excellent poet.* He wrote both Heroic Poems and Elegies, according to *Ovid.* de Pont. l. 4.

Quique vel imparibus numeris, Montane, vel æquis
Sufficis, et gemino carmine nomen habes.

(*g*) He is mentioned by *Tacitus*, l. 5. as one of the clients of *Sejanus*.

(*h*) And alſo a poet.

(*i*) Et cædens longi relegit tranſacta diurni.
Et cædit donec laſſis cædentibus, exi,
Intonet horrendum, jam cognitione peractâ. *Juv.* vi. 484.
Caſts up the day's account, and ſtill beats on;
Tir'd out at length, with an outrageous tone
She bids them, in the Devil's name, begone. Dryden.

(*k*) So *Tacitus* moſt elegantly of *Meſſalina*, the wife of *Nero*. Nomen tamen matrimonii concupivit, ob magnitudinem infamiæ, cujus apud prodigos, noviſſima voluptas eſt.

EPISTLE CXXIII.

On Luxury.

TIRED, *Lucilius*, with a disagreeable rather than a long journey, I came to my house at *Alba* late at night. I found nothing ready, but myself. I stretched therefore my weariness on the couch; and began to reflect with myself; that nothing is grievous, but what may be endured with patience; nothing intolerable, but what we make so by discontent. *My baker has got no bread*; but the porter has got some; as likewise the farmers and the ploughmen. *Yes, coarse bread!* Stay a little, and you will think it fine enough; hunger will soon render it as soft and delicate, as what is made of the finest wheat-flower. We should not eat therefore 'till this incites us. *Well then I will wait, and not eat before I can get white bread, or can relish brown.*

It is very necessary to accustom ourselves to live upon a little. Many difficulties, both with regard to time and place, intervene, and hinder the rich and great themselves from their usual repast (*a*): no one can have at all times what he pleases: but it is always in a man's power to have no mind to that which he knows he cannot have, and chearfully to make use of what he has. A great part of liberty consists in an orderly good-tempered appetite, that can brook a delay, and even contumely. You cannot imagine what great pleasure I take in finding that my weariness can cure itself: I want not unction nor a bath: I ask no other remedy but that of time: for, what labour hath contracted, rest will soon disperse; and a supper at such a time, whatever it may be, will be more delicious than a public feast in the capitol (*b*).

I have sometimes made trial of my mind, by way of surprize; as it is then more sincerely and truly made. For when the mind is prepared and hath enjoined itself patience, it will not so easily appear how strong and firm it is. Thoſe are the ſureſt proofs of it that are made *extempore:* when it looks upon an inconvenience, not only with an equal, but with a pleaſant eye; falls not into a paſſion, nor is litigious: when it ſupplies itſelf, with what might have been expected, only by not deſiring it; and thinks that ſomewhat indeed is wanting to habit and cuſtom, but nothing abſolutely to itſelf. There are many things, which we knew not to be ſuperfluous before we wanted them; for we uſed them, not becauſe we had need of them, but becauſe we had them. And how many things do we ſeek to get, only becauſe others have them, and eſpecially ſome of our acquaintance?

It muſt be reckoned among the cauſes of our evils that we live by example. Neither are we governed by reaſon, but led away by cuſtom. If ſuch a thing is done but by few, we regard it not; nor think of following them therein; but when it becomes the faſhion, we cannot but follow it; as if it were the more fit becauſe more frequent; and error, when 'tis become public, uſurps the place of right. Men cannot travel now but with a troop of *Numidian* horſe (*c*), or a ſtring of running footmen, before them. It is thought ſcandalous to have no one to clear the way; and not to ſhew by a great duſt they raiſe, that a gentleman is coming. All have now their mules to carry their glaſſes, made of cryſtal and tranſparent pebble, cut by the hands of the greateſt artiſts. All have the faces of their minions maſked, leſt the ſun or the cold ſhould hurt their tender ſkin. It is thought a ſhame there ſhould be any among this tribe, whoſe face is not ſo fair as to need no paint (*d*).

Now theſe are the men, *Lucilius*, with whom we muſt avoid all conference. Theſe are they who teach vice, and propagate it from one to another. They have been thought the worſt of men who only carry tales from one to another; but theſe men carry vices. Indeed the converſation of ſuch men is exceedingly hurtful; for though it may not affect us at firſt, yet it will leave certain ſeeds in the mind, which, even when we have ſhook off theſe our companions, will abide with us, to our great detriment. As when we have heard a concert of

muſic,

music, we carry away the modulation and sweetness of an air, that engages our thoughts, nor will suffer us to give attention to any thing more serious; so the voice of flatterers, and of such as commend vice, stays longer with us than the time we give it hearing; nor is it an easy matter to shake off from the fond mind the pleasing sound: it pursues us; will not forsake us; and at times will interfere do what we can. We must shut our ears therefore to frivolous discourse; and indeed to the first attack of such men; for, when once they have made a beginning, and find free admission, they soon grow bolder, and at length come to the following language:

" *Virtue*, *Philosophy*, and *Justice!* what are they but mere empty " sounds! Our only happiness consists in *good living!* to do every " thing we please; and to enjoy one's patrimony. This is to live; " this is to remember that we are mortal: the day fleets from us, and " life irrecoverably passeth away (*e*). Why should we scruple to em- " brace every delight, and to treat life with those pleasures it cannot " always enjoy; but now can, and even demands them? What avails " it to stretch our frugality even beyond the grave? and now to deny " ourselves those things which death will soon deprive us of? What " a poor wretch art thou, who hast no mistress? and no minion for a " mistress to envy! How ridiculous is it to walk the streets sober, " and to sup so early and frugally as if you were to make a diary for the " approbation of a father! This is not to live for yourself, but for " another! What madness is it for a man to sollicit for his heir! and " to deny himself every thing, that the prospect of a large legacy, or " an inheritance may make your friend your enemy! For, the more " he is to receive, the sooner will he desire, and rejoice in your death. " Value not a rush those severe and supercilious censurers of other " men's lives, and enemies to their own; those public pedagogues, " who would fain govern the world! Despise them we say, and make " no scruple to prefer mirth, and good living, to the empty name of " a good man."

Such

Such harangues as these are to be dreaded, as the voice of the *Syrens* whom *Ulysses* would not venture to hear; before he had bound himself to the main-mast. They are altogether as prevalent; they draw us from our country, our parents, our friends, our virtue: and basely inveigle those wretches that listen to them into a scandalous life. How much better is it to walk in the strait path, and to attain this happy end, to think those things alone delightful, which are fit and honourable? And this we should certainly attain, if we suppose and sincerely reflect on two sorts of things, those that have sufficient charms to incite us, or those that are attended with horror. By the former I mean *riches*, *pleasures*, *beauty*, *ambition*, and the like pleasing, sweetly-soothing baits; while such as drive us from them with abhorrence, are *ignominy*, *hard-living*, *labour*, *pain* and *death*. We must therefore be well exercised that we fear not these, nor covet the former. We must fight contrariwise, retreat from those that invite us to them, and make head against those that press upon us. See you not how different is the attitude of those, who ascend or descend an hill? They that go down a steep place bend their bodies backward; they that go up stoop forwards. For if when you descend you stoop forwards, or in ascending lean backwards, this, my *Lucilius*, would be to favour and assist the precipice. Now, we descend into pleasures, but climb up against adversity and hardships: here then must we stoop forward our bodies, and in the former case lean them back, restraining them with all our might.

But think not that these are the only men whose discourse is pernicious to us, while they recommend pleasure, and instil a dread of pain; which is terrible enough in itself. No, there are others whom I think as prejudicial; I mean those who under a pretence of affecting *Stoicism* exhort to vice: for, this is their boast: *that the lover is the only wise and learned man; and that he is most wise, who hath the most skill in drinking and feasting. Let us enquire then*, say they, *to what age young men are amiable.*—No; let us give up those vices to the *Greeks*; and rather attend to the following instructions: *No one is casually good: virtue is to be learned: pleasure is a low and mean engagement; to be held in no esteem; common with dumb animals; the lowest and most contemptible have recourse thereto; glory is something vain, volatile, and more inconstant than the winds; poverty is no real burthen, but to those who repugn it; death is no evil; why do you complain? This is the most just and equal law to all mankind: superstition is a mad error (f); it fears those, who ought most to be beloved; and abuseth those it worshippeth: for what difference is there whether you deny the Gods, or scandalize them?* These are the things, *Lucilius*, that are to be learned; nay, they are to be learned, as we say, *by heart*. Philosophy should never suggest any excuses for vice; the sick man can have but little hopes of recovery, to whom his physician recommends intemperance.

ANNOTATIONS, &c.

(*a*) A diebus optantem: *al.* a diis. *al.* a diu optatis. *al.* octavam, referring to the hour of supper:

Exul ab octava Marius bibit, et fruitur diis
Iratis; at tu victrix provincia ploras.
Marius his fine begs off, contemns his infamy,
Can rise at twelve, and get him drunk at three.
Enjoys his exile, and condemn'd in vain,
Leaves thee, prevailing province, to complain. Dryden.

(*b*) Cœna Diali] al. adjiciali, *sive* adicialL. Ep. 95.

(*c*) Numidarum equitatus] So in Ep. 87. Cursores, et Numidas, et multum ante se pulverem agentem.

(*d*) Desideret medicamentum] So *Juvenal*, of women:

Sed quæ mutatis inducitur, atque fovetur
Tot medicaminibus, coctæque siliginis offas
Accipit, et madidæ, facies dicetur an ulcus? Juv. vi. 470.
But hadst thou seen her plaister'd up, before,
'Twas so unlike a face, it seem'd a sore. Dryden.

(*e*) Una felicitas est, bona vita, facere omnia libere] This is another passage in full agreement with that of St. Paul, *come let us eat and drink, for to-morrow we die.* i. Cor. xi. 32. which in my paraphrase of that admirable chapter runs thus:

Come, let us swim in pleasure; swim at large;
Eat, drink, and with variety of sport,
Indulge the taste of lustful appetence.
For why? To-morrow the eclipse of life
Shall cover us with an eternal shade;
The common period of all earthly beings.

Where I observe that this is no *laconic* proverb, properly so called as some take it; because no people

people were more ſober and frugal than the *Lacedæmonians.*——St. *Paul* certainly took it from Iſ. xxii. 13. but to a different end, &c.

(*f*) Error inſanus, *ab* infantis, *a childiſh error.* "Superſtition is a very dangerous weapon, that cuts with two edges; for while it fills with ſome falſe fears, the abſurdity of thoſe fears drives others into infidelity. Superſtition built the *Pagan* hell and *elyſium*, and infidelity, not content with pulling down the ſuperſtructure, eraſed the very foundations. The extreme errors are, ſuperſtition, which realizes the fire and the worm; and infidelity, which, laughing at theſe, overlooks the analogy. *Melampus*, p. 207.

EPISTLE CXXIV.

Againſt the Epicureans, *that Good conſiſts in Reaſon and not in Senſe.*

POSSUM multa tibi veterum præcepta referre,
Ni refugis, teſtiſque piget cognoſcere curas.

I many ſolid precepts could rehearſe,
Would you attend to the inſtructive verſe.

But you, I know, *Lucilius*, will attend; nor are you diſguſted at the moſt ſubtle queſtion. Such is your elegance of taſte, not to delight only in what is great. And this I likewiſe approve in you, that you reduce all things to ſome uſe and profit; and then only are offended, when a ſubject is not argued with the niceſt ſubtlety imaginable: which indeed is not what I ſhall now pretend to. The plain queſtion is, *whether good is comprehended by ſenſe, or the underſtanding.* And as an adjunct to this, it is ſaid, *that neither infants nor brute animals are capable of it.*

The *Epicureans*, who ſet pleaſure in the higheſt place, affirm *good to be ſenſual:* but we *Stoics*, on the other hand, who attribute it to the mind, ſuppoſe it *intellectual.* If the ſenſes were the ſole judges of good, we ſhould reject no ſort of pleaſure; for there is no pleaſure but what is alluring and delightful: and, on the contrary, we ſhould undergo no pain willingly; as there is none but what offends the ſenſes.

 Beſides,

Besides, they would by no means deserve blame or censure, who are too fond of pleasure, and who live in the utmost dread of pain; whereas we condemn those, who devote themselves to lust and gluttony; and despise those, who dare not engage in any manly exercise for fear of pain. For, how do they sin, or do wrong, who act in obedience to the senses, supposing these to be the judges of good and evil; for to these you have given the power of determining what you shall fly from, or what pursue? But surely *reason* should preside in this affair; which as it ought to determine concerning *life*, *virtue*, and *the fitness of things*; so likewise concerning *good* and *evil*: for otherwise, according to these men, pre-eminence is given to the baser part to judge of the better; if good must be judged of by the *senses*, dull and stupid as they are, and much more imperfect in man than in other animals. What if any one had a mind to discern minute things not with his eye, but his touch? Surely to discern good from evil, no penetration can be more sharp and exact for this purpose than the sight of the eyes. You see then how ignorant of truth they are, and how disrespectfully they trample upon things high and sublime, who make the *touch* the judge of good and evil.

But it is said, *that as every science and every art must have something that is manifest, and comprehended by sense, from whence it may be derived and encrease; so an happy life takes its source and foundation from such things as are manifest and fall under the apprehension of sense.* Well then, you say, an happy life takes its beginning from things manifest; and we say, that such things are happy, or create happiness, which are according to nature. And what is according to nature appears clearly, and at first sight, as whatever is perfect and entire. *What then is according to nature?* Why, it is that which befalleth him, who is just born: I do not call it actually good, but the beginning of good. Whereas you attribute pleasure as the chief good to infancy; as if a child began to have that from its birth, which he obtaineth only when a complete man. This is to set the top of the tree, where should be the root. If any one should say that an infant, while it lies in its mother's womb, of an uncertain sex, tender, imperfect, and unshapen, is already

in

in poſſeſſion of good he would certainly ſeem to be miſtaken. But how little difference is there between him who hath juſt entered upon life, and him, who is as yet a latent burthen in the womb? Both of them as to any underſtanding of good and evil, are alike mature; becauſe an infant is no more capable of good than a tree, or a brute animal. And why is not a tree or a brute animal capable of good? Becauſe they want reaſon: and upon the ſame account infants are not capable; for they as yet want reaſon.

Some animals are irrational; ſome not as yet rational; and ſome rational, but imperfectly: in none of theſe dwells *good*. It is an attendant upon reaſon. What difference then is there between the things before-mentioned? Good can never be in what is irrational; in what is not yet rational, good is not yet; and in what is imperfect, good may hereafter be, but is not now. What I mean, *Lucilius*, is this: good is not found in every natural body; nor in every age of life; and is as far from belonging to infancy, as the laſt is from the firſt; or perfection from a beginning: therefore much leſs in a body, ſcarcely formed in the womb, or whatever prior ſtate it may be in. Again, ſpeaking of the good of a tree or plant; you will not ſay that it is in the firſt leaf that buddeth forth; or that the good of wheat is in the tender blade, or in the ſoft ear that firſt ſprings from the ſtalk; but in the grain, when the ſummer and due maturity hath hardened it. As nothing in nature exhibits good before it is in perfection, ſo the good of man is not in man 'till reaſon is become perfect in him. Now what this good is I will tell you: *it is a mind upright and free, ſubjecting other things to itſelf, itſelf to nothing*. Infancy therefore is not capable of this good; neither can the child, the boy, or youth itſelf expect it, but unjuſtly and in vain. And happy is the old age, that hath attained it by long ſtudy and application, when it becomes a real and intellectual good.

You allow, it is ſaid, *ſome good to be in trees and in herbs*; *why not then in infants?* *True* good is neither in trees nor in brute animals; the good in them is only a precarious good, by conceſſion. *And what is that?* you ſay. Why it is that which is conſonant to the nature of every

every thing. Good can by no means be aſſigned to brute animals; it is of a more noble and happy nature. There can be no good, but where there is reaſon.

There are four ſeveral natures: that of a tree, that of a beaſt, that of a man, and that of God. The former two, being both irrational, have much the ſame nature. The other two have different natures, the one being immortal, the other mortal. The nature then of one, i. e. *of God*, is perfect good in itſelf; and care and diligence in the other, i. e. in man, hath made alſo his (reſpectively) perfect. Other things are ſaid to be perfect in their nature, but not truly perfect, foraſmuch as they want reaſon. For that, in ſhort, is perfect, which is perfect according to univerſal nature; but univerſal nature is rational; other things however may be perfect in their kind.

In what there cannot be a bleſſed life, neither can be that by which a bleſſed life is effected; there is not in a brute animal that whereby a bleſſed life is effected, therefore in a brute animal good is not. A brute animal indeed comprehends things preſent by ſenſation; and remembers things paſt, when the ſenſe is awakened thereto by ſomething preſent. As a horſe remembers the road when he is put into it; but it is not to be ſuppoſed that in the ſtable he remembers any thing of the road, though he treads it every day (*a*). The third degree of time, I mean the time to come, appertaineth not to brute beaſts. How then can the nature of thoſe things ſeem perfect, which have not the uſe of perfect time? For time is divided into three parts, paſt, preſent, and future: that only which is ſhorteſt, and is paſſing, i. e. the preſent, is given to the knowledge of animals; very rare is the remembrance of the paſt, nor ever recovered, but by the intervention of ſomething preſent. The good therefore of a perfect nature cannot be in a nature that is imperfect; or if it naturally hath good, it is of the ſame ſort that plants alſo have.

Nor do I deny but that brute animals are carried with a ſtrong force and impulſe towards thoſe things that ſeem agreeable to nature; but then

then it is in a confused and disorderly manner; but there can never be any disorder or confusion in *good*. *Why then*, say you, *are brute animals moved confusedly and disorderly?* I said this upon a supposition, that their nature was capable of order; they are now moved according to nature. For that is confused, which may not be so at another time; and that not at ease, which at another time may be secure. Vice is in none, but where also there may be virtue. The motion then in brute beasts is such as is according to their nature. But not to detain you too long, suppose a brute animal to have some good, some virtue, something perfect; what then? It is not absolutely good, nor virtue, nor perfection; for these privileges belong only to rational animals, to whom it is given to know, *wherefore*, *how far*, and *in what manner*. So that *good* is in nothing but where there is *reason*.

You ask, *whereunto tends this discourse, and wherein will it profit the mind?* I will tell you; it both exercises and sharpens it: and, as the mind must be employed some way or other (*b*), detains it in a fit employ: it is of service likewise in preventing it from pursuing its natural tendency to ill. But give me leave further to say, that I cannot possibly confer a greater benefit upon you, than by pointing out to you your own good, by distinguishing you from brute beasts, and placing you in communion with God.

Why then, I say, do you take so much pains in nourishing and exercising the strength of your body; as if this was to be boasted of? Nature hath given this in greater perfection to savage beasts. Why so careful to heighten and preserve beauty? When you have done all you can, many animals will excell you herein. Why do you trim your hair with so great diligence and art? Whether you let it flow at full length, like the *Parthians*, or tie it up in a knot like the *Germans*, or frizzle and spread it wide, like the *Scythians*; every horse shall toss about a thicker and more flowing mane; and the lion shall look more formidably noble: and whatever swiftness you pretend to, you are no match for the little hare.

Would

Would you then laying aside these qualifications, in which you are necessarily excelled, as they are foreign to you, return to your own proper good? Know, it is this: *a mind or soul truly reformed, and comparatively pure as God is pure:* advancing itself above all earthly things, and reckoning nothing its own from without. Thou art a rational animal; and what is the good within thee? Perfect reason. Do all you can then to advance this, and carry it to the highest perfection, its proper end. Then think yourself happy, when all joy and satisfaction arise from yourself; when in all those things that men so greedily catch at, so fondly wish for, and so carefully guard, you can find nothing, which, I do not say, you had rather have, but which you at all desire. I will conclude with this short rule, whereby you may examine yourself, and know whether you are as yet perfect. Thou shalt possess the proper good, when thou shalt know and understand, infelicissimos esse felices, *that they are most unhappy, who are happy* (c).

ANNOTATIONS, &c.

(a) If brutes have any *ideas* at all, and are not bare machines (as some would have them) we cannot deny them to have some *reason*. It seems as evident to me that they do some of them in certain instances reason, as that they have sense; but it is only in particular *ideas*, just as they received them from their senses. *Locke*, p. 121.

There is a gradation or scale of ascent of the principle of action among creatures in proportion to their perfection, with regard to the motion of their bodies. But men have further a power of directing arbitrarily their perceptive capacity to, and throughout their past perceptions, which brutes have not: and therefore cannot properly be called thinking creatures. And this is the specific difference betwixt rational and irrational beings, as this power is the foundation of the rational nature. See *Baxter* on Locke, p. 79, &c. *Brown* on the understanding, p. 173.

(b) That there are *ideas*, some or other always present in the mind of a waking man, every one's experience convinces him: though the mind employs itself about them with several degrees of attention, &c. *Locke*, p. 184.

(c) Or it may be rendered, that *the most unhappy are happy*, if they discharge to the best of their power the respective duties of life.

THE END.

www.ingramcontent.com/pod-product-compliance
Lightning Source LLC
Chambersburg PA
CBHW022122020426
42334CB00015B/719

* 9 7 8 3 7 4 3 3 3 5 0 6 6 *